THE PRAEGER PICTURE ENCYCLOPEDIA OF ART

THE PRAEGER

WITH 192 PLATES IN FULL COLOR

AND 416 ILLUSTRATIONS IN MONOCHROME

PICTURE

ENCYCLOPEDIA

OF ART

a comprehensive survey

of painting, sculpture, architecture and crafts,

their methods, styles and technical terms,

from the earliest times to the present day

FREDERICK A. PRAEGER, *Publishers*
NEW YORK, N.Y.

BOOKS THAT MATTER

This venture in international publishing
has been prepared in its English version
with the assistance of
James Cleugh, Stuart Hood,
Peter Gorge and Beatrice Musgrave
under the supervision of
Olive Cook and the Editorial Staff of Thames and Hudson, London

The original German edition
was published by
Georg Westermann Verlag, Brunswick,
with contributions by
Dr Bert Bilzer, Director of the Brunswick Museum,
Dr Jürgen Eyssen, Director of the Municipal Library, Gelsenkirchen,
and Dr Otto Stelzer, Professor at the Academy of Art, Hamburg

Published in the United States of America in 1958
by Frederick A. Praeger, Inc., Publishers
15 West 47th Street, New York, N.Y.
All rights reserved
Library of Congress catalog card number: 58-11404

© 1958 by Georg Westermann Verlag, Brunswick, Western Germany
PRINTED BY GEORG WESTERMANN VERLAG, BRUNSWICK, WESTERN GERMANY

Contents

How to use the Encyclopædia

The work, as can be seen from the Contents, is divided into eight parts. The first is a general introduction dealing with the nature of art, its forms and styles. This is followed by six sections on the great periods, Antiquity, the Middle Ages, the Renaissance, Baroque and Rococo, the 19th and the 20th century, and a final section on Art outside Europe. Each section opens with a survey of the period covered, the sources of its forms and the historical background and is followed by a comprehensive glossary of technical terms, artists and their works, movements in art, etc. An extensive easy-reference index covers every subject dealt with in both the narrative texts and the sectional glossaries, besides providing additional short self-contained entries.

Art – its Nature, Forms and History

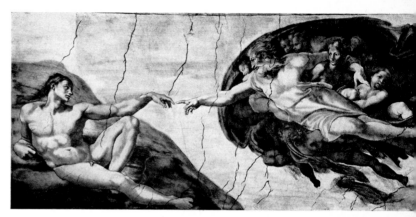

1. MICHELANGELO, *The Creation of Man, ceiling painting in the Sistine Chapel, Vatican, Rome*

It is DIFFICULT to define art in a single sentence. Its aim is to express emotions, experiences and ideas that are beyond the reach of language. There would probably be no painters or sculptors if everything they wished to say could be conveyed in a few well-chosen words. If art, then, is entirely concerned with what cannot be expounded, how can we define its true character? Language can do no more than circle around the kernel of the problem. Nevertheless, there has been no lack of attempts at explanation from Antiquity to modern times.

Medieval thinkers based their interpretation of art on the philosophy of Plato and St Augustine. For them, this meant that there should be a harmonious relationship between the part and the whole. There was no question of the imitation of Nature in either the theory or the practice of art. Such ideas did not come to the fore until the Renaissance, when art was made to reflect man's newly-awakened sensuous approach to the natural world about him. The copying of Nature – based on the philosophy of Plato's pupil Aristotle – has continued in favour up to the present day and prevents many people from having access to wide realms of creative art. It was an entirely misleading theory, which could not truly widen the art of Classical Antiquity or even that of the Renaissance; it was strongly opposed by the protagonists of the Romantic Movement (c. 1800), who rightly maintained that artistic creation depended on the imagination and that the latter was not required for the mere copying of Nature. Nineteenth-century naturalism was, it is true, once again less interested in imagination, and Zola's famous dictum that art was 'Nature seen through the individual temperament' gained ground everywhere. But here the individuality of the artist is at least allowed to inform his work, even though its purpose is still to mirror Nature.

None of these explanations is completely right or completely wrong; each is only a half-truth and can at most characterize the art of a certain epoch; they do not explain the phenomenon of 'art' itself. If we survey the field of creative art, we see at once that, besides the artist who 'forms', there must be substance which can be given form. The raw material – the sculptor's block of marble, the artist's paints, the mason's load of stone – has to be brought to life. A wooden building of necessity differs from one made of ferro-concrete. A rigid Egyptian statue owes its form to granite and basalt just as the Gothic Madonna owes

7

hers to the grain of the wood. The impact made by a fresco derives not only from the painter's skill and purpose, but also from the medium he uses. Primitive art – and modern art, too, when it tries to get to the roots of primitive creation – shows that art begins with the very experience of the material. A beautiful piece of stone or wood engenders inspiration.

We must remember that the theme is as much 'material' for the artist as is the clay, wood or stone. The theme must likewise be brought to life; it, too, must receive form. Its individual components must be integrated into an organic whole. A lump of clay is no entity, but merely part of an amorphous mass. A landscape, likewise, is merely the sum total of its part. A work of art is more than this – it possesses a 'wholeness' of its own. To help us understand such a philosophy of art, we might turn to the constellations of the heavens: add one to the seven stars of the Great Bear, or take one away, and the entire effect would be altered, so rhythmically and tellingly are they grouped.

In the same way, those who look at a work of art should receive the impression that there is neither too much nor too little, that everything is in its appointed place. A work of art must stand up to this test, whether it is large or small, monumental or intimate, impetuous or calm, naturalistic or abstract. In this respect, each true work of art possesses the quality of perfection. Goethe explained how this is possible, even though the artist himself is, like all men, imperfect. The miracle of a work of art, he says, can be compared to the miracle of procreation: just as a child can be greater than its parents, so the work of art – the child of the world outside the artist and of the world within him – can be greater than both.

But what of the actual subject-matter which the majority of sculptures and paintings seek to portray? What of their content? Is this of secondary importance? Certainly not – although we cannot insist that, as a matter of principle, there be a 'subject'. Architecture, one of the noblest of the arts, has no need to imitate anything in Nature. Nevertheless, a specific object can play a very important part in art, for it, together with the theme, often provides the impetus for creative activity by firing the artist's imagination. To those who look at a picture, furthermore, it serves as a bridge that leads them to the work of art. But if the beholder goes no farther and imagines that it is enough to be absorbed in the 'subject' alone, he has merely entered the forecourt of art's temple. We need not be artists to be able to portray an object with pencil or brush; anybody can do that more or less adequately. Art begins only when we can perceive the realm of pure form beyond the outward manifestation, and only those who pay as much attention to the interpretation as to the object portrayed will truly understand a work of art.

STYLES IN ART

Art is as old as mankind. It is present in all stages of civilisation throughout the world. It no more stands still than does Nature, which is constantly in a state of flux. Its face, down the ages, changes with the generations of men. It is the function of the history of art to elucidate these changes.

The writing of history must be more than a listing of consecutive events. It should distinguish important happenings from those of less significance, if it is to give a true and balanced picture. Likewise, the art historian must not only trace and record the works of art of all periods, but also classify them. Since art as an expression of the human consciousness is manifestly linked with the great cultural movements of an era, its designations are derived from the main epochs into which world history is divided. We refer to the art of Antiquity, of the Middle Ages, of the Renaissance and of the Modern Age. This is a very broad classification, but it is still valid. The decline of ancient Greece and Rome and the beginning of a new age between the time of the Barbarian Invasions and Charlemagne can be traced as clearly in art as in other fields. Again, the changes that took place in art during the Renaissance, around 1500, marked the end of the Middle Ages as clearly as did the discovery of the New World and the Reformation.

Variety of artistic 'handwriting' shows up the distinctive
characters of the artists. (Individual style)

But such simplifications also have their drawbacks. Recorded history goes no farther back than the
written word; everything prior to that belongs to prehistory. Civilisations that did not leave written
records used to be overlooked. But the inception of writing is quite independent of the existence of art.
Gradually, the art of prehistoric times has been brought to light by the spades of the archaeologists.
Civilisations that were ignored by historians because they left no writings – such as those of Africa and
Ancient America, the South Seas and the Polar Regions – produced their own characteristic art styles,
and the study of these has contributed much to the development of art today. It is also a mistake to
consider the art of Antiquity – that of Egypt, Crete and Mesopotamia, of Ancient Greece and Rome –
as merely a preliminary stage of medieval art. Nor must we forget the contribution made by the true
racial forebears of medieval Europe – the Saxons, Celts and Illyrians. The art of the Middle Ages seems
retrogressive compared with that of Ancient Greece; in relation to the prehistoric art of its own region,
however, it shows a progressive, organic development. To ignore European prehistoric art is to suggest
that the Middle Ages had no childhood or youth.

The art historian of today must consider all the cultural areas of the globe in relation to each other.
Although influences from other civilisations can frequently be recognised – particularly if they coincide
with a certain development – each area has yet a character of its own. European art is immediately
distinguishable from the no less rich art of the Far East; for that matter, the art of Western Europe is
quite distinct from that of Eastern Europe. The Byzantine influence, emanating from Constantinople,
extended over the Balkan countries and Russia, and lasted until well into the 19th century. Although
there is nothing in the history books to suggest that Europe was ever a cultural entity, the study of art
clearly shows how the transition from the Romanesque to the Gothic, from Renaissance to Baroque and
thence to modern art was experienced in common by all the nations of Europe.

Art is such a delicate instrument that it can **register** still slighter gradations. Despite certain obvious
traits that they possess in common, the different European nations have their own national styles. French
Gothic differs from Gothic in England, Germany or Italy. The expert can without difficulty discover

9

much finer distinctions. He can tell whether a Madonna of about 1500 was made in northern or southern Germany, and he can also readily distinguish between a drawing by Dürer and one by Grünewald (ill. 2, 3). He recognises the artist as the smallest unit in the moulding of a particular period style.

But this question of style goes farther than that. When the question is put to us, 'What style is that?', we tend to think in terms, not of a specific artist or even a particular country, but of the period that gave rise to the work in question. A national or an individual style is determined by certain constant factors. We recognise a master because of something changeless in him, even though an early work will differ from the product of his maturity. The concept of a period style, however, is based on the idea of change. Nobody will speak of an 'early German' or a 'late German' style – but of different phases of Gothic art. True, the arts of some other cultural regions have not tended to alter so much as those of Europe. Egyptian art shows comparatively few changes; certain aspects of Byzantine art, too, altered very little between the 14th century and the 19th. European art, on the other hand, is ever ready to swing from one contrast to the next – it would seem that change is in its very nature.

The Early Christian centuries occupy a key position between the classical and medieval periods. During the 3rd and 4th centuries the Christians began to adapt classical art to their purposes. The earliest works of art were produced in a pagan environment, and their style naturally derived from that of coeval pagan art. But it contained new elements which were soon to develop into a transcendental, abstract style, thus foreshadowing the tendencies of the medieval period. There is often, for instance, a significant neglect of the third dimension and a lack of individuality in the rendering of faces. These characteristics were developed to an extreme in the solemn, unyielding art of 6th-century Byzantium, though Byzantine art, too, exhibited a duality of styles, the hieratic and the classical. Carolingian art (8th and 9th centuries) gave fresh life to late antique forms, transplanting them to the North and merging them with native, Northern, purely abstract traditions. In this way the Carolingian epoch became the basis for the entire post-antique development of style in European art.

The Carolingian style was international, but after the break-up of Charlemagne's empire individual countries began to evolve styles of their own. Ottonian art (10th and early 11th centuries) is characterized by a rather rigid, monumental style which is quite different from that of contemporary France, England, Italy and Spain, although all stem from Carolingian example. English art at that time entered upon one of the most important phases of its history. The foremost place in the art of the Saxon period is perhaps occupied by the Winchester school of painting, which shows an entirely original relationship between figures and ornament, a remarkable fusion of abstract and classical tendencies in a new expressionist style.

The Romanesque style of the 11th and 12th centuries was, above all, an architectural style and marked the beginning of the great medieval building period all over Europe. It represented a complete break-away from dependence on antique models and was accompanied by sculptural decoration on a large scale. It was a monumental style in which all forms were reduced to their simplest elements. The country which more than any other contributed to the clarification and systematic organisation of the Romanesque was France. Though the style varied in different countries, it was, like the Carolingian, international.

The Gothic style (12th to 15th centuries) has a more dynamic character. Diagonal lines and oblique views replace the 'frontal' treatment. Solid masses are broken up and a sense of space is introduced; there is attenuation, particularly in the upward direction, suggesting a desire to counteract the force of gravity.

The Renaissance (c. 1500) seeks to offset this effect of restlessness and dispersal. But the compensatory period of restraint did not last very long. A rigid monumentality was as alien to the Renaissance as it was to the late Gothic. Whereas medieval art was symbolic and 'removed from life', the Renaissance artists now imbued it with their experience of the world about them. The effort to render natural appear-

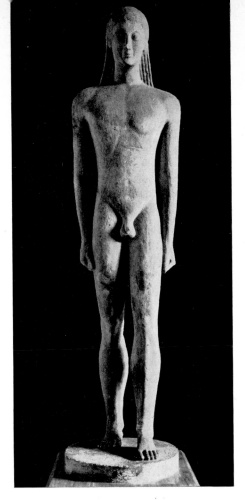

4. *Greek Archaic: Kouros of Melos (6th cent. B.C.)*

5. *Greek Classic: Spear-thrower of Polycleitus (5th cent. B.C.)*

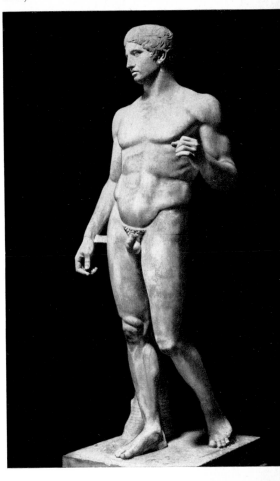

The four pictures show the stylistic evolution of a civilisation from the simple and severe archaic phase through harmonious and balanced classicism to the animated richness of form resulting from a 'baroque' interpretation, and finally to a heightened naturalism, which does not shrink from depicting what is ugly

6. *Greek 'baroque': Nike of Samothrace (c. 180 B.C.)*

7. *Hellenistic naturalism: old market-woman (1st cent. B.C., found in Rome)*

ances, which ended with the decadent photographic realism of the 19th century, had its roots in the Renaissance. But soon there is once more a reaction against this 'classical' phase. The Mannerism of the late Renaissance (second half of the 16th century) already anticipates Baroque art. Forms were interpreted in an ingenious but somewhat convoluted manner.

Baroque art proper (17th and 18th centuries) introduces new movement after the restraint and balance of the Renaissance. But the new dynamism cannot be compared to that of Gothic; the latter rarefied and spiritualised, whereas Baroque emphasises and elaborates, form. It exalts bodily vigour and manages to combine a down-to-earth forcefulness with mystical elements, thereby achieving a certain urgency and impact.

The forcefulness of Baroque art was transformed into grace and a frivolous light-heartedness during the Rococo period. The forms have become very intricate, and thus point to the end of a long process of development. The neo-classic Greek Revival (c. 1800) has all the signs of a spent force, insofar as original architecture ceased to exist. Greek and Roman forms at first continue to be used by capable architects and are still interpreted with a certain vigour, but the eclecticism of the 19th century soon reduced all architecture to an imitation of the antique past. Since style means harmony between the life of the mind and physical existence, and seeing that the human beings of the early machine age could have little in common with the men who built the Pitti Palace or with the Court of Louis XIV, it is hardly surprising that this period of masquerading has no longer any individuality of style. Painting alone made one significant further advance. Impressionism, developing out of the naturalism of the 19th century, produced landscapes that captured light and atmosphere as they are revealed only in fleeting moments. But Impressionism also laid the foundation of the abstract painting of our own times.

It needed the modern art of the 20th century to produce once more a new and characteristic style of architecture. Thanks to the new materials and their potentialities, present-day buildings are quite unlike those of any previous era. Painters and sculptors, what is more, go about their work as if painting and sculpture were something entirely novel. It is not unlike the earliest days of art when all manner of new forms of expression were allowed to evolve naturally from the chosen media. Such daring experiments undoubtedly resulted from a desire to explore virgin territory.

Such a brief and simplified description of the changes that have taken place over the years suggest – not for the first time – that there may be a law of evolution in art corresponding to that which has been found to occur in Nature. This view was strengthened when the same type of rhythm was found to exist in prehistoric art as in that of Ancient Greece and Rome.

Ancient Greek art began between the 8th and 6th centuries B.C. with the so-called archaic phase. The term archaic is now used for the early stages of various cultures, though strictly speaking it should be applied only to Greece. The next phase in Greek art was the classic (5th and 4th centuries B.C.), and this was followed by a development which is now often termed 'baroque'. Finally, we have the Hellenistic phase (4th century B.C. to the Birth of Christ), and a closing phase not altogether unlike the art of the 19th century (ill. 4–7). It betrays strong naturalistic trends; indeed, the painting of that time has sometimes been labelled 'impressionistic'. At the end of this development a repetition of archaic forms can be noticed, resembling the eclecticism of the 19th century. Even the poetry of earlier centuries was imitated in the 2nd century A. D.

Nevertheless, the great differences between the art of Antiquity and that of Western Europe show how much freedom can be exercised even within the bounds of the 'laws of natural development'. Classical Greek art was to dominate the art of the Christian West – with the notable exception of Italy – for a very short time only, during the Renaissance. The culture of Northern and Western Europe is expressed much more aptly by the Gothic. There could scarcely be a greater difference than that between the Greek temple and the Gothic cathedral.

12

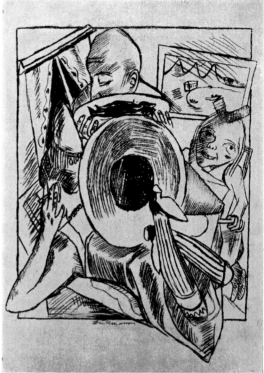

It is difficult to believe that both these lithographs are by the same artist. They demonstrate the evolution from an 'impressionist' early style to Expressionism

8. MAX BECKMANN, *David and Bathsheba (1911)*

9. MAX BECKMANN, *'Woman with gramophone' (1920)*

Where does such a study of the evolution of styles lead us? It opens our eyes to the relationship of works of art to their period, of the artist to his work. It also shows the influences of the various periods upon buildings that it took many decades to complete. The expert can place a work of art, and he can group anonymous works according to different schools and masters. He is also able to identify fakes. But all this is by no means simple, since an artist frequently goes through many stages in his development. Would two plays as different as *Hamlet* and *As You Like It* really both be attributed to Shakespeare had we not been told that he was the author of each? This applies, too, to painters such as El Greco, Goya, Turner, Beckmann, Picasso and many others (ill. 8, 9).

But stylistic criteria alone do not bring us any closer to the true nature of a work of art. An artist's work can only be understood if we open our minds as well as our eyes. We must take this further step without prejudice, and we can achieve the desired end without possessing any specialist knowledge. All the same, it has been proved over and over again that understanding will be all the greater if we know something about a work of art before we look at it. The connoisseur truly appreciates works of art.

FORMS OF ART

We can speak of Art and of the Arts. Art as a concept exists only in the realm of the mind. When it enters the world of the senses a 'work of art' results. It can be three-dimensional, as in sculpture and architecture, or two-dimensional, as in painting and drawing. Additionally, there are music and poetry, whose 'dimension' is time. The arts can further be divided into those that appeal to the eye and the sense of touch, and those that appeal to the ear. Only the former concern us here.

13

Sculpture, painting and the crafts have existed since the earliest days of mankind; architecture as such dates back to the ancient civilisations, such as that of Egypt. The term 'mother of the arts', though often applied to architecture, is therefore not accurate in the sense that architecture gave birth to sculpture and painting; it is only justified to the extent that architecture, when it did finally come upon the scene, took sculpture and painting under its wing and nursed them as a mother nurses her children. Then it was that the sculptural treatment of buildings and wall painting became art forms in their own right.

SCULPTURE

In its simplest form, sculpture requires nothing other than clay. It can most readily be 'grasped', in the literal as well as the metaphorical sense. Sculpture is the art of the sense of touch. When Michelangelo was nearly blind, it is said, he asked to be led to the statue of the Apollo of Belvedere so that he could feel the form with his hands. Sightless Helen Keller frequented the workshops of sculptors to enable her to 'grasp' art in this dual sense. The modern sculptor Brancusi made a statue which he called 'Sculpture for the Blind'. The sculptor of Classical Antiquity worked in such a way that the eye was always controlled by the sense of touch. Only during periods of decadence was this principle discarded. A blind man would not recognise as an 'eye' the jagged socket in a head by Rodin – merely proving that Rodin's work belongs to a peripheral region of sculpture (ill. 10, 11).

Objects meant to be apprehended by touch must have form. When sculpture is in the round we can not only feel it, but we can walk around it. The eye perceives surfaces only. We receive an impression of space through seeing with both eyes, but not an impression of plasticity. If we imagine that we see something three-dimensional (in a shadow, for example), we are actually doing no more than drawing a logical conclusion. We need to walk round a statue in order to derive the fullest enjoyment from it.

All those who have ever picked up a stone on the beach and have held it lovingly in their hands share this three-dimensional experience. So powerful is it that it has led men to build the pyramids in the desert, the huge funeral mounds of the Bronze Age on the Continent of Europe and Stonehenge on Salisbury Plain.

10. Apollo of Belvedere (detail)

In sharp contrast to 'classic' sculpture with its clear, smooth outlines, Rodin's statue, in which the contours are fused, produces an almost painterly effect

11. RODIN, Victor Hugo (detail)

12. Egyptian obelisk in the form of a pointed pyramid (Temple of Amun in Karnak, 16th cent. B.C.)

13. Menhir of Carnac/Brittany ('Abstract stone pillar')

14. Figural stele from Colombia

The 'abstract' stone monolith (menhir) is older than the carved totem pole and proves that monumental sculpture was not inspired by the desire to imitate. The obelisks of Ancient Egypt, the stelae of Peru, the stambhas of India, the Druid stones of Western Europe and even our present-day tombs (ill. 12–14) are all essentially non-representational. When men sought a fuller means of expression, they turned to the human body as the most rewarding motif. No object, and indeed no animal, offers so great a wealth of detail and so much harmony as the nude human form. The round shape of the head, the curves of the muscles, the finely differentiated areas of the back and the flanks, the long narrow arms and legs and the fine tapering fingers provide the artist with unlimited opportunities. At periods when the emphasis was on the spiritual and abstract, the clothed figure was preferred. Thus, medieval sculpture showed superb mastery in the treatment of draperies, though these bore little relation to natural ones.

Until recently it was considered that the task of the visual arts was to accentuate the three-dimensional quality of every object. This can be achieved, for example, by endowing the human figure with even greater rigidity than it normally possesses, whereby it appears stronger and more dignified – as in all Egyptian and archaic sculpture. But the tendency towards greater mobility is ever present. The three-dimensional effect can also be heightened by impelling the beholder to walk round the figure. This the symmetrical Egyptian statues do not do; their very symmetry offers us no encouragement to look from the left when we have already done so from the right.

The Greeks introduced a new feature in Classical times. The legs were made to take up different positions, thereby also causing the shoulders to vary in height. The profile, too, became less rigid. We feel more than ever compelled to walk round a figure if the body is given a bent or twisted posture. Michelangelo's statues are often unnaturally contorted, but they reveal to us the most extraordinary wealth of forms, providing us again and again with entirely unexpected aspects.

Modern sculpture is no longer concerned with the naturalistic representation of the human form, for similar reasons. We know it so well that we can guess what a figure will look like once we have seen it from the front, and this deters many people from walking round a statue. But this does not apply when naturalism has been discarded – as, for example, in Henry Moore's 'Reclining Figure' (ill. 15–17).

15

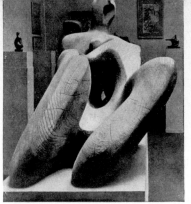

15–17. Henry Moore, *'Reclining Figure' from three different angles*

By walking round this statue, we are vouchsafed a series of impressions such as we should never get from a more orthodox piece of sculpture. The versatility, and hence the vitality, of a work of art thus create a tremendous impact. This is increased further by making use of enclosed spaces and hollows.

Thus, the wide realm of sculpture is seen to extend from serene and monumental calm to a dramatic dynamism. It can even achieve a playful elegance, if the right materials are chosen and they are appropriately handled.

There are two basically different methods of producing sculpture – modelling and carving. It is possible to model without any tools by shaping the malleable material, such as clay, wax and so on, with the hands. But a simple clay figure would very soon warp and disintegrate. It is therefore fired, or a casting (q. v.) is made in a tougher material like plaster, cement and above all, metal (bronze).

A large clay figure cannot be fired if it is solid; that is to say, it has to be sectioned, hollowed out and assembled again. Another and better method is that which was used by the potter before the invention of the wheel. Strips of clay are rolled out and then, by placing one coil upon another and working them together with the fingers, a hollow figure is gradually shaped. It is then ready to be fired. Such figures acquire an even, reddish colour. The fired material is called terra-cotta.

The majority of clay figures are, however, made differently. Statues with delicate limbs and flowing outlines need a wire frame. The clay is put on the frame in small lumps and the form grows as material is added.

Most of the models for bronze statues are made that way. The malleable metal allows a fluidity that could never be attained in the more brittle stone.

Sculpture is sometimes made by beating the metal instead of casting it. The shape is hammered out of a sheet of metal from the inside. This process was very popular for small figures and reliefs in medieval times. Occasionally it was also used for larger statues.

In contrast to modelling, where the desired shape is achieved by adding material, in stone or wood sculpture, and in ivory or alabaster carving, it is arrived at by removing material. If the artist makes a mistake and takes off very much more than he wanted to, he must change his plan and make his 'mistake' the point of departure for a new design. Carving is therefore more arduous than modelling, but at the same time a greater artistic 'adventure'. Stone-carving calls for large-scale and 'four-square' designs since the material is not conducive to fluid outlines. The wood carver, on his part, has to consider the grain of the wood because he cannot cut against it. Shapes projecting at right-angles from the main line of growth, such as outstretched arms, are not possible – they would break off. But if wood is carved with the grain, forms and designs of great delicacy and variety can be produced, as witness the drapery of Gothic sculptures in this material. Bone and ivory are carved in the same way as wood, but there is no grain to be considered. The limits are set entirely by size – large pieces being obviously not available (ill. 18–19).

All these materials are suitable not only for sculpture in the round but also for carving in relief. Whereas sculpture in the round makes the very most of three-dimensioned actuality, the relief plays it down. Yet the relief offers special opportunities of its own, for, in that it approaches the realm of painting, it enables the artist to introduce scenic and dramatic elements. Sculpture in the round must of necessity give preference to the single figure. The relief, by contrast, calls for a series of figures since its surface can be brought to life most effectively that way. Of course, individual figures and portrait busts are sometimes carved in relief, but these do not do full justice to the technique. 'The essence of a relief', in Rodin's words, 'is the procession.'

This applies literally to most historical reliefs, from the Egyptians' representations of sacrifices, the Babylonian animal reliefs, the battle scenes on the Parthenon and the Roman triumphal columns to the rows of the blessed and the damned in medieval cathedrals. The temptation to work in three dimensions and to tell a story at the same time is so great that most sculpture is virtually relief-carving.

The relief palpably shows how much it owes its origin to the two-dimensional arts. It began as a drawing. If the area within the outlines of a figure is hollowed out, we obtain the incised relief of the Egyptians. If we do this also with the areas between the figures, we get a flat surface from which just the outlines stand out. The relief has gone through various other stages, from bas-relief to high relief. The latter comes close to sculpture in the true sense, even though the figures are still attached to their background (ill. 20–25).

18. The Virgin from an Annunciation group in Regensburg (c. 1300). The wood-carver's work is conditioned by the grain of the wood. By following the grain he can achieve appreciably finer modelling than can the sculptor in stone

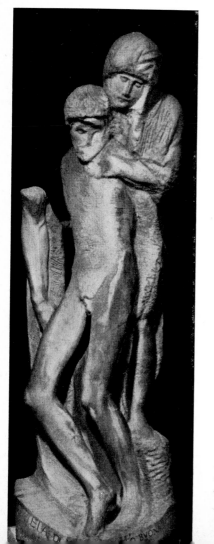

19. MICHELANGELO, *Pietà Rondanini. The disconnected arm from an earlier design is evidence of a complete change of plan while the artist was carving this marble sculpture – one of the most moving works of Michelangelo's old age*

20. *Incised relief: Queen Hatshepsut from obelisk in Karnak (16th cent. B.C.)*

21. *Flat relief: Hornhausen Equestrian Group (Germanic rhinestone, 7th cent. B.C.)*

22. *High relief: metope from Temple of Zeus in Olympia (c. 460 B.C.)*

23. *Spacial relief: Last Supper from the west choir-screen of Naumburg Cathedral (c. 1260)*

24. *Relief with depth through perspective, i. e. using painterly resources:* GHIBERTI, *section of the 'Paradise Gateway' of the Baptistery in Florence (15th cent.)*

25. *Modern relief, which seeks to achieve a new formal simplicity by combining shallow and deep incised lines with flat relief:* KURT LEHMANN, *'Woman resting' (1953)*

THE CRAFTS

Crafts have a certain amount in common with sculpture. Their products are also three-dimensional; indeed, they are often made by exactly the same process as a statue. A clay vessel such as a Greek amphora differs from a statue only in that it can be put to practical use. A candelabra, a brooch and the handle of a sword virtually represent sculpture in the round: a carved door, a carved rood screen and an embossed binding are all examples of relief work. Chests and cupboards, for their part, are closely related to architecture, whilst medieval reliquary shrines constitute miniature churches. Wallpaper, all types of weaving, and lace work belong to the realm of painting, although the processes are different. This also applies to commercial art (q. v.).

We can now see why the so-called applied arts cannot be considered as falling into a separate category; they are invariably linked to sculpture, architecture and painting. Indeed, the division into pure and applied art is as recent as the last century when the crafts were rapidly declining. In earlier times we find no such distinction; Renaissance artists such as Leonardo, Dürer, Verrocchio and Cellini thought it natural to design all manner of things. After all, architecture is strictly speaking an 'applied art', since it has a function.

The problem of distinguishing between an art and a craft presents itself in a different light today. We do not consider that function necessarily excludes or diminishes aesthetic value. Many present-day embroideries and tapestries are hung in frames and treated like paintings (ill. p. 100). But we must also ask ourselves what it is that makes a mere tool a potential work of art. The answer is that beauty should be added to utility. An article or implement does not have to be painted or covered with ornament. A good shape is sufficient for a vessel; ornament, if excessive or applied at the wrong places, often detracts from a vase's beauty and can even destroy it if it is contrary to the laws of form. An object does not become a work of art unless form and ornament supplement one another. Ornament must not only decorate, as the name suggests ('ornare'

26. *Corded beaker from Rathmannsdorf. In this Early Stone Age vessel, no less than in the Baroque Danzig cupboard (ill. 27) of 400 years later, the artistic construction and conformation are enhanced by the use of ornament*

means to decorate), it also has to interpret, and heighten the effect of, the object itself. The horizontal lines on Stone Age pottery stress the shape of a vessel's rim, the vertical lines that of the stem (ill. 26).

The interaction of ornament and form is most obvious in tattooing and personal adornments. A necklace does not merely adorn; by enclosing the neck it stresses its curves and demarcates the head from the body. If it hangs upon the breast it draws attention to man's upright posture. Such decoration would be meaningless in an animal. Tattooing, where it still has its roots in native art, also underlines the body's basic build. It is sometimes done in such a way as virtually to reproduce the skeleton on the skin, thus harmonizing with the anatomical structure.

These principles apply broadly to most objects of everyday life. A Dutch wardrobe, a Danzig cupboard (ill. 27) or a Jacobean court cupboard is certainly lavishly decorated. But the ornament is determined by the basic structure, it merely lends greater emphasis to the different parts. A carpet has usually no naturalistic decoration because it would be absurd to invite people to walk about on scenery, or tread upon human figures. The pattern is usually symmetrically arranged, so that we can enjoy much the same aspect from every corner of the room. Anything else would merely induce a feeling of unrest and would make the house uninhabitable. For a similar reason, wallpapers are usually based on repetition of the same motif.

Thus, function very often determines the artist's approach. As long as this is recognised, a harmonious work is likely to result.

ARCHITECTURE

All these considerations are of such importance because, without them, we cannot do justice to the greatest of the functional arts, the art of building, known as architecture.

Since we could include a shed, a pig-sty or a prison (buildings no one will class as art) under the broad heading of architecture, we must ask ourselves what makes architecture an art. The answer is exactly the same as in the case of the crafts. It is a matter of telling disposition, the ordering of space, mass and planes. Man has a sense of proportion. Proportions can be expressed in numbers, and many great architects from the earliest times to the present day have based their designs on geometry. But only the artist knows what form of construction to use in any given circumstances. Relative proportions also vary with the spirit of the times. Although man is always taken as the measure of architecture, this does not mean that the scale of a building must be commensurate with the human figure. Some buildings are designed to make man feel his smallness and insignificance. Architecture may aim to preserve bulk and monumentality, as in Romanesque art, or it may combat the solidity of the walls and make them 'dissolve', as in the Gothic cathedrals. The architect may emphasise and separate supporting and buttressing components, but he may also integrate them. As in all the arts, everything will depend on the particular cultural level attained. Unlike other works of art, buildings are monuments to an epoch rather than expressions of individual aspiration. Architecture is essentially directed towards the greater public.

28. Karnak, Grand Temple of Amon (c. 1250 B.C.)

29. Cordova, mosque (9th/10th cent.)

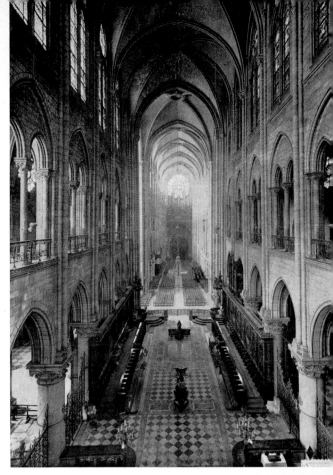

30. Paris, Notre Dame (13th cent.)

31. St. Gallen, collegiate church (18th cent.)

The architecture of a civilisation depends substantially upon the appreciation of space possessed by its people. The massiveness and weight of the Egyptian 'forest of columns' points to a more developed plastic than spacial sense. The mosque at Cordova is admittedly articulated spacially through its numerous pillars and arches, but achieves no over-all spacial unity. By contrast, the starting-point of Gothic architecture is an upward-ranging interior space, while Baroque achieves an effect of endlessly broadening vistas by means of clever lighting and making the walls seem to recede by means of paintings

21

Architecture has much in common with sculpture. Both favour stone, wood and clay. Even ferro-concrete has its antecedent in the iron-framed plaster cast of the sculptor. A column or pillar ranks as a piece of sculpture where it appears on its own – as sometimes happens. Earlier wooden or stone buildings are unthinkable without the work of the sculptor or the wood-carver, even when they are not decorated with actual figures. The architect in the modern sense of one who is only concerned with the structure and so-called conveniences of a building is a product of our age. Most of the early architects were mason-sculptors.

Monumental architecture does not appear amongst the more primitive civilisations although other art forms are often very well represented. Architecture demands an advanced stage of awareness, an ability not only to visualize but to benefit by experience – both conscious and subconscious. It does not appeal to the eye alone. Rooms need walking through and looking at from different vantage points – recourse to what might be called a 'sense of movement'. A sense of distance – even of sound (echoing halls) – matters as much as the sense of gravity.

Early architecture was conceived in terms of volume rather than of space. A veritable forest of pillars crowds the interior of Egyptian temples. The impressive columns of a Greek temple contrast markedly with the very modest hall, the cella; but in the Gothic cathedral the point of departure is the interior space, which the whole complicated system of supports and buttresses is there to serve. (Ill. 28–31)

The doors and windows of an ordinary house are obviously indispensable for daily use. Though they are functional, their proportions and disposition can be such as to result in an artistic design. Rows of windows one above the other, usually – but by no means always (Inigo Jones' Banqueting Hall in Whitehall) – indicate that a building has several storeys. This inner ordering can be made still more apparent from the outside by adding continuous horizontal features – the cornices. The existence of such cornices sometimes indicates that the walls of a building are supporting ones, i. e., that they carry for their entire length the weight of the floors above. This need not always be the case. The roof in a wooden-framed building is carried by posts and the walls merely fill the space between these posts. The walls are usually made of wattle and daub, a mixture of twigs and clay. Obviously, such a wall is not there to support but merely to enclose.

Architecture thus falls into two groups: the building with a framework or skeleton, and the solid structure. Wooden buildings belong in the main to the first category (Norwegian stave churches, q. v.), though we also find solid structures built of logs. Stone buildings are most easily made with solid walls; the Gothic master-builders, however, contrived to achieve what were virtually frameworks of stone by the use of arches and flying buttresses. Not until the introduction of 'skeletal' structures in steel, concrete and glass, was it possible to dispense with such lateral supports. Solid structures are often designed in such a way as to register the distribution of weights and stresses, though this is to a certain extent symbolical. Thus, vertical components are often added to the cornices and architraves though, like pilasters, their purpose is not to carry weight. But once walls have received such additions by way of 'relief', there is a tendency to accentuate it. The vertical members are made progressively stronger until they become genuine supports, the walls recede and we witness the translation from a solid, to a frame, structure. (Cf. ill. 193–196)

The simplest piece of architecture consists of two posts with a beam across the top. When the building is of stone, the posts become columns or piers and the beam the architrave. When men first learned to build an arch upon two supports, they had discovered the secret of vaulting. The means had also been found to separate an interior into rooms without isolating these completely. This led to the colonnades of the great temples, the loggias on palaces and on patrician houses, and the *svalgang* of the Norwegian stave church. The interior can be divided into several aisles – in the case of a church, usually the nave and two aisles.

32. *Alternation of supporting members: St Michael's in Hildesheim (11th cent.)*

With such an 'open' division of the whole area the visitor can be induced to look in certain directions and even to proceed at a certain pace, merely by virtue of the way the columns have been disposed. Places for pausing – similar to the intervals in music – can also be achieved, mainly by placing a square pier after every second column, thereby introducing a rhythmic and harmonious design. But the design would be incomplete were one wall to be considered by itself. There is still another wall opposite, which has been similarly divided up. Responsive people will notice this association as they walk between these walls and thus become aware, not of two facing walls but of a series of rooms. Articulation of surfaces has, so to speak, led to articulation of space (ill. 32).

The integration of the interior area can be materially enhanced by special handling of the ceiling and roof zone. Thus, series of vaultings could be made to look like a row of canopies and so suggest movement (ill. 33). The cupola, on the other hand, which generally surmounts a central structure, gives such a building an appearance of great stability (ill. 34). Pillars, columns, ambulatories and recesses can all be used to advantage to achieve the desired effects.

To ring the changes on such designs is the architect's noblest task. The ancient Egyptians and the medieval church builders often set one hall at right angles to another. Again, a long narrow building may adjoin a central structure; they can even be merged to form an ellipse, as was done in the 17th and 18th centuries (ill. 35). An effect of contrast can be achieved with ceilings of different heights, whereby the light in different rooms is reduced or increased. Many 17th-century churches in Rome have brightly lit domes at the end of a long dark nave. The size and nature of the fenestration are undoubtedly of the greatest importance for spatial effect. But the architect must not rely too much on daylight alone, since his building will also be seen by artificial light.

It is only natural that the character of a building should be expressed in its façade. The façade often reveals the interior arrangement of a building, such as a church's cruciform plan. Not until the 19th century was the façade reduced to a mere disguise. There may be good reasons, however, for making

23

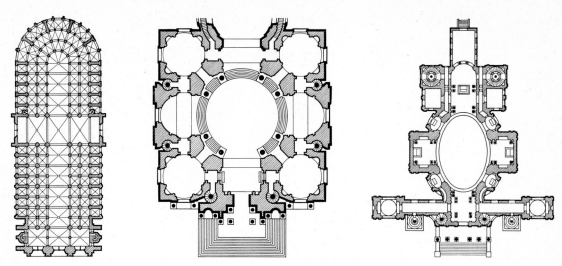

33. Ground-plan of an axial building: Notre Dame in Paris (12th/13th cent.) – 34. Ground-plan of a centrally planned building: cathedral of the Invalides in Paris (17th cent., arch. JULES HARDOUIN-MANSART) – 35. Combination of an axial and a centrally planned building: ground-plan of the Church of St Charles in Vienna (18th cent., arch. FISCHER VON ERLACH)

the exterior differ from the interior – for instance, to introduce contrast and thus heighten the over-all impression. A many-turretted building may harbour very modest rooms like small caves in a huge rock. The sober, indeed almost sombre, exteriors of South German churches of the 18th century often conceal interiors of overwhelming splendour.

It must be remembered that a building is frequently seen from a distance and its outward appearance should therefore not be determined by the interior requirements. Often, it may form part of its surroundings. The arts of gardening and landscape architecture go back to early times. Paths, streets, and avenues may be planned in such a way as to lead up to a building, and form part of the lay-out. The Ancient Egyptians grouped gateway, corridor, courtyard and pyramid so as to form an integrated architectural whole. This treatment came into its own after the Renaissance; it is still much in evidence in modern architecture, of which town planning has become a separate branch.

PAINTING

Monumental architecture influenced and stimulated all the other arts. The painter, no less than the sculptor, made his contribution. Coloured surfaces were indispensable to architecture for the reason that man craves for colour in his daily existence; mosaic work and glass windows were particularly well suited to this end.

But painting as such was soon introduced. Man's desire for colour goes back to prehistoric times. It even became the symbol of life, as several early myths show. Neanderthal man was buried with the ochre that he probably used on his own person. Before long, man was painting everything that would take colour. The walls of Greek and Egyptian temples, and Egyptian, Greek and medieval statues were all decorated with colours. Coloured pottery survives from the pre-dynastic age in China and from the earliest known Mexican civilisations, as well as from the so-called Hallstatt period. Such pottery shows that the sense of colour was already well developed. Although painted objects appeared before pictures, the latter are known to us from as early as the Ice Age and from early Mediterranean civilisations, particularly those of Crete, Greece and the Etruscans. There we find the fresco, the most important method of wall painting, which is still practised, and the now less frequently used encaustic technique (a form of painting with wax).

REMBRANDT: *Head of a Child. Detail from the* Family Portrait. — *Rembrandt's technique already shows the characteristics of 'pure' or 'absolute' painting which is not concerned with realism in details such as the child's dress but concentrates entirely on colour relationships and tone values*

JAN VERMEER OF DELFT: The Milk-maid. – *Vermeer knew how to combine, in the same picture, tonal unity with* **colour** *contrasts (complementary colours: yellow and blue, red and green) so that his paintings have a unique, luminous quality*

LEONARDO DA VINCI: Mona Lisa (La Gioconda). – *The 'sfumato' mist with which Leonardo veils his painting gives it its enigmatic attraction and is – by avoiding hard contours – the first step towards a purely painterly interpretation of the subject*

Lovis Corinth: Walchensee Landscape. – *The thickly-applied colours and clearly visible brush-strokes of 'impasto' painting give this artist his painterly style (colour rhythms in place of linear rhythms, breaking up of light)*

But there was an intermediate stage between mere colouring and true painting. It consisted in filling-in outlined areas with paint, and men contented themselves with this for centuries. Line and colour were placed on an equal footing. Colouring a carefully made drawing in this way led to the art of the medieval illuminator, who worked in water colours. Medieval panel paintings, in tempera, also lent themselves to this technique. Long after Dutch and Flemish painters of the 15th century had fully exploited the new invention of oil colours, German early 19th-century painters like Cornelius, Kaulbach and others reverted to the older method.

We speak of 'pure' painting where the composition is built up entirely of colour and is not based on a pattern of lines. The dress of the child in Rembrandt's 'Family Portrait' consists only of a series of carefully nuanced colours (ill. p. 25). This presupposes a very sure sense of the quality of colour, which is quite a different thing from mere intensity. Each colour of the spectrum has a certain degree of brilliance of its own which, quite apart from its intensity, can be expressed as a shade of grey. But individual colours also produce special effects. Thus, red seems closer to the eye than blue; it belongs to what we call the warm colours (red and yellow), as opposed to the cold colours (blue and green) which are more 'distant'.

True painting relies exclusively upon the qualities inherent in the paints, and does not depend on any other method of representation. Since the outline naturally follows the form of an object, its use introduces a sculptural element, which the 'pure' painter tries to avoid. With this end in view, Leonardo da Vinci invented *sfumato* (ill. p. 26). Its function is to make the picture appear as if a veil had been placed over it or as if it is enveloped in a mist, whereby all the outlines have become blurred and indefinite. An effect of a similar kind is achieved in 'tonal' painting where one basic colour tone is used. In Vermeer's case this was blue (ill. p. 27), whilst Rembrandt and other Flemish and Dutch painters used a golden brown. This basic tone suffuses all the other colours; it is either used as a 'ground' and shines through them, or is laid over them to form a last layer of colour.

But in 'tonal' painting the picture suffers from a lack of colour contrast. In an attempt to retain the full benefit of colour without confining it to clearly defined areas, painters devised a new method (ill. p. 28). The tools – brush or spatula – were used in such a way that they left clear traces on the surface and produced a rough relief-like effect. This notwithstanding, the picture acquires no sculptural attributes, because the depth of the paint has nothing to do with the shapes of the objects portrayed. The areas where it is most thickly applied correspond with the high-lights, and are apprehended by the eye only and not by the sense of touch. This technique was called impasto painting and has been widely used from Titian to the present day. The layman tends to regard it as an unnecessary 'messing about with paint', not realizing that this is the way to teach the eye to experience pure painting.

A heavy impasto can be produced only with oil colours. They also allow continuous over-painting, both in a wet and a dry state. Tempera painting, in which pure egg yolk usually takes the place of oil, is also highly suitable for over-painting, although it does not permit of the impasto technique to the same extent. Here the colour is often put on in many layers which extend from edge to edge of the picture. Tempera was always used in the fresco, the predecessor of oil painting. European painters used this technique until late in the 19th century. But most artists were no longer satisfied with the slow and gradual growth of a work from a rough ground to the final over-all colour layer. They liked to finish one area of a picture complete with detail, before proceeding to the next.

This *alla prima* technique is very suitable for water colours. Although water colours can be applied in layers and so produce what is known as a gouache, pure water colour is best used very thinly. The colour lets the light penetrate it, so that the white of the paper shines through. Since there is no white in water colour, the virgin paper must take its place wherever there are to be light effects. A tinted paper can be used to obtain a 'tonal' effect such as has already been described for oil painting. Using a damp paper causes the colours to merge and the outlines to disappear, and delightful effects can be obtained in this way. The fact that the white of the paper is used in water-colour painting gives it a certain kinship with drawing. It is for this reason that museums usually keep water colours and drawings in the same department, though this does not seem altogether justified, since a pure water colour differs greatly from a drawing. It does not even permit a preliminary pencil outline as this could not be erased, but would remain visible beneath the colour. Water colour painting should therefore be regarded as an independent art form.

Every painted picture leads us into realms where the laws are quite different from those that govern sculpture. Sculpture and architecture have substance. They are what they seem, they occupy space; whereas a painting has a certain intangibility, whether it be a landscape, a still-life or a portrait. Only the dabs of colour are real; everything else is illusion. A painting is as unreal as a reflection in a mirror.

In order to give depth to their pictures painters use perspective (ill. p. 37). It was discovered in Italy about 1400 and can be arrived at by mathematical means (converging lines). But it can also be produced by ranging colours. Brown tints in the foreground, green in the middle and blue at the back create a perspective which – being based on colour – is far more appropriate to pure painting. There are several other ways of conveying depth, such as the atmospheric perspective of the Chinese.

Modern art has discovered many other devices for creating the illusion of space, notably Cubism. It is not, after all, the function of painting to simulate at all costs space as we know it in nature, by means of an optical illusion. A public that seeks and admires such an effect in art is on the wrong track and is unlikely to discover the painter's real intention. Painting should aim rather at creating an ideal space, an archetypal space, that does not vitiate the quality of the plane. This idea cannot be expressed better than in the words of the German painter Max Beckmann: 'We must transfer the three-dimensional world of nature to the two-dimensional world of the canvas ... To transform three dimensions into two is a magic experience for me. In those moments I obtain a brief glimpse of the fourth dimension for which I yearn with all my being.' This fourth dimension is neither illusion nor reality but stands half-way between, and can only be made manifest through art.

DRAWING AND THE GRAPHIC ARTS

It is drawing, perhaps, – the art of the line – that shows most clearly to what an extent and how rapidly art grows beyond the mere representation of objective reality – how all its endeavours are directed towards transfiguring what occurs in nature. To draw means to 'abstract' from nature. Even the simplest drawing of a child – a little man composed of a few strokes – is essentially an abstraction. Any natural object comprises an entity with coloured surfaces, it never consists of mere lines. Without colour, drawing is removed further from nature than is painting. Birds may have pecked at painted grapes, as academicians used to tell, but they will never have pecked at the grapes in a drawing. In days gone by, therefore, men very rarely contented themselves with mere drawing. Cave drawings and the neat outlines on medieval manuscripts were not considered complete unless they were coloured.

Drawings are part of our everyday life, even if we ourselves have no artistic talent. A drawing is used to explain the plan of a house, the streets of a town. Such 'explanatory' drawings also play an important role in art, whether they are the sketches for a painting, for a statue or the plans of a building. Drawing has had this ancillary character for centuries. The drawings of the old masters are rightly called studies. The study was not recognised as a work of art in its own right until the 19th century, when sounding a genuinely original note was considered more important than conformity to the accepted pattern of the age. And, indeed, a rapid sketch has all the appearance of a spontaneous and personal expression of an artistic utterance; it often bears the same relationship to a finished painting as handwriting to copper-plate. The more rapidly the drawing is made, the livelier it appears.

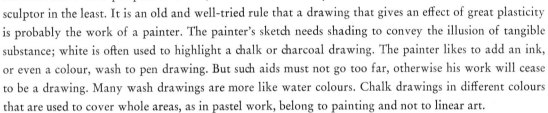

36. Silver-point drawing: RAPHAEL, *Self-portrait*

Even without colour, the potentialities of drawing are considerable. How great is the difference between the smooth line of a goose quill and the hard stroke of a reed pen, between the effects obtained by a wet brush dipped in ink – handled so skilfully by the Chinese and Japanese – and the almost dry brush used by the Greeks on their vases! There are also the various greys of the lead pencil and of the silver-point, chalks of all kinds and charcoal with its broad, crumbling strokes (ill. 36–40).

Indeed, linear art has many techniques at its disposal. The drawings of painters and sculptors are not hard to distinguish from one another. The sculptor is usually content with a close, clarifying outline and is little concerned about light and shade. These show up very much better in the statue. The painter quite justifiably wishes to obtain the effect of light and shade in a preliminary drawing. He must know how perspective works, which does not worry the sculptor in the least. It is an old and well-tried rule that a drawing that gives an effect of great plasticity is probably the work of a painter. The painter's sketch needs shading to convey the illusion of tangible substance; white is often used to highlight a chalk or charcoal drawing. The painter likes to add an ink, or even a colour, wash to pen drawing. But such aids must not go too far, otherwise his work will cease to be a drawing. Many wash drawings are more like water colours. Chalk drawings in different colours that are used to cover whole areas, as in pastel work, belong to painting and not to linear art.

Line can be incisive or undulating, it can be delicate or coarse, hesitant or firm, but it always expresses feelings and emotions. The eye can follow its course and so will retrace the movement of the artist's hand. The beholder can thus experience the artist's moment of insight and partake of the joy of his creation.

Although by the end of the 15th century the possibilities of pure drawing might seem to have been exhausted, further means of expression nevertheless were added to linear art. There is a great difference between drawing and the graphic arts. This distinction has unfortunately been somewhat obscured in recent years but experts consider the term 'graphic arts' to apply only to the art of the hand print (in contrast to the machine-produced print). This art did not have its source in aesthetics. Efforts to reproduce drawings on a large scale led to the invention of the woodcut (c. 1400, though the Chinese had already known it much earlier), the invention of copper engraving, followed by etching in its many forms and by lithography and other techniques (see Graphic Arts). Until the end of the 19th century all these methods had a commercial, rather than an artistic, character because there had been no other way of reproducing paintings or illustrating books before the invention of photography. Their function was to imitate art, as art imitated nature. But from the outset, genuine artists discovered the potentialities of the engraving and practised it as 'peintures graveurs'. No pen could produce the delicate line of the etching, the vigour of the woodcut. Soft ground etching (vernis mou), aquatint and lithography also had possibilities not inherent in the drawing. Indeed, their effect is very much closer to that of water colour.

31

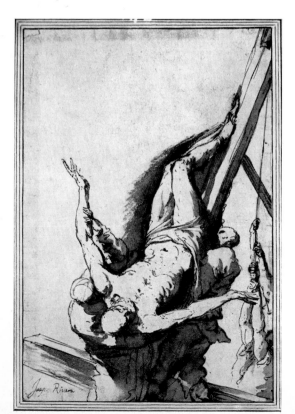

37. Pen and wash drawing: RIBERA, *Crucifixion*

38. Brush drawing: Chinese-Taoist roll-picture *39. Pencil drawing:* MARCKS, *Woman*

The print assumed increasing importance in the eyes of true artists from the time of the Renaissance onwards. This applies particularly to the graphic art of today, when to turn out large numbers of prints is no longer the aim. This is left to the photo-reproductive machine processes. Colour printing, in particular, has come to flourish as never before (ill. p. 38). The colour print of to-day demands the greatest economy, since at most seven plates – sometimes as few as three – are used. One is printed on top of the other. The colours therefore have to be distributed over large areas – a feature that also characterizes modern painting. Thus, the man-in-the-street is now able to possess works of art which can still be considered 'originals' even though several copies of any one picture may exist.

A print made by the artist himself and not by commissioned craftsmen clearly has great instrinsic value, since it bears the stamp of his individuality. Although an etching by Rembrandt may cost less on the open market than one of his paintings, it is no less important. Size, the costliness of the material and the time spent on it do not of themselves add up to a work of art, greatly as these may contribute to its market value. It calls for the exercise of the imagination, the courage to venture into new spheres – in brief, the creative spirit.

Art-lovers should bear these latter qualities in mind when looking at – still more, when judging – a work of art, for they lie at the heart of all artistic creation.

40. Reed pen drawing: VAN GOGH, *Sailing-boats*

ACADEMY. The word derives from a grove near Athens dedicated by the Ancient Greeks to the mythical hero Akademos, where Plato conversed with his pupils. The name was revived during the early Italian Renaissance in idealistic humanist circles, the most influential of which was the group gathered about Lorenzo de' Medici. The term academy was then used of any meeting of cultured and learned men to discuss the problems of science and philosophy. In the 16th century the word came to denote almost any regular gathering.

The earliest official academy of art was the Academia del Disegno founded by Vasari in 1563. Its immediate offspring was the Academia di San Luca in Rome (1593), the organization of which became the prototype of Lebrun's and Colbert's Académie Royale de Peinture et de Sculpture, founded in Paris in 1648. The latter, in turn, with its elaborate order of precedence, its mode of training, its artistic doctrines and its affiliate institution in Rome, was the model for similar enterprises throughout the 17th and 18th centuries.

From the beginning, these official academies differed from such private studio academies as that of Bandinelli (1531) and that of the Carracci in Bologna (c. 1590), by their wider aims and their higher pretensions. Their object was to raise the artist from the level of the medieval craftsman to that of the creator by freeing him from the jurisdiction of the guilds. In order to achieve this, the founders of the official academies usually invoked the protectorate of the reigning monarch, a course of action which often resulted in the subservience of the new academicians to the Crown.

The pedagogic aims of the academy were not much emphasised in the early foundations. The artist still received his elementary training in the workshop of his master and the academy attempted no more than to educate him to fulfil the demands of the grand manner. It was only at the beginning of the 19th century that the academies added instruction in the actual technique of painting to their classes in drawing – first after drawings, then after plaster casts and living models.

The conceptions of workshop and academy were united towards the end of the 19th century when schools of arts and crafts were founded, where not only sculpture, painting and architecture were taught, but also the crafts, typography, commercial art and industrial design. One of the most famous of all such schools in the present century was the Bauhaus (q. v.). The academies themselves, however, did not follow this trend, but persisted in educating artists in the grand manner. The battle between independent progressive artists and the academies fills the annals of the 19th century. Only now are the academies slowly beginning to renounce their tenets and coming to terms with contemporary modes of expression.

ACANTHUS. When objects were first shown in perspective in the art of Ancient Greece (c. 500 B.C.), the palmette also was represented in this manner, its edges apparently contracting. From about 460 B.C. onwards, this form was developed into the acanthus – an adaptation of the leaf of a plant, the Acanthus Mollis, – an ornament which found wide-spread use and became one of the characteristic features of the Corinthian style (ill. 62). The first known examples are on the interior columns of the temple of Apollo at Bassae (420 B.C.). In Roman architecture the acanthus leaves are larger, project farther and often are more deeply undercut, becoming a luxuriant growth. They appear on Byzantine and Romanesque capitals but the earlier exuberance has disappeared and the leaves are kept close to the block. The motif frequently occurs on Renaissance pilasters and borders, where curving tendrils are combined with the acanthus to form the popular rinceau pattern.

AEDICULA. A Latin word, meaning a small temple and used by the Romans to describe a recess for a statue. In medieval architecture, the term also refers to a private chapel. Art historians also use it for porches and any decorative features – standing against or forming part of the wall – where it consists of an architrave, gable or arch supported by columns. These forms have been used since the Renaissance for altar surrounds, funeral monuments and to emphasise windows and doors.

ALABASTER. This is a comparatively soft, crystalline stone varying in colour from white to pale yellow. It was used in Assyria both for small vessels and for large reliefs, but it is generally associated with its wide use in medieval Europe for monuments and retables. The employment of alabaster for these purposes originated in England during the second quarter of the 14th century. After the Black Death its popularity increased and it set the fashion for all other trades in religious and monumental sculpture. The chief centre of the alabaster trade in Europe was Nottingham and from there tombs and retables were exported in great numbers to all parts of the Continent. An enormous number of figures and panels grouped in wooden frames to form retables are to be found all over Europe, as far away as Iceland and southern Italy, and it is only comparatively recently that their English origin has been traced. No alabaster retable remains in its original position in England, but fine complete specimens in their original settings survive in France, Germany and Italy; one of the best is at Yssac-la-Tourette in France. For these retables the panels were grouped in sets of suitable subjects. Thus the Annunciation, Nativity, Magi, Circumcision and Coronation of the Virgin with a central panel of the Assumption would make one set, while a central panel of the Crucifixion would be flanked by scenes of the Passion and the Resurrection to constitute another set. These were the two commonest scenes.

Retables dating from after the close of the 14th century are coarser in handling and mannered in treatment; and in the latest examples, dating from the end of the 15th century, the workmanship is careless. The whole nature of the trade at that time is shown by the record of an action brought in 1491 by Nicholas Hill, an image-maker, against his salesman for the value of 58 heads of St John the Baptist.

ALTAR (Lat. *alta ara*, high place). The earliest altars seem to have been mounds or platforms of unbaked earth or large stones, but these rapidly developed into more ornamental forms. Assyrian altars were of limestone and alabaster, those of the Egyptians were of basalt or polished granite. A Cretan altar found at Cnossus was a slab of black steatite supported by four legs and used as a cover for a sacred stone. Two types of altar were common in Ancient Greece and Rome. One was placed within the temple before the image of the god and consisted of a small, low platform upon which the worshipper could kneel; the other took the form of a table and was intended for offerings or burnt sacrifices in the open air. It usually stood before the principal entrance and was of marble and generally of modest dimensions. Notable exceptions were the altars of the Temple of Zeus and Athena at Pergamon, built by Eumenes II (c. 200 B.C.) and the heroic altar of Augustan Peace in Rome (dedicated in 9 B.C.), which are huge architectural structures richly ornamented with sculpture.

The altar had become an established feature of Christian meeting places by the 3rd century. In England and in Western Europe wooden altars were usual until the 11th century, although stone and marble were common in Mediterranean countries as early as the 4th century. There are records of gold and silver coverings for altars, an extant example of which is that given in A. D. 835 by Archbishop Engelbert to S. Ambrogio, Milan. It covers the four vertical sides of the altar and is made of sheets of gold, silver and silver gilt with designs in engraving and relief, with added decoration of enamels, cameos and precious stones.

The developed altar of the medieval church consisted of (1) the table (mensa) which was usually a stone slab marked with five crosses as a sign of its consecration; (2) the support (stipes) a solid mass or a series of piers or columns and (3) the altar cavity (sepulchrum) which contained the relics of some saint or martyr, a practice developed from a decree of Felix I in the 3rd century requiring Mass to be celebrated above the tombs of the martyrs.

When a church has more than one altar the principal one is called the High Altar, and it is placed against the rear of the chancel or isolated in the body of the church. In Italian churches the High Altar is placed at the crossing (at the intersection of the nave and transepts); in France towards the rear of the choir; in Spain towards the rear of the nave.

Small movable or portable altars have been used in Christian worship since the 7th century. They are usually slabs of stone marked with the five crosses. Since Late Gothic times portable altars have also been formed by altar-pieces (q. v.).

ALTAR-PIECE. A decorated screen, panel or series of panels, movable or fixed, placed on or behind an altar, generally incorporating paintings or reliefs. Few altar-pieces are recorded prior to the 11th century, yet the elaborate design of such works as the Palo d'Oro in

34

41. Königslutter Cathedral, view of choir with apse and side-apses (c. 1135)

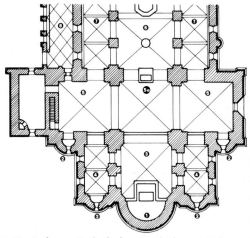

42. Königslutter Cathedral, ground-plan with choir and transept (metrical system)

1 Apse, 2 Side-apses, 3 Choir, 4 Choir-aisles, 5 Transept, 5a Crossing, 6 Nave, 7 Aisles, 8 Cloister

St Mark's, Venice suggests an earlier development. The Gothic altar-piece (13th and 14th cent.) usually consisted of a group of hinged panels, a *triptych* of three panels or a *polyptych* of five or more panels, so arranged that the outer sections or wings would fold over the inner sections. The principal subject was painted on the face of the inner panel, related subjects or a continuation of the principal subject appearing on the outer panels. The backs of the panels were also sometimes painted, the panels then generally being divided into a series of smaller pictures. If the panels were fixed rather than hinged the same formal arrangement was retained. The major panels were usually mounted upon a step or base called the *predella* and this predella was decorated with a series of small paintings or carvings related to the theme of the main panels. The predella was often included in the design of the frame and thus became an integral part of the altar-piece rather than a base supporting it. Frames were of wood elaborately carved and gilded. Examples of the triptych include Duccio's 'Madonna and Child' (London/Nat. Gall.) and Simon Martini's 'Annunciation' (Florence/Uffizi); the 'Crucifixion' by Jacopo di Cione (London/Nat. Gall.) is a typical polyptych. (Ill. 84)

During the 15th century the Gothic altar-piece was gradually replaced by the more typical Renaissance form of a single main panel divided into three or more parts under which in the base of the frame were the predella pictures. Examples include the 'Adoration of the Lamb' by Hubert and Jan van Eyck (St Bavon, Ghent), a multiple central panel with folding wings; the San Zeno altar-piece by Mantegna (Verona), the Frari altar-piece by Giovanni Bellini (Venice), and the 'Coronation of the Virgin' by Fra Angelico (Paris/Louvre). The altar-piece of the 16th century and later was often a single picture attached to a wall behind the altar or set into an architectural frame like Titian's 'Assumption of the Virgin' (Frari, Venice).

ANATOMY. Since the re-introduction of the nude into the plastic arts in the Renaissance a knowledge of anatomy spread everywhere – often through dissection (Pollaiuolo, Leonardo, Stubbs), which was practised by artists themselves. Scenes of such dissections appear in art from the 15th century onwards. Dutch 17th-century painters even created a special subject, the 'Anatomy', where groups of physicians are shown round an opened corpse. The most famous example is Rembrandt's 'The Anatomy Lesson of Dr Tulp'.

ANONYMOUS. (1) Nameless or of unknown name, (2) of unknown authorship. Artists whose names are not known are called after some of their best-known works (Maître des heures de Rohan, Master of the Life of the Virgin) or after the location of an important work of theirs (Master of Wittingau, Master of Flémalle). Antique vase painters are often named after the potter for whom they worked (Brygos painter). Works of art which cannot be ascribed to a particular artist are sometimes named after their former location (Apollo of Belvedere), the place where they were discovered, the finder (Ludovisi Throne), or an owner (Portland Vase).

APSE. The apse, like the plan of the early Christian church, was taken over from the Basilica (q. v.). It is usually a semicircular bay, mostly at the eastern end, but sometimes also at both ends, of the building. Known also as the Concha, Tribuna or Exedra, the apse contained the bishop's throne, with the altar in front of it. Later, the altar moved further into the apse and displaced the bishop's throne. In Carolingian times, the choir developed as a new feature of the church, for

which the apse then became the fitting terminal. The Romanesque apse is usually semicircular, the Gothic polygonal, though sometimes also rectangular. Besides the main apse on the axis of the nave, we sometimes also find an apse on the aisles or at the ends of the transepts. A church with three apses, one at the end of each transept and one at the nave, is called triapsial (St Mark's Venice). Ill. 41, 42, 140

ARABESQUE. Whether used as adjective or noun, this term means 'Arabian' or 'in the Arabian manner'. It describes mural or surface decoration composed of flowing lines and patterns of flowers, leaves, branches and scrollwork fancifully intertwined. The derivation suggests an actual Arabic origin for all decoration of this sort, but actually this kind of ornament was inherited by Renaissance artists from Graeco-Roman work. Flowing, intertwining scroll designs which occur in Moorish and Arabic work are usually distinguished as Moorish arabesques or *Mauresques*. (Ill. 68)

ARCADE. An arch, or a series of arches supported on piers or columns (arcading). Developed by the Romans, it was used in architecture until modern times. Arcades attached to the wall for purely decorative purposes are called wall arcades (Norman churches in England, Romanesque churches on the Continent). Ambulatories with open arcades – often under the eaves of Romanesque churches, particularly above the apse – are called eaves galleries. (Cf. ill. 41, 119, 146, 172, 175, 188)

ARCH. The arch, already known in Antiquity, is of the greatest importance in architecture, both structurally and aesthetically. It can carry heavier loads than the horizontal beam or architrave and performs a useful function above doors and windows. But it also gives distinction to an opening in a wall, and brings movement into a series of such openings. In that both vault (q. v.) and dome (q. v.) are based on the arch, it opened up truly dramatic possibilities in the treatment of interiors. The arch is formed of wedge-shaped stones. It is begun from right and left with stones resting against an abutment, and the keystone completes it. The keystone is as a rule heavier than the other stones, and often carved. The form of the arch is usually derived from the

43. Types of Arch or Opening

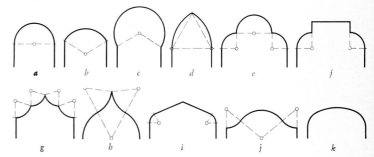

a) Round, b) Segmental, c) Horse-shoe, d) Lancet, e) Trefoil, f) Shouldered, g) Curtain, h) Ogee, i) Tudor, j) Convex, k) Elliptical

circle, less often from the ellipse, and very rarely from the parabola. (The basic shapes are shown in ill. 43.)

ARCHAIC. Literally, this term applies to the beginnings of Greek art (8th to 6th cent. B.C.). But since the characteristic features of this epoch (monumentality, little approximation to real life, straight lines, symmetry) occur in the early art of many civilisations, the expression 'archaic' is also applied to the early stages of art in other countries. An art using 'archaic' features deliberately is called archaistic, as, for example, a school of late Graeco-Roman sculpture, which was a reaction to the naturalism of the Hellenistic period.

ARCHITRAVE. The lowest part of the entablature in direct contact with the abacus on the capital of a column. The term is also used of the mouldings surrounding a door or window opening, including the lintel.

ARCHIVOLT. Both the mouldings on the face of an arch and its profile are called archivolts. Gothic and Romanesque doorways with their succession of receding arches often show several archivolts carved with figures forming terminals to the arches. (Ill. 151, 179)

ART COLLECTIONS. The history of collecting, like that of patronage, reflects the trend of taste and also shows the relation of art to wealth. The earliest collections were associated with religion and the public treasury, as in the Egyptian tombs of the kings and the sanctuaries at Delphi and Olympia. Private collecting was first fully developed among the Romans. A whole quarter of Rome was devoted to art dealers. Among the collectors, one of the first and most prominent was Sulla, who numbered among his treasures the 'Hercules' of Lysippus, which had once belonged to Alexander the Great; a golden statue of Apollo stolen from Delphi; and the first recorded collection of antique engraved gems. Julius Caesar also owned six collections of cameos and intaglios; Sallust owned the 'Dying Gaul' and the 'Venus and Cupid', now in the Vatican.

The suppression of private wealth during the Middle Ages restricted collecting and attention was mainly directed towards the embellishment of ecclesiastical institutions by the work of contemporary artists. In Venice, however, where the merchants and bankers were concerned with the financing of the Crusades, objects brought back by the Crusaders and gifts from Oriental potentates formed the nucleus of the Doges' collections. The Medici in Florence were conspicuous as patrons of contemporary art. But by the time of Lorenzo the Magnificent they were showing equal interest in works of the past. Lorenzo himself formed a distinguished collection of antique gems, cameos, intaglios and marbles. Ghiberti owned among other antique marbles a reclining figure by Polycleitus and some Greek vases. Squarcione, head of the Paduan School, collected on a large scale and actually travelled to Greece bringing back statues and paintings for his pupils to copy. Giulio Romano's house at Mantua was filled with Roman fragments; and Mantegna formed a celebrated collection of classical sculpture.

Among papal collectors of the Renaissance may be mentioned Paul III who owned Byzantine ivories, and Julius II, who with the purchase of the 'Apollo Belvedere' began the collection of antique statuary which made the Vatican famous. Outside Italy, the Habsburgs formed magnificent collections which ultimately became parts of the museums of Dresden, Munich, Vienna and the Prado. Francis I, besides his lavish patronage of living artists, formed the nucleus of the present Bibliothèque Nationale with his collection of Greek, Byzantine and medieval manuscripts, and with his vases, medals, statuettes, drawings, tapestries and sculptures, brought together the core of the national art collections of the Louvre.

The *Catalogue of the King's Pictures,* 1948, records the growth of the English Royal Collections. The elder son of James I, Prince Henry, left a number of pictures and bronzes to his brother Charles which formed the basis of Charles' important collections. His greatest acquisition was the purchase of the collection of the Dukes of Mantua which included the nine 'Triumphs of Caesar' by Mantegna. On the advice of the Rubens, Charles bought the cartoons by Raphael now in the Victoria and Albert Museum. The most important private collectors in Charles' reign were George Villiers, Duke of Buckingham and Thomas Howard, Earl of Arundel. The last-named is chiefly remembered for his collection of antiques, the 'Arundel Marbles', now in the British Museum. In Holland, Rembrandt's collection was of particular interest. He specialized in paintings and drawings of the old masters, antique busts, arms and historic costumes.

The Duke of Marlborough's collection was considered to be one of the finest of the 18th century. When it was dispersed in 1885, the 360 pictures put up for auction included Raphael's 'Ansidei Madonna' and van Dyck's 'Charles I', both now in the National Gallery, and Titian's 'Venus and Adonis', now in the Metropolitan Museum, New York. Horace Walpole is, however, usually instanced as the typical 18th-century collector. He owned Rembrandt's 'Saskia', 'Charles I', 'Henrietta Maria' and 'Archbishop Laud' by van Dyck, Raphael's 'Last Supper' and Michelangelo's 'Rape of Ganymede'. Other notable English collectors were the Duke of Devonshire, the Duke of Bridgewater, the Duke of Northumberland, Earl Temple of Stowe and the Earl of Pembroke at Wilton. Many of their collections were enriched by the sale in 1792–93 of the Orleans Collection, which had been formed in the early years of the century by Philip, Duke of Orleans. Among the painters represented were Titian, Rubens, Veronese, Reni, Poussin, Tintoretto, Correggio and van Dyck. All these great 18th-century collectors preferred 16th- and 17th-century Italian painters and painters like Poussin who worked in an italianate manner.

Of 18th-century amateurs who devoted themselves to the remains of Classical Antiquity, Charles Townley was the most outstanding. His collection consisted of bas-reliefs, sepulchral monuments, inscriptions, cinerary

CARLO CRIVELLI: The Annunciation. – *The development of central perspective and its application to painting was one of the most important innovations of the Italian Renaissance. In this picture the perspective is worked out with mathematical precision*

Imp.Edw.Ancourt à Paris.

Colour lithograph: Henri de Toulouse-Lautrec: The Englishman at the Moulin Rouge

urns, votive altars and statuary. They all came to the British Museum by purchase on Townley's death.

This history of collecting in the 19th and 20th centuries is largely the history of museums. Disrupting changes in the social scale gradually reduced the possibility of the acquisition of great works by old masters on the part of private individuals. Many of the great collections of the previous century were dispersed by sale or made into public museums, until to-day only a few remain in private hands. A growth of national feeling led many collectors – to mention only Angerstein and Sir George Beaumont – to bequeath to public institutions the works they had gathered together. Napoleon's vast collections were established in the Louvre as symbols of national, rather than private, prestige.

The English Royal Collections, however, maintained for a time the great tradition of 18th-century collecting. George IV acquired Rembrandt's 'Shipbuilder and his Wife' and 'Portrait of the Artist and Saskia' and van Dyck's 'Charles I in three positions'. Albert, as Prince Consort, bought interesting early Italian, Dutch, Flemish and German masters at a time when these were entirely ignored.

The new race of collectors brought into existence by the Industrial Revolution were conspicuous for their patronage of contemporary art. One or two collectors in the old tradition eventually emerged, among whom may be mentioned Baron Rothschild, Lords Leverhulme, Crawford, Lee of Fareham and Duveen, Sir Walter Burrell and Sir Samuel Courtauld. The last two possessed fine collections of French 19th-century painting.

In America immense private wealth, such as has become rare in Europe, made possible such collections as the Altmann, Stuart Gardiner, Phillips, Mellon, Widener, Pierpoint Morgan and Rockefeller, though these too have now mostly come to form part of public institutions and museums.

ATLANTES. In Greek mythology, the pillars of the heavens are said to have rested on the shoulders of the titan Atlas. The term atlantes, in its wider meaning, therefore describes male figures who support the entablature of a building in place of columns or piers. The female equivalent is called a caryatid (as in the Porch of Maidens on the Erechteum, Athens, ill. 122).

ATRIUM. (1) The central portion of the Roman house. It has an opening (impluvium) in the centre, with a cistern (compluvium) underneath to take the water from the inward-sloping roof. The hearth was near-by. The rooms are arranged round the atrium. (2) The open court before the narthex of a Christian basilica (also called Paradise) with a fountain for ritual ablutions. This feature was occasionally retained in Romanesque churches (ill. 46, 172).

AULA. The aula was the courtyard of the private house in Ancient Greece. It was sometimes colonnaded and bedrooms and living rooms were grouped round it. In Roman times the Imperial palace was known as the aula, in the Middle Ages the Emperor's residence in the Palatinate. In Germany, the term has been used since the 16th century to describe the assembly halls of schools and universities.

BALDACHINO. Originally a canopy of brocade or other precious material, which was carried in procession above the Sacrament, or a ruler, on special occasions. The term was later also extended to stone or wooden canopies above altars, tombs, statues, porches, fountains, thrones and beds. (Ill. 158, 174)

BALUSTRADE. A balustrade is a parapet, whose handrail or coping is supported by small columns, the balusters, which swell in the centre or towards the base.

BASE. The base, in architecture, is the lowest member of a column, consisting of a plinth and moulding between the shaft and the pavement or between the shaft of a column or pilaster and the pedestal on which it rests. In primitive Egyptian and Greek architecture the base was a raised slab of stone whose function was to insulate the timber column from ground moisture. When stone replaced wood for columns this simple base was retained except in the Doric column. The other Greek orders developed a characteristic base in which the profile varied by different proportions and combinations of torus and scotia mouldings and fillets. An adapted Greek design known as the Attic base is common to all the Roman orders. In each of the Greek orders the base is round, and the Romans, too, adopted this practice. But in Romanesque and Gothic architecture the base assumed many varieties of form. Bases composed of elaborate mouldings occur in Assyrian and Persian architecture at an early date. The term is also used to describe the lowest course of masonry in a building. (Cf. ill. 62, 75)

BASILICA (Gr. from *Basileus*, a king; hence 'Royal Hall'). In Roman times the basilica was a hall of justice and commercial exchange, and occupied a central position. The usual plan, which was probably a Roman development from a Greek temple, was a rectangle twice as long as its width. Either two or four rows of columns, forming three or five aisles, ran the entire length, and above were galleries with upper columns which supported the roof. The entrance was either at the side or at one end. The tribunal at the other end was on a raised dais, generally in a semicircular apse and sometimes separated from the main building by a screen of columns or by a low balustrade. Ranged round the apse were seats for the assessors with a raised seat in the centre for the praetor, and in front was the altar where sacrifice was offered before the transaction of business. The building, which was generally covered with a wooden roof, was, according to Vitruvius, sometimes open along the sides, and the exterior was extremely simple. Roman basilicas included Trajan's Basilica, the Basilica of Constantine, Rome, adjoining the Forum, the Basilica Julia and the Basilica Aemilia. Wherever Rome established her power a basilica for the administration of justice formed an important feature in her town planning and remains of basilicas have been found at Pompeii, Fano, Trier (Trèves), Tingad and at Silchester in England. (Ill. 44)

The Roman basilicas served the Early Christians as models for their churches and thus formed a connecting link between buildings of pagan Classic times and those of the Romanesque period. The term basilica was applied to a Christian church as early as the 4th century. A basilican church was usually erected over the burial place of the saint to whom the church was dedicated and immediately above the burial place or crypt was the

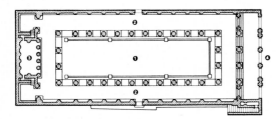

44. Roman basilica: B. Pompeii (ground-plan)
1 Nave, 2 Aisles, 3 Tribune, 4 Forum

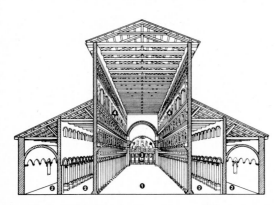

45. Early Christian basilica: Rome, Old St Peter's (cross-section)
1 Nave, 2 Aisles, 3 Apse with altar and bishop's throne, 4 Clerestory

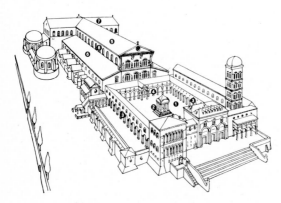

46. Rome, Old St Peter's (reconstruction)
1 Outer court (atrium), 2 Fountain for ablutions (kantharos), 3 Pillared walk (peristyle), 4 Inner vestibule (narthex), 5 Nave, 6 Aisles, 7 Transept, 8 Clerestory

High Altar covered by a ciborium, also known as a tabernacle or baldachino (q. v.). There were 31 basilican churches in Rome alone. The plan of the Christian basilica was as follows: an atrium or open rectangular fore-court surrounded by arcades, formed an imposing approach to the church and in the centre was a fountain for ablutions. Next came the covered narthex between the atrium and the church, which was assigned to penitents. The narthex opened into the nave, lighted by a clerestory (q. v.) of small windows, with an aisle on either side usually half the width of the nave. Sometimes there were two aisles on each side of the nave, as in Old St Peter's (ill. 45, 46), S. Paolo and S. Giovanni in Laterano, Rome. Galleries for women were occasionally placed over the aisles as at S. Agnese and S. Lorenzo, Rome, but otherwise the sexes sat on opposite sides of the nave. The platform in the pagan basilica was retained in some of the Early Christian churches and was the germ of the medieval transept which later converted the plan into a Latin cross. A choir, which became necessary with the growth of ritual, was enclosed by low screen walls or 'cancelli' (hence chancel), and was provided with an ambo or pulpit on either side, from which the Gospel and Epistle were read. In the semicircular apse or sanctuary the bishop took the central place which had been that of the praetor in the Roman basilica, and the members of the Church Council occupied seats on either side corresponding to those used by the Roman assessors. The altar in front of the apse, which in the basilica had been used for libations to the gods, was now adapted for the celebration of Christian rites and a baldachino, or canopy, supported on marble columns was erected over it. The interior of many Christian basilicas, S. Clemente, S. Agnese, S. Maria Maggiore, Rome, and S. Apollinare Nuove, Ravenna, among others, was enriched by the use of glass mosaic in the semidome of the apse.

BAY. One of the compartments into which the nave or roof of a building is divided and which impart a sense of rhythm to it. The bays are marked either by buttresses or pilasters on the exterior walls, by the disposition of the main ribs of the vaulting in the interior, by the main arches and pillars, or by any other leading features that separate the interior into rhythmical portions.

BELFRY (Old Fr. *berfrei,* a tower, not connected with *bell*). The belfry was the last refuge of the inhabitants of the castle in times of attack (ill. 50). More usually, the term denotes the upper room in a tower in which the bells are hung and this sometimes comes to signify the tower itself.

BINDINGS. Antiquity knew the book only in the form of a roll. The Codex which was folded into leaves required solid covers and was developed in the 4th and 5th centuries A.D. The first bindings consisted of leather- or parchment-covered wooden boards, reinforced and decorated at the corners with metal mounts. Books used in the service of the Church were also given jewelled bindings of precious metal, which were often lavishly decorated with filigree enamel, ivory carvings, pearls and precious as well as semi-precious stones. Such books included the Golden Codex of St Emmeram and the Bernward Gospels (ill. p. 47). Leather-covered boards soon began to be elaborately tooled. The principal leathers used were morocco, old calf and pigskin. A book entirely covered in leather is called whole or full-bound. A half-bound book has leather spine and corners, and the sides are covered with cloth or paper. When only the spine is leather the book is said to be quarter bound. The craft of book-binding gained great impetus in France, Italy and Germany (Jakob Krause) when during the Renaissance, as a result of Oriental influences, cardboard replaced wood for boards. Using carefully selected and prepared leathers, Italian Renaissance craftsmen decorated the covers and spines of books in gold with geometric interlaced patterns, arabesques and plant forms. In France and the Netherlands panel stamps were largely in use. English binders of the 15th century were in the habit of decorating their books with a number of small dies arranged in bands and circles. The craft flourished throughout the 17th and 18th centuries, especially in France where it was practised throughout generations of book-binders' families (Padeloup, Derome) and always followed the current style of the period. French book-binding suffered eclipse in the upheaval of the Revolution, though during the 19th century Thouvenin, Trautz and Duric restored the tradition of finished workmanship. In England, Francis Bedford was one of the most noted binders of the 19th century and in more recent times good work has been done through the example of Cobden-Sanderson and Douglas Cockerell. This re-awakened feeling for fine binding also affected the machine-bound, mass-produced book, whose cloth cover is now often designed by artists and made to harmonize with its dust-jacket. Glazed calico was first introduced for book covers in about 1820, and about ten years later cloth began to be specially manufactured for the covering of books.

BOOK ILLUSTRATION. Early illustrated books were modelled on the illuminations of medieval manuscripts, whose style was copied in coloured woodcuts. The first printer to make use of illustrations was Albrecht Pfister of Bamberg in 1461. The illustrations in Breydenbach's 'Peregrinationes in Montem Syon' (Mainz 1486) show a marked advance upon previous efforts in the art of woodcutting. The illustrator, Erhard Reuwich, joined the expedition as special artist to record the pilgrimage. Two other remarkable German illustrated books made their appearance at Nuremberg towards the close of the 15th century. The 'Schatzbehalter' of 1491 and Hartmann Schedel's 'Liber Chronicarum' of 1493. Wolgemut was the artist responsible for the cuts of both. The most remarkable Italian illustrated book of the 15th century was the 'Hypnerotomachia Poliphili' of Francesco Colonna, printed by Aldus. In Paris the printed book kept in closer touch with the art of the illuminator than anywhere else. Books of private prayer

were printed on vellum with borders and pictures gilded in the style of manuscripts. Prominent printers and publishers of these were Philippe Pigouchet, Jean du Pré, Thielman Kerver and Antoine Vérard. The early English press is not outstanding for its illustrations. Caxton, Wynkyn de Worde and Pynson all issued illustrated editions of the *Canterbury Tales.* In the 16th century the talents of the foremost artists found expression in the service of the printed book, among them Dürer, Hans Burgkmair, Holbein and Cranach. Holbein designed book decorations in the form of initials and borders. Towards the end of the century Theodore de Bry and his sons brought out at Frankfurt a wonderful series of illustrated travel books. Foxe's *Book of Martyrs* (1563) was one of the most popular illustrated books of the period. (Cf. ill. p. 50)

The 16th century saw the woodcut at its best, but by the middle of the period a rival craft had begun to assert itself, the art of copper-plate engraving. This belongs to the *intaglio* group of processes, and illustrations executed in this technique cannot be printed at the same time as the letter-press. Sometimes the engravings were printed in blank spaces left for the purpose or on thin paper which was afterwards pasted into the text; sometimes the engravings were worked on separate sheets of paper gathered together at the end of the book. In this form, known as 'plates', the illustrations were no longer an integral part of the printed book. During the 17th century illustrations were rare in English books except for title pages and portraits. The outstanding feature of 18th-century illustration were the delicate engravings of the French 'livres à vignettes'. In the latter part of the century Thomas Stothard was busy with plates for *Robinson Crusoe, Clarissa Harlowe* and *Tristram Shandy.*

The art of the woodcut was revived by Thomas Bewick whose illustrated editions of Gay's *Fables* (1779), *Select Fables* (1784) and *General History of Quadrupeds* (1740) mark a new era in book illustration. New methods and principles were introduced and henceforth we speak of the craft as 'wood engraving'.

In the 19th century the use of illustrations in books of every kind greatly increased. Wood engraving was the principal process employed, but lithography, invented early in the century, also became very popular and was carried to great perfection in France. Soon after 1830 the field for wood engraving was enlarged by the use of illustrations in weekly journals, and additional impetus was given to this movement by the founding of the *Illustrated London News* in 1842. Steel engravings of a fine quality were a special feature of *The Keepsake* and other annuals. (Cf. ill. 262)

Bewick and his contemporaries, Stothard, Blake and Flaxman were succeeded by Cruikshank, Hablot Browne ('Phiz'), illustrator of Dickens, Ainsworth, Lever and John Leech. The 'rural beauties' of Birket Foster, translated in wood by the able Dalziel Brothers, were the delight of the mid-Victorians. The books of Walter Crane, Kate Greenaway and Randolph Calde-

47. *Chorin, conventual church, from W. (begun 1300), brick construction*

cott mark the following period. In the last decades of the 19th century wood engraving, metal engraving, etching and lithography were challenged as methods of illustration by the onset of mechanical photographic processes for reproducing drawings and paintings. But in the early years of the present century Vollard began to commission the leading French artists to illustrate various classics with woodcuts, engravings and lithographs, and Maillol's woodcuts to Virgil's *Eclogues*, Derain's coloured woodcuts to *Pantagruel*, Picasso's great series of aquatints for Buffon's *Natural History* and Chagall's brilliant lithographic illustrations to La Fontaine's *Fables* and the Bible are among the finest book illustrations ever executed. In England Barnett Freedman's lithographs for *Wuthering Heights, Jane Eyre, War and Peace* and *Anna Karenina* marked a new achievement in book illustration. (Cf. ill. 265)

BOOK PLATE (Ex Libris). A decorative name label usually stuck on the inside cover of a book. Its history closely parallels that of printing. The earliest known book plate dates from 1450. Dürer, Altdorfer and Cranach all engraved a number of book plates. The earliest dated English book plate is of 1520. These early examples are nearly all armorial, many of them with the coat of arms only and no name. Later book plates embraced every variety of theme, from wreaths and urns, portraits, humorous subjects, animals and birds to the purely typographical design. Many well-known artists have designed book plates: Hogarth, Bartolozzi, Papillon, Millais, Liebermann, Corinth, Edward Gordon Craig, William Nicholson and Eric Ravilious. The older

examples were all engraved on copper; 19th- and 20th-century designs were chiefly woodcuts or lithographs.

BRICKWORK. As long ago as between the 4th and 3rd millennia B. C. the Sumerians faced their buildings of sun-dried bricks with bricks of fired clay. Brick in its unglazed form, or as tiles, glazed and moulded or carved in relief, was the most common building material in the architecture of Western Asia, Persia and the world of Islam, although it was used less in Greek and Roman Antiquity. The Romans often plastered or faced the façades of their brick buildings, whereas a brick structure in the fullest sense of the term should have its walls left bare. The use of brick was revived in the Lombardic architecture of the early Middle Ages and in the 12th century spread to Bavaria, northern Germany and Denmark. During the following centuries, up to the end of the Gothic period, brick architecture flourished in northern Germany from the Lower Rhine to East Prussia (red brick Gothic). It reached the Netherlands, Scandinavia, the Baltic and Poland through the Hanseatic League and the Teutonic Knights. Churches, abbeys (such as Chorin in the Brandenburg province), castles of the Teutonic Order (Marienburg in West Prussia), town halls (Lübeck, Thorn), hospitals (Heilige Geist Spital, Lübeck), universities (Cracow), city walls (Reval), their gates and towers (Holstentor Lübeck, Tangermünde), were all built in exposed brickwork. But this technique lost its vigour during the Renaissance, when brick walls were mostly plastered. The 19th century saw a revival of yellow (London stock) and red brick. (Ill. 47)

Although England does not on the whole possess buildings which, as examples of brick architecture, can stand comparison with the best work produced in northern Germany and Scandinavia, brick has been continuously used since the 13th century, and Hampton Court is a world-famous 16th-century brick structure. Indeed, at a time when architectural design throughout the world was at its lowest ebb, English architects played no small part in reviving brick, using it in an entirely original manner to suit the English climate (Philip Webb's Red House, built for William Morris, houses in Kensington, in Chelsea and New Scotland Yard by Norman Shaw).

CALLIGRAPHY is the art of writing. In a more restricted use the term is frequently employed to refer to the products of professional writing masters working in Europe from the 16th to the 19th centuries. Specimens of their work appear in the copy books produced as models for students of handwriting. The earliest of these manuals was that of Ludovico degli Arrighi, also known as Vicentino, which was issued in Rome in 1522 and gave an example of a semi-formal script, the chancery hand. In the 20th century there has been a revival of calligraphy in Europe, begun by Edward Johnston in England and continued in Germany by Rudolf Koch. It is, however, in the Far East that calligraphy has been most highly developed, especially by the Chinese. They regard calligraphy not so much as

48. Types of Capital

a) Egyptian palm (sepulchral temple of King Sahure near Abusir, 2563–2423 B.C.) b) Roman composite (Arch of Titus in Rome, A.D. 81) c) Byzantine trapezoid with abacus (San Vitale in Ravenna, c. 547) d) Byzantine folded with abacus (San Vitale in Ravenna, c. 547) e) Romanesque cushion (Abbey church in Alpirsbach, beg. 12th cent.) f) Romanesque multiple cushion (Cathedral of St Mary in Lincoln, mid 12th cent.) g) Romanesque figured (St Michael's in Hildesheim, beg. 11th cent.) h) Gothic capital with conventionalized stiff-leaf foliage (Church of Our Lady in Gelnhausen, c. 1225) i) Gothic foliated capital with naturalistic hawthorn leaf (Naumburg Cathedral, beg. 13th cent.)

good penmanship as a fine art in the fullest sense of the word, very often a higher art than painting, because it is purer and more spontaneous. It is an art of the stroke or the line executed by the use of the brush. Both the strokes themselves and the composition of the whole must be organized according to certain general principles. There are five recognised calligraphic styles: the bronze or seal, the clerical, the formal or modal, the informal or 'walking' and the cursive or 'dancing'. Strokes fall into many categories, each with its own dynamic and characteristic expression. The ideal of the Chinese calligrapher is rhythmic vitality, and the dramatic quality of each stroke and the organic whole of a character must be such as to realize the 'four essentials' of beauty in calligraphy, namely *shun*, a spirited style, *ch'i*, a strong brush stroke, *yun*, rhythm or balance and *wei*, aesthetic quality, interest and taste.

CAMPANILE. In Italy, the bell-tower in contrast to that of churches north of the Alps is usually not part of the main building, but stands a small distance away from it. The most famous of these 'campanile' are the Leaning Tower of Pisa, the campanile of St Mark's, Venice, and that of Florence Cathedral. (Ill. 175)

CANDELABRA. There was little distinction between lamps and candle-sticks in prehistoric times. Artificial light was produced by a wick, burning in an oil-filled clay or stone basin. Wax candles were invented in Classical Antiquity and candle-sticks and candelabra of every kind, often elaborate in shape, have since been developed. The earliest examples are mostly of stone or bronze, less frequently also of wood. They are sometimes shaped like human figures (the 12th-century Wolfram candelabra in Erfurt Cathedral and the angel candelabra of the Renaissance). The altar candelabra for Easter were often given very elaborate forms, as were the seven-branched monumental State candelabra (Brunswick and Milan Cathedrals, both 12th century). The Renaissance and the Baroque used a variety of

forms and materials, including pewter and wrought iron as well as precious metals. Many fine examples of the chandelier – a fitting suspended from the ceiling and capable of holding a large number of candles – have survived from as early as the Romanesque (Hildesheim and Aix-la-Chapelle Cathedrals). The glass chandeliers of Venice are world-renowned.

CAPITAL. The crowning feature of a column, pilaster or pier, effecting the transition from the column to the horizontal architrave course. It projects beyond the shaft of the column and is frequently carved. In *Egypt* the chief decorative shapes used were the conventionalized lotus flower and bud and the papyrus flower and bud. On *Persian* capitals the foreparts of two bulls placed back to back were favoured. *Minoan* capitals were cushion-shaped. The *Greeks* evolved the three types of capital which have since been most widely used in western architecture: the Doric, Ionic and Corinthian. The Doric capital consists of a square crowning block (abacus) and a cushion (echinus), subtly curving into the necking that joins it to the column proper. The Ionic capital consists of an abacus, a double scroll (volute) and an echinus elaborately decorated with bead-and-reel or egg-and-dart ornament. The Corinthian capital is still more elaborate, consisting of a bell-shaped core from which long volutes rise to support the corners and shortened ones merge into a profusion of acanthus leaves in two florid rows. *Byzantine* architects used a form derived from the Corinthian; they flattened it and made it a more compact type of surface decoration. To the acanthus motif they added others based on basket weaving and melon ridges. *Romanesque* capitals are also Corinthian in shape, but display great variety of carved decorative motifs, conventionalized birds, animals and robust foliage designs. The rich carving on *Gothic* capitals is more deeply cut, more naturalistic and even more fertile in invention, and the capitals themselves are diverse in shape. (Ill. 48)

49. *Harlech Castle, Merionethshire, Wales. A concentric castle dating from 1285*

CARICATURE. A drawing of a person or persons in which certain characteristics are exaggerated with the intention of ridicule or burlesque.

This form of satire can be found in Greek vase painting and in the Roman frescoes at Pompeii and Herculaneum; and in the Middle Ages caricature appears in the carving of stalls and capitals, in ornaments and gargoyles and in the margins of illuminated manuscripts. But caricature as an independent art did not come into existence until the time of the Renaissance. A well-known example of that period is the German woodcut by an anonymous artist in the Gotha museum showing a doctor shaped exactly like the urine glass he is holding. The earliest known portrait caricature dates from 1600; it is the work of Annibale Carracci (Stockholm/Nat. Mus.) and depicts an Italian singer and his wife. It was Carracci who first used the word caricature to designate this kind of drawing. Bernini was a skilful caricaturist, though his work in this field is little known. The first caricaturist to make his living entirely from his art was P. L. Ghezzi (1673–1755). But the rapid development of caricature in the 18th century was not due to his influence alone. It was Hogarth, above all, who made it a genuine expression of the age. George, Marquess of Townshend (1724–1807) was the first to apply caricature to politics. His crude, but witty cartoons were acclaimed by an eager public and caricature became a fashion amounting almost to a craze in the late 18th century. The greatest master of the hundreds of political caricatures published between 1780 and 1820 was James Gillray, to whom the whole art is greatly indebted. The Hogarthian tradition of social satire was carried on and developed by Rowlandson. The first comic weekly to reproduce caricatures was published in France in 1830 by Charles Philipon under the title *La Caricature* and this was followed by his daily, *Charivari*. Philipon employed the great French caricaturists, Daumier, Gavarni, Grandville and Doré. Daumier worked for Philipon all his life, producing 4,000 lithographs. *Punch* was founded in 1842 and *Simplizissimus*, whose most brilliant artist was T. Heine, first appeared in 1896. The late 19th-century caricature

began more and more to exploit the effects of simplicity, a tendency which reached its climax in the work of Max Beerbohm. (Ill. 263)

CASTING. This is a means of reproducing three-dimensional objects. Casting in plaster cast implies copying an original, while casting in bronze or some other metal often gives a work of art its final form. In art, bronze and plaster are the most important materials used in this manner. In the 'cire perdu' or 'lost wax' method (the French term is generally used), the clay model is given a coating of wax as thick as the bronze cast it is intended to have. This is covered with a layer of clay. Holes are then made in the clay; these serve the dual purpose of allowing the heated wax to escape and the liquid bronze to enter the intervening space. The bronze having cooled, the outer layer of clay is smashed. The clay core can be removed through an opening. It is of no further use in the 'cire perdu' method. By this method only one casting is possible. In the case of a plaster cast, a 'negative' casting of the model must first be made. This also has to be destroyed after use. If this is to be avoided, the negative has to be removed from the model in parts, reassembled for casting and then removed again. It is thus possible – via a plaster cast – to make a bronze cast without destroying the mould (temporary moulds of sand, piece moulds). Other metals, such as iron, lead, etc. can also be used for casting, as can plaster and cement of all kinds, including various stone substitutes.

CAST IRON, see Ironwork.

CASTLE. Before the 11th century, castles had little architectural character, for they were chiefly earthworks with a wooden tower and palisading. The feudal system necessitated a permanent stronghold for the feudal lord, and castles therefore became most important buildings. These 11th-century castles had keeps of two types, the 'shell' and the rectangular. The shell keep was built on existing earthworks, its walls of masonry circling the mound in which it was built, replacing earlier palisading; it was developed from the 'motte and bailey' castle with its bailey or court at the base of the motte, or mound, and a surrounding fosse, or ditch. Carisbrooke, Pontefract, Windsor and Durham are among castles with 'shell' keeps. The rectangular keep originated in France and was erected on sites other than those suitable for a 'motte and bailey' castle. It was generally four storeys high and stood in a court surrounded by a thick, lofty wall and a deep moat.

50. *The Wartburg from N. E. (begun c. 1200)*

1 *Ramp,* 2 *Drawbridge,* 3 *Defence galleries (encircling wall),* 4 *Battlements (encircling wall),* 5 *Gatehouse,* 6 *Knights' quarters,* 7 *Steward's office,* 8 *Watch-tower (belfry),* 9 *South tower,* 10 *Hall,* 11 *New ladies' room,* 12 *Stairway,* 13 *Porch,* 14 *Heated room,* 15 *Guest house,* 16 *Well installation*

Such is the Château de Châteaudun. The Crusades brought about a change in the planning and building of castles. Instead of relying for defence on the keep, a system of concentric curtain walls with towers at intervals was adopted. This was the plan of the great castles such as the Crac des Chevaliers built by the Crusaders in Syria and the Holy Land. They took the plan from the Turks who had adopted it from Roman military architects. The Tower of London has a rectangular keep in the old style and concentric walls with towers added by Henry III and his successors in the new manner. This new style gave rise to several outstanding masterpieces of military architecture in the symmetrically designed Edwardian castles of Wales: Beaumaris, Harlech (ill. 49), Conway, Caernarvon, Pembroke and Caerphilly. During the 14th and 15th centuries castles were increasingly adapted to provide domestic comfort on the model of manor houses. At Kenilworth, for example, the Norman keep was incorporated into a concentric plan which included a magnificent entrance porch, banquetting hall, kitchens and other offices. Design was still important at Kenilworth, but the principle of symmetry which had made the Welsh castles such splendid works of architecture was gradually lost and the typically late Gothic English castle, like the French *château* and the German *Burg* were picturesque agglomerations of rooms. In France many Gothic castles were pulled down to made room for the Renaissance châteaux such as those along the banks of the Loire. (Cf. ill. 50, 197)

CATHEDRA (Gr. for seat). The cathedra is the high-backed bishop's throne, from which the name of the diocesan church, the cathedral, is derived. In the early Middle Ages the cathedra stood behind the High Altar, in the centre of the apse; since Carolingian times – i. e. since the Mass has been celebrated in front of the altar instead at the back – the bishop's throne has stood at the north side where the Gospels are read.

CENTRAL STRUCTURE. The central structure (see p. 23), as opposed to the longitudinal structure, is not based on a simple axis. A building of this type can be circular (a rotunda) or polygonal. The type was common to the Mediterranean region in prehistoric times (Tiryns, Mycenae, Crete). The Greeks developed the round temple *(tholos)*. In Christian architecture, sepulchral churches and baptisteries were mostly designed as central structures. Occasionally, a 'rotunda' may be fitted into an axial church. (Ill. 34, 35, 141, 142, 191, 224)

CERAMICS, see Pottery, Porcelain and Tiles.

CHALICE. The chalice, one of the most important articles in the service of the church, consists of the foot, the knopped stem (Latin, *nodus*) and the bowl *(cuppa)*. The chalice used in the service of the Mass has to be of gold or must at least be of gilt on the inside. The Romanesque chalice had a semicircular bowl, while the Gothic chalice was funnel-shaped, and had a higher

51. *Tassilo chalice (781) with Anglo-Saxon ornamentation and figural representations in niello*

shaft and a flatter base. The medieval goldsmith often decorated the chalice, particularly the usually hexagonal foot, shaft and nodus, with engravings, scenes beaten in relief, enamel and precious stones. The Renaissance chalice had a round foot, a pear-shaped nodus and a waisted bowl. During the Baroque, the chalice was lavishly ornamented and decorated in relief, while the Classic Revival not only returned to simpler forms, but also disdained any decoration apart from simple garlands. (Ill. 51)

CHAMFER. A chamfer, in architecture, is a projecting, and usually profiled, stone slab between a pillar or pier and the base of the arch resting on it. If the chamfer rests on the capital, it is considered to form a unit with the latter and is called a chamfer capital.

CHANCEL (Latin *cancellus*, a screen), that part of the East end of a church in which the altar is placed, usually applied to the whole continuation of the nave east of the crossing. The chancel of continental churches is usually apsidal, while that of English churches is, with rare exceptions, square ended. (Ill. 186, 187)

CHIAROSCURO. An Italian word, meaning light and dark. While medieval artists only used bright, clear colours, painters from the Late Renaissance onwards – especially since Caravaggio – preferred to create effects of light and shade with intermediate tints of brown, grey and black. This development culminated in the art of Rembrandt.

45

52. 'Figura piramidale' composition:
RAPHAEL, *Sistine Madonna*

CHILD ART. Although the drawings or paintings of a child cannot, strictly speaking, be classed as art, they are yet of great importance to the art historian. They give some indication of the world of primitive or pre-historic artists, whose work shares many features – such as the absence of perspective – with the drawings of children. Child art does not depict objects as they appear but is based on what is known about them; it thus possesses the quality of 'direct expression'. Undoubtedly, modern art, in its desire to return to the springs of creation, has gratefully accepted many an inspiration from child art. The increasing number of exhibitions of child art are a sign of the interest shown in education for art to-day.

CHOIR. The part of the church accommodating the singers or more generally the arm of the cross between the transept and the chancel. In large churches there are usually aisles at the sides of the choir sometimes continued across the east end of the building so as to surround it, especially in churches which have polygonal or apsidal terminations like many continental cathedrals. The choir is often raised one step above the nave and in strictness does not extend further eastward than the steps leading up to the altar where the sanctuary begins, but this distinction is by no means always maintained, and the term choir is very generally applied to the whole space set aside for the celebration of the church services. In English parish churches choir and chancel are one. (Ill. 41, 42, 147, 186, 187)

CHOIRS STALLS. From the 13th century onwards carved wooden choir stalls were arranged on either side of the chancel behind the choir screen to provide seats for the clergy taking part in the offices. In a large establishment the choir stalls would vary in number from about 60, as at Beverley, to 108, as at Lincoln, and occupy about three bays. The choir stalls provided magnificent opportunities for the wood-carver. They often boast carved canopies and elbow rests and they have tip-up seats with curved ledges projecting from under the edges to give support during the long services when the occupants of the stalls were supposed to stand. The underparts are often carved with little scenes, sometimes very satirical, from Bible history, legend or local life. These are called misericords and some of the best can be seen at Gloucester, Wells, Carlisle and Lavenham. The carving of English choir stalls is unsurpassed; among numerous examples, the stalls at Ripon, Sherborne, Beverley, Norwich, Christchurch, Winchester, St George's Chapel, Windsor and the Henry VII Chapel, Westminster, deserve special mention. There is fine German work at Ulm, and in Spain splendidly carved stalls are common, provided with separate canopies and tall spires, as at Avila, Leon and Valladolid.

CLASSIC. Although the art of classical Greece was actually extremely varied, including work which may be classed as romantic, impressionistic and naturalistic, certain of its characteristics are usually considered to epitomize the classical spirit. Broadly speaking these characteristics are (1) the representation of the human form without distortion or abstraction; (2) a strict sense of balance and formal design resulting in a work which is serene and generalized rather than individualized, intellectual rather than emotional in its appeal, subordinating detail to contour and mass. The influence of the Greek ideal on European art has persisted until to-day, but conscious imitations such as those produced by the Romans, by Canova, Thorvaldsen and Flaxman usually exhibit only the negative virtue of restraint. They can be called *classical* but not *classic*. Truly classic works approach the Greek ideal instinctively, although superficially they may have nothing in common with it. Gandhara sculpture, the work of Francesca, Vermeer, Raphael, Maillol and Henry Moore are all essentially classic.

CLERESTORY (derived from 'clear storey'). Usually the windowed nave walls of a church above the roof of the aisles, but the term can be applied to any wall with windows rising above adjacent roofs. (Cf. ill. 45)

CLOTH HALL. The cloth hall was the hall of the weaver's guild. Since medieval weavers, particularly in Flanders, fared extremely well, cloth halls were often lavishly decorated. The long cloth hall at Ypres had a tall tower, as had the cloth hall at Bruges, which was arranged round a square inner courtyard (both 13th/14th cent.). German cloth halls, of which Brunswick's is one of the finest examples, are generally without towers. (Ill. 156)

Book binding: Gospels of Bishop Bernward of Hildesheim *(died 1022). – Gold with filigree and inset jewels. Symbols of the four Evangelists in corner medallions (left part restored in the 13th century). Centre: Christ, with the Virgin and St. John as intercessors; carved ivory, originally the central panel of a small portable altar*

Book illumination: Codex Manesse (c. 1320). Der Schenke von Limburg

Book illumination: LIMBOURG BROTHERS: The Book of Hours of the Duc de Berry *(1411–16). –*
Representation of the month of July; in the background, the castle at Poitiers

wie der man · Heit vnd left den iungē gan · Lutz er
den knabē reitē · Vnd lief den knaben pei der feiten

Daran thet er vil paſz · Do der alt erhoret das · Vō
dem eſel ſaſz er do · Der iung ſaſz auff vnd was fro
Der ein zu dem andern ſprach · Do er den knaben
reitē ſach · wart getreuer geſelle meÿ · Der alt mag
wol ein narre ſein · Das er left reiten den knaben ·
Der ſolt laufen vnd trabē · Vnd ſolt der alt reiten ·
Vil kaum mocht er gepeiten · Das der alt auff den
eſel kam · zu dem knaben vnd reiten hin dan ·

Printing: The 'Edelstein' of ULRICH BONER, *a medieval collection of fables. Printed in Bamberg 1461 by Albrecht Pfister. The first
printed book in the German language*

CLUSTERED PIER. A pier – first found in architecture of the Early English period, and usually of round section – which is partly or fully enclosed by small free-standing shafts (q. v.). Ill. 150

COINS, see Numismatics.

COLLECTOR'S MARK. This is a written or stamped mark on drawings, engravings, etc., to denote the owner. It has been used in Europe since the 17th century, in China at least since the Ming dynasty (1368–1644).

COLONNADE. In contrast to the arcade (q. v.), the columns of a colonnade are linked by a horizontal entablature (q. v.) instead of arches. It was a favourite motif of the architects of the Baroque and the Classic Revival (Bernini's colonnades at St Peter's, Rome, ill. 218, 219).

COLUMN. The column is aesthetically the most satisfying form of support. It generally consists of the round or polygonal shaft, the base and the capital. The lowest member of the base is called the plinth. The capital can be separated from the shaft by the necking; the shaft itself is occasionally further divided by the astragal or torus, a narrow, profiled moulding (Late Romanesque and Early Gothic). The shaft usually tapers towards the capital. Often, the column is made to appear more slender by fluting (q. v.).

COMPOSITION. Composition, in the plastic arts, is the integration of colour, line and plane into a harmonious or dramatic whole. In its simplest form, composition is based on alignment or symmetry. In the Renaissance, the '*figura piramidale*' was a favourite guide to compositions (ill. 52). But composition is by no means tied to any inflexible rules and will in the last resort depend on the artist's sense of order.

CONFRATERNITY. An association of medieval craftsmen and artists, connected with the building of the cathedrals, which already existed in the 12th century and developed to great importance in the 13th and 14th. The confraternity differs from the guild in that members were not restricted to any locality in the practice of their craft. They could move from one workshop to another and were not bound by any local obligations. But they had to subordinate their work to the general plan and had to take their place in the communal task. In the 15th century, the statutes for the different confraternities were written down and we know from these records that the journeymen and apprentices were under the authority of the master and his deputy. The members of the confraternity wore distinctive clothes and had a ritual of their own. The importance of the confraternities decreased from the 15th century onwards in favour of the guilds, and they disappeared altogether in the 18th. The early English trade unions modelled themselves on the medieval confraternity.

COPPER ENGRAVING. The copper engraving (in contrast to the woodcut, q. v.) is based on an intaglio process. The drawing is engraved on a copper plate, exactly as ornament had been engraved on armour, jewellery, etc., for centuries. The plate is then coated with printer's ink, which will cling to the incised lines when the plate is wiped clean. If the plate is then placed on a piece of dampened paper and put into a press, the paper will soak in the colour and the print will be ready. The plate is held against a leather cushion in the course of engraving and the burin is pushed forward very firmly, so as to bring out curved lines with sure strokes. The degree of pressure executed by the hand will determine the thickness of line. The burr of metal turned up in the course of the work must be carefully scraped off before making a trial print. The plate can then be corrected and further prints made, each being slightly different from the other (first state, second state, etc.). Such prints are valued by collectors and are called *avant-la-lettre*, since they were made before the artist finally signed the plate. The signed print is called *après-la-lettre*. Design, drawing, engraving and print can all come from different hands. This applies especially in the case of engravings based on paintings (see p. 341). The name of the 'inventor' is followed by the letters 'inv.', that of the draughtsman by 'del.' (Latin, *delineavit* – drawn), and the engraver's name by 'sc.' (*sculpsit* – engraved). Sometimes we also find the publisher's name preceded by 'exc.' (*excudit* – printed). If design and engraving are the work of one man, we speak of a *peintre graveur*. The first engravings on copper date from shortly after 1400, soon after the invention of paper in Europe. The greatest engraver of all time was Albrecht Dürer. After his day, several variants of the copper engraving were invented, such as the stipple engraving (16th cent.), for which the artist uses a small punch in place of the burin. The mezzotint is an invention of the 17th century. Here the plate is scored all over with a roulette or mezzotint rocker, a steel tool with sharp teeth along its curved edge. The light areas of the drawing are then scraped out and smoothed, so as not to show on the print. Coloured prints, obtained by using several plates, enjoyed great popularity in the 18th century especially in England. The steel engraving replaced the copper print in the 19th century, since it could be produced in greater numbers. The true copper print has generally been superseded by the etching (q. v.) since the 17th century.

COPY. A copy is the repetition or the more or less free interpretation of an original work of art, mostly by an artist of a later age. A copy made at approximately the same date as the original, and made by the artist or a pupil is known as a *replica*. Copies, which are frequently not made of the same material as the original, played an important part in the history of Greek and Roman art. Copies of famous works – mostly statues – were made in Imperial Rome in large quantities (but never in a purely hackneyed manner), for private or public display. These Roman copies are in many cases the only records of the works of the great Greek sculptors of the 5th century B.C., and of the following periods, that have come down to us, since the originals have often been destroyed. The Roman copyists did not faithfully keep to the style of the original, but interpreted their Greek models according to the taste of their own age. This has set a number of problems. Often, parts of different statues were joined into a new work (so-called *pasticcio* or pastiche). In their wall paintings, Roman painters mostly deviated from the original models to such a degree that – with the exception of the Alexander mosaic (ill. p. 149) – we can hardly ever tell the style of the original from a copy. Copies were utterly alien to the spirit of the Middle Ages. They have only reappeared since the Renaissance (mostly paintings); even so, they have never again approached their erstwhile importance. (See also Reproduction)

CORBEL. A bracket projecting from the wall to support a beam or a statue. Corbels are usually carved, often quite elaborately. They can be of stone or wood.

CORNICE. Used to stress the horizontal division of a building, it projects from the wall like a relief and may be elaborately carved. Though originally applicable only to the upper portion of the entablature of the Greek temple, the term now covers any band of projecting masonry on the façade. Many Renaissance buildings have cornices above the base, and are divided horizontally by additional ones above each floor. The main cornice under the roof is always larger and is treated as an important feature, since it also serves to protect the wall below from rain. Doors and windows can be given separate architraves. In Gothic architecture, we often find a plain, slanting cornice. The Baroque cornice was almost turned into a piece of sculpture. Modern architecture dispenses with the cornice almost completely.

CRACKLE. The glaze on pottery often shows fine cracks after firing, since body and glaze do not always expand in the same manner during cooling. These cracks were often produced deliberately, in the glaze of oriental pottery. Crackle also occurs in the painted surfaces of old pictures, the cracks extending right through to the support. Forgeries are often detected by an examination of crackle. Artificially created crackle will usually affect only the varnish and paint film.

CROSS. The cross appears as a decorative or symbolic motif in almost every civilisation; it became the chief symbol of the Christian faith through the crucifixion of Christ, chiefly in the form of the so-called Latin Cross, whose lowest arm is longer than the three others. Numerous important variations of the cross are also found, among them the Greek Cross, with four arms of equal length, the T-shaped Cross of St Anthony, the X-shaped Cross of St Andrew, and the Cross of Constantine as the Sacred Monogram. The foliated cross with the Crucified Christ developed during the Middle Ages and owes its form to the symbolism of the Tree of Jesse and the Tree of Life. (Cf. ill. p. 217)

DAMASCENING. A form of inlaying metal was already known in Antiquity (Mycenae), when silver and gold metal thread was hammered into the engraved ornament of bronze objects. This technique, used to enhance articles made of base metals, is called damascening after the Islamic craftsmen of Damascus, who practised it with great skill. The term is also applied to a type of decoration on steel blades, produced by etching or welding rods of iron and steel together. (Ill. 329)

DANCE OF DEATH. This motif occurs from the first half of the 15th century onwards, chiefly in one of the following forms: either the dead and the living dance a round, during which the live person is grabbed by one of the dead and carried off; or, Death, in the form of a skeleton, takes a living person with him (this is not shown as a dance but as a series of scenes); or, again, the dead execute a dance. Scenes from the Dance of Death appeared on the walls of cemeteries (Saints Innocents, Paris, 1425 and the Dominican monastery in Basle, 1437–41, both destroyed), mortuaries and churches (Church of Our Lady in Lübeck, 1463, with verses in Low German – in copy only). Two woodcut series, 'La danse macabre' (Paris 1491–92) and Hans Holbein the Younger's 'Dance of Death' (1525, but first published in Lyons 1538) are amongst the most interesting interpretations of this theme in the graphic arts (ill. 210). Alfred Rethel took it up again in another form in the 19th century in his 'Auch ein Totentanz'.

DIPTYCH(ON) (Gr. for twice folded). (1) Two panels, generally designed as a single composition (e. g. Wilton Diptych). (2) A pair of tall, narrow rectangular tablets of ivory, bone or metal, coated with wax on the inside for taking down notes, such as were found in the ruins of Pompeii. The so-called Consular Diptychs were ivory panels, elaborately carved in relief, which Roman Consuls of the 5th and 6th centuries A. D. used to give to high officials on their assumption of office. These diptychs – whose borders were decorated with Christian symbols – served in the early Christian Church for taking down names for the Mass. They were occasionally used in bindings for illuminated manuscripts during the Middle Ages. (Ill. p. 206)

DOG TOOTH. A type of carved ornament common in 13th-century English Gothic or Early English architecture. It consists of radiating leaves suggesting the crowns of teeth. Lincoln Cathedral has good examples.

DOME. A dome, or cupola, is a spherical roof; it is ideal for a central structure (q. v.). Corbelled domes have existed since the Stone Age. They are constructed by laying the stones horizontally, each row overlapping the other, until the ceiling is closed by a key-stone. Some of the monumental round buildings of early Antiquity were vaulted in this manner (Treasury of Atreus, Mycenae). The style is still used to-day in some regions (Apulia). Properly vaulted domes probably originated in the Near East and were perfected by the Romans (The Pantheon, Rome, c. A. D. 120). Later, the dome be-

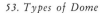

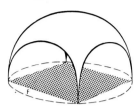
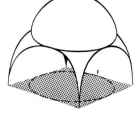

Cushion dome   *Saucer dome*

came an important feature
of Byzantine architecture
(Hagia Sophia in Istanbul,
c. A.D. 530). It was through
Byzantium that the dome
came to affect the architecture both of Islam and of
Italy (Ravenna; St Mark's,
Venice). Occasionally it even
appears in France (Aqui-
taine, Périgueux). Else-
where, the dome has only

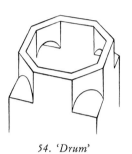

54. 'Drum'

assumed importance again since the Renaissance (Brunelleschi's dome in Florence, Michelangelo's dome for
St Peter's, Rome). Pendentive domes are of two types:
in the one case, dome and pendentives are of the same
hemisphere. The pendentive is simply the curved over-
hanging surface supporting the dome, each dome thus
having four pendentives (cushion dome). In the second
type of pendentive dome, the saucer dome, dome
and pendentive consist of different hemispheres. This is
an advanced form of the dome, already known in Byzantium, and rediscovered by Brunelleschi. Illustration
54 shows how the transition from a square section to
an octagonal 'drum' – to take the dome – is effected.
Often, the dome is surmounted by a small turret-like
structure, the lantern (as in the dome of St Paul's, London). The horizontal segments between the pendentives
are called lunettes. (Ill. 53, 54, 170, 218, 222, 251)

DRAPERY. The folds of a fabric, usually a garment,
and their representation in sculpture, painting or drawing. Drapery was of special importance to Gothic
artists. It was in the garment draped over the curves
of the body that both painters and sculptors found
their most expressive subject-matter. The flowing or
angular lines of drapery, its indentations and bulging
convexities were treated in a different manner by each
generation or school of artists and often furnish the
principle evidence for the dating and localization of
a work.

EASEL PICTURE. The easel picture as distinct from
the wall painting is portable and is executed on either
wood, canvas, or more recently, hardboard. Easel pictures were known in Antiquity (mummy portraits), and
in the Middle Ages from the 12th century onwards. But
the form only began to assume importance when the
private patron superseded the Church as sponsor of the
arts. Among the earliest true easel pictures were van

Eyck's portraits. The portable picture has dominated
painting from the Renaissance to the present day.

ENAMEL consists of a glass flux, coloured with metallic oxides. The earliest known form of enamelling
was practised in Ancient Egypt and, above all, amongst
the Celts and Saxons between the 3rd and the 1st
centuries B.C.: a red enamel was simply poured into
grooves which had been made in the metal. When these
grooves are enlarged into hollows, we speak of champlevé enamel. This technique, already known to the Romans, was brought to a high state of perfection in the
12th and 13th centuries, especially in the regions round
Cologne, Trèves, Verdun and Limoges (reliquary pendants). A great variety of colours was added to the
glass flux. The design is formed by ridges of metal that
have been left standing between the hollows. By contrast, the metal is left intact in the cloisonné technique,
where strips of metal are welded to the base, following
the outlines of the figures. The cells (cloisons) formed
by these strips are then filled with the enamel. This was
the principal method used by Byzantine artists especially during the 10th and 11th centuries. In the cloisonné
of Eastern European popular art the metal strips are
replaced by silver wire. Another technique of enamelling on silver, the basse-taille process, developed in Italy
from the 14th century onwards. The drawing was cut
into a silver plate and everything was then covered in
transparent enamels. Another process known since
Renaissance times used the so-called Grisaille or 'painter's enamel', which cannot be considered a true enamel,
since the picture is simply painted on its enamel background with a brush – as ordinary colours are on a
panel or canvas – and fired. It was Limoges that led in
this technique (Limoges enamels of the 16th century and
earlier), as it had in the case of champlevé enamel in
the Middle Ages. Later, miniature paintings on a white
enamel ground became very popular. Our own age has
shown an increasing interest in the older techniques and
has brought them to life again. (Ill. pp. 192, 194)

ENCAUSTIC. A technique of painting widely used
in Greek and Roman Antiquity, employing pigments
mixed with hot, refined beeswax. Most Greek stone
sculpture had to be painted and the encaustic process
was eminently suitable for this purpose. No Hellenic
Greek specimens exist, though there are many literary
allusions to the process (Pliny the elder, Theophrastus
and Dioscorides). The best-known surviving examples
are the Fayum mummy portraits. Encaustic became
obsolete during the 9th century. (Ill. p. 161)

ENTABLATURE. The portion above the capitals of
the pillars of the Greek temple, consisting of architrave,
frieze and cornice. It occurs again in many forms in
Renaissance and Baroque architecture. (Cf. ill. 99)

ETCHING. Etching, like copper engraving (q. v.) is
an intaglio process. There is little difference between
the two methods, except that the lines, in the case of
an etching, are not engraved directly into the plate
(often also of copper), but are produced with acid

(nitric acid or sulphuric acid). The plate is coated with a thin layer of wax or asphalt, called the *ground* (q. v.). The design is then easily drawn into the soft coating. The acid can only eat into the metal where the needle has pierced the ground, thus producing the drawing. After removing the ground, the prints are made as in copper engraving. The technique of the etching permits the most delicate lines and requires little physical effort. The result is particularly interesting when the plate is exposed to the acid in stages. The finest lines are produced by leaving the plate in the acid for a short time only. Therefore, the plate is taken out of the bath, the lines meant to be delicate ones are covered again with ground, and the plate is replaced in the liquid. The other lines will then come out more strongly. A great variety of tone and chiaroscuro are easy to achieve and it is therefore not surprising that Rembrandt, the greatest master of the etching, should have shown such an interest in this technique. The beginnings of the etching date from the time of Dürer (Dürer himself had etched on iron). The etching has lost none of its importance since the 17th century. Several variants have been developed in the course of time. As in copper engraving, there is a manner of producing a softer effect, called *vernis mou* or soft ground etching. The paper is placed on the soft ground and the drawing made. The pencil presses into the ground, thus exposing the plate, which is then etched; the resultant outlines will appear relatively soft. The aquatint was invented by Le Prince in 1768. Here, the plate is covered with rosin grains and heated, so that the rosin will cling to the metal. Having covered areas that are meant to come out light in the drawing with ground, thus exposing the plate, which is then etched, the latter is put into the acid. It has to be immersed a number of times, depending on the desired effect. Ground and rosin must, of course, be removed before printing. The general effect will resemble that of a wash drawing. The etching needle can also be used directly on the plate without using any acid. Artists like Corinth and the Expressionists liked this method, which is more immediate and more personal. It can be distinguished from the etching by the pointed endings to the lines. As in copper engraving, coloured prints can be produced by using several plates. (Ill. 235, 236, 277)

FAIENCE, see Pottery.

FAKES followed in the wake of art collectors; that is to say, they began at the time of the Renaissance, though it is known that forgers were at work in Ancient Rome, where the private collector first emerged. The application of stylistic criteria and of chemical and physical tests (X-ray photographs) usually brings the truth to light. But even great experts have been deceived by brilliant fakes over comparatively long periods, and enormous sums have been paid for entirely worthless articles. It is a widespread belief that in such instances the faker must be a 'great artist' and that his work must therefore have considerable commercial value. It should

55. *Baptismal font from St Mary's in Wismar (14th cent.), cast bronze*

be borne in mind, however, that the merit of a work of art does not lie in the process of its manufacture, but in its originality and vigour – both qualities of necessity absent in a fake.

FAN. Fans have existed in almost every age and civilisation. Made of peacock or ostrich feathers, they were carried in front of the highest dignitaries as symbols of authority in Babylon and Ancient Egypt. The popularity of the fan in Europe dates from the 16th and 17th centuries, when it came into use amongst the ladies of the Court, either as the circular fan or as a folding fan, based on the Chinese model. During the Rococo, frames of gold or ivory were decorated with paintings on silk or paper after the designs of leading artists, such as Boucher or Watteau.

FILIGREE is lace-like ornament of gold and silver wire, usually welded to a metal base. The technique probably came from the Far East (India, China), was known in Antiquity and has been practised in the West since the Barbarian Invasions. It has been kept alive in popular art until the present day.

FLUTING. Vertical decorative grooves on the shafts of columns or piers. Fluting was used on columns in Greek Antiquity; in the case of Late Gothic and Baroque columns, it sometimes winds spirally round the shaft. (Ill. 102, 171)

FOLLY. An architectural extravaganza, a monument without functional intention, a concrete expression of the builder's private beliefs, an embodiment of his wit and a mirror to his vanity, a house abandoned incompleted, any building which is generally considered to lack utility or meaning. The folly is particularly associated with 18th-century England, when indulgence in this aberration of the art of architecture assumed the proportions of an epidemic. Yet the folly is not confined to any style, period or nationality. Conspicuous examples are scattered throughout the centuries, from the Tower of Babel to the palace and gardens of the Prince of Patagonia, La Bagaria, in Sicily and the artificial ruins on the hilltops of Lower Austria. The unfinished cathedral of the Sagrada Familia by Gaudi in Barcelona is also a genuine folly. The earliest authentic follies in England were built in Northamptonshire by the recusant Sir Thomas Tresham who designed Rushton Lodge (1595) and the unfinished house called Lyveden New Building to symbolize his private views on the Passion; other follies of a religious nature include the Tattingstone Wonder, Suffolk, cottages built in the form of a church to improve the view from the squire's window, and Jezreel's Temple near Rochester designed by James White in 1885 in preparation for the end of the world. The most conspicuous follies took the form of isolated towers; among the more notable examples are Eyre's Folly, Wiltshire, Sir William Chambers' Pagoda at Kew, Stratton's Folly at Little Berkhamsted, Beckford's Lansdowne Tower at Bath and the Sugarloaf Folly above Dallington, Sussex, erected by 'Mad Jack' Fuller to win a bet that Dallington Church spire could be seen from his drawing-room window. Nearly every 18th-century country house could boast its Temple, Artificial Ruin, Triumphal Arch, Pyramid, Tower, Gazebo, Grotto or Ornamental Mausoleum. Some parks, like that at Stowe, were embellished with all these types of folly. The most modest follies were *grottoes*, stemming from the memories of Baroque gardens in Italy and France. Evelyn and Sir William Temple were the first to indulge in grottoes; Pope popularized them with his celebrated folly at Twickenham; the Duchess of Richmond and her daughters built a famous shell grotto with their own hands at Goodwood House. The most magnificent folly Triumphal Arch, known as the 'Gates of Jerusalem' was erected at Shugborough Park in 1763 to the designs of James Stuart. The folly Pyramids were usually intended for tombs; outstanding are the two built by Jack Fuller, one at Brightling for himself and the other on Farley Mount, Hants, for a favourite horse. Sir Francis Dashwood's mausoleum at West Wycombe is another curious sepulchral folly. A strange medley of imitation Roman *tempietta* and sham Gothic ruin is to be seen in the grounds of Colchester Castle.

FONT. The font is always placed at the west end of the church. Fonts vary greatly in design: they may be cylindrical, rectangular or polygonal, rest directly on the floor or be supported on plinths, legs or steps. They are carved in the style of the period to which they belong. During the Middle Ages it was customary to consecrate the baptismal water at certain seasons only. Hence a font cover was generally provided which could be lowered over the bowl and locked. This fitting became a favourite object for the ingenuity of the woodcarver. There are fine examples of covers at Ufford, Castle Acre, Beverley and Durham in England, and a famous one at Notre Dame, Hal in Belgium. (Ill. 55)

56. Romanesque double-basined fountain: Goslar, market fountain

FOUNTAIN. Fountains, as works of art, are a feature of towns and monastic communities, where a supply of safe drinking water was imperative. The fountain of Antiquity was usually a jet fountain, in which the water flowed down over a series of basins. The same type of fountain, simplified or with staggered basins, occurs again in medieval Europe – two-basin fountain at Goslar (ill. 56), three-basin fountain at Maulbronn Abbey, – and was built until the end of the Gothic. (One of the last examples, dating from 1408, is at Brunswick.) But the Gothic also produced its own style of the fountain consisting of a pier or column, and a basin, usually polygonal. The water spouts forth into the basin in thin jets from the top of the column. The Gothic fountain often terminates in a finial or in turreted forms of the Gothic tabernacle (Schöner Brunnen, i. e. 'Beautiful Fountain', Nuremberg, 1386; Jörg Syrlin's fountain in Ulm, ill. 57). The jet fountain continued through-

57. Gothic pinnacle fountain: Ulm, 'Fish-box' of JÖRG SYRLIN, THE ELDER

58. *Baroque fountain: Rome,* NICCOLO SALVI's *Fontana di Trevi (1732–62)*

out the Renaissance and the Baroque, although the Gothic pyramidal form usually grew into a sturdy column, surmounted by a statue. But the Classic fountain with its series of basins also came back into favour (Bernini's fountain in the Vatican forum, Rome), although the water no longer flowed into the basins from narrow pipes, but cascaded down like a curtain. Indeed, the splendour of the Baroque fountain with its sculptures (Salvi's Fontana di Trevi, Rome, ill. 58) is equalled only by the Nymphaeum (q. v.) of Ancient Rome. Fountains for ritual ablutions are to be found in the atrium of the Early Christian basilica and form an integral part of the courtyard of the mosque.

FRESCO. The term 'fresco' is Italian and means fresh, in contrast to dry. In fresco, the most common technique of wall-painting, already known in Antiquity, the pigment, mixed with water, is applied to the plaster while it is still wet. The plaster, therefore, must be prepared in sections from day to day and must be painted immediately. Since the painter has to work very quickly, he first makes a full-scale drawing, which he transfers to the wall. Corrections are impossible, because any over-painted parts will flake off. Colours and plaster combine on a fine enamel-like surface in the fresco, but fade a little in the process – a point the artist must consider in advance. The great masters of Classical times and of the Early Renaissance used this technique. (See ill. p. 59)

FRESCO SECCO is, as the name implies, fresco painting on a dry plaster ground (in contrast to Fresco, q. v.). The artist uses either pigments mixed with lime water – which do not last on a dry ground and are therefore unsuitable for important work of a permanent character – or modern poster colours. (See ill. p. 203)

FRIEZE. In Greek architecture, the frieze is the middle division of the Classic entablature, i. e. the part between architrave and cornice. In its wider sense, the term is used for any relief below the cornice (not necessarily the main cornice) of a building. The frieze is decorated either with figures or patterns, such as the palmette, the acanthus and the rosette, or with sculpture, as on Greek temples. In Romanesque architecture, we find friezes formed by dentils, lozenges, rounded arches (in the manner of Romanesque galleries), chequer-board patterns and other motifs. Gothic friezes are mostly foliated. The Renaissance saw a return to the ornamented friezes of Antiquity, which were rather freely interpreted by Baroque architects. In the interior, friezes are mostly constituted as paintings.

FURNITURE. Chests and cupboards are the earliest surviving specimens of furniture; tables, beds, desks and chairs are later in date. Furniture, in early days, had to serve many functions. Very little furniture survives from Antiquity. Some wooden chairs and chests from Ancient Egypt, and some Roman bronze and marble furniture found in Pompeii are preserved in museums. For the rest, all our knowledge of early furniture comes from vases and wall paintings. Early medieval household furniture – in contrast to church fittings – was very modest indeed. The most important piece was the chest, which was also used as a seat, a travelling trunk, a table and often a bed. The first chairs had box seats and clearly derived from the chest. The increasing wealth of Late Gothic times created a demand for more elaborate furniture. The hollowed-out tree trunks, of which the earliest chests were made, gave way to framework and panelling. Next, craftsmen learned to veneer, or to use thin layers of rare woods to face the more ordinary kinds and to decorate furniture with marquetry (q. v.). Aesthetic, rather than purely utilitarian, considerations became increasingly important from the Renaissance onwards (ill. 204). Architectural forms were used for chests, court cupboards, sideboards and tables. This is very characteristic of English 16th- and 17th-century furniture. It is heavy, solid and, with few exceptions, not particularly elegant. Motifs were widely and sometimes unsuitably copied. During the Baroque, craftsmen began to specialize in various branches. Next to the 'ébénistes' (ebony workers), the makers of solid furniture, there were the 'chaisistes', or makers of chairs. Pieces were no longer made in their entirety by one craftsman, but parts, made elsewhere, were now assembled to a pattern. The middle-class furniture (e. g. the Danzig Baroque cupboard, ill. 27) of the time with its carvings and sculptural forms was already far more elaborate than its Renaissance predecessor. The making of French furniture – dictated by Court fashions – demanded even greater skill. The most celebrated 'ébénistes' were Boulle, Roentgen, Oeben, and Riesener. (Ill. 237, pp. 81, 319). The Wallace Collection in London probably contains more examples of their work than any other museum outside France. Forms were continually changing between the time of the 'Roi Soleil' and the French Revolution. These changes are characterized by the names of the different rulers as the styles of Louis XIV, Louis XV and Louis XVI. In England, Thomas Chippendale created furniture of elegant forms in the Chinese and Gothic manner and was famous for his chair-back designs, particularly the ribbon back. Other English furniture makers, whose names have become by-words, were Hepplewhite and Sheraton. The great tradition of the 18th century lingered on in the Empire, Regency and Biedermeier periods. But while the Empire, as the 'Imperial' Napoleonic style, and the Regency, inspired by the taste of the Prince Regent, have the characteristics of a Court style, the German and Viennese Biedermeier furniture is essentially middle-class (see p. 408). With them, originality in furniture design had come to an end. The 19th century saw veritable orgies of imitation, to which Art Nouveau, or the *Jugendstil,* tried to offer an alternative. In England, William Morris and his circle, to whom Art Nouveau is so greatly indebted, made various attempts to return to good, wholesome craftmanship. Yet recently a number of small craftsmen have appeared both in England and on the Continent in whom the old traditions have not yet died and who are yet open to new impulses. The followers of the Dessau Bauhaus tried to approach problems of design in the spirit of our century and also experimented with new materials such as chromium steel.

GABLE. The portion of the wall between the two sloping sides of the roof is called the gable. The gable – as far as it forms part of the façade – has always been the object of special attention. The flat roof of the temple of Antiquity produced a low triangular gable (pediment, q. v.), which was decorated with sculpture. In French Gothic churches, the gable end of the nave roof is sometimes hidden by a screen linking the two towers above the west front. In German Gothic, however, the roof very largely determined the outline of a building. Here we find the stepped gable (Münster, Lüneburg, Stralsund), which lives on in the German Renaissance (Brunswick Gewandhaus). 'False', or purely decorative, gables, not dictated by the structure of the roof, are sometimes placed along the sides of a building (Copenhagen Stock Exchange, ill. 220).

GARDENS. Famous gardens, often with enclosures for wild animals, existed already in Achaemenid Persia. The Roman Emperor Hadrian in the 2nd century A. D. built a villa with extensive grounds in Tivoli. The Renaissance brought about a revival of the art of garden design, as the examples of Settignano, Bagnaia and Tivoli prove. Germany, too, had famous gardens – often attached to princely palaces – such as the Hortus Palatinus in Heidelberg and the Hofgarten in Stuttgart. During the Baroque, garden design assumed a new importance. The gardens at Caserta near Naples, with their canal, cascades and groups of nymphs, were laid out in 1760. In France, the famous garden architect Le Nôtre created in 1656 the magnificent park of Vaux-le-Vicomte (near Melun) with its carpet bedding. Such

'broderie-parterres', together with trimmed box hedges, formed the frame-work of many a park. In Versailles (1667–88), the central axis with various ornamental pools and groups of sculpture (Latona-Apollo fountain) is intersected by the great canal. More fountains, basins, temples, open-air theatres, pavilions, and miniature palaces are distributed throughout the park. The French Renaissance châteaux of Chenonceau, Valencay, Villandry and Chambord, too, were given extensive gardens during the Baroque. There are more famous gardens near Paris and Marly-le-Roy, Chantilly, Rambouillet, St Cloud (with a remarkable cascade) and in St Germain-en-Laye, the latter also by Le Nôtre (1673). French garden designers also produced extensive parks in Germany. The most famous of these are at Herrenhausen near Hanover, at Schleissheim and Nymphenburg near Munich (Charbonnier, Girard). Others are the Karlsaue in Cassel and the vast, but unfortunately unfinished, Wilhelmshöhe. Where conditions made gardens in the immediate surroundings of the palace impossible, these were laid out in the vicinity (Veitshochheim near Würzburg, and Schwetzingen near Mannheim). In Vienna, the gardens at Schönbrunn and at the Belvedere deserve special mention, as do the gardens of the Mirabell Palace in Salzburg. Towards the end of the 18th century, the informal 'English Garden' – asymmetrical and 'romantic' – gradually replaced the formal, geometrically laid-out Baroque garden. The most famous examples of this type of garden in Germany are at Muskau and Wörlitz. (Ill. 227, 228)

In England, gardens have long played an important role. There are the formal Tudor and Jacobean gardens, of which Hampton Court with its complete 17th-century garden is only one famous example, the 'romantic' garden of the 18th and early 19th centuries, the Victorian gardens of all shapes and sizes, and those of Gertrude Jekyll. Often, gardening was a branch of architecture, and the garden designer, perhaps to prevent him from losing caste, was called a 'garden architect'. Englishmen, even great landscape artists like Humphrey Repton and 'Capability' Brown, were proud to be called gardeners. To create a 'romantic' garden or a landscape effect is no easy task. The carpet bedding will be perfect in two months, whereas the trees will only reach maturity in fifty years or more. Again, the carpet bedding will need careful attention, the trees hardly any. The Baroque garden, with all its splendour, contained no animals except perhaps stone ones; but in the English garden the lawns will be grazed by cattle and horses, thus maintaining the contact with living things that makes it so delightful.

Both Repton and Brown stopped at nothing to achieve their effects. Expense counted for very little. Hills were moved to open up views, underground passages were built, small rivers dammed. Everything was to look as natural as possible, without aping nature. English landscape gardeners allowed their imagination full play, yet they maintained a sense of proportion: '... every circumstance which marks the habitation of man must be artificial; and although in works of art we may imitate the forms and graces of nature, yet to make them truly natural always leads to absurdity', Repton wrote in *Sketches and Hints on Landscape Gardening* (1795). Large-scale gardening was made easier in England by the enclosure of the land formerly held in common. As a result, much of the landscape of southern England was transformed into one vast garden. This pleasing effect was, however, diminished by the Industrial Revolution and by the subsequent spread of built-up areas.

GARGOYLE. Water-spouts, designed to draw rain-water from the roof, were already treated as an architectural feature in Antiquity, when they were given the shape of a lion's head. In the Middle Ages, these gargoyles (Latin *gurgus,* a whirlpool) appear as devils, monsters and chimaerae. The presence of the demonic and grotesque, which the artists engaged by the Church had little opportunity to represent elsewhere, was permitted outside hallowed ground, and so appeared on the church roof.

GENRE PAINTING. Genre painting depicts scenes from everyday life (in contrast to religious or historical painting). It does not deal with any particular stratum of society: there are genre pictures showing life amongst the aristocracy, the middle class and the peasantry. Though examples of genre, parading under religious titles, occur in the Middle Ages and the Renaissance, it flowered in its own right from the 17th century (Dutch and Flemish painters) to the middle of the 19th. (Ill. p. 60)

GLASS is made of silica and metallic oxides, or, more simply, of sand, soda and lime, which are fused together. Glass has always attracted the artist, since in its molten state it is very malleable and will readily take colour. It can be blown, moulded, treated with various tools and further decoration fused to it. By a variety of techniques, glass can be made colourless, given a single colour or several colours. Thin threads of glass can be used to produce the so-called 'twist stem'; this can be elaborated into the 'lace twist', the 'spiral gauze' and many other forms. If the thin threads in the stem are coloured, the result is known as a 'colour twist stem'; if both opaque and coloured, a 'mixed twist stem', and so on. If glass rods of different colours are fused together, cut across and melted into plain glass, the resulting effect is called *millefiore* (literally 'a thousand flowers'). The best-known examples of this kind are the paper-weights of the 19th century. Often, vessels of plain glass are coated – or 'flashed' – with a thin layer of coloured glass, a technique more common on the Continent (Bohemian red glass, red 'Biedermeier' glasses, etc.) than in England. Glass can be painted in enamel colours and gilt, or it can be decorated on the lapidary's wheel, with the diamond point or etched with acids. Glass pastes, as substitutes for jewellery, were already known in Ancient Egypt in the 3rd millennium B.C. Technical improvements led to a mature phase of the glass-maker's art in the Hellenistic period and in Imperial Rome. The Roman tradition was continued by the glassmakers of Islam, who decorated glass with enamels and carvings. The Venetians took up Eastern techniques in the 15th century, developed them and were soon in advance of all their competitors. Venetian coloured glass has held a leading place ever since. It was the Venetian goblet that replaced the simple beaker of plain green glass which had either been decorated with punts or with coats of arms, mottoes and figures – usually enamelled. Glass cutting and facetting flourished during the Baroque and Rococo periods in Germany, Holland and the British Isles. Lead and flint glass, richly facetted, was mostly made in England and Ireland (Bristol, Waterford), flashing was mostly practised in Bohemia, enamelling in England (Bristol) and France. After a decline in the second half of the 19th century, the advent of Art Nouveau brought about a revival of glass-making. Three French artists, in particular, Brocard, E. Rousseau and Gallé began experimenting with glass colouring and decorating and were the forerunners of contemporary French artists. In recent times it is Scandinavian glassware which is of outstanding importance. The Orrefors factory is celebrated for high quality glass designed by Edvald Hald and Simon Gate. The endless possibilities of glass are only now beginning to be realized. A particularly interesting use is being made of the material by architects.

GLASS PICTURES. Glass pictures are paintings on the back of a glass panel. In contrast to stained glass windows, they are not meant to be looked at with the light shining through them, but as ordinary paintings. The usual practice is just to draw or engrave the outlines, then to fill in the individual portions with brilliant colours. The picture is often backed with metal foil, which further increases its characteristic charm. This form of art dates from as early as the 4th century A.D. But its great triumphs did not come until after 1500, when it was practised throughout Europe, mostly to meet the demand for devotional pictures. But the 17th and 18th centuries saw a decline in the glass picture, which degenerated into a mass-produced article. It was rescued from this state by peasant artists, who, using simple outlines and vigorous colours, turned it into a branch of popular art. It attained its greatest importance in this new form in southern Germany, Bohemia and Silesia, although it is by no means unknown elsewhere.

GLAZE consists of metallic and mineral substances and is applied to pottery before firing – or after a preliminary firing – as decoration. It serves also to make it waterproof.

GLYPTIC ARTS. The term 'glyptic' is derived from the Greek. It embraces the arts of carving precious or semi-precious stones in relief. Engraved stones are called intagli (It. *intaglio, -i*) or gems, while those which are worked in high relief are called cameos. Intagli were often used for clay or wax seals and were therefore frequently worn in rings. Cameos served a variety of other purposes, but were often merely made to display the gem-cutter's skill or the beauty of the stone. Cameos

Fresco painting: PIERO DELLA FRANCESCA: *The Court Ladies of the Queen of Sheba.*
Detail from the Legend of the True Cross (S. Francesco, Arezzo)

Genre painting: JAN STEEN: Twelfth Night

and intagli are fashioned on the lapidary's wheel, or with the help of carborundum dust. The glyptic arts were practised with great skill in Mesopotamia as long ago as during the 4th millennium B.C. Cylinder seals, for impressing on some soft material, and used for official or business purposes, were already well known. The Egyptians scarcely knew the intaglio, since most of their seals were made in pottery, often in the shape of the scarab. In the Minoan and Mycenaean civilisations, the glyptic arts were much to the fore. The stone-cutters of this age used both pattern and figure decoration. Gem cutting, mostly in the form of intagli, also flourished in Ancient Greece from the 8th century B.C. onwards. As the making of intagli and cameos became an important branch of the arts, many stone-cutters came to sign their work. Under Greek influence, the glyptic arts spread to Persia, where they assumed great importance between the 6th and 4th centuries B.C.; also, from the Archaic period onwards, to Etruria and thence throughout Italy. Here, too, most of the stones were cut as intagli; the motifs were mostly based on Greek models. Cameos came into vogue during the Hellenistic period only in connection with the art of the Court; they mostly bore the portraits of princes or served to glorify ruling houses. Vessels carved in semi-precious stones were rarer and so were greatly treasured. Since the late Hellenistic period substitutes for intagli have been used, made of glass cast from moulds (pastes). The glyptic arts were very rarely practised in the Middle Ages; but antique gems and cameos were always very highly prized and were used until the Baroque, often to decorate objects employed in the service of the Church. Gem-cutting was only rediscovered as a separate branch of the arts during the Renaissance, and it came into its own again during the Classic Revival. (Gemma Augustea, ill. 117; Lothair Cross, ill. p. 193)

GOLD GROUND. While paintings of Late Antiquity usually have a naturalistic background, Byzantine art from the 4th century onwards often shows figures against a plain gold ground, which is non-spatial and without perspective. This gold ground occurs in Western miniature and panel painting until the end of the Middle Ages. In the case of panels, it is sometimes decorated with embossed or relief-like ornament. Gold is still used to-day in the religious painting of Eastern Europe (see Icon, ill. p. 182).

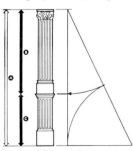

59. Golden section
A : B = B : C

GOLDEN SECTION.
That part of a line or figure in which the size of the smaller part is to the size of the greater part as the greater is to the whole. A system of relative proportions already known in Antiquity. It is used both in painting and architecture (see Brunelleschi).

GOLDSMITH'S WORK. The art of the goldsmith includes chasing, hammered work, damascening, filigree and casting in precious metals, as well as inlaying with precious stones and enamel-work. Jewellery, precious vessels, altar equipment, weapons and suits of armour all fall within its scope. The relatively few instances of larger sculptural works of this kind are mostly made of metal beaten upon a wooden core, like the gold and ivory statues of Antiquity (Pheidias' Zeus and Athene, both lost) or the Romanesque statue of Ste. Foy in Conques-en-Rouergue. The art of the goldsmith had reached great heights in Antiquity, especially in the Egyptian and Sumerian civilisations (see ill. of Tutenkhamon's golden coffin p. 121). The earliest examples of granulated work come from Egypt.

The famous Vaphio Cups illustrate the skill of Minoan goldsmiths, while Greek jewellery includes some of the finest specimens of filigree enamel and granulated work. Geometric motifs prevail but there are many representations of human and animal figures. Roman goldsmiths' and silversmiths' work (discoveries at Pompeii, Boscoreale, Hildesheim, Mildenhall) exhibits the same techniques used with heavy magnificence rather than with the grace and delicacy characteristic of Greek work. Byzantine goldsmiths perfected the art of cloisonné and excelled also in filigree and granulated work. The remarkable Treasure of Petrossa (Bucharest Mus.) is typical of the goldsmith's work produced during the Dark Ages; the style is a decadent form of the classical tradition combined with barbaric elements. Its chief characteristics are a use of conventionalized animal forms, pierced goldwork and a lavish display of stones inlaid in cloisonné fashion. Later and more refined forms of this type of work are to be found in the Merovingian style of the 5th century. The contents of the tomb of King Childeric (Paris/Bibliothèque Nationale) admirably illustrate the goldsmith's craft of this period. Celtic and Anglo-Saxon chalices, plates and jewellery show excellent hammered work full of intricate detail and with interlacing winding scrolls in repoussé with fillings of enamel. A celebrated example of Celtic work is the Tara Brooch, while Anglo-Saxon work is well represented by the Sutton Hoo Treasure (British Mus.). The goldsmith's art flourished during the Romanesque period with its golden altar fittings (Henry II's Basle antependium, Cluny), golden altar panels (Aix-la-Chapelle/Cathedral treasure), embossed reliquary shrines inlaid with precious stones or cloisonné enamel (shrine of the Magi, Cologne; Domed Reliquary of the Guelph Treasure, Brunswick, ill. p. 194) and beautifully worked communion plate, etc.

Medieval work exhibits greater elegance, but still exploits the sensuous appeal of colour in enamel and gems, as in the Chalice of St Remi. The work of the most representative goldsmith of the Renaissance, Benvenuto Cellini, illustrates, both in the design of jewellery and table pieces such as his famous salt cellar, the fine craftsmanship of the period and its tendency to exuberance. The latter quality was characteristic of the

16th century and is nowhere more apparent than in the extravagant gold and silver ecclesiastical vessels of Spain. The richly decorated goldsmith's work of this time even influenced architecture and was the origin of the name given to the *Plateresque* style. Standards of workmanship remained high until the end of the 18th century, though many former techniques were gradually discontinued. Nineteenth-century work was marked by borrowings from historical sources, particularly the Romanesque, Gothic and Renaissance styles. A small group of Italian craftsmen produced work of exceptional quality. These include Castellari, a Roman goldsmith, who rediscovered the technique of granulation. The forgotten art of enamelling on a prepared *guilloche* field was revived by the Russian goldsmith Fabergé at the close of the century. His curious pieces range from boxes, clocks and bell-pushers to automatic toys. (Cf. ill. 51, 205, pp. 192, 193)

Remarkable examples of the goldsmith's art have survived from pre-Columbian America. The Aztecs, the Mixtecs and Toltecs were skilled in all the techniques and used them for both personal ornaments and ritual objects. (Cf. ill. p. 554)

GOUACHE. A form of water-colour painting, in which the pigments – in contrast to pure water colour – are thickened with zinc white and gum and become opaque as a result. Medieval illuminated manuscripts were often executed in this medium. It was used by early water colourists such as Paul Sandby; and Turner excelled in gouache as well as in transparent water-colour painting. Many modern artists, among them John Piper and Graham Sutherland, use this technique.

GRANULATION (Latin, *granulum* – a grain). A technique of decorating objects in precious metal by soldering small grains of gold or silver on to them.

GRAPHIC ART. Although this term, strictly speaking, covers all the arts connected with writing and drawing, it is now principally applied to the processes of printing from various kinds of blocks, plates or type, such as etching, drypoint, lithography, wood and linoleum block printing, etc. Print processes fall into three general classifications: (1) *Relief process,* in which the impression is made by a line or area that stands out from the background of the block, carries the ink and by means of pressing or rubbing transfers it to the paper, as in woodcuts (q. v.), wood engraving, linol-cuts and commercial line blocks. (2) *Intaglio process,* in which the line or area that makes the impression is cut into the metal plate and holds the ink which is drawn out into the paper in printing by the great pressure of the press, as in engraving on metal, mezzotint, aquatint and drypoint. (3) *Flat process,* in which there is no appreciable difference in level between the printing area and the general surface, but in which the area destined for printing has been chemically treated so that it retains ink which transfers to paper under pressure, as in lithography (q. v.). Another flat process is silk-screen printing in which the ink is applied through stencils.

Among the technical terms used in connection with prints the more important are: *edition,* the number of prints issued, often numbered by contemporary artists, as for example, 3/50, 3rd of an edition of 50; *impression,* each print produced; *proof* or *trial proof,* impressions printed while the artist is working on the block or plate to check progress; when the artist prints a number of impressions, alters the plate and then prints others, the first group is said to be of the *first state,* those printed later after revision, of the *second state,* etc. Occasionally, when only one proof of a certain *state* exists, it is known as a unique impression. But there is only one graphic process which limits prints to a single copy – the monotype, which dates from the 19th century. (See also Copper Engraving, Etching)

GRISAILLE, see Enamel.

GROTESQUE (It. *grottesco,* from *grotta*). Human or animal figures or fabulous creatures decoratively combined with garlands, wreaths of flowers or other ornamental devices such as arabesques or scroll-work. The derivation of the word links it with the excavation in Italy of Ancient Roman remains where this style of decoration was common. Grotesque ornaments were widely used by Italian painters, sculptors and engravers after about 1490. Raphael was among the pioneers in the revival of the antique grotesque. From Italy the popularity of the grotesque spread, very largely through engraving, to the North, where it was developed with particular ingenuity by the Flemish and the Dutch.

GROTTO, see Folly.

GROUND. To seal the surface, it is advisable to ground the canvas or panel intended for an oil or tempera painting. The artist might choose a chalk ground or, as in the case of the Dutch and Flemish 17th-century painters, a bolus ground toned with brown or red earth colours. The ground, until very recently, was then covered with a coat of paint, the underpainting, which also adds considerably to the life of a picture. The colours of the underpainting will affect a work decisively. Oil and tempera paintings throughout the Middle Ages, and often until the 19th century, consisted of a series of layers of paint. The final effect was obtained by using transparent colours. The opposite of this technique is *alla prima* painting.

60. *Grotesque by* RAPHAEL *from the Vatican loggias in Rome (1515–19)*

HALF TIMBERING. Vertical posts, horizontal beams and diagonal bracing form the frame of the half-timbered building, which is filled with wattle and daub or brick (brick nogging) and sometimes plastered. Half-timbering occurs throughout England, France and Germany. Methods of construction differ considerably, not only in each country but in each district. The half-timbered town house developed from the cottage and reached the peak of its development between the 15th and 17th centuries. King posts, beam faces and corbels provided ample opportunities for painting and carving, while the plaster was occasionally decorated in sgraffito (q. v.).

HALL CHURCH. A church whose aisles have the same height as the nave, with the consequent absence of triforium and clerestory. Such a church may have three, five or – as sometimes in Austria – two aisles. The hall church seeks to unite the congregation visually as well as spatially. The plan is already anticipated in the hall crypt. Hall churches occur in Bavaria, East Suabia and Westphalia from the 12th century onwards. The parish churches in German towns were predominantly of this type in Gothic times. Hall churches were an early development in southern and western France, Lombardy and central Italy. They also appear as parish churches in Spain and, rarely, in England (St Mary's, Warwick). Bristol Cathedral is the only example of a large English hall church. They became less frequent during the Renaissance. (Ill. 61)

HALL MARK. Craftsmen often mark their work with the place, the name of the workshop, the artist or maker, the year, the gold or silver content, etc. Marks on porcelain (q. v.) and earthenware give the factory, sometimes also the name of the potter, the painter or the enameller (ill. 74). Pieces of furniture are marked less frequently, and then only with the craftsman's name. Tapestries often bear the name of the factory and of the designer. Pewter may display marks of the country or town of origin, of the pewterer or of the silver content. Goldsmiths and silversmiths often impress similar stamps on their work.

HELM. A small turret on the roof of a church, usually above the crossing of nave and transept. It came in with the Cistercian churches of the 13th century. That it originated in the helm above the smoke outlet in Germanic timber buildings seems clearly established.

HISTORY PAINTING. The painting of historical subjects was already common in Antiquity ('The Battle of Alexander') and it was widely practised by Renaissance artists (Uccello, 'The Rout of San Romano'; Titian, 'The Battle of Cadore', 'General del Vasco addressing his soldiers'; Tintoretto, 'The Battle of Zara'; and Leonardo's famous cartoon, since lost, of 'The Battle of Anghiari'). In the 17th century history painting was officially encouraged in Holland for the decoration of the town hall in Amsterdam and historical themes were among the subjects of two of the great painters of the age, Velasquez ('The Surrender of Breda') and Rubens.

61. Hall church: Nördlingen, St George's (15th cent.). Interior, looking E. (pulpit by an Augsburg master 1499, tester by MICHAEL EHINGER *1681, organ 1610)*

Eighteenth-century painters were chiefly drawn to history painting by the desire to excel in the 'grand manner'. Reynolds' least successful works were his historical pictures such as 'Ugolino' and 'Macbeth', and the desire to achieve fame in the heroic field prompted painters like Benjamin West and John Singleton Copley to expend their modest talent on such compositions as 'The Death of Wolfe' and 'The Death of Chatham'. David's 'Oath of the Horatii', despite its startling effect on the revolutionaries of the day, shows the coldness and theatricality to which history painting had sunk by the beginning of the 19th century. Fresh life was, however, imparted to the genre by Delacroix who was inspired by the Greek revolt against the Turks and by the French Revolution. His example did not prevent history painting from degenerating as the century wore on into the composition of mere costume pieces, such as Dyce's 'Baptism of King Ethelbert' and Maclise's 'Death of Nelson'. Yet history painting is not dead; in our own day it has inspired at least one great picture, Picasso's 'Guernica'. (Ill. 259, pp. 69, 149, 385)

ICON (Gr. *Ikon*, image). Within the orbit of the Greek Orthodox Church, mostly in Eastern and South-Eastern Europe, the word 'Icon' denotes the panel painting as distinct from the fresco. Certain themes are particularly favoured by the icon-makers, the Trinity, the three angels at Abraham's Table, scenes from the life of the Virgin, certain types of the Madonna, the archangels and the saints of the Byzantine calendar. The traditional Byzantine form of the icon has scarcely changed since the 6th century. Icons are chiefly found in Russia and the Balkan countries. (Ill. p. 182)

ILLUMINATION. Strictly speaking, the term only applies to manuscript paintings if they are heightened in gold and silver. The texts of some Ancient Egyptian papyri were interspersed with illustrations. The Codex, a book bound in sheets, first appeared in the 4th century A. D. and provided opportunities for a new art, since text and illustrations were kept separate. The earliest illuminated manuscripts belong exclusively to the region around the Mediterranean (Itala MS., Berlin; Iliad Ambrosiana, Milan). The earliest illuminated manuscripts north of the Alps date from the 7th century. Pre-Carolingian illumination (7th and 8th cent.) mostly absorbed late classic Eastern and Byzantine influences and produced some works of the highest order, especially in the British Isles (Hiberno-Saxon illumination: Book of Kells, Lindisfarne Gospels, Book of Durrow; ill. p. 180). The great impetus to all forms of art and scholarship received under Charlemagne also influenced the illuminator's art (see p. 184). Different schools, such as the Aachen Palace School, which was close to the Imperial court, and the schools connected with various abbeys, such as the Rheims, Tours, Metz, Corbie and Canterbury schools, based their work generally on earlier models; these, however, they were often able to transform in a very original manner. In the Ottonian age, which had witnessed the gradual development of a linear style, the illuminator's art reached new heights. The works of the Reichenau School (The Evangeliary of Otto III, the Book of Pericopes of Henry II) and manuscripts from Henry II's capital Regensburg, from Echternach, St Gall, Hildesheim and Fulda, are amongst the finest examples. The scriptoria – as illuminators' workshops are called – of southern and northern France produced an equally vivid art (for example, the St Armand and St Omer schools in the Meuse region). At the same time, the Winchester School flourished in England (Winchester Bible, Grimbald Gospels) and in Italy the school of the Benedictine abbey of Monte Cassino – which was in close contact with the Eastern Empire. A number of important local scriptoria developed during the Romanesque period (for comparison see p. 178). The strict division into text and illustrations was only abandoned during the Gothic, when the hitherto customary borders to the miniatures (ill. p. 48) also became gradually rarer. This change was largely initiated by the Paris school (Psalter of St Louis) and the schools of northern France. Secular scriptoria now appeared and secular subjects like poems, chronicles, etc. (Codex Manesse, Heidelberg) became increasingly popular. The Burgundian miniatures of the early 15th century show a realistic treatment of space and landscape (the Limbourg brothers' 'Les très riches heures du Duc de Berry', ill. p. 49). The Brothers van Eyck and Jan Fouquet (ill. p. 218) took this naturalism further and applied it to panel painting. With the invention of printing, book illumination quickly lost its importance. Outside Europe, we find the miniaturist's art developed in the Islamic world to a high degree from the 12th century onwards (Baghdad school). Secular themes were used almost exclusively. Persian miniatures of the 15th to 17th centuries (e. g. Herat School) and Indian miniatures of the Muslim Mughal Empire (16th cent.), too, are amongst the most famous works of their kind (ill. pp. 521, 533). Illuminated manuscripts also survived from the Ancient American civilisations of the Mixtecs, the Aztecs and the Maya (see p. 543).

INCUNABULA. Books printed before 1500. The art of printing with movable types was preceded early in the 15th century by the production of single pictures printed from wood blocks. Lines of descriptive text were added to these woodcuts and the so-called 'block-book' came into existence, consisting of pictures and text cut on the same wood block. These block-books, of which some 30 separate works have been recorded, were produced chiefly in the Netherlands and Germany. They were popular in character and mainly concerned with religious instruction. Examples include the *Biblia Pauperum*, the *Apocalypse* and the *Ars Moriendi*. It is not known for certain who was responsible for the invention of movable type, though the discovery is generally attributed to Johann Gutenberg of Mainz, c. 1440–50. The immense superiority of movable type lay in the fact that while the earliest blocks could be used only for the particular work for which they had been cut, the movable type, being composed of separate letters, could be used over and over again for any book. The earliest extant piece of printing is an *Indulgence* printed at Mainz in 1454. Three names are connected with it: Gutenberg, Fust and Schoeffer. The first printed edition of the Bible was issued before 1456 and is known as the Gutenberg Bible. In 1457 Fust and Schoeffer, working together, brought out their famous *Psalter*, the first printed book to contain the names of its printers and the date of printing. By 1461 the new art had been carried to Strassburg and Bamberg and a few years later presses were set up at Augsburg, Cologne and Nuremberg. The invention soon spread to other countries. More printers worked in Venice during the 15th century than in any other town. Of these, about 150 in number, the most famous at the end of the century was Aldus Manutius. Paris had become a busy centre of the craft by 1470, and there were important centres of early printing at Deventer in Holland and Louvain in Belgium. William Caxton, England's first printer, worked at Bruges before returning to his native land to introduce the new art. He produced the *Recuyell of the Historyes of Troye,* the first book to be printed in the English language. Incunabula look so much like manuscripts that an unpractised eye might find some difficulty in distinguishing between them. It was customary for the 15th-century printer to leave blank spaces for head-lines and initial letters which were afterwards added by an illuminator. In size, too, early printed books closely resembled manuscripts. (Cf. ill. p. 50)

IRON STRUCTURES. Engineers having proved the great strength and other structural advantages of iron as a material for bridges early in the second half of the 18th century (Lyons 1755, Coalbrookdale 1779), architects could thenceforward no longer ignore it. The London Crystal Palace (1851), railway stations (Liverpool 1852) and libraries (Paris 1861) were the first buildings constructed in iron. Glass – and later, ferroconcrete – was used for the walls. Eiffel's Galérie des Machines and his famous tower, built for the Paris International Exhibition in 1889, represent the first triumphs of the new technique, which had meanwhile advanced from cast iron to rolled iron and thence to steel. Thus the structural basis of the new architecture, as well as its changed appearance, was established.

IRONWORK. From the days of the Egyptians wrought iron and cast iron have provided civilised man with the major part of his tools, weapons and utensils and with many decorative objects. *Wrought iron* can be hammered, drawn or twisted and still maintain its strength. Parts can be completely fused by welding. Even when cold, iron is sufficiently soft to be hammered and bent. *Cast iron* in its moulded form is too brittle for further manipulation but lends itself readily to the finest details of the mould.

It is mainly since the Middle Ages that wrought iron has been developed as a medium of artistic expression. By collaring, or attaching separate units by strips, by rivetting, bolting, threading and mortising, the exacting material could be made to yield astonishing variety. In England ironwork developed from the bar which gave structural strength to windows, door hinges, grilles and screens. Stone tracery was imitated in iron by means of small pieces rivetted and chiselled on a sheet background, as in the grille over the tomb of Edward IV in St George's Chapel, Windsor, the work of John Tresilian. The hinges of the west door of Notre Dame, Paris illustrate the controlled grace and the intricacy of medieval French ironwork.

The quatrefoil grilles and the lanterns of city palaces indicate the use made of iron by Italian craftsmen. In Renaissance Spain wrought iron was magnificently used for monumental screens with vertical columns of hammered ornamentation and horizontal bands of arabesques, the whole crowned with elaborate crests. The iron was coloured and gilded with striking effect in the dim church interiors. The Spaniards also used iron for pulpits and lecterns.

It was, however, in France during the age of Louis XIV that the art of wrought iron reached its greatest heights. Imposing gates for parks, mansion staircases and screens for churches were produced by a succession of fine artists. St Cloud, Fontainebleau, Chantilly and Versailles offer notable examples. In the 18th century, ironwork adapted itself to Rococo forms although Lamour, in the gates at Nancy, reached the limits of the craft as a monumental technique. Jean Tijou brought the French style to England where his exquisite work can be seen at Hampton Court and St Paul's, London. He influenced

but did not dominate the native craftsmen, who produced admirable work during the 17th and 18th centuries for country houses and for the colleges of Cambridge and Oxford.

Cast iron had long been in use in England for fire backs and fire dogs and the railing of St Paul's was an early instance of its architectural use. Further examples are provided by the balconies and porches of the Regency period.

In the Far East, iron was used from about 500 B.C., rapidly replacing bronze for weapons and domestic utensils. From the 9th century in China it even tended to replace bronze for sculpture. Iron pagodas and temple furniture and even iron pictures were ingeniously devised. Medieval Japanese craftsmen showed great sensibility for the material, especially in the decoration of armour and the embellishment of sword handles.

IVORY is made from the tusks of the elephant, occasionally also those of the walrus, and has attracted the carver since prehistoric times. Widely used in Late Antiquity, it was taken up by Byzantine artists who – like their Carolingian and Ottonian contemporaries – carried this art to heights it has never again reached. Ivory carving was revived in the 13th century under French – especially Parisian – influence, with the result that sculpture in the round (chess figures, figures of the Virgin for pocket altars, etc.), supplemented the relief carvings that had hitherto preponderated. Interest in ivory lapsed during the Renaissance, but re-awoke during the Baroque period, when it was widely used, especially in the crafts. (Cf. ill. pp. 47, 194)

JEWELLERY. The earliest surviving articles of jewellery are Egyptian. Many techniques are represented: chiselling, moulding, hammering, inlay, filigree and cloisonné. Egyptian jewellery also includes the earliest known instances of 'granulated' work (see Granulation). The principal ornaments of the bulk of the Egyptian people were beads and amulets of stone and earthenware. Bead-making reached its highest perfection during the 17th dynasty, when necklaces were enlivened not only with scarabs but with little pendants and other ornaments. Glass beads were also introduced during this period. Both men and women wore deep collars of string beads. Large silver loops were worn by the Egyptians through the pierced lobes of the ears. Bracelets were worn on the forearm and the upper arm. Rings of ivory and earthenware were worn by the common people, while gold and silver were reserved for the wealthy. Metal rings were generally set with semi-precious stones. The signet ring of the Paraoh often consisted of a red cornelian cut in the form of a scarab. Babylonian and Assyrian sculptures show men and women wearing necklaces, ear-rings and bracelets, and the discovery of articles of adornment at Ur disclosed that these were made either of gold or of silver.

A vast store of jewellery was discovered during excavations along the shores of the Aegean, the types of ornament including diadems, ear-rings, necklaces, bracelets, pendants, brooches and rings. Where metal occurs it reveals knowledge of the various methods of repoussé (q. v.), twisted wire and granulated work. Ornamental motifs are based principally on the sphinx, the griffin and the bull's head.

Greek jewellery includes diadems, hairpins, necklaces, ear-rings, fibulae, brooches, bracelets and rings. Engraving, gem-cutting and filigree work reached the greatest degree of perfection among the Greeks. The chief decorative designs were geometric motifs, animal and human figures. The Etruscans were noted particularly for their filigree and granulated work in gold. Their methods were lost to the modern world until the 19th century when Castellani of Rome discovered goldworkers in the Abruzzi to whom the Etruscan technique had descended. In its general character Etruscan jewellery resembles that of the Greeks. Cloisonné enamel and repoussé work are frequent methods of ornamentation. Roman jewellery clearly derives from the work of both the Greeks and the Etruscans. But the delicate, graceful designs of the Greeks became heavy and ornate in the hands of the Romans. Where the Greeks and the Etruscans used gems sparingly, the Romans were lavish, and where the Etruscans delighted in intricate patterns of filigree or granulation, the Romans preferred massive, plain surfaces.

Byzantine jewellery derived from three sources: Greece, Rome and the East. The ease with which precious stones could be procured resulted in an even more prodigal use of them than that which the Romans had made. Thus splendour of colour was the keynote of Byzantine work, and this found further expression in enamel, which was mainly cloisonné. Niello (q. v.) work was much used in decorating gold and silver, especially rings.

The barbarian peoples who overthrew the Roman Empire produced remarkable jewellery. That of the Teutonic invaders displays a special type of ornamentation. Instead of the gems being fixed individually in a setting which is burnished or bent over them to keep them in place, the pieces are ground flat and each cemented into a compartment, or cemented into holes pierced in sheet metal. This is known as 'plate' inlaying. The effect produced is of rich, flat colour approaching that of mosaic or cloisonné enamel. The style derived from the East. It was common to all the barabaric tribes though the treatment of the metal surrounding the gems differed considerably in different places. In Scandinavia the decoration consists of entwined and contorted animals; in Merovingian and Anglo-Saxon work the design is usually based on knot work in twisted and beaded wire; the Frankish tribes favoured bird forms. In all the more westerly countries precious materials were used less lavishly. (Cf. ill. p. 152)

T-shaped fibulae were much favoured by barbarian tribes. The Anglo-Saxons produced two special forms of fibulae, the cruciform shape which is found exclusively in Scandinavia and northern England and the disc-shaped variety. The use of enamel constantly increased.

Owing to the gradual abandonment of the custom of interring a man's belongings with him, few specimens survive of the Anglo-Saxon period. Exceptions are the Sutton Hoo treasure and the Alfred jewel.

Magnificent jewellery much influenced by oriental example was produced in Visigothic Spain. The chief articles were votive crowns inscribed with the names of the various Visigothic kings who reigned during the 7th century. The craft of the Merovingian jeweller is represented by the contents of the tomb of King Childeric. Many of the objects comprise thin plates of gold over some baser metal decorated with cloisonné work, almost always in garnets. Celtic metalwork and jewellery, remarkable for their fine craftsmanship, stand apart from the general development of the period. They are distinguished for the skilled use of the hammer and rivets, for the Celts were ignorant of the art of soldering. Early examples of Celtic jewellery are characterized by ornamentation in inlaid enamels and chasing.

The chief article of medieval jewellery was the ring. Both the bracelet and the ear-ring fell out of fashion owing to the vogue for long sleeves and for head-dresses which covered the ears.

During the Renaissance the art of jewellery was highly esteemed. Many outstanding artists of the period designed jewellery, among them Mantegna, Verrocchio, Ghirlandajo, Leonardo and Dürer. Cellini was more celebrated for his jewellery than for his sculpture. Stones were generally mounted in openwork settings and were often chosen for their irregularity of form; thus an odd-shaped pearl became the body of a mermaid and an emerald the fore-part of a sea-horse. Transparent stones in Renaissance jewellery are usually backed with foil and diamonds are backed with black. Elaborate chains and collars composed of massive links were regarded as emblems of wealth and distinction. During the 17th century the ring fell from favour, though the execution of Charles I revived an earlier custom of wearing memorial rings.

Throughout the 18th century two classes of work were common, described by the French as 'bijouterie', the art of working in gold and enamel, and 'joaillerie', the art of mounting diamonds and precious stones. Rococo motifs are used in pieces belonging to the earlier part of the century, whereas classical themes predominate in the later work. To the latter half of the period belong some of the most charming examples of mourning jewellery, nearly all of English origin. Portrait miniatures were surrounded with tiny stones and borders of black enamel, cameos showed figures in classical garb gracefully posed under a tree or porch and gazing at an urn or tomb. Tortoise-shell was often used for hair-slides, combs and waist-clasps and was ornamented by a method resembling inlay, for which purpose gold, silver or pinchbeck was used. The 18th-century 'bijoutier' expressed his skill particularly in the chatelaine, the more costly examples of which were made of gold and enamels.

The industrial revolution changed the art of jewellery into a commercial industry in which individual creation played an ever smaller part. Black onyx and jet were popular in about 1840 for brooches, bracelets and ear-rings. An ornament, instead of being an independent work of art now became one of a set of identical objects. There was a reaction against machine-made jewellery towards the end of the 19th century when the French jeweller Lalique turned for inspiration to the jewellery of the Orient, Egypt, Greece and Italy. He ignored the hierarchy of gems and used any stone, even flint if it suited his design. Platinum jewellery is a 20th-century contribution to the field of ornamentation. Hand-wrought jewellery is still made in small quantities. Salvador Dali has made fantastic ornaments reflecting the same spirit as his paintings, and Calder has composed some interesting pieces of twisted copper wire and hammered brass.

Oriental jewellery strikes quite a different note from both ancient and European forms. Indian jewellery is characterized by profusion of both colour and decoration, a lavish display of gems and gold, though these to European eyes often seem faulty and flawed. The archaic beaten gold of Mysore illustrates the way in which Indian craftsmen elaborate an extensive surface of ornament from an apparently inadequate quantity of material, beating it to the thinness of tissue paper. The Chinese have produced little jewellery for the sake of ornament alone. The most characteristic form of ornament was inlaid featherwork. Japanese jewellery is characterized by great restraint; effects are gained by intricacies of surface and treatment rather than by any display of gems. The metals used are often alloys of little intrinsic value.

LACE. Lace-making falls into two classes: (1) needle-point made by the needle; (2) bobbin or pillow lace made with bobbins and pins on a pillow. Pillow lace may easily be distinguished from Point lace as in the former the ground or réseau is made of plaited thread. That of Point lace is composed of threads made by the use of the button-hole stitch only. Laces made during the last hundred years frequently have a machine-made ground and thus, strictly speaking, are not lace at all, but embroidery or appliqué work. Owing to its fragility very few early examples of lace have survived. A primitive form of lace has been found in Egyptian tombs decorating the edges of garments, and some Coptic embroideries exhibit drawn threadwork. Gold and silver laces of simple design were discovered in the tombs of Mycenae and Etruria. A few specimens of cut work survive from Byzantium. The cloth covering the body of St Cuthbert, buried in 685, was cut and fringed to form a kind of rudimentary lace. All pre-Renaissance lace consisted of drawn work, cut work and darned work. The Venetians were the first to abandon all foundation material (c. 1530) and to rely solely on the needle to create the fabric. The chief varieties of Venetian lace are known as Rose Point, Point de Neige, Gros Point de Venise and Point Plat de Venise. The chief characteristics of Venetian lace are the raised cord outlining the design, known as the *Cordonnet,* the diversity of the fillings worked in button-hole stitch and the starry effect of the *brides* or connections between the various parts of the design. The principal designs for Venetian lace, shown in a pattern book printed in Venice in 1560, were conventionalized floral scrolls. During the reign of Louis XIV lace schools were established in France near Alençon, resulting in the fine laces known as Point d'Alençon, Point d'Argentan and Point d'Argentella. These laces were at first indistinguishable from those made at Venice, except that figures were introduced into the designs. The principal characteristics of the later French laces are the fine, clear ground, the stiff Cordonnet outlining the pattern and the variety of motifs in the fillings.

Meanwhile the bobbin process had developed independently in Flanders towards the close of the 16th century from plaited fringed work. The chief laces of Flanders are known as Flemish Point, Brussels Point and Point d'Angleterre. They are all very much alike, characterized by their gossamer-like texture and the total absence of the Cordonnet. Pillow lace was also made at Valenciennes, which was formerly part of Flanders. In fineness of thread it rivals the Flemish laces and looks more like ornamental cambric. It differs from Flemish lace, however, in the ground, the stitches in the Valenciennes being much closer and thicker in the plait.

The persecution of the Huguenots led to the introduction of lace-making into England. The best-known English lace is Honiton, a coarse copy of Brussels lace. Of Irish laces, the Carrick-ma-cross is more like embroidery than lace and did not develop until the beginning of the 19th century. Patterns outlined in button-hole stitch are applied to a machine-made net. The Irish crotchet is the only true lace made in Ireland. It is a close imitation of Venetian Point made with a fine thread and a crotchet needle.

LAMP BLACK is made of soot (in recent times also of burnt umber) and is processed into sticks, which differ from red chalk only in their dark brown colour. Liquid lamp black used by the Old Masters like drawing ink, is often mistaken for sepia.

LANDSCAPE PAINTING. Landscape is the latest to develop of the various branches of painting. It probably cannot mature until a civilisation is sufficiently advanced for Man no longer to feel Nature as a wholly unpredictable, hostile force. The first manifestations of landscape in Europe occurred in the Pompeian frescoes. Some nine centuries later under the Sung dynasty (A.D. 960–1279) the Chinese found a perfect expression for their pantheistic, meditative philosophy in landscape painting. The chief elements of these pictures are lakes, mountains, torrents, mists, rocks and trees, highly conventionalized, in no way attempting to reproduce an actual locality by always interpreting a definite mood of Nature. (Ill. p. 534)

In Europe, landscape painting has been much more closely associated with particular localities, rendered with varying degrees of realism. The desire of the Renaissance painters to recreate actual appearances inevitably led to a realistic rendering of the background behind figures of Saints and Madonnas. The backgrounds in the large figure compositions of such painters as Pollaiuolo and Francesca are astonishingly faithful renderings of the Tuscan landscape. The study of perspective developed an understanding of the importance of space and light in the painting of landscape and these qualities are emphasised in the works of Perugino and his followers. A more personal attitude towards Nature, the beginnings of an understanding of the power of landscape to convey particular emotions, is displayed in the remarkable backgrounds of Giovanni Bellini, and to some extent in those of van Eyck. The Venetian painters, of whom Bellini was the first, did much to further the development of landscape painting. In pictures such as Titian's 'Noli me Tangere' and still more Giorgione's 'Fête Champêtre' and 'The Tempest', landscape is no longer relegated to the background, but plays an equal part with the figures in the production of the total impression. (Ill. pp. 269, 299)

Such paintings of figures in landscapes paved the way for the 'Landscape with Figures', of which Brueghel in the North and Claude in Italy were the notable exponents. (Ill. p. 330)

So long as figures played even so small a part in the composition as in 'The Tempest', they determined the design. But when they came to play quite an insignificant role, the bones of the design had to be evolved from the landscape itself. Brueghel made the landscape into a flat, decorative pattern; to Claude, on the other hand, light and atmosphere were all-important.

Meanwhile in Holland an independent art of landscape was produced, whose chief merit was the sincerity with which the cool skies, the marshes, the sandy seashore, the waterways and buildings of the Dutch countryside were recorded. With few exceptions these Dutch landscapes fall into the category of topography, rather than of true landscape. The landscapes of Rembrandt and Seghers are exceptions to this generalization. In Flanders, Rubens' great sweeping compositions were isolated achievements in the career of one whose chief business and contemporary appeal as a painter lay in quite other directions. Rubens' importance as a landscapist was not recognised until the 'Château de Stern' was lent by Sir George Beaumont to the British Institution in 1815.

In England by the end of the 18th century, appreciation of natural beauties was considered essential in any person claiming to be cultivated. This was specially propitious to the development of landscape painting. But Gainsborough's early Suffolk landscapes and Wilson's 'Cader Idris' had been painted long before this, and Alexander and J. R. Cozens had already produced pen and wash drawings which had more of the Chinese approach to Nature than anything so far seen in Europe. By 1815 the art had become a matter of intensive study

to such painters as Crome, Constable and Turner. Constable is one of the most important figures in the history of landscape painting. He was the first to paint the colours of nature and the sparkle of light as he saw them. But his work is by no means naturalistic. It expresses far more in its intensity of feeling than the spirit of a particular locality and moment. (Ill. pp. 387, 386) Constable's example was of great importance in the development of French Impressionism. The Impressionists inherited his technique, however, rather than his feeling, and were chiefly concerned with the accurate renderings of effects of light and with the formal problems of painting. Cézanne still further emphasised structural elements and created a monumental landscape art. Van Gogh used landscape as a vehicle for his own turbulent emotions with brilliant results; but his pictures were too individual to exert any but a disastrous influence on the art. (Cf. ill. pp. 72, 418, 419, 437, 439) Constable had little influence on English landscape painting and Turner's great achievements in romantic landscape and his astonishing rendering of effects of light were equally neglected until our own day, when his influence is apparent in the work of painters such as Donald Hamilton Fraser, Peter Kinley and William Johnstone. An interest in Cotman led to the development of one modern English school of landscapists, concerned with style and formal values, of whom Paul Nash was the most distinguished. After the Second World War there was a romantic revival among English landscape painters, the most notable of whom is Graham Sutherland (ill. 324).

LITHOGRAPHY. A lithograph is a flat print, i. e. the lines and areas to be printed are neither raised nor sunk, but entirely level with the plate. This can be made of limestone or slate, which is the reason for speaking of a lithograph (Greek *lithos* – a stone). The particular type of limestone used absorbs both fat and water, both substances that do not mix. If we now draw on the stone with greasy chalk or other greasy colours and wet the entire surface, the water will only cling to the portions of the stone not covered in colour, and will eventually evaporate. The stone is then covered with greasy printer's ink, which will not adhere to the wet areas, but only to the drawing. This can now be be transferred to paper. That is the basic principle of lithography (it is slightly more complicated in practice), the technique invented in 1796 by Alois Senefelder, who saw in it a cheap was of reproducing his own writings. The lithograph was taken up enthusiastically by artists everywhere, since it allowed pen, brush and chalk to be used as they would be on paper. Goya availed himself of this technique occasionally, Daumier used it almost exclusively in preference to any other. Toulouse-Lautrec was one of the first artists to make coloured lithographs from several stone plates. But since this required a fairly large number of unwieldy stones – as many in number as colours – experiments with other types of plates were made and it was soon discovered that zinc can be substituted for slate. The term 'litho-

History painting: Paolo Uccello: The Battle of San Romano (*Victory of the Florentines over the Sienese 1432*), *painted for the Palazzo Medici in Florence. One of three panels*

Interior: PIETER DE HOOCH: Woman Sewing

Still-life: GEORG FLEGEL: Still-life with Candle

Landscape painting: CLAUDE MONET: Regatta

graphy' is also used for printing from zinc plates, although these are not often employed. (Ill. 263, p. 38)

MANNERISM means literally the hackneyed use of accepted forms without any real feeling. But the term has also come to be used for the art of the transitional phase between the Renaissance and the Baroque (see p. 273, 282), which, in its main features, can certainly not be described in any way as 'mannerist' in a derogatory sense.

MARQUETRY denotes the inlaying of wood with other woods of various colours or with materials such as ivory, mother of pearl, etc., to form pictures or patterns. This technique flourished from the 16th to the 18th century, but was already known in Antiquity and still survives. (Ill. 237)

MASON'S MARKS. These are marks – either monograms or geometric designs – which are found on buildings dating from the period between the middle of the 12th and the 18th century. They enabled the stone-mason to identify his work and helped him with his final account. The mason's mark was a sign of distinction in the medieval confraternities (q. v.). Masters used to have boards with their mark on them.

MAQUETTE. A small model (the 'sketch in clay') of a figure, or group of figures, to guide the sculptor in his work. During the Baroque period, artists often supplied only a maquette and left the execution of the work to their assistants.

MEANDER. The meander, or key-fret, is a band-like, rectangular ornament and is probably based on plaiting or weaving patterns. Widely used in the eastern Danube regions in prehistoric times, it reached Greece in the Neolithic Age and became the characteristic feature of the so-called geometric style (Dipylon style, q. v.) of vase painting (ill. 63, p. 151), where it can be studied in many variants. It has since played an important part in the minor arts of Europe and was also often used in architecture. The Classic Revival considered it the Greek ornament par excellence (Fr. *à la grecque;* German *Grek-Kante).*

MEDALS, see Numismatics.

METRICAL SYSTEM. A method of articulating the whole of a church, which probably originated c. 1000 in Saxony and one of the earliest surviving examples of which is St Michael's, Hildesheim. The nave is divided up into three squares and the transepts again consist of a centre square flanked by rectangles. The centre squares are singled out by means of chancel arches not only to the east and west but also to the north and south. In later buildings each transept was square, too, and the aisles consisted of sequences of squares. This system was followed by Central European architects for the two succeeding centuries. It is not known who conceived this 'metrical system', but it is recorded that St

Bernward, the bishop who was responsible for the building of St Michael's, was 'foremost in writing, experienced in painting, excellent in the science and art of bronze founding and in all architectural work'. This suggests that the bishop may have had a hand in the designing of the church. (Cf. ill. 32, 42)

MEZZANINE is applied to a floor situated either between the ground floor and the first storey (the 'bel étage' or 'piano nobile') or under the attic. The expression is of Italian origin and is mostly used in connection with Baroque and Renaissance palaces. (Ill. 212)

MINIATURE PAINTING (the word is derived from the Latin *miniare,* to draw with minium, i. e. red lead colour). Originally, a miniature was an illustration, drawn in red, in an Early Medieval illuminated manuscript. The illustrator usually also lettered the text. Later, when the range of colours was increased, and when the illustrations became more elaborate, the term 'miniature' was extended to initials and illuminations (q. v.). Since these are comparatively small, the expression came to be applied to pictures of the smallest size. This special form of painting – which Hans Holbein the Younger was one of the first to practise – has occurred since the Renaissance and was primarily concerned with the portrait. It assumed great importance in the 18th century, when ivory came into use as a ground, in addition to parchment and metal. Miniatures were painted on decorative objects of all kinds, such as watches and the snuff boxes of the world of fashion. The miniature lived on throughout the Classic Revival and into early Victorian times until it was superseded by the photograph.

MONASTIC ARCHITECTURE. The monks of Early Christendom lived separately in scattered cells, meeting at the monastic church for ritual purposes and in the refectory for meals. Later, the accommodation for the monks in Eastern Christendom was regularly built against the inside of a fortified girdle wall, leaving the church standing free in a central court with the refectory facing it. In Western Christendom the church is usually to the north of the *cloister,* an arcaded garden court which is the centre of the life of the community. The normal arrangement of the various rooms in a medieval monastery is as follows: along the east walk of the cloister were: the *sacristy* (adjoining the church); the *chapter-house,* where the community met daily to hear a chapter of the monastic Rule and to transact business (there was often a chapel extending east from the chapter-house with an infirmary for old and sick monks beyond it); the *parlour* or auditorium for speaking, which gave access to the easterly parts of the monastery; and the *workshop.* Above these rooms was the *dormitory* with exit directly into the south transept of the church or, by stairway, to the cloister. The south walk embraced the *calefactory,* the only heated room in the monastery, the *refectory,* the *pantry,* and the *kitchens,* with shops, bakery, stables and quarters for

73

lay brethren and servants not far distant. The west walk gave access to the cellars and stores and in it, adjoining the church, was the cloister entrance. The north walk ran alongside the church nave and the library, and the scribes used to be installed there. The guest house was often north of the church nave with the porter's cella in it or near-by. There was generally a hospice for poor visitors to the south-west of the church. Conventual structures had a simple rather barn-like character until the 12th century; later they developed fine architectural features, showing the same variations in style as the churches. Many notable monasteries were built in the 17th and 18th centuries especially in France and Austria.

MOSAIC. A mosaic is a design formed by embedding small stones, vitreous or enamelled cubes in cement. The method is an outgrowth of inlay. A remarkable piece of mosaic dating from c. 3500 B.C. was excavated at Ur. Thought to be a standard, it is executed in lapis lazuli and pink sandstone attached to a wood background with bituminous cement. On one side it shows an army going into battle; on the other, a king or noble at a feast. (Ill. p. 106)

Mosaic was a common type of decoration in Greece in the Late Hellenistic period and the name given to it, 'Opus Alexandrinum', points to Alexandria as a centre for the work. But few examples can be dated earlier than the Roman occupation. The Romans excelled in the art of floor mosaic; fragmentary examples are to be found wherever they established themselves, in France, England, Germany, Sicily and North Africa. A few wall mosaics were found at Pompeii and Herculaneum. Roman mosaics were usually simple in colour and generally consisted of all-over geometric patterns or a central rectangular field surrounded by an ornamental border. Large pictorial compositions such as the famous 'Battle of Issus' (ill. p. 149) and the figure compositions at Piazza Armerina in Sicily were rare.

The use of mosaic for interior wall decoration, the full development of the possibilities of the medium in a dimly lit room, were characteristic of the Christian era. Several examples of Early Christian mosaics on the walls of catacombs are preserved in Rome. When the ban on Christianity was removed by the Emperor Constantine the technique of mosaic was used to adorn church walls, and stone cubes were replaced by brilliant pieces of glass, thus making available a magnificent new gamut of colour. The earliest examples of Christian mosaics in churches date from the 4th century. In S. Costanza, Rome, the barrel ceiling is covered by a series of mosaic patterns. The most famous fragment represents a vintage scene with the grape gatherers climbing through the vines which are supported by a geometric lattice. Only two of the mosaics are Christian in subject. From the same century, but late, come the mosaics on the apse wall of the S. Rufina e Segunda Oratory, opening into the Lateran Baptistery, consisting of green acanthus fronds strewn across a blue field; and contemporary with these are the low tinted group of mosaics in the east end of S. Pudenza, Rome. Among the more important mosaics of the 5th century is the remarkable frieze in the church of St George, Salonica which runs all the way round the sloping walls, just below the dome. The frieze is architecturally designed in two columned storeys with an occasional personage, life-size and splendidly apparelled, stationed at the entrance of the lower one. They represent bishops, saints, soldiers, or the months of the year, and one is a flute player inscribed with his name, Philimon. The background of these mosaics is gold, but the rendering of the figures harks back to classical traditions. The masterpiece of early mosaic is, however, the mausoleum of Galla Placida, Ravenna. The interior of the Baptistery, Ravenna, is also dominated by the great 5th-century mosaic picture of the Baptism decorating the ceiling.

By the 6th century the gold background was general in mosaic. The celebrated mosaics at Ravenna in S. Apollinare Nuovo, S. Vitale and S. Apollinare in Classe all testify to the increasing stiffness and abstraction of the mosaic, while S. Vitale, the work of the Emperor Justinian, shows that mosaic – with its jewel-like texture and the ease with which it could render the rigidly monumental and the imposingly monotonous – was the medium which was suited to the Byzantine artist (ill. p. 179). In Istanbul a different school of Byzantine mosaic had developed, of which the decoration of S. Sofia is the earliest (6th century) and most impressive example. The scale is larger than in Italy and the ornament used is oriental in feeling and remote from classical influence. The type of mosaic elaborated by the Byzantines with its glittering gold ground dominated the art for the next 700 years in Istanbul and was responsible for the dazzling interiors of Monreale Cathedral (1170–90), the Martorana and the Capella Palatina, Palermo (12th century). At Monreale a particularly awe-inspiring example can be seen of a motif first used at S. Sofia, the single great head or bust of Christ in the apse. In St Mark's, Venice, the mosaics of the narthex and baptistery are oriental in conception and the vaults and domes of the main body of the church are also eastern in spirit, though the figures, dating from the 12th to the 16th century have been much repaired and disfigured. In Italy, mosaic was gradually ousted by mural painting but in Istanbul and Greece it remained the chief form of church decoration until the fall of Constantinople in 1453.

Mosaics were an extremely common form of floor decoration in medieval Italy. They consisted of small pieces of marble cut to stock shapes and the most frequently used colours were red, dark green, white, black and sometimes creamy yellow. The patterns made were all geometric. Among innumerable examples, those of St Mark's, Venice, and S. Maria Maggiore, S. Maria in Trastevere and S. Clemente, in Rome, deserve special mention. During the 12th, 13th and 14th centuries this type of decoration was used not only for floors but for parapets, choir screens and altar frontals. There are many examples in Rome and southern Italy. When this type of mosaic was used for church furniture there was a gradual tendency for glass or enamel to be substituted for the original stone. Such mosaics are known as Cosmati work, after the name of the family who were the chief exponents of the art during the 13th century. Not only were flat surfaces decorated in this way, but spiral columns, like those in the cloisters of St John Lateran, were ornamented with Cosmati work.

In Mohammedan countries special types of mosaic were evolved. Exterior mosaic decoration used in Persia took the form of small rectangular tiles put together to form geometric patterns deriving in some instances from the shapes of Arabic lettering. The remarkable development of tile decoration in Persia led gradually, however, to the abandonment of mosaic. The Mohammedan architecture of India is often embellished with skilful and elaborate marble mosaics in which intricate curvilinear patterns are further enhanced by the use of precious and semi-precious stones.

Except when the medium was distorted to imitate painting, mosaic art almost completely disappeared in Europe with the full development of the Renaissance.

NATURALISM. Naturalism in art is a form of representation which (in contrast to 'Idealism') aims at reproducing an object as faithfully to nature as possible. Carried to extremes (as it was in the 19th century, when the drive for illusionism begun in the Early Renaissance had reached its climax), naturalism can thus act as a serious curb to the artist's imagination. Naturalism is often equated with realism; there is still much disagreement about the use and meaning of these two terms. Modern art critics are inclined to consider realism as being fundamentally different from naturalism. Some hold that a realistic painting should aim at reproducing an essential quality rather than mere detail. The art of Goya or Käthe Kollwitz is realistic in its portrayal of the horrors of war or poverty but not naturalistic. The paintings of the Pre-Raphaelites whose treatment of colour was by no means conventional or unimaginative, were naturalistic, but not realistic.

NIELLO. Niello is a black alloy (Lat. *nigellum*) of silver, lead, copper, sulphur and boracic, and is used to bring out engraved ornament on metal – mostly silver – more clearly. The term is applied both to the metal and the technique, which was already known in Ancient Egypt. (Cf. ill. 51)

NUMISMATICS. The science of numismatics is concerned with coins. These are pieces of metal with an officially guaranteed weight and gold or silver content (in case of precious metals). This guarantee may take the form of an inscription, a coat of arms or the sovereign's portrait. Apart from early forms, which were not yet coins in the true sense, coins occurred first in the Greek colonies on the west coast of Asia Minor

in the 7th century B.C. Greek coins are distinguished by their excellent design and execution. They are usually decorated in well-modelled relief with human heads, gods, demons, plant and animal motifs. The Greek coins of the 5th century B.C. have never been surpassed. Roman coins usually bear the portrait of the ruler and his name on the obverse, while the reverse is reserved for the figures of deities, personified virtues or political events. In the Middle Ages, there was a short flowering of the art of the coin in the second half of the 12th century, although this was limited to central Germany. Large, paper-thin silver coins were decorated on one side only with handsome representations of sovereigns on horseback, enthroned bishops, lions or eagles. These coins are called bracteatae (Lat. *bractea* – a piece of metal foil) after the bracteatae of the time of the Barbarian Invasions – coin-like, ornamental gold discs, decorated at first with figures, later with interlaced and zoomorphic designs. Coins not intended as currency, but to commemorate an event are called medals. These frequently also bear a sovereign's portrait, were already known towards the end of the Roman Empire (4th and 5th centuries), and became very popular from the Renaissance onwards (Pisanello), first in Italy and since the 16th century also in Germany and the rest of Europe.

NYMPHAEUM. The nymphaeum, in Ancient Greece, was a place of worship – usually near a spring – dedicated to the Nymphs. During the Hellenistic period the term came to include extensive water gardens. In Roman times, the nymphaeum was often decorated with colonnades and recesses and thus became an attractive feature of large cities.

OIL PAINTING. Oil colours have been used for panel paintings – for which tempera colours had up till then been employed – from the 15th century onwards. Oil paint for practical use only had long been known to the medieval craftsman, and Jan van Eyck and his fellow artists in the Netherlands developed this medium as an addition to tempera, which they continued to use as a base. This composite method soon spread – especially through Antonello da Messina – throughout Italy, and from the 16th century onwards it gradually superseded all other techniques. Its great advantages are faster application (*alla prima* technique) and a wide range of delicately nuanced colours.

ORDERS. Columns have been divided into three groups since Antiquity. Certain features of the entablature correspond to these separate groups or orders, which thus represent different styles. The Doric column developed from Egyptian models. Without a separate base, it rests immediately on the stylobate; its capital is formed by a convex or projecting moulding, the echinus, and by a stone slab, the abacus, usually square in shape, above the latter. The Doric order was chiefly used in Greece, where it was known from the 7th century B.C. The Ionic pillar has a composite base,

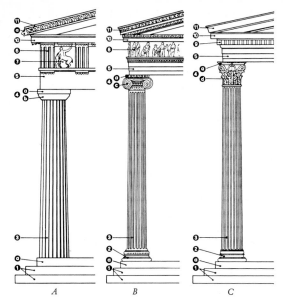

62. Greek orders of columns: A Doric (classic): Parthenon in Athens (448–432 B.C.), B Attic-Ionic: north antechamber of the Erechtheum in Athens, (420—407 B.C.), C Greek-Corinthian: Buleuterion of Miletus (c. 175 B.C.).

1 Base,	4b Echinus,	7 Metope,
1a Stylobate,	4c Ionic volute,	8 Frieze,
2 Attic base,	4d Corinthian volute with	9 Dentils,
3 Shaft,	acanthus leaves,	10 Facia,
4 Capital,	5 Epistyle,	11 Pediment moulding,
4a Abacus,	6 Triglyph,	11a Waterspout

consisting of a convex moulding, the torus, which rests on a concave moulding, the scotia. In the case of the so-called Attic order, there is a second, or lower torus, below the scotia. The capital consists of two parts: a pair of outward-curving volutes grows out of an echinus moulding decorated with the egg-and-dart motif. This is surmounted by a comparatively thin, square abacus. Although the Ionic order was already known in Asia Minor and at Samos in the early 6th century B.C., it did not appear on the temples of Attic Greece until nearly 150 years later. While the Ionic capital is a drawn-out rectangle, the capital of the Corinthian column, developed from the former, possesses four diagonally placed and strongly projecting volutes. These give the Corinthian capital a satisfying form, from whatever angle it may be looked at; whereas the Ionic capital, by contrast, must be seen from one of two sides. The Corinthian capital is further enriched with ornament, usually plant motifs based on the acanthus (q. v.) and the palmette. The Corinthian column has the same base as the Attic Ionic order. It is said to be the invention of the architect and sculptor Callimachus, who was active in Athens at the end of the 5th century B.C. Besides these three orders, mention must also be made of the Tuscan column, frequently used in Rome and Etruria, which combines an Ionic base with a Doric capital. The Romans also developed the composite capital, a variant of the Corinthian capital. (Ill. 48b, 62, 99, 102)

ORNAMENT stems from man's desire to decorate the things around him. The wealth of forms from which ornament derives embraces many realms. It can be abstract and geometrical, like the square form of the meander, which is found in many civilisations. Its rounded variant, the spiral, appears in many forms in the Late Bronze Age and throughout Celtic art. Diapering, zig-zag ornament, billet, chevron and nail-head are all abstract ornaments. The cloud band of Oriental art, the knotwork of Early Medieval art, the strapwork of the Renaissance and the more delicate interlacings of Early Baroque art already mark the transition to naturalistic forms. Indeed, it is to the world of the plant that ornament is indebted more than to any other realm. From the palmette or the acanthus leaf (see ill. 62 C, Corinthian capital) of Antiquity to the native plant forms of early Gothic art (Gothic

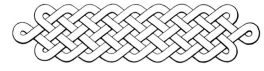

63. Meander (from a bowl by the potter Euphronius, c. 500 B.C.)

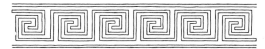

64. Wave (on a funerary stele from Mycenae, 2nd mill. B.C.)

65. Plait (from a shield umbo)

66. Palmette (from a chalice krater of the Niobid painter, 5th cent. B.C.)

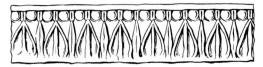

67. Cyma, Frieze from the Treasury of the Siphnians in Delphi, (beg. 6th cent. B.C.)

68. *Arabesque (wall decoration in the Imperial Palace in Delhi, c. 1640). Indo-Islamic*

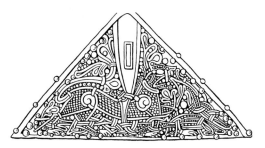

69. *Animal ornament from the so-called 'Ornamental shrine of St Kunigunde' from Lund, c. 1000. Oseberg style*

70. *Shell decoration (Rocaille) from the Throne Room of the prince-abbot's residence in Kempten/Allgäu, 1651–74*

71. *Ear-shell style (ornamental engraving by* FRIEDRICH UNTEUTSCH *c. 1650)*

72. *Art Nouveau or Jugendstil (vignette from the periodical 'Pan' by* OTTO ECKMANN)

foliated or leaf-bud capital, ill. 48h, i), from rosettes of all kinds to arabesques (q. v.), the plant offers unlimited scope. The stylization of animal forms into ornament is more difficult. It is fully achieved only in the animal style of Germanic art, although the sea shell was a popular ornament in Antiquity and from the 18th century onwards (see Rocaille), and the very names of Early Baroque forms of ornament – *Ohrmuschelstil* and *Knorpelstil*, i. e. auricle style and cartilege style – point to its close relation to animal and human forms. The Art Nouveau movement achieved an entirely new synthesis of plant and animal forms in its ornament. The basis of ornament is pattern, i. e. the continuous or rhythmical repetition of the same motif. Without it, a frieze would become a picture, as would a wall-paper. It would be a mistake to attribute decorative qualities only to ornament, although the word (Latin *ornare* – to decorate) encourages such a conclusion. Not only does ornament often have a symbolic significance (spirals as symbols of the sun, etc.), but it also serves to emphasise the structural features of a vessel, a building, etc., which might have remained unnoticed without it. Ornament is often the most unsophisticated form of art and springs from quite undiluted sources of creation. That explains partly why ornament often changes its forms so much more quickly than the object it decorates. It is surprising how rapidly each epoch found its own style of ornament and how fast it spread even before the appearance of the engraved pattern-books of the 17th and 18th centuries. Ornament is an excellent guide in dating works of art.

PALETTE KNIFE. The palette knife, or spatula, originally intended for mixing the colours on the palette, is also used for applying paint to the canvas. Rembrandt painted partly with the palette knife. Constable was perhaps the first artist to paint an entire picture by this means.

PARCHMENT. Parchment is prepared without tanning from the skins of animals (sheep, goat and calf) and was used in Europe for painting and writing from the 4th century until, for general purposes, paper began to replace it in the 13th. Medieval manuscripts were written on parchment and important documents are still occasionally written on it to-day. Parchment is prepared by washing, treatment with lime, removal of hair, successive scraping, paring, rubbing and dusting. The word itself comes from Pergamum and the tradition is that Eumenes II (c. 200 B.C.) was largely responsible for the development of its manufacture.

PASTEL DRAWING makes use of manufactured chalks, called pastels, preferably on a fairly soft paper with a rough surface. Although pastel drawings can be treated with a fixative to prevent smudging, this is not desirable, since it affects the purity of the colours. They are best kept under glass in a dust-proof frame. This highly 'painterly' technique has been practised since the 16th century and flourished in Rococo art,

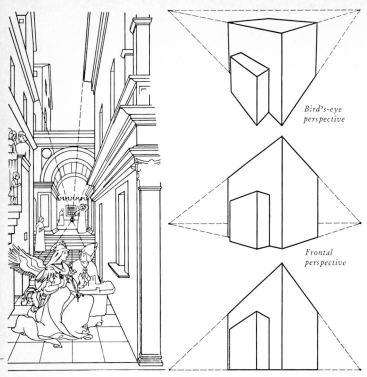

73. Perspective: central perspective (after CARLO CRIVELLI, Annunciation, cf. ill. p. 37)

Bird's-eye perspective

Frontal perspective

Worm's-eye perspective

when it was of great importance primarily in portrait painting (Quentin de la Tour, Liotard and others). In recent times Manet, Renoir and, above all, Degas made excellent use of this medium. (Ill. p. 420)

PENTIMENTI are traces of brush strokes which seemed wrong to the artist and were corrected by him in the course of his work.

PERSPECTIVE. The fact that objects seem to get smaller with increasing distance, and that parallel lines apparently meet, assumed importance in painting when artists first tried to reproduce natural effects (towards the end of the Middle Ages – as also towards the end of Classical Antiquity). A 'correct' perspective can be produced by the use of the imagination or by geometric construction. The lines at a right angle to the visual plane – the vanishing lines – will appear to converge towards one point in the distance, the vanishing point. This coincides with the station point in the case of all lines running at a right angle to the picture plane. The horizontal line drawn through the station point is called the ground line. Thus we speak of a bird's-eye perspective, frontal perspective and worm's-eye perspective. But the painter will only very rarely use the geometrically constructed perspective. It would seem exaggerated to the onlooker, whose mind automatically adjusts the impressions of the eye, and does not register decreasing size accurately. Indeed, painters have other means at their disposal, such as colour perspective and atmospheric perspective by which to represent space. Altogether, perspective is only a necessity if we assume an observer outside the picture, and the artists of many periods and countries certainly did not do so. In

medieval art, the vanishing lines often radiate from the main figure (reversed perspective). Modern painters since Cézanne have rejected mathematical perspective as lifeless and inartistic. (Cf. ill. 73, p. 37)

PEWTER. An alloy of tin, copper, antimony, and, occasionally, lead. The lower the lead and copper content, the higher the quality of the pewter. Pewter vessels were already known in Antiquity and in the Middle Ages; the Chinese are said to have used pewter as early as during the Han dynasty. Pewter gained great popularity towards the end of the Middle Ages, when it began to be made into jugs, plates, bowls, candelabra and so forth. Pewter was gradually superseded by earthenware and had already fallen into disuse before the 19th century. It is eagerly collected to-day.

PICTURE FRAME. Frescoes, miniatures and tapestries usually have no more than a painted or woven border. The panel paintings of the later Middle Ages were given wooden frames that projected slightly beyond the surface of the picture and were ornamented with the crockets and finials of Gothic architecture. The frame as a separate entity dates from the time of the Renaissance. The principal material used was wood, often elaborately carved and gilded with leaf gold in Baroque art. The Baroque type of frame was widely used until the end of the 19th century. The finest craftsmen (such as Grinling Gibbons in England) frequently turned their hand to carving frames.

In the 18th century, in the effort to meet the demand for cheaper frames, a composition which could be moulded to imitate carving was perfected. Such frames, heavy and brilliantly gilded, were characteristic of the Victorian home. In modern art, where a more severe composition holds the picture together far more than would be the case in a naturalistic painting, the frame is reduced to a narrow edge or even dispensed with altogether.

PIER. The pier is a square support, in contrast to the round column (q. v.). Like the latter, it can have a base (q. v.) and a capital (q. v.). The term is occasionally applied to a short and stumpy pillar (see also Clustered Pier).

PIETÀ. Devotional image representing the Virgin mourning over the dead Christ in her lap. The motif first appeared in German art shortly before 1300 and spread thence to other parts of Europe. (Cf. ill. 19)

PILASTER. The pilaster is a slightly projecting strip of masonry with (in contrast to the shaft) both base and capital. (Cf. ill. 194–196)

PORCELAIN. Porcelain consists of non-fusible clay, called kaolin, and fusible felspar, called *petuntse* by the Chinese. These are fired at a temperature of roughly 1400⁰ C. After the first firing, the glass is applied. This will harden when the wares are fired for the second time. Porcelain can be either hard or soft according to the materials used. Both are translucent, but soft porcelain, which is in reality a form of hard earthenware, has a body of ordinary clay and sand, soda or flint, depending on the individual factory. It is fired at a lower temperature than is hard porcelain. Colour is produced by means of metallic oxides which will stand up to very high temperatures. When porcelain is painted, the colours are either applied to the body before glazing (under-glaze painting) or afterwards, over the glaze. In the first case, colours and body are indissolubly fused. In the second, the colours, having been put on after the second firing, are fired again in the comparatively cool muffle kiln. These soft enamel colours can be used in great variety, but are not so durable as under-glaze colours. Other forms of decoration are gilding, a 'crazed' surface (obtained by sudden cooling) and various other techniques of glazing. Porcelain was invented by the Chinese. The actual date is disputed; some authorities consider it to be not older than the T'ang dynasty (A. D. 618–907), others maintain that it was already made towards the end of the Han period (218 B.C. – A. D. 205). Undoubtedly, porcelain experienced its greatest triumphs in China, Japan and Korea. Marco Polo spoke about it in his *Travels,* and when the Dutch East India Company later imported Chinese porcelain, it was soon highly coveted by collectors (ill. p. 547). It should be remembered that Chinese porcelain had been exported to the Middle East since the days of the T'ang dynasty and was already greatly valued even then. The Chinese had always distinguished between wares made for the Imperial Court, those made for the home market and those which had become slightly defective during firing and were used for export. Whole regions, such as Swatow in southern China, made mostly export wares. Some of these have none of the 'delicacy' we normally associate with porcelain. Their decoration is vigorous, handsome and not in any way naturalistic. In Europe, imitation porcelain (Medici porcelain, French artificial pastes) was finally superseded when Johann Friedrich Böttger of Meissen discovered the secret of real porcelain in 1709. The Meissen factory was founded a year later. Employing the painter

Heroldt and the sculptor Kändler, Meissen maintained its leading position for some years, chiefly through its porcelain figures (ill. p. 82). It was soon the ambition of every ruler to have his own porcelain factory. The Vienna factory was opened in 1717. One of its leading artists was the sculptor Grassi (ill. p. 322). The Viennese wares produced during the Classical Revival, usually richly painted and gilt and of graceful forms, are amongst the most coveted porcelains. The Höchst factory, founded in 1746, owes its fame to flower-decorated wares in the Meissen style with characteristic colours of red and pink, and to over 300 statues by Johann Peter Melchior. The factories of Berlin (founded 1751) and Nymphenburg (founded 1753) were soon amongst the most important in Germany – after Meissen. While the shapes of the Berlin wares have always been examplary, Nymphenburg owes its reputation to the work of two sculptors, Bustelli and Melchior, whose delightful figures and groups are amongst the finest works of Rococo art. Other factories were founded in Frankenthal, Ludwigsburg and Fürstenberg. In Italy, a leading manufactory was that at Capodimonte (founded 1743) near Naples. It was later moved to Buen Retiro in Spain. Catherine the Great established a porcelain factory at St Petersburg, and in 1759 Louis XV became sole proprietor of the privately founded Sèvres factory, in which he had already held a third of the shares since 1753. The soft porcelain made there is characterized by a wealth of glowing colours. Famous sculptors like Falconet created small figures in unglazed biscuit and porcelain of a matt and somewhat rough surface, for the royal factory. Special porcelain painters decorated dishes, plates and vases with 'pastoral' scenes after Fragonard and Boucher. England's most important factories were at Bow, Chelsea (already active in 1745), Derby, Longton Hall and Worcester. There is little difference between the early ware of Chelsea and Bow. Both were soft porcelains and at first made use of Japanese patterns, although in time they developed greater originality. Later, Bow wares were made chiefly for use, while the Chelsea factory became famous for its so-called 'Chelsea toys' – small flasks, boxes, flowers, scent bottles and little figures. Transfer printing was used at Bow as early as in 1756. Longton Hall porcelain also resembles the wares of the Chelsea factory, although it is somewhat coarser. Worcester porcelain is still being made. It comprises, *inter alia,* soft porcelain, 'Chinese' decoration, blue and white transfer printing and table ware with Classic Revival borders. The Copenhagen factory, founded in 1775, was soon producing articles for everyday use in excellent shapes. Its 20th-century products have had a fundamental effect on porcelain design. Many factories marked their wares in a special way; these marks were varied from time to time (Chelsea red anchor or gold anchor) and thus give an indication of the date. (Ill. 74)

74. Porcelain marks a) China, Wan-Li (1573–1619, Ming Dynasty), b) Meissen (1725–63), c) Vienna (1770–1810), d) Höchst (1765–78), one of the marks of J. P. Melchior, e) Berlin, Royal porcelain manufacture (1775–1834), f) Nymphenburg (from 1862), g) Sèvres (1760), h) Chelsea (c. 1755), i) Worcester (1751–83), k) Copenhagen (1897)

PORTICO. A portico is a colonnaded space forming an entrance or vestibule with a roof supported at least on one side by columns. (Cf. ill. 150)

PORTRAITURE. The portrait, whether painted, carved or modelled, confronts the artist with a special problem – that of achieving a likeness, pleasing the sitter and at the same time creating a work of aesthetic value. It is usually only when confronted by himself that the artist has the opportunity for perfect sincerity and, though romanticism and sentimentality tend to interfere, the most moving portraits are often self-portraits such as those of Rembrandt (ill. 235) or, nearer our own time, of Munch and Kokoschka. Portaiture is by no means a continuous artistic activity. The age of Pericles produced no portraits, and medieval painters and sculptors have left very few records of features which can be identified with particular persons. Portraiture plays little part, too, in the art of the Far East where the individual is held in light esteem. The art of portraiture persisted, however, throughout 4,000 years in Egypt, fostered there by a fantastic pre-occupation with death and the desire to preserve beyond the grave a recognisable likeness of the individual, motives which were scarcely aesthetic; while in Ancient Rome the most interesting and original artistic manifestation was in the sphere of naturalistic portrait sculpture, which arose from the imitation in more durable materials of the wax effigies used in family cults and in funeral ceremonies. (Cf. ill. 114–116, 120, 124, 127; pp. 115, 122).

After the advent of Christianity with its emphasis on the worthlessness of the material world, interest in portraiture disappeared almost entirely until its revival in Europe towards the beginning of the 15th century, when diminutive portraits of donors began to appear in unimportant corners of Italian altar-pieces, and when Pisanello and Jan van Eyck began to concern themselves with the representation of individual physiognomies. These portraits were very modest in scale, consisting in Pisanello's case of profile medallions and in van Eyck's of small panels. Even when van Eyck ventured a full-length portrait, extremely rare at that period, as in 'Giovanni Arnolfini and his Wife' (ill. p. 261), the picture was of small proportions. In Italy the profile pose, the most naïve and obvious manner of catching a likeness, continued to be favoured until the beginning of the 16th century.

The Renaissance revived the sense of the importance of the human personality which had been stifled by Christianity, and portraits increased steadily in size until life-size or nearly life-size became the rule. Full-length life-size portraits were, however, at first confined to emperors, popes, kings, doges or great nobles. Men of more lowly status satisfied the urge to immortalize their features by commissioning religious or mythological pictures in which they played the part in the composition. Thus Chancellor Rollin kneels before the Virgin and Child in van Eyck's celebrated picture; in Veronese's 'Marriage at Cana' the bride, bridegroom and guests are all portraits of personages of the day, including the painters Titian, Tintoretto, Bassano and Veronese himself, while Botticelli's 'Mars and Venus' presents portraits of Giuliano de' Medici and Simonetta Vespucci.

The introduction of portraits under the guise of religious or mythological composition soon yielded to portrait groups which pretended to be nothing else, such as Velasquez' 'Las Meninas', which consists of likenesses of the Infanta Margarita and her maids of honour and also includes an almost life-size portrait of Velasquez himself. The portrait had by this time – the 17th century – become recognised as one of the major activities of artists, regardless of the social position of the sitter. By a curious reversal of the earlier state of affairs Rembrandt's 'Night Watch', which showed more interest in composition and chiaroscuro than faithful portaiture, was rejected because some of the sitters felt that their features were not readily recognisable. Artists of the greatest imaginative powers, Velasquez, van Dyck, Hals and, above all, Rembrandt now became absorbed in likenesses, almost to the exclusion of other forms of painting. (Cf. ill. pp. 335, 336, 337, 338, 351)

Portraiture was cultivated with particular zest in England from the 15th century onwards. Holbein, on coming to England devoted himself almost exclusively to the painting of likenesses (ill. p. 290). Van Dyck's inclination to become a portraitist was certainly encouraged by his English sojourn, and other foreigners, Lely and Kneller, soon established themselves in England as portrait painters. By the 18th century a galaxy of native portrait artists were at work, including Hogarth, Reynolds, Gainsborough, Romney, Lawrence and lesser artists like Devis and Zoffany (ill. pp. 373, 374). Gainsborough, despite the delicious quality of his brushwork, would sooner have painted landscape, but was compelled to produce likenesses by the taste of the day. No less that 15 presidents of the Royal Academy have been portrait painters. But things have changed; few serious artists to-day devote themselves to portraiture, in the sense of the careful depiction of an individual physiognomy. The photographic means of recording a likeness has not lessened the numerical output of academic painted portraits, but it has encouraged painters of sensibility to seek other modes of expression than the faithful recording of reality. Cézanne was more interested in making a generalized, formal study of his wife's head than in depicting her features or conveying her character; and though Picasso may suggest the salient features of a personality in an abstraction of the actual forms before him, this can scarcely be called portraiture. But it is not only the tendency of the arts towards non-realistic forms of expression which has affected portraiture; man's estimation of his own importance has waned. The optimism of the Renaissance and the 18th century, the romantic attitude of the early 19th century towards the individual, have vanished and it is these which must nourish the art of portraiture.

POSTER. Artists began to design posters in the modern sense round 1890. Toulouse-Lautrec's lithographed coloured posters had been preceded by the work of his compatriot Chèret. The art of the poster continued to develop to a remarkable degree until about 1910, in England (Beggarstaff Brothers) and America no less

Furniture: English wing chair covered with needlework *(c. 1715)*

Porcelain: JOHANN JOACHIM KÄNDLER: Pantaloon and Columbine *(Meissen)*

than on the Continent. But this rapid rise made the subsequent decline all the more noticeable, since the demand for quantity lowered the artistic standard. Modern poster artists do not hesitate to make the widest use of modern, even of abstract, art forms, a public which elsewhere tends to reject them being apparently willing to accept them in this form.

POTTERY. Pottery is one of the oldest crafts and was already known in the earliest agricultural societies, which have often been named after the particular form of pottery they produced (corded-ware, 'Bandkeramik', painted pottery, etc.). The invention of the potter's wheel gave the ceramic arts a new impetus and carried them to great heights – notably the unsurpassed Athenian vase. Some of the greatest potters were the Chinese, the Islamic peoples and also the inhabitants of Ancient Peru. The progress of ceramics is not only marked by more elaborate forms, by painting and ornament, but also by the use of glaze (q. v.). The most important forms of pottery are earthenware (Faience, or Majolica) and porcelain. Faience (named after the Italian city Faenza, where this type of ware was made at an early date) is a form of earthenware, covered with an opaque and non-porous tin glaze. The Italians call it Maiolica, after the island of Mallorca, from which Spanish 'faiences' were imported to Italy. To-day, the name 'faience' is mostly used to describe French earthenware; Italian earthenware is called majolica; Dutch and English earthenware of a similar type are known as 'delft'. Like porcelain, earthenware can be decorated in a few, but brilliant, 'hard enamel' colours; these fuse with the glaze during the second firing, or, having been fired twice, with a wider range of less durable 'muffle colours'. They are fired in so-called muffle kilns, as distinct from the open flame kilns used for coarser wares or where great heat is required. Glazed pottery was already known in Ancient Egypt. The Babylonians invented a white tin glaze. This technique was taken up in the East, especially amongst the Islamic peoples, whose pottery is outstanding (Rhages, Sultanabad, Samarkand, etc.). The Arabs brought Islamic pottery to Spain (Malaga, Valencia), whence it found its way to Italy and the rest of Europe. The most famous Italian workshop was in Florence (della Robbia family, q. v.), where whole paintings, based on the work of famous masters (Dürer and Raphael, amongst others), were used to decorate large platters and bowls. The fame of the Delft potters was based on the imitation of Chinese porcelain (mostly blue and white). The Rouen, and, later, the Moustiers factories, were the most important centres of production in France; in Germany, faience was first made in the region around Hanau, but soon gained popularity everywhere. The most important centres in England were Lambeth, Bristol and Liverpool. English delft was at first based on Dutch models, from which it is often almost indistinguishable. Here, too, 'Chinese' decoration continued until fairly late in the 18th century. A number of typically English designs were already developed in the 17th century, amongst

them the so-called blue dash chargers, i. e. large platters decorated with blue dashes along the edge and with paintings of Adam and Eve, or royal portraits, in the centre. Other types are the tulip chargers, and the brown slipware of Thomas Toft. By 1800, Wedgwood's invention of hard earthenware put an end to 'faience' almost everywhere. In recent times, there have been many attempts at a revival of the old technique (Karlsruhe, Copenhagen). One of the early predecessors of porcelain is stoneware, which becomes non-porous in firing and whose handsome, shiny glaze is produced by the addition of salt, which evaporates in firing. Stoneware, known to the Chinese since the Han dynasty (206 B.C. – A. D. 220) was widely made in Germany during the 16th and 17th centuries. Important centres of production were in the Rhineland (in the region of Cologne), where the so-called 'grey-beards' – jugs with a bearded face near the spout – and the 'Kurfürstenkrüge' with their medallions of local rulers were made.

The 'Schnellen', slender mugs of white stoneware, were made in Siegburg, other types of vessels in the Westerwald region and in Franconia and Silesia. In England, John Dwight of Fulham claimed to have discovered the secret of German stoneware in 1671 and took out a patent. He founded the Fulham factory, which has continued to the present day. Dwight's early wares were statues and jugs copied from German models. Other important pioneers were the Elers brothers, who made red stoneware teapots in the Chinese manner. Hard salt-glazed earthenware was also made by John Astbury and by Thomas Whieldon. This type of earthenware is not a stoneware, but has merely had ground flint added to the clay. Earthenware of this type must not be confused with the so-called 'soft' porcelain, made at Chelsea and Worcester, and also in Persia. Hard earthenware was perfected to the highest degree by Josiah Wedgwood. His vases, tea-pots and medallions, mostly decorated with classical motifs, were often finished on the lapidary's wheel. Experiments were also made with various other techniques. Transfer printing, i. e. the application of transfer pictures, which were secured by firing, came into vogue at the beginning of the 19th century; stone china was invented slightly later.

The ceramic arts have also been used in architecture from the earliest days. The decorations of Gothic red brick churches are often of terra-cotta, as were the statues or ornaments on the roof of the Greek temple (Akroterion). Glazed earthenware played an important part in the prehistoric civilisations of Mesopotamia (Ishtar gate in Babylon, see ill. 94) and, above all, in the architecture of Islam. The walls of the Alhambra (Granada) are faced all over with coloured earthenware tiles, the so-called *azulejos*. Painted pottery has, in fact, existed since the Stone Age; but the term, in its narrower sense, is only applied to the pottery of prehistoric or early historic times. Painted pottery is classified according to cultural epochs. With the exception of an area in the Rhineland in the Early Middle Ages (Pingsdorf ware), it was unknown in the

Germanic North. But it was known in Asia Minor between 3000 and 4000 B.C., and spread throughout the Balkans, the Danubian plain and southern Italy, as early as in the Neolithic Age, although it had fallen into disuse by the Bronze Age, except in the Aegean peninsula and the surrounding islands. Painted pottery only seems to have returned to favour in the Iron Age, when it occurred in Italy, Spain and within the orbit of the Hallstatt and La Tène cultures.

In porcelain (q. v.) – not discovered in Europe until the 18th century, although known to the Chinese at least a thousand years earlier – the dreams of the potters of the past seemed to have been fulfilled. A material suitable both for bowls and jars of all kinds and for small statues hitherto made of terra-cotta had at last been found.

PROFILE. In architecture, a profile is the outline of a projecting portion, such as a cornice, base, etc. Individual forms are shown in the illustration below.

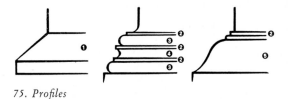

75. Profiles

1 Chamfer, 2 Fillet, 3 Torus, 4 Scotia, 5 Cornice

76. Nicola Pisano, Pulpit in the Baptistery in Pisa (1260)

PULPIT. In northern European churches the pulpit was originally combined with the reading pew, which was placed beyond the chancel screen in the nave as it had to be in a position from which the priest could best be heard. During the 13th century, when preaching grew increasingly popular, the pulpit became a separate piece of furniture placed towards the middle of the nave against one of the pillars or against the north or south wall. Both the reading pew and the pulpit are northern forms of the ambo, which in basilican and Byzantine churches was used for the lessons, the litanies, the giving out of notices, preaching, as a standing place for singers and even as a platform for coronations. Ambos can be seen facing each other, like an English pulpit and reading pew, across the nave in Italian and Spanish churches. No European country is as rich as Italy in carved stone pulpits such as the famous examples at Pisa and Assisi. English craftsmen excelled in carved wooden pulpits which were often three-storeyed and surmounted by elaborate testers as at Lincoln and Canterbury. Spanish craftsmen produced some remarkable hammered iron pulpits, of which the gilded example at Avila is outstanding. (Cf. ill. 76, 61)

RELIQUARY. The reliquary contains Sacred Relics (Lat. *reliquiae* – remains), such as ashes or bone fragments. In Early Christian times, relics were kept in box-like shrines or in the Pyx; from the 6th to

the 8th century onwards, in shrines shaped like a pilgrim's bag *(bursa),* of which the Engern reliquary in Berlin is one of the best-known examples. Reliquaries were made in the shape of an arm, foot or head, according to the nature of the relic. In the Romanesque period, relics were often placed in larger shrines, which were given the form of a basilica (e. g. Shrine of the Magi in Cologne Cathedral) or a domed church (domed reliquary from the Treasure of the Guelphs, ill. p. 194). Cruciform reliquaries – to take particles of the True Cross, – chests, tablets (see Golden Panel), medallions, etc. also occur. Because of their venerable contents, reliquaries were made of gold and silver, decorated with precious stones, pearls and enamels and with chasing, engraved ornament and beaten and cast relief. Many reliquaries represent the goldsmith's art at its finest.

REPLICA, see Copy.

REPOUSSÉ. A technique used both in jewellery and in sculpture. It consists in hammering sheets of metal from the back until the desired form is obtained. Details are worked out with the punch. Not only chalices and bowls, but also monuments can be made in this way. The equestrian statue of Augustus the Strong in Dresden is made entirely of beaten copper. The technique itself is as old as metalwork. The Mycenaean gold masks are made in repoussé work, as is the Basle antependium dating from about 1020. (Cf. ill. p. 554)

REPOUSSOIR. A term used to describe figures or objects placed in the foreground of a painting, where they will seem to move towards the viewer, and so create an illusion of greater depth. Objects of every kind set well in the foreground (as also doorways, trees, etc.), help towards this end, just as they do in a photograph. (See ill. p. 302)

REPRODUCTION. A reproduction, in contrast to the replica, is rarely contemporary with a work of art, and can be made by mechanical means. Before the invention of photography, paintings were often reproduced in copper engravings. Statues can be reproduced in bronze, or in plaster or concrete casts.

RESTORING is the method of bringing a damaged or defaced work of art back into its original state. The condition of buildings, statues, paintings, jewellery and other works depends to some extent on the materials of which they are made. External damage, however small, may seriously affect or even destroy a work of art. For instance, if the eyes in a portrait are blurred so that the sitter's expression is lost, the whole work may be ruined. It may be possible to replace the missing parts from photographs or by comparison with copies, but the essential character of the painting will have gone. Less serious damage, resulting from dirt, or later additions and alterations, can, however, be detected with modern methods (X-ray, ultra-violet rays) and be put right by chemical means. Preservation is related to restoring, but here, too, there are certain limits. Each work of art is subject to natural changes, the rate of decay merely depending on the material. In the case of bronze, the product of oxidization, the patina, actually increases the value, since it has a beauty of its own and is also taken by some people as proof of genuine-

ness (mistakenly, since modern chemistry can achieve almost any surface effect in a matter of hours). The colours of a painting may alter in the course of the years and some painters, taking advantage of such changes, allow for this in their work, thus actually causing it to change for the better over a comparatively long period. But the physical decay of a work of art can only be partially arrested; nothing will stop it completely.

RETABLE, see Alabaster.

ROOD. A cross or crucifix generally standing on the rood screen or attached to the vaulting of the entrance to the chancel of medieval churches. A famous example is the Romsey Rood. The rood screen separated the part of a medieval church reserved for the use of the clergy from that intended for the use of the public. Rood screens were often richly decorated with sculpture. A celebrated example is the one in the West choir of Naumburg Cathedral in the Saale, Germany, dating from about 1250 (ill. 174). A late example is that of St Etienne du Mont, Paris.

ROOF. The roof of a building is an important architectural element, quite apart from its purely utilitarian function. The most importants forms are shown below (ill. 77).

ROSETTE. A stylized, circular flower, which has been known since earliest times. A particular form, the whorl rosette, gives the impression of rotation.

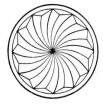

78. Whorl Rosette

RUSTICATION. Stonework with roughened surfaces and

77. Types of Roof

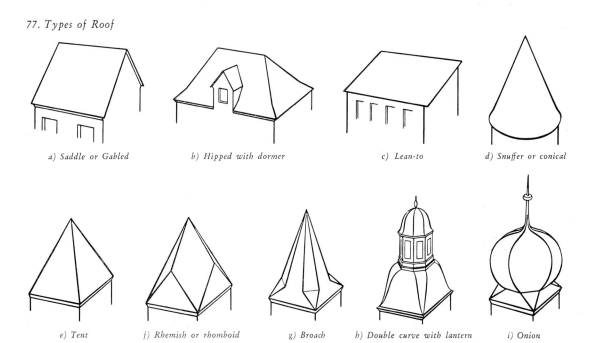

a) *Saddle or Gabled*   b) *Hipped with dormer*   c) *Lean-to*   d) *Snuffer or conical*

e) *Tent*   f) *Rhemish or rhomboid*   g) *Broach*   h) *Double curve with lantern*   i) *Onion*

recessed joints. It was widely used in Baroque and Renaissance architecture to enliven the wall area, particularly on the ground floor. (Ill. 193)

SARCOPHAGUS. A sarcophagus is a coffin – frequently decorated with paintings or sculpture, etc. – of stone or clay or metal. In Ancient Egypt, the sarcophagus was often a replica of the house of the deceased; later, it was given the form of his body, with a realistic sculptured head. The Ancient Greeks usually buried their dead in simple coffins. After the 4th century B. C., these were occasionally decorated in elaborate relief (e. g. Alexander sarcophagus, q. v.) or with paintings (recent finds at Paestum). The sarcophagi of the Etruscans often had lids with a portrait statue of the deceased, while the sides showed reliefs with scenes from Hades or mythological representations. The type of sarcophagus in use amongst the Romans since the 2nd century A. D. is based on the Etruscan model. Here, too, the outside is decorated with scenes from everyday life and mythology, which perhaps have some symbolic reference to death and the dead. During the Late Romanesque period, sarcophagi were decorated with Christian symbols. The sarcophagi in Ravenna, mostly of the 5th and 6th centuries A. D., are in a class of their own and show strong Byzantine influence.

SEPIA, a brown pigment, made from the ink of the cuttle fish, is used mainly for pen and wash drawings. It must not be confused with lamp black (q. v.), which is similar in colour and was often used by the Old Masters in its liquid form.

SEPULCHRAL MONUMENTS. Sepulchral monuments have played an important part in every civilisation since the earliest days of history. They achieved their most monumental aspect, perhaps, amongst the Egyptians (necropolis, pyramids) and amongst the ancestor-worshipping Chinese and Japanese. Architectural monuments – it is debatable, whether the earliest funeral monuments can be classed as architecture, although, in the opinion of the great modern architect Adolf Loos, tombstone and monument are the only forms of architecture that can be classed as pure art – were developed in Asia Minor from the 6th century B.C. onwards and

79. Tomb in the Herbert Chapel, the Priory Church of St Mary the Virgin, Abergavenny, Monmouthshire, Wales. Effigy of a natural son (d. 1510) of the first Earl of Pembroke

80. Funerary stele of Ilissus (3rd or 4th cent. B.C.)

grew into the mausoleum of Late Antiquity and into the memorial chapel (the tomb of Theoderic at Ravenna, ill. 141). The Classic Greek tombs were generally on a more modest scale and confined to a funerary urn *(lekythos)*, a statue or an upright stone slab (stele) – the predecessor of the modern tomb-stone – decorated in relief. The Christian tombs of the Middle Ages were placed both inside and outside the church and consisted of a stone or bronze tablet (ill. 79), often placed on a box-like base, the tumba (hence tomb; Fr. *tombeau*). This, from the 11th century onwards, bore the full-length portrait statue of the deceased. In English parish churches, we often find these tablets made of engraved brass. Later, a canopy and statues of mourners were often added to the tumba. Renaissance and Baroque tombs were often placed against walls and were made into elaborate monuments (e. g. Michelangelo's Medici tombs in Florence). English parish churches contain a great variety of tombs, as do the cathedrals. Interesting examples are the tomb of Henry VII in Westminster Abbey (erected 1511–18) by Pietro Torrigiani, Oliver Goldsmith's tomb by Nollekens, also in Westminster Abbey, and the tomb of Sir William Gore, by John Nost, in Tring parish church.

SGRAFFITO. This term was used in Renaissance Italy to define a popular method of decorating the fronts of stuccoed buildings. A coat of pigmented plaster was laid over a coat of another colour, and before it had dried a design was incised through to the undercoat. Black and white were used in the traditional manner, but as the technique was elaborated many colours were employed, as well as gilding. A famous example is the Palazzo del Consiglio, Verona (1476). The word sgraffito is also used to designate any image incised on a wall, such as the example in Ashwell, Hertfordshire, a 14th-century representation of Old St Paul's, London.

SHAFT. A term used to describe the section of a column between base and capital in Classic architecture. In medieval architecture, this term is applied to entire small columns, such as those enclosing a clustered pier.

SILHOUETTE. The name is usually applied to shades and profiles and derives from that of Etienne de Silhouette (1709–1767), the parsimonious finance minister of Louis XV. He was an amateur cutter of shades but not the originator of the art. As such portraits were cheap they were dubbed à la Silhouette. Although its origins go back to Antiquity, the silhouette as we recognise it to-day dates from the end of the 17th century. The earliest silhouettes were probably scissor-cuts. One was that of William and Mary said to have been cut by Elizabeth Pyburg (c. 1699). Among painted silhouettes, the most prized are those of John Miers (1758–1821) and Isabella Beetham (fl. 1750). The best known practitioners of the cut silhouette were Augustin Edouart (1788–1861), Philipp Otto Runge (1776–1810), A. Farberger (1762–1865) and E. P. Sideau (fl. 1782). Among the large number of American silhouettists, mostly cutters, Charles Willson Peale (1741–1827) was outstanding. The heyday of the silhouette as a form of portrait ended with the invention of photography.

SILK. The mulberry silk moth which produces silk is indigenous to China and the silk industry originated in that country at a remote period. The secret of silk culture was jealously guarded in China and only penetrated to Japan in the 3rd century A.D. Although according to a legend a Chinese princess took silk worm's eggs wrapped in her hair to India, silk culture was never fully developed there owing to the religious ban which forbad the killing of the silk worms. The first country to import silk from China was Persia.

The earliest surviving Chinese patterned silks were discovered in 1910 by Sir Aurel Stein in Chinese Turkestan on the route opened by the Chinese for silk trade with Western Asia in the 2nd century B.C. These fabrics reveal an intricate technique of tapestry weaving and the designs consist of fabulous birds and beasts, scrolls, wave patterns and cloud forms.

Aristotle is the first European writer to describe the silk worm. The material was much prized by the Romans. The Emperor Justinian recorded his interest in the weaving of silk, and Byzantine designs have great strength. The earliest Persian silks belong to the Sassanian period. Sassanian silks were remarkable for their colours. Vegetable, mineral and animal dyes were used, the most prominent colours being dark blue, intense green, red, brown, purple, yellow and black. Syrian weavers adopted the technique and many of the designs of the Persians, and when these latter were conquered by the Arabs, their art vigorously influenced that of their conquerors. Islamic traders carried Persian methods as well as the actual silks both east and west. From the 7th century onwards Persian silks were more generally influential than the Chinese. The fine silks produced in Persia under the Seljuks (1037—1256), a Turkish dynasty, were at first close in design to the earlier Persian textiles. Later, the formerly angular patterns gave way to flowing, scroll-like motifs. The Kufic script played an important part in the development of these designs, which much resemble, and probably stimulated, those later evolved in Europe during the Renaissance. Sicilian silks of the 12th century show an interesting combination of these Seljuk designs with the Byzantine practice of introducing formalized human figures.

Oriental fabrics presented in 800 to Charlemagne by Haroun al Raschid inspired him to establish his own silk industry, but examples of this work have not survived. In the 14th century Lyons became a centre for the production of fine fabrics probably owing to the settlement in that place of silk weavers from Lucca. Etienne Turquet, a cloth merchant of Italian descent was also largely responsible for promoting the silk industry of Lyons by gaining the patronage of Francis I. The industry prospered during the reign of Henry IV (1589—1610) when a silk weaver, Claude Dangon, invented a special loom for more readily weaving patterned silks. In the 17th century Cobert reorganized the Lyons factories and prepared the way for the great activity of the 18th century, when silks for Court use were ordered from Spain, Russia and Prussia. Changes in fashion, which suddenly favoured muslin more than silk, followed by the French Revolution, almost ruined the Lyons industry. It revived, however, under Napoleon, who favoured wall hangings of silk, and commanded women of fashion to wear Lyons silk. Lyons remained the most important centre of the silk industry even after the Jacquard loom, power-driven first by steam and then by electricity, had replaced individual labour.

Apart from its use as a textile, silk has served an important purpose as a particularly durable support for much Far Eastern, especially Chinese, painting.

SILVER POINT. A silver-tipped style will produce a delicate grey line on specially prepared paper (see ill. 36). The silver crayon was the 'lead' pencil of the Old Masters (our 'lead' pencil is made of graphite and is an invention of the last century); it is particularly suitable for studies from nature and for travel sketches. The illustrations in Dürer's 'Travel Sketches in the Netherlands' were carried out in silver crayon.

STAGE DESIGN. This term embraces all the devices by which the audience is enabled to visualize the setting of a play, including the scenery, movable objects and the proscenium.

In Ancient Greece, stage design consisted of but a simple back wall with three doors. By the time of Vitruvius

(1st cent. B.C.) some painted scenery was used. Vitruvius describes standardized decorations for three types of drama, architectural motifs for tragedy and comedy and pastoral designs for satyr plays.

During the Middle Ages, when mystery plays took place inside the church, stage design was at first limited to movable objects. But when, during the 14th and 15th centuries, the play was transferred to the outside of the church and to the market place, settings became more elaborate. The different scenes were called 'mansions' and the decoration was carried out by the guilds.

Renaissance stage design was nourished by three sources: the rediscovery of the works of Seneca, Plautus and Terence, the descriptions of Vitruvius and the festival processions, *trionfi* and masques of the 15th century. By the beginning of the 16th century the use of perspective was common on the stage. The matured Renaissance stage had a background painted in perspective with painted canvas wings to the right and left. Palladio and Scamozzi, who together designed the Teatro Olimpio at Vicenza, transformed the painted perspective into actual three-dimensional architectural settings framed by three triumphal arches. Changeable sets were first used in the Teatro Farnese at Parma, built 1618–19.

Aesthetically, stage design reached its climax in the 17th and 18th centuries. The art was considered so important that copper engravings were made and preserved of the work of all the leading theatre architects and designers. The influence of Italian stage designers spread throughout Europe. Inigo Jones was profoundly affected by what he had seen in Italy and based the designs for his elaborate masques on the Teatro Farnese. Italian artists working in Germany and Austria produced even more complicated settings than those seen in Italy.

Early in the 18th century stage design underwent important changes owing to the examples of the great stage-designing family of Bibiena, four generations of whom worked in various parts of Europe. Instead of a static, symmetrical composition, illusionistic Baroque perspectives became the order of the day. The spectator no longer looked at the stage as if it were a separate room with the fourth wall removed, but he himself was included in the room. Filippo Juvarra, who worked chiefly in Turin, and Giovanni Sernandoni worked in the manner of the Bibiena. But the artist who above all excelled in the style, surpassing the Bibiena in spatial fantasy, was Piranesi.

Complicated prison scenes, romantic ruins and crumbling stairways gave way at the beginning of the 19th century to increased naturalism. This can be observed in the stage designs of the German architect, Schinkel. The tendency led to the development of the 'box set', in which closed side walls replaced the individual side wings. This period was marked by the decline of stage design as an art, despite the improvement in purely mechanical devices and lighting.

Max Reinhardt (1873–1943) was among the first to revolt against complete naturalism. He used devices for movement which were opposed to realism. The work of the artists who designed for him, Alfred Roller, Emil Orlik and, above all, Ernst Stern combined naturalistic detail with stylization. Reinhardt was the first to realize that the demands of the intimate theatre and the theatre for the masses were entirely different. Adolphe Appia (1862–1928), following Wagner, regarded the theatre as a combination of visual, musical and literary impressions united by rhythm. His stage designs were three-dimensional and relied largely on light and colour, arranged rhythmically. Edward Gordon Craig reduced stage sets to pure cubic volumes and later even dispensed with these basic shapes and used only portable folding screens. Meanwhile, in Russia, Tairov tried to abolish stage illusion by the use of scaffold and technical constructions. Tairov's ideas influenced the characteristic settings of the Jewish Moscow Academical Theatre.

Cubism and Futurism greatly influenced stage design, and abstract sets were designed by Picabia, Bagaglia, Prampolini, Moholy-Nage and Oskar Schlemmer. Theatrical machinery such as the revolving stage was used, not for practical purposes, but for the expression of ideas. Bakst replaced the conception of the three-dimensional spatial setting by a two-dimensional fantasy and was followed by various painter-designers, Léger, Matisse, Braque, Picasso and Derain. The influence of Surrealism lingers on in some recent stage design, but it is combined, as in the work of Leslie Hurry, with a return to the three-dimensional set and a revival of something of the spirit and fantasy of the 17th and 18th centuries.

STAINED GLASS. A pictorial or decorative composition of pieces of coloured glass of various shapes and sizes held together by strips of lead. Detail is added afterwards. Except for the wider range of colours available today, the art of stained glass-making is the same to-day as it was in the 12th century.

The origin of stained glass is obscure, but it is thought to come from the Near East and to date from no earlier than the 9th century. By the 10th century, Venice was the centre of the industry. The first record of pictorial windows is a manuscript giving an account of the various windows of Rheims Cathedral rebuilt from 969 to 988. But the history of the art is documented with existing works only from the 11th and early 12th centuries. Windows of this period were usually single and the stained-glass picture was of one monumental figure. There are examples at Augsburg, Le Mans, Canterbury and York. Three lancet windows from the west front of Chartres belong to this period, which are characteristic of the school of glass painting encouraged by Abbot Suger of Saint-Denis. The subjects are the Tree of Jesse, the Infancy of Christ and the Passion. The wide, rich borders vary considerably in design; the armature of iron bars traverses the windows with rectangles, there are many bands of lead and the segments of glass are minute. Multiple leading and small panes increase the refraction of light and the intensity of the colours, particularly the rich blue. (Ill. p. 204) By the beginning of the 13th century two or three windows were generally combined within one frame, and began to increase considerably in size. French glass-making in the north and centre of the country was dominated by the style of Chartres. The style penetrated to England, where it is found at Canterbury and Lincoln, and other examples of it are at Bourges, Sens, Le Mans, Laon and Cologne. Red is preferred to blue as background, and decorative painting in grey mono-tone appears in which leafy patterns are painted in grey, black or brown on large clear areas of glass. To the latter half of the 13th century belongs the Sainte-Chapelle, with the 15 huge stained glass windows from which it derives its chief significance. (Ill. 153, p. 204)

The composition of the windows changed during the 13th century. The grid frame of verticals and horizontals in the iron armature was curved to enclose scenes and figures in circles, semicircles, lozenges and squares.

In technique, the great invention of the 14th century was silver stain, the painting of glass with an oxide or chloride of silver that turned the glass yellow when heated. Larger panes of glass were used, and in the designs the tendency towards naturalism reached its height. In the typical 14th-century composition the window is dominated by a single figure or group, set in the middle of a long lancet of grisaille and standing within a niche of bewildering architecture. Flowing curves are used for the eyes, hair and lips as for folds in the dress, which itself mirrors contemporary fashion. In the 15th century there was less insistence on naturalism. Heraldic designs developed as decoration. Various local schools of glass painting sprang up around talented artists all over Europe, each differing slightly from the others. The tendency of the stained glass workers to rival the painter increased, and persisted indefinitely throughout following periods. In the 16th century stained glass windows were regarded as large pictures. A master of this technique was Bernard Flower, who came from the Netherlands to England to execute the windows for the King Henry VII Chapel, Westminster, as well as for windows for King's College Chapel, Cambridge. Important windows of this period are at Rouen, Antwerp, Amsterdam, Brussels, Liège, Augsburg, Strassburg, Cologne, Rome and Florence.

In the 17th century a type of stained glass was produced in Switzerland to be used in almost every home. It again resembled painting and indeed often took the place of painting on the walls of houses. As it was intended to be seen at close range, the glass design became extremely fine and delicate.

The Gothic Revival in England produced imitations of medieval glass. William Morris and Burne Jones in the 19th century revolted against such imitation and tried to encourage new creative efforts in the stained glass technique. They produced windows for Christ Church,

Oxford, for Salisbury Cathedral, and Birmingham Cathedral as well as stained glass pictures of romantic and literary subjects for domestic use.

The 20th century is marked by a widespread use of glass, and true stained glass window-making, as distinct from pictures painted on glass and inserted in the window opening in an attempt to imitate the canvas, has returned after a lapse of more than three centuries. The best windows now are built in the techniques of the glass-makers of Chartres. The designs are boldly decorative and largely abstract, being used for churches as well as for secular buildings, though so far in a limited way.

STELE. A stone pillar used as a gravestone or to mark a site, decorated with a relief or inscribed. The earliest known stelae to bear a relief are Sumerian work dating from 2550 B.C. One of these represents King Urnammu pouring a libation, another shows him at the head of his army. Chinese Buddhist stelae are adorned with reliefs of the seated Buddha. Mayan stelae bear dated inscriptions and religious reliefs and were set up as 'time-markers'. The finest stelae are the Athenian tombstones of the 5th and 4th centuries B.C. The earliest examples are tall and narrow usually carved with a single figure, but the mid-5th-century slab is wider and allows of a more elaborate relief, generally depicting an episode from the life of the deceased. These Greek slabs were often crowned with a pediment and framed by engaged pillars. In the 4th century the compositions become more crowded and the relief more coarsely cut. The demand for sculptured stelae declined in Athens after the decree of Demetrius of Phaleron against the display of wealth, but they remained popular in the Greek colonies and were also favoured by the Romans. (Cf. ill. 14, 80)

STILL-LIFE PAINTING. Like landscape painting (q. v.) still-life was late to develop in Europe as an independent art. In Chinese and Japanese painting, however, the still-life held an important place from a very early period. Flower and bamboo studies formed a prominent branch of Chinese painting already by the Ch'in period (A. D. 265–420). Though these still-lifes were often related to poetry, they were fundamentally preoccupied with the purely painterly qualities of rhythm and linear design.

Greek and Roman mosaics show understanding of the decorative possibilities of still-life painting. The subjects chosen by the painters of Antiquity appear to have consisted of horns of abundance, festoons of fruits and flowers and designs composed of insects, butterflies and snails. Much of this decorative convention was inherited by the Italians, but with them still-life, like landscape, was subordinated to the principal theme of the picture and the primarily religious purpose of their work. Still-life plays a very great part in Crivelli's paintings. Though religion provided the excuse for his pictures, their most vital interest lies in the extraordinary precision and intensity with which he painted canopies of fruits and flowers, pots and domestic utensils.

As enthusiasm for the human figure began to wane with the approaching decadence of the Italian schools, the still-life detail encroached more powerfully upon the canvas space. Caravaggio produced several examples of independent still-life – an elaborate painting of flowers. Luca Barbieri executed a painting of a dead fish, another of dead game and one of a basketful of flowers, and Paolo Antonio Barbieri painted huge piles of animals, comestibles, fruits and flowers, which entirely overwhelm the landscapes in which they are set.

In Spanish painting still-life often plays an important role. Velasquez lavished all his technical skill, feeling for texture and colour, and sense of design on the still-life groups which take so prominent a place in his compositions. Later, Goya painted a few astonishing independent still-lifes, among them a study of dead game in the Prado, which must have exercised considerable influence on Manet.

It was, however, in Holland and in Flanders in the 17th century that the art of still-life was first most fully developed for its own sake. The Dutch and Flemish painters were inspired by no other motive than to render as meticulously as possible what they saw before them. Among Dutch and Flemish masters of still-life may be mentioned the Van Huysums, De Heem, Heda, Kalf, Bosschaert, Snyders, Van Aelst and Walscapelle. The works of these painters are on the whole more remarkable for their verisimilitude than for their concern with aesthetic problems. (Cf. ill. p. 71)

In France the first most notable still-life painter was Chardin, who delighted in the colour and texture of fruit, in the various ways in which the dark flask, the thick tumbler and the half-cut loaf might be composed, and in the design made by simply folded napery and sparkling porcelain. Fantin-Latour painted flowers with delicacy, but with too great naturalism and too little interest in formal values (ill. 261). The Impressionists, preoccupied with the play of light and atmosphere, did not often paint still-life. Manet's attempts reflect his study of the Spanish masters. A few pictures by Monet and Renoir, however, of both flowers and fruits, show the grace and poetry with which the impressionist technique might be applied to still-life subjects. Van Gogh's intense and asymmetrically composed still-lifes and Gauguin's flat, decorative treatment and brilliant colouring both show in different ways the influence of the Orient, particularly of the Japanese colour print.

In Cézanne's monumental still-lifes, this genre reaches its highest expression. The problems of form, colour and design are here the painter's exclusive study.

In England, where literary interests have always predominated, the art of still-life was not much cultivated for its own sake before the present century, and the work of recent times both in France and in England stems from Cézanne and the Impressionists. Still-life has passed through all the various phases of abstraction, which sprang from Cézanne's simplifications of natural

forms, providing the main theme for the dignified decorative designs of Juan Gris and Braque; and still-life has inspired painters like Bonnard or Matthew Smith in their richly textured and painterly works. (Ill. p. 503)

STUCCO. Plastering or stucco is one of the most ancient crafts connected with building. The Egyptian Pyramids contain plasterwork dating from c. 2000 B.C. used as a ground for decorative painting. Great use was made of the medium by the Aegean civilisations. The Cretans used an exquisitely thin, fine and white lime stucco as a basis for murals; and where they were not built of marble, the Greeks covered their temples both internally and externally with plaster. Very often decorative ornament was painted on this stucco. From a description by Pausanias of the Temple of the Stymphalides (c. 400 B.C.), which had a ceiling ornamented with panels and figures of harpies, it appears that the Greeks used stucco for modelling.

In his work on architecture written c. 16 B.C., Vitruvius describes the methods used by the Romans for plasterwork, and stucco seems to have been used profusely at Pompeii.

The Byzantines did not employ plaster and for more than 1000 years all relics of ornamental stucco work in the Empire were gradually forgotten. But the removal of the capital to Byzantium spread the art of plaster to the Near East where it was enriched with an oriental extravagance the results of which were brought back to Europe in the early part of the 13th century by the Moors, who were responsible for the magnificent plasterwork of the Alhambra. (Ill. 343)

During the Early Middle Ages plastering existed in Europe only as a craft, its highest function being to furnish a painting surface. Not until the time of the Renaissance in Italy was there any sign of the revival of stucco work as an art. Donatello sometimes modelled in stucco (e. g., a group of the 'Entombment' over the sacristy door in the church of S. Antonio at Padua and medallions of the four Evangelists in the sacristy of S. Lorenzo, Florence.) Andrea Verrocchio founded the art of piece moulding in Venice and perfected the craft of plaster casting, making possible the reproduction of the work of Antiquity, and thus greatly stimulating original ornamental plasterwork.

In 1515 Raphael was appointed director and inspector of the search for the buried remains of Ancient Rome. He and his assistant, Giovanni da Udine, were astonished by the discovery of abundant modelled stucco ornaments, still dazzling white. Udine analysed the composition of this Roman stucco and at once it became the most popular form of decoration. Raphael designed the arabesque plasterwork ornament for the Loggia of the Vatican and for the Villa Madama, which after his death were completed by Giulio Romano, Giov. Francesco Penni and Udine. On the sack of Rome by the French in 1527, Udine fled to Florence where he founded a school of stuccoists. They were responsible for the ceilings of the Pitti Palace and the interesting external work on the pillars of the courtyard of the

Palazzo Vecchio. It was in southern Italy in the next century, however, that the Italians produced their finest stucco work.

Giulio Romano went in 1524 to Mantua where he established an important school of plasterers who later influenced all Western Europe. Primaticcio was sent at the request of Francis I from Mantua to supervise the decorations at Fontainebleau. The noble figure work they executed together with swags of fruit and flowers established a canon for the French sculptors, Goujon, Pillon and their followers. Meanwhile Italian stuccoists had come also to England to work for Henry VIII, amongst them Luca and Bartholomew Penni. The art of the plasterer, or pargeter as he was then called, was considered of such importance in England before the advent of the Italians that in 1501 Henry VII had formed them into a separate guild. Little use, however, had been made of ornamental work before that date. The English plasterers soon learned and practised Italian methods but they did not attempt to emulate the compositions and designs of the foreigners; instead, they evolved an indigenous type of decoration based on the familiar groining which had strengthened and adorned the stone roofs of the Middle Ages. Curvilinear and knotted forms succeeded the geometric arrangements, and scrollwork of large dimensions became popular. The plasterer soon considered the ceiling too small in scope for his rapidly developing art; he encroached upon the walls and a deep frieze crowded with relief figures and ornament soon filled the space between wainscot and main cornice, as at Aston Hall. External walls were covered with pargetry and magnificent examples survive. Some fine work was executed during the early years of the 17th century, among which may be mentioned the rich designs of the ceilings at Audley End.

The closer acquaintance with Italian Renaissance architecture which developed under Charles I produced ceilings of a plainer character. Wide compartments were adopted and ornament was concentrated into modelled bands and scrolls as at Coleshill.

When Wren visited Paris in 1665, he specially noticed the plasterwork carried out by van Ostel and Arnoldino. Wren's influence was important for the revival of the art during the reign of Charles II after a partial eclipse under the Protector. Floral motifs now became popular, and it became fashionable, following French example, to leave the main field of the ceiling plain and to drive the ornament into the corners and centre. Cast plaster now came to be frequently introduced, much to the detriment of the plasterer's art. Design was further divorced from craft by the habit of bringing out books of designs for plasterers composed by those who knew nothing of the art.

The interest of the mid-18th century in Classical Antiquity and its remains was of importance in the formation of the style of plasterwork cultivated by the Adam brothers. It had charm but very little work was left for the true artist in plaster. He had only to cast models designed by another artist and to produce monotonously repeating ornaments. Thus Classical Antiquity, which had fostered the art of stucco during the Renaissance, led two centuries later to its decline.

STUCCO LUSTRO. Stucco lustro is a variant of the fresco (q. v.) technique. A layer of stucco (q. v.) is coated with another layer of marble dust. The paint, bound with soap and lime, is then applied to this still damp surface, which is afterwards gone over with a hot iron. The colours have great radiance and a lacquer-like glow. The technique was very popular in the Hellenistic period, lived on in Italy as a form of surface treatment rather than as an art, and has been revived in recent times for decorative work.

TAPESTRY. Tapestry is woven on a loom with several bobbins each used to insert its yarn in the area where the pattern requires that particular colour; it thus permits of a free, non-repeating design and unlimited colour. In the simplest tapestries the warps are vertical in relation to the design, but European weavers almost always rendered the design at right angles on the loom so that the warps would run horizontally when the panel was hung. The earliest known tapestries were found in Egyptian tombs of the 2nd millennium B. C. All textile material is scarce until the early centuries of the Christian era. Examples of silk tapestry survive from the Han period in China; and Chinese weavers settled in Japan and introduced the art there during the 3rd and 4th centuries A. D. Numerous examples of Near Eastern tapestry dating from the 4th and 5th centuries A. D. have been found in Egyptian burial grounds. The bulk of these pieces are fragments from tunics, cloaks, cushion covers and wall hangings woven with wool and linen wefts. After the Islamic conquest, silk was commonly used. Pre-Islamic Near Eastern designs comprise strapwork, plant forms and human and animal figures derived from the popular eschatological cults. During the Islamic period the patterns consisted of small hexagons, lions or water birds, strap patterns and calligraphy arranged in bands or medallions. Traditional forms of tapestry are still being made in the Near and Middle East, mostly with geometric patterns or stylized plant patterns. (Cf. ill. p. 99)

Tapestry was certainly woven in Europe by the 12th century. The oldest extant example is the 12th-century Halberstadt Apostle tapestry, but this shows imperfect control of the medium. The first examples of a fully evolved professional European tapestry art are the tapestries woven at Arras for Charles the Bold and the remnants of the great Apocalypse Series of Angers Cathedral, the work of Paris weavers of the 14th century, based on cartoons by Jean de Bruges. At the beginning of the 15th century the focus of the industry shifted from France to the Low Countries, to Tournai, Bruges, Antwerp and Brussels. The famous Apostle series was designed by Raphael and woven by Pieter van Aelst of Brussels. Purely decorative elements were now relegated to the borders while the main part of

91

the tapestry more and more resembled a painting. Bernard van Orley successfully combined the decorative and the narrative elements of the 16th-century style in the 'Hunts of Maximilian' with their backgrounds of scrolling foliation of acanthus inspiration accompanying birds, butterflies, hounds and lions. (Cf. ill. p. 216) In the course of the 16th century, weavers dispersed from Brussels and Antwerp to many other European cities, and workshops were set up in England (Sheldon works, c. 1560, noted for tapestry maps), in Sweden, at Fontainebleau, Ferrara and later in Paris. Each developed its own style, but all were dominated by the monumental classical ideal which reached its climax in the work of Rubens. Important new centres were founded in England and France during the 17th century: at Mortlake in England (1619), where Lowland influence remained strong; and, in France, in Paris (1667) in a factory built by the Gobelin family after whom the organization was named, at Beauvais (1664) and at Aubusson (1665). Leading painters designed cartoons for these factories, among them Charles Lebrun, Claude Audran le Jeune, Antoine and Charles Coypel, J. B. Oudry, Boucher, Jean Berain and François Desportes. The 18th century again witnessed a dispersal of weavers, both Flemish and French, and looms were set up at Madrid – celebrated for the translation of cartoons by Goya, – St Petersburg and Naples. During the 19th century, with the advent of the machine, the art of tapestry declined. William Morris made an attempt to revive hand weaving and established the Merton Abbey looms in 1887, where cartoons by the Pre-Raphaelite painters were executed (ill. 264). The art has been revived in Paris with Lurçat as the principal designer (ill. p. 100), and many contemporary painters have also worked specially for this medium.

TECTONIC. A term used for the structural elements of a work of architecture and, in a wider sense, for any ornament underlining the form of a vessel or other object. (Cf. ill. 26)

TEMPERA PAINTING. Tempera painting was practised before the invention of oil painting in the 15th century. The colours were bound with an emulsion, preferably egg, instead of oil. The panel paintings of the Middle Ages are tempera work. Tempera colours were never completely abandoned and have again found favour with modern artists, since they are purer than oils and free from the gloss produced by the oil content of the colour. Medieval tempera pictures were given a varnish which increased the glow of the colours considerably.

TEMPLE (Latin *templum*, Greek *temenos*). Originally, a sacred enclosure dedicated to the gods; later, the building within this region. Temples built of sun-dried bricks already existed in Mesopotamia between the 4th and 3rd millennia B.C. The statue of the god to whom the temple had been dedicated stood against the wall facing the entrance. The Assyrian temple comprised a series of buildings and courtyards. The cult-hall itself was built on a longitudinal axis. Many towns possessed lofty temples built on platforms or in the form of stepped structures (Ziggurat, q. v.). Most of the Egyptian temples known to us have the characteristic features of the architecture of the New Empire: a processional avenue, lined by two rows of sphinxes, leads to the gate with its two pylons and, past the courtyard, to the heart of the sanctuary, the pillared temple. The Greek temple (cf. p. 128) developed from the Megaron, and is built on an oblong, rectangular plan (Gr. *naos*, Lat. *cella*), usually on a base of three steps, the stylobate. If the side walls (antae) are lengthened at the front portico, we speak of distyle in antis, in the case of a two-pillared portico, of tetrastyle in antis if there are four columns. The latter type of portico is also called a pronaos. Sometimes, the antae have also been lengthened at the back, thus achieving a distyle in antis at both ends (ill. 100). Whereas the porch in front is called the pronaos, a similar porch at the back constitutes the opisthodomos. Smaller temples only have a simple open portico in front of the building (prostylos), which is sometimes repeated at the other end of the temple, constituting the amphiprostylos. If the cells are surrounded by pillars on all sides, we speak of a peripteral temple (Peripteros, ill. 100), in the case of a double row of columns of a dipteral temple (ill. 101). A temple with half-columns on the naos walls is called pseudo-peripteral, or pseudo-dipteral, as the case may be. It is questionable whether the tholos, a round structure with a ring of columns, can be classed as a temple. Greek temples are called Doric, Ionic or Corinthian, according to the orders of architecture (q. v.). Features common to all temples are the simple span roof and the stone carvings on the tympanum. The cella, which contains the statue of the deity, and serves also as a treasury, relies upon the entrance for its lighting. The cella of Roman and Etruscan temples is about as deep as the front portico. These temples often have a nave and two aisles and stand on a raised base reached by a series of steps. Buddhist temples are round structures, developed from funeral mounds. In India, such a temple is called a stupa (q. v.), in Burma a pagoda (q. v.). These temples often contain sacred relics of the Buddha. Buddhist monasteries and temples in China and Japan – also called pagodas – are built of wood. The sturdy posts support a projecting tiled roof. Often, several receding roofs are placed on top of each other. Cave temples, too, are found in China and Tibet. The Mayan temples in Central America are box-like, plastered-stone structures situated at the top of high, terraced pyramids. In the coastal region of Peru, the base was made of air-dried bricks, while the temple itself appears to have been made of wood. The Incas in the highlands of Peru, however, had temples of several storeys, built in carefully joined stone-masonry.

THEATRE ARCHITECTURE. The Greek theatre was arranged around a circular orchestra. In the middle of the orchestra stood the altar, around which the chorus used to dance and chant. The semicircular rows of seats,

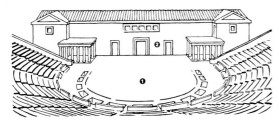

81. Theatre of Dionysus in Athens (reconstruction)

divided by rows of steps into a wedge-shaped section *(kerkides)* and into different tiers by broad passages *(diazomata)*, were invariably hewn into the hillside so as to face a natural landscape. The theatres of Epidaurus, Pergamum and Delphi are prototypes of this kind. The Romans, by contrast, usually built their theatres on level ground in their cities. Enormous substructures below the seats therefore became necessary. The raised stage was backed by a wall, the *scenae frons* (Marcellus theatre in Rome and the theatre at Arles). But there were also intermediate forms, i. e. theatres partly hollowed out and partly constructed (Orange, Miletus and Ephesus). If an elliptic arena is surrounded by rows of seats, it is known as an amphitheatre (gladiatoral combats). Perhaps the most impressive extant amphitheatres are the Colosseum in Rome, the arenas at Verona (Italy) and Pola (Istria), Arles and Nîmes (southern France) and El Djem (North Africa). A special theatre building did not exist in the Middle Ages, since mystery plays were usually performed in the open in front of the cathedral. Palladio alone resumed the antique tradition with his Teatro Olimpico in Vicenza. His theatre, however, was an enclosed room, of a type already known in Antiquity (Odeon – a concert hall). In the Teatro Farnese in Parma, the tiers are framed in a manner that can hardly be justified on functional grounds. The tiered auditorium was further developed in Baroque times. The magnificent theatre at Bologna and many German theatres, particularly those near royal residences (Munich, Bayreuth, Potsdam, etc.), were built in this period. In the 19th century, theatres were built throughout Europe on a scale hitherto unknown, the Baroque tiered theatre remaining the model. The famous Paris opera house was the work of Charles Garnier and the Berlin New Theatre was designed by Schinkel. (Cf. ill. 81, 112, 255)

TILES (Lat. *tegula;* Fr. *tuile*). The term is applied to any kind of earthenware slab applied to any surface of a building. Roof tiles have little artistic interest and art history is concerned with the tiles of floors, walls and ceilings. Decorative tile work was invented in the Near East and was practised there for a longer period than anywhere else. As early as the 4th millennium B.C., the Egyptians used tiles with a surface glaze stained blue with copper. The Assyrians and Babylonians (9th to 6th centuries B.C.) made wall tiles of earthenware with patterns or figures in coloured glazes (ill. 94, p. 106). Under Islamic rule ceramic art in the

Near East reached unparalleled heights. The earliest Islamic tiles date from the 9th century A. D. and include squares with a plain green or brown glaze and decorative designs such as that of a cock within a wreath painted on squares surrounded by oblong hexagons mottled to resemble marble. Quantities of lustre ware with brown or yellow painting executed in a sketchy, broad style found at Rayy include star-shaped tiles. Another important tile-making centre was Kashan, where the tiles were painted in brownish lustre.

The Islamic veto on the representation of living things was observed in the decoration of religious buildings but usually ignored elsewhere. Thus, many Islamic tiles show human figures, birds animals and trees. Carved and glazed tiles were made in the region of Samarkand from about 1369 onwards and adorn the mausoleum of Tamerlane's sister (1371) and buildings in Bokhara. Patterns in gold alone, applied by stencils are found on hexagonal blue or turquoise tiles in the 13th-century Kiosk and Kara Tai Madrasa at Konia.

The brickwork of Persian buildings was often arranged to form patterns or Kufic inscriptions on the outer walls, and these designs or lettering were picked out in coloured glazes. The technique of tile mosaic flourished in Persia during the 15th century, the most famous example being the decoration of the Blue Mosque at Tabriz (1465). Potters from Tabriz were probably the first to make tiles painted in underglaze blue with patterns similar to those found on blue and white Ming porcelain. From Tabriz this blue and white tilework was introduced into Turkey. Blue and white tiles in the Chinese taste were used in the decoration of the Great Mosque at Damascus and similar tiles occur on buildings in Cairo dating between 1495 and 1544. The early blue and white tiles were succeeded by tiles painted in blue, turquoise and sometimes olive green. Seventeenth-century Isnik tiles are painted in scarlet, emerald green, blue and turquoise with a frequent use of black outlines, on the pure white slip which is peculiarly Turkish. The designs are derived principally from plants, flowers and arabesques. Towards the end of the 17th century the tile industry of Isnik began to decline until in 1726 there was a revival in Istanbul itself.

Imitations of Near Eastern tiles were made in Chelsea and at Merton Abbey by William de Morgan (1839–1917) who attempted to reproduce the green, blue and turquoise tiles of Isnik.

Decorated tiles did not come into use in Europe until the second half of the 12th century when they were relegated to the floor. Tile mosaic and inlaid tiles were probably first invented in northern France, their use spreading from there to England and the Netherlands. The tile mosaic consisted of small tiles of red or brown clay cut into shape while soft, and fitted together on a cement bed after firing. The upper surface was always covered with a transparent yellow glaze and this was sometimes stained green, blue or black. Some tiles were coated with pipe-clay. One of the earliest tile mosaic floors is in the abbey of St Denis (c. 1260).

93

A development in the making of tiles occurred when, after the tile had been shaped, a pattern was struck into its surface by means of a wooden block on which the design had been carved in relief. The impression was then inlaid with white pipe-clay. A splendid medieval tile floor of this type has survived in the chapterhouse of Westminster Abbey.

The 15th century witnessed an innovation in technique: the white clay was not so deeply embedded in the surface and seems to have been smeared over the tile before the impression was made. Examples from Malvern Priory are in the Victoria and Albert Museum, London. French tiles of the 13th and 14th centuries differ little from English examples, but towards the beginning of the 16th century they take on a more distinctive character. The pattern appears dark on a light ground and Renaissance ornament is introduced.

Meanwhile in Germany, whose cultural area embraced also Austria, Switzerland, Poland and Denmark, wall tiles decorated in relief were popular. The oldest surviving tiles of this kind were found in the church of St Fides at Schlettstade near Strassburg. Hexagonal and diamond shaped, these red clay tiles are moulded in high relief with fantastic centaurs and birds. They date from about 1150. In the late 15th and 16th centuries the manufacture of stove tiles became more important than the making of floor tiles. Tiles from 15th-century German stoves show decoration moulded in relief including naturalistic designs and geometrical patterns. After about 1520, Renaissance designs were common and figures in classical costume were favoured.

In the craft of tile-making as in all other branches of the arts, inspiration during the Renaissance period came from Italy. Tiles first became popular in Italy during the 15th century when the potter aspired to rival the painter. The earliest existing majolica pavement is at Naples in a chapel added to the church of S. Giovanni a Carbonara before 1427. Bold designs, including profile heads decorate long hexagonal tiles arranged round squares. On the whole, 15th-century Italian tiles are distinguished by bold and rather sombre colour dominated by dark blue. The style of the High Renaissance, on the other hand, is characterized by minute detail and a predominance of orange and pale yellow colouring. Italian potters carried the Renaissance style all over Europe. By the 16th century tin-glazed wares in the Italian manner were being made in Germany, France and the Netherlands. But very soon in the Netherlands tiles began to be used in the form of large pictorial compositions on walls spread over a number of tiles.

During the wars with Spain craftsmen fled from Antwerp to what was to become the Dutch Republic and by the beginning of the 17th century Dutch wall tiles had assumed a highly individual character. Tile pictures often appeared as house signs in Holland, but the usual place was on the interior walls; they were especially used to decorate fireplaces and overmantels or to form a wainscot. The earliest Dutch tiles were painted with arabesques on dark blue or light orange grounds. Later,

owing to the influence of Chinese taste, blue or, less commonly, purple monochrome painting on a white ground supplanted all other colouring. Dutch tiles were exported in great numbers and some of the finest examples of their use are found in the chateau of Rambouillet near Paris and in the Amalienburg pavilion of Schloß Nymphenburg near Munich. In London and Bristol, where Dutch influence was strong, the production of tiles was limited though tile pictures were used as house signs in 17th-century London.

In Spain, the meeting-ground of Christian and Islamic cultures, tile mosaic reached its full development in the south in the 14th century. The finest examples are in the Alhambra and in the church of S. Gil, Seville. Tiles decorated with designs of which the outlines were depressed by means of a relief mould, were made on a large scale in the 16th century at Seville. A special type of tile was made by the creators of the superb Hispano-Mauresque lustreware. The earliest examples show designs painted in blue and including Christian and Islamic symbols; but as the 15th century advanced the oriental motifs were displaced by the foliage and heraldic figures of Gothic art. The technique of majolica was introduced into Spain early in the 16th century and the tile picture painted continuously over a number of tiles became a favourite art form.

In connection with the history of Spanish pottery, mention may be made of the majolica made at Puebla in Mexico from the middle of the 17th century onwards. The style was at first entirely Spanish, then became influenced by the Chinese taste and, by 1700, Indian painters had incorporated a strong native flavour.

TONDO (It. for round; plural, *tondi*). A round picture or relief is called a tondo. This form was very popular during the Italian Renaissance (see ill. p. 279).

TOWN PLANNING. The cities of Ancient Greece were either left to grow naturally in the landscape, while outstanding topographical features were brilliantly emphasised (the Acropolis, Athens), or – as in the later, Hellenistic period – they were built on the gridiron plan with horizontally crossing streets and square or rectangular blocks (Miletus, Priene). This system, used by the town-planner Hippodamus of Miletus, is still to some extent used to-day. It was somewhat modified by the Romans, who were probably influenced by Etruscan examples. Two axial roads, crossing at right angles, divide the otherwise geometrically arranged city into four areas (Trier, Timgad). This axial road-crossing still influenced the planning of certain medieval towns (Rottweil, Villingen). The gridiron was also retained and was mainly used in the cities of the newly colonized regions of eastern Germany. Otherwise, the medieval city is generally a picturesque 'natural' growth, unaffected by any geometrical principles, although it is by no means an aimless sprawl. The Renaissance planners alone tried once again to devise 'ideal cities' on strictly geometric lines, preferably circular, polygonal or square, with a radial street system. But few towns

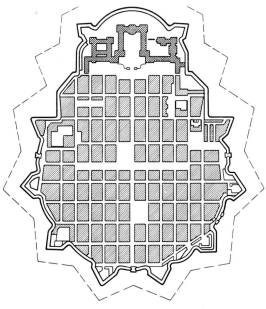

82. Town plan of Mannheim, begun 1652, Palace 1720–60, arch. Hauberat, C. de Froimont, Pigage

were in fact built in this manner (Palmanova, Hanau, Freudenstadt). Town planning gained a powerful new impetus during the Baroque. The Baroque city was not so much arranged round a central square as orientated towards the sovereign's residence, whose gardens either mirrored or slightly varied the lay-out of the streets (ill. 82, 227). In France, the classic example of this kind is Versailles; in Germany we find Baroque lay-outs at Rastatt, Karlsruhe, Ludwigsburg and a number of other cities. In Italy, where an absolutist central power was unknown, emphasis was on the square as the city centre. Michelangelo's re-designed Capitol marked a beginning; this was followed by Rainaldi's Piazza del Popolo (1662) and Bernini's St Peter's Square, Rome (ill. 218), built between 1655 and 1667. In France, the Place Vendôme, the Place Royale and the Place des Vosges (all in Paris) deserve special mention, as does Heré's magnificent Place Royale (1753–55) at Nancy.

In England, one of the earliest examples of town planning is Wren's design for London after the Great Fire, although with the exception of St Paul's and the city churches, it scarcely materialized. But London still has a number of well-planned districts. Regent's Park, with its terraces and crescents, the design of John Nash, was originally part of a very much larger scheme, of which the old Regent Street, Carlton House Terrace and Carlton House itself formed part. Carlton House, the residence of the Prince Regent, was demolished before Nash's work was finished, the colonnades in Regent Street were taken down in 1848 and Regent Street itself was completely re-built in the twenties of this century. Regent's Park fortunately survives, its terraces comparatively undamaged. As a piece of town-planning, it is probably unique. The park with its lake, the light

stucco houses, forming a background to the landscape, the brilliantly produced illusion of the country-side so close to the centre of a big city, have won admiration for well over a century.

Other fine examples in Britain of the town-planner's art are the Royal Naval College at Greenwich (begun by Inigo Jones and completed by Sir Christopher Wren) with Inigo Jones's Queen's House opposite; the large area between the Gray's Inn Road and the Thames, known as the Temple (in parts badly damaged during the Second World War); Edinburgh New Town by the Adam Brothers; and the Royal Crescent at Bath by John Wood and his son.

TRIPTYCH, see Altar-piece.

TRIUMPHAL ARCH. Triumphal arches were built in Antiquity in honour of the returning victorious armies and their commanders. The origins of the triumphal arch are disputed. Its basic form includes a monumental gateway – often surmounted by a quadriga containing a statue of the victorious general – decorated in relief with scenes of war and triumph. There are also triumphal arches with several gateways, and double archways, which were built at street crossings. Some of the best-known and best-preserved arches in Rome are the arch of Titus (completed c. A. D. 80), the arch of Septimius Severus (built at the beginning of the 3rd century A. D.) and the arch of Constantine (A. D. 312, ill. 111). Triumphal arches were also frequently erected outside Rome during the Imperial age (Benevento, Orange, etc.). The bridge of the Emperor Frederick II (d. 1250) in Capua, the Arc de Triomphe in Paris (1806) and the Marble Arch in London (1825) were all modelled on the Roman triumphal arch.

TROMPE L'OEIL. A French expression, meaning to deceive the eye. Since a picture is two-dimensional, it can only create an *illusion* of space and volume. If this is carried to such a degree that the beholder can hardly distinguish between illusion and reality – as in pretended architectural features on Baroque ceilings – we call this effect a trompe l'oeil.

VAULT. An arched covering in stone or brick over any building. One of the earliest examples of vaulting is the chamber of Harem in the Assyrian Palace of Sargon, Khorsabad (722–705 B.C.) excavated in 1864; the entire roof of this palace was probably vaulted with huge blocks of compressed clay, supported on continuous walls. Another early example of vaulting is the ruined palace at Ctesiphon (A. D. 450), where a great central arched porch about 83 ft wide leads into an immense throne room covered with a remarkable vault supported on walls 24 ft thick; it is elliptical in form and obviously based on Assyrian prototypes. Some authorities consider that this great vault of brick is a reproduction of the native Sassanian architecture where such constructions were formed with bundles of reeds and rammed earth. (Cf. ill. 83)

95

83. Types of Vaulting

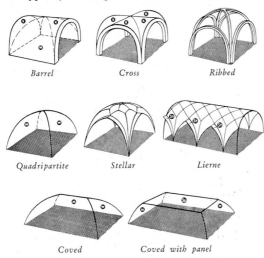

Barrel   Cross   Ribbed

Quadripartite   Stellar   Lierne

Coved   Coved with panel

The Romans excelled in the use of vaults of various kinds. The *barrel* or *tunnel* vault was borne throughout its length on the two parallel walls of a rectangular apartment. The *cross* vault was formed by the intersection of two semicircular vaults of equal span and used over a square apartment. When cross vaults were built over long halls or corridors the hall was divided by piers into square bays, each of which was covered with a cross vault which allowed of the insertion of windows in the upper part of the walls as in the terpidarium of the Baths of Caracalla and the Baths of Diocletian, Rome. The lines of intersection of these cross vaults are known as groins.

The Roman system of vaulting was continued in the Romanesque period, but an innovation was demanded by the necessity to surmount the difficulty of vaulting an oblong church nave where there were differences in height between semicircular arches over spans of varying width. The problem was only satisfactorily solved when the pointed arch was introduced in Gothic vaulting. Gothic vaulting consists of a framework of stone ribs which support thin stone panels. The difficulty of vaulting oblong compartments was overcome by the use of the pointed arch over the shorter spans, while the semicircular arch was for some time retained for the diagonal or longer spans.

It was the solution of the problems connected with vaulting which very largely determined the character of medieval architecture. The problem for the medieval architect was to construct a stone vault over the lofty nave of a church of the basilican type while leaving clerestory windows in the nave walls above the aisle roofs. He replaced the simple groins of the Roman architects by specially constructed ribs on which thin vaulting panels were laid. The weight of the stone vault exerted considerable thrust which resulted in the introduction of such novel features as buttresses and pinnacles to resist it, while the numerous ribs required for their support novel types of piers.

Anglo-Saxon vaulting was based on the Roman, as in the porch at Monkwearmouth. Norman vaulting was either of the barrel type as in St John's Chapel, Tower of London, or the groined cross type as in the crypt of Canterbury Cathedral (1096–1107), while sometimes in oblong bays the vaulting ribs across the shorter span were stilted or slightly pointed. The pointed arch came into general use in the 13th century. The plain four-part ribbed vault primarily constructed as a framework of diagonal and transverse ribs was chiefly used at this period as in the naves of Durham and Salisbury. Intermediate ribs known as tiercerons were later inserted between the transverse and diagonal ribs to give additional support to the panels, as in the nave of Westminster Abbey. Ridge ribs were next introduced to resist the thrust of the opposing tiercerons. The courses of the vault panels meet at the ridge in zigzag lines as at Lincoln, Exeter and churches in south-western France. Vaulting of the Decorated Period is elaborate in character. Lierne ribs were added which merely followed the curved surface of the panel and gave an intricate appearance to an otherwise simple vault. The star-shaped pattern thus produced is known as *stellar vaulting* and examples are to be found at Gloucester, Ely, Wells, Bristol and Winchester. Carved bosses originated as keystones against which the ribs abutted and also resulted from the need for disguising the awkward mitres made by the meeting of moulded ribs. In the 14th century the increase in the number of ribs led to a corresponding increase in the number of bosses which gave to Gothic vaults their extremely ornamental and web-like character.

The intricate stellar vaulting of the late 14th century led gradually to the type known as *fan, palm* or *conoidal* vaulting, first used in the cloisters at Gloucester, in which the rising ribs are formed at equal angles on the surface of the inverted concave cones and are thus of the same arcs, and these are connected at different heights by horizontal lierne ribs. In fan vaulting the ribs and panels are often formed of the same piece of stone instead of the panels resting as separate stones on the ribs, so that fan vaulting represents a return to the Roman method of construction and the ribs lose their structural value. Fan vaulting is confined to England and there are examples at King's College, Cambridge, Sherborne Abbey, the Divinity Schools, Oxford, St George's Chapel, Windsor. (Cf. ill. 169, 173)

VEE CUT. A form of decoration produced by cutting into the material with a vee tool, or in such a manner that the hollow left after removing the surplus matter will have the shape of a V. This type of ornament was used already in the Neolithic Age (see Beaker Culture), and is also found in the Bronze Age in the art of the Hallstatt period (q. v.). It also played an important part in the Germanic art of the time of the Barbarian Invasions and has survived in popular art until the present day. (Cf. ill. 86)

VIGNETTE (Fr. *lavigne* – the grape vine). The term was originally used to describe the drawn or painted decorative borders of medieval manuscripts, and came to be applied to the small arabesque-like drawing (cf. ill. 72) at the end of the chapters of 18th- and 19th-century books (see Book Illustration).

VOLUTE (Lat. *volutum* – a snail). The volute is the scroll or spiral of the Ionic capital (see Orders). It also occurs frequently in Renaissance and Baroque architecture. (Cf. ill. p. 319)

WALLPAPER. The invention of paper came to Europe from the East in the 12th century but it was not until the 16th century that wallpaper was used extensively. The oldest surviving fragments of European wallpaper are English. An early 16th-century example was found in the Master's Lodge, Christ's College, Cambridge which has a large-scale pattern adapted from a contemporary damask. These English papers are not painted, but blocked. In the 17th century in France painted wallpapers became increasingly popular, the more usual designs being diaper patterns, stripes, cartouche and flower arrangements. Occasional landscapes and figures appeared. In none of these papers was there a repeat pattern. Each sheet was painted separately and was not connected with the next. At first these painted papers were only used by country people, but by 1700 their use had extended to the better-class houses of Paris. In England printed papers of small design were now common, though elaborate papers were sometimes painted in oils. Flock papers, produced in the same way as flock prints, were fashionable in both England and France.

In the middle of the 17th century, wallpaper design was subjected to a new influence from the East. Travellers to China brought back sheets of paper painted with designs made up into sets. By the beginning of the 18th century these became one of the most popular of all wall decorations, painted as they were with designs of landscape, birds and flowers and scenes of domestic life. Meanwhile in Germany, where wallpapers until this time had scarcely been used, a unique type of wall covering was being produced known as *gaufragé* paper. The design was printed in outline from a copper plate and impressed in relief.

In France the popularity of the wallpaper was greater than anywhere else. In 1688 Papillon started the first great printing house for wallpapers. He invented continuous patterns and lustre paper, using powdered metals. His device of a repeating design was widely imitated.

The invention of the method of printing from wood blocks is attributed to John Baptist Jackson who had a wallpaper factory in Battersea and published a book on the subject in 1754. Jackson's designs were panels with varied borders. He was particularly proud of his relief effects with statues in niches. The technique of multicolour printing from wood blocks was brought to perfection by George and Frederick Eckhardt in 1750. English techniques in wallpaper design were so popular that they were adopted in France.

English flock papers had always been printed in one colour on a ground; the French in the early 1760's began to print flock patterns in polychrome, thus producing an effective imitation of the elaborate brocades of the period.

During the Revolution two Englishmen, Arthur and Robert set up a paper manufactory in Paris. They specialized in sepia and grisaille prints, the designs consisting of panels with architectural frames enclosing engravings after pictures by Boucher, Fragonard and Hubert Robert. In 1797 the house of Zuber was founded at Rixheim where in 1939 wallpapers were still being produced. In 1893 Zuber began to publish a series of panorama papers, the first of which, Swiss mountain scenes, were painted by Mongin. They were followed by scenes from all parts of the world. Joseph Dufour, a great rival of Zuber, was noted for his grisaille papers. Another firm of the 19th century, that of Dauptain, issued a wide range of designs including Renaissance, Rococo and Pompadour patterns as well as a paper illustrating Molière's *Precieuses Ridicules*. A quaint product of the early 19th century was the commemorative wallpaper. One such was issued in honour of Washington and showed a repeat design of a tomb inscribed 'Sacred to Washington'. Another similar paper intended for the French royalists commemorated the Battle of Waterloo.

With the perfection of mechanical methods of printing, design in wallpaper sharply declined. By 1867 the last of the great scenic papers had been produced. In 1856, when Japan was opened to Western commerce, a new type of paper became known which simulated embossed leather. There was one notable reaction against the degradation of design caused by machinery. Im 1861 William Morris established the firm of Morris, Marshall, Faulkner and Co. at 8 Red Lion Square for the design and execution of mural decoration. The firm attempted its first wallpaper in 1862, the rose trellis design. In all, Morris made between 70 and 80 wallpaper designs, the printing of which he supervised in person. The reaction begun by Morris developed with the Art Nouveau movement. Art Nouveau wallpaper designers included Gussmann, Beckerath, Weigl and Hoffmann of Munich and Gallé, Grasset and Follot in France. Twentieth-century movements in painting were reflected in wallpaper design in the work of Andre Maré, Duchamps-Villon, La Fresnaye, Villon, Marie Laurencin and Laprade. A continous effort is being made in England to maintain a small proportion of wallpaper designs of merit to supplement the regular commercial productions. Designers of ability include Edward Bawden, John Aldridge and E. Q. Nicholson.

WASH. A wash is a layer of sepia, ink, or water colour, lightly applied with a wet brush to a pen drawing to indicate shadows or plasticity (ill. 37).

WAX SCULPTURE. Wax has always been of great importance to the sculptor, both for making models and

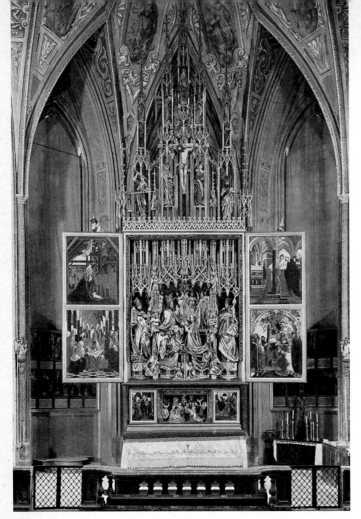

84. Winged altar: MICHAEL PACHER's *Wolfgang altar in St Wolfgang (c. 1480)*

in bronze casting (see Casting). But wax figures were also at all times made in their own right (Renaissance portrait busts). The high malleability of a material that allows the human form to be produced with such likeness makes it a tempting medium. The grossest naturalism became a characteristic of modelling in wax, eventually leading to the figures in wax cabinets or waxworks.

WINDOWS. The windows are a significant feature of any style of building, and their shape and arrangement considerably affect its character. The window area is limited at the sides by the *reveal*, a surface at right angles to the face of the wall, and by the *head* at the top. If the reveal has a slant, it is called a *splay*. The window can terminate horizontally or in an arch. The latter is semicircular in Early Christian and Romanesque architecture and pointed in Gothic buildings, where it is often decorated with tracery (q. v.). The Romanesque circular wheel window, divided by mullions arranged like spokes, was the predecessor of the traceried Gothic rose windows. Windows with semicircular heads were often coupled by central columns in Romanesque churches. Gothic windows are divided horizontally by narrow stone mullions. Although the Renaissance and the Baroque took up the semicircular arch again, windows with a horizontal head, surmounted by a tri-

angular or flat segmental gable (ill. 211, 212) occurred more frequently. Oval windows and windows of no determinate form are by no means rare in Baroque architecture. The wooden window frame has been known only since the Renaissance.

WINGED ALTAR, see Altar-piece.

WOODCUT. The woodcut is a relief process, i. e. one in which the drawing stands out from the background of the block. Areas that are not meant to print off are hollowed out. This technique had already been used in connection with fabric printing, many centuries before the woodcut. The invention of paper – in Europe at the end of the 14th century, in China somewhat earlier – made possible the woodcut as we know it to-day. The first German woodcuts – Germany led in this technique – were devotional pictures, printed on single sheets. The blockbook, invented round 1430, consists of a series of woodcuts, printed from blocks, containing both text and illustrations. It is the predecessor of the illustrated woodcut book, printed with movable type. Dürer was one of the supreme masters of the woodcut. His technique of closer shading rendered unnecessary the hand-colouring that had been used until his day. But from then on, artists only made the drawing and entrusted special craftsmen, called xylographers, with the making of the blocks. The coloured woodcut, as a substitute for hand-colouring, was an invention of the Renaissance (Cranach, Burgkmair). It consisted in printing a layer of green over the drawing with a further block. Another method is to cut lines into this block, leaving white areas on the print (also called chiaroscuro printing). This marks the beginning of the coloured woodcut, printed with several blocks, which plays such an important part in the graphic arts of to-day and which had already reached a very high stage of development in 18th- and 19th-century Japan (see p. 536). In Europe, the copper engraving (q. v.) gradually displaced the woodcut from the time of Dürer onwards. It was revived by Thomas Bewick in the early 19th century. Instead of cutting the wood along the grain, it was now cut across, using a burin or copper engraver. The resulting wood engraving can possess the most delicate tones and lines. This technique is also highly suitable for cheap reproductions (see p. 407), but is for this very reason easily debased. Munch, Nolde and others, dissatisfied with lifeless technical perfection, revived the old form of the woodcut. These artists once again made their own blocks and brought out the characteristic features of this process, such as rough, heavy lines. The modern lino-cut and the brick-cut techniques are variants of the woodcut and only differ from it in that they use blocks not made of wood. Various experiments had already been made by the end of the Middle Ages with the metal cut (steel cut), with the use of a punch in place of a knife on the wood and with printing wood blocks on paper held in position with dough. (Cf. ill. 203, 210, 262, 289, pp. 540, 541)

Textile: Persian silk brocade: Horseman with captive Mongols *(Safavid period, second half of the 16th century)*

Tapestry: JEAN LURÇAT: The Warrior *(Le Guerrier). Wall tapestry*

The Art
of Antiquity

PREHISTORY

THE EARLY STONE AGE

85. *Apollo from the west pediment of the Temple of Zeus at Olympia (c. 460 B.C.)*

In 1868 A HUNTER in the open country near Santillana, not far from the charming little town of Torrelavega in the northern Spanish province of Santander, discovered the blocked entrance to a cave, which was later given the name of Altamira. The lord of the manor of Santillana, Don Marcellino de Sautuola, a keen local antiquarian, began systematic excavation at Altamira in 1879. One day he took his five-year-old daughter with him to the place. The little girl had no need to stoop in the low-roofed cave. She caught sight of some coloured pictures of animals in the rock overhead and her cries of delight at this discovery attracted her father's attention. In the candle-light, he saw to his amazement a number of lifelike paintings of bison, boar, wild horses and female red deer, all faithfully depicted (ill. p. 105). The unknown artists had mixed charcoal and earth-colours – different tones of ochre, red chalk and black manganese ore – with fat or white of egg, painting the walls and roof with the resulting pigments, which had eaten deep into the rock. The lucky finder knew that no one except a few hunters had entered the cave since it had been opened up. As his excavations had brought to light certain stone and bone tools, shaped for human use, which dated from the Ice Age, he deduced that the pictures must be of the same period. The initial enthusiasm aroused by this sensational discovery, however, turned to general scepticism when the genuineness of the paintings was called in question by the learned world.

Ever since the sixth and seventh decades of the 19th century not only tools but also pictures of animals engraved on bone and rock, and even miniature works of art, had been found. Finally, in 1901, two caves in the Dordogne, in southern France, were unearthed, Font-de-Gaume and Les Combarelles, which were both adorned with paintings. In the former, two hundred masterly pictures of animals were found and in the second no less than three hundred, which included representations of human ritual dancers and trappers. The pictures at Altamira were then remembered and subjected to thoroughgoing investigation. To-day thousands of Ice Age paintings, in many caves, are known, which afford evidence of stylistic development.

During the long Early and Middle Stone Ages, when Man subsisted on the proceeds of hunting and food-gathering expeditions, there had not been any representative art. Nevertheless, the flint knives that date from the Old Acheulean Age already reveal, in their definite shape and careful polishing – which exceed purely utilitarian requirements, – a primitive pleasure in modelling and visual beauty.

The late Palaeolithic period, that of the cave-paintings, coincides with the last Ice Age, which ended about 10,000 B.C., and is divided into three principal stages, called after the French places where finds were made. They are named the Aurignacian, the Solutrean and the Magdalenian. Representatives of the cultures of this period were hunters and food-gatherers at a relatively advanced stage of evolution, occupying the ice-free regions of Europe and Asia.

The cave-painters' art centred upon southern France and northern Spain, in the so-called Franco-Cantabrian region, with offshoots in the direction of southern Italy. From its sudden first appearance in the Aurignacian to its end in the late Magdalenian age it retains a homogeneous character. The pictures are artistically true to nature; that is to say, the creatures represented are given, in slightly stylised form, the distinguishing marks of their species.

Cave-paintings have their origin in magic and ritual. They were designed to cast a spell on the game so necessary for survival. The picture was meant to ensure, by its magic, that the weapon or the pitfall used would successfully achieve its object. With increasing dexterity and longer practice came the desire, no doubt often unconscious, to produce something artistic. In art on a smaller scale the main magical object was quite frequently subordinated to a clearly discernible delight in pure decoration.

The first statuettes of human beings and animals belong to the Aurignacian period. They, too, served a magical purpose, that of ensuring either fertility among the clan or a plentiful supply of game. This is how we must interpret the two clay buffaloes found in the Tuc d'Audoubert cave, for instance, and also the exaggerated proportions of the bodies of the many female figurines discovered in France (the 'Venuses' of Lespugue and Brassepouy), Lower Austria (the 'Venus' of Willendorf, q. v., ill. 135), Czechoslovakia (Unter-Wisternitz), as well as in Russia (on the Don and at Kursk, Bryansk and Irkutsk) and elsewhere.

The multifarious flint and bone tools and weapons found were adorned with figures or designs at first composed of lines and dots and later of crosses, lozenges, spirals and so on. Ornaments consisting of the artificially treated shells of fish and snails, of ivory and animal-teeth, were also dug up. It is probable that late Palaeolithic Man also painted his body.

THE MIDDLE STONE AGE

The homogeneous character of the Ice Age cultures disappeared in the climatically warmer Middle Stone or Mesolithic Age. The melting of the Alpine and Scandinavian glaciers left new land available for occupation, while other districts dried out and were abandoned by game. The migrations of mankind began. Stone tools became very much smaller (microliths), and those of bone grew rarer. From archaeological evidence we can deduce that Mesolithic cultures existed in Europe, North Africa and Palestine, as well as, perhaps, in western India, and certainly in the Gobi Desert, Siberia and eastern Asia. Several groups of rock-paintings are to be ascribed to such cultures in eastern Spain (Levant art) and North Africa (Saharan Atlas mountains, oasis district of Fezzan and Ahaggar plateau).

These groups are stylistically related, despite certain differences of detail, though there is uncertainty as to their origin and the migrations affecting their provenance. The faded or monochrome pictures, some simply outline drawings, were not found in caves, but on exposed walls of rock. As distinct from Palaeolithic art, their style evinces no interest in detailed representation, the aim being to bring out the rhythm of movement in animals or groups of animals and human beings by concentrating on essentials. Natural forms become stylised and gradually grow into subjective symbols, convincing in their exclusiveness and reminiscent of the expressionist woodcut in its prime (ill. p. 105).

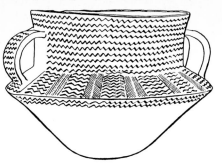

86. Bell-beaker

87. Incised pottery in the 'Grand Style', from Hagebrogaard, Denmark

88. Incised pottery in the 'Refined Style', from Skarpsalling, Denmark

89. 'Bandkeramik' painted ware from Cucuteni, near Jassy, Rumania

THE LATE STONE AGE

The most revolutionary period of the early evolution of mankind was the Late Stone or Neolithic Age. Man, who had hitherto lived from hand to mouth, then began to transform nature to suit his own ends. The cultivation of useful plants, cattle-breeding, the provision of dwellings, technical innovations in the production of masons' tools for sharpening and drilling, the invention of weaving and plaiting and also of pottery fundamentally altered man's standard of living. The harvesting of crops and the need to repel raiders led to the establishment of village or even urban communities. Once set up in fertile districts, such communities proceeded to the division of labour. Handicrafts and trade came into existence.

Agriculture depends upon soil fertility, water supply and sunshine; activities are determined by the rotation of the seasons, sowing and ripening, birth and death. These ideas take visible shape in symbols which can be identified in myth. Art is accordingly no longer applied exclusively to the actual but also to the supernatural.

This cultural revolution began in the 6th millennium before Christ and came to a head, according to our present knowledge, in the Near East. Settlements arose which remained in occupation for very long periods. Q'alat Yarmo in eastern Iraq and the walled city of Jericho have been estimated to date from about 4500 B.C. Pottery, invented during the last third of the 5th millennium, produced both single-colour glazed ware and also vessels with painted geometrical patterns, excavated at Mersin in Cilicia, at Nineveh and at Hassuna on the Tigris.

So well did Neolithic art realise the manifold potentialities of ceramics that this term has quite justifiably been adopted into the language to describe such products. Pots, jars, bowls and beakers had their prototypes in nature, e. g. gourds or skulls. The potter's creative imagination took these simple forms and rang the changes on them. For the production of a three-dimensional vessel both hand and mind had to 'take in' the shape. The potter's inward participation in the productive process came to expression in the adornment of the vessel with painted, impressed or incised patterns. The ornamentation, by which certain parts of the object could be rendered conspicuous or subordinate, indicated the feeling Neolithic culture had for design (ill. 86–89).

Many female statuettes, made of clay, stone or other materials, have been found, either in the abstract form of small, flat chopping-boards, or in the round as somewhat gross figures, with the hands placed below their breasts. They constitute idols of the *magna mater*, the Mother Goddess, symbol of life and fertility. These products precisely chart the direction and distribution of Neolithic culture.

This culture in all probability spread from its source in the Near East, in waves to all points of the compass. It flowed into central Asia and followed the course of the Nile towards central Africa. It also extended through Asia Minor and the lands bordering the Danube to central and eastern Europe, as well as along the shores of the Mediterranean, to the south, west and north of the continent. Encounters with the locally established Mesolithic cultures led to the formation of new cultural groups. The further the distance from the movement's original source, the later did the change take place. By the time Neolithic culture first appeared in northern Europe, the early advanced cultures of the Near East and Egypt were already in existence in the Mediterranean region.

On the mainland of Greece, about the middle of the 4th millennium, a culture arose at Sesklo in Thrace which was conspicuous for its miniature sculptures in clay and stone, notably of female idols, as well as for its pottery with painted angular patterns and for its dwellings erected on rectangular foundations. Neolithic culture spread from Greece and Asia Minor into the Balkans, whence several of its components returned, during the first half of the following millennium, to the Eastern Mediterranean, for instance the Danubian variety, characterised by 'Bandkeramik' ware. They introduced, in architecture, the oblong type of house or *megaron* and in painted pottery the meander and the spiral, found at Dimini in Thrace.

In Crete, influences from Syria and Egypt intermingled, producing dwellings with several rooms and much more lifelike idols. Cretan engraved pottery and stone vessels appear to have been based on Egyptian models.

In the early Neolithic period a crudely engraved pottery was manufactured in Italy. But it was later replaced by vessels painted in the Danubian manner. About 2000 B.C. a culture arose at Matera in the south of the peninsula, undoubtedly under the influence of Egypt and the Near East. It produced earthenware painted in several colours and also bearing plastic ornament. Spain enriched European Neolithic art with the culture characterized by bell-beakers (q. v.), which penetrated the north of the continent and far into the East after 2000 B.C.

Megalithic architecture (q. v.) came from the south-eastern shores of the Mediterranean. It appeared in southern Italy, Malta and Africa, reaching Spain after 2500 B.C. and France and England some time later. North Germany and Scandinavia were its ultimate limits.

In Europe north of the Alps a number of large cultural areas can be identified. The western group is distinguished by a megalithic-style architecture and an industry producing vessels almost entirely lacking in surface decoration.

The northern group in Scandinavia and northern Germany, comprised the corded-ware and megalithic peoples, who were characterised by a simple pottery with incised (q. v.) or corded ornament, giving it a rigidly symmetrical form.

The 'comb-stamped' culture, so called on account of its style of decoration, centred upon the Baltic and eastern Scandinavia.

The Danubian, also known as the 'Bandkeramik', culture owing to the peculiar ornamentation of its earthenware, produced a great many figurines, thus proving its close relationship to the eastern Mediterranean sphere. The western sub-groups manufactured pottery with engraved meander and spiral patterns while the others turned out, for the most part, finely painted vases.

THE BRONZE AGE

Copper and gold had already been much used in the Neolithic period for personal adornment and for the manufacture of tools. But the far harder and technically more adaptable metallic alloy of bronze was the only really satisfactory substitute for stone tools and weapons. Bronze Age culture continued the developments of the Neolithic with no visible break. The transition may be dated in southern Europe at about 2000 B.C., in the north some 300 years later and in eastern Europe about 1200 B.C. The demand for metal – since bronze consists of 90 % copper and 10 % tin – ushered in mining and gave a great stimulus to trade with lands where minerals were scarce.

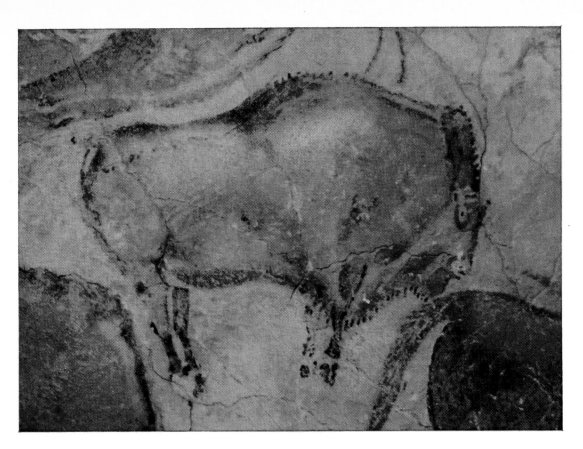

Old Stone Age cave painting from Altamira, Northern Spain: Representation of a bison *(Franco-Cantabrian period)*

African rock painting at Kargur Talah (New Stone Age)

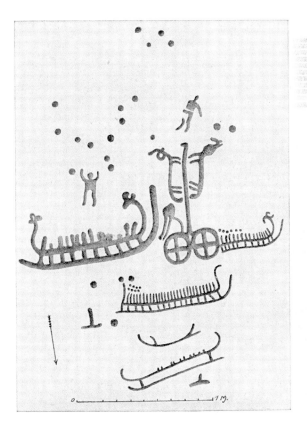

Nordic rock painting at Bohuslän, Sweden (Bronze Age)

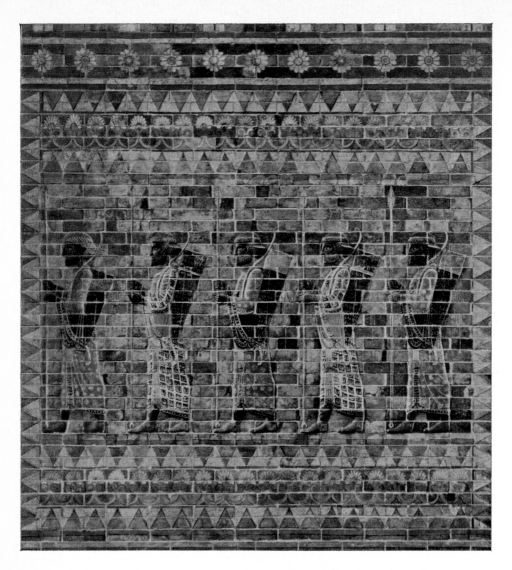

'The Immortals'. *Bodyguard from the palace of Artaxerxes II in Susa. Frieze of archers (405–362 B. C.) Glazed tiles*

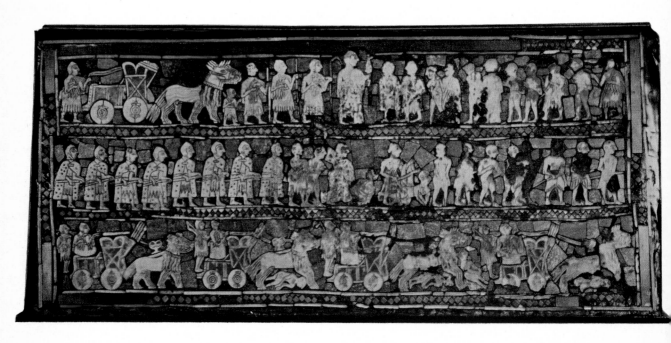

'Standard' *from Ur in Sumer (2450 B. C.) Asphalt on a wooden background with inlaid shells, lapis lazuli and sandstone*

90. La Tène Period. Bronze mirror from Britain

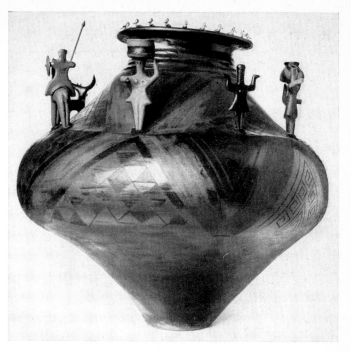

91. Hallstatt Period. Sepulchral urn (cinerary urn) from Gemeinlebarn, Lower Austria

The new and improved implements caused a further rise in the standard of living. Their shapes became increasingly varied. Sword-blades and lance-points, helmets and shields, razors and fibulae, as well as personal ornaments of all kinds, came into use and were artistically fashioned. The emphasis was unmistakably on the crafts, rather than the fine arts.

The northern, Germanic, peoples had a particularly high reputation as workers in bronze. They replaced the hitherto prevalent ornamentation in straight lines with curves that formed circles – perhaps solar symbols – spirals and waves. Geometric decoration gave way to organic and freely flowing shapes in this Germanic art (q. v., ill. 133).

The megalithic architecture of the culture of western Europe continued far into the Bronze Age. In Ireland, the El Dorado of the period, the goldsmiths' art flourished, with a knowledge of the processes of casting, embossing and wire-drawing.

The central European group spread, together with its sub-groups, from eastern France and from Italy as far as Hungary. Barrow-culture is regarded as mainly represented by Celtic tribes. Pottery showed a great variety of chip-carved decoration. The metallurgical technique of breaking up surfaces by punching was known, in addition to that of incrustation, inverting background and pattern.

The Urnfield culture, the northern division of which is known as the Lausitz culture, involved the inhabitants of Illyria. The Illyrian cultural groups spread across central and south-east Europe, sending out offshoots to England, Spain and northern Italy. They produced at first embossed vessels of clay and subsequently pottery usually unpainted and little decorated, but exhibiting a very great variety of shapes, such as high-necked jugs with convex sides, bowls with turned-down rims, beakers and basins.

The Bronze Age of Italy was represented by the Apennine culture, which adorned its clay vessels with incised spiral and meander patterns resembling those of the Balkans. In the south of the peninsula, about 1000 B.C., the Ausonian culture, modelled on that of Crete, produced embossed pottery, while in the north the Terramara culture built lake-dwellings protected by dikes and manufactured bronze ornaments and tools of fine quality.

THE IRON AGE

Iron had been in use for a long time in the advanced cultures of the Orient and the Aegean. The new metal began to be increasingly used in the Balkans and in Italy after about 1200 B.C. for the manufacture of weapons and other implements, though not in central Europe until after about 800 B.C. No thorough-going transformation of cultural life ensued, however, though the economic and consequently the cultural centres of gravity shifted as a result of the opening up of new mining districts.

In central Europe, from France to the northern Balkans, between the 9th and 5th centuries B.C., the Hallstatt (q. v.) group of craftsmen, so called from the place in the Salzkammergut district of Austria at which discoveries were made, was represented by Illyrian peoples in the east and Celts in the west. They produced large clay urns designed partly in relief, sometimes portraying the heads of animals, at others with small figures of human beings, horsemen or beasts, circling the shoulder-rim (ill. 91). This taste, hinting at the Baroque, is also shown in the employment of different techniques such as decorative paint, scalloping, incrustation and stamping on one and the same vessel. Metallurgy produced fanciful bronze ornaments, fibulae in the form of serpents or tympana, bracelets resembling knots and so on.

The *situlae*, ceremonial buckets or urns from Venice and the Tyrol, were adorned with embossed or engraved processional scenes, columns of chariots or animal friezes.

During the late Iron Age, from about 500 B.C. till the beginning of the Christian era, the La Tène (q. v.) Celtic style in art spread over large parts of Europe. Celtic merchants introduced Greek and Etruscan applied art, which stimulated the native product. Eastern influences were initiated by nomadic invasions, as is testified by the find of gold objects at Vettersfeld (q. v.) in the Guben district. The Hallstatt style of animal representation was first adopted, then the Greek palmette and acanthus-tendril type of ornament, both being eventually transformed into fantastically ravelled shapes which bore little resemblance to nature. Goldsmiths' work of an unusually high standard of craftsmanship was discovered in the royal graves. The importance of the La Tène style arises from its successful blend of abstract Nordic ornament with the figural art of the Mediterranean cultures (ill. 90).

During the 3rd and 2nd centuries B.C. the plant type of ornamentation grew more and more conventional. At last all surface decoration was abandoned on the continent, though in the British Isles the application of a subtle style of linear design resulted in a late maturity of Celtic art. La Tène pottery produced rotund pitchers and slender beakers, with painted decorations of simple geometrical patterns and curved, stylised plant motifs.

In the Germanic north of Europe a largely independent Iron Age culture developed, though it did not remain uninfluenced by the Hallstatt and La Tène styles. Its simplicity distinguished it from the previous Bronze Age cultures. It gradually penetrated as far as the Vistula and central Germany. The Nordic rock-drawings, which had begun in the Stone Age with depictions of game, continued during the Bronze Age with pictures of ships and in the Iron Age most often represented ships and rafts as well as human figures.

MESOPOTAMIA

The region enclosed by the rivers Tigris and Euphrates is known as Mesopotamia, the 'land between rivers'. Both overflow every year after the snow melts, flooding wide areas and leaving a fertile muddy soil behind them when they recede. But everything which remains above water is parched by the heat of the sun. The fertility of the river valleys, which Herodotus regarded as superior to that of Egypt, can be augmented by means of irrigation works and a system of dikes to protect it against the frequently devasting inundations. These conditions had prevailed for thousands of years. But the task of counteracting them could only be achieved by communal labour; this, in its turn, required the creation of a single State, the foundation on which advanced cultures are built.

The early history of Mesopotamia dates back to the 6th millennium B.C. and the recognisable beginnings of art to the 5th (Halaf and Obaid periods).

SUMER AND AKKAD

The Sumerians, occupying the south of the region between the rivers, are the first cultural group in this area to enter history, at the beginning of the 3rd millennium B.C. How talented these people were shows in their production of the earliest kind of writing, cuneiform. It was taken over by the Akkadian Semites, the Babylonians, the Assyrians and other peoples speaking different languages. The many finds of inscribed clay tablets provide some idea of their religion, their literature, which set forth the myths of the Creation and the Flood (Gilgamesh epic), their codes of laws, systems of computation and astronomy. To this day we follow the Sumerians' division of the hour into 60 minutes and the circle into 360 degrees.

Sumer comprised, politically, a number of city-states. Each was ruled in theory by its own god, though in practice the 'lugal', the 'great man', exercised power.

Architecturally this dual authority was made manifest by the erection of temples. At Erech on the Euphrates the so-called 'White Temple' of the sky-god Anu is regarded as the prototype of the high temples built on graduated terraces (Ziggurat q. v., Tower of Babel q. v.). A temple dedicated to the Mother Goddes Inanna had a long interior apartment, a court or hall, flanked on each side by a succession of smaller rooms. The extra length required for ritual processions was attained by a serial arrangement, of recesses in the exterior walls. Air-dried bricks were used as building material. They were covered with thick layers of loam, pegged with clay nails, the red, white and black heads of which formed an interlacing pattern resembling mosaic.

During the Jamdat Nasr period (2800–2650 B.C.) an artistic style came to maturity which was destined to last a long time. It owed its strength to two sources, the warlike mentality of the Sumerians, who delighted in battle, hunting, and the exercise of power, and the piety of the subject peasantry devoted to agriculture and their flocks and herds. These two creative currents fertilised one another and intermingled. But in the Jamdat Nasr period the masterful Sumerian element, concerned with representation, obtained the upper hand. Stone cylinders for seals were carved in realistic style, the composition often resembling that of heraldry, to depict fabulous creatures, ritual scenes or the pleasures and risks of cattle-breeding. Their large-scale sculpture, once so important, is to-day only exemplified by the marble head of a woman, almost life-size, whose noble features radiate earnestness and dignity.

In the reign of King Meselim of Kish (c. 2600 B.C.) the Sumerian culture was permeated by eastern Semitic nomads. The new blood is conspicuous in the sphere of art, where an abstract phase becomes noticeable, as evidenced by the twelve alabaster statuettes, votive offerings, from Eshnunnak. The human figure is divided into geometrical components, thereby being stripped of its material aspect and spiritualised. Reliefs on votive plaques with figural subjects or on seals grow shallower. Vessels, from being rotund, now assume straight-sided, triangular shapes. Industrial art had to take a more refined aesthetic into consideration by utilising the precious metals and brilliantly coloured inlays. In architecture, the rigid axial form was abandoned. The inroads of barbaric peoples from the highlands, so characteristic of the cultural history of the Near East, became noticeable for the first time. The evolution of art, which led elsewhere to classicism, was here interrupted and archaic styles returned.

109

92. Bronze head of a ruler of Akkad from Nineveh (probably Naramsin, 2270–2233 B.C.)

The period of the first dynasty of Ur (2500–2400 B.C.) coincided with a relaxation of the Sumerian social structure, involving the breaking-away of ecclesiastical from royal power, the separation of temple from palace. The material prosperity of the time found expression in a more refined artistic style (ill. p. 106). The votive statuettes of the great personalities of the realm, exhibited to do honour to the gods – male standing and seated figures, with shaved heads, and naked torsos, clothed from the waist downwards in flounced skirts, or robed female figures – were once more given a more rounded appearance, with more complex modelling. Relief work now takes in the politico-religious memorial, which from now on becomes a striking feature of the art of the Near East and a valuable source for its history. The 'Stele of the Vultures', representing King Eannatum of Lagash, is an example of such a monument.

After 2350 B.C. the warlike, Semitic Akkadians usurped Sumerian sovereignty. Sargon I and his grandson Naramsin, operating from Kish and Sippar, subjugated the Sumerian city-states, the region of Elam to the east, the Bahrein Islands, northern Syria and perhaps even Cyprus. The capital of this empire was established at Akkad, near the site of the future Babylon. The new State was the work of strong, masterful personalities. It was governed with the aid of a well-organized bureaucracy. The sparse minority of Akkadian conquerors entered upon the intellectual inheritance of Sumer and used the cuneiform script.

The monuments of Akkadian art, of which only few have survived, celebrate the heroic deeds of the victors ('Victory Stele' of King Naramsin), or depict their kings and military leaders (bronze head from Nineveh, ill. 92). The specific Akkadian style appears particularly clearly in the statue of King Manishtusu, a torso in diorite. Quite apart from the difference in costume – the flounced skirt having been replaced by a heavy mantle – the diagonal rendering of the folds reveals the artist's interest in movement, affording the strongest possible contrast with the still and timeless air of the Sumerian figure. Little is known of Akkadian architecture. A palace excavated among foundation-walls in the Tel Brak-Chabur neighbourhood had been erected, significantly enough, on older temple ruins. The consecrated area of the temple had been taken over for the palace. The Akkadian king was held to be divine, not merely, as in the last period of Sumer, the representative of divinity.

About the year 2150 B.C. the Akkadian empire was overrun by the Gutaeans, a barbarous tribe from the Zagros Mountains; literary and artistic evidence ceases for a hundred years. The expulsion of the savage conquerors was followed by the restoration of Sumerian rule. But this period was characterised by cultural and religious reaction rather than by new creative effort. Many institutions, including the language, remained Akkadian.

At Lagash a rich artistic legacy was unearthed. Statues of the priest-king Gudea (2050–2000 B.C.), reliefs and specimens of stone-engraving bear witness to a style based on religious sensibility. Akkadian restlessness had been replaced by Sumerian serenity.

During the ensuing three centuries the Sumerian empire again split up into city-states and eventually succumbed as a result of continual warfare with Semitic invaders, Elamites from the east and Amorites from the west.

BABYLONIA UNDER AMORITES AND KASSITES

After 2000 B.C. the Amorites occupied central Mesopotamia, superimposing on its ancient civilisation the First Dynasty of Babylon, named after the capital. The sixth king of this line, Hammurabi (1727–1686 B.C.), established an empire stretching from the Persian Gulf to Assur. The Babylonian language, in the course of its development, took over the cuneiform script. Science, literature and art flourished. A stele found at Susa in 1901 bears the text of the oldest code of laws in existence, prepared by Hammurabi.

The high level of subsoil water has hitherto prevented excavation of the palace. But at Mari on the central Euphrates the massive royal residence of Zimrilim was found, a conglomeration of various systems of courts concealing the monarch's own quarters, their fortifications, administrative offices and storerooms. The western Semitic artists naturally made use of a number of Sumerian and Akkadian motifs, though their figural stelae and clay tablets betray a certain urgency and religiosity. The deities of the Empire, Marduk, Shamash and the war-god Ishtar appear, as well as winged beings, on reliefs, frescoes and roller-seals. The dynasty of Hammurabi soon fell and the empire became disrupted. About 1450 B.C. an Iranian highland people, the Kassites, settled in Babylonian territory for three hundred years, bringing artistic activity to a standstill. Their *kudurru,* boundary-stones which also provided evidence of deeds of gift, are carved in clumsy relief with religious emblems, fabulous creatures and scenes with human figures.

ASSYRIA

The rise of Assyria, a country of peasants between the Tigris and the Zab, which had been colonised by the Semitic Akkadians, began in the 14th century B.C., when King Eriba-Adad (1390–1364 B.C.) forced Babylon to acknowledge his independence. His successors conquered extensive tracts of land and created a large empire, which was firmly established by mass deportations. But they did not succeed in weakening the dominant position of Babylon as a centre of civilisation in the Near East, even when they destroyed the city itself in 689 and plundered the holy places. Continual warfare crippled the power of the Assyrian empire. Assur, its capital, was destroyed by the Medes, an Iranian people, in 614. Two years later, Nineveh fell and the Assyrian power was apportioned between the Medes and the Chaldaeans.

Assyrian civilisation at first showed Sumerian and Akkadian characteristics, later modified by Hurrian influences. In sculpture these elements blended to form a style peculiar to Assyria, which began in the 14th century B.C. Warlike and heroic motifs were preferred in these works. Kings, official dignitaries and warriors were represented in the guise of athletes with terrifying expressions and muscular limbs. Military expeditions, sieges, encampments and hunting-scenes, in short, events taken from the king's life, were depicted by the Assyrian artists in relief on great stone slabs placed in position on the walls of the palaces.

These pictures give us precise information about the customs of the time – for example, the breed of horses in vogue and the clothing, weapons and tools in use – but also indicate the uniformity of type among ordinary citizens. Their precise movements are like those of puppets, though there is something admirable in the way they are subordinated to a single will and directed towards a distant goal. In the hunting-scenes the animals are shown in full career. The national military virtues are expressed in the severe style of the reliefs, which approaches that of engraving in the clarity and descriptive power of the line. Despite the muscular nature of the human beings and animals depicted, these low reliefs, often with writing superimposed, are of extreme delicacy, though for that very reason more decorative

93. Lioness. Alabaster relief from the hunting-scenes in the palace of King Assurbanipal at Nineveh (c. 669–633 B.C.)

than plastic in effect. The predilection of the Near East for ornament is readily discernible in the careful treatment of the robes and their embellished borders, in the dressing of hair and beards and in the stylized vegetation. In the late period, represented by the reliefs in the palace of Assurbanipal (669–633 B.C.) at Nineveh, the soldierly severity of this style is modified by the introduction of genre features. Realistic pictures of court life alternate with vivid delineations of nature as in the relief of the dying lioness (ill. 93). This naturalism is perhaps to be referred to Egyptian influence, though the archaic style taken over from Sumerian and Akkadian art still survives.

Assyrian art, especially in its late phase, favoured the use of colour, both in impressive frescoes of tinted enamel and brightly painted earthenware. Its technical accomplishment is apparent in metallurgy, bronze casting and embossed work.

Temples were built with transverse members in addition to the rigid oblong. Twin temples with ziggurats of several storeys rose high above the battlemented walls and their gate-towers surrounding the sanctuary area. The palaces consisted of many courtyards with several subdivisions and were continually being extended by annexes. Assyrian art did not produce any novel, constructive ideas in architecture.

NEW BABYLON

Ever since 1200 B.C. the Near East had been overrun by Aramaic peoples. They included the Chaldaeans, who can be traced in southern Mesopotamia from about 850 B.C. In combination with the Medes, they shook off the yoke of Assyria. Under Nebuchadnezzar II (604–562 B.C.), the king who destroyed Jerusalem in 587 and caused the Jews to enter into the 'Babylonian captivity', the Chaldaean empire comprised Babylonia, Elam, some districts east of the Tigris, western Mesopotamia, Syria and Palestine. In 539 B.C. Babylon became a province of the rising Persian power.

The Chaldaeans and the inhabitants of Ur felt bound to support the venerable civilisation of the country. The cult of Marduk, formerly a city-deity of Babylon and now a universal god, rose to its zenith. Science flourished, especially in the fields of astronomy and astrology. The rulers sought glory, not as warriors, but as princes of peace. Chaldaean art endeavoured to combine Aramaic mentality, the ideas bequeathed by the western Semites and the Sumerian heritage. It was no wonder that the artist of New Babylon, who felt himself to be a link in a chain of tradition, worked with more subtlety of feeling and greater composure and assurance than his Assyrian kinsman. The celebration of Man and his deeds gave place to glorification of the Divine. Ritual sculpture and reliefs were made to express tender and deep emotion. The pictures in relief are manifestly no longer earthbound.

Nebuchadnezzar II, who had a passion for building, changed the whole aspect of Babylon. The Greek historian Herodotus described the magnificent palace as it was c. 450 B.C., the 'hanging gardens', the Marduk sanctuary called Esagila, with its tower, called Etemenanki, the Ishtar Gate and the splendid architecture of the Street of Processions. The walls of the palaces, the gates and the bases of the battlemented walls of the processional way, with their towering buttresses at intervals, were adorned with brick reliefs enamelled in brilliant colours, usually yellow and light blue on a dark blue ground. There were friezes representing pacing lions, in decorative series, while the doorways were guarded by bulls and fabulous beasts set one above another (ill. 94).

THE PERSIAN EMPIRE OF THE ACHAEMENIDAE AND SASSANIDS

The Persians belong to the Indo-Germanic family of peoples. Their westerly migrations took them to southern Iran, where they settled. Their earliest artistic products may have been the Luristan bronzes of chivalric type dating from the 2nd millennium B.C. and taking the forms of idols, bridle-bits, chariot fittings, weapons and personal adornments. Contacts with the civilisations of the Near East, Egypt and Greece greatly stimulated Persian art. Cyrus II (559–529 B.C.) created an empire which stretched from the Indus to the Mediterranean. His successors annexed Egypt and even Libya. Darius I and Xerxes I subjugated the Greek cities of Asia Minor but failed in their attacks on the Greek mainland, losing the battles of Marathon in 490 and Salamis in 480 B.C. Darius (521–486 B.C.) organized his empire by dividing it into twenty provinces, building postal highways and establishing a centrally directed administration with an elaborate system of taxation and coinage. In religious and cultural affairs the imperial rule was marked by magnanimous toleration.

Massive palaces were erected in the large cities of Babylon and Susa, as well as in the newly built capital, Persepolis. They no longer resembled fortresses, but offered easy access to the visitor by stairways and anterooms. The great halls were roofed over with the aid of closely ranged, tall and slender pillars, as in the Hall of a Hundred Columns at Persepolis. The Persians delighted as much as did the Chaldaeans in artistic ornament, decorating the walls of their palaces with reliefs of enamelled tiles and representations of the ten thousand 'Immortals', the crack troops of the army, on the march (ill. p. 106). Here and in the rock reliefs of the Achaemenid kings at Naksh-i-Rustum (q. v.) there is evidence of a new style, smoothly flowing and organic, superior to the art of Assyria and New Babylon.

94. Processional Way in Babylon. Part of approach to Ishtar Gateway between walls of main citadel (c. 580 B.C.).
Glazed brick

Applied art, for example that of metalworking and glyptography, was technically flawless and attained a high artistic standard with the collaboration of the Greek masters.

The disadvantages of oriental despotism – the employment of eunuchs and favourites in public affairs, cruelty and routine bureaucracy – brought about the ruin of the empire despite its sound organization. Alexander the Great and his Macedonians crushed the Achaemenid power within a few years (334–327 B.C.). Alexander ascended the throne of the Great Kings of Persia.

As a result of the Greek and Macedonian occupation Persian art was subjected to strong Hellenistic influences. In the second half of the 3rd century B.C. the Parthians, nomadic horsemen from the northeast, invaded the highlands of Iran, bringing with them a lifelike and energetic style in the depiction of animals. Parthian, Persian and Hellenistic elements blended to form a single manner, which is clearly reflected in decorative work.

In A. D. 226 the ancient Persian dynasty of the Sassanids overthrew the Parthian sovereignty and founded the Sassanian empire, which extended, by A. D. 625, to western Asia Minor and the Nile delta. The Sassanid kings were zealous builders of cities, castles and palaces. The form of architecture preferred was the *ivan,* a rectangular, barrel-vaulted structure. Rock-reliefs celebrated the deeds of the rulers. Chivalric tournaments and hunting-scenes were depicted in monumental frescoes. A rare degree of refinement was reached in the minor arts. Richly decorated gold and silver plate, jugs and jars of silver and bronze, as well as clay and glass vessels, seals, coins and textiles of all descriptions were produced by artistically gifted craftsmen. Sassanid art outlasted the empire itself, which fell to the Arabs in A. D. 642, and greatly stimulated the art of the West.

EGYPT

In the year 1798, Napoleon attempted to conquer Egypt for France, so as to strike a blow at the most vulnerable point in the British imperial system. His army was accompanied by scientists and technicians who began studies of the country and its inhabitants, thereby rediscovering the civilisation of ancient Egypt. They laid the foundations of the science of Egyptology, solidly based on the deciphering of the hieroglyphic script. The investigation of it was begun in 1822 by François Champollion.

The narrow valley of the Nile constitutes a prolonged oasis in the North African desert. Below the first cataract at Syene-Aswan the river-bed deepens and widens, often splitting up. The current flows through a strip of fertile territory, called in the ancient Egyptian tongue Kemet, or the 'black land', and in Greek Aigyptos. This tract is at most 16 miles across and some 530 miles in length. It is bounded on the east and west by the mountain ranges of the desert, called Teshret or the 'red land'. To the north, below Cairo, lies the wide alluvial district of the delta, intersected by many tributaries and canals. Every year, from July to October, a great volume of water is carried downstream from the melted snows and precipitates of the Abyssinian highlands. The river overflows, depositing a dark crust of exceedingly fertile mud.

The Neolithic agricultural workers who multiplied in the Nile valley during the 6th and 5th millennia B.C. began by exploiting the 'brink' of the river, that is to say, the fertile muddy soil deposited by the annual inundations. Just as in Mesopotamia, the cultivation of the soil, which required the building of irrigation works, could only be successfully carried out by communal labour. Such was the origin of the establishment of national States. A number of villages combined to form a district. In historical times there were twenty-two such districts in Upper, and twenty in Lower, Egypt. Whenever

rince Rahotep and his wife Nefert *(Egypt, 4th Dynasty). Painted limestone, eyes made of clear and opaque quartz in a dark setting*

Egyptian wall painting from the tomb of Queen Nefertari at Thebes (19th Dynasty): Isis accompanying the Queen into the next world

the central power weakened they increased their own authority. The Egyptian nation arose from a mixing, which had already taken place in the prehistoric period, of Hamitic and Semitic stocks. Each district had its god, generally represented in animal form or with an animal's head – a cow in the case of Hathor in Dendera, a hawk in the case of Horus at Hierakonpolis, the Bull Apis at Memphis and so on. In addition to these deities there were nature-gods, such as the fertility god Osiris, and a large number of idols of obscure significance. A powerful priesthood organized these deities, according to their districts, into systems with a strict order of precedence. Consequently, different divinities acquired outstanding importance at different times, depending on the current distribution of political and cultural centres of gravity. The belief in physical survival after death led to the preservation of bodies by embalming, their protection in tombs and their endowment with the necessities of life. Osiris, the god of the dead, weighed souls in the balance and pronounced judgment on them.

About 280 B.C., the priest Manetho wrote a history of his country, enumerating thirty dynasties between that of the most ancient of the kings or Pharoahs, Menes, and 342 B.C., when the Persian king Artaxerxes III subjugated Egypt. This division into periods is still in general use to-day. The tendency of modern criticism is to allocate later rather than earlier dates. But as investigations in this field are not yet complete the present work will adhere to the dating hitherto in force.

The Old Kingdom, comprising the first to the tenth dynasties (2850–2052 B.C.), owed its unification to Upper Egypt. The Pharoahs of the first dynasties ruled from Memphis and were worshipped as embodiments of the hawk-god Horus. But the authority of this patriarchal monarchy was weakened during the period of the fifth dynasty by the land-owning officials and the power of the priesthood. The realm was disorganised by social revolution and the inroads of Bedouin into the delta from Mount Sinai. The south of the country forced Memphis to acknowledge its independence and the district governors acquired far-reaching powers. Political reconstruction caused the supersession of Horus by the sun-god Re and the Pharoah was declared to be the latter's son. External dissolution led to a relaxation of the sanctified bonds of magic. Individuals assumed more importance. It was by no means an exception for an artist to add a self-portrait and his own name to reliefs and frescoes. The collapse of the State and the political confusion that ensued during the period between the seventh and tenth dynasties involved the arts in decline.

The Middle Kingdom (eleventh to seventeenth dynasty, 2052–1750 B.C.) was first unified by the rulers of the eleventh dynasty, resident at Thebes in Upper Egypt. Under the twelfth dynasty

95. *Guide to the Art of Antiquity*

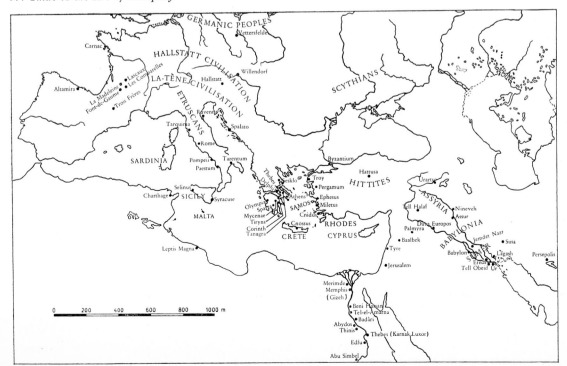

(1991–1792 B.C.) the Government was transferred to Memphis, the southern frontier extended to the second cataract of the Nile, a firm system of administration established and fresh territory, the province of Fayum, acquired for development. The sun-god Re came to be associated with the ram-god Ammon and gained in importance. The worship of Osiris spread further and the cult of the dead, hitherto reserved for the Pharoah and the chief men of the realm, began to be practised by the lower classes of the population. Internal disorders led to yet another collapse of the realm. The thirteenth and fourteenth dynasties in Thebes and Xois could not stop invasion by the Hyksos from the Near East about 1670 B.C. The newcomers took over the superior civilisation of the nation they had conquered. The Egyptian princes of the contemporary seventeenth dynasty, who had at first been tolerated as vassals by the victors, carried on a war of liberation, directed from Thebes, against the foreign usurpers.

The New Kingdom (eigtheenth to twenty-fourth dynasties, 1570–715 B.C.) began with the final expulsion of the Hyksos, driven back into Syria by the kings of the eighteenth dynasty. Thutmosis III (1480–1448 B.C.) raised Egypt to the level of a world power. From Nubia to the Euphrates he ruled over an empire 2000 miles long, though its fertile strip averaged only 12 miles in width. Egypt grew economically rich and began to maintain widespread commercial and cultural relations with foreign countries. A brilliant Egyptian civilisation developed. The Pharoah was regarded as the son of Amon-Ra, the State god, whose priests came to occupy important posts. Amenhotep IV, called Ikhnaton (1377–1358 B.C.), endeavoured to reform the State religion. The political crisis thus brought about endangered the position of Egypt as a world power. The Pharoahs of the nineteenth dynasty restored allegiance to the ancient tradition. Ramses III (1197–1165 B.C.), belonging to the twentieth dynasty, was the last important ruler of the New Kingdom. Under his successors it declined. Libyan mercenaries and the priests of Amon engaged in a struggle for power.

During the Late Period (715–332 B.C.) Libyans and Ethiopians, Assyrians and Persians dominated the country. Psammetichus I (663–609 B.C.) founded the twenty-sixth dynasty, based on the city of Sais. He introduced a new unification of the realm and a national renaissance, known as the Saite (q. v.), modelled on the civilisation of the Old Kingdom.

ARCHITECTURE

Egyptian architecture reached its highest level in the Old Kingdom. The founder of the first dynasty, King Menes, built himself a detached tomb, surrounded by a brick wall, at Nagada. Other royal tombs, at Abydos, consisted of walled underground chambers roofed with massive baulks of timber and sand. Simple tombs built of sun-dried bricks and wood evolved into complex structures of limestone, with several chambers and raking sides, the original *mastaba* (q. v.) form. Zoser, who founded the third dynasty, had a stepped pyramid built for him by the legendary architect and priest Imhotep. In this structure both sepulchral forms were used – the detached and the underground chamber – in six dimin-

96. Sphinx of Gizeh and Pyramid of Cheops (mid 3rd millennium)

97. *Temple of Luxor. View of forecourt and temple building (18th dynasty). Papyrus-stem columns with papyrus-bud capitals*

ishing mastaba storeys, with the tomb itself at the centre below ground. The pyramid was surrounded by a walled area enclosing a number of communicating courtyards and chambers. Thus men sought to reproduce for the dead, in the more permanent material of stone, the ordinary wood and clay buildings used by the living.

The Old Kingdom has bequeathed to posterity those unique and characteristic monuments, the pyramids, which were given their final, geometric form under the rulers of the fourth dynasty. At Dashur a pyramid was erected for King Snefru, having a mastaba base and raking side-walls. This angled type of structure represents the transition from the step-mastaba to the true pyramid. The nucleus of the building comprised an irregular pile of roughly dressed blocks of stone, enclosed in a casing of carefully smoothed and accurately fitted limestone cubes. An ingeniously planned corridor led from the north to the sepulchral chamber.

The pyramid territory of the fourth dynasty extended for nearly 90 miles in a line from north to south, to the west of Memphis along the edge of the desert. The three most famous pyramids, those of Cheops, Chefren and Mycerinus, are situated in the Gizeh district (ill. 96). They each marked the boundary of a complex of buildings and comprised the temple placed in the valley and the pyramid itself. The temples, now almost wholly ruined, must once have made a profound impression on the multitudes of worshippers, by their great splendour and solemnity, by virtue of the structural simplicity of the square blocks of stone and the exact proportions observed. The impression would be reinforced by the succession of broad and lofty halls, separated by pillars of granite.

The pyramids of the fifth and ensuing dynasties were not so carefully designed as their predecessors. The various sections of the temples were rearranged and the monolithic columns – single upright blocks of stone – were rounded off into pillars with carved capitals representing leaves or flowers, the pillars themselves being given the shapes of plants, papyrus stems, palms and even lotus-stalks, so that they resemble natural growths under the timbering of the roof (ill. 28, 97).

The Pharoah, in his character of 'Great God', chose the site of his eternal home immediately after his accession, and for the rest of his reign the entire nation contributed to keep the building in repair. Dignitaries sacrificed daily in the temple of the dead, uttering the magic formulae that should secure perpetual life for the King. He in his turn allotted these officials graves near to his own massive monument, so that a city of the dead arose to encompass the pyramid.

It is difficult for us to visualize the important architecture of the Middle Kingdom. The buildings extolled by ancient travellers – for example, the 'Labyrinth', the temple of the dead at Fayum under Amenemhet III, which Herodotus considered the most magnificent specimen of architecture in Egypt – have been destroyed. By dint of much effort and labour it has been possible to piece together certain portions of the ruins, and thereby obtain some idea of what these ancient Egyptians achieved. The funerary temple of Nebhepetre Mentuhotep III near Thebes had a pyramid set on two stepped bases (ill. 121). There was a hall with columns in front of the substructure, while the temple itself was situated

119

in the upper storey. The pyramid above was supported on several rows of octagonal pillars of the so-called proto-Doric order. In this way, the stolid pyramid of the Old Kingdom, utterly expressionless on all four sides, became, owing to its front elevation, a structure with an open countenance facing in a certain direction. The sun-god Re was worshipped in the open air, in the presence of towering stelae. The obelisks (ill. 12) were now given the form of a tapering pyramid.

In the New Kingdom temples were built with an eye to the ritual procession. Accordingly, the king's tomb was placed some distance from his funerary temple. An avenue of sphinxes led to the portal, flanked with pylons (q. v.), separating the natural from the supernatural world. The processional route continued through courtyards and pillared halls, as well as through other dimly lit chambers, columned and multi-aisled, on its way to the sanctuary of the god. The great scale of the architecture, with its gigantic pillars in the form of sheaves of papyrus, and the colossal statues of gods and kings, inspired in the faithful a mood of religious devotion which may have resembled that induced by medieval Christian cathedrals. The brilliantly-conceived ground plan of the New Kingdom temple, already used for the terraced temple at Deir el-Bahri, facilitated alteration and enlargement to truly enormous dimensions, as at the holy places of Karnak and Luxor (ill. 28, 97, 121), as well as at Medinet-Habu and Abu Simbel.

The architectural monuments of the Late Period have been destroyed. But during Greek (after 332 B.C.) and Roman dominion (after 30 B.C.) temples were built in Upper Egypt which earn our respect. Subsequently the vigour of Egyptian architecture was eclipsed.

SCULPTURE

Sculpture was called into being through the cult of the dead. The soul of a deceased person was supposed to reside in the commemorative statue. Such is the explanation of the austere attitude, the rigid and, as it were, timeless character of the figures, as well as their naturalism and tendency to portraiture (for example, the seated statue of King Zoser, third dynasty). The seated figures of Prince Rahotep (fourth dynasty) and of his consort Nefert, the 'Fair', though almost identical in their attitudes, are nevertheless individualised not only by their clothing and hair style but also by the way their features are carved and by their colouring (ill. p. 115). Technically and artistically the diorite statue of Chephren (fourth dynasty, c. 2500 B.C.), represents a culmination of development in this manner. The body, with its uncomplicated lines hewn from the hard stone, rises, austere and dignified, from the royal throne.

At the foot of the pyramids of Chephren there lies, subject to repeated burial by the desert sand, the Great Sphinx, hewn out of the natural rock in the form of a recumbent lion's body, 228 feet long, with a hooded human head of regal aspect, constituting a truly monumental work of art (ill. 96).

In addition to the royal portraits more life-like statues of the chief men of the kingdom have survived, of which the best known are the 'Squatting Scribe', at the Louvre in Paris, and the 'Village Headman', in the Cairo Museum (ill. 131). In these cases it almost seems as though sculpture were about to cast off its archaic quality and pass over into realism. The figures are endowed with a certain wayward power of expression, akin to that of portraiture. In the case of the naturalistic statue of a court dwarf, for example, the emphasis is on physiognomy. Yet they remain faithful, throughout the whole period of Egyptian art, to the laws originally laid down.

The sculptures of the Middle Kingdom recall, in their austere conformity, those of earlier times. Their aspect of unapproachable majesty seems deliberately assumed, indicating the political difficulties both domestic and foreign which these princes saw themselves having to face. Their features are often of a melancholy cast and bear convincing witness to the burden of the duties of a sovereign. In order to preserve the cubic style prevalent under the Old Kingdom, the sculptured figures of kings and private personages were usually represented robed, which conveyed compactness without suppressing the rounded

120

Golden coffin of King Tutankhamen (Egypt, 18th Dynasty). – Amarna period (mirror photograph)

Queen Nefertiti, *wife of Amenhotep IV Ikhnaton (Egypt, 18th Dynasty). – Amarna period. Painted limestone*

forms of torso and limbs. Hunting scenes, groups of wrestlers and figures of drovers were realistically represented, to adorn the tombs at Meïr; they were, moreover, obviously based on technical manuals. Egyptian sculpture of this era possesses a convincing power of imagery, coupled with complete mastery of the sculptor's art; it is calculated to appeal to man in every age.

The sculptors of the New Kingdom gave their figures the appearance of both a freer and a more harmonious movement, at the same time endowing them with a subtle touch of life. A break with the tradition of pure profile or full-face representation meant that beautiful effects of a new kind could be achieved, as exemplified by the lion from Soleb, dating from the time of Amenophis III, which turns its head towards the beholder. Even the conventional motif of the die squatter (ill. 137), is freely and sensitively treated in the Berlin statue of Senmut with a child.

Under the influence of Ikhnaton (1377–1358 B.C.), who sought to introduce the worship of the sun-god Aton as the State religion, an over-refined style arose at the king's new palace of El Amarna (head of his Queen, Nefertiti, ill. p. 121) which showed both in a tendency to mannerism and decadence and in an exaggerated naturalism. The longing for a closer approximation to truth even seduced the sculptor Thutmosis into taking plaster casts of ugly and coarse faces to use as models.

The changed political and religious conditions and the minor wars that, during the nineteenth and twentieth dynasties, resulted in a new outward prosperity, are reflected in the colossal statues, in combination with columns, in the rock temple at Abu Simbel. The sculptural style here is rude and almost barbarous in its severity.

During the Late Period sculptors produced, in addition to technically faultless but uninspired works, a few portrait busts, including the 'Green Head' in Berlin, admirable for their liveliness and versatility (ill. 124).

RELIEFS AND FRESCO PAINTING

Tombs were being lavishly furnished even at the time of the Old Kingdom. The embalmed body was placed in a funerary chamber, serving as a residence for it. The often numerous statues of the deceased person were set up in a temple of the dead to enable the spirit to find a home there. Storerooms were constructed to accommodate the sacrificial offerings. Information concerning the dead man and his rank, and also as to the arrangements made for the cult of the deceased, was deposited. Under the fifth dynasty the walls of the chambers began to be decorated with reliefs and paintings representing life and work at court and in the country districts. These pictures were not meant to be looked at by all and sundry. They were supposed to develop magic powers and assure the deceased the same degree of authority and the same possessions in the life beyond as he had enjoyed on Earth. Consequently, the dead man is to be seen at the altar and the banqueting table. Long processions bring him nourishment, fruit, poultry and domestic animals. Finally, details of the management of his estate are represented, such as the tilling of the soil and the harvest, the breeding and tending of cattle, fishing and hunting, craftsmen and scribes at work, furniture and equipment. The object was to enable the deceased to continue his former life in Eternity.

There is no attempt at three-dimensional representation in Egyptian reliefs. People, animals and objects are accordingly ranged in rows, upon a single base-line. But if a crowded scene does not admit of this treatment, it is broken up into groups, standing one above the other, each on its own level. Overlapping is avoided in the early reliefs. Objects are always shown at the angle which gives the least dimension in depth. This is the reason why, in human beings, the head is presented in profile, though the eye is seen from the front, and both shoulders are visible. In the same way a table is either drawn from one side or from above. Just as there were rules for what could be legitimately represented, so there was

123

engendered a convention as to how the figures should be portrayed; though, admittedly, pictorial clarity and intelligibility took precedence. Work in shallow relief was painted in various colours and really only differed from the less numerous frescoes of the Old Kingdom in the deeply incised outlines.

The wall-paintings and reliefs produced at the time of the Middle Kingdom no longer exhibit the animation and rich pictorial content characteristic of the Old. The Beni Hasan tombs have frieze-like ornamentation, combining to form a single composition full of movement. For decorative purposes the individual pictures, drawn with particular delicacy, are set close together, so as to retain the smoothness of the wall surface.

Serial arrangement of the figures also prevailed at the time of the New Kingdom, though their noble bearing and rhythmic gestures introduced an air of greater refinement (ill. p. 116). These representations, taken from private life – normally so carefully screened by Orientals – breathe all the charm of an almost overbred way of life. Husband and wife are shown at the family festal board, slender-limbed girls play musical instruments and dance, young people attend sacrificial and funeral ceremonies. With the abandonment of strict tradition by a wealthy and luxurious imperial people went a similar freedom in art. The achievement of beautiful form rather than tragic sublimity had become the object of artistic ambition.

THE CRAFTS

The applied arts reached an astonishingly high standard. The custom of providing the dead with a proportion of their personal possessions to take with them into the grave, with a view to their comfort in the after-life, has left to posterity numerous specimens of craftsmanship. There are clay vessels that date back to prehistoric and early historical times; subsequently, such 'ordinary earthenware' was, however, despised, only to come into its own again at the time of the New Kingdom by virtue of the imaginative shapes and variegated colouring it was given.

The art of polishing and scooping-out stone, whether alabaster, dark green diorite, basalt or slate, flourished particularly in prehistoric times and during the period of the Old Kingdom, though the technique continued to be employed right down to the Roman period. Vases, jars to hold ointment and palettes for mixing cosmetics were produced. Semi-precious stones of various colours were shaped into cylindrical seals and engraved with figures representing human beings and animals.

Natural pearls or semi-precious minerals were used by the Egyptian goldsmiths in conjunction with precious metals at all periods to fashion ornaments of great splendour, mirrors or articles for the toilet. The manufacture of decorative weapons began at the time of the Middle Kingdom, with outstanding results in the Late Period. At a very early date faience or glass beads, or paste, began to be substituted for the natural pearl. Lastly, glazed earthenware was used for the manufacture of belts, necklaces, rings and amulets, though receptacles also were made of faience, as were, in particular, the miniature funerary figures, generally glazed green or blue, of which great numbers were deposited in tombs for the performance of agricultural work on behalf of the deceased person in the after-life.

Joiners and carvers constructed veneered bedsteads, headrests, tables and chairs, chests and jewel-caskets. Small anointing spoons, rouge-pots and domestic utensils were carved out of wood and ivory. During the eighteenth dynasty especially, with its love of refined manners, man's artistry was applied to the production of gorgeous objects, very many of which came to light in the tomb of Tutenkhamon, the son-in-law of Ikhnaton. The combined labours of joiners, workers in stucco, goldsmiths and sculptors were devoted to producing superb works of art, often by the most ingenious methods. The throne of Tutenkhamon and his gold coffin are particularly famous (ill. p. 122).

The Egyptian people's artistic capabilities endured for more than three thousand years – an achievement without historical parallel. Even after the loss of the country's political independence Egyptian art continued to influence neighbouring civilisations, especially the Hellenistic and the Roman. Even

98. Palace of Cnossus. Throne Room with wall paintings (c. 1550 B.C.)

Early Christian and Byzantine art is often inspired by Egyptian models. It was not until the rise of Islam that Egypt lost contact with the antique cultural centres of the West and disappeared from the European horizon for twelve hundred years.

CRETE

Our knowledge of the art of ancient Crete is due primarily to the tireless researches, from 1899 onwards, of the British archaeologist Sir Arthur Evans, excavator of the palace of the legendary king Minos at Cnossus. It has been suggested by Sir Arthur that the ancient Cretan civilisation may be divided into three periods, the Early, Middle and Late Minoan, each of which is in turn subdivided into three stages.

In the Early Minoan period (2700–2000 B.C.) the Neolithic tradition persisted. Domestic architecture – characterised by contiguous apartments, like the cells of a honeycomb, set on stone foundations, and by main walls which were generally straight – remained typically Neolithic. It was apparently from the North African megalithic centre that the circular tomb with projecting stone ledges was adopted, occasionally attaining an over-all diameter of some 43 feet. The most usual type of pottery was the beaked jug, decorated towards the end of the period with spiral patterns. The technique of stone-polishing, derived from Egypt, was characteristic of this era, being responsible for its thin-walled and beautifully veined vessels. Cretan art of the period stays wholly within the Anatolian-Aegean cultural field. It was only at the third stage of Early Minoan that an independent direction was first taken.

In the 'Older Palaces' epoch (Middle Minoan I and II, 2000–1700 B.C.) extensive buildings of palatial type were erected on hillsides at Cnossus, Phaistos and Mallia. Storerooms, living apartments, halls of state, corridors, staircases, light-wells and verandas surrounded a courtyard in such bewildering profusion that they gave rise to the legend of the labyrinth. The pillars which came into use for building construction tapered off towards the base. Wooden props and timber-work were painted in various colours. The palaces were not fortified, thus implying that the island as a whole could be defended by a strong fleet. There were no temples, except for a few chapels in the palaces. The mainly female divinities were worshipped in caves or on mountain peaks.

Applied art reached a particularly high level. Pottery was characterized by spiral and stylized plant-patterns, painted in various colours. It is known as Kamares ware from the place at which it was chiefly found, a cave on Mount Ida. In addition to vessels of stone, faience pots and statuettes, also of variegated hues, were produced. About 1700 B.C. the older palace-buildings were destroyed in a war which may have had some connection with the invasion of Egypt by the Hyksos.

During the period of the 'Later Palaces' (1700–1200 B.C.) the arts came to their first maturity at the third stage of Middle Minoan. The rebuilt palaces were decorated with frescoes and stucco-work representing plants, animals and human beings. The idea behind these works, that of life in its unending varieties of movement, was artistically conveyed. The fully developed style of the 'Older Palaces' was superseded by a new vision. Ancient Cretan art thus took a step which had not occurred to the artists of Egypt and the Near East (ill. 98).

About 1580 B.C., at the first stage of Late Minoan, an earthquake caused great destruction, and annihilated the fleet. Thereafter art flourished yet again in the island, finding particularly characteristic expression in ceramics. Vase-painters covered their rotund clay vessels with paintings of octopus tentacles, grotesquely shaped branches of coral or luxuriating plant growths.

During the second stage of Late Minoan, up to 1400 B.C., the powerful State of Mycenae, situated on the Greek mainland, first equalled, then surpassed Crete in the political, military and cultural spheres. At Cnossus everyday life and artistic activity became permeated by Mycenaean ideas. In fresco painting and pottery this transformation is to be observed in the adoption of a strict scheme of composition, whereby the component parts of vessels are clearly contrasted, as well as in a tendency to ornament.

At the beginning of the third stage of Late Minoan, about 1400 B.C., the Achaeans, Greeks from the Peloponnese, destroyed the palaces and colonized the island. A final wave of destruction, towards 1200 B.C., ended ancient Cretan civilisation. Its legacy passed to the Greeks.

GREEK ART

The Homeric poems had a far-reaching effect upon the history of the mind. The Iliad related the Greek assault upon Troy and the Odyssey the fabulous home-coming of the warriors. Both epics uniquely influenced later Greek civilisation, its religion, its national consciousness – for the language of Homer was no tribal dialect but a literary tongue intelligible to all Greeks and giving them a sense of unity, – its poetry and its intellectual development. It was long supposed that the Iliad and the Odyssey merely transmitted antique myths and sagas. But the exavations of Heinrich Schliemann undermined this premise. For now it became surprisingly clear that the poems described historical events and a rustic and chivalrous Greek society, full of heroic grandeur, which had already vanished by Homer's own time at the turn of the 9th and 8th centuries B.C. The discoveries at Troy in western Anatolia and at the cities of Mycenae and Tiryns in the Peloponnesian province of Argolis revealed a flourishing civilisation dating back to the 2nd millennium B.C.

It is known to-day that in prehistoric times the Greek mainland was the scene of a number of migrations. In the course of the 2nd millennium B.C., Ionians, Aeolians, i. e. Achaeans, and Dorians – in other words, Indo-European tribes from the north – entered the country and mingled with the probably more numerous native population. The power of the Aeolians, who penetrated to the south of the Greek peninsula, is evident in the residential buildings at Mycenae and Tiryns. Their massive, cyclopean stone walls and beehive tombs with 'false', or projecting, lintels are magnificently, if also gloomily, impressive and differ sharply from the casual, attractively dispersed style of architecture in Crete. Objects of applied art were to some extent imported from the latter country. Cretan artists came to work on the mainland. But in time a native style in art developed, marked by more carefully balanced composition in fresco, a severer line and soberer colouring. An ornamental, geometrical feature made its appearance; it is recognisable in vase-painting and on sepulchral stelae in relief. The gold death-masks found in Mycenaean

126

shaft-graves or the famous gold beakers from Vaphio have an impetuous artistic expressiveness which far exceeds anything the Cretans were capable of. The southern migration of the Dorians, prior to 1000 B.C., annihilated Mycenaean civilisation (ill. 128).

The first wave of colonization that followed the Dorian immigration covered the Aegean Islands and the west coast of Asia Minor. A second wave, lasting from the 8th to the 6th century B.C., resulted from the increased population of Greece, which the rugged country could not support. Colonies were then founded along the coast of the Black Sea, in southern Italy and in Sicily. The results for the intellectual development of Greek civilisation were momentous. On the one hand, solidarity among the heirs to the cultural 'estate' began to decline and, on the other, countless new ideas were taken up in the colonies and returned to stimulate the mother-country.

The Greeks had in early times been a pastoral and agricultural people with a very small class of craftsmen. Sovereignty was exercised by kings. But gradually the leading families, rendered independent by the ownership of land, came to form an aristocracy which eventually obtained power. By the beginning of the 6th century B.C., the Greeks had begun to be a nation of traders within which craftsmanship was able to expand. The political and economic centre of gravity shifted from the orbit of the great landowners and agriculturalists to that of the urban population. Despotic rulers or 'tyrants', supported by the lower orders of citizens and peasants in their struggle with the aristocracy, arose in almost all the Greek cities, with the exception of Sparta, where the military regime formed during the prehistoric migrations, with its two warrior kings, lasted a good deal longer. The Greek races produced a great many specimens of the small city-state, the *polis*. This compact unit was apparently regarded by its inhabitants as the most perfect of all possible forms of the State. During the 5th century B.C., democracy, in which the privileges of birth and rank were largely abolished, made more and more progress. At the same time the decay of the ancient piety, the beginnings of which had been noticeable at an even earlier period, was accelerated. The educated classes looked to philosophy for consolation and support, while the general run of the people turned to foreign deities from the East and Egypt, worshipping them in secret rituals and 'mysteries'.

Persia subjugated the Ionian cities of Asia Minor and made two attempts to subdue the Greek mainland by assault. But the Persians were defeated in 490 B.C. at Marathon and in 480 and 479 at Salamis and Plataea. It may be a mere coincidence, but it is not without significance, that at the same time the Carthaginian invasion of Sicily was checked by the Greek colonial cities of the West. Although the Persians had devastated Attica, Athens emerged victorious from the Persian wars and became the leading Power in Greece, a position which the city endeavoured to maintain by fierce fighting against Sparta. Scholars, poets and artists poured into Athens from all the Greek lands, inaugurating that high level of civilisation which was to be of such importance for the destiny of the West, and to which we are still so deeply indebted to-day. But the power of Attica was destroyed by Sparta in the Peloponnesian War of 431–404 B.C. The bloody civil wars which ensued rendered Greece an easy prey to foreign dominion. Philip II of Macedonia put an end to the independence of the city-states in 338 B.C. But the intellectual and artistic talents of the Greek people were not spent, despite their political ruin. The Asiatic and African conquests of Alexander the Great, and the great Hellenistic cities that sprang up as a consequence, relegated the Greek homeland to the fringe of events. The old centres of civilisation in Greece became islands of tradition, sending out cultural influences to affect such new political and economic capitals as Pergamum and Alexandria. Greek civilisation penetrated the Near East and Egypt, and was subjected to Oriental influences. The resultant Hellenistic culture was cosmopolitan, not national. Its scholars, poets and artists lived at the courts of princes, as in the Baroque Age. Art was no longer produced by the people as a whole but depended entirely for its maintenance or decline upon the personality of the ruler.

ARCHITECTURE

Little is known of the more ancient religious buildings of the Greeks. They were erected in open country, wherever the divinity had manifested himself in some outward event such as a clap of thunder. The temple was the god's residence. The community assembled in front of the building to offer sacrifice. The archaic form of the temple was still that of the antique *megaron* (q. v.). The ritual image inhabited by the deity stood in the 'holy of holies', the *adyton* or *cella*, facing east. The eastern vestibule or *pronaos* contained two pilasters, the *antae*, posted between the two extremities of the flanking walls. Archaic temple architecture included, as well as the *antae* type, the peripteral, with a circular colonnade surrounding the *cella*. The colonnade added to the majesty of the building and enhanced its representational character by the impressive contrast between plain wall and serried columns. The porch admitting the visitor to the consecrated ground gave a diagonal view of the temple, so that its full plastic effect could be grasped. The Greeks attributed less importance to the interior, their sense of space not equalling their sense of form. The *cella* was therefore provided, for the sake of symmetry, with a rear vestibule, the *opisthodomos,* resembling the *pronaos.* The original rigidly orientated oblong of the main hall was transformed, by symmetry and colonnades on all sides, into a plastic entity complete in itself (ill. 99–102).

The change from construction in sun-dried brick and timber to stone architecture proceeded slowly. The development can be traced in the older temples at Olympia, where wooden columns were gradually replaced by stone, so that their appearance cannot have been uniform. The substitution of stone for timber was made with exemplary fidelity to the general character of the building. Even the application of a roof of large and heavy slabs of clay to the stone temple was successful. The original steep thatched roof was flattened, being given gabled form.

Greek sculpture, like architecture, was rooted in plastic sensibility. The stone temple with its hewn blocks, its pillars consisting of separate drums and the various shapes of its timber-work, was carved by a sculptor. The building, like the statue, seems to pulse with vitality and to breathe in space. Justifiably, the Greek temple has been regarded as an organism, resembling a human body with individual limbs only to be appreciated when working in combination. Its proportions, the relations between its measurements, were derived by the Greek architect from those of the human body.

There were at first two main orders (q. v.) of temple architecture or types of columns (ill. 62). These were the Doric and the Ionic, which the writers of late Antiquity were already able to distinguish. It was not until later that a third order, the Corinthian, was added. But since the mainland was for centuries ruled by the Dorian race, the principal temples in any of its cities had to be erected in the Doric style. It is certain, however, that the difference between Doric and Ionic temples is based on the difference of character between these two mutually fertilising sections of the Greek people.

A Doric building is erected on the *krepidoma*, a substructure consisting originally of several, and eventually of three, high steps. The rows of columns at once conceal and reveal the sanctuary. The Doric column has no pedestal. It rises straight from the stylobate (the upper step) and carries a number – increasing from 16 to 20 in the course of time – of closely set flutes or grooves, separated by sharp edges. The column swells as it rises (entasis) and then tapers to receive the weight of the roof-tree on its slenderer top section. The ratio of thickness to height is fixed. The original squat and powerful shape in time developed into a lighter and more lofty form.

The Doric temple achieves its effect by the precision with which its proportions are worked out. This largely accounts for the harmonious impression conveyed. For the rest, it is due to the interplay of support and weight, of vertical and horizontal members, of swelled columns and the cubic form of the *cella* and foundations. Mortar was not used; instead, each architectural component was integrated with another with the greatest care. Each existed in its own right and yet blended with the building as a whole. The structure was enlivened by colour, especially in its upper portions. As a rule the pillars were

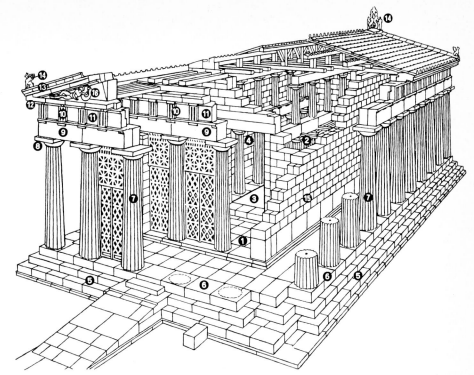

99. *Temple of Aphaea in Aegina.*
Beginning of 5th century B.C.
Doric Peripteros. Reconstruction

1 *Pronaos*
2—4 *Naos or cella divided into*
3 aisles by 2 rows of columns
each on a different level
5 *krepidoma or krepis (3-step-*
ped substructure)
6 *stylobate (top step)*
7 *Doric columns*
8 *Doric capital, consisting of*
the echinos (convex mould-
ing) and abacus (roofing slab)
9 *epistyle (Latin architrave*
i. e. beam)
10 *triglyph (slab with 3 slots)*
11 *metope (space decorated with*
architectural sculpture)
10 and 11 *Doric frieze*
12 *geison (cornice)*
13 *cyma (gable moulding with*
gutter)
14 *akroterion (ornamental fea-*
ture of roof)
15 *exterior wall of cella*
16 *sculptured gable*

covered by yellow stucco, and the larger temples, especially after the Classical period, were provided with marble roofs. The buildings seemed to be self-contained, miniature worlds, full of a hidden vitality, confronting the grandeur of Nature, to which they were essentially akin (ill. 102).

The Roman architect Vitruvius, writing in the time of the Emperor Augustus, described the Doric order of architecture as masculine and the Ionic as feminine.

Only scanty traces remain of the huge Ionic structures of the Archaic period. At Ephesus the temple of Artemis, the virgin goddess of the chase, which had been erected shortly before the Persian Wars, i. e. prior to 490 B.C., was burnt down in 356 B.C. by Herostratus, in the hope that this act would make him famous. The temple of Hera at Samos, the Heraion (ill. 101), was destroyed by the Persians. But it is possible to infer that the Ionic temple, like the Doric, owed its origin to the megaron. At Ephesus the vestibule still had a rear annexe. But at a later date the more ample *pronaos* alone, with four rows of columns, was preferred. While the supporting function of the Doric column is obvious, the Ionic seems merely decorative. Ionic temples are predominantly *dipteroi,* in other words, structures surrounded by two rows of columns.

The Ionic column is one of the most marvellous fruits of the Greek genius. It was originally designed to suggest a plant growing in marshy soil, such as a reed, papyrus or lotus, native to Meso-potamia and Egypt, but not to the rocky land of Greece. But the Ionian Greeks were not content simply to reproduce their Oriental model. They would have considered it blasphemous so much as to suggest

100. *Temple of Zeus at Olympia (470–456 B.C.) Doric*
peripteros. Nuclear construction with double antae.
Ground plan. Architect, Libon of Elis.

1 *Pronaos*
2 *Naos*
3 *Opisthodomos*

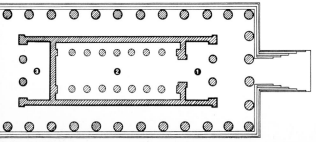

101. *Temple of Hera at Samos (mid 6th century B.C.)*
Ionic Dipteros. Ground plan. Architects, Rhoecus and
Theodorus.

1 *Pronaos, 3-aisled, 2 cella (probably never roofed)*

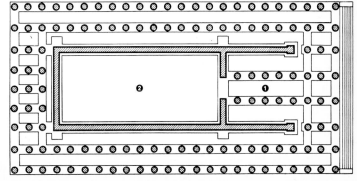

102. Parthenon on the Acropolis at Athens, from N.W. (448–432 B.C.). Architect Ictinus

the stalk of a plant in constructing the supporting components of their temples. They accordingly gave their columns a symbolic, instead of an architectonic function, not regarding them as supports but as images of human nature, human in form and therefore figural sculpture. Thus the Attic-Ionic temple of the ancient snake-god, Erechtheus, the Erechtheum, on the Acropolis, was actually provided with a Porch of Maidens, the entablature being supported by female figures, or korai (ill. 122).

The city-states of the Greek mainland, the Sicilian colonies and those in southern Italy used the Doric style in their building during the Archaic period, the 6th century B.C. But in the following century, the Classical period, the more subtle, decorative, Ionic style replaced the Doric. Athens eventually constructed the last of her ritual buildings in the purest Ionic manner. For example, the Parthenon, the marble temple erected by Ictinus and Callicrates between 448 and 432 B.C. in honour of the tutelary goddess of the city, belongs to the Doric Order, though Ionic elements have been added to it (ill. 102). Classical features are evident in the masterly stonemasons' technique, in the perfect balance of architectonic forces – measurements of supporting members and weight being precisely calculated – and in the noble proportions of the building. An animated artistic effect is produced by the use of curves. Thus stylobate and architrave do not run horizontally but on a slight curve, the corners of the four exterior sides lying on a lower level than the centre. The walls of the *cella* and their surrounding columns incline inwards, the deviation from the vertical of the columnar axis at the top amounting to 2.7 in., while the corner columns incline diagonally towards the corners of the *cella*. These subtleties are scarcely apprehended by the eye; the observer becomes aware of them intuitively, so that he has the impression that the building is a living organism.

During the last quarter of the 5th century B.C., the Doric and Ionic language of form coalesced, at Athens, into an Attic-Ionic style; this gradually absorbed and replaced the hitherto clearly differentiated divisions in the realm of Greek art. The small Temple of Victory and the Erechtheum on the Acropolis are works in the new manner, which is also responsible for the invention of the Corinthian capital. The acanthus leaves of the latter inaugurate the botanical style of decoration destined to become so important. In the Erechtheum we notice a manner of conceiving space that differs from that of the mature Classical period (450–430 B.C.). It is true that architectural concentration of several centres of ritual involved a departure from the traditional form of the temple, yet the modifications seem to have gone beyond what was necessary to serve the purposes of the centre. The columns, for instance, are not placed all round the core, as in the case of the *peripteros*, but emphasise distinct parts of it.

This new conception of space continued to be influential in the post-Classical epoch, the 4th century B.C., when the Corinthian capital attained its full development (cf. ill. 62). Columns with this type of capital were first used in the interior of circular buildings such as the *tholos* at Epidaurus, which were popular on account of the solemn and inspiring character of the area enclosed. The decorative element, clearly visible in the lavish employment of ornamental plant-forms, was also applied to strictly architectural components. Building found new outlets in the erection of theatres, gymnasia and assembly halls (ill. 81).

Important results were achieved in the large-scale planning of cities. Markets and squares were encircled by rows of columns and halls. But there was no consciousness in this connection, as there was in Rome, of a rhythmic association between individual buildings, markets and streets. Massive temples arose, but no truly creative progress was made. A characteristic form was the *pseudodipteros*, which omitted interior columns and thus consisted of a single ample hall surrounding the *cella* on all sides. An important feature of this architecture was the correspondence of the exterior articulation of the building with its interior conformation. The semicircle was only used tentatively and then simply as the rounded termination (apse) of a longitudinal space and as detached arches for gates and windows. The vault was known, but as yet it played no part as a medium of expression.

SCULPTURE

There had been miniature anthropomorphic sculpture, representing human beings, on the mainland of Greece and its islands in prehistoric times, as also in the 9th and 8th centuries B.C. Monumental sculpture, which most clearly expresses the character of Greek art, could not have been directly derived from these early statuettes. We must assume that new principles were adopted. The Homeric poems had described the gods as resembling human beings both mentally and physically. In due course men wanted to see images of these deities, which would bring them nearer. But it was in particular the idea of equating mental and physical qualities – a conception which gave a peculiar significance to the Olympic Games established in 776 B.C. – that led to the rise of monumental sculpture. This resulted in two types of images: the *kouros*, the standing naked boy or youth, and the *kore*, the clothed female figure.

It is no accident that legend ascribes the invention of large-scale sculpture to Daedalus – his name means 'ingenious-moulder' – who worked, like the similarly named inventor of flying, on the island of Crete – an island that had played the part of intermediary, ever since early times, between the East and Europe. Accordingly, in the 'daedal' art of the middle of the 7th century B.C. and after, we find the *kouros* represented in a straight-legged, striding posture, the arms hanging at the sides, with clenched fists. The hair of his head is gracefully curled. The eyes gaze straight ahead and the lips smile enigmatically (ill. 4, 104). Behind the symmetry and the severity of the frontal presentation of the figure stands Egyptian sculpture, which must have been the model for it. Yet despite all the exterior signs of kinship the decisive advance made by Greek art remains recognisable. The daedal statue is an isolated work, not associated, like the Egyptian, with architecture. The *kouros* is completely rounded and can be viewed from all four sides, like a column. The Egyptian figure, on the other hand, cannot be seen from the back. The Greek statue of the Archaic period (650–500 B.C.) is a ritual image, intended to represent a god or hero, or still more frequently a sacred or memorial figure on a tomb. It is full of vitality, feeling and determination, held in check by the severity of its shape and thus facilitating the expression of inner steadfastness and dignity.

During the 6th century B.C. the art of sculpture was practised throughout Greece. Instead of limestone or other porous materials the artists used the hard marble which they found on the islands and in Asia Minor. Very clear differences can be seen between the styles of the various localities. The Cheramyes female statue dedicated to Hera in Samos about 560 B.C. is a typical work in the Ionic style, columnar in form. The subtle folds of the garments fall in fluted, flexible lines, softly moulding

131

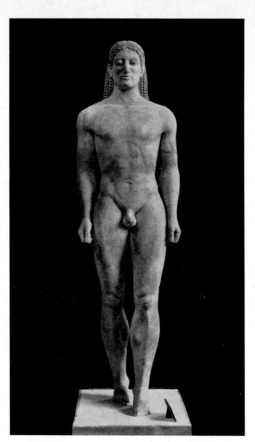

103. *Kore, dedicated to the Samian Hera by Cheramyes (c. 560 B.C.)*

104. *Kouros of Anavyssos (c. 520 B.C.)*

105. *Charioteer from Delphi (c. 474 B.C.). Bronze*

the curves of the figure to indicate its beauty. If this Ionic image, rising like the tall, slender trunk of a tree, is compared with that of a standing youth at Anavyssos in southern Attica, which may have been made about 520 B.C., the regional difference of style can be recognised in the powerful build and greater structural rigidity of the latter (see ill. 103).

The custom of dedicating statues of young women to the sanctuary on the Acropolis grew up during the second half of the 6th century B.C. After the destruction of the city and its citadel by the Persians under Xerxes in 480 B.C. the ruins, including the fragments of many statues, were used to level the site for rebuilding. Modern excavation has recovered a number of these Kore figures. The graceful, girlish forms, in festal garb, radiant with youth, are infinitely fascinating, full of the bright, imperishable magic of femininity. The paint – for both Greek sculpture in the round and also reliefs were painted – is still well preserved in places and adds considerably to the effect produced.

Early Classical art, the austere style of 500–450 B.C., owed its origin to man's release from the bonds of myth and his recognition of the value of the individual personality. The gable sculptures from the Doric temple of the goddess Aphaea on the island of Aegina, which – as restored by Thorwaldsen between 1815 and 1817 – are among the principal works preserved in the Glyptothek Museum at Munich, provide tangible evidence of the new outlook, in that the stature of the warriors is no different from that of the deities. By their nobility they break the formerly prevalent rule of frontal presentation.

The individual art styles of the various regions are still maintained. At Athens the statue of a boy, ascribed to the sculptor Kritios, instinct with naturalistic animation, solved a problem that was new to sculpture at the time, namely, that of ponderation, or the harmonious distribution of weight in the body. The art of the Greek colonies in Sicily and southern Italy is represented by the life-size bronze figure of a charioteer (ill. 105). It was part of a group portraying a four-horse chariot, a votive gift that stood in the shrine of Apollo at Delphi. The inner power of this monument was concentrated in its

132

106. MYRON, *Athena (mid 5th cent. B.C.).* Copy

107. PRAXITELES, *Aphrodite of Cnidos (c. 350 B.C.).* Copy

108. LYSIPPUS, *The Scraper (Apoxyomenos). Marble copy based on bronze original (c. 330 B.C.)*

vertical axis, from which the impressive tranquillity of the tall, erect figure derives. The folds of the long robe seem designed to keep the outside world at a distance; yet the steady forward gaze and the outstretched fist that grasps the reins penetrate the surrounding space.

Since the 8th century B.C., games had been held at Olympia in honour of the god Zeus. Every four years the most prominent of the Greek communities competed against one another in peaceful athletic rivalry. Between 470 and 456 B.C., a Doric temple of large dimensions, enclosed by a colonnade (ill. 85, 100), was erected in honour of the god. It had been designed by the architect Libon of Elis. The plastic ornament not only marks the highest level attained by the austere style but is also a masterpiece of Greek art. The legendary events depicted are made to seem like real ones. The complete correspondence here achieved between the language of art and that of Nature serves to define the Classical manner. But we must not take the realism in question to be merely a matter of naturalistic representation, which is evident. An inward truth also permeates these works of art, which accordingly have to be rendered with precise harmony and in obedience to natural law.

The mature Classical art of Greece (450–430 B.C.) is practically identical with the Attic style. For during this period Athens, led by the eminent statesman Pericles (499–429 B.C.), acquired the status of a Great Power in the Aegean. The city was built up on a lavish scale. The Parthenon on the Acropolis was decorated, under the artistic supervision of the Attic sculptor Pheidias, with architectural carvings that mirrored the entire Greek world of the 5th century B.C. (ill. 130). Ninety-two metopes depicted the battles and heroic deeds of legendary times, whereby an orderly existence for mankind was ensured. The frieze, well over 500 feet long, showed the ritual procession in honour of the goddess, which amounts to a self-portrait of the Attic people. On the gables the birth of Athena and her struggle with Poseidon for possession of the land of Attica were represented, implying the eternal rule of the gods. Mature Classical art is expressed by the complete identification of a natural object with its

133

portrayal as contrived by art, of psychological experience with its artistic shaping. The sculptures must have presented a most animated appearance when adorned with colour.

Pheidias made a colossal gold and ivory (chryselephantine) statue of Athena, completed in 438 B.C., for the Parthenon. It later fell a victim to lean times. This artist's fame rested mainly upon this work and the equally colossal statue of Zeus at Olympia.

During the short-lived period of the mature Classical style two other important sculptors, Myron at Athens and Polycleitus from Sicyon in the district of Argos, were active. Two of the many bronzes by Myron, the Discobolus, representing an athlete hurling the discus, and the group of Athena with the satyr Marsyas, have survived in Roman copies (ill. 106). In the Discobolus Myron exhibited sheer movement. It is significant that Hellenistic critics found his works lacking in emotional power. But Classical art was not able to reproduce just physical and mental effort, since the ideal human being had to be shown in all his outward and inward beauty. The Greek of the Classical period equated the beautiful with the divine. The works of Polycleitus are known to us through marble copies dating from the Roman imperial period. For example, the Doryphorus, the youth carrying a spear, has a rhythmic character, from the slightly bent head to the feet, which comes from the counterpoising shift of the weight of the body almost entirely from the relaxed to the supporting leg (ill. 5). The body is given a slight curved flexion, thus restoring the equilibrium lost by the forward stride. The proportion of the powerfully built limbs in relation to one another and to the frame as a whole are exactly right. This statue was known as the 'canon' of the human figure, possibly, because Polycleitus had composed a treatise on the symmetrical features of the body.

Movement and feeling are never expressed for their own sake in the Classical figure, nor are they dissipated in space. They are always subordinated to the principle of the self-sufficient and circumscribed image.

The art of the late Classical period (430–400 B.C.) continued to adhere to the traditional style of the Parthenon. The majority of the artists who had taken part in the construction and sculptural adornment of that mighty edifice scattered to the four winds as soon as the work was completed. Just as the Ionic spirit had influenced the building of the Parthenon and the Propylaea, the gateway to the Acropolis, during the maturity of Classical art, so in the next period Ionian artists came under Attic influence; this is seen, for example, in the hovering figure of Victory, by Paeonius, placed in front of the temple of Zeus at Olympia about 420 B.C., and in the sculptures of a sepulchral monument at Xanthus in Lycia, dating from about 400 B.C. and known as the 'Nereid Monument'. The architectural style of sculpture derived from the Parthenon here competes to admirable effect with the Ionian mastery of movement. The impulsive forward movement of the figures is reinforced by the abundance of subtle folds of drapery clinging to the bodies and fluttering backwards.

The post-Classical period of the 4th century cannot be precisely dated. Transitions are less clear-cut. Where godlike human beauty used to be represented by means of self-sufficient, circumscribed images, 'baroque'-type animated figures now appear, in which physical beauty is subordinated to the expression of inward feelings. At the time of exhausting conflict between the Greek city-states, ending with their loss of freedom and subjection to Macedonia, art took to the portrayal of emotion. Special attention was paid to the face, the mirror of psychological tension. Where the head of a Classical statue had formed part of a whole, it now expressed the personality, thus inaugurating portraiture.

From the point of view of Classical art the emphasis on the individual features distinguishing a certain person or type leads to a weakening of the plastic element. The all-embracing aspect of the figure is lost. On the other hand, through the accentuated movement and the shift of the centre of gravity from the middle axis to the peripheral region it grows out into the surrounding space. The Hermes of Praxiteles holding the child Dionysus, from the temple of Hera at Olympia, needs support, owing to

134

the displacement into space of the figure's centre of gravity. In such cases the statue abandons its self-absorption and declares itself to the beholder, enlisting his collaboration.

Three masters and their schools are of decisive importance for 4th-century Greek sculpture. They are Scopas of Paros, Praxiteles of Athens and Lysippus of Sicyon. Scopas participated in the construction of the massive sepulchral monument at Halicarnassus, commissioned by King Mausolus of Caria (d. 353 B.C.). This sculptor's statue of Heracles with a club, unfortunately only known to us through later copies, turns towards the beholder with a gaze that seems to solicit interest in the suffering of the figure.

The Cnidian Aphrodite, like most Greek sculpture, survives only in a Roman copy. It was regarded in Antiquity as the masterpiece of Praxiteles and was in fact the first large-scale statue of a female nude (ill. 107). The modest attitude and half-closed eyes of the figure, shown stepping into a bath, as well as the subtly handled marble surfaces designed to catch the light, suggest maidenly rather than divine sensibility. In the Hermes, mentioned above, we possess an original work by Praxiteles.

The Apoxyomenus of Lysippus, a youth removing the oil and the dust of the arena from his body with an iron strigil, masters space with an outstretched arm (ill. 108). The same sculptor is said to have made a number of statues of Alexander the Great (ill. 126). Greek art of the 4th century B.C. was capable of portraying both the outward aspect and the character of a particular person; but it invariably took the form of a statue, for Greek portraiture never attempted a bust.

The representational resources of art in the post-Classical period enabled sepulchral sculpture to reach a high level. The numerous figures in scenes of mourning families illustrate the whole gamut of emotions from hopeless grief to the relief of resignation. Admittedly, the relief loses its basic character, for the figures become more and more rounded and finally break away from their 'ground' to become virtually free-standing (ill. 80).

Hellenistic sculpture, beginning in the 3rd century B.C., went to extreme lengths in its desire to express passionate emotion. To this end it cultivated a close correspondence with nature and did not shrink from exhibiting ugliness, as in the 'Old Drunkard' of the Glyptothek Museum at Munich and the 'Old Market Woman' of the Metropolitan Museum in New York (ill. 7). The Hellenistic style reached a peak at Pergamum. The struggle with the Celts of Galatia inspired such realistic, space-challenging groups as the 'Dying Gaul'. The frieze of the great altar of Zeus at Pergamum, representing the battle of the gods against the giants, displays a tumultuous affray between massive figures whose faces are distorted by frenzy. Both Greek plasticity and Oriental fantasy characterize the work.

By the middle of the 2nd century B.C., talented craftsmen were also beginning to produce attractive genre sculpture, as exemplified by the 'Boy with the Goose', the 'Thorn Extractor' and 'Beggar' motifs. Portrait sculpture exhibits an integrated interpretation in its main classifications representing rulers and intellectual leaders. But it grows more and more personal in style, revealing the most intimate emotions, often in repulsive fashion. The extremes to which art can carry the horrors of naturalism are illustrated in the bronze 'Boxer', by Apollonius of Athens. A further attempt to present legend in art was made by the Rhodian sculptor Hagesandros and his sons in the 'Laocoon' group (ill. 125).

PAINTING, VASE-PAINTING AND THE CRAFTS

The great paintings of Greece have disappeared. But that such works existed is proved by many references in literature which praise them very highly. Until about 400 B.C. the colours used were white, black or dark blue, red, yellow and their various blendings. Green, pink, violet and other delicate secondary hues were then added to the palette. The most important masters of the pre-Classical period were Polygnotus, active between 475 and 450 B.C., whose compositions with many figures had a great

135

reputation, and Parrhasius, who worked in Classical and late-Classical times, and is said to have been the first to achieve the effect of emotion in his pictures. He and his contemporaries Zeuxis and Apollodorus tried to improve delineation in depth. But it was the Theban school of painting, which flourished in the first half of the 4th century B.C., that first taught perspective. In the second half of the century the most influential painters, only familiar to us through literary sources, were Apelles and Nicias. Hardly anything is known of Hellenistic painting.

The greatness and importance of the art are reflected in vase-painting. In the 11th and 10th centuries B.C. amphorae of definite shape, i.e. vessels of spherical form tapering to the base, with a narrow, projecting neck and two handles, were already being produced. Their decoration not only suited the structure but actually dictated it. The geometrical ornament composed of straight lines and circles lent a lively effect to the plastic organisation of the vase (cf. ill. 136).

The mature geometric style of the 9th and 8th centuries B.C. introduced the decorative motif of the scroll, giving a rhythmic animation to the body of the vessel. Friezes of animals, and also of human beings, were inserted in the geometrical ornamentation. As the vessels were intended to serve as cinerary urns, the subjects depicted were funeral ceremonies and burials. The definitely geometrical shape of the vases clearly indicates the starting-point of a development culminating during the next century in the Classical style of Greek sculpture and architecture, imbued as the latter also was with sculptural feeling (ill. p. 139).

The style of the 7th century B.C., characterized by Oriental influence coming by way of imports of textiles and metallic work, added foliage and rosettes, beasts of prey, sphinxes and griffins to its decoration. In water-jars from Athens, vases from Corinth, large amphorae from the island of Melos and jugs from Rhodes the idea of man's defeat by ubiquitous Nature can be traced, as well as the liberation of artistic talents long repressed (ill. 109).

Towards the end of the 7th century the black-figured style developed in Corinth and Athens. Pictures of gods and heroes were painted by the glazing method, in black, on a reddish-brown ground. After the middle of the 6th century B.C., the potteries and studios of Athens come unmistakably to the fore. It was then that artists began to sign their works. The potter Ergotimus and the painter Clitias are named on the François Vase in Florence, named after its finder. One of the chief masters of the black-figured style was the potter and painter Exekias, responsible for a bowl displaying a splendid picture of the sea-voyage of the wine-god Dionysus (ill. p. 151).

The red-figured style, in which the background was given a black glaze and the picture portion left free, flourished in the last third of the 6th century (ill. p. 151). The figures themselves were painted in with a fine brush. The new technique permitted more precise delineation, and so enriched the pictorial content. The Attic vase-painters were mainly interested in the narrative depicted. They enjoyed reproducing the human, the all too human, features of their gods and heroes. About 510 B.C., Andocides painted Heracles eating, and Euthymides showed the hero Theseus in a scene of rape. Vases by the painters Cleophrades and Brygos are known which illustrate the wild orgies of Dionysus and his troop of worshippers.

In the 5th century B.C., vase-painting came to its most mature expression, particularly in Athens. The names and pseudonyms of the painters are legion, and they decorated countless vessels. As, however, vase-painting was unable to keep pace with the further development of fresco and panel-painting, which eventually achieved composition in depth and characterization in figure-drawing, it declined into mass-production at the beginning of the 4th century B.C. and so lost its creative power. Later, it flourished for a short time in southern Italy and Etruria.

The clay of which the vases were made could be put to manifold uses. Baked, as terra-cotta, it served for roof and gutter tiling, gable facing, roof capitals and metopes. Great numbers of miniature

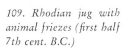

109. Rhodian jug with animal friezes (first half 7th cent. B.C.)

110. Niobid painter (c. 450 B.C.). Niobid bowl, red figured style

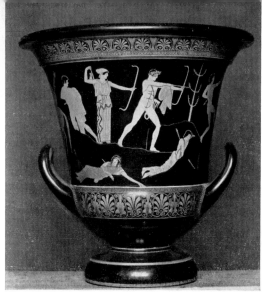

figures of animals and human beings in terra-cotta were produced, the most beautiful being the robed statuettes of Tanagra in Boeotia, dating from the 4th century B.C.

Since the 7th century B.C., bronze had been employed for the manufacture of cauldrons on tripods, water-jars, personal ornaments, such as bracelets and fibulae, and hand-mirrors. Gold was used for the production of small decorative fillets or headbands, embellished with granulation after geometrical motifs had come in, as well as for ear-rings, diadems, pendants and ingeniously intertwined belts and chains. Granulation was replaced in the 5th century by enamelling in various colours and in the Hellenistic era, after 300 B.C., by precious and semi-precious stones.

During the 7th century B.C., coins were struck in Lydia, Asia Minor, and subsequently throughout Greek territory. They are distinguished, especially during the 6th and 5th centuries, by the beauty of their polymorphous images. Greek execution was also outstanding in the other handicrafts, such as the glyptic arts (q. v.), glass-blowing, textile weaving and cabinet-making.

Greek art really came to an end when the Greek world was absorbed into the Roman Empire. But it long survived to perform its new task. It is still a beneficial influence in modern times.

ETRUSCAN ART

At the beginning of the last millennium B.C. the indigenous population of the Apennine peninsula, consisting of many races, had not achieved any cultural success worth mentioning. The Etruscans were the first, in the 8th century B.C., to maintain a high standard of civilisation, during which an art derived from Greek sources evolved.

The early history of the people is still unknown. Scholars conjecture that the tribe emerged from a mixture of races. This supposition would explain the various elements, ancient Aegean, Italian, Oriental (from Asia Minor), ancient Central European, Greek and finally both Indo-European, and non-Indo-European, to be met with in Etruscan civilisation. The Greek alphabet it employed is certainly decipherable, but the meaning of the inscriptions can only be understood in a few cases. Etruscan rule extended in the 7th century B.C. over western Central Italy as far south as the Tiber and in the following century from Salerno to the river Adige in the north. From the 5th century onwards, the political and economic power of Etruria declined steadily, in the face of Greek and Carthaginian pressure and owing to the rise of Rome.

The term 'Etruscan art' has only been in use for about a generation. Archaeologists recognised, in the early years of the 20th century, that the finer works of art excavated in Etruria could definitely not be regarded in every case as imports, but to a considerable extent as of native, in other words of Etruscan, origin. In many of the discovered paintings, sculptures and works of applied art it was believed that elements recalling modern practice could be identified. Hence such epithets as impressionist, abstract, cubist or surrealist were hastily applied to them. This assumed affinity influenced contemporary art and still does so. It also spurred archaeologists on to further studies of Etruscan art. Such research has become almost a popular pastime. For the fascination of the enigmatic and strange invariably arouses curiosity and a desire to participate.

No logical development of style can be traced in Etruscan art. It undoubtedly owes much to, and participates actively in, Greek artistic developments. But the model is not slavishly copied, in a continuous way. We find, in addition to crude but very close imitations, magnificent works of art showing only formal Greek influence but otherwise typically Etruscan. Indigenous, ancient Italian characteristics are very frequently combined, in the same work, with Greek elements of various stylistic tendencies.

The deposits of mineral ore in Etruria are the material source of many bronze statuettes, defensive and offensive weapons and tools of all descriptions. Large-scale carvings also exist, such as the Capitoline she-wolf or the Todi Mars. But the Etruscan artists preferred to work in clay. Temples were adorned with life-size figures on the gables. The Apollo of Veii, dated about 500 B.C., powerfully formed and quite un-Greek in its vigour, comes from one such group.

One of the main objects of modelling in clay was the production of sarcophagi or urns. The marked Etruscan cult of the dead may be of Egyptian origin. At all events the sepulchral art of Etruria is highly significant. The dead man is represented on the lid of the sarcophagus or urn, reclining as on a couch, often in the company of his wife. The demand for a pictorial reminder of the deceased inaugurated portraiture (ill. 114). The Hellenistic portrait, which had a different origin, may have provided the final impetus in this direction. There is no suggestion of Greek formal austerity and idealism in the Etruscan heads, where individual features are treated with such merciless realism that the effect is almost terrifying. Yet, the so-called head of Brutus, in bronze, conveys the man's character as well as his features. Etruscan portraiture is one of the greatest achievements of this people.

The underground sepulchral chambers are adorned with wall-paintings in fresco (ill. p. 140). They depict scenes of daily life such as banquets, festivals and funeral ceremonies. Greek vase-painting may have inspired the pictures of mythological character. But the figural element is often subordinated to profuse botanical ornament. There is no attempt at any illusion of space. The forms are sharply outlined and remain two-dimensional.

The rectangular funerary apartments dug into the earth are surmounted on the surface by conical heaps of soil. The temple architecture is not of Greek origin, at any rate in its ground-plan, but peculiarly Etruscan in character. The ground-plan is practically square, consisting of a long *cella* in three sections and a pillared vestibule. The columns line the walls of the *cella*, resulting in three naves, the central one being wider than the lateral ones. The temple is surrounded on three sides by a colonnade and has no rear elevation or aspect. The building is orientated towards the congregation.

ROMAN ART

The Etruscan legacy remained influential in Roman art long after the destruction of the power and capabilities of the nation. But Roman civilisation depended for its development above all on the force of the Greek example, derived from the Greek colonies founded, from the 8th century B.C. onwards, in central and southern Italy and in Sicily. It was reinforced in course of the 3rd century B.C. by the Roman conquest of all Italy. The subjugation of the Hellenistic lands of the eastern Mediterranean gave Roman civilisation a 'Graecianised' cast.

138

Attic amphora (c. 800 B.C.). – Geometrical style

Etruscan wall painting: Flute player *from the Tomb of the Leopards in Tarquinia (480–470 B.C.)*

In the 2nd century B.C. Rome, as the capital of a powerful empire, became the centre of the then-known world. Greek works of art were imported to adorn the city. Greek artists either produced original works in Rome or copied Greek masterpieces at the orders of the State or private patrons. Side by side with this Greek art in Rome, which soon assumed a Roman colouring and official status, a popular Roman art, barbarous from the Greek point of view, practised naturalistic portraiture and a primitive, crudely descriptive type of painting.

ARCHITECTURE

A specifically Roman type of architecture had already come into being in republican times from the fusion of Hellenistic and Etrusco-Italian characteristics. Temples were built on the Etruscan ground-plan, comprising the *cella* and the pillared vestibule. Orientation of the edifice was achieved by stressing frontal elevation. The heart of the building, planned on Etruscan lines, was both disguised and enriched by Greek ornament. Roman architects preferred the Corinthian order of columns (q. v.) on account of its lively detail. By means of an apse invisible from the outside the ritual image was kept well within the interior chamber, where recesses and columns, sometimes on several levels, were used to break up the space. For centuries, the conservative Romans would not allow arcades or vaulting in their temples.

The ground-plan of the temple was repeated in the square or forum. The longitudinal axis of the forum coincided with that in the temple, while the lateral halls ran parallel to the walls of the *cella*, only offset (ill. 123).

Basilicas were situated by the forum, serving the purposes of courts of justice and markets. The basilica was made up of several aisles, the central one of greater breadth and height (ill. 44, 45). Light entered by a series of windows above the roofing of the side-aisles. The Basilica Julia, built in republican times, had two flanking floors, and three – with galleries at intervals – in the loftier central aisle. The use of mortar eventually led to the construction of the arch and vault, as in the Pantheon (ill. 113). The sober and practical Romans were very interested in technical problems.

They made use of rows of arches supported upon pillars in their engineering works, aqueducts (ill. 119) and bridges, and also used this principle in their theatre construction. The piers had columns superposed – of the Doric Order at ground level, of the Ionic on the first floor and of the Corinthian above that, as in the Colosseum (ill. 112). The triumphal arch belongs to the same type of architecture, employing arch and architrave, as in the Arch of Constantine (ill. 111). The final phase of Roman basilica building is represented by the Basilica of Constantine, dedicated in A. D. 315, which was essentially a covered-in forum. The middle aisle had cross-vaulting with a span of some 80 feet, and the adjoining rooms barrel vaulting of about 63 feet.

The Roman architects, technicians and engineers, were able to give their imaginations free rein in the construction of the huge imperial palaces

111. Triumphal Arch of Constantine, Rome (A. D. 312–315)

112. Colosseum, Rome (Flavian amphitheatre, second half 1st cent. A. D.)

113. Pantheon, Rome (A. D. 120–125)

and public baths. In such building complexes the changes were rung with axial and transverse arrangements of rectangular and circular rooms, while flat roofs alternated with domed, barrel or cross-vaulting.

SCULPTURE

Roman sculpture begins with the portrait, based ultimately on the cult of the dead. At one time a wax impression of the features of the dead person was taken, shown to those participating in the obsequies and preserved for posterity. It was therefore natural for the Romans at an early date to employ the methods evolved by the Greek artists for perpetuating the images of their ancestors in stone or bronze. Likenesses were portrayed during the period of the republic by precise reproduction of the outward aspect of the model, by a grasp of the characteristic features (ill. 115) and by reference to the career of the deceased. The hard faces, of peasant type, seem to confront the world with gloom and anxiety. The aura of death imposes respect upon the beholder. Representative portraits are those of Augustus (31 B.C. – A. D. 14), which clearly reveal the influence of Classical Greece. The splendid memorial to that ruler, the so-called Augustus of Primaporta, imitates the style of the Classical Greek sculptor Polycleitus, yet the deliberate idealization and lifting of the subject out of time and space, in the Hellenistic manner, is unmistakable (ill. 120). The reliefs of the Altar of Peace, dedicated to the Imperial goddess of peace in A. D. 9, illustrate a procession and sacrificial scenes, as well as botanical motifs. The somewhat stiffly designed figures suggest dignity and a talent for unemotional description.

The Flavian style of the last third of the 1st century A. D., so called after the emperors who belonged to the Flavian family, Vespasian, Titus and Domitian, is pictorially effective. The portraits are extremely life-like, owing to the subtle treatment of surfaces. The curling hair of the female heads and the many folds of the togas worn by the men cause the interplay of light and shade, so loosening the plastic form.

The enormously long strip of reliefs on the Column of Trajan relates the emperor's achievements and those of his troops (ill. 134). This chronicle in stone is inscribed in popular style. As a story in pictures has to be told concisely and clearly, purely pictorial effects are avoided. The romantic taste of the emperor Hadrian for Greek art arose from his realization that a cultural phase was then drawing to its close. In the statue of Antinous, the handsome Bithynian boy beloved by the emperor, the formula of Praxiteles is revived in Roman guise.

Art in the second half of the 2nd century A. D. expressed heightened emotion. Refinement of sculptural technique enabled portraits to be rendered with more impact. The treatment of the marble surfaces in the representation of hair and beards contrasts with that employed on the parts indicating flesh, which are meticulously polished. Eyes are chiselled with particular care. The portrait bust of

142

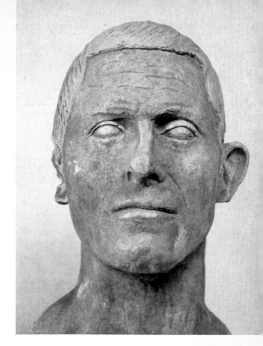

Caracalla (ill. 116), with its spiteful and suspicious look, gives a very clear idea of this pictorially effective manner. But in addition to such refined statuary, less 'finished' works were also produced.

The sculptor of the equestrian statue of Marcus Aurelius, erected prior to A.D. 180, is no longer interested in the shaping of elaborate interstitial details. He prefers to aim at a serene monumental effect produced by bold outline. The outstretched arm, the mild amiability of the sorrowful gaze, express the desire to have done with a clamorous, restless world. The suggestion of an anguished sensibility is enhanced by the sculptor through careful stylization of the separate parts of the composition (ill. 127).

At the beginning of the 4th century A.D. sculpture again attained a higher artistic level. The head of the colossal statue of Constantine the Great does not wear the features of an individual; they are impersonal and timeless.

PAINTING

In the 2nd century B.C., Roman wall-painting took over from the Greek East a certain formal articulation. This so-called 'First Style', known from Pompeian survivals, contrived to depict a stone base surmounted by architectural features giving the illusion of space.

In the 'Second Style' of the 1st century B.C., the imitation of architecture appeared to open out the wall and afford a deceptive view of landscape. The art in this case consisted neither in decorative nor in pictorial ornamentation but rather in the resolving of inner space. It proves the high standard of technical perfection to which the Greek painting here imitated had attained. Scenes with figures, arranged in the fashion of a frieze, as in the 'Aldobrandini Wedding' (ill. p. 150), served the same purpose of spatial enlargement.

The 'Third Style' flourished under Augustus. In this case the wall was again used to limit space, the architectural features being represented as slender and fragile, in straight lines, without space in depth. They framed small, paradisal landscapes and mythological scenes, which appeared to hang on the wall like panels (ill. p. 162).

In the 'Fourth Style' the 'loosening-up' characteristic of Flavian times, and already noted in connection with sculpture, is to the fore. Typical elements are taken from the second and third periods of Pompeian fresco painting and employed to simulate Baroque-like architectural features, which advance and retreat. The painted building components, and also the figures are small. They play no real part in the pictorial organisation and amount to nothing more than *décor*.

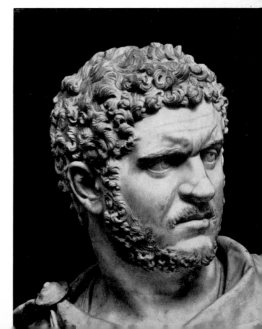

114. Portrait of an elderly man. Etruscan (1st cent. B.C.). Terra-cotta, found in Cerveteri
115. Julius Caesar (B.C.). Marble
116. Caracalla (Roman Emperor, A.D. 211–217). Marble

THE CRAFTS

The crafts in all their forms were applied to the improvement and fitting-out of the Roman palaces and villas. Their floors were made of marble slabs of various colours or mosaic, as in the Alexander Mosaic (ill. p. 149). Furniture and utensils were made of carefully chosen materials. Chafing-dishes, lamps and mirrors were of bronze, with embossed or engraved ornament. Household silver of the kind found at Boscoreale and Hildesheim was in use by many middle-class citizens. Goldsmiths employed the most refined technique on the precious metals and on jewels, beads and enamel. Gem-cutting flourished under Augustus and during the following decades to an extent never again equalled (Gemma Augustea, ill. 117). Roman glass and pottery (*terra sigillata*, q. v.) were exported to all parts of the Empire.

Once ancient art had lost its distinctive national life and become cosmopolitan owing to the absorption of foreign influences, its creative powers quickly waned. The line of evolution led from the Greek Archaic to the mature Classical style, whence it gradually became dissipated in the wilderness of late antique fashions. Chronologically, Roman art replaced Greek, taking over its formal language without reaching its classical level.

117. Gemma Augustea (time of Birth of Christ). Stone carving (slightly less than actual size)

ABU SIMBEL is in Lower Nubia, 164 m. south of Assuan. Two temples were erected at the place by Ramses II (19th Dynasty, 1301–1234 B.C.). The frontages are cut out of the vertical rock rising from the desert, the interior chambers penetrating 185 feet into the heart of the mountain. At the entrance to the larger temple, dedicated to the gods Amon-ra and Ra-harakht, four seated figures of the king, each 65 feet high, are chiselled out of the sandstone of the cliff. The walls and columns of the interior chambers are richly adorned with reliefs and inscriptions dealing with the exploits of Ramses II, including his military campaigns.

ABYDOS, one of the oldest Egyptian settlements, is about 350 m. south of Cairo. It was part of the district of Thinis, whence the kings of the 1st and 2nd Dynasties came. Traces of the tombs of these kings have been found at the place. One of them was supposed in later times to be the tomb of Osiris, whereupon it became the chief centre of the worship of that god. After the 2nd millennium B.C. the kings erected a cenotaph near the tomb. The ruins of the temples built by Seti I and Ramses II in honour of the dead are still considered the most important of their kind.

ACROPOLIS. The Greek word means 'hill-town' or 'citadel'. It is used especially of the Acropolis of Athens, which in prehistoric times was the fortress of the kings. From the 6th century, at latest, it served, together with Eleusis (q. v.) as the religious centre of Attica. The tyrant Peisistratus and his sons, who lived in the Acropolis at the same time, built a number of temples there which were nearly all destroyed in 480 B.C. by the Persians. Themistocles then used what remained of the architecture and sculpture to level the site and erect new fortifications. Cimon and, in particular, Pericles constructed more temples. The supervision of all those set up in the time of Pericles was entrusted to Pheidias, assisted by the architects Ictinus (in the building of the Parthenon between 448 and 432 B.C.) and Mnesicles (in the building of the Propylaea between 437 and 432 B.C.). The Temple of Nike (or Victory), enclosed by a balustrade adorned with reliefs (now in the Acropolis Museum), was erected, like the Erechtheum, during the Peloponnesian War (431–404 B.C.). Ill. 102, 118, 122, 130

AEGINA, an island between Attica and the north-east Peloponnese, is famous for the temple of Aphaea, erected about 500 B.C. Its gable-sculptures are to-day in the Glyptothek Museum, Munich. They illustrate battles between Greeks and Trojans, including those described by Homer in the *Iliad.*

AGORACRITUS, the Attic sculptor, lived in the last third of the 5th century. He was a pupil of Pheidias and collaborated with him in the Parthenon sculptures.

AGRIGENTUM in Sicily, a very rich city in ancient times, contains to-day the ruins of several extensive temples, chiefly of the 6th and early 5th centuries B.C. There is also the so-called tomb of Theron, a late Hellenistic memorial to an unknown dignitary.

118. Plan of the Acropolis

1 Roman entrance to citadel, 2 Old entrance to citadel, 3 New rampart (restored after 479 B.C.), 4 Old rampart, 5 Old royal palace, 6 Old temple, 7 Parthenon (448—432 B.C.) Doric Peripteros. Nucleus with double prostyle. Architect Ictinus, 8 Propylaea. Built by Mnesicles (437—432 B.C.) Doric, 9 Temple of Victory. Built by Callicrates (430—421 B.C.), 10 Erechtheum (420—408 B.C.) Ionic, 10a Porch of Maidens of Erechtheum, 11 Statue of Athena (Athena Promachos), 12 Asclepieum. Temple enclosure dedicated to god of medicine Asclepius 420 B.C., 13 Enclosure sacred to Dionysus, 14 Theatre of Dionysus. Rebuilt about 330 B.C., 15 Orchestra, 16 Stage, 17 Hall of Eumenes II of Pergamum (197—159 B.C.), 18 Odeum of Herodes Atticus (c. A. D. 160)

ALCAMENES, an Attic sculptor of the last third of the 5th century B.C., who was a pupil of Pheidias. The group of Procne and Itys preserved in the Acropolis Museum at Athens is an original work by Alcamenes, who may also have collaborated in the sculptures on the Parthenon (q. v.).

ALDOBRANDINI WEDDING. The name of a wall painting of the later 1st century B.C., so called after its former owners. It was found in Rome and is derived from a Greek original of the later 4th century B.C. The subject is the first stage of a ritual ceremony representing the mystical marriage of the god Dionysus to the wife, called the *Basilinna* or Queen, of the Athenian High Priest, Aphrodite being shown seated next to her on the marriage bed (ill. p. 150).

ALEXANDER MOSAIC. This pavement, artistically the finest of all antique specimens of its kind, was found at Pompeii and is to-day in the National Museum of Naples. It represents a battle between Macedonians and Persians, including an – unhistorical – encounter between Alexander the Great and Darius. The mosaic may be a late Hellenistic copy of a picture by Philoxenus of Eretria (c. 300 B.C.) and is considered the best surviving reconstruction of a Greek monumental painting (ill. p. 149).

ALEXANDER SARCOPHAGUS. A marble sarcophagus decorated by Attic sculptors towards the end of the 4th century B.C. with coloured reliefs representing among other subjects the deeds of Alexander the Great and hunting-scenes. It is to-day at Constantinople. Found at Sidon among other marble coffins of a more remote date.

AMARNA, preferably Tel-el-Amarna, in Upper Egypt, is the ruined site of a city founded about 1370 B.C. by

119. Roman Aqueduct, Pont du Gard at Nîmes in southern France

King Ikhnaton. Excavations in this region not only provided a wealth of information on the planning of an ancient Egyptian city, with its temples, palaces and private residences, but also revealed certain outstanding works of art differing substantially in style from those of other periods of Egyptian history. These works are distinguished by an astonishing naturalism and animation. The most famous and important is the bust of Queen Nefertiti (q. v.), the wife of Ikhnaton (Amenophis IV), now in Berlin (ill. p. 122).

APELLES, Court painter to Alexander the Great, and one of the most famous painters of Classical Antiquity, flourished in the middle of the 4th century B.C. We can form no clearer idea of his work than of that of other painters of Ancient Greece. Literary tradition informs us that he sometimes painted allegories. A surviving picture of Alexander as a youthful Zeus may perhaps be a copy of a work by Apelles. It is to be found in the 'House of the Vettii' at Pompeii.

APOLLODORUS of Damascus built the Forum of Trajan at Rome in the first quarter of the 2nd century A. D. It was planned on a vast scale and served as a model for similar lay-outs in the Baroque period. He also erected baths and a circus in Rome, as well as a bridge over the Danube.

AQUEDUCT. The Romans specialized in this method of piping water, which took the form of great arched structures when spanning valleys (ill. 119).

ARA PACIS AUGUSTAE. The name of an altar-building erected by the Roman Senate between 13 and 9 B.C. in the Field of Mars near Rome and dedicated to the personification of Peace after the pacification of the Empire by Augustus. The altar itself was surrounded by a stone wall with reliefs on each side representing among other scenes the procession of members of the imperial family and officials of the highest rank on the inauguration of the building. Legendary scenes from early Roman history were depicted on the side-walls of the porch. The altar itself was reached by a flight of steps and was adorned with reliefs of sacrificial ceremonies. Some of these reliefs, including a

number of ornamental slabs of great beauty, are in the National Museum of Rome and in the Louvre.

ARRINGATORE. The name of an Etruscan statue of an orator, dating from about 100 B.C. Preserved in the Archaeological Museum of Florence.

AUGUSTUS OF PRIMAPORTA. The name of a statue of the emperor Augustus (27 B.C.–A. D. 14) which is a masterpiece of the Court art of the time. It was found in a villa owned by the emperor's wife at Primaporta near Rome, and is to-day in the Braccio Nuovo room at the Vatican (ill. 120).

BAALBEK in Syria was an important city in Roman times owing to its situation. Extensive ruins remain. Of these the most important is the enormous Temple of Jupiter Heliopolitanus, dating from the 1st and 2nd centuries A. D. and partly constructed in the megalithic style. A small, well-preserved circular temple dates from the 2nd century. The plan of the Jupiter temple in particular includes certain non-Roman features of native origin, which may have influenced Western architectural theory in the later ages of Antiquity.

BABYLON, on the Euphrates, was the centre of the civilisation of the Near East and the capital of Babylonia during the second and the first half of the 1st millennium B.C. The city was several times partially destroyed by the Assyrians. It flourished under Nebuchadnezzar II (604–562 B.C.), and the German excavations begun in 1899 have revealed many buildings from his time (cf. p. 112, ill. 94).

BANDKERAMIK is the name given to neolithic earthenware made by an agricultural community of south-eastern and central Europe. The vessels are decorated with wide bands often of spiral or scroll (meander) pattern. The south-eastern groups produced highly ornamental vessels, painted in various colours,

120. Augustus of Primaporta (time of Birth of Christ)

under influence from the Near East. But in the North colour tended to disappear. Isolated examples of variously painted pottery continued to be produced in the Bohemian and Moravian regions but there as elsewhere in the distribution area vessels in monochrome predominated, decorated with bands, which were at first scratched in and later incised (ill. 89).

BARBERINI FAUN, also called the 'Sleeping Satyr' (Glyptothek Museum, Munich), is a masterpiece of Hellenistic sculpture executed about 200 B.C. by a sculptor of Asia Minor or Rhodes.

BELL-BEAKERS. The name given to gracefully curving beakers with much deeply incised patterning, often emphasised with a white inlay. They were native to Spain. Thence they spread, at the end of the Neolithic Period, northwards to England and eastwards to Hungary. They occur in association with metal utensils, bronze daggers and axes. Bell-beakers developed, under the influence of geometric pottery, into beakers with zonal decoration. (Ill. 86)

BENI HASSAN, in Central Egypt, is well known to Egyptian archaeologists and art historians on account of the rock-tombs of princes and dignitaries of the Middle Kingdom (2000 B.C.) found there. Not only is the architecture of the tombs, with their pillared frontages, interesting, but their inscriptions and painted scenes illustrating the owner's private life have rendered them some of the most attractive of all Egyptian monuments.

BERLIN PAINTER. One of the greatest of the Attic vase-painters of the early 5th century B.C. His real name is not known.

BORGHESE WARRIOR. The marble statue now in the Louvre was made by Agasias of Ephesus. It is a late Hellenistic version of an original to be referred to the school of Lysippus. The figure, which confronts an imaginary adversary, has served as a model for sculptors and draughtsmen of the last three centuries, owing to the precision of its anatomical detail.

BOSCOREALE. The name of a villa near Pompeii where a treasure of silver, now in Paris, was discovered. The collection consisted of a valuable dinner-service which had belonged to an eminent Roman, individual items dating from the 1st century B.C. and just after.

BRICK RELIEFS are clay slabs fired and enamelled in colour, with decorations in relief of animals such as pacing lions and bulls, or human figures such as warriors. They were found as decorative wall-facings in temples and palaces in Mesopotamia, south-western Persia and elsewhere at the time of the Assyrian, Babylonian and ancient Persian empires. (Ill. 94, p. 106)

BRYAXIS. A Greek sculptor living in the mid and late 4th century B.C. who collaborated in the sculptures of the Mausoleum at Halicarnassus. The Demeter of Cnidos at the British Museum is perhaps an original

work by him. The images of the Graeco-Egyptian god Serapis, which are preserved in many museums, relate to one of his works, carried out for Alexandria at the command of kings of the Ptolemaic dynasty.

BRYGOS PAINTER. An attic vase-painter of the early 5th century B.C. working for a potter named Brygos.

BUCCHERO WARE. Clay vessels of a black or greyish-black colour both on the surface and at fractured areas, manufactured, especially in Etruria, during the 7th and 6th centuries B.C.

CAECILIA METALLA. The tomb of this name in the Appian Way adjacent to Rome was built about the time of the birth of Christ. It is a typical funerary monument of leading Roman families of the Imperial age and in medieval times was used by the Roman nobility as a fortification.

CALLIMACHUS, a Greek sculptor of the late 5th century B.C., is supposed to have invented the Corinthian capital. No works that can definitely be attributed to him are known. According to writers of Antiquity they were remarkable for mannerist elegance and excessive refinement.

CANOPIC JARS are vases for holding the viscera which had to be removed from a corpse during the embalming process in Egypt. The vessels were at first simply closed up. Later they were given lids in the form of a human head, which were changed, after the beginning of the New Kingdom about the middle of the 2nd millennium B.C., to represent the heads of the tutelary deities of the internal organs. Such heads might be human or those of baboons, hawks or dogs. The name derives from the god worshipped at Canopus near Alexandria in the form of a vessel shaped like a human being.

CAPITOL. The name of one of the seven hills of Rome, on which the most sacred of ancient Roman sanctuaries, the temple of the Capitoline divinities, was built. The temple, frequently reconstructed, was originally of Etruscan design and erected in the so-called Tuscan style, on a high platform, practically square, with only frontal and lateral colonnades. The rear half of the ground floor contained three parallel, narrow, rectangular apartments for ritual ceremonies. The central chamber was sacred to Jupiter Capitolinus, that on the left to Minerva and that on the right to Juno.

CAPITOLINE SHE-WOLF. This bronze in the Conservatorio in Rome is the work of an Italian artist about 470 B.C. It is probably to be identified with the ancient Roman emblem struck by lightning in 65 B.C. The figures of Romulus and Remus at the wolf's udder were added in Renaissance times.

CASSEL APOLLO. The original of this statue was made about 450 B.C., perhaps by Pheidias. Of the many copies in existence that in the Museum at Cassel is the best rendering.

CATACOMBS. The name given to underground burial-places, often very extensive, found in Italy, Sicily and elsewhere. In early Christian times they were called cemeteries. Catacombs of this period – the 1st to the 4th centuries – exist in Rome. They often comprise passages of various lengths on several floors. The dead were buried in recesses *(loculi)* set in parallel rows along the side-walls and blocked up with stone slabs. These catacombs are of importance on account of the many relatively well preserved wall and ceiling paintings of scenes and symbols of great significance for primitive and Early Christian iconography. Antique, pre-Christian pictorial themes, such as that of Orpheus among animals, and decorative features given a Christian orientation, are conspicuous and have contributed to the development of later art by carrying on the traditions bequeathed by Antiquity.

CEPHISODOTUS, a Greek sculptor of the early 4th century B.C., was the father of Praxiteles. He made the statue of the Goddess of Peace erected at Athens in 374 B.C. There is a copy of it in the Glyptothek Museum at Munich.

CHORAGIC MONUMENTS are those erected in Antiquity to commemorate victory in musical contests and dedicated to the deity presiding over the event. The best preserved is the Monument of Lysicrates at Athens, set up in 334 B.C. A circular substructure in Corinthian style formerly supported a tripod, actually the prize awarded, which is now lost.

CIST. 1. A wickerwork or bronze receptacle, usually cylindrical, with a lid. Wickerwork cists were often used by the ancients, for ritual purposes, the sacred vessels being carried in them. They very frequently appear on votive reliefs dedicated to chthonic and fertility deities. Bronze cists were customary in central Italy during the period from the 5th to the 2nd century B.C. The sides of the vessel were adorned with engraved scenes and the handle of the lid often represented a human figure. The so-called Ficoroni casket, decorated with scenes from the legend of the Argonauts and dating from the second half of the 4th century, is well known. It is to-day at the Villa Giulia in Rome. 2. A small, rectangular, stone or clay urn for ashes, used in Hellenistic times, especially in Etruria, and adorned with mythological ornament.

CLEOPHRADES. The pseudonym of one of the most important Attic vase-painters, active in the early 5th century B.C.

CNOSSUS. This city, in Crete, was the centre of the 'Minoan' civilisation (cf. p. 125). The great palace installations were several times reconstructed during the first half of the 2nd millennium B.C. They prove that Cnossus was formerly the capital of a great empire. It was the residence, according to legend, of King Minos. An extensive courtyard, mainly intended for ritual purposes, is surrounded by a honeycomb arrangement of many rooms of different sizes. The apparently chaotic and wholly non-European, pre-Greek plan is reflected in the non-architectural, haphazard nature of the building itself, extensive parts of which have been restored in modern times. The several floors are interconnected by great staircases. In the magnificently equipped state apartments remains of impressive paintings were discovered. The intricacy of the planning gave rise to the legend of the labyrinth. (Ill. 98)

COLOSSEUM. An enormous amphitheatre in Rome, built under the Flavian emperors in the second half of the 1st century A. D. It derives its name from a colossal statue of Nero erected close by. (Ill. 112)

COLOSSUS. A more than life-size statue, such as were often placed in Egyptian temples and especially on each side of their entrances. Those of Ramses II in front of the rock temple at Abu Simbel and the so-called Memnon colossus are splendid examples of the type. The Hellenistic world was acquainted with the Colossus of Rhodes, a bronze statue of the sun-god Helios, 102 ft high, set up at the port in 285 B.C. and considered one of the Seven Wonders of the World. A figure of Nero as the sun-god, also cast in bronze and 108 ft high, stood in Rome. The Flavian amphitheatre built alongside the latter colossus was accordingly called the Colosseum in late medieval times. The Colossus of Barletta in Apulia, 13½ ft high, was erected to represent an emperor of the later antique period.

COLUMBARIUM, the Latin for a dovecote, is the name of an Ancient Roman and Early Christian burial place in which the cinerary urns were kept in a large number of recesses resembling those in a dovecote.

COMB-STAMPED POTTERY is a coarse type of earthenware with stamped comb ornament, produced in north-east Europe during the Neolithic Age.

CORDED-WARE. Towards the end of the Neolithic Age corded pottery began to occur over wide areas of Europe. Its chief forms are amphorae and slender beakers. Ornament, which always strongly emphasises the construction of the body of the vessel, is effected by laying twisted cords round the neck and upper section of the vessel before firing, so that they make a deep impression in the still soft clay. At a later period, genuine cord decoration was counterfeited by pricking. Finely-made perforated battle-axes were found in association with this pottery. This culture appears to have been concentrated in Thuringia and Jutland (ill. 26).

CORINTH was an important Greek port already in ancient times and had a flourishing art in the archaic period. From the 8th to the 6th century B.C. it was the leading pottery-making centre in Greece. In the 7th century B.C., Corinth was one of the first places to produce monumental architecture and the double-gabled temple is said to have derived thence. A large temple of Apollo survives from the 6th century B.C. In 146 B.C. the city was destroyed by the Romans. Rebuilt in 44

The Battle of Alexander, floor mosaic in the House of the Faun in Pompeii (probably c. 50 B.C., after a Greek prototype c. 300 B.C.)

'Aldobrandini Marriage', *Roman wall painting (1st century B.C., after a Greek prototype of the 4th century B.C.)*

Chalice of Duris: Athena pouring
wine for Hercules
(Attic, c. 480–470 B.C.)
Red figure style

Chalice of Exekias: Sea voyage
of Dionysos *(Attic, c. 530 B.C.)*
Black figure style

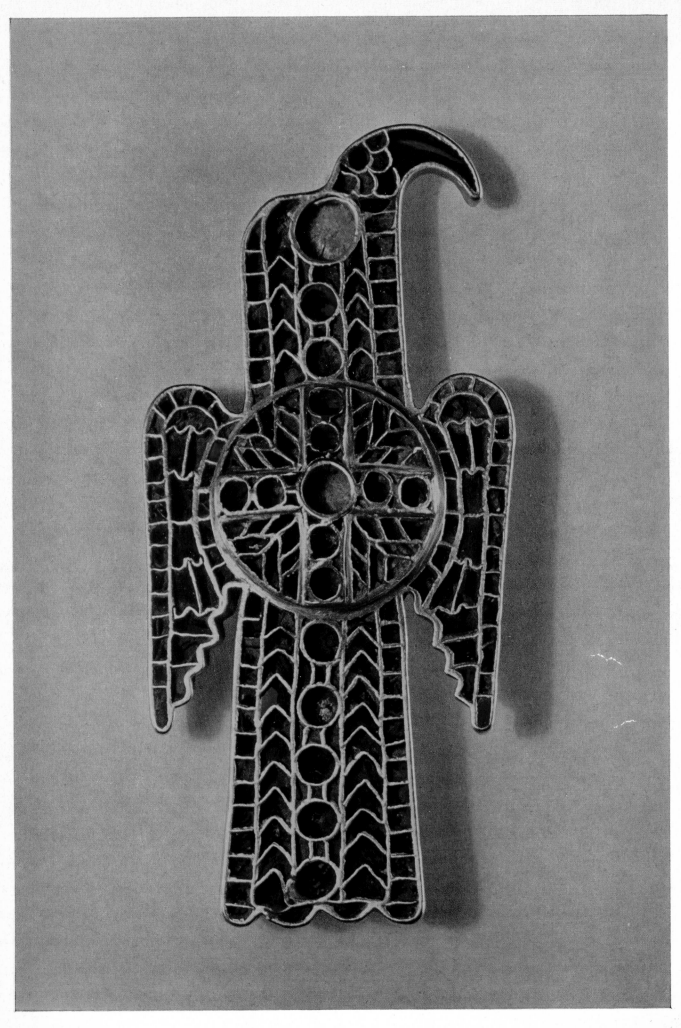

Brooch with eagle motif inset with alamandine, from the time of the Barbarian Invasions. North Italy (c. A. D. 500)

BC., it rapidly regained its former size. Most of the surviving structures date from the Roman period. They include covered markets, public assembly halls, administrative buildings, temples, baths and well-known fountains such as the Peirene.

COSMETIC SLABS or palettes were found in prehistoric (4th to 3rd millennia B.C.) Egyptian tombs in vast numbers. They were often flat slates, lozenge-shaped or in the shape of an animal, sometimes also circular or quadrangular, and were used for the application of cosmetics obtained from malachite, galena and vegetable juices.

CRESILAS, a Greek sculptor of the 5th century B.C., is famous for his portrait of Pericles, made about 430. Another work of his is the statue of an Amazon for the temple of Artemis at Ephesus. The figure was executed in competition with Polycleitus and Pheidias. There is a Roman copy in Berlin.

CRITIUS, a Greek sculptor active about 480 B.C., is supposed to have executed among other works the marble statue of the standing youth found on the Acropolis at Athens. He collaborated with Nesiotes in the bronze group of the tyrannicides Aristogiton and Harmodius, set up in 477 at Athens to replace the group made by Antenor for Delphi some twenty years before and carried off by Xerxes in 480. The later, less well composed, group survives in Roman copies.

CYCLOPEAN WALLS are megalithic ramparts such as surrounded the citadels of Mycenae and Tiryns shortly after the middle of the 2nd millennium B.C. They consist of irregularly shaped stones like fragments of rock, closely stratified (ill. 128). As later generations could not believe that such walls had been erected by human hands, they were attributed to the Cyclopes, assistants of the god Hephaestus. Similar masonry has been noted in the buildings of the Incas of Peru. It is known as polygonal masonry.

DEIR EL-BAHRI is situated west of the ancient Egyptian capital, Thebes. A rocky arena formed by vertical cliffs rising from the desert contains the ruins of two funerary temples. One of them was built by Mentuhotep III, founder of the Middle Kingdom. The other was the famous terraced temple built by the architect Senmut for Queen Hatshepsut between 1501 and 1480 B.C. (ill. 121). The edifice rises in three terraces, connected by ramps and adorned with colonnades, against the grandiose background of the cliffs. The sanctuary is built into the mountain-side. The colonnades and interior apartments are adorned with reliefs showing scenes from the life of the queen, in particular her expedition to the 'land of incense', Punt, perhaps to be identified with the Suakin area on the Red Sea.

DELOS. An island in the Aegean Sea reputed to be the birthplace of Apollo and containing one of the most important shrines in Greece. Ruins are abundant. Temples, halls and living quarters have been unearthed.

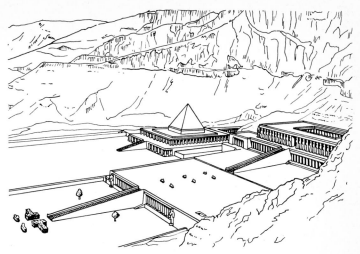

121. Deir el-Bahri. Terrace temple of Queen Hatshepsut; in the background, that of Mentuhotep III. Reconstruction

There are fine mosaic pavements and traces of Hellenistic frescoes; also architectural sculpture of the late 5th century B.C. and Hellenistic portraits.

DIE SQUATTER is the name given to a figurative convention of Egyptian sculpture by which a man squatting on the ground is so enveloped in his robe that his body forms a die (for throwing). This mode of representation became general under the New Kingdom in the middle of the 2nd millennium B.C. In the Late Period of the 1st millennium B.C. the die was often completely covered with inscriptions (ill. 137).

DIPYLON VASES were found in a large cemetery in front of the Dipylon Gate at Athens. They are early Attic clay vessels decorated in geometric style. The Dipylon style prevailed in Greek vase-painting from the 10th to the 8th centuries B.C.

DOCUMENTARY RELIEFS denote official inscriptions of ancient Athens, adorned with reliefs, in which State decrees and similar pronouncements of a political nature and of public interest were published. Since the reliefs, executed in the second half of the 5th and in the 4th century B.C., are all precisely dated, they are important for the determination of the chronology of other Greek works of art, though their own artistic merit is relatively slight.

DURA EUROPOS, a town on the upper course of the Euphrates, was a frontier fortress of the Roman Empire for defence against the Parthians after the time of the emperor Trajan (round about A.D. 1000). There are important ruins in good preservation, with many frescoes in predominantly provincial style. They may be early specimens of late antique and Byzantine painting.

DURIS. An Attic vase-painter of the early 5th century B.C. (ill. p. 151).

EBERSWALDE GOLD HOARD. During building operations at Eberswalde in Brandenburg a large clay vessel was unearthed which contained a amazing collection of gold articles. There were eight goblets, a

153

number of rings, spirals of wire and an ingot, all of gold. The goblets were small rotund vessels with the outward-turned rims, made of thin gold-foil. The entire pot, even its base, was covered with embossed knobs, concentric circles, parallel lines and stars. The hoard dates from early in the 1st millennium B.C.

ELEUSIS was an important cult-centre in Attica where since prehistoric times fertility and chthonic deities had been worshipped in ritual 'mysteries'. The focus of the cult and of the celebrations of the mysteries was the *telestrion* or house of initiation, a quadrangular building, often restored, with an interior chamber of many columns and ascending rows of seats placed against the walls, whence the congregation could watch the dramas performed. There was a opening in the roof of extremely complicated construction to enable the ritualistic lighting effects to be achieved. Lateral staircases were also used in the ceremonies. Owing to the special demands of the cult, the structure as a whole has no parallel in the history of ancient architecture. The final restoration of the *telesterion* was carried out by Ictinus, builder of the Parthenon. Many votive reliefs and statues, some of great importance, have been found at Eleusis.

ELGIN MARBLES. The name given to sculptures from the Parthenon, brought to London by Lord Elgin at the beginning of the 19th century (British Museum).

EPHESUS. A town on the coast of Asia Minor, formerly Greek. The ancient city is now being excavated. It appears to have been planned in the 7th century B.C. in the style later used by Hippodamus (q. v.) of Miletus, an architect of the 5th century B.C. The temple of Artemis, one of the Seven Wonders of the World, was an enormous building in the Ionic style, several times reconstructed. Another temple begun about the middle of the 6th century B.C. was never completed. The so-called *columnae caelatae,* high pedestals for columns, adorned with figures in relief, are characteristic of both buildings. This is a peculiar, non-Greek architectural feature, derived from the Ancient East. Remains of the buildings and their sculptures are to-day in the British Museum. The Hellenistic, Roman and Byzantine cities erected on another site have left extensive architectural traces, especially of the Roman period. The ruins of a theatre, a nymphaeum (monument to the nymphs) and a library exist. Among the Byzantine buildings, St John's Cathedral is outstanding. It commemorates the death of the Evangelist at Ephesus.

ERECH, the modern Warka, in Mesopotamia, was the Sumero-Akkadian capital at the beginning and end of the 3rd millennium B.C. (cf. p. 109). The earliest city surrounded the ziggurat temple dedicated to the goddess of the heavens, Inanna. Near-by were other temples and palaces. Excavations, which still continue, have unearthed many works of art dating from the 3rd millennium B.C., as well as cuneiform texts giving information about ancient Babylonian civilisation (cf. ill. p. 106).

154

122. *Porch of Maidens of the Erechtheum on the Acropolis at Athens (420–408 B.C.)*

ERECHTHEUM. An Ionic temple on the Acropolis at Athens, built 420–408 B.C., and dedicated to the Snakegod Erechtheus, the former tutelary deity of the city, to Athena and to Poseidon. This multiple dedication accounts for the complicated ground-plan of the temple, differing from all other antique structures. Several ancient cults were recalled by the mark of Poseidon's trident in the rock, made to release a salt spring, by the tomb of King Cecrops, who was revered as a god, under the Porch of Maidens, and by the adjacent sacred olive tree, one of the emblems of Athena (cf. p. 130, ill. 122).

EUPHRONIOS. An Attic vase-painter of the end of the 6th century B.C.

EUTYCHIDES. A Greek sculptor living at the turn of the 4th and 3rd centuries B.C. A pupil of Lysippus, he was responsible for the statue of 'Fortune', the tutelary goddess of the city of Antioch on the Orontes in Syria. The goddess is represented seated with crossed legs on a cliff, at the foot of which the river-god Orontes, in the form of a youth, appears. Roman copies of the group survive, as for instance in the Vatican.

EXEKIAS. The masterpiece of this Attic vase-painter of the third quarter of the 6th century B.C. is the amphora in the Vatican, showing two heroes playing draughts, which is one of the finest of Greek vases. A goblet by Exekias illustrating the sea-voyage of Dionysus (in Munich) is also well known (ill. p. 151).

FARNESE BULL. The well-known group of this name in the National Museum in Naples represents the Theban queen Dirce being bound to a bull by her stepsons Zetus and Amphion. The work is a Roman copy of a lost original by the sculptors Apollonius and Tauriscus, made about the middle of the 1st century B.C. The composition has been changed by the copyists.

FARNESE HERCULES. A colossal statue of the hero at rest, made in the 2nd century A. D. by Glycon. It is possibly a free imitation of an original by Lysippus. The statue is now in Naples.

FIBULAE are metal brooches for fastening robes. They first appeared in Europe during the Bronze Age: those in one piece, resembling the modern safety-pin, in Italy, and those in two pieces, with the flat part and pin fastened together, in the Northern territories. Both types were widely distributed and were later also manufactured of iron and the precious metals (ill. p. 152).

FORUM. The Latin name for the market-place of an Ancient Roman city. In large cities there were several. In imperial times the forum was the focus of commercial and political life, as well as of jurisdiction. Genuine markets were either held elsewhere in special areas devoted to meat, fish and vegetables or were operated close to the Forum. The best-known Forum in Rome is that between the Capitoline, the Esquiline and the Palatine hills, laid out on the site of a burial-ground (*via sacra*), and is called the Forum Romanum. It contains temples and public buildings, such as the house of the High Priest (*regia*) and the senate-house, as well as basilicas and triumphal arches. The so-called Imperial Fora (ill. 123) adjoined the Forum Romanum.

FRANÇOIS VASE. An Attic clay vessel, named after its former possessor, which was made by the potter Ergotimus about 560 B.C. and painted by Clitias in the black-figured style with a number of friezes. Now in the Archaeological Museum at Florence.

GALLEHUS GOLDEN HORNS. In 1639 and 1734 two large golden horns with rich figural decoration were found at Gallehus near Tonder, Jutland. In 1802 they were stolen and probably melted down. Reconstructions of these famous objects, which had been copied from old models, are on view in the National Museum at Copenhagen. Rings with semi-plastic human and animal figures soldered on to them enclosed the smooth surfaces of the horns.

GERMANIC ART. The Germanic peoples came from a mingling in the first half of the 2nd millennium B.C., in southern Scandinavia and what is now Schleswig-Holstein, of Nordic builders of megaliths and indo-germanic producers of corded ware. The race subsequently spread in the directions of the Vistula, Danube and Rhine. Wooden architecture reached quite a high level in the 1st millennium A. D., exemplified by farmhouses 90 to 150 feet long, with sloping roofs and clay-roughcast wattled walls, by the mercantile buildings of

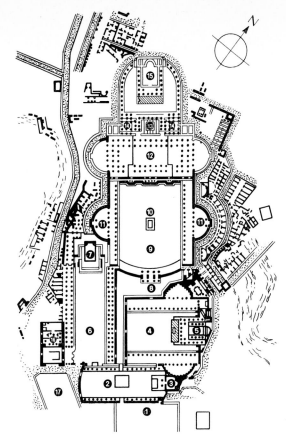

123. Plan of the Imperial Fora at Rome

1 Forum of Peace or Vespasian's Forum, 2 Forum of Nerva, 3 Temple of Minerva, 4 Forum of Augustus, 5 Temple of Mars the Avenger, 6 Julian Forum, 7 Temple of Venus Genetrix, 8 Triumphal Arch of Trajan, 9 Forum of Trajan, 10 Equestrian Statue of Trajan, 11 Hemicycles (semicircular recesses), 12 Basilica Ulpia, 13 Trajan's Column, 14 Libraries, 15 Temple of Trajan, 16 Curia, 17 Basilica Aemilia (no longer part of Imperial Fora)

the ports of Haithabu and Trelleborg and by churches with astragal mouldings. Plastic work comprised crudely-hewn wooden idols, bronze statuettes and artistic carvings, as in the Oseberg Treasure (q. v., ill. 69). We can form some idea of what has been lost in the way of paintings from the rock-pictures (ill. p. 105) and vase-painting, as well as from some tapestry and embroidery. Striking evidence of Germanic aesthetic feeling is given by the ornamentation of tools, weapons and personal adornments. In the Bronze Age, patterns of straight lines changed to stamped spiral motifs and these in their turn, later, to whorls and waves, as in the sun-chariot of Trundholm (ill. 133). From about 700 B.C. (Iron Age) until the Christian era there was little or no Germanic art; but thereafter the adoption of foreign methods brought about a rebirth. In the North, after the 6th century A. D., an abstract animal ornamentation (Animal Style I) developed, which became associated with southern Teutonic banded wickerwork in the filling of plane surfaces (Animal Style II). In Scandinavia, in the 8th century, a special form of eddying animal motif (Animal Style III) occurs. Germanic art also adopted pictorial representation after 600 A.D., as in the Hornhausen equestrian monument (ill. 21). While in central Europe and England, on the advent of Christianity, medieval art began, with its monumental architecture,

155

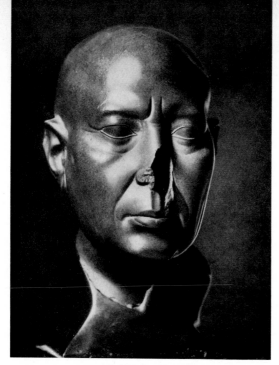

124. *Head of a priest, the so-called 'Green Head'* *(c. 500 B.C.)*

sculpture, manuscript illumination and industrial production, in still heathen Scandinavia Animal Style III evolved into Viking art.

GOD FROM THE SEA. The name given to an antique bronze statue salvaged off Cape Artemisium in Euboea, Greece, in 1928. It is now in the National Museum at Athens. The statue is of a naked, bearded god, either Zeus or Poseidon. It is an original Greek work of about 460 B.C. by an unknown but outstanding sculptor.

GOLD AND IVORY STATUES (in Greek *chryselephantine*). Statues of enormous size were periodically favoured in Ancient Greece. The core was of wood, overlaid with ivory to represent the flesh and plates of thin gold foil, the clothing. This extremely expensive technique was used mainly for cult-statues like those of Athena Parthenos and of Zeus at Olympia, both by Pheidias. As a substitute, the cheaper acrolith method was sometimes used, in which stone represented the unclothed parts and wood the clothed, so that the latter could be covered with precious metals.

GREEN HEAD, THE. The name given to a fragment of a statue of a priest in hard greenstone. It is one of the most important works of the late period of Egyptian art (26th–27th dynasty, about 500 B.C.). The head, about 8½ in. high, represents an elderly man with a lined countenance. A special peculiarity of these late portraits is their affinity, despite the stylisation due to the formal austerity of Ancient Egyptian art, with the expressiveness of Roman portraiture (ill. 124).

GUNDESTRUP SILVER CAULDRON. This hemispherical silver vessel was found in marshy soil near Gundestrup, Jutland. Its upper portion, both without and within, is profusely decorated with large human heads and smaller forms of human beings and animals. The figure of a stag-deity reveals the place of origin. It is East Celtic work of the 1st century B.C.

HADRIAN'S VILLA is the name given to an extensive establishment which the emperor Hadrian erected for his personal use near Tivoli. Several palaces, private baths, libraries, theatres, a stadium and gymnasium, as well as large parks, form parts of it.

HALLSTATT CIVILISATION. In the first half of the 1st millennium B.C. a wealthy and frivolously elegant society flourished in the south of central Europe. It was discovered by excavations at Hallstatt in Upper Austria. Richly decorated weapons of bronze, and at a later date of iron, brooches, ring ornaments of bronze and pearl, fibulae in the forms of drums, boats, snakes and birds, magnificent pottery, frequently painted, and figures of animals in bronze and clay, all point to delight in formal organisation and wealth (ill. 91). There is evidence of a strong influence of southern upon central European agricultural society resulting from the many imports from the South in the shape of bronze vessels, armour and masks and the intermingling of geometrical and naturalistic elements of style.

HAMMURABI STELE. A basalt monument found in 1902 at Susa in Mesopotamia (now in the Louvre) depicting, in relief, the Ancient Babylonian king Hammurabi (1728–1686 B.C.) as he prays to the sun-god Shamash. The stele is inscribed in cuneiform with the text of a code of laws which exceeds in importance all those previously or subsequently collected from the records of Ancient Mesopotamia.

HATTUSA, or Chattusa, was the capital of the Hittite empire. Its ruins date from the 14th and 13th centuries B.C. They were found near the Turkish village of Boghazkeui, about 95 m. east of Ankara. Remains of ramparts with gates decorated in relief and of palaces and temples, as well as a clay tablet of archives with a cuneiform text, supply data for Hittite art and civilisation. Near Boghazkeui is the sacred enclosure of Yasili Kaya, with rock-reliefs of gods, some standing on animals, and also of kings and warriors.

HERCULANEUM. A city in the Campania destroyed in A. D. 79 by an eruption of Mount Vesuvius. Excavations began in the first half of the 18th century (see also Pompeii). In addition to public buildings a few luxuriously fitted dwelling houses and villas were found. Important frescoes were discovered in the *basilica*. The 'Villa of the Piso Family' contained, as well as other works of art and further items many excellent bronze portrait-busts and papyrus rolls of the writings of otherwise unknown Greek philosophers.

HERM. The name given to a high rectangular pillar surmounted by a human head. As a rule two small rectangular stumps project from the sides, to suggest arms. This type of image, originally sacred to Hermes, began to be used for portraiture towards the end of the Hellenistic period. The double herm comprised two such portraits placed back to back, usually representing writers or poets having certain affinities.

156

HILDESHEIM SILVER HOARD. As in the case of the similar find at Boscoreale (q. v.), this buried treasure of table-silver belonging to an eminent Roman, which was found near Hildesheim in the last century, dates from several periods, but mostly from the 1st century B.C. The majority of the items were manufactured in Italy, though some came from Alexandria, and a few are of Celtic origin.

HIPPODAMUS OF MILETUS. This Greek architect of the mid-5th century B.C. is regarded as having introduced the system of town planning in broad main streets intersecting at right angles, with parallel side-streets, as at the port of Piraeus near Athens and Thurii in southern Italy.

HORNHAUSEN EQUESTRIAN GROUP. This stone carving dates from about A.D. 700. It was found on a tomb near Hornhausen in the Oschersleben district of Saxony (ill. 21). An armoured warrior is represented riding over a snake. The figures are shown in low relief, and are composed in so masterly a manner that the whole surface springs to life.

HYPAETHRAL TEMPLE. The Greek word *hypaitros* means 'open to the sky'. The name is applied to a type of temple structure so extensive that the temple proper is replaced by an open precinct. The only roofed building was a kind of chapel, containing the sacred image. The most noted example of such a temple is the shrine of Apollo at Didyma near Miletus.

ICTINUS, a Greek architect of the second half of the 5th century B.C., built the Parthenon at Athens, the shrine at Eleusis and the temple of Apollo at Bassae near Phigalia in the Peloponnese.

IDOLINO (It. diminutive for 'idol'). This name has been given to the bronze figure of a standing boy (Florence), which is a Roman copy of a Greek original dating from the end of the 5th century B.C.

IMAGINES (Latin: 'pictures') are ancestor-portraits in wax, perhaps taken from casts of the dead. The portraits were placed in the houses of the Ancient Romans and borne by actors at the funerals of important families to represent the ancestral line of the deceased. It is not clear whether this custom influenced the portraiture of ancient Rome.

INCISED POTTERY is the name given to the beautifully shaped earthenware of Neolithic times in the northern area of megalithic architecture. As the name indicates, ornament is deeply incised with separate perforations by means of a wooden splinter, the edge of a shell or some other instrument. The chief forms are funnel-beakers, amphorae and 'collared bottles', the latter having high, narrow necks expanded just below the lip to a 'collar'. The vessels are characterised by strict devotion to shape. Each separate section is clearly differentiated. Ornament emphasises structure. The incised patterns are brought out by the occasional insertion of a white chalk inlay (ill. 81, 88).

JEMDET-NAZR. A group of hills in central Mesopotamia, covering the ruins of the ancient Babylonian city of Kid-nun. The Jemdet-Nazr period (3000–2700 B.C. succeeded that of Obeid or Tell Obeid (q. v.) and is distinguished by an astonishingly high level of artistic production. A nearly life-size marble head and a tall stone ritual vessel, 3 ft high and adorned with reliefs, both from Erech and now in Bagdad, as well as variously coloured pottery, reach a surprising artistic standard and are technically perfect.

KAMARES WARE. Prehistoric Minoan earthenware named after the place of its discovery in Crete. The sides of the vessels are often as fragile as egg-shells. They were usually given a thin coating of black clay and then painted with plant patterns in various earth-colours. Production flourished in the Middle Bronze Age of Crete, about 1800 B.C.

KARNAK. The ancient Egyptian capital, Thebes, was formerly situated between the village of Karnak and the city of Luxor in Upper Egypt. Extensive ruins of temples sacred to various divinities still survive near Karnak to-day to bear witness to the former civilisation of the land of the Pharoahs. The most splendid building was the national temple of Ammon, the erection of which was carried out by many generations of Egyptian kings after the inauguration of the Middle Kingdom about 2000 B.C. The temple is still well-preserved. The great hall of 134 columns in 16 rows, standing nearly 70 feet high, is particularly impressive (ill. 28).

KHORSABAD is the present name of the Assyrian settlement at Dur Sharrukin, the Palace of Sargon, 10 m. north of Nineveh. The palace was built by King Sargon II between 713 and 708 B.C., and abandoned after his death. A turreted wall surrounded the place. To the north-east, on a terrace separated from the city by a wall, stood the palace, several temples and a ziggurat. The apartments of the royal palace were adorned with reliefs, now in London, Paris and elsewhere, representing the martial deeds of the king.

KIVIK TOMB. This Early Bronze Age tomb at Kivik in southern Sweden is built of separate stone slabs with incised pictures of human beings and animals. The figures are highly stylised, like those in the Nordic rock-paintings. Each slab bears a picture with wide borders, illustrating scenes from the cult of the dead, as can be deduced from the rows of draped and undraped human figures, musicians and horses, including a two-wheeled chariot and its driver.

KORE (Greek: maiden) is the name given to a certain type of archaic Greek statue, representing the standing figure of a maiden in long robes. They were dedicated to various sanctuaries, though their exact significance is no longer understood. Well-known examples are in the Acropolis at Athens. The caryatids in the Erechtheum (q. v.) at Athens are also called korai (ill. 103, 122).

KOUROS (Greek: youth) is the name given to a type of archaic Greek statue, representing the erect figure of a naked youth or boy with one foot slightly advanced, which it was the custom to dedicate in Greek temples as votive offerings. Statues on tombs or portraits of the gods were also of this type. A striking example is the Apollo of Tenea, made shortly after the mid-6th century B.C., and preserved in the Glyptothek Museum at Munich. (Ill. 4, 104)

LAGASH, now called Tello, is in southern Mesopotamia, between the rivers Euphrates and Tigris. The site was in occupation as early as the 4th millennium B.C., and in the course of the 3rd became prosperous, flourishing towards the end of that period under the rule of the High Priest Gudea, statues of whom, preserved in the Louvre, are among the finest works of Sumerian art (cf. p. 110).

LAOCOON. This group, executed during the late Hellenistic age, about 40 B.C., by the Rhodian sculptor Agesander and his sons Polydorus and Athenodorus, is now in the Vatican. It represents the Trojan priest Laocoon and his sons, who were killed, according to the legend, by snakes sent from the gods as a punishment for warning the Trojans not to admit the Wooden Horse to the city. It is doubtful whether the Vatican group is to be identified with the once highly celebrated original or whether it is a good copy. It exerted great influence on Renaissance and Baroque art. (Ill. 125)

LA TÈNE CULTURE. The Celtic culture, so called after the place in Switzerland where it was discovered, spread from France, south-west Germany and Switzerland, during the last 500 years B.C., over wide areas of Europe. It produced iron brooches and weapons, at first of a somewhat elaborate nature, afterwards plain and strictly practical in design. But in the decorative sphere a sumptuous native art developed. Individual techniques, such as that of enamel inlay, as well as botanical and zoological motifs, were borrowed from Greek and Scythian art. But they were treated in a novel, rhythmically vital, ornamental style. The curves, fish-bladder and scroll forms on stone and metal, for all their active whirling, are kept in check and proportioned. Human beings and animals are sculptured in relief and also free-standing. On the continent of Europe the native art was obliterated by the advance of Rome. But in the British Isles it continued to flourish for a further period during the first millennium A. D. (ill. 90).

LEOCHARES, a Greek sculptor of the mid-4th century B.C., participated in work on the Mausoleum (q. v.) and executed many statues of the gods, including one of Zeus. The celebrated Apollo Belvedere in the Vatican is probably his, as well as the Versailles Artemis in the Louvre. The Rondanini Alexander in the Glyptothek Museum at Munich is considered a Roman copy of the famous statue made of the young Alexander by Leochares. Another Roman copy of his work is the Vatican group of Ganymede seized by an eagle.

158

LEPTIS MAGNA, capital of the ancient Roman province of Tripolitania in North Africa, was adorned with splendid buildings during the later imperial period of the 2nd and 3rd centuries A. D. A ceremonial avenue, bordered by colonnaded halls and spanned by triumphal arches, led from the old Forum, with its surrounding temples, to a pentagonal open space. The Imperial Forum, the Courts of Justice and extensive baths were situated close to the avenue.

LUDOVISI GALATIANS GROUP. The name given to a monument executed about 230 B.C. and erected at Pergamum to commemorate the Galatian wars in Asia Minor. The group represents a Galatian supporting his mortally wounded and expiring wife and about to stab himself. The statue of the 'Dying Gaul' by Epigonus, of which there is a copy in the Capitoline Museum at Rome, is also associated with these wars.

LUDOVISI THRONE is the name given to a magnificent original Greek work produced in southern Italy about 460 B.C. and found near the Villa Ludovisi. It is a three-sided relief, shaped like the back of a throne, the largest section possibly representing the birth of Aphrodite from the sea and the two smaller probably priestesses of the goddess. The original use to which this object was put has not been determined. A work similar in form, though it may not be a primary example, is at Boston.

LURISTAN BRONZES are cast weapons, ornaments and utensils, particularly portions of harness and chariot-fittings, which take the forms of animals or human beings or are given abstract figural decora-

125. Agesander and his sons. Laocoon group (c. 40 B.C.). Marble

126. *Lysippus, head of Alexander the Great (second half 4th cent. B.C.). Marble copy*

tion. They were manufactured by a people settled in the highland province of Luristan in western Persia during the 2nd and early 1st millennia B.C.

LUXOR is situated in Upper Egypt, on the east bank of the Nile, on the site of the ancient capital, Thebes. A large temple to Ammon, built by Amenophis III (1413–1377 B.C.) and Ramses II (1301–1234 B.C.), is extensively preserved in the town (ill. 97). The national temple of Ammon at Karnak, the 'Valley of the Kings', containing the burial grounds of the Pharaohs of the New Kingdom, is nearby and used to be connected to the Luxor temple by a paved road.

LYSIPPUS, the renowned Greek sculptor active during the middle and second half of the 4th century B.C., was Court sculptor to Alexander the Great, of whom he made many portraits, including works representing the king as Zeus. According to ancient writers Lysippus introduced a new theory of proportion, based on a closer study of Nature. He attempted a more pronounced use of perspective in composing sculpture in the round. The 'elegance' of his work is also stressed, referring probably to a new elasticity of movement in the rendering of the human form. The 'Scraper' (in Greek *apoxyomenos*, cf. p. 135), a figure executed about 330 B.C., probably gives the best idea of his style. A Roman copy is preserved in the Vatican (ill. 108, 126).

MALTA. Round about 2000 B.C. a unique culture, responsible for magnificent stone buildings on an elliptical ground-plan, developed in Malta. A strong feeling for the plastic was exhibited in stone reliefs depicting animals and spiral ornaments as well as in corpulent nude female statuettes of stone, erect or seated. The discoveries at Hal Saflieni probably date from a later period. The figures are of clothed women lying in a sleeping posture on couches shaped like shallow bowls.

MARCUS AURELIUS, Roman emperor, reigned from A. D. 161 to 180. The bronze equestrian statue of him in the Piazza of the Capitol at Rome was erected in his lifetime and is the only extant equestrian statue of Antiquity (cf. p. 143, ill. 127). The raised foreleg of the horse probably once rested on a human figure symbolizing a province subjugated by the emperor.

MASTABA (Arabic: embankment) is the name given to a certain form of Egyptian tomb of the Old Kingdom, whose rectangular upper portion, walled in brick or faced with limestone blocks, with raking side-walls, has the appearance of an embankment. The underground burial chambers were reached by a vertical shaft, closed after the body had been deposited. Surviving relatives performed the ritual of the dead at the east wall of the superstructure, originally a simple tombstone. In later mastabas the ritual chamber extended from, or was contained in, the superstructure.

MASTER OF THE BATHS is the name given to a celebrated bronze statue in the National Museum of Rome. It is excellently preserved and represents a ruler or general. It was executed at the beginning of the 1st century B.C. and is a masterpiece both of late Hellenistic art and of antique portraiture as a whole. It may originally have been part, together with the 'Boxer' of Apollonius in the same Museum, of an allegorical group in commemoration of the victory of Sulla over the Bithynian king Mithridates.

127. *Equestrian statue of Marcus Aurelius, in Rome (A. D. 161–180). Bronze*

MAUSOLEUM. The tomb of the Carian king Mausolus (d. 352 B.C.) and his wife Artemisia at Halicarnassus in south-western Turkey was among the Seven Wonders of the World. The architects Pytheus and Satyrus built a hall of columns, on a quadrangular foundation, surrounding the actual funerary chamber. The roof was pyramidal, with a four-wheeled chariot at the apex. The most eminent Greek artists of the day were employed on the rich plastic decoration. They were Timotheus, Leochares, Scopas and Bryaxis. Of the surviving sculptures, preserved in the British Museum, the statues believed to be those of Mausolus and Artemisia – though they may represent other members of the family – are of special importance. This type of building, indigenous to the region, had a decisive influence on later sepulchral monuments in ancient times, which were also called 'mausolea'.

MEDINET ABU. The name given to certain Egyptian temples situated on the west bank of the Nile opposite Luxor. The main building is a large temple of the time of Ramses III (1197–1165 B.C.), comprising the funerary temple of the king, his palace, administrative offices, residential accommodation and stabling. In front of the large temple stands a smaller one dedicated to the god Ammon by Queen Hatshepsut (1501–1480 B.C.) and Thutmosis III (1480–1448 B.C.). Both buildings are surrounded by a battlemented rampart which is as excellently preserved as the temples themselves.

MEGALITHIC STRUCTURES. 'Megalith' is the Greek for 'large stone'. Such buildings are to be found in the coastal regions of Western Europe, southern Scandinavia and northern Germany. They also occur on the islands of the Mediterranean, in Eastern Mediterranean countries, in the Near and Far East, in India and the Indonesian and Melanesian archipelagos. Megalithic cultures were based on the ritual of ancestor worship, expressed in a cult of the dead. Megalithic architecture is therefore sepulchral and funerary. The chief styles are the dolmen (or Celtic tabular), comprising between 4 and 6 slabs set edgewise and from 1 to 3 laid horizontally, to form a roof; the tunnelled tomb, with several edgewise and horizontally set slabs, accessible through a tunnel; the galleried tomb, consisting of one long tunnel, often cut through actual rock; underground tombs of rectangular or beehive shape, roofed in corbelled masonry. Megalithic ritual structures consisting of arrangements of perpendicular stones are found in Brittany, England and Ireland. The stones are set up in isolation (menhir, ill. 13), or so as to form a circle (cromlech) or in long rows, as at Stonehenge (ill. 132).

MEGARON. The longitudinal principal apartment of the ancient Greek house, usually accessible through an antechamber of equal width. In the Mycenaean age the centre of the megaron was occupied by the hearth. The roof was supported on four pillars. The main chamber (Greek: *naos;* Latin: *cella*) of a Greek temple was also laid out in accordance with the ground-plan of the megaron. The latter evolved from a longitudinal wooden structure and was only built of stone at a later stage.

MEMNON COLOSSI. The name given to two seated statues of the Egyptian king Amenophis III (1413–1377 (B.C.), believed in later Antiquity to be memorials to the Ethiopian king Memnon, slain by Achilles before Troy and made immortal by Zeus. The ancients regarded them as of special interest because one of the statues used to emit a musical sound at daybreak. The phenomenon is attributed to the fact that cracks in the stone resulting from an earthquake caused the air in the interstices to vibrate when the sun warmed it. After the statue had been restored by order of the Roman emperor Septimius Severus (A. D. 193–211) the sounds ceased.

MILETUS. In modern times extensive architectural ruins have been discovered in this former Greek city on the coast of Asia Minor. Until 494 B.C., Miletus was the principal commercial centre of Ionia, and it regained importance on the advent of Alexander the Great. The ruins include those of a large theatre and temples of the Hellenistic and Roman eras. The gate of the South Market, built in the second half of the 2nd century A.D., has been reconstructed in the Pergamon Museum at Berlin.

MUMMY PORTRAITS were in Roman times – from the 1st to the 3rd century A. D. – almost exclusively produced at Fayum in central Egypt. They were painted in wax on wood, as substitutes for the ancient Egyptian mummy-masks, being fastened to the face of the deceased by the mummy-bandages. They include some of the best examples of Roman portraiture (ill. p. 161).

MYCENAE, a city and fortress in Argolis in the north-eastern Peloponnese, was according to Homer the residence of Agamemnon. It was the centre of 'Mycenaean' civilisation. The older part of the citadel was confined to the top of the hill. The, still extant, extensive installation was erected in the 14th century B.C. and prospered until some time in the 12th. It was during this period that the 'Lion Gate', with its famous relief, was set up (ill. 128). A royal cemetery of the 16th century B.C. adjoins it, containing the 'Grave Circle', enclosed by stone slabs, where Heinrich Schliemann discovered shaft graves in which gold offerings of unprecedented value were stored. A second and older 'Grave Circle', some distance away, was recently excavated, but yielded offerings of lesser worth. Of the 'beehive tombs' (q. v.), dating from the 16th and 15th centuries B.C., the most famous is the 'Treasury of Atreus'. Its enormous inner chamber, without supporting pillars, is only exceeded in size by that of the Pantheon at Rome. The megalithic (q .v.) ramparts of the citadel are Cyclopean (q. v.).

MYRON was an Attic sculptor of the mid-5th century B.C. His Discus Thrower, or Discobolus, has come down to us in many Roman copies. He executed, for the Acropolis at Athens, the group of the youthful Athena, depicted after throwing away the flutes she has just devised, and the satyr Marsyas hastening to pick them up. A copy of the figure of Athena is in the Liebighaus at Frankfurt (ill. 106), and one of the Marsyas statue in

Mummy portrait of a noble warrior *(from Fayum, Egypt, beginning of 2nd century A.D.) Encaustic painting on wood*

Roman wall painting: Putto drawn by Dolphins, *Pompeii, House of the Vettii (A.D. 63)*

S. Giovanni in Laterano at Rome. Pupils of Myron collaborated in the metopes of the Parthenon.

NAKSH-I-RUSTAM is the name given to the perpendicular walls of rock near Persepolis (q. v.), close to Shiraz in southern Persia, in which the tombs of the ancient Persian kings of the Achaemenid dynasty were hewn (cf. p. 112). These kings were Darius I, Xerxes I, Artaxerxes I and Darius II, who reigned during the 6th and 5th centuries B.C. The cliffs are adorned with pictures in relief.

NEREID MONUMENT. This sepulchral monument to an unknown ruler of Xanthus in Lycia, south-western Turkey, dates from the beginning of the 4th century B.C. and anticipates the Mausoleum in its architectural style. The many fragments of the relief sculpture which probably adorned the lower section of the memorial are to-day in the British Museum. Female figures darting across water were set up between the columns, and are believed to have represented nereids. The architectural ornament in particular reveals a close affiliation to Attic art of about 410 B.C., though its artistic quality, of the sculptures especially, is very uneven and parts of it are frankly provincial.

NICIAS. This Greek painter, a contemporary of Apelles, probably influenced a number of Pompeian and Roman frescoes, for example, the 'Io and Argos' in the National Museum at Naples and the copy of it found on the Palatine in Rome and now in the National Museum of that city, as well as the equally often copied picture of 'Andromeda and Perseus' of which several replicas are to be found in the Museum at Naples.

NINEVEH, on the Tigris in Mesopotamia, opposite the modern city of Mosul, is proved by pottery finds to have been already in occupation in Neolithic times. As the capital of the Assyrian Empire it was adorned with palaces and temples by kings Sennacherib (705–681 B.C.) and Assurbanipal (669–633 B.C.). The city, destroyed by the Medes in 612 B.C., has been undergoing excavation since the middle of the 19th century.

NIOBID PAINTER. This designation refers to an important Attic vase-painter of the mid-5th century B.C. His chief works are the 'Argonaut' and 'Niobid' bowls, both in the Louvre (ill. 110).

NEFERTITI. The portrait bust of Nefertiti (ill. p. 121), wife of King Amenophis IV Ikhnaton, is one of the most impressive works of the Amarna period (q. v.). It is in the National Museum of Berlin.

OBELISKS are tall, four-sided columns, usually cut in one piece, tapering towards the summit and ending in a pyramidal point. In Egypt they were regarded as emblems of the sun-god, before and in whose shrines they were placed. Countless obelisks survive in Egypt to-day. The tallest, nearly 100 ft high, is that of Queen Hatshepsut in the Karnak (q. v.) temple (ill. 12, 20).

OLYMPIA. An important centre of ritual in Ancient Greece, situated on the west coast of the Peloponnese.

128. Lion Gate at Mycenae

The sacred enclosure is known as the Altis. In association with pre-Greek cults, games began to be held there in honour of Zeus in the 8th century B.C. The oldest shrines served for the worship of Pelops, the eponymous hero of the Peloponnese, and a mother-goddess later identified with Hera. In the early 7th century B.C. a temple was built to the latter deity. The edifice was originally of wood, which was gradually replaced by marble. The great Temple of Zeus was constructed in the second quarter of the 5th century B.C. by Libon, a local architect (ill. 100). The well preserved sculptures illustrate, in the metopes, the deeds of Heracles, on the east pediment the myth of Oenomaus and Pelops, the former occupants of Olympia, and on the west pediment the battle between the Centaurs and the Lapithae in the presence of Apollo. The style is mainly Peloponnesian, though Ionian sculptors also participated in the work (ill. 22, 85). In the thirties of the 5th century, Pheidias executed the statue of Olympian Zeus for this temple. The figure was regarded by ancient writers as the most splendid of all works of its kind. Nothing remains of it but parts of the mould from which the gold for the god's robe was cast by Pheidias and his assistants. The many architectural remains excavated include: treasure-houses dating partly from the 7th and partly from the 6th century B.C., with rich sculptural decoration; the Philippeum, a circular edifice of the 4th century B.C., dedicated by King Philip of Macedon as a memorial to his family; the Leonidaeum, a kind of guest-house; several official buildings and halls. Many individual

163

129. Pantheon, Rome. Interior (A. D. 120–135). Engraving of 1829

works of art, some of the highest aesthetic value, have been found at Olympia. They include, in particular, the sculptures of the Temple of Zeus, the statue of the Goddess of Victory by Paeonius of Mende erected about 420 B.C. and the well-known Hermes of Praxiteles. In addition, remains of bronze memorials set up in honour of victorious competitors in the Games have been preserved, as well as countless votive weapons of the period from the 7th to the 5th century B.C. Innumerable small bronzes in geometric style, mostly representing animals, more rarely human figures, as well as metal tripods and kettles with geometric and early archaic ornament, gave Olympia in olden times a unique character, these objects being publicly exhibited votive offerings to Zeus.

OMPHALOS APOLLO. A famous statue of Apollo dating from about 460 B.C. The original may be by Calamis, one of the chief masters of the pre-classical style. Roman copies only are extant, of which the best is in the British Museum.

OSEBERG TREASURE. About A. D. 850 Queen Ose, the grandmother of Harald the Fair-haired, first king of Norway, was buried in a ship under a massive sepulchral mound at Oslo Fjord. By good fortune the wooden funerary offerings, such as the sledge, chariot, bed and so on, have been preserved. They prove the excellence of Viking sculpture in wood. The broad exterior portions of the chariot, for instance, are completely covered with carvings in which the animal forms echo ancient German whorl-decoration.

PAESTUM, to the south of Naples, was originally a Greek city called Poseidonia. It is famous for three excellently preserved temples in the Doric style erected in the late 6th and in the 5th century B.C. Recent excavations have revealed the city itself; among the valuable finds was a richly furnished underground shrine. Also precious bronze vessels of about 500 B.C.

PAINTED POTTERY in the literal sense has existed ever since the Stone Age. But the term is commonly restricted to ceramics of the prehistoric and early his-

torical periods, and these enable various cultural groups to be identified. There is no painted pottery in the Germanic north, apart from a Rhineland group (Pingsdorf ware) of the early Middle Ages. But coloured ceramics were known in the Near East as early as the 4th millennium B.C. In the Neolithic Age they reached the Balkans, the Danube area and southern Italy. In the Bronze Age they were only to be found in the Aegean island region. Further distribution did not begin until the Iron Age, when such pottery was found in Italy, Spain and in the area of the Hallstatt (q. v.) and La Tène (q. v.) civilisations. (Ill. 90, 91)

PALMYRA. Extensive ruins bear witness to the importance of this former trade centre in Syria, which flourished in the Roman imperial epoch. The huge temple dedicated to Baal was completed in the 2nd century A. D. Its plan shows affinities with the older architectural style of the Near East. The sepulchral reliefs from Palmyra, executed in the 2nd and 3rd centuries A. D. and now distributed in museums throughout Europe, represent a provincial variant of a style which later informed Byzantine art.

PANTHEON. This building, in Rome, is the largest domed edifice of Classical Antiquity, the diameter of the dome measuring nearly 130 feet. In A. D. 27 Agrippa, the most eminent minister of Augustus, built enormous baths on the site, to which a temple dedicated to all the gods – hence the name Pantheon – was added. Hadrian erected the present building about A. D. 120, renovating Agrippa's inscriptions. It is composed of two parts, a pillared entrance-hall and a circular structure over 140 feet high at the summit, in which an opening admits the light (ill. 112, 129). Its excellent state of preservation is due to its having been transformed into a Christian church (S. Maria Rotonda) in which, as in the Pantheon Church in Paris of similar construction, national celebrities, such as Raphael, were buried.

PAPYRUS CLUSTER COLUMNS, or simply 'papyrus columns', were much used as supporting structures in Egyptian architecture. Their shafts represented sheaves

164

of papyrus stalks and the capitals open or closed papyrus blossoms (ill. 97).

PARRHASIUS was an important Greek painter of the second half of the 5th century B.C. His works are known to us only from literary sources, according to which he was the first Greek to suggest the personality of his models by the way he drew or painted their faces. He is said to have brought the mature Attic classical style of drawing to an artistic peak.

PARTHENON. The temple of Athena Parthenos on the Acropolis at Athens became the supreme example of classical Greek architecture when it was erected by the architects Ictinus and Callicrates under the super-vision of Pheidias, in the Doric style, between 448 and 432 B.C. Much of its fine sculptural ornament has been preserved, as for example the Elgin Marbles (q. v.) in the British Museum. In the metopes, battles between gods and giants and of heroes against barbarian powers, such as Amazons, Trojans and Centaurs, are represented; these symbolize the great struggle of the Greeks against the Persians in 480 B.C. The festal procession of the citizens of Athens, the Panathenaea, which took place every four years in honour of the goddess Athena, decorated the extensive frieze. The pediment sculptures depicted, on the east side, the birth of Athena and, on the west, the dispute between Athena and Poseidon for the possession of Attica. These sculptures were the joint products of a large workshop but were probably design-ed, without exception, by Pheidias himself. Within the temple stood the gigantic statue in gold and ivory of Athena Parthenos, unveiled in 438 B.C., also the work of Pheidias. We possess a number of small-scale copies of the figure by his hand, as for instance the Varvakion statuette in the National Museum at Athens, though they only render its most superficial features. In the 6th century A. D. the temple was transformed into a Christian church and in 1456 rebuilt by the Turks as a mosque. A cannon-ball fired by Venetian troops in 1687 exploded a magazine within the Parthenon, causing extensive damage. Till then it had survived in good condition. After the First World War, M. Balanos re-constructed part of the building (ill. 102, 130).

PASITELES, a Greek sculptor of the end of the Hellen-istic age, worked in the classic, or 'New Attic', style and trained many pupils, of whom the best known to-day is Stephanus. Pasiteles wrote a book about the famous sculptures of former times.

130. Parthenon. Athens. West frieze. Horsemen from the Panathenaic Festival Procession (c. 440 B.C.). Marble relief

PASQUINO GROUP. The name given – after an antique torso in Rome – to a well-preserved group of statues, do-day in Florence, representing Menelaus with the body of the slain Patroclus. The group only survives in Roman copies of an original that dated from about the middle of the 2nd century B.C. and was produced on the island of Rhodes or in some other centre of Hellenistic art. The torso in Rome, in poor condition, was placed in front of the Palazzo Braschi in 1501, and derives its name from a satirical versifier of the 16th century, who was accustomed to affix his abusive political poems to it.

PEGGED MOSAIC. In Sumerian and Babylonian archi-tecture, pillars and columns were erected in the form of bundles of reeds projecting from walls composed of rushes matted with loam. The resultant prominences and recesses were taken over, for no very good reason, by the later bricked architecture of Mesopotamia. Nails and conical or hollow tubular wedges of fired clay were employed to secure the loam-matted rushes of the wall. The tops of the wedges, coloured black, red and white, were arranged to form various geometrical patterns. 'Pegged Mosaic' of this kind gave animation to the loam walls and remained in use long after the end of the 4th millennium B.C.

PERGAMUM. This city in Asia Minor, first founded in 283 B.C., was a centre of Hellenistic culture and art. Its rulers collected old Greek works of art and had them copied; they also patronized contemporary art – such monuments as, for instance, the 'Galatian' groups. German excavations at the end of the last century in Pergamum brought to light an unsuspected quan-tity of original sculptures, some of great importance, for the most part dating from the middle Helle-nistic period. Nearly all the items are in the Pergamon Museum in Berlin. The best-known monument is the enormous 'Pergamum Altar', with a wealth of reliefs – there were probably also many statues, – which may be dated between 180 and 160 B.C. It is adorned with two extensive friezes in relief. The larger presents the battle of the gods and the giants allegorizing that of the Pergamenians against the Galatians. The second frieze illustrates the life-history of the mythical founder of Pergamum, the hero Telephus. The frieze of the giants is an outstanding example of mature 'baroque' Hellen-istic sculpture. The slightly later Telephus frieze re-presents the transition to an academically more restrain-ed phase of that epoch.

PERISTYLE. The colonnaded courtyard of the ancient Greek dwelling-house. The Romans took over this type of structure and combined it with their own traditional form of dwelling by adding the peristyle to its rear elevation. They also turned the peristyle into a garden and surrounded it with a chain of reception-rooms.

PERSEPOLIS (Greek: 'Persian City') was founded by the Persian king Darius I as a fortified town of palaces. Its ruins are situated near Shiraz in southern Persia. The extensive palaces, administrative offices and warehouses were erected, mainly between 518 and 460 B.C., on a vast, artificial terrace of earth. The city was destroyed by Alexander the Great in 330 B.C.

PHEIDIAS is the most important of all Greek artists. His activity coincided with the culmination of Attic classicism in the 5th century B.C. He was especially famous as the creator of the statues of Athena Parthenos at Athens and Zeus in the latter's temple at Olympia, both constructed by the gold and ivory method (q. v.). Pheidias was in charge of all the work undertaken on the Acropolis at Athens by order of Pericles and is supposed to have been responsible for the design of the Parthenon and its architectural sculptures. Of his other statues we only know for certain of one which he made in competition with Cresilas and Polycleitus, the figure of an Amazon. The best copy of it, the so-called Mattei Amazon, is in the Capitoline Museum in Rome. The Cassel Apollo (q. v.) and a helmetless statue of Athena, of which the body is in Dresden and the head in Bologna, supposed to be the sculptor's famous Athena Lemnia, are ascribed to him. Pheidias was also active as a painter. He trained many pupils, among them Agoracritus and Alcamenes. As to his life, we only know that he was an Athenian citizen, the son of an otherwise unknown Charmides. Contradictory accounts are given of his last years. He was prosecuted in 435 B.C. for alleged misappropriation of the gold used for the statue of Athena Parthenos. But he must have been acquitted, for he later continued his work at Olympia on the statue of Zeus. Recently his workshop, which had survived into later Antiquity, was discovered at Olympia, and in it were the original models employed by Pheidias and his assistants for casting the robe of thin gold-foil worn by the statue of Zeus. These models, from their style, are to be referred to about 430 B.C. (cf. ill. 102, 130).

POLYCLEITUS is the second most famous classical Greek sculptor, after Pheidias, of the 5th century B.C. A native of Argos, he headed the Argive school of art which flourished from the early 5th century until well on in the 6th. Ancient writers state that his statues followed a pattern and figural ideal that hardly varied. They always gave an impression of strength and athletic prowess. In composing the human figure he introduced the principle of balance, taking the weight off one leg and offsetting this by a corresponding movement of one arm, thus imposing a hitherto unknown rhythm on his statues. Only a few of his many works are definitely known to us. The most famous was the 'Doryphorus' of about 440 B.C., representing a youth carrying a spear. The best copy is in the National Museum at Naples. There is an excellent reproduction at Munich University by the sculptor Roemer (ill. 5). It is doubtful whether the statue is of a victorious athlete or a hero. Around it, Polycleitus wrote a treatise on proportion for sculptors. The statue of Cyniscus, an Olympic prize-winner, is also well known (copy in the British Museum, London). The figure of an Apollo binding a chaplet of victory on his head (best copy in the National Museum, Athens) may be a decade later in date than the spear-carrier. In competition with Pheidias and Cresilas, Polycleitus also executed the statue of an Amazon for the temple of Artemis at Ephesus, known to us through many Roman copies (best replica in the Capitoline Museum, Rome).

POLYGNOTUS, an important Greek painter of the pre-classical epoch, was a native of Thasos. He executed many paintings between 475 and about 450 B.C. of which we only possess written accounts, some of considerable length. A group of contemporary Attic vases enables us to form some idea of the nature of his art. Both sources suggest that Polygnotus arranged the many figures in his compositions in superimposed rows of closely packed individuals, and avoided dramatic treatment. The noble appearance of his figures has won particular praise. His colour range was restricted to the traditional red, yellow, dark blue and white and their mixtures, though he did not use green.

POLYGONAL MASONRY. In ancient Greek architecture, walls, especially those of a town or citadel, were sometimes built of rectilinear cubes of hewn stone polished on the exterior face. As a variant, the curvilinear polygonal style was employed, in which individual blocks retained their chance contours but the adjacent stones were carefully adjusted to fit the irregularities, as in the polygonal wall at Delphi. Polygonal masonry was not only decorative but also served to counteract displacement of the blocks through earthquakes, for mortar was never used in the Greek wall.

POMPEII, a city in Campania, southern Italy, was at first under Etruscan and later, Italo-Greek or Alexandrine influence. At the end of the 2nd century B.C. it was romanized. Partially destroyed by an earthquake in A. D. 63, it was immediately rebuilt. But 16 years later it was completely overwhelmed, together with Herculaneum and Stabiae, by an eruption of Vesuvius. Systematic excavations began in 1748. They have provided more detailed information about the cultural, private and artistic life of a small Italian provincial town than is available from any other source. Many public and private buildings have already been unearthed and the work is still going on. The development of the Roman dwelling-house and its equipment, over many generations, can be followed with precision. Apart from a number of mostly second-rate sculptures and a great variety of products of the applied arts, it is the many surviving frescoes that are of particular artistic value (ill. p. 162). They present us with a picture of Italic development in this branch of art from about 80 B.C. to the date of the destruction of the town. The Pompeian paintings are predominantly the work of craftsmen, though they include several copies and alternative versions of older Greek pictures. The way in which a whole room or even a whole building was decorated with paintings can also be traced at Pompeii. The numerous mosaic pavements, among which the Alexander Mosaic (ill. p. 149) is conspicuous, are of similar importance.

Some of the works found are in the National Museum of Naples, but of recent years the majority have been left in situ.

PRAXITELES, a Greek sculptor of the mid-4th century B.C., is a forerunner of Hellenistic art (cf. p. 135). His special character as an artist resides in the peculiar softness with which he moulded form, so that he was qualified, in particular, to represent youthful, feminine divinities. He was the first Greek artist who ventured to portray Aphrodite undraped. The figure of Hermes at Olympia is probably an original work by him. We possess copies of his statues of Apollo piercing a lizard on a tree (best replica in the Vatican), of the Arles Aphrodite (in the Louvre) and of the Cnidian Aphrodite (copies at Munich and in the Vatican, ill. 107).

PRAYING BOY. This bronze, formerly in the State Museum of Berlin, is a Roman copy of a Greek work of the end of the 4th century B.C. The arms have been restored in the wrong position. The figure may have represented a ball-player. The original was by a sculptor of the Lysippus circle.

PROPYLAEA are monumental entrances giving access to major precincts. In Greek Antiquity the type is first found in sanctuaries, as at Eleusis. The famous Propylaea on the Acropolis at Athens were erected in their present form by Mnesicles, under the supervision of Pheidias, between 437 and 432 B.C.

PROTODORIC COLUMNS are the cylindrical pillars, fluted or provided with eight or more faces, which are found as early as the time of the Egyptian king Zoser (about 2500 B.C.) and recall, thought at times only distantly, the form of Doric columns.

PYLON (Greek: entrance-gate) is used to designate the porticoes of Egyptian temples, consisting of two massive gate-towers with raking sides. The door between them is relatively small and low. Flagstaffs were formerly placed in the symmetrically arranged recesses of the front elevations of the towers.

PYRAMID. In the Old and Middle Kingdoms the royal Egyptian tomb customarily took the form of a pyramid. Later it was occasionally also used for the tombs of private citizens. It originated in the superimposition of several mastabas (q. v.), as still seen in the sepulchral monument of King Zoser dating from about 2500 B.C., the so-called Step Pyramid near Sakkara, considered to be the immediate predecessor of the pyramid proper. Shortly afterwards the famous pyramids at Gizeh were erected, of which the largest, that of King Cheops, has an area of upwards of 13 acres and a height of nearly 480 feet. It was regarded in Antiquity as one of the Seven Wonders of the World (ill. 96).

PYRAMID OF CESTIUS. The tomb, near the Porta San Paolo in Rome, of a Roman who died in 12 B.C.

RAMESSEUM is the name given to the funerary temple of the Egyptian king Ramses II (1301–1234 B.C.) situated west of Thebes, opposite Luxor.

RHODES, a Greek island and traditional centre of ancient art, under Egyptian and Near East influence until the middle of the 1st century B.C. These features, mingled with others from eastern Greece, gave Rhodian art a special character. In the 7th and 6th centuries B. C. pottery was manufactured on the island, as on the adjacent Ionian mainland, and widely exported to the eastern territories of Greek civilisation, where it was variously imitated, as in Rhodo-Milesian or Fikellura ware. For political reasons Rhodes, like most of the eastern centres of Greek art, entirely lost its importance in the 5th and 4th centuries B.C. But in the Hellenistic period it prospered again, producing a particularly notable sculpture, such as the Laocoon (q. v.) group and the Victory of Samothrace (ill. 6, 125; cf. ill. 109).

ROCK PAINTINGS or Cave Paintings. Many paintings, drawings, engravings and reliefs on rock, either in caves on exposed surfaces, have survived from prehistoric times. Palaeolithic cave paintings have been found in southern France at Lascaux, Combarelles, Trois Frères, Niaux, etc., and in northern Spain at Altamira and elsewhere (cf. p. 101). They are of magical import and depict animals of the chase. For the paintings, mineral colouring matter mixed with charcoal and a binding medium such as fat was used, while the drawings were scratched with stone tools. In mesolithic times rock-paintings were executed on exposed cliffs. In eastern Spain the Palaeolithic manner developed into more highly stylized hunting and fighting scenes, man being shown as dominant. These pictures are ritualistic or mythical rather than magical in significance (cf. p. 102). They are related to those of North Africa, often engraved on the rock, which continued into the Neolithic Age. Similar rock-drawings have been discovered in France, Italy, Scandinavia, northern Russia and Siberia. In Sweden, at periods including the Bronze Age, human beings, animals and such objects as ships, chariots and sledges were reproduced in simplified forms, sometimes as symbols, but also in scenic composition. Such rock-pictures were still being produced in Scandinavia during the Iron Age. (Ill. p. 105)

ROMAN MASONRY. In addition to the methods still employed for building walls of hewn stone blocks or superimposed layers of bricks, the Ancient Romans used rubble construction, faced externally with varied ornament. Two parallel walls were built, with layers of small rectangular stones or bricks set diagonally to achieve a trellised effect (*opus reticulatum*), or else common stones, roughly shaped, were held in place with great quantities of mortar, thus giving the wall an irregular aspect (*opus incertum*). The gap between the two walls was then filled up with pieces of stone of different sizes, and mortar. The corners and edges of walls built in this way were lined with horizontal courses of stones or bricks.

RUNIC STONES are inscribed fragments and slabs of rock set up in Northern Europe as memorials to fallen heroes, between the 4th and 12th centuries. The inscription is usually brief, merely stating for, and by, whom the memorial was erected. Many runic stones are also lightly engraved or bear designs in low relief. As well as ornaments and such emblems as the wheel-cross, spiral and, later, the Christian cross, animals, weapons and ships are delineated. Pictures of warriors and horsemen occur more rarely and are usually highly simplified. Of special interest is the portrait of Christ on the large, richly decorated Jellinge stone in Jutland.

SAITE RENAISSANCE. In the 7th and 6th centuries B.C., under the 26th dynasty of Sais, a town on the Rosetta tributary of the Nile delta, a conscious classical revival took place which affected all Egyptian activities, but especially art. Interest in the Old and Middle Kingdoms grew so strong that, for example, reliefs on tombs of the Old Kingdom were copied down to the smallest detail. On the other hand, in portraiture a frank naturalism developed, bearing witness to an amazing faculty for anatomical observation. Portraits were executed which exceeded practically all previous work in their powers of expression, as for example the so-called 'Green Head' (q. v., ill. 124).

SAMOS. This island in the Aegean Sea possessed a very old sanctuary. It was renowned for the enormous temple of Hera, erected by Rhoecus and Theodorus in the Ionic style by order of the tyrant Polycrates in the mid-6th century (ill. 101). The bases of the columns were turned on a lathe. In the sanctuary, German excavators found costly votive offerings, mostly of early Greek or ancient oriental workmanship, including some important archaic statues, such as the Kore of Cheramyes, now in the Louvre (ill. 103). After the end of the 6th century B.C. the importance of the shrine declined. It did not revive until Roman times.

SARDINIA was occupied in the Early Bronze Age by people of the bell-beaker culture. Formally designed stone idols are probably to be ascribed to this period. Megalithic architecture developed, producing large circular buildings with domed roofs, called *nuraghi*. The numerous expressive human figures found, including warriors with weapons and ornaments, may be dated at about the middle of the 1st millennium B.C. This characteristic native culture gradually disappeared under Roman rule.

SCARABAEUS. One of the most popular Egyptian amulets, in the form of a carved stone 'apothecary' beetle. The insect was considered sacred, as it was believed to have come into being out of nothing. The fact that eggs had been laid in the ball of dung from which the larvae emerged had not been noticed. As the sun, too, appeared each morning of its own accord, the scarabaeus was made sacred to the sun-god.

SCENOGRAPHY, or the painting of landscapes and architecture on theatrical backcloths or the wings of theatres, was developed in Athens about the middle of the 5th century B.C. by Agatharchus of Samos, obviously on mathematical principles, which led to a method of representing perspective no longer completely intelligible. 'Scenography' was identified in later Antiquity with the teaching of perspective.

168

SCOPAS was a Greek sculptor of the mid-4th century B. C. who won renown for the pathos with which he invested his figures. Original works from his studio, designed by him but at most given only finishing touches by his own hand, are extant on certain slabs from the frieze of the Mausoleum at Halicarnassus and in fragments of the gable sculptures of the temple of Athena at Tegea in southern Greece (now in the National Museum, Athens). A youthful work, the statue of an adolescent Heracles (copy in the Lansdowne Collection, London) and also a masterpiece, the racing figure of an intoxicated maenad (copy in Dresden) have not survived as originals.

SCRIBES. Egyptian sculptors of the Old Kingdom (3rd millennium B.C.) gave much prominence to representations of the male scribe or reader squatting on the ground or on a mat. The most famous statue of a 'squatting scribe' is that in the Louvre. It is of limestone, nearly life-size, with inlaid eyes which lend the figure an extraordinarily lifelike aspect (ill. 131).

SCYTHIAN ART. The nomads of the steppes of southern Russia were called 'Scythians' by the Greeks in the 1st millennium B.C. In the burial mounds (*kurgans*) of Scythian chieftains, which were of great size, magnificent objects made of bronze, gold and silver, were found. The principal subjects depicted were animals. Individual species, in particular, stags, birds and fish, as well as groups – animals fighting, for example, – appeared in relief work or filigree. Each figure, despite its simplification and decorative form, remains naturalistic and vigorous. Scythian art had a strong influence for a time on Chinese and European cultures, as in the goldsmiths' work found at Vettersfelde (q. v.).

SEALING CYLINDERS are perforated stones or semi-precious stones, from $^3/_8$ to $2^3/_8$ in. long, used for sealing documents and, when of clay, for sealing storage jars. The stones were engraved with figural or botanical

131. 'Squatting Scribe'. Limestone, eyes inlaid with alabaster, black stone, silver and quartz (Egypt, 5th Dyn.)

designs, mostly of religious significance. They spread from Mesopotamia, where sealing cylinders had been in use ever since the early 3rd millennium B. C., over the ancient East as far as Egypt.

SELINUS. A Greek colony in Sicily which flourished in the 6th and 5th centuries B.C., when some temples were erected in the Doric style. A number of temple metopes of the end of the 6th century B.C. illustrate among other scenes the slaying of Medusa and Heracles with the Cyclopes. The metopes of a somewhat later temple of Hera depict mythological scenes such as the mystic wedding of Zeus and Hera. All these finds are to-day on view in the National Museum of Palermo.

SITULA. The name of a bucket-shaped metal vessel with a handle. Fine specimens, embossed with representations of human beings and animals, were manufactured in Italy and the Hallstatt region during the 1st millennium B.C.

SPALATO, to-day Split, Yugoslavia, was originally a vast Roman palace which Diocletian (A. D. 295–305) had built on the plan of a Roman legion's camp. It is surrounded by a rectangular, turreted wall. An important feature is the emperor's mausoleum, now used as a cathedral. Octagonal outside, the building has a circular interior, fitted with recesses. The architecture of both later Antiquity and the early Middle Ages was influenced by it.

SPHINX. This Greek word is applied to representations of Egyptian kings as a lion with the Pharoah's head, symbolizing the power of the monarch. A famous example is the great sphinx placed in front of the pyramid of Cheops (c. 2500 B.C.) near Gizeh. The natural rock was used in its construction. It is some 60 ft high and 189 ft long (ill. 96). In Greek art the sphinx is a female hybrid, a virgin with the body of a lion. Examples are the winged sphinx from Delphi (c. 590 B.C.), which is seated on an Ionic pillar, and the sphinx on the temple of Apollo at Aegina (about 460 B.C.), serving as an acroterium, i. e. an ornamental feature surmounting the pediment of a temple. The sphinx also occurs as a motif in medieval, Baroque and Classical architectural sculpture.

STONEHENGE. The massive megaliths of the ritual and funerary precincts at Stonehenge in southern England were set up in three major stages of construction from just before, until towards the end of, the Bronze Age. A rampart and trench enclose a circular space some 350 feet in diameter. In the middle of it stand concentric rings of huge stone columns. A continuous architrave covered the outer circle of about 38 stones. The nucleus has five pairs of stones with a roofing stone for each pair. Some of the massive blocks used came from quarries over a hundred miles away. A road led from the ritual area to a kind of racecourse which, it is assumed, served, as in Ancient Greece, for sham fights and chariot races (ill. 132).

SUSA, the ancient Persian capital, on the river Karkha, south of the Zagros mountains, exists only as a great

132. Stonehenge (c. 1500 B.C.). Reconstruction

heap of ruins in which much pottery and also the remains of Achaemenid palaces were found (cf. p. 111). Brick reliefs enamelled in various colours, representing armed men, bulls and lions, were unearthed (ill. p. 106).

SYRACUSE was founded as a Greek colony on the east coast of Sicily in the 7th century B.C. The cultural maturity of the city lasted from the 5th to the 3rd century B.C. Remains of the 5th-century temple of Apollo have been built into the modern cathedral. The Greek theatre, the largest of its kind, is well preserved. Extensive fortifications indicate the former importance of the harbour. The enormous quarries (*latomie*) which often served as prisons, are famous. A notable system of catacombs is of early Christian date. Syracuse struck in the 5th century B.C. the handsomest of all antique coins.

TANAGRA, in Boeotia, central Greece, has been the source of countless clay figures. In common with the rest of Boeotia, it enjoyed during the 4th century B.C. a boom in an industry producing so-called terra-cotta figures, such as had flourished, especially in central Greece, since very early times. Formerly, terra-cottas had mostly been manufactured to provide votive or funerary offerings. But after the 4th century they also came to be used for room decoration.

TARENTUM became a centre of Greek culture in southern Italy after the 7th century B.C. The excavation of extensive burial grounds from archaic and classical times has yielded great numbers of clay figures, often showing great independence of style. The 'Seated Goddess' in Berlin is a most notable example of Late Archaic Tarentine monumental sculpture. Abundant remains of limestone carvings have survived from the 4th century B.C. The freedom of their execution is characteristic of Italo-Greek art in this area. Tarentine pottery came to maturity at the same period and differs markedly from Attic both in style and subject. Greek tendencies in Etruscan art originated in Tarentum.

TARQUINIA, a town in Tuscany, was founded by the Etruscans. Adjacent burial-grounds contain funerary chambers of the Archaic and later periods in which very many works of art were discovered. The tombs are noted for their frescoes, in part well preserved, mainly dating from between 500 and 300 B.C. (ill. p. 140).

TELL HALAF, the Assyrian Guzana, was situated on the Chabur river in northern Mesopotamia. Coloured pottery of the early Chalcolithic (Stone-Copper) Age, from 3500 to 3250 B.C., is termed Halaf ware. It is characterized by *boukranion* (bull's head) motifs and pictures of the sacred ox, which suggest an agricultural

169

civilisation. Contemporary chromatic pottery from Samara on the central course of the Tigris and from Tepe Sialk in central Persia, on the other hand, indicates, with its geometrical and abstract designs of animals, a people dominated by conceptions derived from hunting and magic.

TELL OBEID (or Ubaid), on the lower Euphrates, north-west of Ur, provided evidence of early Neolithic (post-5th-millennium B.C.) settlement and also occupation at later periods. The Obeid Age refers to a late Chalcolithic civilisation in Mesopotamia between 3250 and 3000 B.C. To symbolize the cosmic order, these people erected monumental temples, occasionally terraced, with walls already suggesting the typical Mesopotamian projection of pillars. They were the first to make bricks, and invented the potter's wheel and the wheeled chariot.

TERRA SIGILLATA is the name given to Roman clay vessels, mostly of the imperial era, and predominantly manufactured in Italy itself though later also in Gaul and Germany. The vessels were treated with red oxide and often seem to have been polished on the outside. They were frequently stamped by the manufacturer. The best specimens, often with rich ornament in relief, were produced at Arezzo about the time of the birth of Christ and are called Aretine ware.

THESEUM. This temple, erected at Athens in the Doric style in 440 B.C., is the best preserved in Greece. It was dedicated jointly to Hephaestus and Athena Hephaestia. Its metopes illustrate the deeds of Theseus and Heracles. The west frieze depicts the battle between the Lapithae and the Centaurs and the east frieze an unidentified conflict watched by the gods.

THORN EXTRACTOR. The name of a bronze at the Capitoline Museum in Rome which is a leading example of late Hellenistic classicism, probably dating from the 1st century B.C. The motif was taken from older figures of street-urchins extracting thorns – masterpieces of Hellenistic naturalism in their own right. This particular statue, known as the Capitoline Thorn Extractor, was often imitated in the Middle Ages and later.

TIRYNS. A citadel near Mycenae, mainly erected in the Mycenaean Age, about the middle of the 2nd millennium B.C. A large circular building of still undetermined significance is of earlier date. The plan of the citadel is in two parts, surrounded by a massive cyclopean (q. v.) wall. The part not built over served as a refuge for the population of the neighbourhood in time of war. The palace, on a separate site, has two *megara* (see, Megaron). They were once adorned with frescoes of which only traces remain. A very old-fashioned temple of the 7th century B.C. is built into one of the *megara*, showing how the Greek temple evolved from the Mycenaean *megaron*. Historically and culturally Tiryns belongs to the same type as the Mycenae citadel.

TOWER OF BABYLON. The building referred to in the Old Testament as the 'Tower of Babel' appears to be identical with the tower called *Etemenanki,* meaning approximately 'Foundation of Heaven and Earth'. The base, ascended by a ramp with steps, occupied an area of about 100 sq. yds. Above this were six further storeys, rising to a height of 295 ft. The topmost storey containing the sanctuary of the tutelary god of Babylonia, Marduk. There were similar temple-towers at Borsippa and Ur.

TRAJAN'S COLUMN. In A. D. 114, Trajan had a gigantic column, decorated in relief and surmounted by his statue, erected in the Forum he had built in Rome. The frieze of reliefs, some 650 ft long, winds spirally up the shaft, providing a continuous narrative of the Dacian wars of Trajan. The ashes of the emperor were deposited within the pedestal (ill. 134). Marcus Aurelius followed this example when he erected a second column in Rome about A. D. 190, illustrating his campaigns against the Marcomanni in the same way.

TROY. The repeatedly destroyed and rebuilt city of Troy became conspicuous in the 3rd millennium B.C. among the settlements of western Asia Minor. The town of fair Helen, celebrated in Homer's Iliad, was found by Heinrich Schliemann under the mound of ruins of the city of Hissarlik on the coast of the Dardanelles, the entrance to the Hellespont. The rich finds of pottery, the embossed vessels of gold and silver foil, the form of the *megaron* house with its long rectangular hall and open forecourt indicate affinities with the cultures of the islands of the Eastern Mediterranean and the mainland of Southern Europe. Troy probably acted as an important intermediary between East and West. During the 2nd millennium B.C., buildings of hewn stone were laid out on circular terraces. The Mycenaean Greeks (Aeolians) destroyed the city about 1200 B.C., the period of the saga of the Trojan War. The settlement lost its importance in Greek and Roman times.

TRUNDHOLM SUN-CHARIOT. This famous six-wheeled ritual chariot was discovered in a Jutland marsh. A stylized, hollow cast bronze horse, of archaic type, stands on the front pair of wheels. The rear wheels carry a large, round bronze disc, coated with thin gold foil on one side, where it is decorated with regular and complex ornamentation: three concentric circles are filled with spiral and ring patterns. The spiral occurs repeatedly in the Germanic North during the Bronze Age as a symbol of the sun, which is also represented, as the supreme deity, by the disc. The horse retained its ritual significance even among the later Germanic peoples. The Trundholm find dates from the 2nd millennium B.C. (ill. 133).

TUTENKHAMON, an Egyptian king of the 18th Dynasty (1358–1349 B.C.) was the son-in-law of King

133. Trundholm Sun Chariot

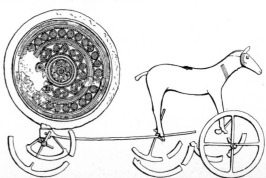

Amenophis IV Ikhnaton. He came to the throne as a child and died young. The discovery in 1922 of his almost untouched tomb and its rich treasures caused a considerable stir (ill. p. 121).

UR (to-day Mugheir), in southern Mesopotamia, flourished in Sumerian times in the middle of the 3rd millennium B.C. and again about 2000 B.C. In the centre of the oval site of the town stood the shrine of the moon-god and goddess, together with a ziggurat temple of which two terraces can still be identified. Many important finds, including a beautiful statuette of a ram, were made in the royal cemetery by Sir Leonard Woolley, the distinguished excavator of Ur. (Cf. ill. p. 106).

URNS are clay vessels in which the ashes and the remains of the bones of deceased persons were deposited. In prehistoric and early historical periods special forms of urn were developed. 'Face Urns' have a human countenance, partly moulded and partly engraved, on the neck of the vessel. Sometimes the body of the vessel bears some resemblance to a human form. Such urns were known in Troy after about 2000 B.C. and occur in northern Germanic regions, mainly in West Prussia and central Germany, at the beginning of the Iron Age. 'House Urns', in the shape of a house, appear in the area of Etruscan civilisation, in Scandinavia, in central and eastern Germany during the Late Bronze and Early Iron Ages and in Carniola, a district of Slovenia, in Roman times.

USHABTI, meaning, in ancient Egyptian, 'answerers', are small, mummy-like figures of faience, wood or stone placed in the tomb of a deceased person. They were supposed to 'answer' when the dead man was summoned to work in the fields of the Other World, i. e. they were to do the work for him. For this reason they carry mattocks in their hands and sacks on their backs.

VAPHIO in the Peloponnese is the place at which two celebrated gold cups, with embossed reliefs, were found. They were probably produced in Crete in Late Minoan times, and are masterpieces of Minoan art, illustrating the capture and taming of wild bulls.

VASES (Latin *vas*, vessel) were made of clay and used for multifarious purposes in Ancient Greece. Their forms, which were occasionally native to certain districts, varied frequently in accordance with the taste of the period and changing requirements (ill. 136). The *hydria* was used for holding water and the *krater* for mixtures of wine and water. Wine and oil were kept in the double-handled *amphorae* which also held the ashes of the dead. Winners in the Panathenaic Games, celebrated in honour of the goddess Athena, were given amphorae as prizes, filled with oil from the sacred olives of Athena. Oil in small quantities, required for anointing the body, was kept in *alabastra* and *aryballoi*. The *lekythos* also contained oil, for instance that used in anointing corpses and in funeral rites. Barrel-like vessels, often of enormous size, for storage purposes, were called *pithoi*. Drinking vessels were the *kulix* (cup), the *cantharos*,

134. *Trajan's Column, Rome (A. D. 114). Relief frieze, 600 ft long*

the *skyphos* and the *cyathos*. Greek earthenware was often finely painted. In the Hellenistic Age impressed pottery, decorated in relief, was often used instead of painted ware. In the Early Roman imperial period the sometimes beautiful Aretine vessels, of *terra sigillata* (q. v.), came into fashion. For daily use the Romans seldom employed ornamented ware.

135. *Symbolic female figurine. The so-called 'Venus of Willendorf'*

VENUS OF MEDICI. The name given to a statue which at one time belonged to the Tuscan Grand Dukes of the Medici family (now in the Uffizi, Florence). The figure is a Roman copy of a Greek original made about 300 B.C. and modelled on a somewhat earlier statue of Aphrodite, also now only preserved in copies, e. g. the 'Capitoline Venus' in Rome.

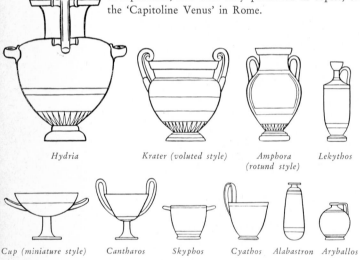

Hydria   Krater (voluted style)   Amphora (rotund style)   Lekythos

Cup (miniature style)   Cantharos   Skyphos   Cyathos   Alabastron   Aryballos

136. *Antique vessel forms*

VENUS OF MILO, one of the most famous of existing Greek statues of Aphrodite. It is a work of the 2nd century B.C., which seems to indicate the influence of Scopas. It was found on the island of Melos, Aegean Sea, in 1820, and is now in the Louvre.

VENUS OF WILLENDORF, the name given to a Palaeolithic limestone carving only 4³/₈ in. high. A standing female figure of exaggeratedly exuberant development, it probably represents a fertility goddess. Such naturalistic or highly stylized female figurines, of stone or ivory, have been found in regions extending from France to Russia (ill. 135).

172

VETTERSFELDE GOLD FIND. At Vettersfelde (Brandenburg) a tomb was discovered which contained among other offerings some splendid gold ornaments. They include a golden quatrefoil with friezes depicting lions and panthers, a golden fish 15³/₄ in. long with an enclosed design of animals and a fish-tailed human figure. These are Scythian works executed about 500 B.C.

VICTORY OF SAMOTHRACE. This masterpiece of Hellenistic 'baroque' sculpture, in the Louvre, is probably a work of the Rhodian sculptor Pythocritus. The statue shows the goddess of victory (Nike) standing on the reproduction, in stone, of the prow of a ship. It was erected shortly after 190 B.C. on the island of Samothrace, to commemorate a victory of the Rhodian fleet over the Syrians. (Ill. 6)

VITRUVIUS. The architect and engineer Vitruvius Pollio, who lived about the time of the birth of Christ, wrote a multi-volumed work, *De Architectura* (Concerning Architecture), which is the only one of its kind to have survived from Antiquity. Rediscovered in Early Renaissance times, it profoundly influenced Renaissance and Baroque architecture.

ZIGGURAT is the name of the Babylonian elevated temple, erected on a terrace of one or more levels. A ziggurat built about 3500 B.C. has been unearthed at Eridu. In the 2nd millennium B.C. the ziggurat occurs also in the form of a stepped tower with brick walls and diminishing storeys (see, Tower of Babylon).

137. *Die Squatter. Statue of squatting priest (650 B.C.). Black granite*

Medieval Art

138. 'Ecclesia' in Strassburg Cathedral (c. 1230)

EARLY CHRISTIAN
PERIOD

THE PREVAILING MOOD towards the end of Classical Antiquity was one of pessimism. As belief in the old gods waned, the idea that man must determine his own fate caused widespread anxiety about life on Earth and uncertainty concerning the after-life. Men began to have profound doubts about the salvation of their souls and this meant that they no longer had much interest in the classical idea of physical perfection. In time, this turning away from Nature and its presentation in the round led to a schism between the human body and the soul. The artistic manifestations of this change in attitude are evident in a preference for relief sculpture, a new interest in the spiritual element shown by greater emphasis on the eyes in the portraits of this period, the gradual disappearance of three-dimensional space in painting, and the contrast between sober, functional exteriors and elaborate interiors in architecture (Pantheon, ill. 129).

Spiritual uncertainty, which was by no means confined to the Hellenist world alone, produced a number of religions featuring redemption. Among these, Christianity came to occupy first place. In less than three centuries it had spread across the entire Roman Empire. The Edict of Milan in the year 313, under the Emperors Constantine and Licinius, granted Christians freedom of religious worship and the Edict of Theodosius I in 380 established a united Western Church.

The Early Christian attitude towards art was not always a sympathetic one. Strict dogmatists were able to defend their hostility by citing St John the Evangelist who had said that God should be worshipped in spirit and truth only. In spite of this, the beginning of the 2nd century saw the development of a Christian art which had its origins in Roman native tradition. It is true that the art of Greece had been taken over by Rome and its provinces, but the spirit of classical art was never fully understood by more than a small cultured minority. A native art which used Greek idioms to express Roman ideas had, however, always co-existed with it. This can be seen in many of the Pompeian frescoes and in the narrative relief bands round Trajan's column (ill. 134). After the beginning of the 2nd century this art found its way into the increasingly 'barbarianized' Imperial Court and the new-rich aristocracy. Being a product of the Late Classical era, Early Christian art welcomed the simplification and stylisation of the Roman native tradition, its emphasis on meaning rather than on form and its anti-classical attitude, as revealed by rejection of the physical element and an increased emphasis on spiritual expression.

The Early Christians met for worship in each other's homes. In Dura-Europos, Mesopotamia, there is a shrine dating from the 3rd century which consists of two chambers, one for Communion, the other for Baptism. This shrine cannot be called a temple as it did not contain an image. The Christian com-

173

munity needed a proper hall in which to assemble and celebrate Mass, and the type of building considered most suited to these needs was the Roman basilica which housed the halls of justice and commercial exchanges.

The Christian saw in the typical basilica (ill. 45, 46) the path to salvation. Symbolically, the entrance gateway, or propylaeum, received the worshipper into the sacred domain. Thence he stepped into a square colonnaded court (atrium, q. v.) where he washed off the sins of this world in the fountain (kantharos). Inside the basilica he found himself in an oblong hall divided by rows of columns into a number of avenues which led him to the semicircular presbytery (apse, q. v.). The cruciform plan of the basilica with transept was likened to Christ's Cross, the columns to the prophets and apostles, and the roof to Heaven. The columns were of vari-coloured marble, the floor was richly encrusted and the walls of the nave below and between the window openings, as well as the apse, were adorned with mosaics. (Cf. ill. p. 179)

From the 4th century onwards many of the larger churches were built with five aisles. The old basilican church of St Peter in Rome (ill. 45, 46) was constructed this way, the colonnades on either side of the nave (155 ft long and 55 ft broad) being surmounted by architraves, while S. Paolo fuori le mura, also in Rome, and many later basilicas had arcades. During the 5th and 6th centuries the basilica, while keeping to the general plan, underwent a number of regional changes. In North Africa more aisles were added. Syrian church architecture in the region behind Antioch produced a variety of highly individual features which are thought to have influenced medieval architecture, such as an entrance flanked by towers, and barrel-vaulted interiors. Originally the basilica was built without a tower but later a bell-tower or campanile was placed next to the main body of the church; this had a square base in Rome and a circular one in Ravenna.

The Christian rites of baptism and burial supplied the need for baptisteries and tombs. Since the congregation assembled either round the baptismal font or the sarcophagus, the Roman circular or octagonal form of building with cupola was adopted. The simple rotunda was later developed into the monumental domed church, characteristic of Byzantine art, by the addition of vaulted niches (Mausoleum of Theodoric at Ravenna, q. v., ill. 141) or the introduction of a ring of arcades to support the dome (S. Costanza in Rome, q. v.). The possibility of developing the domed church into a centrally planned building of square or cruciform type, or of combining the circular or polygonal rotunda with the basilica to achieve a balance of vertical and horizontal units was explored only in later times.

In the realm of sculpture, Early Christian art was impoverished by the increasing lack of interest shown in the human body during Late Classical times. The symbolical figure of the 'Good Shepherd' (ill. 139) is still imbued with classical feeling. But in its concentration on the front view, figure sculpture was beginning to move more and more in the direction of relief sculpture. The reliefs on the sarcophagi, handed down by Roman tradition, gave new scope to sculptural representation. Mythological figures were turned into Christian ones. The transition from the three-dimensional rendering of space to relief, and a gradual coarsening of forms after A. D. 400, mark the break with the classical tradition of figure sculpture.

The oldest examples of Early Christian painting are to be found in the catacombs. These subterranean chambers with their connecting passages were used for burial. As there was no room for the architectural treatment of walls, these were decorated with frescoes in the manner of Roman wall paintings. But they differed from their Roman counterparts, known to us above all from Pompeii, in being less sophisticated and more the product of skilled craftsmanship. Amoretti, peacocks, flowers and landscapes, delicately applied, create a happy world below ground, made even more sunny by the light from many small lamps. After the end of the 2nd and the beginning of the 3rd century, classical themes were gradually replaced by Christian ones. Miracles, as in the stories of Noah and the Ark, Jonah and the

Whale and Daniel in the Lions' Den, were used as allegories representing the salvation of the soul. New Testament subjects and Christian symbols also appear. Pictures are no longer narrative representations, as in Late Classical times, but allegories pointing to the spiritual reality of the next world.

The typical 4th-century church demanded a severely monumental kind of painting, brilliantly coloured and effective from a distance. These practical requirements were all met by the mosaic which had been developed in Hellenic times. Coloured stones and pieces of glass were set in damp mortar to make up representations of Christ, the Virgin, the apostles and saints. Gradually, Christ was given imperial attributes. The preacher of the doctrine of love became the universal ruler (Pantocrator), enthroned among his apostles like a Caesar in the senate, as in the magnificent apse mosaic in S. Pudenziana, Rome (c. 390). In SS. Cosmo and Damian in Rome the apsidal mosaic (c. 530) barely gives the illusion of space, its figures being almost flat in effect. The triumphal arch of S. Maria Maggiore, also in Rome, has by about 440 replaced the blue of the sky by a gold background which lends the scene a spiritual quality. Byzantine art contributed rows of motionless figures, completing the transition from the narrative to the allegorical picture, which could only be understood with the help of explanatory verses, or tituli.

BYZANTINE PERIOD

The legacy of Hellenism and oriental influence both contributed to the evolution of Byzantine art. It was a national art employed in the service of the Church and the State, whose every utterance proclaimed orthodox religious teaching and the idea of a Christian empire. The subjects portrayed were not man and his experience of the world but the beliefs of the devout Christian. The function of the artist was, in fact, similar to that of the priest. It follows that theological art of this kind had to be impersonal and anonymous.

As very few secular buildings have survived, Byzantine architecture is today known mainly for its churches. These, although differently planned, were at first of the basilican type, as in Early Christian architecture. In and around Ravenna (q. v.), which had already been subjected to strong Byzantine influence as a West Roman (403–476) and Ostrogoth (493–539) residence, and later as the seat of the Exarch of the Byzantine Emperors (until 739), two great arcaded basilicas, S. Appollinare in Classe and S. Apollinare Nuovo, were built during the first half of the 6th century. The altar used by the bishops and clergy was moved down into the nave and screened off from the rest of the congregation. The developing technique of brickwork construction in dome-vaulting led to a predominance of domed churches after the 6th century. Their evolution is well shown in Ravenna. The Mausoleum of the Empress Galla Placidia (d. 450), with its plain exterior and rich mosaic decorations inside, is a small cruciform building with a domical vault on pendentives. S. Vitale (q. v.), built between 525 and 547 and consisting of an inner octagon surrounded by a two-storeyed enclosure, shows a further stage of development.

Another important form is represented by the church of S. Sophia (Hagia Sophia) in Constantinople (ill. 170), which the Emperor Justinian had built between 532 and 537 on the site of an older basilica. The fundamental principle of Byzantine architecture – to balance mass against mass, space against space and vault against vault – finds its most perfect expression in this church. Thus, on the outside only the unembellished brickwork, taking the form of functional blocks, cylinders and spheres, is visible.

140. St Mark's, Venice (11th/12th cent.). View of crossing and choir   141. Theodoric's Tomb, Ravenna (c. 520)

The longitudinal plan which is still evident in S. Sophia was dropped in favour of the cruciform plan in the Church of the Apostles, Constantinople, also begun in the Justinian period and destroyed in 1463. Nave and transept are of the same length and are covered by five domes. A similar architectural effect is created by St Mark's (q. v., ill. 140) in Venice, built mainly between 1063 and 1085, and is still to be traced in S. Front at Perigueux (q. v.).

Later Byzantine church architecture confined itself to smaller and more humble cruciform domed churches with central cupola, or, following the Church of the Apostles in Constantinople, with a further cupola over each of the four arms of the cross. This type of building spread across all the Eastern Christian countries, including Asia Minor, the Balkans and before the end of the 11th century, Russia.

Byzantine sculpture was represented by a few figural sculptures, at first cube-shaped, later more columnar and stylized. Portrait busts were handed on from Late Classical times and became more expressive in the 5th century, when features came to be treated with a greater degree of realism. In architectural sculpture the Corinthian capital, which had already lost some of its delicacy in the course of the centuries, was further modified in a number of ways, the realistic acanthus leaf becoming a flattish, abstract ornament which is largely of Eastern origin (ill. 48 c, d).

Byzantine art is usually associated with mosaic work. This is not surprising, as the striking and often breath-taking effect of many church interiors relies largely on their mosaic decorations. Figures in luminous colours, ranged against a blue – later a gold – background, relieve the weight of walls, columns and vaulting and give an impression of movement, as if surfaces and vaults were dissolving into each other. The development of this art is clearly shown in Ravenna, where examples range from a still fluid Hellenist treatment to the severe manner of the 5th and 6th centuries which uses larger pieces of glass and stone and fewer colours. In S. Vitale there are groups representing the Emperor Justinian and Bishop Maximian, with attendant clergy and soldiers, and the Empress Theodora with her Court ladies (ill. p. 179). The Court followers appear like a hierarchy of angels. Their majestic figures, seen against a fathomless background, are haughty and immobile. The view is strictly frontal and symmetrical, giving the picture a feeling of lucidity and breadth.

Many sculptures, mosaics and pictures have been lost as a result of the iconoclastic persecution (726–843), which forbade figural art in the central Byzantine area. Iconoclasm, perhaps partly influenced by Islamic hostility to art and certainly triggered off by a reformatory movement, was directed against all religious imagery. By this measure the Imperial Court hoped to weaken monastic influence. But

176

iconoclasm did not succeed in putting a stop to artistic activity; what is more, it led to changes which encouraged a freer and more naturalistic treatment and in a new flowering of Byzantine art.

In painting, evidence of this new and revitalizing spirit is shown in the anecdotal style of wall painting which replaced the costly mosaic towards the end of the Byzantine era. But with the victory of the monasteries over the iconoclasts art became lifeless once more. Icon-painting (ill. p. 182), especially after the fall of the Byzantine Empire, passed on the new conservative attitude to the Balkan countries and Russia. For centuries Russian painting continued in the Byzantine tradition, only admitting Western influences after the beginning of the 18th century.

The high standard of the crafts in Byzantine times was encouraged by the Church with its requirements for display, the Imperial Court, and the fabulously wealthy merchant class. The exquisite work of the goldsmiths relied on all kinds of native and foreign techniques, among them cloisonné work (see, Enamelling). In ivory carving Late Classical motifs lived on for a long time, as is shown in many thrones and caskets, writing-tablets and boxes. Strong Oriental influence prevailed in textile art.

THE DARK AGES

For centuries Germanic tribes had been a threat to the Roman frontiers. Their warlike and nomadic spirit, their rapidly increasing population, and the magnetism exercised by a culturally flourishing empire provided the motives for tribal migrations. The first of these took place around 375, when the Huns moved westwards from Mongolia, crossing the Volga and the Don and overthrowing the Ostrogoths. The East Roman Empire was involved in bitter struggles with the migrating tribes but survived the onslaught. West Rome, however, fell in 476. In its place there arose a number of Romano-Germanic nations whose individual character gradually became more distinct by virtue of their customs and speech. In Eastern Europe the Slavs took over the territories vacated by the Germans.

Late Classical and Early Christian art, although recognised as superior by the invaders, soon became 'barbarianised'. One of the reasons for this was that the cities of the Western Empire became impoverished and deserted during the long struggle. In Rome itself the number of inhabitants dropped from one-and-a-half million to 300,000. In Northern Italy wars, famines and pestilence resulted in the devastation of vast areas. Furthermore, the citizens of small towns pulled down such classical temples, palaces and theatres as were left standing and used the stone for building fortifications. Art treasures had been plundered, destroyed and scattered. Roman administration, which had been excellent in its day, no longer existed and commerce ceased. On the other hand, the Germanic invaders, who were themselves not uncultured, began to take an interest in Late Classical art. The Church became the intermediary, handing on the tradition to the Northern nations. This permeating process, although it resulted in much destruction, also bore some fruit. Western European culture was beginning to take root.

Germanic houses and palaces were rectangular wooden structures. After about A. D. 560 cities along the Rhine, which in Roman times had used stone for their building, adopted the wooden construction of the Franks. Nevertheless, stone gradually established itself once more for the building of churches and palaces. The existence of arcaded basilicas in France is proved by the remains of the 5th-century church of St Peter in Vienne.

Little now exists of the famous Visigothic architecture in Spain. Mention should, however, be made of the churches of S. Juán de Baños, Castille, consecrated in 661, and S. Maria de Naranco near Lino in Asturia, which was originally a Visigoth palace and demonstrates the application of methods used in wooden construction to stone buildings.

In Italy, the two great churches of S. Apollinare Nuovo and S. Apollinare in Classe were built at Ravenna around the end of the reign of Theodoric, the Ostrogoth ruler. Both are imbued with the Early Christian and Byzantine spirit. The Mausoleum (q. v.) of Theodoric (ill. 141), on the other hand, which has affinities with the work of Eastern Mediterranean countries, shows features characteristic of wooden building and has a frieze incorporating the Northern tongue ornament. The few remains of Langobard, or Lombard, architecture in Italy during this period show little more than the tentative endeavour to use a foreign idiom for the expression of native ideas.

The Germanic hall survived longest in England. Until the 15th century the great halls in manor houses retained the raised dais from where the Lord of the Manor administered justice as in ancient times. The open timber rood did not disappear until much later. In Scandinavia longitudinal building developed its counterpart in tall, upright steeple building which found its most perfect expression in the Norwegian stave church (q. v., ill. 181).

Northern decorative art in the Dark Ages was based on the animal style (Germanic Art, q. v.), in which the visual world was reduced to fanciful surface patterns. After coming into contact with the art of the Mediterranean countries it began to admit more general subjects but these were always translated into decorative terms (Fibula, ill. p. 152). Themes included the stricken deer, man threatened by demons, even an lancer (Hornhauser equestrian group, ill. 21), though the desire to transform three-dimensional reality into the flat sketch remained. Hence the Northern races had to translate Late Classical and Early Christian figural art into their own fundamentally different and less highly developed artistic idiom. This may partly explain why old Oriental motifs, transmitted through Sassanian, Coptic and Byzantine crafts, were taken over. The salver with the Evangelists' symbols donated to the baptistery at Cividale by Sigwald in 770, which is highly characteristic of Lombard art, represents Mesopotamian trees-of-life. The Irish Book of Kells of the early 8th century makes a Syrian design into a flat, stylized decoration (ill. p. 180). Celtic art in Central Europe (La Tène culture, q. v.) was driven further and further west by advancing Germanic tribes and was seriously hampered in its development by the Roman occupation of Gaul. Ireland was the only place where it was preserved with any degree of purity. Goldsmith's work and manuscript illumination reached their highest peak there in the 7th and 8th centuries (Books of Durrow and Kells, both at Trinity College, Dublin). Celtic influence is evident in Anglo-Saxon art and, on the European continent, can be traced as far south as Italy. But the Northumbrian Gospel of Lindisfarne (British Museum, London) already reveals a different artistic intention. Here the human figure, although decoratively, almost abstractly, treated, has been endowed with a new kind of human dignity and intellectual quality. With this another phase of development has begun.

CAROLINGIAN PERIOD

The Western Roman Empire was the cradle of our Western civilisation. Spain, North Africa and Egypt, Syria and Armenia fell under Islamic rule. Byzantium withdrew more and more from Rome and remained outside the cultural sphere gradually formed by the Romano-Germanic peoples. The Frankish kingdom in Gaul, having subdued the Thuringians and other Germanic tribes, became, after Charles Martel's victory over the Saracens, a power comparable with Byzantium and the Islamic world. By military and peaceful means Charlemagne (768–814) built up and extended this kingdom into a strong and politically united empire. The Church became a national institution while science, literature and art were encouraged not only because of the Emperor's own leanings but because he saw in them a means of encouraging the cultural solidarity of the State. His favourite palace at Aix-la-Chapelle became the meeting place for the most learned men of his day who helped him to plan and carry out a definite

Mosaic from San Vitale, Ravenna: Empress Theodora. *Detail*

Irish book illumination from pre-Carolingian times: Page with initial from the 'Book of Kells' *(early 8th century). Parchment*

iniature painting from a Reichenau evangelistary (c. 1000): The Adoration of the Magi

Icon: Enthroned Madonna with Child. *Byzantine School, c. 1200*

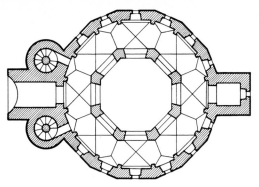

143. Charlemagne's imperial chapel
in Aix-la-Chapelle,
the choir as seen from the octagon

142. Charlemagne's imperial chapel in Aix-la-
Chapelle (c. 800), built by Odo of Metz. Ground
plan

cultural programme. His political ideal was to create another Roman Empire. In this learned atmosphere the word 'renasci' was sometimes mentioned in conjunction with the glories of Ancient Rome and hence the term 'renaissance' has with some justice been applied to Charlemagne's cultural revival. The Emperor and his Court were well aware that their task was not simply to continue the classical tradition, but to rediscover and recreate Classical Antiquity as a living experience. But it was not always practicable to draw directly from the source itself as was done when adopting the decorative forms of Augustan times dating from around the Birth of Christ; often the idiom of Late Classical and Early Christian or Byzantine art proved easier to assimilate, being already closer in character to the flat, two-dimensional character of Carolingian art. In spite of their own departure from naturalism, the figural and representational elements that were taken over from this earlier period were strong enough to infuse new life into the flat, ornamental art of the Northern peoples and Celts.

Although little remains of 8th- and 9th-century architecture, everything affirms its high quality. The cathedral at Aix-la-Chapelle (q. v., ill. 142, 143) was built by Charlemagne as a Court chapel and mausoleum attached to his palace. There is a resemblance, which may have been intentional, to S. Vitale at Ravenna, though the Carolingian church achieves a greater balance of units and shows a firmer control of the cumulative effect of its detail than does the Byzantine monument. The central plan found at Aix was adopted in a number of other churches in the 10th, and as late as the 11th, century, among them Nymwegen and Essen Minster. Apart from a few smaller central structures (St Michael's Chapel in Fulda, q. v.) the church of S. Germigny-des-Prés (Loiret) offers one of the best examples of the West Frankish Carolingian style.

The majority of churches and cathedrals built in Carolingian times, however, did not adopt the central plan but preferred the axial, orientated building. Here three distinct types can be distinguished: the rectangular hall without aisles and with eastern apses which dates from pre-Carolingian times; the basilica with three chapels (Einhartsbasilika, Steinbach in the Odenwald, 821); and lastly, the basilica made up of symmetrical units (convent church of Centula, q. v., ill. 144).

The exterior grouping corresponds to a new internal order. The transept, now the same width as the nave, crosses the latter as it leads up to the square choir at the eastern end. The square crossing serves as a basic unit, repeated throughout the building, which can now be divided into a number of clearly defined compartments ('metrical' system, q. v.). This development culminated in the addition of a second altar at the west end, replacing the doorway, which was moved round to the side. The plan for St Gall (q. v.) in Switzerland (820), a project for what was to be the perfect monastery, combined these new ideas. The Early Christian longitudinal building, with its piers and arcades between which the devout Christian made his way to the altar, had been the symbol in stone of the path to salvation. The more complex building which encompassed worshippers on all sides approximated more closely to the German and Celtic conception of God's love on Earth.

The crafts, while moving in the direction of three-dimensional representation, still lacked the necessary technical and intellectual prerequisites for full-scale figural sculpture. Stucco reliefs from the North have not been preserved, but in their stead we may cite the earlier (mid-8th century) examples in S. Maria della Valle at Cividale, which are of the same Lombard or Byzantine stylistic type. The once numerous altar frontals (antependia) of gilt metal have mostly disappeared due to the trading value of the metal (Pala d'Oro at Milan, donated 835).

Goldsmiths, held in high esteem in northern countries, produced bindings for the Holy Scriptures worked in precious stones. The chased reliefs on the Codex Aureus (q. v.) from St Emmeram in Regensburg (now in Munich) portray elongated, immobile figures that must have been derived from classical examples. The gradual replacing of the flat decorative style by the introduction of figures in relief is clearly shown in the carved ivory diptychs.

Manuscript illumination of the period has been preserved in a large number of liturgies, gospels, prayer books, psalters and scriptural texts. It had its origin in the monasteries where scribes copied out material needed for ritual purposes. The illuminations were commissioned by the Emperor and his Court, and given to favourite monasteries. In style they followed Roman examples, showing figures in architectural settings. In Germany there were two distinct schools, one represented by the Ada group which is thought to have originated in Trier, the other by the Court school which probably had its centre at Aix-la-Chapelle. The school of Tours, by virtue of a larger output, addressed itself to a wider audience, which extended beyond the Court. At Rheims the work of a group of artists probably active at Hautvillers outside the town, represented a zenith of artistic achievement. The miniature of the Gospels of Epernay are passionately animated and expressive (ill. 145). Byzantine prototypes, which were popular at Rheims, can be recognised in the Utrecht Psalter (c. 830) which contains pen drawings of verses or verse fragments of a high artistic standard. But the most splendid and sumptuous examples of Carolingian manuscript illumination came from Metz and Corbie near Amiens during the second half of the 9th century (San Paolo Bible in Rome, Codex Aureus). The many monastic schools of calligraphy in the West Frankish realm, Echternach, Canterbury, Fulda or St Gall were all either developing Celtic and Anglo-Saxon interlacing ornaments incorporating human and animal motifs with great skill and distinction, or using Early or pre-Carolingian ideas.

Wall painting, which was practised throughout this period, has disappeared without a trace in the North. But from S. Vincenzo al Volturno near Monte Cassino, the church of a large Benedictine monastery destroyed by Saracens in 882, a fresco cycle has been handed down. This reveals affinities with the art fostered by Charlemagne, who was there in 787, but it also shows the influence of Early Christian painting in Rome as well as of Byzantine mosaic work. Rome, too (e. g. S. Clemente), produced wall paintings in the 9th century which reflect the pictorial style of Late Classical times. Recently a Carolingian fresco cycle has been discovered in the church of St John at Münster in the Grisons, the work of a North Italian master who must have been acquainted with Byzantine art.

145. Evangelistary of Bishop Ebo of Rheims (Rheims school of 9th cent.). St Matthew

ROMANESQUE PERIOD

In the course of the 9th century the empire of Charlemagne split up into number of kingdoms. These later became the great Romano-Germanic nations of France, Italy and Germany. They, with the neighbouring Spanish, English, Scottish, Irish, Scandinavian, Magyar peoples and a section of the Slavs, were the exponents of the art of the Middle Ages. A settled peasantry formed the social foundation of the Western nations. Administration was based on the feudal system. Bound up with this system was a strong hierarchical order which manifested itself in many different spheres and was considered to be divinely ordained. At the head of the Holy Roman Empire stood the German Emperor. During the 10th and 11th centuries, however, the Church obtained its freedom against imperial domination with the help of the Cluniac reformatory movement, which had its origin at the Benedictine abbey at Cluny. Intervention from outside was no longer tolerated by the Church, which was now aiming at complete spiritual supremacy, or theocracy. The peasant economy, the feudal system, the hierarchical structure of society and the undisputed authority of the Church all led to a feeling of order and continuity which made itself felt in every sphere of life. Only an age in which thought and endeavour functioned within these narrowly defined limits could engender such a harmonious spiritual and religious attitude to life.

Romanesque art, a term that was first used by M. de Gerville in 1823 to describe this style in connection with Romance languages, was a sacred art dedicated to the service of God. Architecture was first in rank, and sculpture, painting, decoration and church furnishings were incorporated as necessary or ornamental additions. The entire church building with all its component parts was regarded as the worldly representation in stone of a divine order, a symbol whose deeper meaning was not always revealed immediately. But in spite of the closely-knit, spiritual nature of the Romanesque style the end of the 12th century saw the creation of works of art that were both highly expressive and imbued with deep feeling: these reflect in some measure the civilisation of the court, the birth of the towns and a new ascetic movement whose leader was Bernard of Clairvaux (1090–1153).

ARCHITECTURE

Bequests and endowments enormously increased the wealth of the Church and enabled monasteries and abbeys to erect sacred buildings on a scale that often made them more a symbol of the glory of God and the might of the Church than a suitable place of worship for a small congregation. Church and State, nobles and merchants all vied with one another in the foundation of monasteries, cathedrals and churches.

The architectural forms of Carolingian times continued to be used in church building, but the reformatory spirit of the Cluniac Order did not permit their direct adaptation. They had first to be reduced to their structural and stylistic elements, stripped of all trappings and then re-developed in accordance with new ritual requirements. Thus the atrium was generally dropped in favour of the more impressive square composition with pairs of towers (St Kastor, Coblenz) or with staircase towers (St Pantaleon, Cologne) at the west end. The nave of the basilica, whose height had once equalled its width, now became taller and narrower. Slender columns gave way to strong piers and columns with massive, cube-shaped capitals, necessitated by the increased weight of the walls. Often columns alternated with piers in a rhythmic sequence (ill. 32). The greater weight and thickness of piers and columns divided the nave from the aisles in a more emphatic manner. Transept and nave, now of the same width, intersected at the crossing which was clearly marked out from the rest of the church or defined by arches supported by piers. This new method of construction was sufficiently strong to carry a crossing tower of the kind already existing at Centula, where, however, it was of wood.

The increasing number of clergy whose duties included the daily reading of Mass required more room for the choir and a greater number of altars. To meet this need, subsidiary choirs were sometimes placed parallel to the main choir (Saint Rémi, Rheims, q. v.), or the aisles were continued behind the choir to form an ambulatory from which radiated a number of chapels (chevet), as at S. Sernin, Toulouse (q. v.). The crypt, a development of the earlier burial chamber and now frequently three-aisled, had become so large that in many 11th- and 12th-century churches it occupied the entire area below the chancel, which had sometimes to be raised several feet above the ground.

The preference of the Romanesque builders for clearly defined grouping and articulation led to increased interest in wall construction. Walls, which had been made of rubble and mortar were now built of ashlar. These matched and squared stones repeated on a small scale the cubic principle used in the building itself. Every detail was carefully considered in relation to the whole. Doors became portals, wider on the outside and approached by steps. Greater importance was attached to lighting, and windows were made larger. Piers, shafts and columns, as well as decorative elements, received more scientific forms and proportions. Impost capitals, billet and chevron ornaments, and intersecting semi-circular or pointed arches are the result of this rationalized use of forms (cf. ill. 48 e, 168). The range of decorative forms was widened by the use of clustered shafts, engaged columns, wall arcading and miniature triforium, or galleries. Capitals were carved with abstract, later with plant, decorations. Finally, sculpture, wall painting and glass painting were called in to enrich architecture by creating a comprehensive picture of the world. Plants and animals, demonic creatures, man himself and the heavenly powers all appeared in the symbolic rank assigned to them by their Maker.

French architecture around the year 1000 had already developed a much more elaborate form of basilican church. The flat-roofed church of S. Rémi at Rheims and the five-aisled cathedral at Orleans have three-aisled transepts whose arms terminate in a number of apses facing east. The aisles, also in the transept, have tribune galleries. In Normandy (Jumièges, q. v.; Caen, q. v.) during the second half of the 11th century the nave walls are articulated vertically by pilasters, and horizontally by three separate storeys – arcade, tribune gallery and clerestory (ill. 146, 147).

In 1090 the chancel at St Trinité (Abbaye-aux-Dames), also at Caen, was given a vault, and ten years later the nave was covered with an intersecting sexpartite ribbed vault. The upward thrust of the vault, where the ribs spring from the shafts, makes a lively contrast with the massive supporting piers. The more intricate recessed treatment of walls and the introduction of ribbed vaulting around 1100, both of which contain the seeds of the Gothic style, are characteristic of Norman basilican architecture which was to influence church building in England (cf. p. 188).

French architecture in the Royal Domain, north of the Loire, developed a related style or continued the classical Norman style with variations. The wall of the barrel-vaulted choir at St-Benoît-sur-Loire, and the nave at Le Mans Cathedral were given a blind arcade below the clerestory. The compound or clustered pier necessitated by ribbed vaulting which required a greater number of shafts, and the triforium galleries, produced greater variations of depth in the walls and resulted in a more animated interplay of light and shade. In many churches a triforium gallery was added below the window storey, making a fourth horizontal division (Laon Cathedral, q. v.).

The façade of St Étienne at Caen, divided into three sections in a way that was to become characteristic of later French architecture, has plain windows with rounded arches. Above a narrow cornice moulding rise two square towers in arcaded stages. Towards the top, the walls with their tall blind

146. *Abbey church in Jumièges, Normandy (1040–67), north wall*   147. *Saint Étienne, Caen, Normandy (1066–77), choir with triforium*

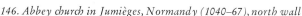

arches, small pierced openings and windows divided by shafts take on an increasingly hollowed-out appearance. The west façade at Laon and the cathedral at Tournai (q. v.) in Belgium with its five massive towers, mark the end of this style.

The region south of the Loire is usually divided into a number of areas corresponding to the different styles of the period, each having its distinctive character. In the duchies of Poitou and Saintogne hall churches predominate; these have a continuous barrel vault covering the nave (as in St Savin on the Gartempe, built c. 1080 and Notre-Dame-la-Grande at Poitiers, built c. 1100). Their façades are decorated in a fanciful sculptural style. Notre-Dame-du-Port, Clermont-Ferrand (q. v., c. 1100) is the classical example of Auvergne church architecture of this period. The smaller Provençal churches of which the abbey church at Montmajour is an example, are distinguished by fine proportions and many features that recall the Late Classical period. To the classicist style of the western portals of St-Gilles-du-Gard (q. v.) and the lovely cloister of St-Trophîme at Arles (q. v., 1170–80) the term proto-Renaissance has been applied. In Aquitaine and Languedoc the domed church finally made its appearance (St Front, Périgueux).

In Burgundy the activities of the reformed Cluniac and Cistercian Orders were to have far-reaching influence on the whole of Romanesque architecture. The great abbey church at Cluny (q. v.) (1088–mid 13th cent., ill. 167), built on the site of several earlier churches, reflected the importance of the Order that created it. The largest church in Western Europe, it had two eastern transepts, a chevet of five apsidal chapels, pointed arches in the nave arcades and a great barrel vault over the nave. Its design influenced that of many later churches. As in Provence, the classical heritage is evident in the decorative treatment of Autun Cathedral (q. v.). The nave of the pilgrimage church of St Madeleine at Vézelay (q. v., after 1120) has pilasters with shafts from which spring the arches supporting the groined intersecting vault. The Cluniac monks decorated their churches generously with carvings and sculptures, whereas the severe, ascetic nature of the Cistercians demanded plain structures without any form of

187

ornamentation. The abbey church at Fontenay was built without towers and shows the characteristic rectangular apse of Cistercian churches, but this austerity is offset by its lucid proportions.

In its variety, Romanesque architecture in France mirrored the many facets of political and cultural life. The different styles flourished in the provinces during the 12th century, at a time when the first Gothic buildings went up in the Ile de France, the heart of the country.

The Romanesque or Norman style in England was preceded by a flourishing Anglo-Saxon period (449–1066). No single large building in wood has survived as evidence of this form of Anglo-Saxon architecture, but the pilaster-strip ornamentation on the stone tower at Earls Barton (Northants) is reminiscent of earlier timber construction. Bradford-on-Avon, built slightly earlier than Earls Barton (c. 700), is the most perfectly preserved Saxon church in England and, though it is small, it is one of the best examples of mason's work of the whole period. The plain nave arcades of All Saints, Brixworth, Northamptonshire, dating from the 7th century, suggest the existence, at least in the south of England, of a broad basilica type of church based on models from Ravenna or Rome. The narrow church of St John at Escomb, Durham, built about 700 and still in an excellent state of preservation, and the Rhenish spire of Sompting, Sussex, indicate, on the other hand, that the Anglo-Saxon style in the north of England owes something to Gallic influence.

Norman architecture is sharply differentiated from that of the Anglo-Saxon period. Saxon towers are tall, Norman towers are short and massive. There are no buttresses in Saxon architecture, whereas Norman churches are distinguished by flat buttresses similar to those found in Normandy. The Norman pier is short, ponderous and cylindrical and Norman arches are enriched with a variety of mouldings, while Saxon arches are plain. Examples of smaller churches in the Norman style include St Bartholomew, Smithfield, London, Barfreston, Kent and Iffley, Oxford.

The earliest cathedrals were built in the cruciform basilican manner with tribune gallery, crossing tower, a long east end and two western towers. In contrast with continental churches, where exteriors give the impression of being composed of a number of square compartments and interiors rely on a rhythmic succession of individual spatial units, the English cathedral of this period makes its effect by an endless interplay of vertical and horizontal elements (Norwich). Ely (begun 1083, q. v.) and Peterborough (q. v.) show the bold and varied use of moulding that was to distinguish English work especially during the succeeding periods. The Transitional style of the second half of the 12th century pointed the way to Gothic architecture. The choir at Canterbury Cathedral (q. v.), built by the French architect William of Sens, belongs to this period.

The fortified castle, serving as a permanent stronghold for the feudal lord, is closely associated with Norman building and is represented almost exclusively in England where examples include Durham, Colchester and the Tower of London (q. v.).

Spain, after it was conquered by the Moors (711 onwards), became an outpost of Islamic culture. But gradually areas like Asturia, which had remained Christian, began to recapture the Moorish territories. Toledo was won back as early as 1085, Granada not until 1492. During the period of occupation Moorish art had erected a number of monuments and had also left its mark on the style of Christian Spain. But the prevailing influence in northern Spain during the Romanesque period, not only in artistic but also in political and military matters, was France, although in the north-eastern province of Catalonia there is evidence of Lombard influence also. The cathedral of the Cluniac shrine of St James at Santiago de Compostella (q. v.), in Galicia, begun in about 1075, forms a group with the pilgrimage churches in the south of France which include S. Sernin in Toulouse (q. v.). The fine sculptured portals of this barrel-vaulted hall church left their mark on French sculpture (ill. 149). The knightly spirit of Spain is attested by the sombre-looking city walls at Avila in Castile, erected shortly before 1100; these harbour the church of S. Vincente, one of the finest examples of the mature Romanesque style.

In Italy the basilican church plan lived on well into Romanesque times. But Italian Romanesque was compounded of many different elements: a close link with classical and Byzantine art, the formation of countless small city-states and territories owing their existence to political unrest, variety in the landscape and the existence of different racial groups which did not merge until later times – these all helped to give it its rich and varied character. In Tuscany, and more especially in Pisa (q. v.), these different elements met. The cathedral at Pisa, begun in 1063, already shows evidence of the beginnings of a national style. In the basilica of S. Miniato (q. v.) and the baptistery of S. Giovanni in Florence (q. v.) the spirit of Classical Antiquity is reflected in purity of form, finely balanced proportions and restraint in the use of sculptural decoration.

Towards the close of the 11th century southern Italy and Sicily saw a revival of building activity under Norman rule which did not, however, have any significant effect on Western European architecture. The cathedrals of Taranto (begun 1072), Bari (1087) and Trani, the Cappella Palatina (1143) in Palermo and the cathedral at Monreale (c. 1182) are the triumphant products of a mixture of styles compounded of classical, Lombard, Saracenic and above all Byzantine elements, but also showing some Norman influence.

In northern Italy, the cathedral of Torcello (begun 1018) was built without a transept in the Early Christian tradition. In near-by Venice, the church of St Mark followed the Byzantine style when it was rebuilt in 1063 (cf. p. 176). Lombard architecture is well represented by the church of S. Ambrogio in Milan (q. v.), which was largely completed before the middle of the 12th century. This basilican church, with its massive piers, tribune gallery and bold quadripartite vaulting gives an impression of great weight and solidity. This feeling is heightened by the absence of a clerestory. The cathedral at Modena was built mainly between 1099 and 1184 and, like S. Ambrogio and other Lombard churches it originally had no transept. Blind arcades and eaves galleries give the exterior walls a deeply recessed appearance. At the entrance to the crypt there are pillars supported by figures seated on lions. Many Lombard churches of the 12th century followed the model at Modena although a great number of variations were introduced.

While northern Italy formed part of the same empire as Germany, a close political and economic relationship existed between the two countries which was also reflected in their architecture. There was a continuous exchange of ideas as well as of architects and masons. It is even likely that Saxon and Rhenish styles penetrated into Italy during the 11th century; a hundred years later, again, Lombard art had a certain influence on architecture in Germany.

During the second half of the 10th century a period of great building activity began in Germany. The convent church at Gernrode (begun 961) shows a new and severe architectural approach whereby the various components, such as nave, transept, west end, the semicircular eastern apse (the apse at the west end is a later addition) and the circular towers, are handled like a set of building bricks. The most striking achievement of German architecture of this period is the monastic church of St Michael in Hildesheim (q. v.), which shows originality in its plan, its construction and the treatment of its detail. The interior with its flat wooden roof does not convey an impression of movement towards the altar but rather one of repose (ill. 32).

Under the Salian emperors the Rhine area became the centre of building activity. Salian architecture differs from that of Ottonian times in a number of ways: a feeling of grandeur, created by massive but harmonious and ordered proportions, a rhythmic articulation of walls, and, above all, the vaulting of spacious interiors. Even the ruined churches of Limburg a. d. Haardt (1025–1045) and Hersfeld (after 1037, q. v.), both arcaded basilican types, still convey the solemn monumental spirit of Salian architecture, although their walls are devoid of decoration. The same spirit is expressed, though more ceremoniously, in the west front of Trier Cathedral (1040–1050, q. v.) with its projecting round towers and apse, and the deep relief of its miniature triforium galleries. The first cathedral in Speyer (q. v.) had a tall nave with narrow arcades formed by piers. Engaged columns supported blind arcading which ran almost as high as the flat roof and linked the two storeys. During the second period of construction (1082–1112) the massive nave was covered with a vault. Transept, crossing tower and the eastern apse with miniature triforium gallery (ill. 148) all date from this period.

The evolution of the large vaulted church was slowed down by the reformatory movement of the Benedictines at Hirsau, whose influence in Germany was stronger than that of the parent order of Cluny in France. Like the Cistercians later, the Hirsau monks insisted on simplicity in church design. The plain, methodical construction at Alpirsbach testifies to the severe, ascetic spirit of these builders.

German Romanesque architecture reached its zenith under Hohenstaufen rule. The cathedrals in Mainz (q. v.) and Worms (q. v.) and the abbey of Maria Laach (q. v.) further develop the features found at St Michael's, Hildesheim: the two apses, one at each end, the metrical system, and the effective grouping of towers. With their fine vaulting, great refinement in the treatment of detail and sculptural decoration they convey an atmosphere of wordly dominion as well as of spiritual beauty and harmony (ill. 172, 188). A significant development was the introduction of ribbed vaulting at Speyer (1151), and Worms (1171), a step which had been taken much earlier in England (Durham). This enabled walls and vaults to become an organic whole for the first time. At this period, too, structural masses came to appear less inert, while the different spatial units began to combine into a more obvious whole. Both external and internal walls became more deeply recessed, the moulding of piers, columns, shafts and ribs more accentuated. The feeling of solidity and unbroken mass previously conveyed gave way to a more open treatment which made the stone appear less heavy and dense. The cathedrals at Bamberg (q. v.) and Naumburg (q. v.) and the minster at Basle (q. v.) mark the end of the style as far as the handling of mass and space is concerned.

To round off the achievement of architecture under the Hohenstaufens, mention must also be made of fortresses and castles, such as Castel del Monte (q. v., ill. 166) in distant Apulia, the castle formerly belonging to the Counts of Flanders in Ghent, the Wartburg (ill. 50), Gelnhausen, or the imperial castle in Goslar (q. v.).

PAINTING

Romanesque painting appeared either inside the churches, where it adorned the walls, or in illuminated manuscripts which were used in connection with church services. It was not an art that appealed to the eye so much as to the spiritual and intellectual nature of man, and in order to draw a clear distinction between Heaven and Earth, inanimate nature and the lower orders of Creation were sometimes sketched in when representing the terrestrial sphere. The art of mosaic was largely discontinued.

Unfortunately, only fragments of Romanesque wall painting have withstood the passage of time. Examples from France are the frescoes at St Savin and at Berzé-la-Ville in Burgundy. These paintings, with their simple forms, broad and generous treatment, flat appearance and predominant use of reds and yellows on a light ground, do not give the impression of being direct copies from Byzantine models. In Italy, dependence on Byzantine art is still apparent in the wall paintings at S. Angelo in Formis near Capua (1068–1086) although the end of the 12th century saw the gradual breaking-away from the Greek-Byzantine style. This

148. Speyer Cathedral (11th cent.), nave with King's Choir

Lectern from Alpirsbach (c. 1150) with the four Evangelists and their symbols made to embody the four cardinal points whither the Word of God had been spread. Coloured woodcut

GERMAN IMPERIAL CROWN. *Goldsmiths' work from the 10th century. The 11th-century band bears the name and title of the Emperor Conrad II in pearl letters. Eight gold plates with pearls and precious stones with figural enamelled inlay show Christ enthroned between angels. The words 'per me reges regnant' (Kings reign through me) indicate the sacred nature of the ruler's status*

Cross of Lothair from the treasury of the Emperor's palace at Aachen *(Aix-la-Chapelle). Late 10th century. – The front of it is richly ornamented with jewels, pearls and filigree; in the centre is a cameo of Indian sardonyx (1st century) with a portrait of the Emperor Augustus symbolising the Prince of Peace. – Height of the cross: 19½ inches.*

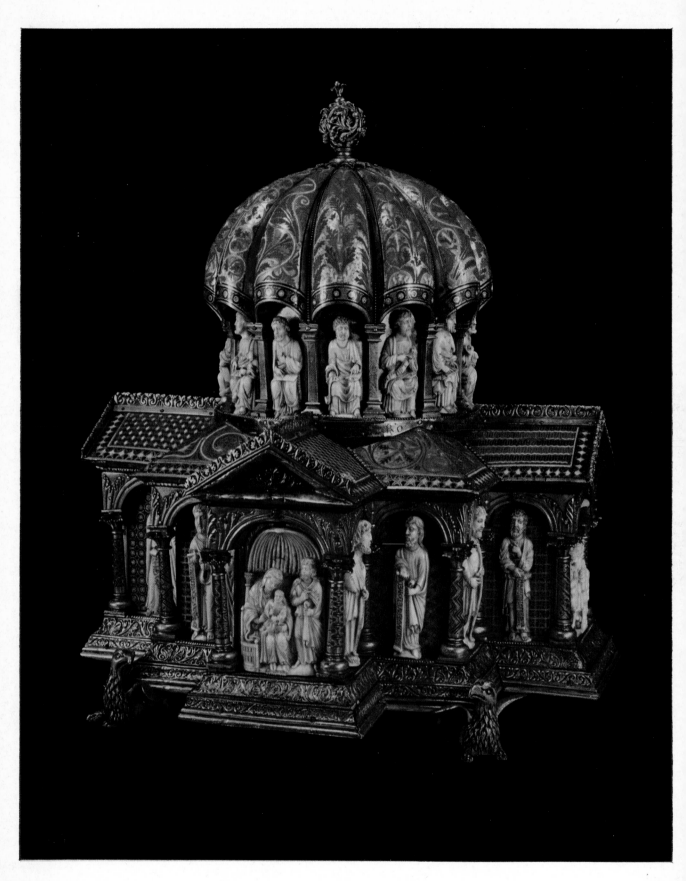

Reliquary from the Treasure of the Guelphs in the form of a Byzantine centrally-planned church. Cologne, c. 1175. Oak overlaid with champlevé enamel, richly ornamented; silver, copper and bronze, gilt; the figures are carved from walrus tusks

process is well illustrated by the narrative frescoes in the lower church of S. Clemente or in S. Maria in Trastevere, both in Rome. German wall painting was flourishing on the island of Reichenau, Lake of Constance, around the year 1000; in the Rhine district and in Lower Saxony, during the 12th and 13th centuries (Brunswick Cathedral, ill. p. 203). In England, fragments of Norman wall painting survive in Ely and St Alban's Cathedrals.

Manuscript illumination in Germany reached a high level of achievement during the second half of the 10th century (ill. p. 181), with some of the best examples coming from the monasteries at Reichenau and Regensburg, while St Gall, Echternach, Cologne, Fulda and Hildesheim were also well represented. Boldly drawn, with bright luminous colours, these miniatures showing figures against different coloured bands, Oriental carpet patterns or a plain gold ground, were influenced by classical, Early Christian, Carolingian and Byzantine models. Manuscripts prepared for the Archbishop of Trier, Otto III and Henry II, all survive.

It would scarcely be possible to conceive of a style more strongly opposed to that of these German miniatures than that of the English work of the period. The foremost place in 10th- und 11th-century illumination is taken by the Winchester school of painting, which between about 960 an 1040 produced a series of splendid illuminated manuscripts. The artists used Carolingian works as models to obtain entirely original effects. There is a new relationship between figures and ornament; the broad borders in the early Winchester manuscripts are not merely frames for figure-scenes, they form an essential part of the composition. A feeling of movement and vigour pervades both figures and foliated ornament, giving an almost expressionist character to the work. This expressionist tendency is a fundamental quality of the English style around the first millennium A. D. The source of this nervous animation has been thought to lie in the illustrations of the Utrecht Psalter, but there are no signs of any direct connection with the early manuscripts of the Winchester school. It is only in its later stages that the Winchester school of coloured, full-page miniatures shows the direct influence of the Utrecht style.

French manuscripts around and after 1000, especially those from the Maas region, favoured figural compositions framed by ornamental lilies, while Italy and Spain adhered to Byzantine models with their characteristic flat and static treatment. After a comparatively barren period, manuscript illumination reached new heights in the 12th and 13th centuries. In Italy and France, more graceful and natural figures replaced the elongated, unrealistic representation of former times, while colours became more intense and luminous. Gradually. too, the Romanesque miniature style gave way to lively Gothic shapes.

In England, too, after the Norman Conquest manuscript painting was characterized by a new realism; figures were heavier in appearance and of more massive proportions with clearly defined outlines. It was during this period that the Bestiary made its first appearance. The early examples were illustrated with delightful realism, combined with a clear, flawless sense of composition.

SCULPTURE AND THE CRAFTS

The Early Romanesque period which liked the appearance of large, smooth stone surfaces, produced relatively little sculpture. But as architectural forms became more complex towards the end of the 11th century, sculpture soon assumed immense importance.

In France the shallow relief work at S. Sernin in Toulouse (ill. 149) and of the figures of the apostles in the transept of St Pierre, Moissac (c. 1100) was inspired by Byzantine and Carolingian carved ivory panels, since artists had no full-size native sculpture to go back to. Two decades later saw the creation of the tympanum above the portal at Moissac with its superb relief of Christ in Judgment, enthroned among the evangelists and surrounded by twenty-four elders. The contorted limbs, grotesque

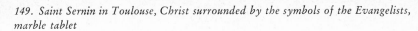
poses and ecstatically raised heads reveal the religious fervour and deep spiritual aspirations of those times. There is evidence of an abundance of fantasy and creative vigour in Romanesque sculpture. Façades, portals and capitals were adorned with biblical, legendary and mythological subjects as well as plants, animals, dragons and evil spirits. These representations were at first intended simply as illustrations of scriptural themes, but soon artists began to invest them with symbolical meaning, to show God's kingdom, His laws and the workings of His will.

Like French Romanesque architecture, sculpture of this period can be divided into different schools (cf. p. 187). The Languedoc school, represented by Moissac and Beaulieu-sur-Dordogne, is related to that of Burgundy, which is responsible for the sculptural decoration on the portals of St Lazare Cathedral at Autun and the pilgrimage church of St Madeleine at Vézelay (ill. 185). Both show animated figures with elongated bodies and delicately modelled heads, limbs and robes, in shallow relief. The carving on the three portals of St Gilles near Arles shows the influence of Late Classical works of art, of which many were found in the district.

Carved free-standing crosses were the most popular form of sculpture in England before the Norman Conquest. The most important examples are the crosses at Bewcastle and Ruthwell on the Scottish border. They bear carvings in high relief and show the obvious influence of Mediterranean prototypes. The two outstanding examples of Saxon sculpture are, however, the 'Raising of Lazarus' and 'Christ coming to the House of Martha and Mary' in Chichester Cathedral (c. 1000). Compared with the refinement and feeling of these noble works the first efforts of the Norman sculptor were crude indeed (capitals of the chapel in Durham Castle, c. 1070), but sculptors developed increasing technical skill with the ever greater demand for architectural sculpture; Norman sculpture, in fact, initiated the movement which produced the fine Gothic building sculpture of the following century. For small country churches elaborate doorways and fonts were favoured. The most conspicuous and celebrated example is the church at Kilpeck, Herefordshire. By the middle of the 13th century the Romanesque style was fully developed and the use of figure-work on a large scale was common (tympanum of Prior's Door, Ely; south porch, Malmesbury; Lady Chapel, Glastonbury; and, above all, the west front of Lincoln).

In Spain, the pier reliefs in the transept of S. Domingo de Silos, with their strong spiritual appeal, show evidence of the traffic in artistic ideas with the south of France. The sculptures, still Romanesque in spirit, on the Pórtico de la Gloria at Santiago de Compostella, the work of Master Mateo in 1188, can be compared in quality with those at Chartres (ill. 158).

Twelfth-century sculpture in Italy did not show as much consistency of development as did that of France. The reliefs and portal sculptures at Modena (c. 1100), the porch at Ferrara (1135), and work in the Parma district are associated with the names of different sculptors, but relatively little is known about them. The presence of barbaric elements in this school resulted in a fanciful and vigorous style characterized by such themes as dragons in combat, fighting men and lions tearing their prey.

Unlike French sculpture, which is mainly associated with façades and portals, German work is best represented inside the churches. France specialized in sculptured scenes that formed an integral part of the structure; in Germany, where workshops were unknown, individual sculptures were more popular and we find such diverse subjects as seated madonnas (Imad Madonna, q. v.), memorial tablets, or the Brunswick Lion (q. v.) of 1166, an exceptional example and the first free-standing sculpture of medieval

150. *Cathedral of Santiago di Compostella, Spain, Pórtico de la Gloria (Master Mateo c. 1180–90)*

times (ill. 165). Even pulpits (ill. p. 191) and the fairly plentiful carved choir-screens retained an individual quality. Thus the figures of the apostles in the Church of Our Lady at Halberstadt appear not as a homogeneous group but as a number of individuals, each of whom has his own spiritual existence.

Among the crafts, the goldsmith's art occupied first place. The magic of gold and precious stones led men to use these costly materials in the service of the Church. During the 10th and 11th centuries magnificent altar frontals of wrought gold or silver representing figural subjects were produced, such as the still extant Pala d'Oro given to Basle Cathedral by Henry II. From this period also date the statues of saints enclosing relics, made of wood and covered with precious metals, of which the fine statue of Sainte Foy (c. 980) at Conques-en-Rouergue is one of the best surviving examples. Churches usually had the walls of apse and nave decorated with wall paintings, while altars and doors were adorned with reliefs. The massive bronze doors of St Michael's at Hildesheim, dating from about 1000 (Bernwardskunst, q. v.), representing vivid descriptions of the Creation and the life of Christ, are perhaps the finest among these door reliefs, which can be found over an wide area (including S. Zeno in Verona, Monreale, Cologne and Novgorod). Goldsmith's, among them Godefroid de Clair from Huy and Nicholas of Verdun (before and around 1200), vied with one another in the production of the finest altar frontals, tabulae, reliquaries, monstrances and chalices. Limoges, the Maas region (Dinanderie, q. v.) and Cologne were centres of this craft in Romanesque times, and many treasures of the period are still preserved in the sacristies of cathedrals and monasteries (Treasure of the Guelphs, q. v.; Aix-la-Chapelle Cathedral Treasure, ill. 194, 193). Walls, floors and benches in churches and castles were often covered with woven or embroidered tapestries (Bayeux tapestry). Woven silks for ceremonial robes were imported from Byzantium and, after the 12th century, also began to be manufactured at Lucca in Italy. The silk coronation robe of King Stephen the Saint (1031) is a magnificent example.

GOTHIC PERIOD

The mid-medieval period was darkened by the struggle between popes and emperors. Pope Gregory VII (d. 1085) enforced a tyrannical theocracy while one of his successors, Innocent III (d. 1216) took the title of Vicar of Christ. The emperors, on the other hand, insisted on the equality of Church and State in the eyes of God. The conflict, carried on with political, military and spiritual weapons, resulted in much bitterness. After the death of Frederick II in 1250 and the downfall of the Hohenstaufen dynasty, the pope became the unchallenged ruler of the Christian world. In the absence of a united Western Europe it was not possible to place the government of Church and State in the same hands as had, for example, been done in Byzantium. Furthermore, the concept of an ordered political hierarchy in which emperor, kings and princes all took their place and which was supposed to mirror the divine order, had never been completely realized and disintegrated rapidly after the second half of the 13th century. Central Europe split up into a number of small States surrounded by larger nations which included France, England, Scandinavia, Poland and Hungary. These latter all strove for independence and sovereignty.

Meanwhile a new cult of chivalry, which grew up at the French Court in the 12th century, spread rapidly throughout the Western Christian world. The Christian knight was endowed with certain virtues: loyalty to his lord, courage, chastity, continence and nobility. Every aspect of the chivalrous life was invested with profound symbolism, and this was most eloquently expressed in the songs of the troubadours. The chivalrous ideal, which as a creative force was beginning to lose its impact after the middle of the 13th century, left its mark on all the arts, especially on sculpture.

At the same time, scholarship became another powerful influence. New discoveries in the realms of theology, philosophy, the natural sciences and law were taught and discussed at cathedral schools and other centres of learning. In Paris in 1202 the faculties of philosophy and theology combined to form the 'Universitas'. With the entry of many Franciscans and Dominicans into academic life and the submission of Christian doctrine to logic and controversy, learning soared to new heights.

Parallel with the rise of scholarship was the growth of mysticism which developed out of an intense spiritual longing for union with God, a desire for mystic participation in the cult of Christ, the Virgin Mary and the Passion. This found artistic expression primarily in a large number of devotional images and representations of the Virgin. But mystic experience gave rise to strange states of mind, and these in turn led to heterodoxy and heresy. The papacy, politically weakened by the exile in Avignon (1309–1378) and further reduced in power by the Great Schism of 1378–1417 in which two, sometimes even three, popes challenged each other's authority, was unable to stem the spread of heretical beliefs. The government of the Church was temporarily vested in reformatory councils, composed of the most learned men of the times, who attempted to stamp out heresy, resolve the Schism and imbue the Church with a new Christian spirit. But despite the changing face of the medieval world after the 13th century, made manifest in the formation of individual nations, economic development, the emergence of a 'middle class' and impassioned attempts to revive the dwindling faith in God's kingdom on Earth, the idea of a united Christianity persisted until the 16th century. It is the Church, with its teaching and its continued use of Latin as a devotional language that we have to thank for the steady cultural development of the later Middle Ages in Western Europe, a development which triumphed over all national differences.

ARCHITECTURE

Gothic art was a product of the Christian faith. It found its noblest expression in the Gothic cathedral, which reflects the clarity of thought evident in the theological and philosophical teaching of such men as Albertus Magnus and Thomas Aquinas. It is not surprising, therefore, that Gothic architecture originated in the Ile-de-France, Champagne and Picardy, the district around Paris which was then the intellectual centre of the medieval world. Artistic enterprise had moved from the country monasteries to the towns where bishops had their residences and where the prerequisites for building on a large scale could be found: accommodation for members of the building confraternities, artists and labourers, as well as provisions, technical aids, transport and money. The building of a cathedral was an event in which the whole population participated; Robert de Mont-Saint-Michel relates how, in 1144 at Chartres – we paraphrase – 'the faithful were for the first time to be seen pulling carts laden with stones, wood, wheat and other supplies needed for the building of the cathedral. The towers sprang up as if by magic. And this did not happen at Chartres alone but all over France, Normandy and elsewhere. People every-

where humbled themselves, did penance and forgave their enemies. Men and women were seen carrying heavy loads through bogs, singing and praising the wonders of God which were happening before their very eyes.' Since the cathedral was the symbol of God's omnipotence, participation in its construction became something akin to a mystic experience. This explains the popular character of the Gothic style; it is the element that distinguishes it from the sacred art of Romanesque times and to which Viollet-le-Duc (1814–1879) gave the name *style laïque*.

Gothic architecture retains many stylistic features associated with Romanesque: the elaborate chancel with ambulatory and radiating chapels, the use of several towers, the three portals of the west front, the sexpartite intersecting vault and some characteristics of wall articulation. And yet the Gothic style is more than merely a development of Romanesque forms. Its earliest phase, represented by the choir of the abbey church of St Denis (q. v., 1140–1144) and the cathedrals of Sens (1140–1164), Senlis (1153–1191), Noyon (choir 1157, nave 1170), Laon (q. v., begun 1160) and Notre-Dame (begun 1163) in Paris (q. v., ill. 30, 33), did not follow on from the end of the Romanesque period but coincided with its peak in the provinces of France. We can therefore conclude that the emergence of the Gothic style was the result of a creative force which, like all other movements and styles in art, had its roots in the intellectual climate of the times. It has already been shown how the narrow metaphysical and religious ideology of Western Christianity gradually began to expand and become more fluid after the middle of the 12th century. And with the dissolution of an accepted order there began a conflict between acceptance and rejection of the world, between religious fervour and agnosticism, between desire and achievement. This tension was mirrored in the Gothic style.

By contrast with Romanesque churches in which the various elements exist side by side in quiet harmony, Gothic cathedrals strive for spatial unity. To this end equal importance is given to nave, transept and chancel which, as in the case of Bourges, sometimes seem to dissolve into each other. Crypts and tribune galleries disappear, capitals are redesigned to support a new system of vaulting. The sexpartite vault, the alternate treatment of piers and the 'metrical' system are usually dropped: where in Romanesque times the nave had one compartment to two of the aisles, the Gothic church generally has no such subdivision so that a succession of small oblong nave compartments correspond in number to those of the aisles. To overcome the difficulties caused by vaulting oblong compartments with semicircular arches, which rose to different heights over spans of varying width, the pointed arch was introduced to keep the crowns of intersecting vaults level. The horizontal division of nave walls in Early Gothic architecture usually consisted of arcades, tribune gallery, triforium and clerestory (Laon and Noyon). In the new cathedral at Chartres (begun 1194) there is no gallery, but the great clerestory windows, consisting of two wide lancets with a rose above, almost equal the nave arcades in size and weight, while the triforium serves as the link between the two. This typically Gothic solution was used again at Rheims and Amiens (ill. 152) and finally ended in simple horizontal division into two parts. In 1240, the architect of St Denis, Pierre de Montereau, built a triforium with lights into the nave of this abbey church. Thereby, and by equating the proportions of triforium and windows, it became part of the clerestory.

In classical architecture a harmonious relationship existed between weight and support, which found its expression in column and entablature. Gothic church architecture, on the other hand, tried to conquer the heaviness of stone and began to increase the height of the nave. In Laon this was 79 ft, in Paris 115 ft, while at Chartres, Rheims and Amiens the crowns of the vaults reached a height of 120, 125, and 138 ft respectively. The even greater height of the choir at Beauvais (q. v., 1247–1272), which rose to 157 ft, with a corresponding span of 51 ft, resulted in the collapse of the vault only a few years after its completion. This, the first of a series of similar disasters, eventually put a stop to such endeavours.

The horizontal articulation of walls played an important part in the attempt to counteract the heaviness of the materials. The Romanesque builders pierced or hollowed-out their walls. In Gothic times this principle was discontinued and, instead, heavy walls were transformed into a host of ascending shafts, vertical ribs and clustered and cylindrical piers. The spaces in this screen of verticals were aglow with coloured glass panes veined by delicate tracery (cf. ill. 153, Sainte-Chapelle). The result was a continuous interplay of energy, of movement flickering and leaping from shafts to ribs and along the ribs to the crests of vaults. This created a feeling of weightlessness, of everything being suspended in the air, an impression that was heightened by the fragile appearance of the walls. For now the complicated mechanism that served to support them and to receive the thrust of the vaulting had been moved to the outside of the building in the form of flying buttresses, and was not visible from within. In Early Gothic cathedrals in France the tribune gallery was still a supporting member. During the mature Gothic period, however, the enormously tall interior, now without its tribune gallery, seemed suspended within a vast and beautifully constructed framework. Strong piers with pinnacles rose along the outer walls above the aisle roof to the full height of the nave, taking the weight of the crested buttresses (ill. 152).

Apart from flying buttresses, the appearance of the Gothic exterior was determined by a careful distribution of the principal features, the towers and façades. Chartres was originally planned to have nine towers, including two at each end of the transept arms. With a reduction in the number of these, interest could be concentrated on the west front with two towers and three portals, and artistic emphasis was focussed on its sculptural decoration (cf. ill. 151).

French architecture in the provinces developed several characteristic forms but architectural activity almost came to a standstill during the Hundred Years' War (1339–1453). Kings, princes, bishops and citizens built churches in the Flamboyant (q. v.) style. Fortified castles were given a 'donjon' or keep. The original Louvre château in Paris, many bishops' residences (e. g. the Palace of the Popes at Avignon), as well as town halls, were a development of the hall building.

In Spain, the cathedrals of Léon (begun 1199) and Burgos (q. v., begun 1220) were built under French influence. With the Christian conquest of the peninsula the Gothic style penetrated farther south, as is shown by the cathedral at Seville (q. v.), built 1402–1506 in the form of a hall church on the site of a mosque, and by the beautiful church of S. Juan de los Reyes in Toledo. Gothic and Moorish elements mingled in the Mudéjar style which flourished in Toledo and Andalusia in the 14th and 15th centuries and was characterized by stalactite vaulting and elaborate surface ornamentation.

Under the influence of French Gothic the Early English style developed in England between the late 12th and early 14th centuries (1189–1307). The Galilee porch at Ely (1198) is one of the earliest examples, while the cathedrals at Lincoln (q. v., 1192–1233), Salisbury (q. v., 1220–1266), York (transepts) and Wells (q. v., nave and west front), as well as the greater part of Westminster Abbey, London (q. v.), whose choir and transept date from 1245–1270, show the style approaching its zenith. Ribbed vaulting, pointed

152. Gothic construction (as in Amiens Cathedral, 13th cent.)
1 Nave, 2 Aisle, 3 Piers with arcades, 4 Triforium, 5 Clerestory, 6 Cross vaulting,
7 Flying buttress, arches, 8 Flying buttress, pier, 9 Finial

arches and oblong instead of square vaulting compartments, each complete in itself, were used early on, but the triforium was slow to replace the tribune gallery. Tall, narrow lancet windows, often grouped in two's and three's, deeply channelled mouldings, foliated capitals and bosses and groups of slender shafts are other features characteristic of this period. The square east end, typical of English cathedrals, already appears at Salisbury. Choirs are often extended by the addition of a Lady Chapel while exteriors are marked by a massive central tower and a wider west front with two towers.

The Decorated 14th-century style, shown in Exeter Cathedral (q. v., completed 1369), the three bays east of the octagon at Ely (q. v., begun 1235), the nave at Lichfield (q. v., completed 1361), in Wells (ill. 154) and Southwell, is much more ornate than the Early English. Windows are filled with magnificent geometrical and flowing tracery, sometimes crowned with an ogee arch. Vaulting becomes more elaborate; clerestories are enlarged at the expense of the triforium.

The Perpendicular Style marks the end of the Gothic period in England and is characterized by the vertical lines of window tracery and the upright panelling of interior and exterior walls. Walls were treated as mere framework for the immense windows. The triforium practically disappeared, while clerestory windows were greatly increased in height. The complicated fan and pendant vaulting, a peculiarly English feature, is seen at its best in the Chapel of Henry VII, Westminster Abbey and in King's College Chapel, Cambridge. The cloisters and choir at Gloucester (q. v., ill. 169), dating from 1377, and the nave and west front at Winchester (q. v., 1371–1460) belong to this period.

The masterpieces of military architecture were designed by Englishmen; they are the great Welsh castles of Edward I, Harlech (ill. 49), Conway, Beaumaris and Pembroke. English architecture of the late Middle Ages is, apart from the Royal Chapels, best represented by manor houses and parish churches. Between the period of the Welsh castles (13th century) and the building of Penshurst nearly a hundred years later, military defence had ceased to be of importance in the design of the nobleman's house and more thought was given to domestic comfort. Penshurst, Ightham Mote and Sutton Courtenay are typical 14th-century manor houses. Each has a fine central hall with a screen at one end and a dais at the other, and an open timber roof. Haddon Hall, Derbyshire is famed as the *beau idéal* of historic medieval manor houses, while Compton Wynyates, with its turretted walls of rosy brick built round a courtyard and originally moated, embodies all that is most characteristic of secular architecture of the Tudor period. Countless small medieval houses survive up and down the country, and Lavenham, Suffolk is an almost perfectly preserved little town of the Perpendicular period with a fine guildhall and market cross.

Architecture in the Netherlands was influenced by France, Germany and England. In ecclesiastical architecture there was a tendency towards economy of form, shown in the church of St Gudule, Brussels, begun 1220, and this is shown even more clearly in the brick buildings of Holland (St Peter's, Leyden). In Late Gothic secular architecture there is greater emphasis on ornamentation, as in the cloth halls, town halls and residential buildings of Bruges, Ghent and Ypres (ill. 156).

The Romanesque spirit lingered on in the architecture of Germany until the middle of the 13th century and only gradually did individual Gothic features establish themselves. The cathedrals of Bamberg (q. v., consecrated

153. Sainte Chapelle in Paris, upper church. Built by Pierre de Montreaux (1243–48)

1237) and Naumburg (q. v., begun 1207) and the collegiate church of St George at Limburg a. d. Lahn (q. v.) represent the style of the transitional period which shows the influence of Laon Cathedral on German Romanesque planning. St Elizabeth's, Marburg (q. v.), a typicall hall church begun in 1235, is Gothic in idiom. But by retaining the triple apsidal termination, it opposes the Gothic idea of unified space in much the same way as does the central portion of the Liebfrauenkirche, Trier (q. v.). Cologne Cathedral (q. v., choir 1248–1322) was from the start based on Amiens, and Strassburg Cathedral (q. v., after 1250) took many of its ideas from French cathedral building. (Ill. 155)

The Gothic cathedrals and minsters in Freiburg i. Br. (q. v.), Regensburg, Breslau and Ulm (q. v.) were built in quick succession. The hall church, spreading from Westphalia, possibly under influence from the west and south-west of France, became a specific form of German Gothic. Represented in Westphalia by Paderborn Cathedral (after 1230) and the Wiesenkirche at Soest (1314–1376), its development is also shown in South Germany and Austria in St Stephen's Cathedral in Vienna (q. v.), St Martin's, Landshut, and the Franciscan choir in Salzburg (q. v.). The Cistercian and Mendicant orders were responsible for its establishment east of the German border. It was given final expression in the church of St Anne at Annaberg (1499–1520), where the division between nave and aisles is largely eliminated.

North German brick building became a feature of Gothic in the Cistercian abbeys of Lehnin and Chorin (begun 1243, ill. 47), while the Marienkirche at Lübeck, built in the French cathedral style, is a fine example of architecture in the Baltic region. The 14th century saw the introduction of brick into secular building, when the knights of the Teutonic Order began to use this material for their fortresses and castles (Marienburg, q. v.) as well as for their churches. The noble proportions of halls and refectories not only bear testimony to the power wielded by this Order but also represent the culmination of brick architecture (ill. 173).

The German medieval town with its houses, town halls, walls and towers received its characteristic appearance during the Gothic period. Towns like Rothenburg, Dinkelsbühl, Goslar and Celle still carry the imprint of medieval civic endeavour and bear testimony to the aesthetic awareness of their builders.

Gothic elements found their way into Italy through the Cistercian and Mendicant orders. S. Francesco at Assisi (after 1228) and the Florentine churches of S. Maria Novella (q. v.) and S. Croce (q. v.), with their spacious interiors in the classical manner, absorbed the Gothic spirit and blended it with the national style. In the cathedrals of Siena (q. v., after 1225), Orvieto (q. v., 1285) and Milan

154. Wells Cathedral (begun at end of 12th cent.). Nave, looking towards the choir. One of the remarkable buttress arches of the crossing (1338). – 155. Cologne Cathedral, from the choir end (1248–1322)

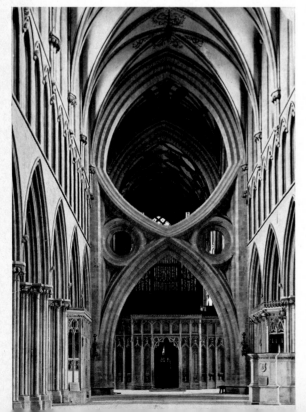

Romanesque wall painting from Brunswick Cathedral (13th century) Detail: Resurrection of Christ

Romanesque stained glass from Augsburg Cathedral (12th century): The Prophet Hosea

Early Gothic stained glass from Chartres Cathedral (13th century): King David with his Harp

MASTER OF THE UPPER RHINE, *c. 1490:* The Dangolsheim Madonna. *Part of the painted wood-carving*

156. Cloth Hall and Town Hall at Ypres (finished 1380)   *157. Cà d'Oro, Venice (1424–1437). Late Gothic palace façade*

(q. v., 1386), French influence is largely resisted (ill. 179). Instead of the organic use of sculptural orna-ment, pieces of coloured marble are combined into geometric surface decorations. Italian secular archi-tecture produced imposing strongholds with massive walls and corner towers, such as the castles at Ferrara, the Hohenstaufen castles in Bari, and Castel del Monte (q. v., ill. 166). The square palazzi (Palazzo Vecchio, Florence, q. v.) and mansions show bare walls to the outside world. Venetian Gothic, under Byzantine influence, produced an exotic style of its own (Cà d'Oro, ill. 157), characterized by elaborate window tracery and arcading on the façades.

SCULPTURE

Like Gothic architecture, Gothic sculpture originated in the Ile-de-France. It was not satisfied with merely playing the role of decorative adjunct; its aim was to represent in stone the entire Christian scene. Chartres Cathedral has over 8000 sculptures, of which the rigid draperied figures on the portals mark the earliest phase. Gradually, heads were imbued with life and soon the rest of the body, too, became animated. The sculptures on the Portal of the Virgin at Notre-Dame, Paris (1210–1220), the transept porches and portals at Chartres (1200–1240) and the west portals at Amiens are characterized by a feeling of sublime calm reminiscent of the figures on the temple of Zeus at Olympia (ill. 158, cf. ill. 22, 85). A classical perfection is reached in the noble sculptures on the west portals at Rheims (ill. 176). The figure of Christ, from the Last Judgment in the gable, familiar from reliefs over Romanesque door lintels (cf. p. 195), now becomes the Son of God on Earth, the most impressive figure in Western art.

The characteristic Gothic statue differs from that of Classical Antiquity by virtue of the highly skilful handling of the draperies, which are wound about the figures in curving folds. The draped figure was a creation of Gothic art and it offered the sculptor infinite scope for variation and experiment in the centuries to come (ill. 18 and p. 205).

Sculptors of the 13th century, having mastered the art of rendering emotion and spiritual expres-sion, were thus able to achieve the ultimate aim of plastic art – to portray divine spirituality in the perfection of the human form. But in the process the creative energy of the artist spent itself, and architectural sculpture in France became empty and devoid of meaning. Its place in the 14th century was taken by tomb sculpture. The portrayal of the deceased became the sculptor's assignment; the painted stone tomb of Philippe Pot, Grand Seneschal of Burgundy (c. 1480, now in the Louvre, Paris) is one of the finest examples of this art. In 1385 the Netherlandish sculptor Claus Sluter began working for Philippe le Hardi at Dijon (ill. 180).

158. Chartres Cathedral (13th cent.), draperied figures in the north doorway of the west front (Balaam, Queen of Sheba, King Solomon)

In Spain as in France, sculpture was employed largely on the exteriors of cathedrals. Spanish sculptors – among them a Master Bartolomé, who was connected with work on the main portal of Tarragona Cathedral in 1278 – worked side by side with foreign artists. Compared with French sculpture, the treatment of the portals is generally more austere and attitudes and gestures are more rigid, although there is a more harmonious blending with the over-all architectural scheme. Inside the cathedrals the 'trascoro', a choir in the nave reserved for the clergy and enclosed by tall screens, as well as the reredos, offered ample scope for lavish ornamentation in the form of figures, reliefs and pictures. The Italian artist Giuliano Fiorentino was responsible for the Late Gothic alabaster reliefs on the rood-screen of Valencia Cathedral, which were completed between 1413 and 1423, while Pere Johan de Vallfogona (between 1426 and 1439) carved the large number of individual figures and reliefs that make up the reredos behind the main altar at Tarragona. These stone *retablos* have the same function as the winged altar-pieces carved in wood that are found in Germany and the Low Countries.

Flemish and German masters left their mark on Spanish tomb sculpture, which reached its culmination in the work of Gil de Siloe (royal tomb of Juan II and Isabella in the Carthusian church of Miraflores, 1486–1493). During the 14th century, assimilation of Moorish elements resulted in the Mudéjar style from which, in turn, developed the Plateresque. With its dependence on classical motifs and its delight in elaborate ornamentation, this stands somewhere between the Late Gothic and Renaissance periods. Its decorative exuberance is well illustrated on the west front of Salamanca University and the façade of the town hall at Seville.

Owing to systematic destruction by Puritan reformers, there is far less figure sculpture in English cathedrals of this period than we find in the Ile-de-France, for example. The principal gallery of 13th-century sculpture is the glorious west front of Wells Cathedral. The lovely carved angels (second half of the 13th century) in the spandrels of the choir windows at Lincoln Cathedral bear the universal characteristics of the Gothic style, especially in the graceful and rhythmic flow of their poses and draperies. But the severe and rigid row of royal figures on the façade, which is of later origin, is more characteristically English in manner.

The same development is noticeable in tomb sculpture (ill. 79). The Purbeck marble effigy of Robert de Ros (d. 1227) in the Temple Church in London shows the reclining figure of a knight in armour with his legs crossed. In the 14th century, however, poses became more rigid. Wood was used as well as stone (tomb of Archbishop Peckham, Canterbury Cathedral). But the most popular materials in the 14th and 15th centuries were bronze, used by William Torell for his tombs of Henry III and Queen Eleanor in Westminster Abbey (1291 and 1292), and alabaster, which features in the sculptural decoration of altars. The memorial statue of Edward II (d. 1327) in Gloucester Cathedral might be given as an example of the high degree of technical and artistic skill that could be achieved in this medium.

Italian sculpture of the second half of the 13th century was influenced by the classical tradition, especially relief decorations on sarcophagi. The pulpits in the baptistery at Pisa (c. 1260) and the cathedral at Siena (q. v., 1265–1268), both by Nicola Pisano, have Gothic ornaments, as well as acanthus mouldings on the capitals. At Pisa there are also sculptured corner figures in the classical style (ill. 76), while the figural reliefs at Siena are more forceful and realistic. In the work of Pisano's son Giovanni, there is evidence of a serious attempt to evolve a personal style (ill. 177). The fountain in Perugia (1278) is still adorned with somewhat static figures. But in such works as the ivory statuette (1299) in the sacristy of Pisa Cathedral, where human beings are shown in a state of heightened spiritual emotion, he reveals a Gothic temperament. The work of Andrea Pisano, especially the twenty-eight bronze panels on the south door of the baptistery at Florence with scenes from the life of John the Baptist, stresses the fact that the Gothic idiom expresses the spirit of this age much more faithfully than the style of Classical Antiquity. With its emphasis on the emotions, it is infinitely more suited to solving the problems of the times, to help the individual to gain his freedom from the bonds of medievalism. In Pisano's work men are endowed with an ideal beauty and grace. Indebtedness to the Gothic style is still noticeable in the work of Andrea Orcagna (d. 1368), and even Lorenzo Ghiberti's (d. 1455) shows traces of it; although both artists already point the way to the Renaissance (ill. 159, 24).

In northern Italy, Matteo da Campione (d. 1396) is generally accredited with the elaborate sculptures on the façade of the cathedral at Monza, while Bonino da Campione was responsible for the magnificent tomb of Cansignorio della Grande with its fine equestrian statue, in Verona. The building of Milan Cathedral (q. v.) gave an impetus to sculpture in this part of Italy, carrying it over to the beginning of the Renaissance period.

The German cathedrals of Bamberg, Paderborn and Freiberg (Golden Portal, q. v.) have many interior sculptures in addition to those on the portals. From 1220 on, some of the finest German works were produced in quick succession: the statues of the Church (ill. 138) and the Synagogue, the Coronation and Death of the Virgin and the Last Judgment, at Strassburg; the Visitation and Horseman (ill. 164) by a master trained in Rheims, at Bamberg. Beneath the supple, flowing robes the bodies seem to be imbued with a strong vitality: the eyes, focussed on some distant point, the noble features and contours, all express deep spiritual insight. The work of the Naumburg (q. v.) Master represents the zenith of German architectural sculpture (ill. 174); the statues of the founders in the west choir are not only vivid portrayals of Teutonic chivalry but highly revealing characterizations of human nature as well.

In the 14th century, under the influence of mysticism, German sculpture concentrated its energies on a specifically German product, the devotional image. Christ and St John as an intimate group, Christ as the Man of Sorrows, and the Pietà, showing the dead Christ in the arms of his mother are among subjects portrayed.

During the second half of the century an element of realism began to invade German sculpture, of which Peter Parler's figures on the triforium of St Vitus' Cathedral in Prague (ill. 160) are an example. The 'soft' style, which originated in the south-east of Germany around 1400, produced the lovely, sweetish madonnas whose broadly flowing draperies bear more evidence of modelling than the bodies beneath. Realism has given way to an elegant, almost urbane spirituality.

The winged altar-piece, a joint creation of painter and sculptor, is the most splendid and com-

159. Orcagna, Death and Ascension of the Virgin. Relief on the rear of the tabernacle of San Michele, Florence (1348–59)

160. Cathedral of St Vitus, Prague, self-portrait bust of the cathedral architect Peter Parler in the triforium gallery. – 161. Krafft, self-portrait statue in front of the tabernacle in the church of St Lawrence, Nuremberg (1493–96)

prehensive product of Late Gothic art. Mounted on a predella, it sometimes ascended pyramid-wise as far as the roof. Many famous artists were engaged in making these winged altar-pieces, while sculptors found a more specific demand for their services in the production of memorial statues, tombs and tabernacles (ill. 84, 161, 178).

PAINTING

With the gradual disappearance of wall surfaces as a result of Gothic architectural development, wall painting in France became less and less important, until it was confined to the decoration of choir screens and sections of vaults.

Stained glass, however, achieved its greatest triumphs within the framework of Gothic architecture (ill. p. 204). The increased size of windows and the striving for transparent surfaces called for glass painting in strong colours. The 12th- and 13th-century windows of Chartres, St Denis, Canterbury and Sens have never been equalled for richness of colour and vigour of line. They show such resemblances to each other that there can be little doubt of common origin; they were probably the work of a group of people. The three windows over the west door of Chartres date from between 1145 and 1150. Two contain scenes from the life of Christ, while the third is filled with a Jesse Tree. Most of the rest of the glass in Chartres dates from the 13th century. There are 124 great windows, 3 great roses and 47 lesser windows. It is only at Chartres that the full, overwhelming effect of 13th-century stained glass can be felt, for it is here alone that it survives in such entirety. In style the windows show an increased use of mosaic diaper pattern in various shades of blue which was peculiarly French. The choice of subject does not appear to be governed by any connected idea, but was probably left to the various donors who are conspicuously represented in the windows by their portraits. The five complete windows in Rouen Cathedral, one of which is signed by Clement de Chartres, equal the work of Chartres in beauty of design and execution. The late 13th-century glass which fills the Sainte Chapelle, Paris (q. v), shows the great esteem in which the art was held, for the whole building was designed to set off the stained glass. The compositions, however, cannot be compared with those at Chartres or Rouen; they are cramped and the borders are narrow and uninteresting. The fine church of St Ouen, Rouen is very rich in 14th-century glass and illustrates the tendency of the period to subordinate figures to ornament and to fill backgrounds with quarries or small diamond-shaped panes. These windows are some of the last great works in stained glass in France. The country was devastated by war towards the end of the 14th century and the art declined.

Panel painting began to flourish in the 14th century, especially in the Burgundian-Flemish realm which had its centre at Dijon. The wings of a carved altar-piece (Dijon Museum) painted around 1400 for Duke Philippe le Hardi by Melchior Broederlam, are Flemish in feeling. The painting of the Holy Trinity by Malouel (Louvre, Paris) on a gold ground, on the other hand, shows Italian influence. Jean Foucquet (c. 1420–c. 1480), the most important representative of the school of Tours already foreshadows the Renaissance in his realistic portraits of Charles VII and Juvenal des Ursins (both in the Louvre).

The University town of Paris greatly fostered the development of manuscript illumination. During the 13th and early 14th centuries a flat, decorative miniature style prevailed, although the work of Jean Pucelle already shows an attempt to create an illusion of depth in the treatment of figures and background. After 1400 a vital new influence was introduced through the work of certain Flemish artists, among them the Limbourg brothers who produced work for the Duc de Berry in Bourges. Jean Foucquet, famous for his easel paintings and even more significant as a manuscript illuminator, marks the end of Gothic miniature painting in France (ill p. 49, p. 218).

After the 13th century, French and Tuscan influences met in Spanish art. Among foreign artists working in Spain there were numerous painters, especially Italians. In Catalonia, Ferrer de Bassa (c. 1287–1348) made known the discoveries of Giotto. A few decades later, Pere Serra and his brothers tried to fuse the Sienese style with the native idiom. The Catalan school was speeded in its emergence from the Middle Ages by Luis Borrassá, who had studied the work of Hubert and Jan van Eyck. The same process was at work in Valencia under the leadership of Luis Dalmau, and in Castile under Ferdinand Gallegos. The latter's altar-piece in the cathedral of Zamora is reminiscent of the work of Dirk Bouts.

In England, glass painting reached a high artistic level. Some of the windows of Canterbury Cathedral (q. v.) are probably among the earliest extant examples in Western Europe, dating from about 1178. The surviving glass is to be found in the north choir aisle and in the Trinity Chapel east of the choir. These windows resemble the work at the great abbey of St Denis (q. v.), though the style is more developed at Canterbury. Where possible, as in the deep, rich blue of the background, the glass is left quite clear. The folds of the drapery and the features are drawn in bold, expressive line. The subjects are scenes from the life of Christ and incidents from the Old Testament which illustrate it, thus forming one of the first and most complete instances of 'type and antitype' windows. The Trinity Chapel at Canterbury contains not only 12th-century but also early 13th-century glass. The 13th-century windows are all devoted to the tale of the posthumous miracles of the Blessed St Thomas and delightfully portray every-day life in medieval England. There are other extensive remains of 13th-century glass at Lincoln (q. v.). During this period a new style of stained glass window was evolved – the grisaille window. The finest grisaille windows in Europe are the five great lancets at the end of the north transept of York, known as the Five Sisters (c. 1260). Fourteenth-century glass was conspicuous for the extraordinary develop-ment of the architectural canopy in the design, this becoming more important than the figures beneath it. Other characteristics were the mannered drawing of figures in an S-like pose and the predilection for natural plant forms. Good examples can be seen at Merton College, Oxford and in Exeter Cathedral (q. v.), but the best work of the period, showing an unbroken progression in style from the late 13th to the early 15th century, is at York. The huge Perpendicular east window of the choir of York Minster (q. v.) is one of the major achievements of English glaziers. It was the work of John Thornton in 1405, a fine draughtsman and one of the first artists to make use of colour as a means of expression. This is the most significant work of the 15th century, a period particularly rich in stained glass in England. The celebrated windows at Fairford, which owe much to Flemish influence, magnificent though they are, mark the beginning of a decline in the art which is still more obvious in the 16th-century windows of King's College Chapel, Cambridge (q. v.).

The Early English period was one of great achievement in the field of illumination. One of the foremost painters of the Middle Ages was working at this time: Matthew Paris, a brilliant historian who illustrated his own work with delicately tinted pen and ink drawings. To this time also belong the Arundel and Queen Mary's Psalters, the former an East Anglian work. They are characterized by rich borders with naturalistic leaf designs and life-like studies of birds and animals. During the 14th century English illumination deteriorated in quality though the flow of work was greater than ever. Even the Luttrell Psalter with its enchanting scenes of domestic and sporting life is inferior in workmanship and inspiration to contemporary French illumination.

Great advance in wall painting was made during the Gothic period in England. The finest extant painting is the Chichester Roundel in the Chapel of the Bishop's Palace at Chichester, a tempera painting on stone of the Virgin and Child. It was a splendid period also for panel painting, especially in East Anglia (retable in Norwich Cathedral with scenes of the Passion, Thornham Parva retable and Ranworth screen). But the greatest picture of the age which is left to us is undoubtedly the Wilton Diptych (ill. p. 206), showing Richard II accompanied by three patron saints kneeling before the Virgin and Child and a company of angels.

Until the end of the 13th century Italian painting continued in the flat Byzantine style or 'maniera greca'. But Pietro Cavallini's frescoes in S. Cecilia and Torriti's apsis mosaic in S. Maria Maggiore in Rome, dating from shortly before and around 1300 respectively, and, above all, the Enthroned Madonna formerly attributed to the Florentine master Cimabue (d. 1302), were preparing the way for a less rigid, more natural style. It was Giotto (ill. p. 228) who finally broke away from the conventions that had by this time become meaningless. With the figures in his frescoes in the Arena Chapel, Padua, he succeeds in suggesting the roundness of the human body, and a third dimension is introduced by the use of light and shadow. Man, still intimately linked with God but already a creature in his own right, becomes a subject worthy of portrayal. Giotto's discoveries, carried on in the work of such artists as Taddeo Gaddi, Barnardo Daddi and Giottino, were to have the most far-reaching effect.

At about the same time Simone Martini (ill. p. 230) was active in Siena. He was more indebted to the Gothic manner than were the Florentine painters, more interested in the pursuit of an ideal beauty than in conveying dramatic intensity (ill. p. 230). His followers, among them the Lorenzetti brothers, attempted a fusion with the style of Giotto and the trend towards realism in the work of such painters as Gentile da Fabriano (ill. p. 227) prepared the way for the spectacular development of Italian painting during the Early Renaissance period.

In Germany glass painting did not take the place of wall painting to the same extent as it did in France. After the middle of the 14th century, however, panel painting occupied an increasingly important position both in Germany and in neighbouring countries. The 'soft' linear style from France and the art of Giotto both played their part in the formation of a naturalistic school of painting which had its centre at the Court of the Emperor Charles IV in Prague but could also be traced throughout Bohemia. Its chief exponents were the Masters of Hohenfurt and Wittingau, and Theodoric of Prague (ill. p. 240).

The work of the Westphalian Master Bertram, active in Hamburg between 1367 and 1410, shows the influence of both the new Italian and Bohemian styles. Master Francke, an artist of some sophistication who is thought to have trained in Paris around 1400, manifests a delight in nature in his 'Englandfahrer' altar of 1424 in Hamburg (ill. p. 239). Schools of painting in Westphalia and Cologne, the middle and upper Rhine district (ill. p. 215), Suabia, Nuremberg and the Tyrol, all have their more or less individual styles. Konrad von Soest from Westphalia and Stephan Lochner from Cologne were exponents of the 'soft' style, concerned with spiritual expression. But in the south of Germany there was already a strong movement in the direction of Late Gothic realism (ill. p. 229, p. 242), highly significant for the future of German painting and represented by the work of Lukas Moser (Tiefenbronner altar), Konrad Witz (Geneva altar, 1444), and Hans Multscher. In Nuremberg, Salzburg and the Tyrol, Alsace and Ulm, under the influence of Burgundian, Flemish and Italian art, the foundations were being laid for a golden age of German painting, represented by such names as Grünewald, Albrecht Dürer and Hans Holbein the Younger. (Ill. p. 241)

THE CRAFTS

After the end of the 12th century the Church gradually ceased to be the sole patron of the crafts; princes, nobles and burghers took its place. Goldsmiths and other craftsmen were set a number of new tasks that called for even greater skill. The technique of champlevé work (see Enamel) and enamelling, mainly practised in Limoges, was perfected. Metalworkers began to adopt the more intricate decorative idiom of Gothic architecture, and vessels and implements had their surfaces chased and pierced.

Dinant in Flanders specialized in the production of bronze and brass candlesticks, ewers and water stoups (ill. 162), while chased bowls and basins came from the workshops of metal-beaters. Wooden domestic utensils were replaced by pewter; smiths turned their hand to the elaborate ornamentation of weapons and suits of armour.

The 14th and 15th centuries also saw the development of the textile arts. Northern Germany and Switzerland produced white embroidered linens, at first for use in churches, later for domestic purposes as well; England and Florence specialized in beautiful embroideries in delicate colours, sometimes on a gold ground. Pictorial tapestries and hangings, after designs by Burgundian and Flemish artists, were woven in North Germany and Paris, and later in Arras, Tournai and Brussels, to adorn the walls of churches and castles (ill. p. 216). After the 12th century silk-weaving was practised in Sicily and, later, in Venice, Genoa and Lucca. Ceremonial robes for princes and vestments for church dignitaries were made of silver and gold brocade on a plain or multi-coloured ground (ill. p. 217).

Instead of the simple earthenware pottery of early medieval times, beautifully fashioned and technically perfect stoneware vessels now came from workshops near Cologne and Aix-la-Chapelle. Southern Germany and the Tyrol, as well as England and France, produced gaily painted and glazed pots with relief ornamentation. The technique of faience, of Moorish origin, was practised in Spain and spread across to Italy in the 15th century.

In the 12th and 13th centuries furniture was still crudely made, strictly utilitarian and limited to a few essential pieces. Carpenters produced box-shaped beds, square chairs with high backs, chests, and table-tops placed on trestles at meal-times. Although few new items came into use in Late Gothic times, the cutting of wood into thin strips resulted in lighter and more graceful pieces that could be decorated with delicate carving and paintwork.

Ivory as a decorative material remained popular in Gothic times and was used for mirror-cases, jewel caskets, book covers, and the crooks of bishop's crosiers. Leather was decorated by various methods which included engraving, chasing, pressing and punching: it was used for covering books, caskets and chests. Venice once again became a centre for the manufacture of glass.

In summing up, it can be said that the aim of medieval art was to represent the glory of God's Kingdom on Earth. Gothic art, coming right at the end of the Middle Ages, gradually dissociated itself from this aim and sought to serve a new purpose. This was to help man in his emergence as an individual, to strengthen his awareness of his own dignity and to assist him in the discovery of Nature.

162. Aquamanile in the shape of a lion (N. German, 13th cent.), bronze

AETHELWOLD BENEDICTIONAL. St Aethel-wold (d. 984), Bishop of Winchester, revived the art of the Anglo-Saxon illuminated manuscript, which had such a proud tradition. The 'Aethelwold Benedictional' is one of the early works of the 'Winchester School'. It was written about 980 by Godeman, later Abbot of Thorney; it was probably he who painted the numerous miniatures, which are in the late Carolingian style adopted from northern France but developed in the Anglo-Saxon manner.

AIX-LA-CHAPELLE (AACHEN) CATHEDRAL. About 800 Odo von Metz built a two-storeyed chapel for the Imperial Palace. This has been preserved as the nucleus of the modern cathedral. Internally the ground plan is octagonal; externally, a 16-sided polygon. In the lower storey, sturdy piers with arcades separate the central space from the ambulatory. A pronounced cornice marks the beginning of the upper story. The arcades of the tribune galleries rest on classical columns. The lofty central space is covered by a dome rising above the clerestory to form a tower. To the west, an entrance flanked by two towers and rising above the galleries, was added. (Ill. 142, 143)

ALCÁZAR (*Arabic*). A term used in Spain to describe a number of castles and fortresses. A well known example is the Alcázar of Seville built in the so-called Mudéjar style (14th cent.).

ALPIRSBACH, BENEDICTINE ABBEY. Of this former Benedictine Abbey in the Black Forest, which was founded in 1095, the flat-roofed, cruciform pillar-ed basilica of the first half of the 12th century is still extant.

AMIENS CATHEDRAL. The construction of this classic Gothic French cathedral began in 1220. The west façade and the nave were completed in 1236, the choir in 1270. The proportion of width to height of the nave is 1 : 3; of the west front, 1 : 2. The aisles are half as high and half as wide as the nave. The body of the church, the three-aisled transept and the choir with ambulatory and seven chapels, communicating through arcades with high pointed arches, seem to flow into each other. The western façade is in the classic pattern: two great towers, three doorways with a rose window above the central one. Compared with Rheims (q. v.), there are signs of a certain rigidity in the sculptured figures and the decoration, but the severe 'Beau Dieu' and the 'Golden Virgin' are among the most admired master-pieces of French Gothic. (Ill. 152)

ANGOULÊME CATHEDRAL. St Pierre, begun in 1105, is a typical example of the domed church of the Romanesque school of architecture in Aquitaine (south-western France). The aisleless nave consists of three domed spaces. The central dome rises above a drum pierced with windows. The short arms of the transepts are also covered by domes. These were to have been surmounted by towers, of which only the northern one – now restored – was actually built. In spite of

163. Angoulême Cathedral (first half 12th cent.), west front

irritating additions in the 19th century, the façade, dating from about 1170, is one of the most important achievements of Late Romanesque French architecture and sculpture (ill. 163).

ANTELAMI, BENEDETTO, is the most important sculptor of the Late Romanesque period in northern Italy. His earliest known work is the 'Descent from the Cross' of 1178 from the pulpit formerly in Parma Cathedral; its clear and orderly composition is rooted in the local Lombard tradition but the style betrays southern French training. In the sculptures of the Baptistery in Parma (from 1196 onwards) and, above all, in the whole conception of the main door of the cathedral at Borgo San Donnino, Antelami attempted to transfer to Italian buildings the conventional sculptural cycles familiar to him from Arles and Saint-Gilles-du-Gard.

APOCALYPSE OF ANGERS. Duke Louis I of Anjou ordered a series of tapestries depicting the Apocalypse of St John from the Paris tapestry weaver, Nicolas Bataille. These were executed between 1375 and 1381 after cartoons by Jan Bandol (q. v.). About seventy scenes of the 413-feet-long series have been preserved in the Tapestry Museum at Angers.

AQUAMANILE (from the Latin *aqua* – water and *manus* – hand) is a term for a medieval ewer or stoup used for the ritual ablutions of the higher clergy and later also for profane purposes. The vessels were artist-ically made in the form of animals, generally of lions, but also of griffons, dogs, stags, etc. They were made of bronze or brass. (Ill. 162)

214

MASTER OF THE UPPER RHINE, *c. 1410:* The Paradise Garden

French tapestry: 'The Nine Heroes and Heroines' *from the studio of* Nicolas Bataille, *Paris (c. 1385). Detail*

Cloth used at Mass with a representation of the Crucifixion. *The crossed bough as the symbol of the Tree of Life bears a particular relationship to the sacrifice of the Mass. German needlework on Italian gold brocade (15th century)*

JEAN FOUQUET: St Martin and the Beggar. *Illuminated manuscript page from the Book of Hours of Étienne Chevalier. In the background, a view of Paris*

ARLES CATHEDRAL. The cathedral of St Trophîme in Arles (Provence), built mainly in the second half of the 12th century, is a three-aisled basilica. The nave has pointed barrel vaulting; the extremely narrow aisles have half-barrel vaults. In the wonderful doorway in the west façade, the Roman tradition – which never completely died out in Provence – comes to life again. Life-size figures of the Apostles stand between columns, which are covered with a closely knit frieze of figures. The beautiful cloisters, built in the 13th century, are also richly decorated.

ARNOLFO DI CAMBIO (c. 1245–1302). Architect and sculptor, is first mentioned in documents in 1266 as assistant to Nicola Pisano (q. v.), who was then working on the pulpit in Siena Cathedral. In Rome, he left various pieces of sculpture, among them the tomb of Boniface VIII, in which we can detect Roman tradition, French influence and Tuscan sensibility, these having here come together to form a national style. From 1296, Arnolfo was active as architect on the Badia (abbey) in Florence and on the cathedral there, the façade of which he also decorated with sculptures.

AUTUN CATHEDRAL. St Lazare in Autun (Burgundy) was built between 1116–1132 as a three-aisled basilica covered with a pointed barrel vault. The porch was begun in 1178. The walls are divided horizontally into three; between the arcades of the ground storey and the clerestory windows is a triforium in which the elements, like the superimposed fluted pilasters that take the place of semicircular shafts and support the arches of the vaulting, are borrowed from the Roman remains in the town (Porte d'Arroux). The decoration is important, e. g., the tympanum of the main door with the Last Judgment.

AVIGNON, PAPAL PALACE. From 1309 to 1377, the Popes resided in Avignon. Benedict XII (1334–1342) began the construction of a four-winged castle to which his successor Clement VI made additions. German and Italian artists (e. g. Simone Martini) worked on the decoration of the interiors along with French artists.

BAMBERG CATHEDRAL was founded by the Emperor Henry in 1004. It was rebuilt and extended to the west under Bishop Egbert of Merano (1203–1237), using the remains of the original building which had been destroyed by fire. The east choir with apse and crypt together with the lower storeys of the two east towers belong to an earlier Late Romanesque structure. Subsequently, the nave and west transept were added, followed by the west choir and the two west towers. From about 1215 to 1220 building continued, using Early Gothic forms. The sculptures, executed at the same time as the building or a little later, are among the greatest achievements of German art. The rails of the St George Choir in the east are decorated with apostles and prophets. The 'Bamberger Reiter' – that quintessence of the high knightly ideal of the imperial age of the Hohenstaufens – together with the sculptures

164. The 'Bamberger Reiter' (13th cent.)

of Mary and Elizabeth (the 'Visitation'), or the 'Ecclesia' and 'Synagoga', were originally conceived as decorations for the exterior of the cathedral but are today haphazardly displayed (ill. 164).

BANDOL, JAN, also known as Jean Bondol or Hennequin of Bruges, was a native of that town and became, in 1368, Court painter to King Charles V of France. He designed the cartoons for the tapestries of the 'Apocalypse of Angers' (q. v.). A title page miniature of Charles V's illustrated Bible shows that the artist was a masterly draughtsman.

BARCELONA CATHEDRAL. The construction of the three-aisled basilican cathedral with transept, choir and small choir chapels began in 1298. The spacious interior with its high aisles, slim piers and narrow clerestory broken by a triforium with circular windows above, is typically Spanish.

BASLE CATHEDRAL. The three-aisled (earlier five-aisled) Romanesque basilica with its intersecting vaulting was begun in 1185, on the remains of an earlier building destroyed by fire. The tribune galleries seem to have been executed after Lombard models. The transition to Gothic – of which there are indications in the vaulting – is complete in the polygonal choir.

BEAUNEVEU ANDRÉ, native of Valenciennes, is first mentioned in documents in 1360. He died in 1403 or 1413. He entered the service of Charles V of France and worked as painter, sculptor and architect. Beauneveu created the statues of the King and his wife (now in the Louvre) and the stained-glass windows of the Sainte-Chapelle in Bourges. From 1396 onwards, the

165. *The Brunswick Lion (1166), bronze*

artist worked as miniature painter for Duke Jean de Berry.

BEAUVAIS CATHEDRAL. The Gothic cathedral was begun in 1247 on the ruins of an earlier building destroyed by fire; 158 ft high, it was the climax of a desire to build upwards. The choir, completed in 1272, collapsed in 1284. Its buttresses had to be considerably reinforced when it was rebuilt. This first great building disaster, which was followed by others, brought the Gothic mania for height to a tragic end. In 1500 Martin Chambige, architect of Troyes Cathedral, began to build the three-aisled transept. The 502-ft-high central tower by Jean Vaast collapsed in 1573. The cathedral remained unfinished.

BERNWARDSKUNST (German: 'Bernward's art'). Bernward, Bishop of Hildesheim 993–1022, was equally important as Prince of the Church and patron of the arts. He was himself a creative artist. The church of St Michael in Hildesheim (q. v.) appears to be his personal creation. During his tenure of office, many works of art cast in silver and bronze, and fashioned from wood and stone were created in Hildesheim. The bronze doors of St Michael dating from 1015, later placed in the cathedral (the Hildesheim Bronze Doors), and the bronze triumphal column of Christ are outstanding examples of *Bernwardskunst* (cf. Bernward's Evangelistary, ill. p. 47).

BOHEMIAN SCHOOL. Emperor Charles IV (1316–1378), who became King of Bohemia in 1346, made Prague his residence and encouraged the arts by attracting to the city numerous artists from Germany, France and Italy. French influence was disseminated through the art of book illumination, which was brought to Bohemia by monks; it was later superseded by the Italian influence. Bohemian altar painting, which rapidly grew to be the most important branch of the school, is represented by the Master of the Hohenfurth Altar (q. v., Višší Brod), Tomaso da Modena (q. v.), Nicolas Wurmser (q. v.) and Theodoric of Prague (q. v., frescoes

in Schloss Karlstein) and by the Master of Wittingau (q. v., Třebon), who is the most accomplished of the school (ill. p. 240).

BONNINO DA CAMPIONE, a sculptor and architect from Campione on Lake Como, was active in northern Italy and died in Milan in 1397. His main work, the monument of Can Signario, is to be found among the tombs of the Scaligers, the ruling family of Verona.

BORASSÁ, LUIS, was one of a family of painters in Gerona, Catalonia. In 1390 he transferred his studio to Barcelona, where he remained until his death in 1444. The altar with scenes from the life of John the Baptist in the Musée des Arts Décoratifs in Paris shows his easy style, which was certainly influenced by French painting. Borassá brought Spanish painting, particularly the Valencian school (Marsal de Sax, the Perez family, etc.) into contact with the northern school of painting as represented by the van Eyck brothers (q. v.).

BOURDICHON, JEAN, 1457–1521, worked in Tours as illuminator and painter. The miniatures in the prayer book of Anne of Brittany (Paris, Biblioteque Nationale) constitute his main work.

BRADFORD-ON-AVON, St Lawrence. This church in Wiltshire was probably built round about 700 and is therefore one of the oldest churches in England. The interior is high and narrow; in the west there is a rectangular chancel.

BRUNSWICK CATHEDRAL. Duke Henry the Lion had the collegiate church of St Blasius built between 1173 and 1195 on the site of an older building. It was a cruciform Romanesque basilica built on the square plan. In accordance with custom in Lower Saxony, the alternation of supports – in this case of main piers with a cruciform plan and simple intermediary piers – was adhered to. The nave is covered with a pointed broken barrel vault. Under the choir and the crossing there is a crypt. Between 1322 and 1346, a second aisle was added in the south and a similar aisle in the north was completed by 1474. The two northern aisles have, however, been amalgamated into a double-aisled hall with spiralled pillars and stellar vaulting. In the interior, large sections of the wall paintings dating from about 1220–1250 have been rediscovered (ill. p. 203). Of the furnishings the wooden crucifix of Master Immerward, dating from 1194, as well as the Treasure of the Guelphs (q. v.) has been preserved.

BRUNSWICK LION. In 1166, Duke Henry the Lion had his badge, a gilt bronze lion, erected in front of his castle at Dankwarderode in Brunswick. It is a fine piece of secular monumental sculpture (ill. 165).

BROEDERLAM, MELCHIOR, a Flemish painter from Ypres, was active between 1381 and 1409 as Court painter to the Counts of Flanders and Duke Philip the Bold of Burgundy. Duke Philip commissioned him to paint the panels of an altar carved by Jacques de Baertze (in Dijon Museum) with a 'Presentation in the

Temple' and a 'Flight from Egypt'. His style shows signs of Flemish bourgeois and Burgundian courtly taste. The broad sweep and clarity of the draughtsmanship of the Paris school combines in his painting with the vivid colouring of the Sienese painters.

BRUGES TOWN HALL. This cubical building with its steep gabled roof and three turrets was begun in 1376. It is decorated with statues set on the outer wall between the doorways and windows. The building's rich decoration produces the effect of a Gothic stone reliquary.

BRUEGGEMANN, HANS (c. 1480–1540). The Late Gothic altar with its numerous carved figures, which this master originally made for the monastery church at Bordesholm, is now in the cathedral at Schleswig. The relief panels show great symmetry of composition; they are unpainted and are partly based on the drawings in Dürer's 'Little Passion'.

BURGOS CATHEDRAL. The building of the Early Gothic three-aisled cruciform basilica at Burgos in Castile was begun in 1221. The polygonal choir (c. 1230) has an ambulatory and chevet. The high walls of the nave are divided into three storeys. The vaulting is supported by multiple buttresses in the French style. The façade and the two towers, decorated with tracery, were completed in the middle of the 15th century by Master Hans of Cologne.

CAEN. The town occupies a peculiar place in the history of architecture. In St Étienne (c. 1065–77) and St Trinité (basic structure 1059–1066) we find innovations of importance for the emergence of the Gothic style. The wall is divided horizontally into three – ground floor arcades, tribune gallery and clerestory – and vertically by shafts running the whole height of the building. The choir of St Trinité has cross vaulting. A little later, in St Étienne sexpartite vaulting was used. The west façade of St Étienne (1080) with its twin towers and three doorways, is also indicative of future developments. (Ill. 147)

CAMBRIDGE, KING'S COLLEGE CHAPEL. Built 1446–1515 on an unusually long, narrow plan, its rectangular choir is barely distinguishable from the body of the church. Low chapels with ribbed walls (see Perpendicular Style) are inserted between stepped buttresses of the external wall. Above them are large windows divided into a number of lights. The interior is aisleless; shouldered arches rise from moulded piers to support fan vaulting.

CANTERBURY CATHEDRAL. In 1174 fire destroyed the sanctuary of the Romanesque building. In the following year, William of Sens began the building of the Early Gothic (Early English) choir which was finished round about 1185. The east end of the choir was enlarged after the French model (Sens Cathedral) to form an apsidal chapel. The fluidity of spatial relationships shows that Gothic architecture in England is not merely a direct descendant of French Gothic but developed in its own way. The restoration of the nave,

166. Castel del Monte in Apulia (1240), hunting lodge of the Hohenstaufen emperor Frederick II

built 1379–1400, was carried out in the 15th century when the towers were also completed.

CASTEL DEL MONTE. This hunting lodge of the Emperor Frederick II stands on a hill near Corato in Apulia. It was built between 1240 and 1250 on a regular octagonal plan with two storeys and eight projecting towers (ill. 166).

CAVALLINI, PIETRO (c. 1250–1330), a Roman painter, was active at the Neapolitan Court from 1308. In the 'Life of Mary', a series of mosaics executed in 1291 (in S. Maria in Trastevere, Rome) and in the fresco of the Last Judgment (in S. Cecilia, Rome), the painter produces, through the use of chiaroscuro, figures which emerge from the plane of the picture. Like Giotto, whom he influenced and by whom he was in turn influenced, he freed Italian painting from its Byzantine ties.

CENTULA. This monastery at Saint Riquier, near Abbeville, had a main church which was erected between 790 and 799 and later destroyed. It was one of the most important products of Carolingian architecture. It was a basilica with an east transept, a domed central tower and a square choir. In the west the basilica had a westwork (q. v.) with a central tower and two staircase towers flanking the entrance hall. The new spatial organization at the east and west ends influenced future church architecture (ill. 144).

CHARTRES CATHEDRAL. All but the western part of the Romanesque cathedral was burnt down in 1194. The new building took the form of a cruciform basilica with three-aisled nave and transepts. These and the choir with its double-aisled ambulatory were for the first time combined to form a spatial entity. The round piers have four attached shafts which run halfway up the clerestory and there support the transverse arch of the intersecting vaulting. This has the effect, on the one hand, of stressing the rapid succession of the arches and thus unifying the interior; on the other, of connecting all three storeys of the nave walls, so that the arcading of the lower storey is included in the soaring movement.

The west façade with its triple doors was preserved from the old building although with alterations. For the first time the external fabric is 'suspended' in a complete supporting system. From 1224 onwards, porches were added to the transepts, first in the south and later in the north, in place of the towers which had been planned. The consecration took place in 1260 in the presence of St Louis. The cathedral is famous for its stained glass, which has been preserved almost intact (ill. p. 204), as well as for its sculptured figures and reliefs. Christian doctrine and human knowledge, in so far as it is centred on God, are expounded in more than 8000 pieces of sculpture (ill. 158).

CIMABUE, whose real name was Cenni di Pepo, was born in Florence in 1240 and died in 1302. His many works include the great painting of the Madonna enthroned between angels and prophets from S. Trinità in Florence (now in the Uffizi) and the frescoes in the upper and lower church of S. Francesco in Assisi. In the ceremonial pose of his figures and his use of abstract colours on a gold ground, he clings to the rules of the older school of painting, which was influenced by Byzantine art; but he attempts to create an impression of space by bolder movement and free use of line.

CLERMONT - FERRAND, NOTRE - DAME - DU - PORT. This church, dating from the 11th century, was built on a cruciform plan. The nave is barrel-vaulted; there are galleries over the aisles. The central dome, the arms of the transept, the choir with its ambulatory and chevet are charmingly stepped. (Cf. p. 187)

CLUNY. The Benedictine abbey of Cluny in Burgundy, founded in 910, became, in the 10th and 11th centuries, the starting point for a powerful movement of Church reform, which also influenced church architecture. In 1089, the third reconstruction of the church was begun – the first began in 910, the second, some time after 981. The huge five-aisled basilica with its great barrel vault had two transepts in the east, a main choir with ambulatory and five chapels, as well as several towers. The east arms of the transepts had round apses. To the west was a three-aisled entrance set between two towers (ill. 167). The building was destroyed during the French Revolution.

CODEX AUREUS (Latin: golden book), is the name given to various medieval manuscripts which are noted either for their gold script or their gold covers. The Latin word 'codex' originally meant 'trunk of a tree'. It was applied in ancient times to books consisting of wooden tablets treated with wax and bound together; later it was used for parchment manuscripts consisting of single pages. The name *Codex Aureus* is applied, *inter alia,* to the following: a book of the Gospels written and illuminated in Canterbury, c. 760–770 (now in Stockholm); an evangelistary in gold uncials from St Emmeram Ratisbon (now in Nuremberg), commissioned by Emperor Charles the Bald from St Denis in western France; a manuscript in gold minuscules written at the Echternach monastery, Luxemburg, between 983 and 991 or perhaps some time after 1020 (now in Nuremberg).

COLOGNE CATHEDRAL. The foundations of Cologne Cathedral, the largest Gothic church in Germany, were laid in 1248. The building was begun at the east end under Master Gerhard, who planned the cathedral on the model of the great French cathedrals, especially Amiens. In 1322, the choir with ambulatory and seven chevet chapels was consecrated. In the interior the shafts of the clustered piers, unbroken by capitals, were made to run through to the base of the vaulting, thus contributing towards an unrivalled adaptation of the Gothic to structural design. The pierced triforium and the tall, closely-spaced windows above it have fine tracery. Work continued with interruptions on the rest of the building – the three-aisled transept, the five-aisled, basilican body of the church and the west façade with its two towers – until 1560, but the building was not completed. In 1880 the cathedral, including the towers, was at last finished on the basis of the rediscovered plans (ill. 156).

COLOGNE, ST MARY-IN-CAPITOL. The Church, as its name suggests, was originally erected on the remains of an ancient building. The present structure (1040–1065) is a basilican three-aisled building with a westwork (q. v.) connected to a centralized east end. From the crossing, the two wings of the transept and the choir extend outwards, each ending in an apse with ambulatory, to give a trefoil pattern. Above the crossing is a hanging dome; barrel vaulting covers the arms of the transept and choir.

COLOMBE, MICHEL, born in Brittany in 1430, died in Tours some time after 1512, was a sculptor whose work places him at the point of transition between Late Gothic and the Renaissance. Mention must be made of his tombs of Francis II and his wife in Nantes Cathedral (1507) and of Roberta Légendre in the Louvre.

COSMATI is the accepted description for a series of Roman decorators and sculptors of the 12th to 14th centuries, who produced particularly fine work in mosaic and marble for pulpits, altars and tombs. They appear very often to have been called Cosmas. To-day this group of artists is also called the 'Marmorarii Romani'.

DADDI, BERNARDO, was active in the first half of the 14th century in Florence as a painter of frescoes

167. Church of the Benedictine abbey of Cluny (1089 to mid 13th cent.) reconstruction

1 Twin-towered west entrance, 2 Three-aisled projecting nave, 3 Five-aisled basilican main nave, 4 Main transept, with crossing tower (4a) and two subsidiary towers, 5 Eastern transept with crossing tower, 6 Chancel, 7 Apse, 8 Ambulatory, 9 Apsidal chapels, 10 Subsidiary chapels

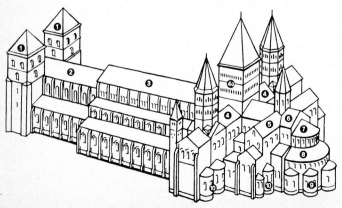

and panels. His frescoes in S. Croce in Florence (Martyr-
dom of St Lawrence and St Stephen) or his diptychs
and triptychs in the Uffizi show that, in spite of his
own narrative powers, Daddi followed the tradition of
Giotto in composition and choice of colours.

DANZIG, MARIENKIRCHE. St Mary's, the largest
church on the Baltic, is a brick hall structure with transept and rectangular choir. All the building's arms have
three aisles. In front of the west wall of the nave stands
a massive tower articulated by corner buttresses and
windows; it contains two twin-storeyed side-chapels.
The interior is made more spacious by the chapels added
in the north and south, which stretch up to the net vaulting. The building was begun in 1343 as a basilica and
finished in the 15th century as a hall church.

DECORATED STYLE is the name for the prevailing
ornate style of English Gothic between c. 1250 and
1350 – it is also called Foliated or Curvilinear.

DINANDERIE is the term for chased copper – and in
particular bronzeware – from Dinant on the Maas. The
style flourished between the 13th and 15th centuries.
The term is also used for chased metal objects in general.

DREIKÖNIGSSCHREIN. This shrine in Cologne
Cathedral contains the relics of the Magi, which Archbishop Rainald of Dassel brought back as booty from
Milan in 1164. The oak casket is shaped like a basilica
and is completely covered with rich metal panels set
with enamels, precious stones or filigree. The decorative
Romanesque figures are of chased gilt silver or gold
plate; they were executed c. 1220.

DUCCIO DI BUONINSEGNA, born c. 1260, was
active in Siena and died there in 1319. In his earliest
dated work, the Ruccellai Madonna (1258), the strong
accent on flat planes, the abstract colouring and the
stiffness of the main figure, show that the artist was
still working in the Byzantine tradition, which was then
common in Italy. In the Maestà, his last signed work
(1308–1311) – a Madonna seated amidst angels and
saints now in Siena Cathedral, which shows a feeling
for plastic values – Duccio, although he lacks Giotto's
(q. v.) expressive power, is gradually freeing himself
from medieval ties.

DURHAM CATHEDRAL. This reconstructed galleried
basilica (begun in 1092) with alternating cylindrical
and composite piers, was roofed in the 12th century.
Between 1235 and 1289 the original sanctuary was
replaced by a transept. The west façade was built in
the Romanesque period, while the two towers and the
upper lancet-windows date from the 13th and 14th
centuries. In front of the façade is the porch (1175), on
which the Lady Chapel (q. v.) was erected. (Ill. 168)

EARLY ENGLISH is the term for the English version
of Early Gothic between c. 1190 and 1250.

ELY CATHEDRAL. The cruciform, three-aisled, flat-
roofed, galleried basilica was begun in 1089 on the site

*168. The vestibule of Durham Cathedral (1175) with
Norman zigzag ornament*

of an older building. The body of the church was completed in 1180. The walls of the nave are divided into
three storeys. The Romanesque choir was demolished
in the second quarter of the 13th century and replaced
by an Early Gothic rectangular choir. An octagonal
lantern spans the nave instead of a central tower. The
single-aisled Lady Chapel – a beautiful and rich Gothic
structure, built between 1321 and 1349 by John Wys-
beck – is exceptional in that it lies parallel to the choir.
Only the southern part of the west façade with its high
central tower was completed.

ENSINGEN, ULRICH VON, born c. 1359, was the
architect who directed the building of Ulm Cathedral
(q. v.) between 1392 and 1417. In the same period the
octagonal tower of Strassburg Cathedral (q. v.) rose
under his supervision.

ERWIN VON STEINBACH. A Master Erwin is mentioned as being in charge of work on Strassburg Cathedral (q. v.) between 1284 and 1293. The plan of the
west façade, which by 1277 had reached the top of the
side doorway, is attributed to him.

ESSEN MINSTER is a triple-aisled hall church with
a rectangular choir. Of an older building, constructed
in the last quarter of the 10th and first half of the
11th century, there remains, besides part of the crypt,
the westwork (q. v.), which is considered important in
the development of early German Romanesque architecture. In the central space the nuns' gallery – in plan
it is half a hexagon – rises upon three arcades. The
façade is flanked by two octagonal semi-projecting
staircase towers. The central part of the façade rises
into an octagonal tower.

EXETER CATHEDRAL. The building of the Gothic
cathedral of St Peter was begun in 1224 on the remains
of a Norman Romanesque church. The single-naved,
triple-bayed east chapel was constructed first; it was
followed by the choir, completed in 1300. The east
transept extends very little beyond the aisle. In the
14th century, the nave was built in the Decorated Style
(q. v.). A low triforium is broken by composite shafts
rising from strongly modelled piers; at the level of the

windows, they spread up into the vaulting in the form of fan-shaped ribbing and meet in the straight ridge rib, which is typical of English Decorated. The three-doored west façade – it has no tower – with its large traceried window has a porch containing a profuse cycle of sculptured figures.

FERRARA CATHEDRAL. The building of the cathedral was begun simultaneously from west and east in 1133. The original building was a five-aisled basilica with an open timbered roof and transept, a central tower and a small east tower between the apses. The interior was completely altered during rebuilding between 1712 and 1724. The projecting main doorway, decorated with figures and relief (two lions bear human figures supporting the first two pillars of the porch), is the work of Master Nicholas; in the upper storeys, the eaves galleries which run round the exterior of the building belong to the 14th century. The campanile was begun in 1452.

FINIAL. An architectural ornament surmounting a pinnacle, bench-end or gable. The form the ornament took followed the various Gothic styles and was based on foliage, flower or animal motifs.

FLAMBOYANT is the name given to Late Gothic stonework composed of flame-like curved lines. It predominated in France in the 15th century. In Germany and England it appears in the form of the vesica piscis, which had already been used ornamentally by the Celts.

FLORENCE CATHEDRAL. The construction of the cathedral of S. Maria del Fiore by Arnolfo di Cambio on the site of an older edifice began in 1296. The architect died when the first west bays had been completed. All energies were now devoted to the erection of the campanile which was begun by Giotto (1334–36) and continued by Andrea Pisano (1336–43) and Francesco Talenti, who worked on it until 1358. It is decorated with reliefs and marble inlay and rises wonderfully lightly to a height of 269 ft. In 1357 the plans were changed. Francesco built the nave in the form of four huge square bays; the bays of the aisles are of the same length but only half as wide. In the width of the bays, in the piers, which have attached pilasters, and in the console cornice with parapet above the pointed arcades i. e. just below the intersecting vaulting, we can detect a new feeling for space and construction, which is a precursor of the Renaissance. Between 1380 and 1421 the east part of the building, including the dome, was added to the main body. It is built on the central plan with triple apses in a trefoil pattern. The dome which spans the central space was executed between 1420 and 1436 by Filippo Brunelleschi (q. v.); it is a masterly double-shelled vault. The exterior of the cathedral is decorated with white, green and red marble. The façade, designed by de Fabris, was constructed between 1868 and 1887. The most valuable work of art in the cathedral – the Pietà which Michelangelo began in 1550 – is in a chapel in the north transept.

FLORENCE, PALAZZO VECCHIO (Ital.: old palace), or Palazzo della Signoria (rulers), is the name given to the town hall in Florence. According to tradition, Arnolfo di Cambio was the architect of the fortified freestone building with its beautiful fenestration, machicolations and battlements, and its slender, battlemented tower. The most important additions are by Buontalenti and Vasari.

FLORENCE, SAN MINIATO AL MONTE. A three-aisled basilica, with a semicircular apse and a crypt but no transept, set on a vantage point on the left bank of the Arno. It was begun in the first half of the 11th century and mostly completed in the 12th. The façade with its triple doorways is divided into five blind arcades on the ground floor and surmounted by a gable. The basilica is decorated inside and out with marble inlay. Because of the archaising styles employed, S. Miniato is one of the main examples of the Tuscan proto-Renaissance (q. v.).

FLORENCE, SANTA CROCE. This three-aisled Franciscan church, begun in the second half of the 13th century, has a short transept and east chapels. The width of the nave – it is 62 ft – allowed only of an open timber roof. The horizontal articulation of the nave, which is divided into three equal parts by the capitals of the piers and a console, gives it an un-Gothic, layered effect. There are signs of an architectural approach clearly foreshadowing the Renaissance. As well as frescoes by Giotto, the church contains a large number of tombs, such as the tomb of Michelangelo by Vasari (1507), the cenotaph to Dante erected in 1829, and the tombs of Alberti, Machiavelli, Rossini and Galileo.

FLORENCE, SANTA MARIA NOVELLA, the main church of the Dominican order, was begun in 1278 by Brothers Sisto and Ristoro as a cross-vaulted three-aisled building with a short transept and rectangular chapels. It was completed in 1360. The marble-inlaid façade was completed between 1450 and 1470 after plans by Leon Battista Alberti. The main doorway also dates from this period. In the interior there are frescoes by Masaccio and Filippino Lippi, the Ruccellai Madonna by Duccio, a Crucifixion by Giotto and a wooden crucifix by Brunelleschi.

FOUCQUET, JEAN, also known as Foucquet (c. 1420–1480) was a French miniaturist and painter. The only work authenticated by documents is the series of eleven miniatures in the French edition of Josephus's Jewish War (Paris, Bibliotèque Nationale). But Fouquet also illuminated a prayer-book and various literary works (ill. p. 218). Of his pictures, mention should be made of the Melun diptych – the Madonna is in Antwerp, the second leaf with St Stephen and the donor, Étienne Chevalier, in Berlin – and his portraits of Charles VII and his Chancellor, Juvénal des Ursins, which are examples of Renaissance art.

FREIBURG IM BREISGAU CATHEDRAL. The cathedral was begun in 1200 as a three-aisled basilica. The transept has the Romanesque elements of the period. In 1250, work began on the nave, which is modelled on Strassburg Cathedral (q. v.). It was not until 1354 that the Romanesque sanctuary was replaced by a three-aisled choir and chevet with almost the same dimensions as the body of the church. In 1275 work was begun in the west, on a great tower standing in front of the nave; its pyramidal, octagonal spire is decorated with tracery. The cathedral contains sculptured ornaments of about 1300, 14th-century stained glass windows, and a High Altar painted by Hans Baldung (Grien) between 1512 and 1516.

FROMENT, NICOLAS (c. 1435–1484), was born at Uzés in Provence and died in Avignon. He is one of the main representatives of French-Provençal painting in the second half of the 15th century. The triptych with the Resurrection of Lazarus and the 'Altar with the Burning Bush' in the cathedral in Aix-en-Provence are attributed to him; the latter depicts the biblical story in an idyllic landscape.

FULDA, ST MICHAEL'S CHAPEL (c. 820). One of the great monuments of German architecture, it has a circular, domed central space with eight pillared arcades surrounded by a vaulted ambulatory with an east apse. In the main chamber of the crypt, which lies beneath the apse, the vaulting is borne by a central pillar. The ambulatory is divided into a series of cells.

GADDI, TADDEO (b. before 1300, d. in Florence in 1366), was the most important pupil and collaborator of Giotto (q. v.). His frescoes of the life of Mary in the Baroncelli Chapel in S. Croce, Florence, or the 28 pictures of the legend of St Francis on the sacristy cupboard in the same church (the latter, with the exception of two in Munich and two in Berlin, are in the Florentine Accademia), as well as his pictures, e. g., the Madonna in the Uffizi painted in 1335, are distinguished by the exact observation of light and – compared to Giotto – by their greater naturalness.

GENTILE DA FABRIANO, an Italian painter and representative of the Late Gothic 'soft style' was active in Venice, Brescia, later in Florence and Siena, and finally in Rome where he died in 1427. His main work is the colourful Adoration of the Magi (1423) in the Uffizi (ill. p. 227).

GERHAERT, NICOLAUS, also known as Nicholas of Leyden, was born between 1420 and 1430 and died in 1473 or later in Wiener-Neustadt. Of the many works attributed to him the following can be said with certainty to be his: 1. The tomb of Archbishop Jacob von Sierck in Trier (1462); 2. Two busts from the old chancery in Strassburg (1463–64) – the fresh young Barbel von Ottenheim and a bearded man with cold eyes, the Count of Hanau-Lichtenberg – of which fragments are preserved in Strassburg and Frankfurt-am-Main but which are otherwise known only from plaster casts; 3. A crucified Christ in Baden-Baden (1467), and 4. The tomb of Emperor Frederick III (after 1469) in St Stephen's Cathedral, Vienna, which was completed by other hands. Nicolaus Gerhaert is the forerunner of the great sculptors of German Late Gothic round about 1480; he anticipates their style with its flowing interpenetration of forms, its anatomical accuracy and the incorporation of space.

GERMIGNY-DES-PRÉS near Orleans was founded by the Visigoth Bishop Theodulf and consecrated in 806. The square interior is divided by four piers into square compartments of varying heights. The tower rises over the central space. Germigny-des-Prés is constructed on the Byzantine system, which was apparently used by the Visigoths in Spain.

GERNRODE, CONVENT CHURCH. The convent church of St Cyriacus was built between 960 and 989 as a flat-roofed, three-aisled galleried basilica with transept, square choir over a crypt and three east apses. In the nave, piers alternate with pillars. In the west there is an entrance bay which connects the body of the church with a structure – resembling a westwork (q. v.) – flanked by round towers. Here a west choir was added in the 12th century. (Cf. p. 189)

GHENT, GRAVENSTEEN. The castle of the counts of Flanders contains, within a fortified wall, both apartments and store-rooms. The lower part of the rectangular donjon dates from the first half of the 12th century. Count Philip of Alsace built the gatehouse in 1180. An extension of the castle and the building of the outer ring of walls date from the 13th century.

GIOTTO DI BONDONE, one of the most famous of Italian painters – he was also an architect – was born in 1266 or 1267 at Colle di Vespignano near Florence and died in Florence in 1337. The great frescoes in the upper church of S. Francesco in Assisi with 24 out of the 28 paintings from the Legend of St Francis, together with the Crucifixion in S. Maria Novella in Florence, must be considered early works. In 1300 the artist was in Rome, as is proved by a fresco in S. Giovanni in Laterano and perhaps also the mosaic of Christ and Peter walking on the waves in the entrance to St Peter's. The great altar-piece from Ognisanti in Florence with the Madonna in glory with the Child and angels, now in the Uffizi, probably dates from 1302. Giotto's main work dates from between 1304 and 1306 – it is the frescoes in the Arena Chapel in Padua, which at that time belonged to the Palazzo Scrovegni (ill. p. 228). They show scenes from the life of the Virgin, from the life and works of Christ and from the Last Judgment as well as illustrations of the Virtues and Vices. The frescoes in S. Croce, Florence, must be dated c. 1317; they show the Legend of St Francis and scenes from the life of John the Baptist and St John. From 1334, Giotto was cathedral architect in Florence and was responsible at least for the relief decorations on the ground storey of the campanile. From his work, it is clear that Giotto owed a debt not only to the Florentine-Byzantine school and therefore to Cimabue (q. v.) but, apart from certain antique and Early Christian elements which he may have acquired in Rome, to his Roman contemporary Cavallini (q. v.); he probably also had links with French artists. Inspired with deep earnestness and yet full of simple humanity, Giotto presents Christ and the Virgin, saints, men and sinners. It is little wonder that his contemporaries, such as Dante, hailed him as the liberator from the Byzantine yoke and an innovator in the arts. His work had a formative influence on the Italian painters of the 14th century. Even his successors, like Vasari and Ghiberti, said of Giotto that he had discovered and reproduced the truth about man.

GLOUCESTER CATHEDRAL. Of the structure begun in 1089 the three-aisled basilican body with its great round piers and low round arcades has remained. In place of a tribune gallery, with which only the ambulatory is provided, there is a passage which in each bay opens on to the nave through two low double arcades. The high windows are robbed of some of their effect by rib vaulting inserted in 1240 to replace the flat roof. Between 1318 and 1377 the transept and choir were rebuilt. A stone tracery was superimposed on the old wall, and fan vaulting was introduced (ill. 169). The round choir was replaced by a huge window. Behind this straight east wall is the single-aisled Lady Chapel (q. v.), which was completed in 1499 and is almost completely detached. It is the most important example of the Perpendicular Style (q. v.).

GOLDEN DOOR is the name of the doorway from the Marienkirche in Freiberg in Saxony, which was destroyed by fire in 1484. It was built into the new cathedral, erected as a hall church between 1484 and 1501. The doorway is decorated with more than 50

169. South wing of cloister of Gloucester Cathedral (c. 1400), fan-vaulting

figures, which were once gilt; they are believed to date from between 1230 and 1240.

GOLDEN MADONNA is the name given to a statue of a seated Madonna with Child (c. 1000) in the treasure of Essen Cathedral. The core is overlaid with gold plate set with enamel, filigree and precious stones.

GOLDEN PANEL is the name given to a carved and painted panelled altar made c. 1420 in Lüneburg for the church of St Michael there. The panels of the lost shrine are in the Landesmuseum, Hanover. The name comes from a Golden Panel, which was contained in the shrine along with a collection of reliquaries; it was pillaged in 1698. The 36 paintings of the story of Christ and the Virgin on the outside of the inner panel and on both sides of the outer panels are one of the peaks of contemporary North German art.

GOSLAR, IMPERIAL PALACE. The imperial residence within the precincts of the imperial palace founded by Emperor Otto III c. 970 is composed of three communicating buildings – a central hall is flanked on its north side by a dwelling and on its south side by a passage to the Ulrichskapelle. The twin-aisled ground floor served as an assembly room; it could be heated. The main floor contains a hall, which originally had a timbered roof and contains a gallery to the front.

GRASSER, ERASMUS (1450–1518), sculptor and architect, was born in Schmiedmühlen in the Upper Palatinate; from 1474 until his death he was active in Munich. In 1480 he fashioned 16 Morisca dancers for the ballroom of the Town Hall, Munich; of these lively figures ten have been preserved. A Morisca (Ital.: Moorish dance) was a dance performed both by the people and in society, which appears to have been based on the wars between the Christians and the Moors. The marble tombstone of Ulrich Aresinger in St Peter's Church, Munich, the Lamentation over Christ (sandstone) in Freising Cathedral and the Reichersdorfer High Altar are attributed to the artist.

GURK CATHEDRAL. The Romanesque cathedral at Gurk in Carinthia was erected between 1160 and 1200 as a three-aisled basilica with transept. The porch is decorated with frescoes and flanked by two towers; a carved portal leads into the nave. The choir is raised; under it lies the hall crypt supported by 100 pillars.

GUELPHS, TREASURE OF THE, is the name given to a collection of reliquaries which until 1671 was kept in Brunswick Cathedral but is today exhibited in the castle of Henry the Lion in Brunswick. The treasure consisted of more than 80 receptacles for holding holy relics and altar equipment of which in all 41 pieces have been preserved. The reliquaries – they are in precious metals and are all the work of artists – were mainly produced between the 11th and 15th centuries (ill. p. 194).

HAGIA SOPHIA (Greek: Divine Wisdom), or the church of S. Sophia, is the name of the splendid domed

GENTILE DA FABRIANO: The Adoration of the Kings. *Detail: The Procession of the Kings*

GIOTTO DI BONDONE: The Flight into Egypt. *Fresco in the Arena Chapel, Padua*

STEFAN LOCHNER: Presentation of the Christ Child at the Temple

SIMONE MARTINI: The Annunciation. *The saints on both sides are probably by Lippo Memmi*

basilica in Istanbul, erected under Emperor Justinian between 532 and 537 by the architects Anthemius of Tralles and Isidor of Miletus. The building is a fusion of the basilican model with a centrally grouped structure. A dome 107 ft across and supported by four pendentives rises above the square central space. To the east hemicycles crowned with semi-domes take the lateral thrust of the central dome. In the transept aisles, galleries decorated with pillars perform the same task. The impressiveness of the interior is increased by marble facing and inlays. (Ill. 170)

HALBERSTADT (Saxony), **LIEBFRAUENKIRCHE.** Work on the cruciform, three-aisled piered basilica began in 1135 using, in part, an older building dating from 1005. This impressively simple church, built under the influence of the monastery church in Hirsau (q. v.) has a wide nave, to which the flat roof has been restored in modern times, and a three-aisled choir. It has no distinct crossing, being built on the metrical system (q. v.), unlike other churches in the Romanesque period. There are twin towers in the west and a further pair are inserted between the aisles and transept in the east. The stucco reliefs on the choir screens are important; they are believed to date from 1200. They are in seven arcades and represent Christ and the Virgin, each flanked by six apostles.

HANS VON TÜBINGEN, an artist trained in France and Burgundy, had a strong influence on Austrian art. There is evidence that he was in Wiener-Neustadt from 1433 onwards and he died there in 1462. Parts of a Passion Altar in Vienna, the votive painting from St Lambrechts (1430), now in Graz, and the Linz Passion of 1450 show his dramatic handling of vigorous figures.

HERSFELD, ABBEY (Hesse), was built as a flat-roofed Romanesque basilica on a cruciform plan after a fire between 1138 and 1144. (It has been in ruins since 1761.) The nave had nine pillared arcades on either side; they are now destroyed. The long arms of the transept are enlarged to the east by high apses. The three-aisled crypt lies under the apse, which is divided by niches, and the choir. In the west, between a pair of towers of which only the southern one is preserved, there is a square entrance hall projecting boldly from the façade; it serves as an apse for a west choir.

HESDIN, JAQUEMART DE (d. 1410–1411), a French painter, was active in Poitiers, a residence of the Duke de Berry. From 1384 until his death he worked on the decoration of several Books of Hours for the duke; they are decorated with miniatures. The colours used include delicate pink, dull green and violet. He liked to surround the pictures with foliage and birds.

HILDESHEIM, ST MICHAEL'S. In this church, built under Bishop Bernward and consecrated in 1033, Ottonian architecture in Germany achieves truly epoch-making expression. The balancing of the structural groups in east and west by corresponding choirs, transepts and crossing towers, the alternation of supports in the in-

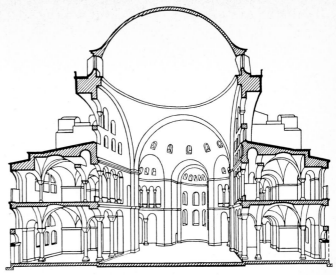

170. Hagia Sophia in Constantinople (532–537, a mosque since 1453), cross-section

terior, whereby a pair of columns is followed by a pillar (ill. 32), the separation of the nave and aisles by arcades running round into the transepts and the provision of the transepts themselves with double galleries ('angels' choirs') – all bear witness to a new and confident feeling for space as compared with earlier church architecture. The flat wooden roof of the hall church with its painted genealogy of Christ dates from the beginning of the 13th century. The structure, with its six towers and choir was well preserved until it was damaged severely in the Second World War; it has since been restored.

HIRSAU, MONASTERY CHURCH of SS. Peter and Paul. The monastery at Hirsau in the north of the Black Forest adopted the Cluniac reforms in the 11th century and became the mother house of many new German foundations. In this way the simplified but clearly articulated pattern of the monastery church, as it was built between 1082 and 1091, came to be widely diffused. The church – burnt down in 1692 – was a three-aisled, flat-roofed basilica with transept and three-aisled, raised choir, which like the entrance hall in the west, reverts to Cluny. The supports are columns with square capitals. Piers are only to be found in the most easterly bay of the body of the church; they mark off the 'chorus minor' reserved for monks who did not sing, from the true choir and the 'chorus major' in the crossing.

HOLY SEPULCHRE. The tomb of Christ in Jerusalem, near Golgotha, was enclosed in the 4th century by a rotunda which was later much restored. In the Middle Ages it was the model for many circular churches built round tombs. The carved replicas of the sarcophagus, common in Germany and England from the 14th century on, were also called 'Holy Sepulchres'.

HORTUS DELICIARUM (Lat.: garden of delights) is the name given to an illustrated manuscript composed and probably also illustrated by Herrad von Landsperg (1107–95), abbess of an Alsation convent, as a book of instruction and devotion for her nuns. Byzantine influences can be detected in the richly figured illustrations, as can the influence of tapestry work. The original was burnt, but copies exist.

171. Königslutter Cathedral, cloister (second half 12th cent.), cross-vaulting

HOUSEBOOK, MASTER OF THE. This is the name given to a draughtsman, engraver and painter who was active on the Middle Rhine in the last quarter of the 15th century. His name is derived from the illustrated manuscript of a 'Housebook' in Schloss Wolfegg in Upper Suabia.

IMAD MADONNA. A carved limewood statue of a seated Madonna with Child in the Diocesan Museum at Paderborn dates from the time of Bishop Imad of Paderborn (1051–1076). The decoration of gold-plate, semi-precious stones and filigree, was removed in 1762 and melted down.

JUMIÈGES, NOTRE DAME (Normandy). The main church of the old abbey, founded by St Philibert in 654, was erected between 1040 and 1067 as a three-aisled, cruciform, galleried basilica with a three-aisled choir, east apses in the transept wings, central tower, and twin towers in the west. Parts of older structures were used in the building. The church, which has been in ruins since the French Revolution, is notable for the sharp division of the bays. The stress on the dividing line between the bays is achieved by making the half-columns attached to the piers on the walls of the nave run through the gallery and through the clerestory to the foot of the flat wooden roof with its open beams (now destroyed). The division of the walls adopted here and in other Norman churches was important for architectural development, above all in England (ill. 146).

KIEV, CATHEDRAL OF ST SOPHIA. The cathedral was built in the 11th century as a five-aisled structure, which was furnished, on the Byzantine model, with shallow main and subsidiary domes and two west towers. Baroque rebuilding in the 17th century has almost entirely obscured the original. The important mosaics in Greek style belong in part to the 11th century.

KÖNIGSLUTTER CATHEDRAL (Lower Saxony). The church of SS. Peter and Paul was endowed by Emperor Lothair in 1135. It was built on a cruciform plan as a pillared basilica. There is no doorway in the west end, which has little articulation and is crowned with two low, octagonal towers. It is typical of Lower Saxony. The sculpture on the exterior of the apse – a hunting frieze – on the capitals of the choir, in the transept and cloisters, as well as the remains of a doorway, show signs of ties with Lombard architecture (ill. 41, 42, 171).

KONRAD VON SOEST, a Westphalian painter active in Dortmund between 1394 and 1425, derived from the Burgundian school. In his main works – such as the Wildunger altar (1404), the High Altar from St Mary's, Dortmund (fragments in Schloss Cappenberg) – he emerges through his elegant forms, his delicate, soft draperies and his strong colours, as the main representative of the 'soft style'.

KRAFFT, ADAM (c. 1460–1508/09). The works of this Nuremberg sculptor, which are all in stone, are characterized by clear, spacial composition and convincing portrayal of individuals. Examples are the 62-feet-high tabernacle (q. v.) in the church of St Lawrence, Nuremberg (1493–96; ill. 161), with its wealth of tracery, figures (self-portrait) and reliefs, as well as tombs and reliefs for the Stations of the Cross in St Sebald's. In his work, Krafft always took the architectural requirements into consideration. His artistic sensibility, though he used Late Gothic forms, took him to the threshold of the Renaissance.

LADY CHAPEL is the name given to the rectangular chapel which, in English Gothic churches, is generally added to the east of the choir. It was used for the worship of the Virgin and was often richly appointed.

LANDSHUT, HEILIG-GEIST-SPITALKIRCHE (Lower Bavaria). This Late Gothic brick church, built after 1407 by Master Hans Stetthaimer of Burghausen (d. 1432), is a three-aisled hall church. The undecorated exterior is given tautness by high windows. In the interior, the nave and the choir, which has no ambulatory, lead into one another. Slim columns support the star vaulting, which no longer has transverse arches. As a result, there is no demarcation into bays. The ambulatory consists of five sides of a dodecagon, while the choir ends in two sides of a hexagon, so that a single column stands in the central axis of the space in front of the east window.

LAON CATHEDRAL. This vaulted galleried basilica, which is three-aisled throughout and was erected on a cruciform plan, was chiefly built between 1160 and 1230. Originally the choir and ambulatory was apsidal but the choir was later extended to the east and made rectangular. To balance it, the arms of the transept, which has a tower over the crossing, were each given a porch. The porches were to have been crowned by two towers of which only the western one was completed. The façade with its deep relief, has three doorways with porches, surmounted by an arcaded gallery. The wall of the nave is built in four storeys — arcade, gallery, triforium and clerestory. The twin two-storeyed towers, with upper tracery, have lost their open-work spires.

LICHFIELD CATHEDRAL. The Gothic cathedral of St Mary and St Chad was erected as a cruciform basilica on the remains of older structures. Work on the three western choir bays was begun c. 1220; during the next decades the transept and body of the church followed. The eastern part of the choir and the adjoining Lady Chapel (q. v) were finished by the middle of the 14th century. The arcades of the gallery spread above the clustered piers. The rib and panel vaulting dates from c. 1300. The effect of the west façade with its three doorways, begun in 1280, its centre window and the sculptured figures in niches (restored in the 19th century), combined with the two spired towers, is somewhat ponderous compared to continental Gothic.

LIMBURG-AN-DER-LAHN CATHEDRAL. The church of St George was chiefly built between 1213 and 1242. It is a three-aisled, cruciform pillared basilica on the metrical system (q. v.). The short nave consists of only two double bays with sexpartite vaulting. The arrangement of the walls into arcade, gallery, columns and windows, is influenced by the Early Gothic style of Laon Cathedral (q. v.). The outer structure with its two arcaded west towers, its central tower (the spire dates from 1774) and the two pairs of smaller towers on the transept arms form a group that owes much to the Romanesque of the later Hohenstaufen period.

LIMBURG, THE BROTHERS OF. The brothers Pol, Jean and Armand of Limburg came from the Netherlands to Paris and trained there – and perhaps in Italy – as painters of miniatures. They were active at the Court of Duke Jean de Berry in Bourges at the beginning of the 15th century. Their main works are the miniatures in two Books of Hours, which were still unfinished at the death of the Duke in 1416: 'Les très riches heures du Duc de Berry', now in the Musée Condé in Chantilly, and 'Les très belles heures de Notre Dame'. The miniatures are distinguished by their lively colours, by the exact rendering of all details and by the purity of the landscape and architectural drawing (ill. p. 49).

LINCOLN CATHEDRAL. Geoffrey de Noyers began work on the cathedral of St Mary, a Gothic basilica, in 1192, using parts of a Late Romanesque façade. First to be built were, apparently, the east choir transept, the fore-choir to the west of it, and the great main transept. The eastern rectangular 'Angel Choir', built between 1256 and 1320, is a richly ornamented example of the Decorated Style (q. v.). The west front, the Romanesque part of which was built c. 1150, was completed between 1220 and 1230 by a screen wall. The two west towers stand behind the west front.

LOCHNER, STEPHAN, one of the most important representatives of German medieval painting, was prob-
ably born in Meersberg on Lake Constance and shortly after 1430 came to Cologne, where he died as a respected member of the Council. His principal works are the Last Judgment Altar (c. 1435), the Adoration of the Magi (c. 1442–44) and the Presentation in the Temple (1447) in the Landesmuseum, Darmstadt (ill. p. 229). Lochner paints his substantial figures on an abstract gold ground. His composition, his exact drawing, the glowing quality of his colours and the way he presents an anecdote, point to his origins on the Upper Rhine, to the tradition of the school of Cologne and to Flemish influences (the Master of Flémalle, the van Eyck brothers).

LONDON, TOWER OF, is a walled and towered pentagonal fortress in the old part of the city. The White Tower was erected in 1078 by William of Normandy as a keep or donjon. To-day it houses a collection of weapons. The Crown Jewels of England are kept in the Wakefield Tower.

LONDON, WESTMINSTER ABBEY, was begun in 1245 on the site of a small church; it is a cruciform basilica with three-aisled transept, polygonal choir with ambulatory and choir chapels. The eastern part was completed in 1258, while building continued on the body of the church until the beginning of the 16th century. Between 1503 and 1519, the Henry VII chapel was erected to the east of the choir in the Perpendicular Style (q. v.). The towers were not completed until 1722–40. French influence makes itself felt, in spite of the traditional English extension of the nave, in the extreme desire for height, in the shape of the choir, in the narrow bays and in the tracery. To the south lie the cloisters and an octagonal chapter-house.

LORENZETTI, AMBROGIO, younger brother of Pietro, was a Sienese painter, whose earliest extant dated picture – the Madonna of Vico l'Abate – dates from 1319. While the Madonna is placed in a strange supernatural setting in which spatial depth is still lacking, his frescoes of 'The Consequences of Good and Bad Government' (1337–40) in the Palazzo Pubblico at Siena are splendidly realistic. In a series of scenes, which are at once spatially arranged and anecdotal, the frescoes deal in an arresting manner with the common fate of mankind. Ambrogio probably died in Siena in 1348.

LORENZETTI, PIETRO, Sienese painter and elder brother of Ambrogio, is believed to have been born between 1280 and 1285, and to have died in 1348. His first dated work is a large altar-piece in the Pieve di S. Maria, Arezzo (1320). The glowing colours recall Duccio; the powerful draughtsmanship, Simone Martini. He is chiefly known for his frescoes in the left (south) transept of the lower church of S. Francesco at Assisi. The Gothic element in Italian painting nowhere finds such powerful expression as in the passion and dramatic tension of the scene of the Crucifixion. The altar painted 1328–29 for S. Maria del Carmine in Siena (now in the Pinacoteca, Siena) or the Birth of Mary (1342, in the Opera del Duomo, Siena), indicate by their handling of space, the harmony of the figures and their freedom of movement, that Pietro had seen Giotto's work in Assisi and Florence.

LORSCH, GATEHOUSE. The so-called gatehouse which stood in the courtyard of the monastery basilica (consecrated in 774 but no longer extant) is probably of the same date: it is a two-storeyed building on a rectangular plan with round staircase towers at either end. At the sides the ground floor opens through three round arches into a flat-roofed open hall. The building is decorated with archaising attached columns and pilasters and faced with stone slabs.

LÜBECK TOWN HALL was begun in the second half of the 13th century. It consists of two rectangular wings. The older north wing has a large turretted decorated wall of brick with, in front of it, a Renaissance arbour. The south wing or ballhouse was extended by the addition of the so-called 'Kriegsstubenbau' with richly decorated walls.

MAGDEBURG CATHEDRAL. The present cathedral is a three-aisled basilica with a single-aisled transept and a choir with ambulatory and five polygonal chapels. Round about 1240, an architect whose route can be traced here from Burgundy by way of Maulbronn and Walkenried, built a gallery storey in the choir – the impressive 'Bishop's Gallery'. The nave of the church was completed in 1363. Work continued on the west façade with its two towers until 1520. The 13th-century decoration on the capitals on the lower ambulatory has particularly beautiful and imaginative plant ornaments into which figures of men and animals are harmoniously introduced. About 1250, the 'Wise and Foolish Virgins' – masterpieces of their period – were produced for the portal of the north transept.

MAGI, SHRINE OF THE, in Cologne. See Dreikönigsschrein.

MAINZ CATHEDRAL. The first cathedral, erected under Archbishop Willigis, was burnt down when being consecrated in 1009. After a second fire in 1081 only

172. Church of the Benedictine abbey of Maria Laach with west choir and atrium (consecrated 1156)

the east towers of the structure rebuilt under Bardo remained standing. Between the towers there was what appeared to be a transept but was in reality an entrance with galleries and an apse which were inspired by Speyer and were set between the two entrances. The construction of the building with its arched nave was not completed until 1118. At the end of the 12th century, cross-vaulting was added. Only then were the west portions begun – a choir of heavy design on a trefoil pattern was consecrated in 1239. After a third fire in the Baroque period, the church was given a new west tower by F. J. Neumann the Younger. The stiffer east tower dates from the 19th century. Among the artistic furnishings of the cathedral are the fragments of a relief for a rood-screen representing the Last Judgment, as well as various tombs of Archbishops of Mainz.

MAITANI, LORENZO, was an Italian architect. Probably born in Siena shortly before 1275, he died in Orvieto in 1330. He designed the façade of Orvieto Cathedral (q. v.) in 1310 and was responsible for part of the decoration on the doorway.

MARBURG-AN-DER-LAHN, ELISABETHKIRCHE. This church was begun in 1235, four years after the death of St Elizabeth. It was the first building in Germany in pure Gothic style. The eastern portion follows the trefoil pattern common in the Rhineland. There is evidence of a certain dependence on French building in the plan, in the external fabric with its closely placed buttresses and in the severe west façade with its two great towers. But these borrowings were modified in accordance with the German style, as is evident from the alteration, which took place from 1249 onwards, of the originally basilican nave into a three-aisled hall church (q. v.). The richly decorated reliquary of St Elizabeth dates from the time of the first building.

MARIA LAACH. The church of the Benedictine Abbey, founded in 1093, was built as a three-aisled vaulted basilica with two choirs and two transepts; it was consecrated in 1156 (ill. 172). The larger, east, transept with its octagonal central tower has two east apses. Over the west crossing, there is a square tower. Two pairs of towers increase the ponderous effect of the east and west groups of the building. In the west, there is a courtyard or atrium (c. 1220), which encloses the west choir and the cloister.

MARIENBURG, on the east bank of the Nogat, was founded c. 1276 as the headquarters of the Teutonic Knights. Like the other castles of the Order it was an enclosed fortress, arranged in a square, round an inner courtyard and defended by walls, ditches and gatehouse. Since it served as the residence of the High Master from 1309 onwards, the monastery, completed in 1280, was enlarged into the so-called 'Mittelschloss', the great halls of which, with their star vaulting supported on columns, form one of the finest interiors of Northern brick Gothic. The elegantly vaulted Lady Chapel has on the exterior of its choir a stucco statue of the Virgin with a blue, red and gold mosaic setting; it is 26 ft high.

173. *Marienburg, castle of the Teutonic Knights: refectory in the High Master's residence (second half 14th cent.), star vaulting*

MARTINI, SIMONE (1284–1344), was, after Giotto (q. v.), the most important Italian painter of his time. He was born in Siena and was mainly active there until 1340, but at various times he worked in Naples, Pisa, Orvieto and Assisi. In 1340, Martini went to the Papal Court at Avignon. His earliest known work is the Maestà – the fresco of an enthroned Madonna and Child under a baldachino borne by angels and saints (1315) in the Palazzo Pubblico in Siena. Simone breaks away from the Byzantine tradition and adopts the courtly French style, which he combines with Giotto's aim – to represent human beings in space. Between 1320 and 1330, he painted the S. Martino chapel in the lower church of S. Francesco at Assisi with frescoes showing scenes from the life of St Martin. The space, which he achieves with the help of light and perspective, is rhythmically arranged. The figures are drawn with sweeping lines and take their intense life from the tender colours. As a result we have pictures not filled, as with Giotto, with dramatic tension, but expressing poetic feeling in a harmonious and beautiful manner. Simone's pictures, e. g., an altar-piece for St Catherine in Pisa and the Annunciation (1333) in the Uffizi (ill. p. 230) express in the courtly elegance of their gestures, in the exact reproduction of physical phenomena and in the delicate, almost fragile, graceful bearing of the figures, a feeling of concentration and rapture in typically Late Gothic terms. The polyptych, dating from some time before 1339, the panels of which are preserved in Antwerp, Paris and Berlin, are examples of this dynamic style. Martini's stay in Avignon stimulated French painting and paved the way for West European painting of the Renaissance.

MASTER OF THE BARTHOLOMEW ALTAR is the name given to an unknown painter active in Cologne between 1480 and 1510. The name comes from the Bartholomew Altar in the Munich Pinakothek.

MASTER BERTRAM, one of the first German artists known to us by name, comes from Minden in Westphalia. There is documentary evidence that he was in Hamburg between 1367 and 1410; he probably died there in 1414 or 1415. Master Bertram was a painter and organizer of a workshop, which produced paintings and carvings. The shrine of the High Altar in the church of St Peter in Hamburg (1379), now in the Hamburg Kunsthalle, must be regarded as the most important product of this workshop. The painted panels are considered to be the work of the artist's own hand.

MASTER E. S. is the name given to an engraver known only by his monogram. He must have been active on Lake Constance and on the Upper Rhine (Strassburg) between 1466 and 1467. Attributed to him are 318 engravings and some drawings, which were often used by sculptors and painters as models.

MASTER FRANCKE. There is evidence in documents that he was in Hamburg between 1424 and 1425 when the *Englandfahrergesellschaft* ordered a St Thomas altar for the church of St John. Such painted panels as have been preserved are in the Kunsthalle, Hamburg. An early work, a St Barbara altar, is in the National Museum in Helsinki. Of his two paintings of the Man of Sorrows, one is in Leipzig and one in Hamburg. Master Francke grew to maturity under the influence of the Paris school. The Hamburg altar shows him at the peak of his powers, as can be seen in its decorative effect, in its unified composition and in the fine gradations of the palette (ill. p. 239).

MASTER OF HOHENFURTH (Vyšší Brod), a painter of the Bohemian school (q. v.), in 1350 painted nine paintings in tempera – Scenes from the Life of Christ (Prague National Gallery), intended for the collegiate church in Hohenfurth. Using carefully graduated colours, he places figures which move stiffly and without depth on an abstract gold background.

MASTER OF THE LIFE OF THE VIRGIN is the name given to the unknown painter of an altar of which panels are in Munich and London. He was active in Cologne between 1465 and 1490.

MASTER OF THE TUCHER ALTAR is the name given to a Nuremberg painter who c. 1445 painted an altar for the Tucher family in the Nuremberg Frauenkirche. It is not to be confused with the Tucher Altar by Hans Süss of Kulmbach. Its sweeping and powerful style points away from the 'soft' style of Late Gothic.

MASTER OF WITTINGAU (Třebon) is the name given to the most important representative of the Bohemian school (q. v.) of the second half of the 14th century. It is derived from his paintings of the Passion (c. 1380) from Wittingau, now in the Prague National Gallery. The scenes constituting the main action are detached from the dark background by mysteriously glowing colours, which transfigure them (ill. p. 240).

MECKENEM, ISRAEL VAN, was a Flemish or Low German engraver born c. 1450, who was active in Bocholt from 1480 and died there in 1503. His engravings – they number about six hundred – are mostly taken from works of contemporary artists.

MEISSEN CATHEDRAL was begun as a basilica in the 13th century, but finished in the 14th as a hall church. In the Princes' chapel which was added to the twin-towered west façade, the Princes of Saxony are buried. The capitals and leafed friezes, the articulation of the choir wall, and the figures of Otto and Adelheid in the east choir, point to affinities with the sculptors in Naumburg Cathedral (q. v.).

MILAN CATHEDRAL. The cathedral, which was begun in 1386, is a five-aisled basilica with a three-aisled transept, choir with ambulatory and central tower. Clearly an attempt was made to fuse Northern Gothic idioms and forms with local ones. The practice, which was already established in Italy, of staggering the height of the aisles was combined with the French mode – as exemplified at Bourges – of setting the supports close together. The whole of the exterior, which is faced with white marble, is ornately overlaid with Gothic decoration. Work on decorative details went on until 1858. The bronze doors in the west front (finished in the 18th century) were mounted in 1951.

MILAN, ST AMBROGIO. The main parts of this three-aisled galleried basilica were built in the second quarter of the 12th century. A large atrium with covered pillared arcades is connected to a two-storeyed narthex, which opens into arcades. The broad nave with its great piers is covered with domed ribbed cross-vaults. The tribune gallery opens over the ground floor arcade through round arches on short piers. The massiveness of the architectural elements is emphasised by the poor lighting, which is due to the lack of a clerestory.

MIRROR OF SALVATION (speculum humanae salvationis) is the name given to a manuscript produced in Strassburg in 1324. It collates episodes from the Old and New Testaments and illustrates them with a series

of pictures. In the second half of the 15th century it was very widely disseminated in Holland and Germany as a book of woodcuts.

MULTSCHER, HANS (c. 1400–1467), was born in Reichenhofen in the Allgäu and was active in Ulm as sculptor and painter. The delicate 'soft' style of his early works, e. g., the Man of Sorrows in stone on the main portal of Ulm Cathedral (1479), became more sober and more realistic under the influence of Sluter (q. v.). His only signed paintings – eight panels of the Wurzacher Altar (1437) in Berlin – are dramatic works with the accent on realism.

MUNICH, FRAUENKIRCHE. With the public funds of the by no means wealthy town of Munich the great parish church was built 1468–88, to the designs of the State architect, Jörg Ganghofer. With its twin 325-foot octagonal towers, surmounted by copper cupolas, the Frauenkirche has become the architectural symbol of Munich. It was heavily damaged in the Second World War, but has since been restored.

NAUMBURG CATHEDRAL was planned in the early 13th century on the site of an older building as a three-aisled, Romanesque basilica on the square plan with two choirs and four towers. The building was constructed from east to west, a process which allows us to follow the transition from Romanesque to Gothic step by step. It must be borne in mind, however, that the east choir, which was originally pure Romanesque, was converted into mature Gothic c. 1300. The west choir, erected after 1250 in Early Gothic style, probably by the Master of Naumburg himself (q. v.), is one of the most beautiful buildings of this period. In the interior, the cathedral contains the rood-loft and the figures of the Founders by the Master of Naumburg (ill. 23, ill. 174). Functional, but immensely imaginative decorations are to be found on capitals, corbels and consoles.

NAUMBURG, THE MASTER OF. About 1250 a sculptor began to work on Naumburg Cathedral whose name and origins are unknown. His artistic development can, however, be traced. Trained in France, where the quatrefoil reliefs on the west front of Amiens Cathedral are attributed to him, he passed through Metz (reliefs on the portal of the cathedral) and Mainz (where he perhaps was responsible for the reliefs on the rood-loft in the cathedral and the relief of St Martin with the Beggar – the 'Bassenheimer Reiter') and so came to Naumburg. His greatest achievements, which are amongst the finest things in German sculpture, are the reliefs on the rood-loft depicting the Passion – here the entirely new elements are, in terms of sculpture, the dramatic expression and, in terms of form, the introduction of space between figures arranged in depth (ill. 23), – a Crucified Christ with the Virgin and St John and the figures of the Founders in the west choir (ill. 174). Since both stylistically and in expression and posture there are considerable differences between these figures, several hands must be presumed to have worked on them (see Meissen Cathedral).

174. Naumburg Cathedral, west choir with figures of the Founders and rood-loft (second half 13th cent.)

NEVERS, SAINT ÉTIENNE, built between 1063–1097, is a three-aisled, cruciform, galleried basilica with a three-aisled choir, ambulatory and three choir chapels. The nave, transepts and choir are covered, daringly, with barrel vaulting. There is a windowless dome above the crossing. Both west towers were demolished in 1792.

NICHOLAS OF VERDUN, a goldsmith from Lorraine, made the base of the altar in Kloster Neuburg, originally intended as an altar-frontal, containing 51 pictures in champlevé. In 1183 Nicholas worked on the 'Anno shrine' in the parish church in Siegburg and in 1186 on the 'Albinus shrine' in St Pantaleon in Cologne. In 1205 he was in Tournai for the last time; there he produced the shrine of the Virgin.

NOTKE, BERNT (c. 1440–1509), woodcarver and painter, was born in Lassan in Pomerania. He was first in Lübeck, then 1483–1498 in Stockholm, and finally once more active in Lübeck until his death. His main work is the group with St George which he completed in 1489; it is 10 ft high and is now in the Storkyrka, Stockholm. Notke carried realism so far that he gave the saint's steed real horse-hair and the dragon elk's horns, and yet out of the tension between the divine atmosphere surrounding the saint and the demoniacal powers of the underworld, embodied in the dragon, there emerges a unique work of art. Notke's work, which is mostly preserved in the Annen Museum, Lübeck, long influenced art in the Baltic territories.

NUREMBERG, SAINT LAWRENCE'S. The three-aisled nave from the 14th century was terminated by a choir begun by Konrad Hinzelmann in 1439 and finished by Konrad Roritzer of Regensburg between 1445 and 1472. The choir which is the same width as the nave gives the effect of being higher and broader because of its slim piers, its wider bays and complicated star vaulting. The wall of the choir is divided into two storeys, each with a row of windows, by a cornice and balustrade. The spire of the stone tabernacle by Adam Krafft (1460–1508/09) reaches the base of the vaulting. In front of the High Altar hangs the Annunciation by Veit Stoss (ill. 161; 182).

ORCAGNA. Andrea di Cione, known as Orcagna (It. *arcangelo* – archangel) was an architect, painter and sculptor known to have been active from 1344 in Florence, where he died in 1368. He was employed as architect on the building of the cathedrals in Florence and Orvieto and painted several frescoes in S. Croce in Florence as well as the altar-piece in the Strozzi chapel in S. Maria Novella in 1357. The only piece of sculpture which can be attributed to him with certainty – the tabernacle in Or San Michele, Florence – shows Orcagna to have been, along with Andrea Pisano, one of the most important sculptors of the Florentine Gothic school. The numerous marble reliefs on the tabernacle show his artistic development from flat sculptures to scenes where the figures are plastically grouped in depth (ill. 159).

ORVIETO CATHEDRAL. The cruciform basilica with its openwork roof was built before 1285 in the place of an older building. Above the round-arched arcades of the nave there runs a wide clerestory with narrow windows. The ornate west front was designed in 1310 by Lorenzo Maitani of Siena in the form of a Gothic triptych. The base has three porches with pointed gables. The façade is richly decorated with figures in relief, mosaics and inlay. In the interior, numerous frescoes have been preserved. In the Capella Nuova in the right transept are the frescoes of the Last Judgment and Resurrection painted by Fra Angelico in 1447 and continued by Gozzoli, Perugino and, above all, by Signorelli.

PACHER, MICHAEL (c. 1435–1498), was a painter and woodcarver. He seems to have been born at Neustift near Brescia and probably died in Salzburg. There is evidence that from 1467 he was a citizen of Bruneck (Brunico), where he was head of an important workshop producing altars. Michael Pacher was an example of that rare phenomenon, a man with two talents; for, although he is always referred to as a painter, the stylistic harmony between paint and carving in his works makes it clear that he was also responsible for the latter. He was a pioneer in his visual grasp of space and objects, in his mastery of perspective and his power of design. His main works are the altar in the parish church at Gries near Bolzano, the High Altar in St Wolfgang which, in its combination of sculpture and painting, represents once of the high points of the genre (ill. 84), and the painted altar with the fathers of the church from Neustift (c. 1480–1483) now in the Alte Pinakothek, Munich.

PALA D'ORO (It.: golden leaf) is the name applied to golden or gilt antependia (front coverings for altars). Famous early medieval examples are those from S. Ambrogio in Milan (835), from St Mark's in Venice (10th century) and the Basle antependium of Henry II (c. 1020).

PARIS, NOTRE DAME. The foundation stone of the cathedral is said to have been laid by Pope Alexander III in 1163. By 1177 the choir, and in the course of the 13th century the whole huge building, were finished. Compared with the Early Gothic cathedrals of Sens and Noyon, the plan shows a further unification in the building concept. The transept which barely projects from the nave lies in the middle. The nave itself is five-aisled as is the choir, which has an ambulatory. The choir chapels and the chapels inserted between the buttresses of the nave are later additions. Instead of being divided into four storeys, as they were in the Early Gothic period, the walls of Notre Dame are divided into three – arcade, tribune gallery and clerestory. There are three doorways in the west front. Above them runs a band of 28 statues of the Kings of France (restored). In the middle storey is a large rose window and above it rise two towers connected by a gallery. (Ill. 30, 33)

*175. Pisa Cathedral from S.W. with the 'Leaning Tower'
(11th/12th cent.)*

PARIS, SAINTE-CHAPELLE. St Louis had the royal palace chapel erected between 1243 and 1248. The two-storeyed building contains a low, vaulted lower church for the retainers and a high, single-aisled upper church – with a polygonal apsidal termination – for the Court, in which the Crown of Thorns was to be exhibited as a relic. Windows, divided into lights by fine vertical ribs, open above an arcaded base. They have fine stained glass which places no barrier between the interior and the space beyond (ill. 153).

PARLER, PETER (1330–1399), was the leading master of the family of architects and masons of that name, which derives from the word 'parlier', i. e., speaker – the term applied to the chief assistant of the master-builder in the Gothic period. Peter Parler seems to have been born in Schwäbisch-Gmünd, where his father had been in charge of the building of the hall choir of the Kreuzkirche; he died in Prague. As an incription on his bust in Prague Cathedral (ill. 160) states, he was summoned to Prague by Emperor Charles IV when he was 23 years old to take over the building of the cathedral from Matthew of Arras. The same inscription lists his works as follows: the choir of All Saints Church on the Hradčany hill, the Charles Bridge over the Moldau (Vltava) in Prague, and the choir of the town church at Kolin on the Elbe. Documents show that Parler was also active as a sculptor and, in addition to statues such as the monument of King Ottokar I, was responsible for at least the design – if not for the execution – of the rich sculptures that decorate the cathedral of St Vitus. By his work on this cathedral, Peter Parler gave a decisive impulse to architecture and sculpture throughout Germany – an impulse which was to last until the end of the Middle Ages.

PÉRIGUEUX, SAINT FRONT. The church of Saint Front in Périgueux in the Dordogne was erected in the second quarter of the 12th century on the model of the Church of the Apostles, Constantinople (mid 6th cent., cf. p. 176), which is no longer in existence. Round a central square, four other squares are grouped to form a cross, all being covered by domes. Apart from some blind arcades, the interior is undecorated. The exterior has been marred by later accretions.

PERPENDICULAR STYLE is the name given to the dominant style of English Late Gothic architecture. It is distinguished by the stress laid on vertical ribbing and by fan-vaulting.

PETERBOROUGH CATHEDRAL. The reconstruction of the abbey church began in 1118; in 1541 it became the Cathedral of St Peter. The three-apsed choir was completed in 1143; the three-aisled nave and transepts in 1197. The nave of the galleried basilica is flat-roofed, while the aisles have arched ribbed vaulting. Between 1483 and 1500, a rectangular retro-choir was added to the semicircular choir, the walls of which had to be pierced by passageways whereby it lost its adjoining apses. The retro-choir is covered with unique fan-vaulting. The Romanesque west front was covered, between 1201 and 1222, by a portico of three pointed arches crowned by gables.

PILGRAM, ANTON (c. 1450/60–c. 1515). This architect and sculptor, though he had his roots in the Late Gothic, was receptive to Renaissance ideas. He was active in 1485/50 in Heilbronn on the Neckar, and after 1500 in Brünn. As cathedral architect of St Stephen's Cathedral, Vienna, he finished the organ in 1511 and the candelabra with relief-busts of the four Church Fathers, introducing his self-portrait in each case.

PISA CATHEDRAL was begun in 1063 under the direction of the Greek architect Busketos. To-day it is a five-aisled, cruciform basilica with a three-aisled transept. The choir and the central aisles of the transept arms terminate in apses. Galleries run above the aisles of the nave and of the transept. The nave and central aisle of the transept are flat-roofed; the aisles are cross-ribbed. There is an elliptical dome above the crossing, the ground storey is decorated with wall arcading and the façade by four tiers of open arcades and by marble inlays. The campanile or 'Leaning Tower', begun in 1173, has several storeys of arcades running around it.

PISANO, ANDREA, was probably born at Pontedera c. 1295 and died in Orvieto in 1348 or 1349. He was a goldsmith, sculptor and architect. In 1330 he came to Florence and fashioned one of the bronze doors of the Baptistery; on it, there are 20 scenes from the life of John the Baptist and eight enthroned Virtues framed in Gothic quatrefoils. Parts of it reveal the influence of Giotto. In 1343, Andrea Pisano succeeded Giotto as architect of the campanile of Florence Cathedral and probably worked on the marble reliefs of the lowest parts of the tower. Not later than 1347, he began to work as a cathedral architect in Orvieto. Here his son Nino (c. 1315–1368), who was also a goldsmith, sculptor and architect, succeeded him.

PISANO, GIOVANNI (c. 1250–1314), sculptor and architect, was a pupil of his father, Nicola Pisano, and collaborated with him on the pulpit in Siena (1265–68) and on the fountain in Perugia (1278). His main works are the pulpit in S. Andrea in Pistoia (completed in

MASTER FRANCKE: The Nativity. *Panel from the altar of St Thomas for the 'Englandfahrer'*

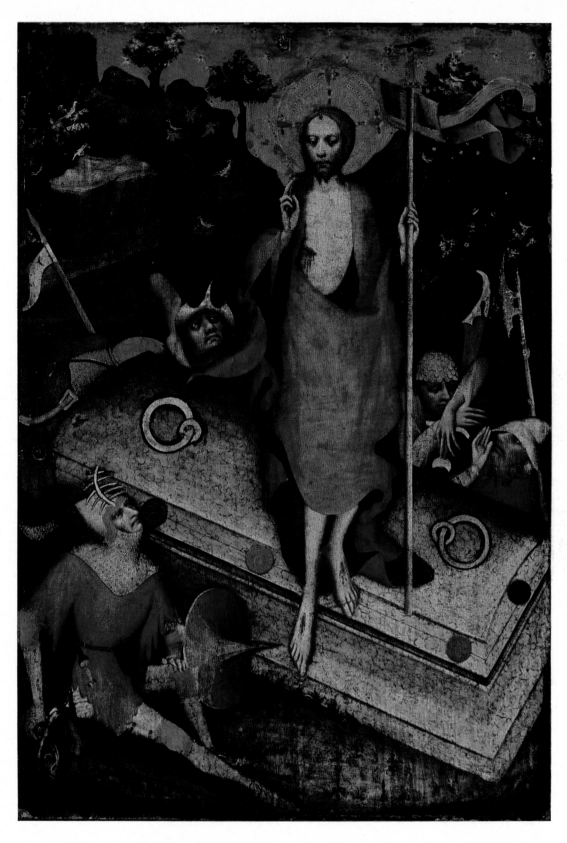

MASTER OF THE WITTINGAU ALTAR: The Resurrection

Martin Schongauer: The Nativity

Conrad Witz: 'The Miraculous Draught of Fishes' *with the Lake of Geneva constituting the land-scape. Panel from the altar of St Peter's Cathedral, Geneva. Detail*

1301), the highly ornamented pulpit in Pisa Cathedral, on which he worked from 1302 until at least 1310, the Madonna in the Camposanto, Pisa, the Madonna on the Altar of the Arena Chapel, Padua (ill. 177), the ivory statuettes in Pisa Cathedral and the alabaster Madonna in Prato Cathedral. From 1284 he was probably active in Siena as chief architect of the cathedral, where he also produced several figures on the façade. In 1297 he went to Pisa in the same capacity. Giovanni Pisano, continuing the art of his father, completed the Gothicization of Italian sculpture.

PISANO, NICOLA (Niccolò), was probably born in Apulia c. 1220–25 and died some time after 1278. In his work, he united classical and Byzantine elements with Gothic. His main works are the pulpit in the Baptistery in Pisa (1260), which by its harmonious marriage of architecture and sculpture, created a new type (ill. 76); the pulpit of Siena Cathedral, which is a richer development of the one in Pisa; the tomb of St Dominic in Bologna; and the fountain in the Market Place, Perugia (1278). The latter, like the Siena pulpit, were produced in collaboration with his son. It is not possible in every case to distinguish the work of the father from that of the son.

PLEYDENWURFF, HANS. There is evidence that this painter was in Nuremberg from 1457 and that he died there in 1472. He introduced into the Nuremberg school a realism inspired by Flemish models. His main works are the portrait of Count Georg Löwenstein and the fragments of the High Altar for St. Elizabeth's, Breslau – now in Nuremberg (Germanisches National-Museum).

PRAGUE, CATHEDRAL OF SAINT VITUS. Charles IV, who became King of Bohemia in 1346 and was crowned Emperor in 1355, brought the architect, Matthew of Arras, with him from Paris to his residence in Prague. Under Matthew's direction, the building of the cathedral began with the choir in 1344. After his death in 1352, Peter Parler (q. v.), who had been brought from Schwäbisch-Gmünd, completed the choir, with its ambulatory and chevet chapels. The walls are three-storeyed with pointed arcades and clearly articulated piers. There is a pierced triforium with a tracery balustrade projecting sharply out from the shafts, which run up to the net vaulting and the high windows with tracery in the heads. There is a tower alongside the south transept. The front of this arm of the transept has a portico and a large traceried window begun in 1344. The five-aisled nave was completed in 1929.

PROTO-RENAISSANCE is the name given by the Swiss art historian, Jacob Burckhardt, to archaisms in Romanesque and Early Gothic art. Thus, when discussing certain Florentine buildings, e. g., S. Miniato (q. v.) or the 12th-century sculptures from the South of France, we speak of a proto-Renaissance.

PUCELLE, JEAN, was active in France in the first half of the 14th century as a book illuminator. He progressed from the Gothic mode of flat stylization to a more solid manner of representing figures. In the borders of the books, he wove naturalistic flowers, animals and figures into grotesque patterns.

RAVENNA, SAN APOLLINARE NUOVO. Theodoric the Great had this three-aisled columned basilica built at the beginning of the 6th century as an imperial church. We can still form a clear impression of the original building, although the floor was later raised, the apse restored, a double window pierced in the façade and the aisles vaulted. The mosaics on the walls of the nave show Christ and the Virgin, saints, and a procession of virgins and martyrs. The campanile dates from the Early Middle Ages.

RAVENNA, SAN VITALE, erected on the orders of Justinian and dedicated in 547, is an octagon with a two-storeyed octagonal gallery, and a projecting apsidal chancel at the east end. Seven other arches enclose columns placed on a half-circle carrying the gallery. The impression of floating, of unreality, is increased by rich marble slabs, by splendid capitals in low relief and by mosaics. The portrait in mosaic of the Imperial Court with Justinian and Theodora is famous (ill. p. 179).

RAVENNA, TOMB OF THEODORIC. The tomb of Theodoric, the Gothic king who died in 526, consists of a lower decagon enclosing a cruciform crypt, and an upper decagon which is circular internally and is covered with a huge megalithic dome-shaped stone. Some people see in it a late derivation of the old Mediterranean circular buildings and, in the huge domed covering, a harking back to the dolmen graves of the Bronze Age. The steps were added in modern times (ill. 141).

REICHENAU. Three churches have been preserved of the once famous Benedictine monastery on the island of Reichenau in Lake Constance. The minster at Mittelzell contains remains of a Carolingian structure as well as early Romanesque portions; the Church of St George at Oberzell has frescoes from c. 1000, and the church at Niederzell some dating from c. 1100 (for Book Illumination, q. v., cf. p. 195; ill. p. 181).

RHEIMS CATHEDRAL. The building of Rheims Cathedral, which along with Chartres, Notre Dame and Amiens, is one of the greatest marvels of Gothic architecture, was begun in 1211. The choir was consecrated in 1241, while work on the nave and the west front continued into the 13th century. The towers were still being built in the 15th century, but they never received the spires, which must surely have been planned for them. The plan follows the classic Gothic cathedral design, in which the transept and the broad five-aisled choir and chevet constitute a single architectural block. As in Chartres, a system of buttresses was developed in order to take the thrust of the vaulting, which, in the nave, meets 125 ft above floor level. The three-storeyed design of the walls replaces gallery and ambulatory by a triforium. The west front with its three portals still shows – in spite of the fluid treatment of the wall surface – distinct signs of horizontal division into a portal tier, a middle tier with rose window, and a gallery. The decoration of the portals is of immense importance for the history of art. The sculptures on the portal of the transept, with its scenes from the Last Judgment (dating from after 1211), the classical Visitation of Mary by Anne of 1230, and the numerous other figures, form a vast body of religious art (ill. 151, 176).

RIEMENSCHNEIDER, TILMAN (c. 1460–1530), born in Osterode in the Harz, was active as a sculptor and woodcarver in Würzburg from 1483 until his death. Because he was on the side of the peasants during their revolt, he was tortured in 1525 and was deprived of his offices – he had become a member of the town council in 1504 and burgomaster in 1520–21 – and of some of his property. His earliest authenticated work is the Münnerstädt altar of 1490–92, which has been partially preserved. Then come, *inter alia,* the stone figures of Adam and Eve for the Lady Chapel in Würzburg (now in the Mainfränkische Museum) and the tomb of Bishop Scherenberg in Würzburg Cathedral (1496–99). The carved altars in the Jakobskirche in Rothenburg ob der Tauber (1501–1505), in Creglingen (1505–1510. ill.178) and in Dettwang, and the High Altar in Würzburg Cathedral, which is preserved only in part, represent the zenith of Riemenschneider's art. He attempted to replace the fussy Late Gothic style by clarity of composition, by finely made, gently moving figures, and restrained spirituality. For this reason he also rejects a coloured setting for his figures and lets light and shade speak instead. The Windsheim altar (now in Heidelberg), the tomb of the Emperor Henry II and his wife in Bamberg Cathedral, together with other tombs and statues, bear witness to the far-reaching influence of the artist and his workshop.

ROGERUS VON HELMARSHAUSEN lived c. 1100 in the Benedictine monastery of Helmarshausen, where he was both monk and goldsmith. Among the works attributed to him – they point to stylistic influences from the Rhineland and the Maas — two portable altars in the cathedral and the Franciscan church in Paderborn are fairly well authenticated. Some authorities identify him with Theophilus Presbyter (q. v.).

ROME, SANTA COSTANZA or, more accurately, the Mausoleum of Costanza, was probably begun in the lifetime of this daughter of Constantine the Great before or c. 1350. In accordance with the purpose for which it was built it is a circular structure. Round a large drum, which rests on twelve arcades borne by double columns, runs an aisle with niches. The dome of the drum, the barrel vaulting, the niches in the aisle and the floor of the central space, all had mosaics of which those on the vaulting of the aisle are preserved.

ROME, SANTA SABINA. This three-aisled basilica on the Aventine, founded under Pope Celestine I (422–432), is one of the oldest and best preserved of Early Christian buildings. The plain brick building is entered through a porch in the east. Twelve pairs of fluted columns with arcades support the walls of the nave; these still have colourful facings and once had mosaics, of which only fragments remain. Eighteen wooden reliefs with biblical scenes on the main doorway date from the foundation of the church; they were originally 28 in number.

ROUEN, SAINT MACLOU. This little church, begun in 1434, is an example of the Flamboyant style (q. v.). The five-aisled basilica has a transept, which does not project beyond the nave, a central tower, a rectangular choir screen, an ambulatory and chevet. The easternmost

176. Rheims Cathedral, Visitation group from the central west portal (c. 1230). – 177. Giovanni Pisano, Scrovegni Madonna from the Arena chapel at Padua (beg. 14th cent.), marble. – 178. Riemenschneider, Ascension of the Virgin, on the altar in the Church of Our Lord at Creglingen (1505–10)

column of the choir stands, as is sometimes the case in Late Gothic churches in Germany, on the axis of the nave. In accordance with Late Gothic views on unity of space, there is a three-sided entrance hall.

SAINT DENIS. Abbé Suger, famous as Imperial Vicar and Chancellor, laid the foundation stone in 1137 for the new abbey church at Saint Denis near Paris, which became the burial place of the kings of France. The three-aisled basilica was laid waste several times and in part restored. Of the original building the two-storeyed ambulatory and the choir chapels (1140–1144) have been preserved together with the crypt and the heavily restored west front, a three-portalled development of the double-towered façade of Caen (q. v.) The architectural innovations and the new forms dictated by a change in aesthetic taste made the choir of St Denis the first Gothic church construction – one which was epoch-making in its effects. The expanse of wall between the choir chapels is replaced by narrow buttresses. In accordance with the Gothic tendency towards spatial unity, the two ambulatories are scarcely separated by the slender columns. The chapels give the effect of niches set out in the ambulatory and a single vaulting connects the various spaces.

SAINT GILLES DU GARD. Of the Romanesque-Gothic church of the former Benedictine Abbey in Provence, which was destroyed in 1562, only the west façade remains. The three portals, of varying heights, are united by pillars and a frieze of figures in relief in the style of Late Classical triumphal arches. In general, many Late Classical elements were subsumed in its architectonics, ornamentation and sculptures (proto-Renaissance, q. v.). The date of origin is debated, being either 1120 or 1170, unless one accepts a long period of development, which would explain both dates.

SALISBURY CATHEDRAL. The cathedral of St Mary was built between 1220 and 1260 as a three-aisled basilica with two-aisled transept, choir and small choir-transept, retro-choir (ambulatory) and a rectangular Lady Chapel (q. v.) projecting to the east. The nave has round piers, surrounded by shafts, a low tribune gallery which has several arches in each bay and which opens under a compressed arcade and high clerestory windows. There is a tall central tower.

SANKT GALLEN. In the monastery library at St Gallen in Switzerland, there is preserved a parchment with the drawings for the plan of a monastery dating from c. 820. To the south of the large church, which has already two choirs, there is a cloister round a square courtyard with dwelling quarters and kitchens. Immediately adjacent to the east choir of the church is the library and writing room. Round this central cloister are grouped the secondary buildings – hostel, schools, hospitals and bath-houses. Since no entire monastery has survived from such an early date, the plan is of particular importance.

SANTIAGO DE COMPOSTELLA. The cathedral of Santiago in the province of La Coruña was built be-

179. Siena Cathedral from S. W. (13th cent., west front and tower end 14th cent.)

tween 1075 and 1128 as a three-aisled cruciform, galleried basilica. As the burial place of the apostle James the Greater, it was one of the most important pilgrimage churches of the Middle Ages. The double arches of the galleries, supported by a central column, open – after the pattern of the French Romanesque school of the Auvergne – above the high ground floor arcades. The semi-columns attached to the piers support transverse arches which divide up the barrel vault of the nave. Behind the three-aisled transept lies the choir with ambulatory and five chapels. The porch – Pórtico de la Gloria – with its dynamic figures is the work of Master Mateo c. 1180–90 (ill. 150).

SCHONGAUER, MARTIN, famous both as engraver and painter, was one of the most influential artists of his time. He was probably born in Colmar c. 1430, the son of a goldsmith who had come there from Augsburg. He was a citizen of Breisach and died there in 1491. Among the pictures attributed to him – on which the influence of Rogier van der Weyden is noticeable – only the more than life-size 'Madonna in the Rosebower' (1473) in St Martin's, Colmar, is fully authenticated. The frescoes of the Last Judgment in the cathedral at Breisach are from Schongauer's hand, as are several drawings. In his signed etchings, of which there are more than a hundred, and in which he showed the way for Dürer, he not only perfected the technique but surpassed all his predecessors in the symmetry and natural grace of his cleanly designed compositions. They are conceived with insight and imagination and use landscape and architecture only with great restraint, while the individual figures, which are given almost sculptural values, stand in the foreground of the work (ill. p. 241).

SCHWÄBISCH-GMÜND, HEILIGKREUZKIRCHE. This church had a Late Romanesque basilican nave, which was replaced in 1330 by a three-aisled hall. Work on the three-aisled apsidal hall choir was begun in 1351 under the direction of the Parlers (q. v.), a family of architects from Cologne. Slim round piers, which run into the close ribbed net-vaulting, give to the choir a

245

180. Sluter, figure of Moses on the 'Well of Moses' in the Chartreuse at Champmol near Dijon (finished 1406)

strong, soaring appearance. A console divides the choir wall into two equal storeys. In the ground storey, arcades lead into niched chapels; in the upper storey, there are lancet windows decorated with tracery. The choir hall of Schwäbisch-Gmünd had a great influence on the development of German Late Gothic (Ulm, Nuremberg, Prague and Milan).

SEVILLE CATHEDRAL was erected on the site of a mosque between 1402 and 1519 as a five-aisled basilica surrounded by chapels. The plan is rectangular with proportions of 2 : 3, so that the arms of the transept are barely distinguishable. The choir ends in a shallow apse. Only the domes of the nave and transepts rise above the aisles. The impression is rather that of a spacious hall.

SIENA CATHEDRAL was begun in the second half of the 12th century and completed in the 14th century. It therefore still has Romanesque piers dividing the three basilican aisles; otherwise the forms used are Gothic. A dome, completed in 1269, rises above the hexagonal crossing. The interior, like the campanile, is faced with black and white marble. The Early Gothic façade, which is richly decorated, was probably designed by Giovanni Pisano, who was architect from 1284 to 1299 (ill. 179). Of the furnishings, the beautiful pulpit by Nicola Pisano, a painting on glass by Duccio, and the inlaid pavements are outstanding.

SLUTER, CLAUS, who probably came from Haarlem, was from 1385 assistant at Dijon to Jean de Marvilles – whom he succeeded in 1389 – in the service of Philip the Bold. He died in Dijon in 1406. The three main works on which Sluter collaborated were the portal of the Chartreuse at Champmol, the so-called Well of Moses – originally a larger than life-size Crucifixion, of which only the base is preserved (ill. 180) – and the tomb of Philip the Bold of Burgundy. In these works, Sluter

246

was ahead of the contemporary developments in sculpture. He freed sculpture from its connection with architecture and gave his figures a power of expression unknown before his time. This applies not only to the realistic faces of his statues but to the impassioned dynamism of their draperies. Thereby, Sluter made the transition from the Middle Ages to modern times.

SOISSONS CATHEDRAL. Work began c. 1180 with the erection of the south arm of the transept. The three-aisled nave with the choir, ambulatory and chevet, was apparently tackled c. 1200. The walls of the tall and narrow nave are divided as in Chartres (q. v.) into three storeys – pillared arcade, triforium, high windows – while the older south transept, with its semicircular apse, still has a fourfold division of the walls and sexpartite vaulting. The vaulting of the ambulatory and the chevet chapels run into each other.

SPEYER CATHEDRAL. The basic structure of the cathedral was begun c. 1030 under Emperor Conrad II as a flat-roofed piered basilica, in which the walls of the nave were divided by shafts that, in the clerestory, met in an arch over the windows. The second stage was finished between 1082 and 1112 under the direction of Bishops Benno of Osnabrück and Otto of Bamberg. The nave, which was divided into four square yokes, was vaulted by the employment of reinforced shafts on every second pier; the eastern portion of the cathedral was also completed – particularly the eaves gallery on the east apse, and the strikingly large crypt. After 1159 certain parts of the vaulting were restored and the eaves gallery extended round the transept and nave. The present western portion dates from 1854 (ill. 148).

STAVE CHURCH. A stave church is a wooden structure with walls consisting of perpendicular jointed

181. Stave church in Borgund, Norway (12th cent.)

planks. The fully developed type dates from the 12th century and is preserved only in Norway; there are about 20 examples (ill. 181). The stave church consists of a main area surrounded by four lower aisles; the adjoining 'svalgang' is open to the exterior but invisible from the interior. The inner beams carry the open roof of the main area and are anchored to the aisles by a kind of arched buttress. These wooden structures utilize the principle of supporting a lateral thrust by inclined buttresses and may have influenced the stone structures that led to Gothic architecture.

STETTHEIMER, HANS (also Stethaimer), the most important Bavarian Late Gothic architect, was born c. 1350–60 in Burghausen and died at Landshut in 1432. He is credited with several hall churches, e. g. the early 15th-century Heilig-Geist-Spitalkirche, Landshut (q. v.).

STOSS, VEIT (1440 or 1450–1533) was active as sculptor, engraver and painter. He was probably born in Nuremberg but abandoned his citizenship and went to Cracow. In 1496 he returned to Nuremberg. Veit Stoss owed much to the work of Nicolaus Gerhaert (q. v.) and the Master of the Nördlingen High Altar, but his early work, the great carved altar in the Marienkirche, Cracow (1477–89) already shows him at the peak of his powers. Here the depth of expression in the wonderfully carved faces and the intricacy of the draperies is in strong contrast to the strict composition of the whole. Other principal works of the master are the Annunciation in St Lawrence's, Nuremberg (1517–18), the Crucifixion in St Sebald's (1520) and the High Altar in Bamberg Cathedral (1520–22). Ten etchings and four altar panels from the parish church at Münnerstädt are also known to be by him.

STRASSBURG CATHEDRAL. An older building was erected under Emperor Henry II as a spacious basilica. After a fire in 1176, rebuilding began on the old foundations. The choir was constructed in Late Romanesque style, while the transept, built during the first half of the 13th century, was already under the influence of French Gothic. The nave was quickly erected between 1250 and 1275 and is the earliest High Gothic church building in Germany. The west front, with its three sculptured doorways, was executed from 1276 after plans by Erwin von Steinbach. The north tower – one of two planned – was begun in 1399 by Ulrich von Ensingen (q. v.), and completed in 1439. The carvings in the south transept are among the finest examples of German sculpture; they include the Last Judgment, the figures of Ecclesia (ill. 138) and Synagoga, and the relief in the doorway of the death of the Virgin.

TABERNACLE. The tabernacle contained the receptacle for the Host. Originally the receptacle was generally suspended above the altar, but since the 12th century it has been kept near the altar in a niche in the north wall of the chancel. In front of this wall, the Gothic architect placed the tabernacle. The receptacle

182. Stoss, Annunciation in St Lawrence's, Nuremberg (c. 1500)

stood on a support in a shrine. A towered structure rose above it. The tabernacle in St Lawrence's, Nuremberg, by Adam Krafft (q. v., ill. 161), c. 1500, is 62 ft high and that in Ulm Cathedral (1467–1471) 92 ft.

THEODORIC OF PRAGUE is the name by which we know a master of the Bohemian school of painting, of whom there is evidence between 1359 and 1381. His main works are the 133 altar panels – saints, a Crucifixion and Man of Sorrows – in the chapel in Burg Karlstein. His heavy, gloomy style, with its low-keyed colours, has great expressiveness.

THEOPHILUS PRESBYTER is the name given to the author of the most important medieval technical manual of the arts, the *Diversarum Artium Schedula* ('Summary of various arts'). In it he describes the preparation of colours, painting, metalwork, glassmaking and painting on glass, the construction of organs, and work with ivory, jewels and pearls. (See Rogerus von Helmarshausen.)

TOLEDO CATHEDRAL. The foundation-stone was laid in 1227. The plan of the building seems in many respects to have been influenced by the Bourges and Le Mans cathedrals. It is five-aisled with niched chapels round the walls. The transept is short and there is a semicircular apse from which a chevet of chapels extends. The triforium of the nave wall is amalgamated with the clerestory. The wide interior with graduated aisles is typically Spanish and contrasts with the French desire to build upwards.

TOULOUSE, SAINT SERNIN. The church of the former Benedictine abbey of St Sernin (Saturnin), which belongs to the Romanesque school of architecture of the

183. Tracery

1 Triple mouchette, 2 Trefoil, round, 3 Trefoil, pointed, 4 Quatrefoil, pointed, 5 Cinquefoil, round, 6 Flamboyant (as in Sens Cathedral, rose window in south transept, 1490—97)

Auvergne, was begun in 1075. The choir was consecrated in 1096. The huge five-aisled, 12th-century nave has a barrel roof; shafts attached to the piers support the transverse arches. The transept, which projects considerably, the crossing, the choir with ambulatory and chevet, are of varying heights; the exterior is particularly pleasing (ill. 149).

TOURNAI CATHEDRAL. In the Cathedral of Notre Dame, Tournai (Belgium) possesses a splendid example of the Romanesque architecture of Northern Europe. The three-aisled basilica was begun in 1140 and the division of the nave walls into four storeys – arcade, gallery, triforium and windows – derives from northern France. The transepts with their semicircular apses, ambulatory and chevet, relate it to the French-Rhenish group of 'trefoil' churches. Among its appointments is the Shrine of the Virgin by Nicholas of Verdun, which is chased and enamelled.

TRACERY. In Gothic architecture, ornaments traced with the compass appear on the upper parts of church windows, on gableboards, triforia, balustrades and so on. By adding together several three-quarter circles, trefoils, quatrefoils and cinquefoils are obtained. In Late Gothic, the tracery becomes richer and more complicated, and through the adoption of the *vesica piscis,* which was already known in Celtic art, and various combinations of it, acquires new forms of expression (Flamboyant, q. v.). (Ill. 193, cf. ill. 151).

TRIER CATHEDRAL was developed from a Late Roman, square central building. Archbishop Poppo of Stablo (1016–1047) and his successors had the cathedral extended to the west; there it ends in two square towers, two round staircase towers and a semicircular apse. Above the two west doorways are two-storeyed, round-arched loggias, which must be considered the forerunners of the eaves gallery. The east choir was built c. 1200; the sanctuary chapel (treasure-house) was added in the 18th century. The vaulting dates from the 13th century. The cathedral was drastically altered

by the conversion of the hall into a basilica with transept (1719–35).

TRONTHEIM CATHEDRAL (Norway). The reconstruction seems to have been begun some time after 1152. The flat-roofed transept, with its Anglo-Norman articulation, gives an idea of this phase of its construction. Between 1186 and 1230 the long choir, which resembles that in Lincoln Cathedral (q. v.), was built. In 1232 the three-aisled body of the church, with its division of the nave wall into three storeys was begun. The vaulting and curtain façade (1248 onwards) also remind one of English Gothic.

ULM CATHEDRAL. In 1377 the citizens of Ulm decided to rebuild their parish church. The first architect – one of the Parler family — planned a hall church. But when Ulrich von Ensingen took over the construction in 1392, he erected a basilica without a transept, and a west tower in front of the nave. Surrounded by a veil of tracery, the tower, with its stress on the perpendicular, rises to the height of 528 ft – higher than that of any other church. The choir stalls are by Jörg Syrlin. The Man of Sorrows by Hans Multscher on one of the piers of the main door is a masterpiece of German sculpture. (Ill. 184)

VENICE, DOGE'S PALACE. The ducal palace of government was erected in the 14th and 15th centuries as a four winged structure arranged round an inner court. The two lower storeys – wide arcades surmounted by delicately traceried arcades – are an effective constrast to the high, patterned walls with their few windows. This effect is used in other Venetian palaces – usually in the inverse order.

184. Ulm Cathedral from S. W. (1377–1543)

VENICE, ST MARK'S. In 1063 work began on the construction of a central building on the foundations of an older church; the Church of the Apostles (now destroyed) erected in Constantinople by Justinian was taken as model. Over a Greek cross rise five domes – one above the crossing and one above each arm of the cross. The various domed spaces are divided from each other by barreled arches. The interior has been enriched by additions in the course of the years. The wonderful mosaics were carried out mainly in the 12th and 13th centuries and in the first half of the 14th (ill. 140).

VERONA, SAN ZENO MAGGIORE, a three-aisled, flat-roofed basilica with a simple alternation of supports, was constructed between 1123 and 1139 partly on the remains of an older structure. In the nave, semi-circular shafts attached to the piers and running up to the base of the roof, where they bear the transverse arches, divide up the space. The west façade has a portal with a gable supported on columns; these rest on lions. Near the portal are figures in relief by Master William and Master Nicholas. The wings of the doors are faced with figured bronze panels from the end of the 11th, and from the 12th, century.

VÉZELAY, SAINTE MADELEINE. The monastery church of St Madeleine at Vézelay in Burgundy was erected as a three-aisled, cruciform basilica after an older church had been burnt down. The nave, which was completed in 1120 and is groin cross-vaulted throughout, has no triforium. Above the arcades is a high clerestory. The aisles and bays are sharply separated. A three-aisled, three-bayed porch leads to the main doorway on the model of Cluny (q. v.). The portals are ornamented with sculptured figures. The tympanum of the main portal with the so-called Pentecost, c. 1132, is a mature work of Burgundian sculpture (ill. 185).

VIENNA, ST STEPHEN'S CATHEDRAL. Of an older Late Romanesque building only the west façade with the great tower and two smaller towers remain. The three-aisled, Gothic hall choir was built between 1304 and 1340; work on the nave began in 1359. The latter was also planned as a hall but, owing to the centre of the nave having later been raised, became a transitional form between hall and basilica (pseudo-basilica). In the early 15th century, Hans Stettheimer built the sharply tapering south tower, the 446-feet-high 'Steffel', which became the symbol of Vienna. The badly lit interior contains artistic treasures of the highest order, such as a huge Byzantine painting of the Crucifixion, the tomb of Frederick III by Nicolaus Gerhaert (q. v.), the base of the organ and a pulpit by Master Anton Pilgram (c. 1512) as well as numerous Gothic and Baroque altars.

WARTBURG, THURINGIA. The three-storeyed castle is a monument dating from the time of St Elizabeth and the conflicts of the Minnesingers (c. 1200); it is arranged round a courtyard and has three rows of windows with round arcades and small double columns.

185. Sainte Madelaine in Vézelay, southern France: tympanum of the main portal of the narthex (12th cent.)

The other buildings including the 'Vogtei' in which Martin Luther lived in 1521–22, date from the end of the Middle Ages or later (ill. 50).

WELLS CATHEDRAL. St Andrew's in Wells is a three-aisled, cruciform basilica (ill. 154). The nave, completed c. 1240, has cruciform piers with a thick cluster of 24 shafts, a pierced triforium and simple clerestory windows. The crossing piers are supported by fantastic flying buttresses, which cross each other diagonally. Behind the five-bayed choir lies a low, wide and light rectangular retro-choir (1320–63). The somewhat higher Lady Chapel (q. v.) adjoins to the east. The west front with its two towers (1220–39) has a wonderful figure cycle consisting of 250 niche statues. The two-storeyed chapter-house (1319), the Vicar's Close – a row of houses for the choristers – the huge cloisters, and the episcopal palace are all worthy of note.

WESTWORK. Monastery churches of the early Middle Ages were often given what is known in German as a 'Westwerk'. It refers to a construction at the west end, usually consisting of a tower over the crossing, flanked by two smaller staircase towers and short transepts (cf. Centula, ill. 144). In the interior, above a low entrance hall, is a chapel, open towards the nave.

WITTEN, HANS, a sculptor active in central Germany at the beginning of the 16th century, was known earlier as Master H. W. His main works are a stone figure of St Helen (1502) in the Town Hall of Halle an der Saale, the striking wooden 'Vesper Picture' in Goslar (1508–10), the unique, fantastically shaped tulip pulpit in Freiberg Cathedral, Saxony, the sculptured portal of the Church of St Anne in Annaberg in the Erzgebirge and the group showing the Scourging of Christ in the Schlosskirche at Chemnitz in Saxony (c. 1515).

WITZ, KONRAD, is one of the greatest masters of Early German painting. Probably born in Rottweil between 1400 and 1410, he was made a member of the artists' guild in Basle and died there or in Geneva

186. *York Minster (13th–14th cent.), aerial view from N. E.*

1 Three-aisled nave, 2 Three-aisled transept, 2a Crossing with open central tower, 3a–d Choir, 3a Westernmost section, with choir stalls, enclosed by choir screens, 3b Choir transept, 3c Retro-choir, 3d Altar to Our Lady, 4 Chapterhouse

187. *York Minster (13th–14th cent.) ground plan*

c. 1445. In his depiction of the human figure in space, mainly by the subtle use of shadow and reflex lights, he is far ahead of anything known till then in Upper Germany. His exact observation finds its most remarkable expression in the 'Draught of Fishes' (1444) from the Geneva Altar, which reproduces the first exactly recognisable landscape in late medieval painting – the Lake of Geneva (ill. p. 242). Other important works are the panels of the Heilsspiegel altar now in the Kunstmuseum, Basle. Witz is also believed to have worked as a wood-carver.

WOLGEMUT, MICHAEL (1434–1519), from Nuremberg, was painter, draughtsman for wood-carvings and Dürer's teacher. Whilst still under Flemish influences, he fashioned the high altar at Zwickau (1476–79); together with Wilhelm Pleydenwurff he produced some 2000 woodcuts for Schedl's *History of the World* – the most extensive collection of woodcuts dating from the last years of the 15th century. Lastly, he carved the High Altar of the parish church at Schwabach (1506–08), which is one of the best preserved carved altars of the Late Gothic.

WORMS CATHEDRAL. The Imperial Cathedral at Worms, one of the main examples of Rhineland Romanesque, replaced an older building in the second half of the 12th century. It is a three-aisled basilica on the metrical system (q. v.) with a double choir. Above the crossing – in the east – is a tower; the east choir with its apse and the pair of flanking towers was consecrated in 1181. The nave has arcades with square piers. The wall is divided into round-arched blind niches. There is cross-vaulting in the nave and ribbed cross-vaulting in the aisles. The west choir tower, the two staircase towers and the apse, together with its niches and round windows were probably completed c. 1220 (ill. 188).

YORK CATHEDRAL: York Minster, the Cathedral of St Peter, is one of the largest churches in England. A new Gothic building was begun in 1232 on the re-

mains of a Romanesque-Norman structure begun in 1080, of which there is evidence in the crypt. The cruciform basilica – the nave has eight, the choir nine, bays – is three-aisled throughout. The great crossing tower is open within. The nave, constructed between 1291 and 1324, has strongly moulded piers with pointed arches. The quintuple triforia are used as a base for the windows. In the choir, the fifth bay forms an east transept, for its aisle bay is the same height as the central one. The east wall is rectangular. The west front with three portals and a large central window is flanked by two towers from the 15th century. (Ill. 186, 187).

ZÜRICH, MINSTER. The Romanesque three-aisled pillared basilica was erected between the 11th and 13th centuries on a plan laid out on the metrical system (q. v.). The cross-vaulting begins above the galleries. The choir is square. The two towers were built in the Gothic period.

188. *Worms Cathedral (1170–1230), west choir*

250

FRA ANGELICO: Christ glorified in the court of Heaven. *Central panel of the predella of the High Altar of San Domenico near Fiesole*

MASACCIO: The Tribute Money. *Fresco in the Brancacci Chapel, Santa Maria del Carmine, Florence. Detail: St Peter gives the coin to the* tax collector

Fra Filippo Lippi: The Madonna adoring the Child *(The Adoration in the Wood)*

MELOZZO DA FORLÌ: *Lute-playing Angel. Detail from the* Ascension of Christ
(Fragment of a fresco from the church of Santi Apostoli, Rome)

DOMENICO VENEZIANO: Portrait of a Young Lady

Sandro Botticelli: Primavera

Renaissance
and Mannerism

Thy will is free and whole and upright
And now it would be wrong to rein it in.
Be thine own Emperor and thine own Pope

189. VERROCCHIO, equestrian statue of Colleoni, Venice

IN THESE WORDS Dante had already expressed the spirit of the Renaissance and of the modern age, although he still felt and wrote as a man of the Middle Ages. His *Divina Commedia*, which leads the reader from the depths of Hell to the mystery of Heaven, is yet rooted in the medieval concept of a Christian, divinely ordained universe resting on the twin pillars of Pope and Emperor. The transition from the Middle Ages to modern times was a very gradual process, extending over centuries.

It began with Humanism around 1300 and was not complete until the advent of the Age of Enlightenment in the 18th century. Historians generally consider the period round 1500 as representing the end of the Middle Ages. This break is also marked by the discoveries of new continents, the advance of the Renaissance spirit into Northern Europe, and the Reformation.

The medieval picture of the world was beginning to show cracks, which grew progressively wider from the 13th century onwards. The apparently solid structure of the Roman Empire collapsed and with it went the idea of a universal sovereignty. This was replaced by the different national States. The Church also had exhausted itself in the struggle between Pope and Emperor, and finally the Pope found himself politically dependent on France during his exile at Avignon. The year 1409 saw three Popes, and a year later three kings ruled on German soil, each staking his claim. The Turks in the Balkans hammered against the outer bastions of Europe and breached one after another, while Western Christendom was divided and exhausted itself in fratricidal strife. The Byzantine Empire was finally conquered in 1452. The medieval feudal system disintegrated and the nobles withdrew to their Courts or into the growing cities, whose wealth and power was increasing steadily. The aristocracy of wealth now took its place beside the nobility by birth. There was an early flowering of capitalism in Northern Italy and in the Netherlands, a forerunner of the modern system of commerce and banking. Sober commercial calculations very soon entered into politics. The 'Condottieri' – the Italian soldier-adventurers – were no longer subject to any particular ruler. On the contrary, they were shrewd business men who practised the trade of war and who offered their services to the highest bidder.

Political and economic convulsions merely reflected a spiritual upheaval that the Italians of the 13th and 14th centuries regarded as a Rinascita or a 'Rinascimento' – a renaissance and a conscious resumption of the traditions of Antiquity which had never died completely in Italy. Humanism prepared the way for the development of European thought during the succeeding centuries. Poets like Petrarch and Boccaccio glorified the authors of Antiquity and revived the art of poetry in the classical spirit. The youth

257

of Europe met at the Universities of Bologna and Padua to study the philosophers of Ancient Greece. The ideal of Humanism is the 'uomo universale', the human being versed in all the arts and sciences. The philosopher Pico da Mirandola, who was active in Florence, said of him, 'I have placed you in the centre of the world, so that you can survey your kingdom more easily. I have made you subject neither to heaven nor to earth, neither mortal or immortal, so that you shall be a sculptor who carves his own features. You can degenerate into an animal but you can also grow into a godlike being by your own free will.'

Man could never have been conceded such freedom in the Middle Ages. Although he remained rooted in the Christian concept of the world, his adventuring spirit could no longer be restrained in its search for 'the discovery of the world and man' as Jakob Burckhardt, the historian of the Italian Renaissance, wrote. Man's native surroundings were now fully explored and an interest in travel awakened. He entered into an entirely new relationship with nature. Petrarch's ascent of Mont Vidoux marks the beginning of mountaineering. Such an undertaking would have appeared completely senseless to medieval man. The extent of the earth's surface was discovered at the same time. Prior to 1300 already, Marco Polo, a Venetian, travelled in Mongolia and China, the realms of the almost mythical Ghengis Khan. The discovery of America in 1492 opened the gates to a new continent.

This discovery of the world had its counterpart in the discovery of man. His portrait now appears in sculpture and painting, the story of his life is told in numerous 'vite' – as the biographies and autobiographies of famous men are called. Giorgi Vasari compiled a series of biographies of artists and thus initiated the writing of art history. Man became interesting as an individual – interesting for what he was. He tried to awaken all his inherent faculties in order to approach the ideal of the 'uomo universale'. The Florentine banker and merchant Lorenzo de'Medici was far more than a mere business man; as a cultured humanist he collected a circle of brilliant men and women around him. Lorenzo himself was a scholar, and spoke several languages fluently – including, of course, Greek and Latin. He was also an art collector and a patron of the Florentine artists.

The artist, too, often mastered several subjects. It was usual for great painters and architects to distinguish themselves in many fields of science. The Florentine architect Leone Battista Alberti was also a sculptor and painter und the leading theoretician of art in 15th-century Italy. He developed a fine physique as a skilful gymnast and horseman. Even musical compositions, elegant novels and Latin prose were not beyond him. In addition, he made a reputation as a capable lawyer and a talented mathematician. And yet beside Leonardo da Vinci's even mightier genius this remarkable man was a mere novice. In Burckhardt's words, 'Leonardo da Vinci was to Alberti as the finisher to the beginner, as the master to the dilettante'.

This awakening of the forces of individuality made the age one of cheerful, ready acceptance of life on Earth. Ulrich von Hutten's paean 'O century, O sciences, it is a joy to live!' is characteristic of this exalted feeling. Through it, Humanism overcame the terrible pessimism which had affected Europe so greatly after the epidemics of the 14th century, when more than 25 million people had become victims of the plague. Mankind felt itself reverting to a happier and fuller life. If the works of the Italian Renaissance seem to breathe this new joie de vivre, the Reformation in Germany and Northern Europe was inspired by similar motives. It, too, was based on a new self-knowledge and an increased awareness; it, too, sought to regenerate the present out of the spirit of a better past. Both movements underline the importance of the individual, both alike appeal to the dignity of man. But Luther's Reformation made the Renaissance image of the free individual subject not only to the Divine Will, but also to the rule of the temporal authorities and thus unwittingly paved the way for the absolutism of later years. But the fundamental difference between the two movements lies in the spirit that informs each. The Reformation, as a purely religious movement, had no understanding for the aesthetic aims of the Renaissance. Indeed,

258

it fundamentally rejected the arts as a form of religious expression. Luther even wanted to 'tear pictures from the heart through the word of God'. In consequence, the Church lost its foremost position as a patron of the arts in Northern Europe.

Protestantism's hostility to art was carried to extremes by Calvinism. A fanatical iconoclasm swept across Northern Europe and destroyed the art treasures of centuries, especially in the Netherlands. But the Catholic Church began its counter-offensive after the Council of Trent (1543–63) before Protestantism had been able to consolidate its position fully in Northern and Western Europe. Europe north of the Alps now became the scene of religious wars for a whole century. Both sides fought with increasing determination. War and strife soon shattered the balance Humanism and the Renaissance had created between the forces of faith and reason.

The fanaticism of the Counter-Reformation also produced an accentuated religiosity. The feeling for nature, the Renaissance delight in every aspect of life and in the harmony between man and the world around him were readily sacrificed. Paintings and statues now acquired a restless, unnatural expression. This Mannerism, as it was called, was a mixture of recollections of medieval mysticism and of growing love of splendour, entirely in the spirit of the Counter-Reformation. It represented a genuine style and not merely a degeneration of the Renaissance tradition, as used to be believed. Such debased art did also exist, but the best artists found their own forms of expression and succeeded in resolving the conflict between spirit and matter, between ideal and reality, between the Middle Ages and modern times no less than the poets of this age who created immortal characters such as Don Quixote or Hamlet. The conflict and feverishness of Mannerism were only overcome through the vitality of Baroque art.

ARCHITECTURE

Gothic architecture in Italy did not undergo the same development as in Northern France, Germany or England. The vision of the virtually untrammelled use of space that found its expression in the heavenward-rising forms of the cathedrals, was not shared in the South. Here, the aim was always – balance. Most of Italy's Gothic buildings contain a horizontal element to curb the dynamic upward movement. The tradition of Antiquity is still clearly visible. The memory of a classic past – fully awakened during the Renaissance – eventually led to violent rejection of the Gothic. 'Cursed the man who invented this miserable Gothic architecture', wrote the sculptor and architect Filarete. Yet Gothic methods continued to be used for the time being. Brunelleschi had to use Gothic techniques of construction for the rib vaulting of the cupola of the cathedral in Florence. But the new style of the Quattrocento was inspired by the numerous buildings of Antiquity and of early Christianity, and it was considered the highest praise to say of a building that it was in no way inferior to those of Classical Antiquity. The works of Greece and Rome were not studied for the purpose of copying, as they had been to some extent during the Classic Revival, but because there was a desire to create new buildings in the spirit of the past and to do even better than the Greeks and Romans. Bramante, one of the greatest architects of the Renaissance, wanted to 'place the cupola of the Pantheon on top of the Basilica of Constantine to surpass two buildings, already perfect in themselves, through a synthesis of both.'

This interest in the architecture of the past is also reflected in an extensive literature. The writings of the Roman architect Vitruvius were found in the abbey of Monte Cassino in 1415. They inspired a flood of books based on the principles of the Ancients in which the rules of architecture were expounded. The first of these works was Leone Battista Alberti's *Ten Books of Architecture* (1485). All these treatises exerted great influence throughout Europe.

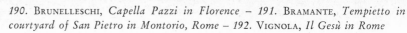

190. BRUNELLESCHI, *Capella Pazzi in Florence* – 191. BRAMANTE, *Tempietto in courtyard of San Pietro in Montorio, Rome* – 192. VIGNOLA, *Il Gesù in Rome*

Vasari said of Filippo Brunelleschi, the father of the new architecture, that he had only been motivated by two thoughts; the first was to recall the good architecture of the Ancients to new life; the second, to vault the dome of the cupola of Santa Maria del Fiore (Florence Cathedral). Harmonious proportions are a characteristic feature of the new architecture (see Brunelleschi's basilica of San Lorenzo – begun in 1421 – and his Capella Pazzi, built on the principle of the 'Golden Section'). The plan is now based on the square and the rectangle. The façades and inner walls are divided by the architectural elements of Antiquity and Early Christian art, such as piers, arches, pilasters, semicircular mouldings and cornices. The emphasis is again on horizontal lines in contrast to the Gothic. The beauty of such buildings is based on the carefully balanced relationship of all components, as the Italian Renaissance architects demanded (ill. 190).

Brunelleschi's great follower Alberti coined for this the term *concinnitas*. This means a harmonious balance that can be calculated mathematically.

'Beauty is manifest law.' The ideal of the Renaissance is the vaulted central building of the type known in the Mediterranean since Antiquity. Brunelleschi already used it in his Capella Pazzi and other architects, like Giuliano da Sangallo in his church of Santa Maria della Carceri – built on the plan of a Greek cross, – developed it further. This motif appears at its purest and most beautiful in Bramante's Tempietto in the courtyard of San Pietro in Montorio in Rome (built between 1500 and 1502). This architectural jewel owes its harmony to the most perfect geometric form, the circle. Carried by sixteen granite pillars resting on a circular platform, the light and elegant parapet of the gallery winds round the drum, which is closed by the hemisphere of the dome (ill. 191).

The concept of a central building is contrary to the needs of the church, since nave and altar should be separated. We therefore find the basilica continued throughout history. Central structures are comparatively rare. But there was always a desire to unite both principles. Alberti tried to do it in his church of San Andrea in Mantua, when he added a nave to a central composition. San Andrea is the prototype of the late Renaissance church. Vignola's Il Gesù – the church of the Jesuits in Rome – was built between 1568 and 1575. Its architect created it as one vast hall the whole of which one could take in when seen from the entrance. The windows are so placed as to emphasise the region round the altar. While the nave remains dark, the light floods into the large dome and draws the eye and thoughts of the visitor to the altar below (ill. 192). Il Gesù influenced the form of Baroque churches everywhere. Its design was developed by architects north of the Alps soon afterwards. The church of St Michael in Munich – the work of the Dutchman Sustris, who had studied in Italy – has a very similar ground-plan to that of Il Gesù, althought the absence of a dome and the uniform barrel-vaulting emphasise the longitudinal axis. St Michael's was begun in 1583.

The conflict between basilica and central composition is well illustrated in the history of St Peter's, Rome. Bramante had begun it as a central

JAN VAN EYCK: Giovanni Arnolfini and his Wife

ROGIER VAN DER WEYDEN: The Adoration of the Kings. *Central panel of the St Columba altar*

Hans Memlinc: St John the Baptist and St Lawrence

DIRK BOUTS: The Nativity

building in 1506, and Michelangelo had continued it in the same manner. But when the cardinals decided to finish the church in 1605, they found in favour of a nave. Carlo Maderna now added three enormous bays to the central hall and gave the entrance its gigantic portico. Lorenzo Bernini's colonnades underline the horizontal effect even further. The vast square in front of St Peter's was given a processional avenue of stone to prepare the pilgrim for the entry into the greatest sanctuary of Christendom (ill. 218, 219).

Many important tasks were also awaiting the architect in other spheres. The wealthy merchants and bankers demanded ostentatious palaces. The 'palazzo' – as this type of building is called in Italian – consists of a series of rooms, which are grouped round courtyards. The rooms are usually intercommunicating and are distributed over several – usually three – floors. The monumental façade is often faced with irregular rustications and these, like the battlements of the period round 1400, often recall the fortified castles of the aristocracy. Often, each storey is given a different type of rustication and a separate cornice to emphasise the horizontal division. Sometimes, this horizontal effect is balanced by vertical elements. This led Alberti to frame the windows of the Ruccellai Palace in Florence with pilasters and so cover the façade with a network of rectangles of equal size. (Ill. 193, 194)

But this dividing up of the façade – taken from the buildings of Antiquity – is still purely decorative and has no structural character. With the coming of the High Renaissance round 1500, the pilasters swell into half-columns. These rest on a base and already reveal more of the load-carrying function of the wall (Farnese Palace). Michelangelo went a step further and extended one order of pilasters over several storeys of his buildings on the Capitol, thereby making the walls look as if they consisted of filled-in panels (ill. 195).

A third type of façade was developed in Venice. Jacopo Sansovino used the orders of Antiquity in such a way that the arcades, interspersed by half-columns seem to lead those who approach it into the building. The almost aggressive ostentation and splendour of the Roman and Florentine palaces have thus been transformed into a calm and hospitable dignity that would become a seat of learning (ill. 196).

Another characteristic building of the time was the villa, the country house outside the city walls. The Renaissance architect treated it as an adaption of the villa of Roman Antiquity. The house, surrounded by loggias and terraces, stands in a formal garden which leads into the landscape beyond and – despite its severe outlines – forms an entirely

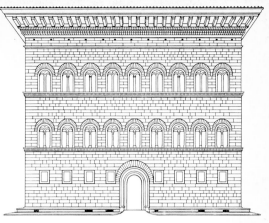

193. Palazzo Strozzi in Florence (BENEDETTO DA MAIANO *and others)*

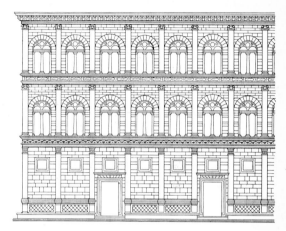

194. Palazzo Ruccellai in Florence (ALBERTI)

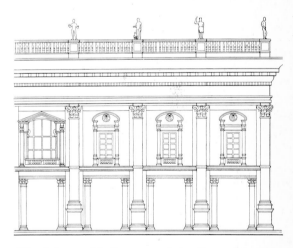

195. Palazzo dei Conservatori in Rome (MICHELANGELO), *one half of frontage*

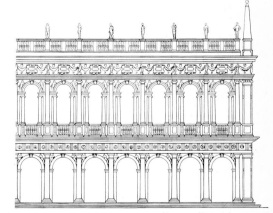

196. Library of St Mark in Venice (JACOPO SANSOVINO), *one third of frontage*

197. Château de Chambord on the Loire from N., built by Pierre Nepveu *called* Trinqueau *(from 1519)*

harmonious relationship with it (Villa d'Este, Tivoli). Andrea Palladio created a fine example of pure architecture in his Villa Capra (also known as the Rotonda) outside Vicenza, although the fact that the building was meant to be lived in seems not to have concerned him overmuch. The central cube, surmounted by a flat dome, is surrounded by four porticos – all exactly alike – above flights of steps (ill. 215). There are a number of copies of the Villa Capra in England and on the Continent, the most famous being Chiswick House, designed by William Kent for Lord Burlington (1729) and Meresworth Castle, Kent, built by Colin Campbell (1723).

North of the Alps, the Renaissance only made slow progress. Its basic forms were not properly understood and were combined with those of the Late Gothic. A strange transitional style developed in most countries. It was thus considered the highest compliment if it could be said of a French architect of the reign of Francis I that he was able to 'faire à la mode française et à l'Antique', i. e. that he could design both in the manner of Antiquity and that of the Middle Ages.

Chambord was one of many castles built at that time in the royal hunting preserves in the Loire valley. It is a characteristic example of the French Gothic interpretation of Renaissance architecture. From a rectangular ground-plan, it soars into the sky like some fairy-tale castle. Finials and pilasters, turrets and chimneys crowd round the central tower with its staircase – surmounted by the fleur-de-lys, the emblem of the French Bourbons – like courtiers round a prince (ill. 197).

The bizarre forms of this transitional period were only gradually disciplined into the powerful monumental classic architecture. The earliest wing of the Louvre, the palace of the French kings built by Pierre Lescot, is an example of this new style. The other portions were finished by later generations. The façade radiates energy and clarity and is a dignified manifestation of royal power in all its self-assurance. Bulging stair turrets and other features no longer interrupt the long frontage, which is given only a gentle, almost imperceptible movement by the slightly projecting and receding portions of the building (ill. 212).

That austere palace of the kings of Spain, the Escorial, is even freer from decoration ('Desornamentado style'). Built by Juan de Herrera in the solitude of the stony Spanish landscape, 'el Monasterio de San Lorenzo del Escorial' was meant to be part royal palace and part monastery. One half of the vast structure was to serve the Court, the other the Church and its servants. Here the close link between Church and Crown – the basic principle of Spanish world rule – is reflected in the architecture and lay-out of the buildings (ill. 207).

A real understanding of Renaissance forms did not follow immediately upon their adoption in Germany, the Netherlands and England, or indeed in France or Spain. Geometrical and mathematical concepts – the very basis of Renaissance art – only gained ground very slowly, and the Classic and Gothic ornaments were at first mixed freely. The Dutch architect Cornelis Floris, a theoretician of great influence, invented strapwork and used it on the otherwise severe façade of his Antwerp City Hall. Strapwork was taken up enthusiastically by architects all over Germany and the Netherlands and remained one of the most popular decorative features until the end of the Baroque.

The secular princes were the most important patrons of architecture at that time, since the Protestant Church in Northern Europe was as yet content to take over existing churches.

The irregular plan of the medieval castle was retained for a long time, and often endowed loosely grouped buildings like the ruins of Heidelberg Castle with a romantic charm. But all this had little in common with the mathematical thinking of the Italians, although in some of the buildings great efforts were made to incorporate the play of the ornaments in the rhythm of the façade.

Saxon castles like those at Hartenfels near Torgau and in Dresden and, in Southern Germany, the Alte Schloss in Stuttgart and particularly the Elector's residence at Aschaffenburg, are amongst the first examples of a clearer and more austere plan. The palace at Aschaffenburg especially forms a clearly defined block of impressive dignity with its four wings that, grouped along the sides of a square courtyard, almost appear as if they had been cast in one piece. This severe style could nevertheless acquire individual features, as can be seen in Denmark, where architects from the Netherlands often decorated the roofs of castles such as the Kronborg with a row of evenly projecting dormers (ill. 220).

The wealthy patricians in the cities of Central Europe also had their large handsome houses; but the most important buildings were those of the community. Magnificent city halls were built in Antwerp, Ghent and Bremen in the North, down to Rothenburg and Augsburg in the South. The Guilds also had their own halls (Brussels). Most of these buildings have severe façades covered with elaborate ornamentation in the characteristic transitional manner.

Only Elias Holl's Augsburg City Hall (finished in 1620) is devoid of such decoration (ill. 211). Its clear and harmonious proportions make it one of the finest examples of German Renaissance architecture. But the Thirty Years War came immediately after its completion and curtailed all building activity for many years.

In England, the Gothic continued until well into the 16th and even the 17th century (Thomas Holt's tower of the Bodleian Library at Oxford). Classic and Gothic details were freely mixed. Audley End, in Essex, has many Gothic features but also boasts of a complete Renaissance loggia. Buildings like Knole House or the south front of Hatfield House (1605 and 1607–1611 respectively) could easily be attributed to the 15th century. But despite their Gothic character, there is an attempt at typical Renaissance grouping that gives Tudor and Elizabethan buildings their special quality (Woollaton Hall, Notts., Hardwick Hall, Derbyshire). But the finest examples of the English Renaissance are the colleges of Oxford and Cambridge. Nowhere have Gothic forms, water, trees and lawns, been blended as happily or as consciously. Everything is on a delightfully intimate and human scale. This quality is characteristic of English architecture and landscape gardening and is not found anywhere else. Some of the buildings (the Pepys Library at Magdalen College, Cambridge) are almost Italian, others (Trinity College and King's College at Cambridge) are typically Gothic, although they, too, show the use of a few Classic motives.

SCULPTURE

It was pointed out at the beginning of this book that 'sculpture is the art of the sense of touch' (see p. 14). The Florentine sculptor Lorenzo Ghiberti was expressing a like opinion when he said that 'the perfection of such works escapes the eye and can only be understood if we pass over the planes and curves of the marble with our hands.' He was speaking of one of the numerous Greek and Roman statues that had been excavated in the period round 1400. Through them, the sculptors of the time were able to regain a sense of volume, which had been lost since the days of Greece and Rome. Now statues were freed from their rigid architectural background. They were at first still placed into semicircular niches, but only one step more was needed to arrive at sculpture in the round in the full sense of the term.

The influence of Antiquity is also reflected in the more catholic choice of themes. Figures like that of Bacchus, or classical scenes like the Judgment of Paris carved in relief, now take their places beside biblical subjects like the Pietà or David. An increasing realism went hand in hand with the advent of secular themes. Already Peter Parler had aimed at personal likeness in his portrait busts of 1380 in Prague Cathedral. But he was mostly portraying princes. His figures were still essentially part of the church build-ing, as were the naturalistic figures of the Dutchman Claus Sluter, whose most important work, the Moses fountain, was made for the cloisters of the Carthusian Monastery of Champmol near Dijon round 1400. It was the Italians who severed the connection with sacred art completely and created portrait busts of ordinary human beings, which were intended for the dwellings of their patrons. (Ill. 161, 182, 206)

Realism extended even to the statues of saints. Here, even disfiguring ugliness is not avoided. Sculp-tures thereby gain in dramatic expression. The figure of the prophet Job, by Ghiberti's contemporary Dona-tello, was called by the people 'Zuccone' (pumpkin-head) and looks like an old and extremely ugly man of the people (ill. 198).

But Donatello also exalted the beauty of the human form. His David is considered the first freshly-interpreted nude statue since Antiquity, his 'Gattamelata' (1453) the century's first equestrian statue in its own right. Comparison with the equestrian portrait of the Swedish Regent Sten Sture – who is still represented as an altar figure of St George, entirely in the medieval spirit – shows how revolutionary was Donatello's statue, though the earlier of the two by several years. The Italian Renaissance sculptors glorified the great *condottieri* in equestrian statues that revived the Classic Roman tradition. Donatello's 'Gatte-melata' no longer wears a saint's robes; he is essentially of this world and, with his baton as a Marshal of Venice, is representative of the man of power, whose thoughts and actions are determined by the utmost realism. This element is further developed in the second great equestrian statue of the Quattrocento, Andrea del Verrocchio's 'Colleoni.' Here power has turned to compulsion in the fierce gaze and gesture of the rider; it is further emphasised by the strength he displays in reining in his horse, yet it unites the move-ment of both man and animal (ill. 189).

With Donatello, sculpture began to move out of the orbit of the Church and to assume more secular attributes. His fellow-pioneer Ghiberti's two bronze doors for the baptistery in Florence – they took him 20 years to complete – show that his work was still more firmly rooted in the old tradition (ill. 24, 208). But on the second door Ghiberti took advantage of the new discoveries made by the painters, and set the biblical scenes of the fire-gilt bronze reliefs against a landscape with perspective and an architectural background.

The connection between sculpture and church architecture, which had existed throughout the whole of the Middle Ages, gradually loosened. Only the interior of the church still provided opportunities – in the decoration of pulpits or tombs. But secular sculpture grew correspondingly in importance. In addition to portraits busts (Settignano, ill. 206; Verrocchio), thousands of small bronze figures were now made for the houses of wealthy collectors (Pollaiuolo, Verrocchio).

The Florentine sculptor Luca della Robbia conquered new realms when he began to use the old technique of coloured glazes. His reliefs with their light blue backgrounds found particular favour and were used to decorate portals, altars and tombs (ill. 217). Their delight in new discoveries often tempted the masters of the Quattrocento to lose themselves in a wealth of detail. But here, too, greater clarity eventually triumphed and led towards the end of the century into the High Renaissance.

Michelangelo's monumental figures must have appeared to the Italians of the 16th century as strange as Donatello's realism had done to their antecedents of a hundred years before (ill. 199). Michelangelo overcame the realism of his predecessor by means of an idealization of the human form, based on certain

GIOVANNI BELLINI: Sacred Allegory

Antonello da Messina: Portrait of a Man

JAN GOSSAERT, *called* MABUSE: A Little Girl

HIERONYMUS BOSCH: The Haywagon. *Central panel*

198. DONATELLO, *the prophet Habakkuk ('Zuccone') – 199.* MICHELANGELO, *statue of Moses from the tomb of Julius II in Rome, marble – 200.* GIOVANNI DA BOLOGNA, *Rape of the Sabine ('Figura serpentina')*

rules of proportion, which he had found in the statues of Antiquity. In place of naturalistic copies he created images of human perfection that were endowed with a truly heroic quality. His figures always transcend their theme. His 'David' is more than the biblical shepherd-boy, he appears as the prototype of the young hero; in his 'Moses' he seeks to portray even more than the biblical prophet – here is a figure whose prophetic rage is the embodiment of a powerful masculinity. But with all their intensity of expression and with all their wealth of complicated movement, Michelangelo's statues always have a compact form. The artist is said to have claimed that they could have been rolled down a precipice without suffering serious damage.

Masters like Michelangelo or Jacopo Sansovino had perfected the technique of the sculptor to such a degree that the human body could now be portrayed while engaged in every kind of intricate action. Their successors looked for a solution that would allow them to give a strong and balanced form to intense movement, and thus Mannerism was born. The Gothic 'figura serpentina', the 'S'-shaped or serpentine twist of the body, shows us that such a solution had already been found. It was Giovanni da Bologna who brought this Mannerist style to perfection. His statue of Hermes seems to wind into space, each movement has a corresponding counter-movement. The figure, standing on tip-toe, is brilliantly balanced: viewed from any angle, it is an admirable example of free-standing sculpture. But the artist does not primarily aim at making a realistic copy of nature as did the sculptors of the Quattrocento, or seek to idealise the human form as did the artists of the High Renaissance. He is concerned above all with the visual; it is the artistic potentialities of the human body that interest him (ill. 200).

Mannerism extended far beyond the frontiers of Italy. Giovanni da Bologna's Dutch pupils Hubert Gerhard and Adriaen de Vries brought it North, where it was received enthusiastically – especially in Germany – since it seemed to breathe the spirit of Late Gothic sculpture. German sculptors like Hans Reichle and Jörg Zürn took up Mannerism and developed in further. Berruguete, in Spain, super-imposed upon the accentuated Mannerist gestures the passion of religious ecstasy, as did El Greco as a painter. French sculpture remained closest to the Classic spirit. Benvenuto Cellini had brought Mannerism to France already before Giovanni da Bologna and had greatly inspired the Frenchman Jean Goujon, whose work was marked by movement and elegance similar to that of the Italian Mannerists (ill. 205, 212).

273

PAINTING

When Giotto, the greatest master of Gothic painting in Italy, introduced 'space' into his pictures, he took the first step towards a fundamental change in the artist's mode of expression. A century later, Masaccio painted figures that stand out almost three-dimensionally from a background which has 'depth' and actuality. Masaccio's Northern contemporaries, the brothers Hubert and Jan van Eyck, on their famous Ghent altar, set the 'Adoration of the Lamb' against an extensive landscape.

The new realism of the Renaissance, then, found expression in painting in two quite separate areas – in Florence and in the Flemish cities. Masaccio continued in the tradition of the Italian fresco painting, the brothers Hubert and Jan van Eyck (ill. p. 261) drew their inspiration mainly from Burgundian miniature painting. The new flourishing art of panel painting in the Netherlands owed its intensely glowing colours to illuminated manuscripts. The colours are mixed with oil and applied to oak panels – these having previously been covered with chalk – in several layers and thus acquire their warm glow. This technique also enables the most delicate nuances of colour to be lent to the smallest detail. Such selfless devotion to the most insignificant features and a close relationship with nature are characteristic of the painters of the Netherlands. Their way of using colour led to the discovery of atmospheric perspective, in which the colours, from the dark brown in the foreground, by way of green, to misty blue in the distance, lead the eye into the picture and thereby create an illusion of depth.

Italian painting since Masaccio achieved these effects above all through Brunelleschi's linear perspective. Masaccio's figures, recalling Giotto in their powerful monumentality, stand out with great clarity in front of the recession of the scenery. While Giotto's figures still resemble those in a relief, Masaccio's seem about to step out of their frames as do Donatello's statues from their niches (ill. pp. 228, 252). They create such a powerful impression, even to-day still, that we can understand Vasari's claim that 'everything made before Masaccio looked as if it was painted, but that everything made by him was alive, true and natural.'

Masaccio's emphasis on the representation of the human figure resulted, in the case of his successors, in pictures of an increasingly secular character. Renaissance artists rejoiced in the beauty and abundance of the earth and paid more and more attention to the landscape in the background. Saints become human beings who, like St Jerome in his cell, were now shown in their home surroundings. Figures are no longer shown in varying sizes – as was the custom of medieval artists – according to their rank. All are now equally important and appear in correct size in relation to each other. The saints in 'Santa Conversazione' are no longer grouped according to iconographic rules, but in natural attitudes, indeed informally conversing. The Coronation of the Virgin becomes a festive spectacle in the delightful and almost gay paintings of the artist-monk Filippo Lippi. The procession of the Three Kings is turned into a gaily-coloured picture of a hunting trip of the Medici family, in the hands of Benozzo Gozzoli.

These painters of 'narrative' pictures used Masaccio's discoveries, without however developing them any further. This was left to another group of artists. Amongst them was Paolo Uccello, who tried to solve the problems of perspective foreshortening (ill. p. 69); Andrea del Castagno, who translated Donatello's energetic gesture and dramatic realism from sculpture into painting, which hitherto had been characterized by calm precision; and Domenico Veneziano, who experimented with new techniques, such as the use of oil to bind his colours and with the effect of light on his compositions (ill. p. 255).

The Umbrian artist Piero della Francesca carried the experiments of these three Florentine innovators further (ill. p. 59) and, above all, elaborated on Domenico's discoveries of light. Light seems to suffuse his almost transparent colours – although no source of light is indicated – and bridges the gap between the picture's foreground and background. The figures are no longer crowded together in the foreground as if they were on a stage, but are distributed in groups extending well into the background which is seen as a continuous landscape. Here the influence of Dutch oil painting is already very noticeable.

274

The fame of the artists of the Netherlands had already reached Florence, the brothers van Eyck and their generation having been followed by Rogier van der Weyden, who no longer paid loving attention to detail but concentrated on expression in his figures and on dramatic composition (ill. p. 262). He visited Italy in 1450 and probably painted several pictures there. So deep an impression did they make that Francesco Sforza, the Duke of Milan, sent the painter Bugatti to Brussels as much as ten years later to serve as van der Weyden's apprentice. Italian merchants now ordered altar-pieces from Bruges through their agents. Tommaso Portinari, the representative of the Medici family, commissioned Hugo van der Goes in 1472 to paint a large altar with an Adoration, which caused a great stir in Florence (ill. 209). Hans Memlinc's altar-piece, 'The Last Judgment', was 'captured' on its journey to Italy by Paul Beneke, a native of Danzig (the picture hung in the Marienkirche there until the end of the last war). But patrons were not content merely to order paintings, they induced the Dutch and Flemish painters to come South. In 1468, Joos van Wassenhove of Ghent, called by the Italians Justus of Ghent, came to the court of the Dukes of Urbino, where he painted the frescoes in the Duke's palace together with Melozzo da Forli.

The art of the Netherlands also reached Italy in another way. Sicily and southern Italy having been under the rule of the House of Aragon since 1442, Spanish painting, like that of the rest of Europe, was greatly influenced by the art of the Netherlands. Rogier van der Weyden was entrusted with many important commissions by the Spanish Court. The Sicilian master Antonello da Messina now also learned how to apply the Northern technique of oil painting; this knowledge he brought to Venice in 1475. The brothers Bellini combined Northern mastery of colours with Italian vision and technique and thus laid the foundation for the great flowering of Venetian art. (Ill. pp. 269, 270)

The painters of the second half of the century completed the early Quattrocento's 'discovery of the World and of Man'. Careful anatomical studies lent authenticity to representations of the human body. The Florentine painter Pollaiuolo was the first artist to dissect corpses in order to acquaint himself with the human organism. Painting from the nude model was the logical outcome of such anatomical studies (cf. ill. 216). Allegorical themes from classical mythology – introduced by the Humanists – provided welcome subjects. Such pictures now began to appear upon walls of private houses, and their popularity grew. Sandro Botticelli, the court painter of the Medici, invested the figures of legend and mythology with a dreamlike life in his harmonious compositions (ill. p. 256). Signorelli was bold enough to introduce nude figures into his frescoes, which were characterised by a dramatic intensity in their execution. Like Andrea Mantegna, Signorelli was a master of perspective, which both painters used for the most daring fore-shortening effects (ill. 201). The delineation of space in depth had been mastered completely by the end of the century and a representation of the human form was no longer a problem.

The Flemish painters of the second half of the century, too, sought in practice to make the most of the discoveries of their predecessors. Many of these painters were not Flemings, but went to settle in Bruges. Dirk Bouts came from Haarlem, Hans Memlinc from the region of Frankfurt-am-Main, Gerard David from Oudewater. For them, as for Hugo van der Goes, the smallest detail needs to be portrayed with a loving care and a pious devotion that recognises the hand of the Creator even in the smallest and most insignificant object; nor does this entail – especially in the case of David – any sacrifice of over-all dramatic effect. But the work of the great individualist Hieronymus Bosch shows that this world of medieval piety was already overshadowed and convulsed by fears and doubts. Bosch gives free rein to a

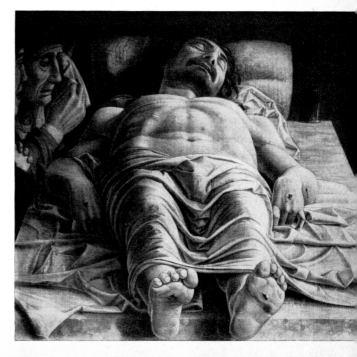

201. MANTEGNA, *Lamentation*

daring and bizarre imagination and a profound pessimism, so that his pictures evoke a veritable witches' sabbath. (Ill. pp. 263, 264, 272)

The Quattrocento's down-to-earth search for truth was transfigured during the High Renaissance and found expression in a new idealism. Masaccio's saints, it will be recalled, looked like honest peasants or small traders, while Filippo Lippi even used simple women from among the common people as models for his Madonnas (ill. p. 253). These were now no longer considered adequate. Raphael wrote to Count Castiglione in 1516, 'To paint a beautiful woman, I would have to see more beautiful women ... but since there are so few beautiful women and competent judges of beauty, I use the ideal picture of a woman that I carry in my mind' (ill. p. 279). The 'realistic model' is replaced by the 'certa idea', a figure of the imagination representing a timeless ideal of beauty. Since artists have by now learned precisely how to paint or draw the human body in motion, slavish copying of nature is no longer necessary. The painter can adapt reality to his concept of a perfect picture.

The Quattrocento saw the human figure either clearly and sharply outlined in an attitude of calm and repose (Masaccio, Piero della Francesca), or advancing in a lively manner (Mantegna, Signorelli). The High Renaissance sought a harmonious balance between the two attitudes. Each movement is offset by another movement, all straight and hard outlines merged into the curved, flowing lines of the human body. The figures no longer stand by themselves but are arranged in the form of a pyramid, the 'Figura Piramidale', the base of which extends well into the picture (cf. ill. 52). But larger groups, too, are arranged in geometric patterns. Leonardo's famous fresco of the 'Last Supper' in the convent of Maria delle Grazie in Milan shows the Apostles in four groups of three, each set of three occupying a fifth of the length of one side of the table, while the fifth in the middle is filled by the figure of Christ. 'Sfumato', the veil-like merging of from and colour, gave Leonardo a means to link the different background bases: 'Between light and shade there is an intermediate state, something twofold, belonging to both, resembling a light shadow or a dark light. This it is that you must seek, for it holds the secret of perfect beauty.' The light in the pictures of the Quattrocento was evenly distributed. Leonardo set brightly illuminated planes and points of light against sections that are bathed in deep shadow (ill. pp. 26, 277). He thereby achieved a loosening of the all too rigid character of the perspective. The landscapes in the background also no longer comprise an assortment of individual features, but are treated as an entity. The composition is studied in many sketches, until every object accurately fits into a predetermined plan based on spacial and surface diagonals. Even the colours are now balanced to fit into the concept of the picture, the 'certa idea'. Leonardo's and Raphael's paintings have attained that complete interpenetration of reality and imagination, that balance of parts demanded by Alberti when he wrote, 'the state of perfection has been reached when not the smallest part can be changed without destroying the beauty of the whole.'

Michelangelo regarded such a complete balance as no more than a transition stage. This sculptor amongst painters, who held that 'the more relief there is in painting, the better,' was above all concerned with man and his strivings and his passions. Unlike Leonardo, he was not interested in uniting man and nature through his art. His tremendous frescoes in the Sistine Chapel, particularly 'The Last Judgment' and the scenes from the Old Testament, such as the 'Creation of Adam,' break through the newly-found harmonious balance of Renaissance art. These works already show the power and movement of the Baroque, and Michelangelo has for this reason been called the 'Father of Baroque'. (Ill. 1; p. 278)

Leonardo, Raphael and Michelangelo between them put Italian painting into the forefront in Europe. European painters now went to Rome instead of to Bruges. If Dutch and Flemish artists had been drawn to the South in the 15th century, Italian masters were now fetched North. Leonardo spent the last years of his life at the French Court of Francis I. Jan Gossaert, called Mabuse, went to Rome in 1508 and it became customary for Northern artists to journey to Italy for the next hundred years. Where formerly Italian painters had marvelled at the Portinari altar of Hugo van der Goes, Dutch painters

LEONARDO DA VINCI: The Virgin of the Rocks. *Detail*

MICHELANGELO: The Libyan Sibyl. *Fresco in the Sistine Chapel, Rome*

RAPHAEL: Madonna della Sedia

Andrea del Sarto: Portrait of a Sculptor

now studied Raphael's cartoons in Brussels – where they had been sent as sketches for tapestries ordered by the Vatican. A Northern artist, Jan van Scorel, was made Raphael's successor as keeper of the Vatican collections in 1524. His fellow-painters in the Netherlands banded themselves together into the so-called 'Romanist' brotherhood. Painters like Jan Gossaert, Quentin Matsys and Jan van Scorel tried to fit the lovingly portrayed world of van Eyck into Renaissance compositions (ill. p. 271).

The art of Pieter Brueghel alone was unaffected by his travels in Italy. Though he painted country-folk at work and at their celebrations (ill. p. 311), his is by no means realism on a 'popular' level. His paintings were meant for cultured and discriminating people in Flemish towns, who used to visit painters in the studio to choose pictures. Public and private patrons no longer gave artists commissions with set themes. Furthermore, with Protestant Northern Europe no longer providing a market for religious pictures, the landscape and the genre painting with its portrayal of everyday life presented artists with new opportunities.

A number of great artists who made a significant contribution towards the development of painting and the graphic arts were active in Germany at the same time as the great High Renaissance masters in Italy. Their art was rooted in the medieval tradition. But the Reformation, with its appeal to the individual to look into his soul, coupled with Renaissance and Humanist influence, aroused in these artists a feeling of greater responsibility and a heightened self-awareness. Their ability to conceive a painting as a whole allowed them to rise above the realism of the 15th century with its attention to countless details. These German artists, like their Italian contemporaries were concerned with clear composition, with the unity of the picture in which everything has its appointed place. But they achieved this unity less through a formal balance of the different components than by making the theme pervade their pictures.

Albrecht Dürer, the greatest German painter of this epoch, was closest to the Italian Renaissance in that he tried to fathom its laws and to make them manifest in his art. One of the first theoreticians of German painting, his constant struggles with the ideas of the Renaissance led him from the bizarre and tortuous forms of the Late Gothic to the beauty and calm of classic art. His fame spread far beyond Germany's frontiers and he was greatly admired in the art centres of Italy and the Netherlands. 'If this exceptional, zealous and universally gifted man had been born in Tuscany instead of Flanders, he would have been the greatest among our painters,' wrote Vasari with an enthusiasm not altogether matched by his knowledge of geography. (Ill. p. 286)

A contemporary of Dürer, though the elder by a decade, was Mathis Gothard-Neithardt, called Grünewald. He was less concerned with harmony and beauty, his overriding purpose being to reveal thoughts and feelings and to achieve the utmost intensity of expression. Indeed, symbolism and expression are the pillars of his passionate, deeply felt art – an art that cannot be measured by the formal aesthetic standard of the Italian Renaissance (ill. p. 285).

By comparison, the works of Albrecht Altdorfer and the Danube School (the early Lucas Cranach, Wolf Huber, etc.) seem almost romantic in conception, for the theme is integrated with harmonious and almost practical surroundings. Man's closeness to nature, shown also in the paintings of Giorgione in Italy and Patinier in the Netherlands, was interpreted with great beauty and feeling by these German masters. (Ill. p. 287)

While Dürer had to acquire his mastery of classic form through continuous training in theory and technique, such hard-won knowledge had already become an established tradition a generation later at the start of Hans Holbein the Younger's career. This artist's sense of reality and the technical perfection of his almost international style, make him one of the greatest portrait painters of all time, for whom life harbours 'neither magic nor mystery' (ill. p. 290).

During the time of the Reformation, German painting still concentrated mainly upon religious themes. It was with the portrait (Dürer, Holbein) that the first approach was made to secular painting.

Dürer himself introduced the self-portrait as a work in its own right, while Altdorfer did the same for the landscape. The historical painting – the Emperor Maximilian had commissioned battle-scenes such as Altdorfer's 'The Battle of Alexander on the Issus River' – also now appeared, although it did not as yet achieve as much popularity as mythological themes.

Secular subjects, and the formal influence of the Renaissance, affected the graphic arts far more than painting. Nearly every German painter of the first half of the 16th century was actively engaged in drawing and engraving. Occasionally, as in the case of Hans Baldung Grien, these drawings are far more important than the artist's paintings. Scenes from mythology and the occult world, the nude figure in all its classic beauty, everyday scenes, soldiers and lovers – and, not least, the landscape – offer great scope to the artist, in addition to the religious themes. No description of German painting would be complete without mention of the graphic arts (these are dealt with separately, see p. 283).

By the beginning of the 16th century Venice had become as important as Rome as a city of painters. Perhaps her special position as a lagoon-city, the silvery glow of her atmosphere and the contacts with the East, helped to bring about the 'Venetian style' in painting. Michelangelo called colour a harlot whose flattery he was able to resist. The Venetian masters abandoned themselves to colour whole-heartedly. Illumined bodies stand against dark, mysterious backgrounds; the colours play and interweave in every conceivable blending of shades. The composition is not determined primarily by the picture's mathematically calculated 'architecture' but by the painter's choice of colours. This effect is closely connected with the technique. Titian applied layer after layer of colour to the canvas without letting it dry. The wet colours therefore seem to merge and do not stand out sharply as on the wooden panels of the Dutch artists. Giorgione had made the Venetian style of the Bellini brothers the classic style of his age; Titian brought it to perfection (ill. pp. 299, 300). In the course of his long life of nearly a century he seemed to follow the same path as the three great Roman masters: from measured beauty, through balanced movement and counter-movement, finally, to the beginnings of a Baroque vigour in colour, form and composition.

We find a last echo of the Italian High Renaissance in the worldly art of Paolo Veronese, who extols the joys of life on earth in his gay and festive pictures of great banquets. But Veronese's time was already a period of transition, although his work was unaffected by the changes taking place around him. It is apparent still earlier on in Correggio, whose pictures – and particularly his ceilings (with their trompe l'oeil effect) – already point to the coming age of Baroque in their dramatic movement. (Ill. pp. 301, 312)

The great masters of the Renaissance had visualized a harmonious balance between outer form and inward feeling. The Mannerists of the ensuing generation concentrated above all else on their ideal of beauty and held that art should not be limited to copying nature but should obey its own laws. They believed, that is, in an art that avoids slavish observation of nature. Painters like Pontormo, Bronzino or Parmigianino, created in the 16th century a style that makes use of heightened aesthetic effects. All forms are deliberately exaggerated, narrowed and elongated, whilst Leonardo's 'sfumato' is used brilliantly to produce clever light effects (ill. p. 313). Magnificent fabrics, jewellery and ornate weapons are made to exist in their own right, thereby contributing not a little to the very individualistic beauty of Mannerist painting. This technique scored great triumphs at the elegant French Court, where the school of Fontainebleau was active. French artists were taught by Italian masters who introduced them to the treasury of Renaissance ornament.

Whilst the tendency here was for the artist to be concerned solely with form, whereby he ran the risk of emptying his pictures of all feeling, painters like Tintoretto and El Greco placed Mannerism at the service of their religious beliefs, endowing it with the passion of the Counter-Reformation. Spain – where El Greco worked – was a particularly fertile soil for such an art, and it was El Greco who carried

282

Mannerist painting to new heights. His excessively elongated figures seem the living embodiments of religious ecstasy, whilst their supernatural aspect is frequently enhanced by a strange triad of colours: sulphury yellow, palish green and deep strong red. (Ill. pp. 302, 314)

Where the Mannerists had experimented, searching for a new style, Michelangelo da Caravaggio succeeded in achieving this in Italy at the end of the 16th century. But his gross realism was very different from the early exaggerated aestheticism. His art marks the beginning of Baroque painting.

THE GRAPHIC ARTS

Italian Renaissance painters concentrated upon large-scale altar pictures and frescoes. The graphic arts were not nearly as important to them as to the artists north of the Alps. Gutenberg had invented printing in 1450 and the woodcut, previously used mainly to illustrate pamphlets and as a substitute for votive pictures for the poor, now became the ally of the 'black art' and shared its triumphs all over Europe. The number and quality of illustrated books increased rapidly. In addition to Nuremberg and Augsburg, Florence and Venice, Paris and Basle, soon became centres of printing where the graphic arts flourished collaterally. Schedel's *World History* was published in 1493 and contained over 2000 woodcuts by leading masters of the calibre of Dürer's teacher Michael Wolgemut. The Emperor Maximilian commissioned a great many woodcuts which were mostly executed by Hans Burgkmair of Augsburg.

Series of woodcuts without accompanying texts now also appeared. Reading had not yet widely spread amongst the people and these woodcuts told the stories of the Bible to those to whom the printed word meant nothing. Albrecht Dürer brought the art of the woodcut to a peak of perfection. The vigorous linear style of the 'Apocalypse,' of the 'Life of the Virgin' or the scenes of the Passion, lent the woodcut such power of expression, that colour, used widely before Dürer's time, became superfluous. The woodcut had now veritably become a 'black-and-white art'. Dürer's influence spread beyond the frontiers of his native country to Switzerland, the Netherlands and Italy. But amongst those German painters who practised the woodcut (Lucas Cranach, Albrecht Altdorfer, Wolf Huber, Hans Burgkmair) at about this time, Hans Baldung Grien alone, after Dürer, developed a truly individual style. The art of the German and European woodcut reached its peak with 'The Dance of Death' cycle by Hans Holbein the Younger (published 1538). It handles with supreme mastery the medieval theme of Death as the victor over all living things. Space has been exploited in the most brilliant manner, for most of the scenes cover an area only a few inches square (ill. 210).

Efforts had already been made at that time to find other ways of exploiting the art of line drawing, since the woodcut did not allow the imagination much scope. Urs Graf simply reversed the process and cut the outlines into the wooden block instead of leaving them raised as before. This 'white-cut' causes the lines to stand out white against the black background (ill. 203). Attempts to produce woodcuts in colour were already made, towards the end of the 15th century, by men like the printer Radolt, a native of Augsburg, who was active in Venice, and who used three or more blocks. The aim was to print all the areas of one colour simultaneously. But more often, just one plate of another colour – yellow, for example, – was used besides the black etched plate. Cranach, Burgkmair and Hans Baldung Grien used an additional plate to obtain

202. DÜRER, '*Knight, Death and the Devil*'. *Copper engraving*

a coloured background. The process of the light-and-dark print was carried further in Italy by Ugo da Carpi, who added green or blue plates to the grey or brown of the Germans, eventually dispensing with the black plate altogether.

These very difficult techniques obviously were scarcely suitable to illustrate books or to produce picture-cycles. It is characteristic of the time that individual woodcut drawings now appeared in addition to costly paintings, and could, by means of reproduction, reach a wider public that was clamouring for pictures. These graphic techniques opened up quite a new field for the artist, and he went to work on them with as much zeal as he devoted to paintings. They also allowed him to experiment with a number of themes that painting was not yet ready to embark on. Thus the woodcut became a means of experimenting with representations of secular and temporal subjects.

The copper engraving, having far greater potentialities than the woodcut, had begun to supersede the latter already in Dürer's time. It was used for the first time on a large scale in 1440 by the 'Master of the Playing Cards.' The 'Master E. S.' and, above all, Schongauer, excelled in the art. The engraved ornament was of the utmost importance to the craftsman and later to the architect, until well into the Rococo period. Ornaments, designs for jewellery, and for whole façades were duplicated in this manner and spread all over Europe. Many of the engravers like Schongauer or Dürer came from long-established families of goldsmiths and the Italian painter Pollaiuolo worked also as a goldsmith all his life.

Mantegna had at an early stage achieved a great deal in this new sphere; the Netherlands produced a great engraver in Lucas van Leyden. But in general, Germany led in the graphic arts. German copper engravings were in demand all over Europe and were even copied as an exercise by Raphael and Michelangelo. Dürer perfected the copper engraving, as he had perfected the woodcut. The cycle of 'The Passion', engraved on copper, or the famous engravings, 'Ritter, Tod und Teufel' ('Knight, Death and the Devil'), 'St Jerome in his Cell' and 'Melancholy' are amongst the most famous examples (ill. 202).

The engraving was also used increasingly during the ensuing centuries to reproduce the paintings of great masters. It was Marcantonio Raimondi who took the first step in this direction by making copper engravings of Raphael's paintings.

The etching increased in importance in the second half of the 16th century and tended to oust the engraving. Where Dürer, Altdorfer and the masters of the Danube School like Cranach, Urs Graf and others had made a beginning, Hirschvogel concentrated upon etching. This art was also practised by Pieter Brueghel in the Netherlands and by Parmigianino and Barocci in Italy. But it was to attain its greatest triumphs in the centuries following.

THE CRAFTS

The Italian Renaissance affected everyday life in all its aspects as much as it did architecture and the plastic arts. The clean proportions of architecture were applied to furniture. Chests (*cassone*), which later developed into settles (*cassapanca*), heavy refectory tables and magnificently finished desks were all designed with their purpose in mind. Rooms often used to be dominated by a piece of furniture such as a chest, which was often decorated with inlay, carving or even painting (ill. 204, p. 319).

Elaborate silver, and gold, dishes were displayed on large sideboards. Masters like Pollaiuolo, Verrocchio or Cellini made pieces that are works of art and are yet exemplary in their shape from a purely

MATHIS GOTHARDT NEITHARDT, *called* GRÜNEWALD: Crucifixion, *from the Tauberbischofsheim altar*

ALBRECHT DÜRER: The Nativity. *Central panel of the Paumgartner altar*

ALBRECHT ALTDORFER: Landscape near Regensburg in the Danube valley

Lucas Cranach the Elder: St Jerome in his Study

HANS BALDUNG GRIEN: Portrait of Count Löwenstein

Hans Holbein the Younger: Portrait of the merchant Georg Gisze

functional point of view. Cellini's famous salt cellar embraces every technique known at the time (ill. 205) and is a piece of Mannerist sculpture in miniature. Rock crystal, ivory and semi-precious stones enjoyed great popularity. A flourishing branch of the goldsmith's art was the fashioning of gold and silver portrait medals. These were commissioned by princes, the nobles and wealthy patricians, and displayed on the obverse the profile in relief, and on the reverse the armorial motto and a suitable allegoric picture.

The Italian ceramic arts also became famous by virtue of the products of the Majolica factories of Faenza, Urbino and Venice. Undoubtedly, Italian ceramics owed a great deal to the Islamic East. The interplay of ornament, coloured painting and shiny glaze was used to produce decorative effects of the greatest charm. Venetian mirrors in elaborately carved frames were as much in demand as Venetian glasses, which had no peer in delicacy of design and transparency despite many imitations. The skill of Italian craftsmen became a by-word all over Europe. Some of them went to Spain and France where most of the furniture, plate, pottery, silks and brocades show a strong Italian influence. Independently of these, however, the Frenchman, Bernard Palissy, developed his own form of ceramic art. His dishes are decked with life-like casts of plants, snakes and small animals in addition to elaborate ornaments (ill. 214).

The Northern interiors developed on somewhat different lines, not least because of the cold climate. The smaller rooms of the German, Dutch or Flemish houses are often panelled and contain enormous tiled stoves in place of the chimneys of the Italian palazzi. These stoves offered the potter interesting opportunities. Kitchens and corridors were also often tiled, the tiles being decorated with various subjects in colour, largely in blue and white. Delft tiles were even then greatly coveted. Enormous wardrobes, magnificently carved, stood in the corridors since there was no space for them in the small rooms.

The English interior of the time was little different from that of France or Italy. Large houses called for large pieces of furniture. On their dissolution, Henry VIII had distributed the monasteries amongst his closest followers and those who had not shared in the spoil built themselves equally large houses. The chair, hitherto reserved for the head of the household, now became a more common piece of furniture, though it was usually far from comfortable or beautiful. Architectural forms were applied to chairs and table legs with but little understanding, although a certain amount of good carving was done – sometimes the work of French or Italian craftsmen (King's College, Cambridge) – and some fine inlaid work. Other important articles of furniture were the court cupboard – a kind of large sideboard with accommodation for plate – the table settle (a settle that could be converted into a table by turning the back down to rest on the arms) and the extensible table. Most of these pieces were solid, heavy and over-decorated. Their forms only became lighter and more elegant in the following century.

The German craftsman produced his finest work in the wealthy South German cities of Nuremberg and Augsburg. Masters like Peter Flötner and Conrad Meit or the Jamnitzer family were famous far beyond the borders of their homeland. Gold and silver plate and elaborate vessels of the most fantastic shapes often incorporated exotic materials like coral or ostrich eggs. Miniature statues of bronze, covered with precious stones and gold enamel were commissioned by princely collectors. German weapons of the time, ornate suits of armour, engraved with arabesques, were unsurpassed anywhere in Europe.

At the same time, tapestry weaving flourished in the part of Flanders centred upon Brussels. The great Renaissance painters made designs for these carefully wrought pictures, which now often had gold and silver thread woven into them. Although they usually decorated churches and royal palaces, these Flemish tapestries also appeared in the houses of splendour-loving patricians.

The achievements of the European craftsman of the 16th century are almost without equal. It speaks for the genuine feeling for beauty of Renaissance Man that he also wanted to be surrounded by beautiful objects in his everyday life. The great masters of the time, such as Dürer, did not think themselves above designing furniture, plate, coins, jewellery, or even clothes. It was the last beautiful flowering of the truly universal culture of the Renaissance.

AACHEN, HANS VON (1552–1615), was born in Cologne and can be regarded as an exponent of Low German Mannerism. He worked in Italy, at the Court of the Duke of Bavaria in Munich, and at the Court of Rudolph II in Prague.

AERTSEN, PIETER (1508–1575), a genre painter from Amsterdam, was active in Antwerp for over twenty years. He painted mostly domestic and market scenes ('The Egg Dance', Amsterdam/Rijksmuseum) and lush still-lifes with fruit.

ALBERTI, LEONE BATTISTA (1404–1472). This universally gifted and cultured Italian Renaissance theoretician and architect wrote a ten-volume work on architecture *(De re aedificatoria)*. In many of his buildings, he drew greatly on classical examples (the façade of S. Francesco in Rimini, inspired by the Arch of Augustus there, is a case in point). The articulation of the façade of S. Maria Novella in Florence by means of different coloured marbles was inspired by the works of the local proto-Renaissance. In the Palazzo Ruccellai in Florence, he divided the storeys by superimposed pilasters using the classical orders (cf. p. 265, ill. 194). In the church of S. Andrea, Mantua, he produced an effect of unity quite exceptional for his time.

ALDEGREVER, HEINRICH. Born in Paderborn in 1502, and active in Soest until 1555, this German artist executed, in addition to a few altar pictures and portraits, some 300 copper engravings of small size representing biblical and secular subjects ('The Anabaptist'). He specialized in ornamental engraving (Renaissance decoration).

ALTDORFER, ALBRECHT (c. 1480–1538). This painter from Regensburg is the most important master of the Danube school (q. v.). He was responsible for the first 'pure' landscape in European painting (1522, ill. p. 287). In his paintings, human activity is integrated into the framework of a landscape which is both all-embracing and analytical – and frequently overpowering. Nature has become an essential part of pictorial composition, which reflects and emphasises the mood of the action depicted, e. g. the 'cosmic struggle' of clouds and sea and the triumphant sun in the 'Battle of Alexander' (Munich). Apart from his paintings, which mostly deal with religious, and less frequently with mythological subjects, Altdorfer left a great number of woodcuts and engravings, some etchings and a series of drawings, which also deal with landscape.

AMBERGER, CHRISTOPH (c. 1500–1561/62), a painter who was active in Augsburg, painted frescoes on the Venetian model and excellent portraits (e. g. his portrait of the cosmographer, Sebastian Münster, in Berlin).

AMMAN, JO(B)ST (1539–1591). This Zurich painter went to Nuremberg where he became one of the most prolific illustrators of his time (cartoons for woodcuts for the Book of Guilds by Hans Sachs, for editions of the Bible, etc.). His large output is an important source for the study of his period.

AMMANATI, BARTOLOMMEO (1511–1592). In the Piazza della Signoria in Florence, there stands a monumental fountain by this Mannerist sculptor. It shows Neptune, surrounded by graceful bronze figures of nymphs, satyrs and fauns, who recline on the edge of the basin.

ANGELICO, FRA, or more precisely Fra Giovanni da Fiesole (1387–1455). His paintings and frescoes (Dominican monastery of S. Marco in Florence, Chapel of St Nicolas in the Vatican) recall that he has his origins in Sienese painting. Although he was completely assured in the handling of perspective and plastic modelling, in his piety he still belonged to the spirit of the Middle Ages, and retained the Gothic rhythm and sensitive stylization of figures (ill. p. 251).

ANTONELLO DA MESSINA (c. 1430–1479) studied and copied the Dutch, probably in Naples, so that he was able, during a stay in Venice (1475/76), to introduce to local painters the technique of improving egg tempera by adding oil. This led to a new era in Venetian painting. The main product of his stay in Venice is the 'St Sebastian' in Dresden, a picture which unites Dutch and Italian concepts without any apparent discrepancies. He was also an excellent portraitist ('Condottiere', Louvre, Male portrait, London, ill. p. 270).

BACKOFFEN, HANS (c. 1470–1519). This sculptor, who worked in stone, was in the service of the Court at Mainz. He exercised a far-reaching influence on numerous successors in the central Rhineland. He is considered to be one of the leading masters of Late Gothic during the transition to the Renaissance (Tomb of the Bishop of Gemmingen, Mainz, Cathedral; Crucifixion groups).

BALDUNG, HANS, called Grien (c. 1480–1545), is one of the most outstanding German artists of the Reformation period. He had his workshop in Strassburg. He was at first influenced by Dürer, but subsequently found his own personal style and discovered how to use a light palette. His altars (Freiburg Cathedral), his religious paintings with their strong worldly features, his allegorical pictures and portraits (ill. p. 289) are, however, surpassed in importance by Baldung's extensive graphic work. His fantastic studies of witches and his Dances of Death are full of powerful movement and are among the greatest achievements of the German woodcut. He also produced cartoons for stained glass (e. g. the choir of Freiburg Cathedral).

BARBARI, JACOPO DE (c. 1440/50–1515/16). This Venetian painter and draughtsman, who was active at the princely Courts of Germany and Burgundy, was one of the artists who introduced the Italian Renaissance to Germany and the Netherlands.

BAROCCI(O), FEDERICO (c. 1535–1612), who was trained in Rome but worked chiefly in his native town of Urbino, was one of the painters who carried Mannerism to its logical conclusion and went beyond it. He painted with pious devotion and great care, using light pastel colours, Madonnas and Saints in voluminous, fluttering robes. The 'Madonna del Popolo' in the Uffizi is one of his famous paintings.

BARTOLOMMEO, FRA (1472–1517). Under the impact of the fanatical sermons of Savonarola 1496/97, this pious Florentine painter burned all his pictures of secular content. A few years later he entered the Dominican monastery of S. Marco. Possessed of a remarkable talent for composition, he sought to build up his altar pictures with their many figures into monumental pieces of great solemnity (Pietà, Florence). He left to posterity a greater legacy of graphic works (composition sketches, studies of draperies, etc.) than any other artist of the Italian Renaissance.

BASSANO, JACOPO or Giacomo (1510/15–1592), whose real name was da Ponte, was a Mannerist painter who achieved particular fame through his brilliant colour, which was influenced by the Venetians (Titian), and by his masterly, lively composition. The rural setting in the background of many of his paintings is the mark of the 'Bassano style', which ultimately became the main feature of the pictures of peasant life and particularly of animals produced by the great family workshop. Of Jacopo's sons, Francesco (1549–1592) and Leandro (1557–1622) deserve mention.

BEHAM. The brothers Barthel (1502–1540) and Hans Sebald (1500–1550) were masters of the small-scale painting. As Court painter to Duke William IV of Bavaria, Barthel produced numerous portraits of princes, but he is chiefly known as an engraver of allegories and portraits. Hans Sebald, who flourished when book production was just beginning to develop, produced more than a thousand woodcuts as illustrations for numerous works. He left a series of etchings and engravings.

BELLINI, GENTILE (c. 1429–1507). Venetian painter, and brother of Giovanni. Among his important works are the portrait of the Turkish Sultan Mohammed II (National Gallery, London) and the large paintings of the 'Legend of the Miracle of the Cross' (Venice).

BELLINI, GIOVANNI (c. 1430–1516). Son of Jacopo, brother of Gentile, is the founder of the High Renaissance in Venice. Giorgione and Titian were his pupils; Albrecht Dürer visited and admired him. Antonello da Messina, who was in Venice in 1475, introduced him to the use of oil paint and the Dutch technique. Thereafter, Bellini succeeded in painting quiet devotional pictures – such as Madonnas with Saints, frequently half-length treatments – sometimes with beautiful landscape backgrounds of great softness and brilliant colouring. One of the painter's favourite themes is the dead Christ supported by angels. The portrait of Doge Loredan in the National Gallery, London is one of the most beautiful portraits in the world. (Ill. p. 269)

BELLINI, JACOPO (c. 1400–c. 1470), the father of Giovanni and Gentile. Most of his frescoes and paintings have been lost. Two sketch-books, each with about 100 drawings are in the Louvre and the British Museum.

BENEDETTO DA MAIANO (1442–1497), whose real name was Benedetto di Leonardo, was a Florentine sculptor. He mostly produced decorative sculptures for churches, chancels and tombs, as well as outstanding portraits (e. g., the terra-cotta bust of Filippo Strozzi). In 1489, the Palazzo Strozzi in Florence was begun from his designs (ill. 193).

BERRUGUETE, ALONSO (c. 1490–1561). During a journey to Italy, Berruguete was deeply impressed by Michelangelo's work. On his return to Spain, he sought to realize these impressions in his marble and wood sculptures. He tried again and again to combine Italian forms of composition and the Spanish desire for expression. ('The Sacrifice of Isaac', Valladolid, Museum).

BOLTRAFFIO, GIOVANNI ANTONIO, also known as Beltraffio (1467–1516) is considered to be the most important of Leonardo da Vinci's Milanese pupils.

BORDONE, PARIS (1500–1571). This painter, who was influenced by Titian, produced portraits and altarpieces of great importance both technically and in terms of colour.

BOSCH, HIERONYMUS (c. 1450–1516), was also called after his home town, s'Hertogenbosch. His best-known works apart from the 'Adoration of the Magi' in Madrid, are the allegorical triptychs with the 'Triumph of the Haywain' and the 'Garden of Delights', both in the Escorial. In dark-toned parables, Bosch demonstrates that, because of original sin, the life of man is fundamentally evil; he reflects this life in a diabolical distorting mirror full of devilish imaginary creatures and apocalyptic visions. Today it is almost impossible to interpret these pictures, but as the same phantom-haunted world is to be found in other artists of his time – above all in Peter Brueghel – it may be assumed that their symbolism was quite intelligible to all initiates. (Ill. p. **272**)

BOTTICELLI, SANDRO (1444/45–1510), brought one early Italian Renaissance mode to its peak of perfection. It was the decorative trend with its lovely line, which still maintained contact with the Gothic, and which had, with Filippo Lippi, his teacher, acquired a tender, sensual humanity. Particularly in his characteristic representations of the feminine, Botticelli added a slight melancholy, which is also evident in his fine portraits or when he depicts the flower of the Florentine aristocracy in mythological or religious scenes. His was a profoundly poetic nature, attracted to all that is vernal ('Birth of Venus' and 'Primavera', Uffizi, Florence, ill. p. 256). He was also a man of great piety. In his 94 pen drawings for Dante's *Divine Comedy,* he shows his serious attitude to the fundamental things of life – an attitude which led him to become a follower of Savonarola and burn his paintings with his own hands. Thereafter, he painted only a few more pictures, in a completely different style.

BOUTS, DIRK (c. 1415–1475), was active in Louvain and owed much to the example of the two 'old masters' of the period – Jan van Eyck and Rogier van der Weyden. He developed an individual style, however. His figures are calm and serious, sometimes, indeed, distributed on the canvas in a rather wooden manner. He painted space and landscape with great care and even attempted difficult light effects, such as the evening sky or sunset (Altar in St Peter's, Louvain). Ill. p. 264

BRAMANTE, DONATO (1444–1514), the Italian Renaissance architect was at first interested in painting, through which he attempted to discover the laws of perspective. In the Milan of Ludovico Sforza some time after 1479, he was responsible for the chancel of S. Satiro which is designed in perspective to simulate a choir, and later for the great domed church of S. Maria della Grazie (1492–1498). In 1499, Bramante came to Rome, where he laid the foundation for that city's unparalleled development during the High Renaissance period. He first built the courtyard of S. Maria della Pace (1500), then the Tempietto in the courtyard of S. Pietro in Montorio (cf. p. 260; ill. 191), and finally, between 1503 and 1514, parts of the Vatican Palace with the Octagonal Court, the Belvedere courtyard and the Cortile of S. Damaso. His most important undertaking was the plan of St Peter's which became the basic theme for subsequent development by Michelangelo.

BRONZINO, ANGELO (1503–1572). This Florentine painter is regarded as one of the chief representatives of Mannerism. He was a pupil of Pontormo and became in 1540 Court painter to Cosimo I de' Medici. In addition to religious and mythological paintings, he chiefly produced numerous portraits of Florentine society.

BRUEGHEL, PIETER, THE ELDER, also known as Bruegel or Breughel. His dates – 1525/30–1569 – place him in the generation of the Mannerists and his pictures do, in fact, show elements of Mannerist composition, e. g. the diagonal lines in his famous painting 'The Blind' (Naples) or his preference for dramatically painted, slightly overcrowded scenes (The Passion, Vienna). Otherwise, his is an unclassifiable genius. His love for coarse peasant scenes rightly earned him the name of 'Peasant Brueghel'. His 'Peasant Wedding' (Vienna, ill. p. 311) and pictures such as 'Proverbs' (Berlin), 'Childrens' Games' (Vienna) introduce us to the life of the Dutch people in a surrealist manner which is not found again until the Dutch genre painting of a century later.

204. Cassone: Medici-Strozzi Chest. Bridal chest of Maria de' Medici with carving and painted view (1512)

Brueghel visited Italy (Rome, Naples, Messina), but the basic traits of his great North European talent were not in the least influenced thereby. His sense of the grotesque and the tragi-comic in human existence derives from a non-Mediterranean preoccupation with the topsy-turvy state of the world. His love for inventing monstrous creatures, in the 'Dulle Griet' (Antwerp), in the 'Triumph of Death' (Madrid) and in the 'Fallen Angel' (Brussels), he shares with Hieronymus Bosch. His ability to plumb the spirit of a landscape is also typical of the North. He is the first artist to depict the seasons of the year, e. g. 'The Hunters in the Snow' (1565, Vienna). Little is known of Brueghel's life. He worked in Antwerp and later in Brussels, where he died. Of his two painter sons, Pieter the Younger (1564–1637/38), known as 'Hell-Brueghel', continued to specialize in nightmare scenes, whilst Jan the Elder (1568–1625), Court painter to Archduke Albert and a friend of Rubens, devoted himself, apart from other subjects, to the flower-painting. Neither attained their father's stature.

BRUNELLESCHI, FILIPPO, also Brunellesco (1377–1446), the Florentine architect of the Italian Early Renaissance, built the 298-ft-high dome of Florence Cathedral as well as the famous domed sacristy of S. Lorenzo and the Capella Pazzi. His two pillared basilicas — S. Lorenzo and S. Spirito – are distinguished by the harmony of their proportions. Brunelleschi's greatest achievement in civic architecture is the Foundling Hospital with its famous entrance hall (1421), and the familiar medallions of foundlings. His discovery of central perspective was of great importance for Renaissance painting. (Ill. 190)

BRUYN, BARTHOLOMÄUS (1493–1555). This painter from the Lower Rhine produced, as the portraitist of the city fathers of Cologne, paintings of ceremonial dignity.

BURGKMAIR, HANS (1473–1531). This Renaissance master from Augsburg was one of the artists whom Emperor Maximilian I engaged for the woodcut illustrations to the *'Theuerdank'*, the *'Weisskunig'* and the *'Genealogie'*. Apart from his important graphic work, he left a number of altar-pieces and portraits.

CARPACCIO, VITTORE (1455–1525), used in an extremely lively manner the active Venetian scene as a background for his religious paintings. His pictures, in which he overcomes the stiffness of many of his predecessors, are logically constructed to produce a unity of treatment (cycle of the Legend of St Ursula, Venice/Accademia).

CASSONE is the name applied to an Italian Renaissance chest. In the Quattrocento it was frequently decorated with coloured pictures; later, these were replaced by rich carvings and precious inlaid work. (Ill. 204)

CASTAGNO, ANDREA DEL (1423–1457), was chiefly active in Florence. In his works, which are mainly frescoes, he attempted a more plastic treatment of the human figure. He achieved this by accentuated gestures and foreshortened perspectives. His monumental realism carries on the art of Masaccio and Donatello (e. g. the frescoes in the refectory of S. Apollonia, Florence).

CELLINI, BENVENUTO (1500–1571). Cosimo I de' Medici, Grand Duke of Florence, commissioned this Renaissance sculptor and goldsmith to fashion the elaborate bronze statue of Perseus in the Loggia dei Lanzi, Florence. His virtuosity – he designed medals and cut intaglios – made him extremely popular in Court circles. His famous salt cellar was made for Francis I of France (Vienna, ill. 205).

CERTOSA DI PAVIA (It. certosa, Chartreuse). The plan (1396–1497) follows the system of a Carthusian monastery in which each monk had his own small house. The church is noteworthy on account of the extremely elaborate decoration of its wide marble façade (completed in 1540).

CHRISTUS, PETRUS (c. 1420–1472/73), was active in Bruges from 1444. His painting (religious works and portraits) was strongly influenced by Jan van Eyck. He painted carefully ordered interiors, such as the 'Goldsmith's workshop of St Eligius' (Cologne). His 'Portrait of a Young Girl' (Berlin) is outstanding.

CLOUET, JEAN, called Janet, was Court painter to Francis I and died in Paris in 1540/41. Over 130 drawings and some portraits from the royal entourage can be attributed to him. Of his son François (c. 1522–1572), who succeeded him as Court painter, we have two signed portraits – 'The Apothecary Pierre Cutte' (Louvre) and 'Diane de Poitiers in her Bath' (Richmond).

CORREGGIO (c. 1494–1534), whose real name was Antonio Allegri, was an Italian painter of the High Renaissance, whose work, however, in many ways anticipates certain characteristics of the Baroque. He uses extremely daring foreshortened perspectives, particularly in the paintings on the ceiling of the dome of Parma Cathedral or the dome of S. Giovanni Evangelista. As well as frescoes, he painted pictures with religious or intensely mythological themes (ill. p. 312). He causes light, which he sometimes uses to produce dramatic effects ('Holy Night', Dresden), to play upon all forms; his colours are brilliant, his figures full of graceful movement. His Jupiter cycle is well known ('Io', Vienna; 'Leda', Berlin).

COSSA, FRANCESCO (1435–1477), was an Early Renaissance painter from Ferrara, who came under the influence of Piero della Francesca. The most important of his relatively few preserved works are the allegorical frescoes depicting the Months, in the Palazzo Schifanoia in Ferrara.

CRANACH, LUCAS, THE ELDER (1472–1553), came from Kronach, Upper Franconia (hence his name). After 1500 he painted some magnificent portraits in Vienna (Dr Cuspinian, Winterthur) and religious

205. CELLINI, *salt cellar for Francis I of France. Base of ebony, vessel and figures of gold*

paintings with idyllic landscapes, which are among the first products of the Danube school (q. v. 'Rest on the Flight to Egypt', Berlin). The freshness and colourful quality of these early works was modified by Cranach, once he became Court painter in Wittenberg; the style becomes calmer, turning progressively more Mannerist. Apart from pictures for churches and castles, Cranach also painted portraits (e. g. of Luther) and produced numerous drawings, woodcuts and copper-plates. Cranach's sons, Lucas the Younger (1515–1586) and Hans (died in 1537) also worked in their father's very productive studio, which from 1520 on specialized chiefly in Bible illustrations (woodcuts). Ill. p. 288

CRIVELLI, CARLO (c. 1430–1495), who was born in Venice, provided a long series of altar-pieces and paintings of the Madonna, which are full of profound piety (to-day they are to be found in Milan, Verona, London, Berlin). The 'Annunciation' (London/National Gallery, ill. p. 37) is an example of perspective logically applied.

DANUBE SCHOOL, or Danubian style, is used to describe a trend in painting in the first thirty years of the 16th century which flourished in Bavaria and on the Danube (Albrecht Altdorfer, q. v., Wolf Huber, q. v., Rueland Frueauf the Younger, q. v., Michael Ostendorfer, etc.). They were all strongly influenced by Lucas Cranach, who was active in Vienna after 1500. They have in common a feeling for Nature, a love of light and colour and of detailed and highly decorated anecdotes. A large number of pure landscape drawings by these masters have been preserved. (Ill. p. 287)

DAUCHER, ADOLF, also known as Dauher or Dauer (1460/65–1523/24), was an Augsburg sculptor of the Renaissance period (choir stalls in the Fugger family chapel; the marble altar in the Annenkirche at Annaberg in the Erzgebirge). His son Hans (c. 1485—1538) is principally known for his stylistically excellent small sculptures and medallions.

206. Desiderio da Settignano, *portrait bust of Marietta Strozzi, marble*

DAVID, GERARD (c. 1460–1523). A Flemish painter who, at the turn of the century, gathered together once more all the artistic threads from van Eyck to Memlinc. From 1483 he worked in Bruges. By preference he painted saintly figures grouped together in quiet meditation (Virgin and Saints, Rouen).

DELORME, PHILIBERT (c. 1515–1570), whose real name was de l'Orme, was a French Renaissance architect. His buildings have mostly been destroyed (Châteaux of Anet and Meudon; part of the Tuileries). His writings on architecture exercised great influence.

DESIDERIO DA SETTIGNANO (1428–1464). This Tuscan sculptor was a pupil of Donatello. In his charming busts of young girls and children he expressed his ideal of pure, tender beauty. His careful handling of marble gave it a soft shimmering finnish (ill. 206).

DEUTSCH, NIKLAUS MANUEL (c. 1484–1530), came from Berne and fought passionately for the Reformation as both poet and statesman. His brilliantly coloured altar-pieces and mythological pictures, as well as his woodcuts and drawings, were chiefly produced between 1510 and 1520.

DOMENICO VENEZIANO (b. before 1438, d. 1461), was one of the Florentine Quattrocento masters who investigated the problem of perspective and light as a means of plastic representation in space. Domenico was the first Florentine artist to use oil as a binding material for paints. He thus increased the intensity of his colours. His chief works are: Madonna with Saints, frescoes in S. Croce (both in Florence), and portraits (ill. p. 255).

DONATELLO (1386–1466). This pioneering sculptor of the Florentine Quattrocento learnt how to cast bronze from Ghiberti, and sculpture in the workshop of the cathedral. He also worked in Siena, Padua and Rome. He aimed at strict realism, as is proved by his 'Zuccone' (It.: bald pate, ill. 198, cf. p. 268). During his study of classical art in Rome he was influenced less by the severe classical canons of beauty than by the classical

feeling for ponderability: he was the first to make full use of 'counterpoise' in his statues, since Antiquity. The scope of his art ranges from the dancing children on the Singers' Gallery in Florence Cathedral to the boyishly graceful David and the monumental power of the 'Gattamelata' outside S. Antonio in Padua, which was to become the archetype for all future equestrian statues. He also produced portrait busts, Madonnas, Prophets, reliefs from Biblical history and finally his dramatic altar-pieces ('Judith and Holofernes', Florence, and 'John the Baptist', Siena).

DOSSI, DOSSO, whose real name was Giovanni di Lutero (c. 1479–c. 1542) worked chiefly for the Dukes of Ferrara. His religious and mythological scenes are set against a background of evocative landscapes in colours of Venetian splendour.

DÜRER, ALBRECHT (1471–1528), the son of a goldsmith from Nuremberg, was a pupil of Michael Wolgemut and spent his years of apprenticeship in Upper Alsace and Switzerland. A first visit to Italy (1494/95) was followed by a second (1505/07). In 1520/21 he travelled to the Netherlands. The tension between Late Gothic and Early Renaissance, the two poles between which he and his vast opus stand (cf. ill. 2, 202, p. 286), is evident if we compare the self-portrait which he drew in 1492 (Erlangen) with the self-portrait he painted in 1500 (Munich). If the former, with its thoughtful expression, suggests nagging doubts, the latter looks at us with the fixity of a legislator. Dürer's stubborn search for the 'kingdom' of beauty lay between these two poles. His work unites a craftsman's zeal, inexhaustible powers of imagination and the keen eye of the searcher after truth. He left hundreds of water colours, studies of landscapes and from nature, drawings (e. g. that of his Mother), sketches, designs for ornaments, etc. (the Prayer Book of the Emperor Maximilian). Among his paintings are altar-pieces like the Paumgartner Altar (Munich, ill. p. 286) and the Festival of the Rosary (Prague), the great paintings of the Four Apostles (Munich) and the fine portraits (Jakob Muffel, Hieronymus Holzschuher, both in Berlin). In his drawings, whether for woodcuts (the Apocalypse, the Life of the Virgin, the Passion) or etchings (the 'Knight, Death and the Devil'; 'Melancholy') he made important technical and formal innovations – hence his reputation as one of the greatest masters of the Renaissance. (cf. p. 281, 283)

ERHART, GREGOR (c. 1468?–1540). This Suabian sculptor in wood and stone, to whom an extensive and important corpus of work must be attributed, developed from being a follower of the Late Gothic tradition of Multscher into a true Renaissance master. His most important works are the five beautiful figures on the Blaubeur High Altar which have been preserved with their original painting, the Madonna with the chaplet of roses from Frauenstein, and the figure of Mary Magdalene in the Louvre, known as 'La Belle Allemande'.

ESCORIAL. This monastery and royal residence was erected near Madrid between 1563 and 1589 by the architect, Juan de Herrera, on the instructions of Philip II. It consists of a rectangle (176×226 yds) having four angle towers and enclosing 16 courtyards. The domed church, which is the burial place of the Kings of Spain, forms the central point. The whole is an example of absolute but unworldly splendour, in keeping with the character of its royal builder. Today the Escorial contains a fine library and a famous collection of paintings. (Ill. 207)

EWORTH, HAUNCE, whose real name was Hans Ewoutsz, was a portrait painter who came to London from Antwerp shortly after 1540. From 1550–1570 he was one of the leading masters of the Elizabethan Age. In his style of painting there is an unmistakable hint of Mannerism.

EYCK, HUBERT VAN (c. 1370–1426) and **JAN VAN** (c. 1385/90–1441) lived at various Courts in Holland and Burgundy at the time when the art of illumination was in its last flowering. The altar in St Bavo, Ghent, which was probably begun by Hubert, was finished by Jan in 1432. In this, his first work, he at once became a pioneer of the new style of painting. With him, Northern Europe breaks with the medieval tradition. Jan van Eyck imported the technique of oil painting, developed perspective, observed the anatomy of the human body and discovered the tangible world of the interior as well as of the landscape. These he painted in pictures of great brilliance (e. g. 'Giovanni Arnolfino and his Wife' in the National Gallery, London, ill. p. 261). The human face loses its idealized qualities but gains in realism (e. g. the 'Man with the Carnation', the Donor of the 'Madonna of Canon Paele' or the 'Madonna of Chancellor Rolin').

FILARETE (c. 1400–1469), whose real name was Antonio Averlino, was active in Rome, Milan and Florence as an architect (*inter alia,* the Hospital in Milan) and sculptor (bronze figure of St Peter, ornamented with reliefs, in Rome). The *Trattato d'architetture* is an imaginative work in 25 volumes with daring plans.

FLORENCE, PALAZZO MEDICI. This palace, which was begun by Michelozzo in 1444, is grouped round a pillared cortile. The three storeys of the façade are differentiated by the decreasing height of the floors and by varied handling of the stone-work. The bottom storey has heavy rustication.

FLORENCE, PALAZZO PITTI. The palace was begun in 1458 and is remarkable for its large dimensions and its massive bossages. The building was frequently altered (by the later addition of wings at the side, and so on). Since 1870 it has housed one of the most important Italian art collections.

FLORENCE, PALAZZO STROZZI. The palace, which was begun in 1489 by Benedetto da Maiano, presents, in the unity of its rusticated façade, an impressive example of Italian Renaissance domestic architecture (ill. 193).

207. Escorial, convent-palace of Philip II near Madrid, from N. W. Built by JUAN DE HERRERA

FLORENCE, UFFIZI. The Palazzo degli Uffizi was erected by Vasari between 1560 and 1574 as an extension of the Palazzo della Signoria. Its parallel wings frame a narrow street which runs up into the Piazza della Signoria from the Arno and, as entrance to the main square, is of great importance in terms of town planning. The Uffizi, like the Pitti, today houses one of the finest Italian art collections.

FLORIS, CORNELIS (1514–1575). This Flemish architect and sculptor from Antwerp exercised great influence with his drawings of architectural ornaments, and gave his name to a particular style. He developed the Roman grotesques and framed fantastic figures with scrolls and ribbons. His most important building, the Town Hall, Antwerp (1561–1565) is, however, a work notable for the clear articulation of the façade; it influenced later buildings on the North German coast (Town Hall, Emden).

FLORIS, FRANS (1516–1570), brother of Cornelis, became – after his return from Rome – a leading figure among the Flemish 'Romanists' of Antwerp (cf. p. 276). Excessively slim figures with tiny heads are characteristic of his religious and mythological pictures in the Mannerist style. His portraits are distinguished by their faithfulness to the models.

FONTAINEBLEAU PALACE. This extensive building, which is grouped round several courtyards, was chiefly built under Francis I (1515–1547) and Henry II (1547–1559); the two splendid galleries are called after these monarchs.

FONTAINEBLEAU, SCHOOL OF. So that the Palace of Fontainebleau should be decorated in a manner worthy of its nature and function, a number of Italian artists were called in, with the result that it became a flourishing centre of artistic activity in the Mannerist style. The leaders were Il Rosso (1490–1540), Francesco Primaticcio (1504–1570) and Niccolò dell'Abbate (1512–1571). The motifs exploited by this group, which later developed into a 'school', were mythology, allegory and landscape. It succeeded in superimposing French elegance and lightness upon the elongated figures of Mannerist tradition.

297

208. GHIBERTI, *'Paradise Gateway' Florence, Baptistery*

FOPPA, VINCENZO (1427/30–1515/16), was the leading artist of the Lombard school of the Early Renaissance, which he founded.

FRANCESCA, PIERO DELLA (c. 1416–1492), from Borgo San Sepolcro, was always regarded as the head of the Umbrian School but has only recently been recognised as one of the greatest of all Italian painters. He succeeded in solving all the representational problems of his time and in particular in uniquely synthesizing the pictorial vision of the Venetians and the plastic sense of the Florentines. There is no doubt that he was aided by his stay in Florence and by his teacher, Domenico Veneziano, who made him familiar with the way in which light reveals form. But Piero went far beyond his master by observing the effect of sunlight and painting it in bright, cool colours (the 'Baptism of Christ' in London; the 'Resurrection', Borgo San Sepolcro) – particularly in the lightly indicated landscapes of the background (portraits of Duke Federigo da Montefeltro and his wife in the Uffizi). This ability is also evident in his frescoes in S. Francesco in Rimini, and particularly so in the great cycle of St Francis in Arezzo, where in his 'Constantine's Dream', he for the first time produces in a fresco a credible version of nocturnal illumination. He was a great master of perspective, on which subject he published a book. He chose compositions of masterly simplicity. His figures, with their statuesque bearing, are both serious and dignified and have therefore the same true monumentality that we find at an earlier date in Masaccio and – earlier still – in Giotto (ill. p. 59).

FRANCIA, FRANCESCO (c. 1450–1517). This Bolognese painter began as a goldsmith and maker of coins. It was only at a late date that he came to painting, in which medium he expresses sensitivity and a deep piety. His pictures are chiefly to be found in Bologna and Munich. His large circle of pupils carried his influence into northern Italy.

FRUEAUF, RUELAND THE ELDER (c. 1445–1507), was active in Salzburg and Passau. Four pictures of the Passion by him have been preserved in Vienna. His son, Rueland the Younger (c. 1470–after 1545) painted the panels representing the 'Legend of St Leopold' in Klosterneuburg with their sensitive, fairy-tale landscapes (see, Danube School).

GALLEGOS, FERNANDO (c. 1440–after 1507), lived in Salamanca and was the most important master of the Castilian school of the 15th century. His realistic style of painting was strongly influenced by Flemish art. Works by him are to be found in Salamanca, Madrid and Zamora.

GEERTGEN TOT SINT JANS (c. 1460/65–1490/95), was a lay brother of the Order of St John (hence his name). He was born in Leyden and worked in Haarlem. He is an important figure in Early Renaissance painting in Holland, painting nature, men and objects from direct observation. His chief works are altar-pieces, now in Vienna (the 'Lamentation' and the 'Burning of the Bones of John the Baptist') and the picture in Berlin showing the John the Baptist in a spacious landscape.

GERHARD, HUBERT (c. 1550–1620), was a Dutch sculptor chiefly active in southern Germany. Influenced by Giovanni da Bologna, he was responsible for, *inter alia,* the splendid Augustus fountain in Augsburg and the bronze group of St Michael triumphing over Lucifer in St Michael's, Munich.

GHIBERTI, LORENZO (1378–1455), was trained as a goldsmith and was for a short time also active as a painter. His main works are the bronze doors of the Baptistery in Florence. Between 1403 and 1424, Ghiberti worked on the 28 reliefs on the North door which depict scenes from the New Testament and figures of the Evangelists and Fathers of the Church. The softly modelled figures and groups, each in its quatrefoil, stand out plastically from the background. Between 1425 and 1452, he completed the East door which Michelangelo called the Gateway to Paradise (ill. 24, 208). In ten compartments there are scenes from the Old Testament, surrounded by statuettes and busts. Here the tension of the compositions of the North door, which are still partly Gothic in style, is abandoned for a more pictorial and, at the same time, more epic style. The relief ranges from the finest bas-relief to high relief. Ghiberti also produced, *inter alia,* the bronze figures of John the Baptist (1404), St Matthew and St Stephen (1428) for the church of Or San Michele. His memoirs are important for an understanding of the history of Florentine art.

GHIRLANDAJO, DOMENICO (1449–1494), belongs to the last generation of the Florentine Early Renaissance. His simply composed frescoes in S. Maria Novella

GIORGIONE: Concert Champêtre

TITIAN: The Tribute Money

PAOLO VERONESE: The Adoration of the Kings

TINTORETTO: The Adoration of the Kings

and S. Trinità, Florence, impart an air of earnestness and dignity. In his paintings – particularly those from his early period – he endeavours to replace stiffness and seriousness in handling by greater tenderness ('Grandfather and Grandchild'; altar-pieces, portraits).

GIORGIONE (1476/77–1510), whose real name was Giorgio del Castelfranco, is one of the most important of the Venetian painters of the High Renaissance. He was a pupil of Giovanni Bellini, whose influence can still be felt in the 'Virgin of Castelfranco'. But he soon outgrew him and reached that pitch of perfection where body and mind, nature and art, form and content, are in constant harmony. Only a few of the paintings which have been ascribed to Giorgione are considered to-day by art critics to be certainly attributable to him – 'Judith' (Leningrad), 'The Three Philosophers' (Vienna), 'Portrait of a Young Woman' (Vienna), 'The Storm' (Venice). The following are very probably by him: 'The Judgment of Solomon' (Florence), the 'Sleeping Venus' (Dresden), in which the background was perhaps completed by Titian; 'The Concert' (Florence) and the 'Fête Champêtre' (Paris, ill. p. 299). Particularly in the last of these paintings, we see Giorgione's especial skill in 'spiritualizing' landscape and making of man and nature an indissoluble unity. Giorgione had a strong influence on Titian and on both Venetian and Italian painting.

GIOVANNI DA BOLOGNA (1529–1608), also known as Giambologna, was born in Douai but emigrated to Florence by way of Antwerp. As the leading master of the Mannerist school, he was the most important sculptor of his day in Italy; thanks to his large circle of pupils, his influence spread far beyond its frontiers (see p. 273). Technically, he was unaware of difficulties and never sought to avoid them; thus he aimed to make his free-standing sculptures equally effective and equally surprising from all angles (e. g. the 'Rape of the Sabine'). His work is varied – fountains (the Neptune fountain, Bologna), equestrian statues (Cosimo I, Florence), statuary for gardens and ornamental pieces. (Ill. 200)

GOES, HUGO VAN DER (c. 1440–1482), was born in Ghent and died in the Roode Clooster, Brussels. He is one of the most important early Flemish painters. His Portinari Altar (Uffizi) is world-famous. It had a strong influence on Italian painting (cf. Ghirlandajo's 'Adoration' and Piero della Francesca). His contemporaries were astonished and delighted by the pastoral feeling which surrounds this 'Birth of Christ', by the combination of elegance and brittle delicacy with country realism (ill. 209). His 'Montforte Altar' in Berlin was earlier believed to be by Rubens because of its brilliant range of colour.

GOLTZIUS, HENDRIK (1558–1617), who was, in his day, a famous Dutch draughtsman and engraver, is the father of the reproduction engraving (cf. p. 284).

GONÇALVES, NUNO (fl. 1450–1471). Only a few works by this Portuguese painter are known but they stand comparison, in their power and glowing colour, with their Flemish models. In the National Museum, Lisbon, there are two triple altars painted on oak and dedicated to St Vincent, which bring together Portuguese of high and low degree – knights, monks, scholars and simple fishermen – round the figure of the patron saint of Lisbon.

GOSSAERT, JAN (c. 1478–1533/36), also known as Mabuse, was one of the first Flemish Romanists (see p. 276). In his composition and his use of light, as well as in his employment of architectural motifs, his pictures, while still preserving certain Flemish and Late Gothic traits, reveal Italian influence. In his drawings (woodcuts, etchings and engravings) Mabuse owed much to Dürer. (Ill. p. 271)

GOUJON, JEAN (1510/14–c. 1568), was a French Renaissance sculptor who worked chiefly in Rouen and Paris. In his life-size reliefs of nymphs (Fontaine des Innocents, Paris) and his architectural decoration, e. g. of the façade of the Louvre by Lescot (q. v., ill. 212), he combined classical tradition with the natural grace of French taste. His work was a model for his successors.

GOZZOLI, BENOZZO (1420–1498), was one of the most sought-after fresco painters in Florence. He worked on his commissions with unwearying energy. Their uninhibited delight in narrative, their gaiety and vividness can be seen in the Old Testament cycle in the Camposanto in Pisa or in the frescoes in the Medici Chapel in Florence (Palazzo Medici-Riccardi).

GRAF, URS (c. 1485–c. 1527), the Swiss goldsmith and draughtsman, left a number of brilliantly sketched pen drawings and woodcuts depicting rough soldiery and military scenes; they are partly in 'white-cut' (cf. p. 283, ill. 203). The only picture known to be by him – 'War' – is in Basle.

209. VAN DER GOES, *Nativity. Centre part of the so-called 'Portinari Altar'*

GRECO EL (1541–1614), whose real name was Domenico Theotocopulos, was born in Crete, but came to Venice at an early age, where he became a pupil of Titian and was strongly influenced by the work of Tintoretto. In 1570 he was in Rome and Viterbo; from 1577 he lived in Toledo. He, more than any other painter, contrived to express in his religious Mannerism the fanatical religious zeal of the Spaniards. His pictures are the visions of a being passionate in his belief – the products of religious ecstasy. The exaggeratedly long bodies seem incorporeal; a shimmering alternation of light and shade, together with colours that are phosphorescent, strengthen their other-worldly appearance ('The Burial of Count Orgaz', Toledo/Santo Tomé; 'The Scourging of Christ', Madrid/Prado, etc.). El Greco also produced a number of portraits in which the sitters' serious eyes look beyond the things of this earth. (Ill. p. 314)

GRÜNEWALD (c. 1460/70–1528), whose real name was Mathis Gothardt-Neithardt or Nithardt, was born in Würzburg. About 1500, he founded a workshop in Seligenstadt, Aschaffenburg. He collaborated closely with the Archbishops of Mainz and finally became Court painter to the Cardinal Prince Albrecht of Brandenburg (Archbishop of Mainz and Bishop of Halle). In his religious works, Grünewald displays a mystical piety. His representations of the Crucifixion are the expressions of a heart laden with pity, which re-lives fearlessly and with immense passion, the death on Golgotha (Isenheim Altar, Tauberbischofsheim Altar, ill. p. 285). His main work is the Isenheim Altar in Colmar – a triple altar which when shut, shows the Crucifixion, when open, (1) Christmas and the Angel Concert with the Annunciation and the Resurrection at the sides, and (2) portraits of saints with Hagnower's carved figures in the centre. Other important works by Grünewald are Christ Carrying the Cross and the Crucifixion from the altar at Tauberbischofsheim, Stuttgart, the Stuppach Madonna, the 'Mocking of Christ', the 'Meeting of St Maurice and St Erasmus' (Munich) and portraits (Cologne). There are important drawings by Grünewald in Berlin. His expressive colours and his mystical ecstasies place Grünewald somewhere between Reformation and Counter-Reformation – too modern for the Middle Ages and too primitively Christian for the Renaissance. He was therefore virtually forgotten until this century. There are works by him in Basle, Karlsruhe, Munich and famous crayon drawings in Berlin. (Ill. 3)

HERING, LOY (1484/85–after 1554). More than 100 works by this Renaissance sculptor can be authenticated, including drawings and life-size wooden crucifixes. His finest work is undoubtedly the more than life-size seated figure of St Willibald in Eichstätt.

HERRERA, JUAN DE (c. 1530–1597), was born in the Asturias and was employed after 1563 on the building of the Escorial under Juan Bautista de Toledo, whom he followed as master of works (ill. 207). He was designated Court architect and was responsible for the south façade of the Toledo Alcazar; rebuilt the castle of Simancas; drew up the plans for the Bourse in Seville and for Valladolid Cathedral; and erected the Segovia bridge in Madrid. He is considered to be the originator of the bare, strong "desornamentado" style.

HILLIARD, NICHOLAS (c. 1547–1618/19), was the most important English miniaturist and also a goldsmith and jeweller. His miniatures are distinguished by their clear outlines and by the careful rendering of all the details of clothing and jewellery. There are many examples of his work in the Royal Collection, Windsor Castle.

HOLBEIN, HANS, THE ELDER (c. 1465–1524), belonged to the transitional period between German Late Gothic and the Renaissance. He worked mostly in his native town of Augsburg and painted a series of great altars (e. g. the St Sebastian Altar, Munich). Numerous drawings by him – particularly portraits – have been preserved (Berlin, Kupferstichkabinett).

HOLBEIN, HANS, THE YOUNGER (1497–1543), from Augsburg, became a citizen of Basle in 1520. Here he obtained his first big commissions – portraits of the Burgomaster Meyer and his wife, the decoration of the Council Chamber and paintings for churches. In 1526, he travelled to London for the first time and spent two years there. In 1532, he finally settled in London, where he became Court painter to Henry VIII. Holbein is one of the greatest of portrait-painters. He incorporated in his entirely personal style the new discoveries of Renaissance painting and assimilated German, Dutch, Italian and French innovations. Holbein looks at his models objectively and with detachment. He paints them mostly from a slight angle and sets them in their characteristic surroundings ('The Ambassadors', London; portrait of Erasmus, Louvre; portrait of the merchant Gisze, Berlin, ill. p. 290). All the details such as the sheen of a costume (Henry VIII, Windsor), the gay patterns on the 'Holbein carpets', flowers, books, instruments and metal-ware are painted with great skill. The personal style of the artist is perhaps even more pronounced in his drawings in Windsor Castle than in his paintings; their delicate line achieves a very high degree of characterization. Holbein also did important work in the field of the woodcut (ill. 210).

210. HANS HOLBEIN THE YOUNGER, *The Pedlar. Woodcut from the 'Dance of Death'*

304

HOLL, ELIAS (1573–1646), was one of the few German architects of his time to achieve the pure formal style of the Renaissance (Palladio). As town architect of Augsburg, which was then a flourishing commercial city, he constructed a number of secular buildings, in particular the massive Town Hall (1615–1620) which is distinguished by the excellence of its articulation (ill. 211). On either side of the central buildings, turretted staircases were built and smaller rooms for offices inserted in the angles. The focal point of the whole edifice was the Golden Hall which was more like a town square than an internal room. It was burnt out in World War II but is to be rebuilt.

HUBER, WOLF (c. 1485–1553). In 1515, Huber began to work in Passau and later became Court painter to the Bishop there. Next to Altdorfer, he is one of the most important representatives of the Danube school (q. v.), with whom he shares his love for painting his native landscape, in which he sets his human figures. Few of his paintings are known to us (scenes from the Passion, e. g. in Munich; 'Rest on the Flight into Egypt', Berlin). A large number of his woodcuts are preserved; they, and even more his drawings, reveal a lyrical and romantic sensibility.

JAMNITZER, WENZEL (1508–1584). The work of this goldsmith, who along with his brothers, sons, and sons-in-law, ran the most famous workshop of his time in Nuremberg, decorated the chambers and tables of the nobility. His precious vessels, goblets and services were extravagantly decorated in a host of variations with chased or applied ornamentation, with figures, semi-precious stones and animals.

KULMBACH, HANS VON (c. 1480–1522), whose real name was Hans Süss, was called after his birthplace. As a painter and draughtsman he was linked with Dürer who provided him with the rough sketches for his most impressive work, the Tucher Altar in Nuremberg. He painted fine glowing portraits and drew cartoons for stained glass.

LAURANA, FRANCESCO (c. 1420/25–1502), was a sculptor from the Dalmatian coast whose travels took him from Court to Court through Italy to Sicily and southern France. His works include the reliefs on the Triumphal Arch in Naples, a series of statues of the Madonna in Sicily and female portrait busts (Berlin, Florence, New York).

LEINBERGER, HANS (c. 1480/85–1531/35). Stylistically, the work of this sculptor and wood-carver falls between decadent Late Gothic and an anticipated Baroque. His monumental figures are hung with heavily draped robes, under which, we feel, the limbs have been formed by the Renaissance attitude towards the human body. (Virgin and Child, Landshut; altar at Moosburg; James the Elder, Munich, and the 'Resting Christ', Berlin – both sitting figures). His work is close to that of the Danube school (q. v.).

211. ELIAS HOLL, *Augsburg Town Hall*

LEONARDO DA VINCI (1452–1519). It was not only in painting that the genius of Leonardo was a seminal force – he also made very advanced architectural designs and astonished the world in 1493 with his huge equestrian monument in Milan, of which the clay version was completed only to be destroyed by French troops in 1499. He was a musician and a virtuoso of the lute; as scientist, engineer and inventor, he was indisputably in the vanguard of his age. Of his paintings, only half a dozen pictures have been preserved, but he nevertheless introduced a new epoch in the history of the art. In the 'Last Supper' (1495–98) in the refectory of S. Maria delle Grazie in Milan, he succeeded, by using a daring technique, in applying to an old theme a new composition in the spirit of the High Renaissance. Unfortunately, the years have taken heavy toll of the fresco. In the 'Battle of Anghiari', which he painted for Florence, he produced highly animated scenes with riders, which anticipated Baroque and influenced Rubens, who copied part of the cartoon. Da Vinci's unfortunate addiction to technical experiment ruined the painting while he was still at work on it. In his 'Madonna of the Rocks' in the Louvre (ill. p. 277) he already employed the sfumato technique (cf. p. 29) and thus opened the way for a remarkable style of painting which later blossomed in Venice. The sweetness and grace of this picture is intensified in the wonderful harmony of his 'St Anne, Virgin and Child' in the Louvre, which is one of his most beautiful works. Here, the same wise, and yet secret smile plays round the features of St Anne, as was to enchant the whole world in the somewhat later Gioconda (ill. p. 26). The smile of Mona Lisa and its soft, blurred technique was copied by many imitators, but never again equalled. After his apprenticeship in Florence to Verrocchio, Leonardo was summoned to the Court of the Sforzas in Milan, which he left in 1499. He was in Florence until 1506 and then returned to Milan. In 1512, he was

305

in Rome; in 1517, he answered a call from Francis I of France. There, he occupied his last years with problems of drainage and hydraulics. He died at the Château of Cloux, near Amboise in his 67th year.

LESCOT, PIERRE (c. 1510–1578), was a Renaissance architect who, in collaboration with the sculptor Goujon, built the oldest wing of the Louvre (cf. p. 266, ill. 212). In 1544, he had concurrently begun the Hôtel Carnavalet; later, he erected the Fontaine des Innocents, an architecturally well-proportioned decorative fountain. Lastly, he produced the rood-screen for St Germain Auxerois of which some portions are to be found in the Louvre.

LEYDEN, LUCAS VAN (c. 1494–1533), was a Dutch painter and etcher, whose work was encouraged by his meeting with Dürer and his studies in Italy. His etchings are his best-known works; he produced his first considerable etching when only 14. Leyden was one of the leading Renaissance masters of his day in Holland.

LIPPI, FILIPPINO (1457–1504), was the son of Filippo Lippi and a pupil of Botticelli. He completed Masaccio's frescoes in the Brancacci Chapel. Probably under the influence of Flemish painting, he concentrated more and more on introducing rich detail into his paintings; although of considerable beauty, it has a somewhat disturbing effect on the composition as a whole.

LIPPI, FRA FILIPPO (c. 1406–1469), became a Carmelite at an early age and, from that date, painted almost exclusively angels and Madonnas, as Fra Angelico, the Dominican, had done before him; but his pictures, in spite of their pious radiance, are more realistic and earthy. He peoples Masaccio's empty spaces with a wealth of detail. Often in Lippi, Masaccio's solemn, statuesque calm is broken up – by a throng of common people, for example. Lippi flourished in Florence during the Early Renaissance; his works are to be found in Florence, Milan, Tarquinia, London, Paris, etc. There are frescoes by him in Spoleto (ill. p. 253).

LOTTO, LORENZO (1480–1556), was born in Venice and was a contemporary of such great Venetians as

212. The Louvre in Paris, oldest wing. Built by LESCOT, *architectural sculpture by* GOUJON

Giorgione and Titian. An unsettled, wandering life led him all over Italy and exposed him to a variety of influences. His sensitive nature made him concentrate lovingly on tiny details. He painted landscapes and portraits as well as religious and allegorical themes in a lively, naturalistic style.

MANDER, KAREL VAN (1548–1606). After his apprenticeship in Italy, this Dutch painter and author became head of the school of drawing in Haarlem, where one of his pupils was Frans Hals. He became famous less for his portraits in the Mannerist style than for *Het Schilder Boeck*, his collection of biographies of artists on the lines of Vasari (1604).

MANTEGNA, ANDREA (1431–1506), is the most important north Italian painter of the Quattrocento. He based his work firmly on the advances in the handling of form, space and perspective made in Florence during the Early Renaissance. His pictures are full of dignity; his figures are treated monumentally and drawn with a clear line. He used his knowledge of perspective and anatomy to produce daring foreshortenings ('Lamentation over the Dead Christ', Milan, ill. 201). As Court painter to the Gonzagas, he decorated the walls and ceilings of the Camera degli Sposi in the castle of Mantua with frescoes in which, by his illusory extension of space, he anticipates Correggio and the Baroque. He also produced outstanding etchings. Other important works are the frescoes in the Eremetani Chapel in Padua (largely destroyed in the Second World War), and the altar in S. Zeno Maggiore, Verona.

MASACCIO (1401–1428), whose real name was Tommaso di Giovanni di Simone Guidi, painted, in collaboration with Masolino who was twenty years his senior, a number of chapels, among them the Brancacci Chapel in Florence, in which the 'Expulsion from Eden' and the 'Tribute to Caesar' are probably Masaccio's most important individual works (ill. p. 252). He was a contemporary of Brunelleschi, whose theories on space and perspective are evident in Masaccio's work. In the limpid space of his paintings impressive figures, conceived plastically, arrange themselves in groups and seem to be held together by a secret inner relationship. The decorative ornamentation of Late Gothic has disappeared from an empty scene in which the only force at work is the expressive power of Masaccio's men and women (cf. p. 274).

MASOLINO (1383–1447), whose real name was Tommaso di Cristoforo Fini, was active as a painter in Florence, Hungary, northern Italy and Rome. He was an assistant to Ghiberti and probably Masaccio's teacher. His main works are the frescoes in the collegiate church in Castiglione d'Olona on Lake Como and in S. Clemente in Rome.

MATSYS, QUINTEN or **METSYS** (1466–1530), was one of the Flemish masters from Antwerp who allowed themselves to be influenced by the Italian High

Renaissance and attempted to subdue their own spiritual unrest through the clarity of Italian art. His paintings and great altars are distinguished by their balanced composition, their precise draughtsmanship and their brilliant colouring ('The Moneychanger and his Wife', Louvre).

MASTER OF FLÉMALLE. In the first half of the 15th century, another artist was active alongside Jan van Eyck and Rogier van der Weyden; he occupied a position midway between them and, like them, is one of the true founders of Flemish painting. He derives his name from the altars in the abbey of Flémalle near Liège (now in the Städel Institute, Frankfurt), and is perhaps indentical with Robert Campin, who was born in Tournai in 1375 and died in 1444 at Doornik. Important works by the artist are the Mérode Altar (New York) and the altar of Canon Werl (Madrid/Prado). His painting is distinguished by strong realism and extremely plastic treatment of motifs from nature (Madonna in the Nat. Gall., London). Ill. 213

MAÎTRE DE MOULINS (fl. after 1480) was in the service of Duke Peter of Bourbon; he painted for the cathedral of Moulins a triptych with the Virgin and Child and the kneeling donors. Its deeply felt piety and the natural freshness of the portraiture are typical of his work. Other works are the 'Birth of Christ with Cardinal Rolin' (Autun Museum), 'Virgin and Child' (Brussels); portrait of Cardinal Charles II of Bourbon (Munich/Pinakothek) and the 'Annunciation' (Chicago/Art Inst.).

MEIT, CONRAD (c. 1480–c. 1550), came from Worms and was Court sculptor to Margarethe, Stattholder of the Netherlands, in Malines and Antwerp. In his favourite materials – alabaster ('Judith', Munich/National Museum), beechwood and bronze – he produced beautiful, polished sculptures. His larger works (e. g. the monuments for Margarethe and her family in Brou) are distinguished, for all their realism, by their unfailing charm.

MELOZZO DA FORLÌ (1438–1494). This Umbrian painter of the Early Renaissance was active in his native town Forlì, in Rome, Urbino and Loreto. In his paintings for walls and ceilings he aimed at spatial unity. He did not conceive of the walls as planes but attempted to include them in the spatial effect by using foreshortened perspective (e. g. the 'Ascension' in S. Apostoli, Rome). In this respect, Melozzo is a predecessor of Correggio and the illusionist painting of the Baroque. (Ill. p. 254)

MEMLINC, HANS (1430/40–1494), born in Seligenstadt near Aschaffenburg, lived in Bruges from 1465. He is one of the best-known Flemish painters of the 15th century; about 100 of his paintings have survived. Memlinc employed a careful style and delighted in perfect reproduction of precious materials, gleaming jewels and paradisial gardens. His main works are the altar with the 'Betrothal of St Catherine' (Bruges); the

213. Master of Flémalle, Male portrait

'Last Judgment' (Danzig); the 'Legend of St Ursula' (Bruges) and admirable portraits. (Ill. p. 263)

MICHELANGELO BUONARROTI (1475–1564). Michelangelo was born at Caprese in the upper valley of the Tiber, of an old Florentine family. He was apprenticed in Florence to Ghirlandajo but left him when he was fourteen in order to become a sculptor. After youthful works like the 'Bacchus' in Florence and the intensely sad 'Pietà' in St Peter's, he established himself with the colossal statue of 'David' (Florence), ranking thereafter with Leonardo as the most important master of his day. Michelangelo was at one and the same time sculptor, architect, painter and poet; all he attempted was on an enormous scale, for which reason much of his work remained fragmentary. He frequently had to defend his original plans by laborious arguments with his patrons in order to carry them through. Before his death he was able to complete for the tomb of Julius II – originally planned with forty figures and begun in 1505 – only the great statue of Moses (Rome/S. Pietro in Vincoli, ill. 199) and some figures of slaves. A similar fate befell the original concept of the Medici tombs. In his sculptures a titanic will seems to be struggling with the sheer weight of the material; he attempts to express himself in terms of sculpture by the use of 'counterpoise' and daring devices of overlapping. When asked why he gave even women and saints the stature of giants, Michelangelo is said to have replied that they would otherwise have been incapable of bearing the burden of their fate. In his last work, the 'Rondanini Pietà' (Milan, ill. 19), the stone was intractable and broke, but, by radically altering his plans, Michelangelo was able to create a work expressing a sorrow not of this

*214. PALISSY, faience dish with cast representations of
plants and animals (so-called 'Palissy ware')*

world – a peak of spiritual grief. In his painting,
Michelangelo could not conceal that he was a
sculptor. From 1508 to 1512 he painted – lying on his back on
a high scaffolding – the frescoes of the Sistine Chapel
in Rome. The immense figures of his sibyls, prophets
and figures from the story of the Creation, conceived in
completely plastic terms, seem to belong to a race of
Titans (ill. 1, p. 278). The same is true of the vision of
the 'Last Judgment', painted between 1534 and 1541 on
the wall of the chapel, with its youthful, heroic Christ
standing in judgment over the surging mass of the
damned and the blessed as they ascend or fall. Thereafter,
Michelangelo remained in Rome in his capacity as architect. Between 1524 and 1534, before leaving Florence,
he had built the Biblioteca Laurenziana with its daring
staircase; subsequently, he drew up the plans for the
great dome of St Peter's and built the Palazzo dei Conservatori on the Capitol, which he laid out as the first
planned square of modern times (cf. p. 265, ill. 195).

MICHELOZZO (c. 1396–1472), whose real name was
Michele di Bartolommeo, was a Florentine architect and
sculptor who in 1446 succeeded Brunelleschi as Cathedral Architect of Florence. He built monasteries and
palaces for Cosimo de' Medici, and was undoubtedly
the most sought-after architect of his time. In the
Palazzo Medici-Riccardi in Florence he left a greatly
admired prototype for the palaces of the future. A large
number of marble Madonnas (e. g. in Berlin), of terra-
cotta figures, friezes and ornaments for doors are
ascribed to him.

MINO DA FIESOLE (1430/31–1484) is one of the leading Florentine sculptors of the Quattrocento. He was
responsible for pulpits, altars, tombs and eloquent portrait busts (Niccolò Strozzi, Berlin).

MO(O)R, ANTHONIS (1519–1576/78), alias Antonio
Moro, was a Flemish painter who trained under Jan
van Scorel. He was, after Titian, one of the leading
portrait painters of his time: his cool and calculating
style of portraiture was prized by the Courts in Brussels, Lisbon, Madrid and London.

MORALES, LUIS DE (c. 1500–1586). In the work of
this Spanish painter of biblical themes, particularly
scenes from the Passion, Italian (Leonardo) and Flemish
influences unite with the typical religious intensity of
Spanish painting to produce pictures with an ikon-like
quality and power.

MORETTO (c. 1498–1554), whose real name was
Alessandro Bonvicino, was born in Brescia and worked
for some time in Venice. In his altar-pieces he painted
charming Madonnas (Brescia, Verona, Milan) and scenes
from the Lives of the Saints (S. Francesco, Brescia).

MORONI, GIAMBATTISTA (c. 1525–1578), was one
of the best Italian portraitists of his age. He painted the
well-to-do middle classes with great psychological insight, preferably setting them against a domestic background.

NANNI DI BANCO (c. 1375–1421). Along with Ghiberti and Donatello, this Florentine sculptor, who portrayed calm figures in controlled, dignified poses, made
an important contribution to the plastic art of the
Quattrocento ('Quattro Coronati' in the niches of Or
San Michele; the seated figure of St Luke in Florence
Cathedral).

OLIVER, ISAAC (c. 1556–1617), came from Rouen and
as a young man travelled to London, where he was
apprenticed to Hilliard (q. v.) as a painter of miniatures. His works depict the great figures of the age, such
as Queen Elizabeth, Mary Queen of Scots and the
family of James I.

PALISSY, BERNARD (c. 1510–1590), worked as a
potter for Catherine de' Medici. He produced vessels
decorated with casts of snakes, plants, fruit and shells,
and richly ornamented china decorated with reliefs, as
well as plates and saucers painted with copies of contemporary prints, and ornamental plaques (ill. 214).

PALLADIO, ANDREA (1508–1580), was the most
important architect of the Italian Late Renaissance. He
also wrote four books on architecture (1570). His most
important work, the so-called 'Basilica' in Vicenza
(1546), has two storeys of arcades, surrounding an older
ceremonial hall. He built a large number of palaces in
his native town, Vicenza (e. g. the Palazzo Chierigati).
His Teatro Olimpico was an attempt to give new life
to the tradition of the classical theatre. In the environs
of Vicenza, Palladio built a number of country houses
(e. g. the Villa Rotonda, ill. 215). His two famous Venetian churches, S. Giorgio Maggiore and Il Redentore,
are remarkable for their striking façades. Palladio had
a great influence on the architecture of England (see,
Inigo Jones), as well as that of Scandinavia, and in the
classical period was also much admired in Germany
(Palladianism).

PALMA, JACOPO (c. 1480–1528), known as Palma
Vecchio, was a Venetian painter of the High Renaissance. In style he has much in common with Titian and

Giorgione. His portraits of women were much sought after ('Violanta', Vienna; 'The Three Sisters', Dresden). In them, we see his womanly ideal – the blond, ample, sensually attractive Venetian. His main work is the triptych of St Barbara in S. Maria Formosa, Venice.

PARMIGIANINO or **PARMEGGIANINO** (1508–1540), whose real name was Francesco Mazzola, was one of the founders of Mannerism. His Madonnas are great ladies with slim figures, beautiful hands and refined gestures, holding the Child nonchalantly in their laps, (e. g. his Madonna in the Uffizi, ill. p. 313). His colours are brilliant and glittering, but cold. His painting is as well-bred as the society for which it was intended. The same applies to his portraits.

PATENIR, JOACHIM, also known as Patinier (1475/80–1524), was born in Antwerp and was one of the first Flemish painters to produce landscapes. Admittedly, he did not paint 'pure' landscapes, but his wide panoramas, seen from an elevated point of vantage, and peopled with numerous tiny conventional figures, are remarkable for their loving concentration on geological and botanical details.

PERUGINO (c. 1445/46–1523), whose real name was Pietro Vannucci, was called after the town of Perugia in which he settled after having worked in Florence and Rome. In Rome, he collaborated on the painting of the Sistine Chapel. His ideal of calm beauty is expressed in his frescoes and paintings with their clean construction and spacious landscapes. As the teacher of Raphael, he was greatly admired by the Nazarenes and Pre-Raphaelites.

PINTURICCHIO (c. 1454–1513), whose real name was Bernardino di Betti di Biagio, was born in Perugia. His frescoes with their wealth of figures frequently seem to give a glimpse into open country or into the depths of a landscape patterned with architectural elements (the Borgia apartments in the Vatican; the frescoes in the Cathedral Library, Siena).

PIOMBO, SEBASTIANO DEL (c. 1485–1547), who was of Venetian origin, was the painter of the High Renaissance responsible for introducing the style of Giorgione to Rome and attempting to strengthen it by the addition of Michelangelo's monumental, plastic power. His fine portraits are well-known (London, Hanover, Budapest).

PISANELLO (1395–1450), whose real name was Antonio Pisano, was born in Verona. He worked in several towns of northern Italy as a painter and maker of medallions. There are frescoes by him in S. Fermo, Verona; his paintings are to be found to-day in Verona and London. He progressed from the 'soft' Gothic style to a much clearer grasp of reality, which finds particular expression in his fine-lined drawings (in the Louvre) and in his astonishingly realistic animal drawings. His great skill as a miniaturist is demonstrated in the clear outlines of his portraits in profile (Paris, Bergamo).

215. PALLADIO, *Villa Rotonda in Vicenza*

POLLAIUOLO, ANTONIO DEL (1429/32–1498), worked as painter, sculptor, engraver and goldsmith. He concentrated particularly on the study of human anatomy (cf. p. 275). He liked to use mythological scenes in order to display the naked human body in movement. He was preoccupied with the same problem in the only one of his engravings to survive (ten nude men fighting, ill. 216) and in his numerous statuettes and small plastic figures. His finest pieces of sculpture are the bronze tombs for Popes Sixtus IV and Innocent VIII in St Peter's.

PONTORMO, JACOPO DA (1494–1556), whose real name was Jacopo Carrucci, was born in Florence. He aimed to achieve something more than the imitation and glorification of Nature. He arranged his figures decoratively in a solid system of straight and curved lines. His colours with their clear, shadowless tones have an unreal effect particularly when compared with the Venetian technique of using light to achieve modelling. The stages in the development of Pontormo's style also mark stages in the growth of Mannerism. He was, besides, an excellent portrait-painter.

PORTA, GIACOMO DELLA (c. 1537–1604). The most important commission entrusted to this extremely active Roman master was the vaulting of the dome of St Peter's on the basis of designs by Michelangelo. He built the façade of the Il Gesù, the Jesuit church in Rome, and worked on S. Maria dei Monti and S. Luigi dei Francesi as well as on the Palazzo Chigi and the Palazzo Farnese.

216. POLLAIUOLO, *ten nude men fighting, copper engraving*

217. LUCA DELLA ROBBIA, *Virgin and Child, faience*

QUERCIA, JACOPO DELLA (1364 or 1367–1438), was a Sienese master of the Early Renaissance. Into his sculpture he sought to introduce a new element of exalted and magniloquent solemnity (reliefs on the Fonte gaia, Siena; bronze reliefs on the font in Siena Cathedral; reliefs for the main door of S. Petronio, Bologna).

RAPHAEL (1483–1520), whose real name was Raffaello Santi, was born in Urbino and was a pupil of Perugino. At an early age he went to Florence and under the influence of Leonardo and Michelangelo soon lost all his provincial limitations. In 1508, he went to Rome where his amiable temperament and his art, which was 'pleasing' in the best sense of the word, soon gained him one effortless success after another. He painted Le Stanze – the apartments of the Pope – for Julius II (the 'School of Athens', the 'Disputa' and the 'Expulsion of Heliodorus'). After the death of Bramante, he took charge of the building of St Peter's, drew the cartoons for the tapestries in the Sistine Chapel, supervised the decoration of the loggias in the Vatican and worked, simultaneously, on the 'Galatea' cycle in the Villa Farnese. He also produced the great portraits of Julius II, the famous 'Sistine Madonna' (Dresden, ill. 52) and the 'Madonna della Sedia' (Florence/Palazzo Pitti) in which the circular shape of the picture – the tondo – makes the impression of the close bond between Mother and Child still stronger (ill. p. 279). The model for Raphael's Madonnas was no earthly beauty; he said that, in his work, he followed *'una certa idea'* – that is to say, an inner vision deriving from his inspiration. In Raphael, painter of the High Renaissance, the aspirations of an age find fulfilment. Thanks to his deep understanding of art he was able to construct his works according to the laws of the classical canons. A rich intuitive sense provided him with an abundance of ideas and his talent allowed him to give complete expression to them. Hardly any other artist has been so loved and cherished over the centuries. In him the connoisseur has found a degree of artistic perfection such as has seldom been attained; while the pious have found in his work an expression of divine gentleness and beauty. (Cf. ill. 36)

RAIMONDI, MARCANTONIO (c. 1480–c. 1534). This Italian engraver left more than 300 engravings of Raphael's paintings. He was one of the inventors of the reproduction.

RICCIO, ANDREA (c. 1470–1532), whose real name was Andrea Briosco, came from a goldsmith's family in Padua. He cast great, richly decorated candelabra for the choir of S. Antonio in Padua. He was chiefly known for his bronze figurines – shepherds with their beasts, satyrs, nymphs, etc.

ROBBIA, LUCA DELLA (1399–1482), is one of the most important artists of the Florentine Early Renaissance. Among his most important works are the reliefs on the *cantoria* (singers' gallery) in Florence Cathedral. He found his own style by applying the technique of faience to large-scale sculpture. The soft, glazed, brilliantly-coloured material allowed him to give the most immediate expression to his warm artistic temperament. He chiefly produced architectural reliefs with Madonnas (ill. 217), prophets, saints, etc. (Capella Pazzi, Florence). His family carried on his workshop. Andrea della Robbia (1435–1525), for instance, was responsible for the medallions with babes in swaddling clothes on the Foundling Hospital in Florence.

ROME, PALAZZO DELLA CANCELLERIA. This palace, which was built between 1486 and 1496, is one of the few Early Renaissance buildings in Rome. In this impressive edifice the upper storeys of the façade are divided by pilasters into rhythmical travées; it is grouped round a *cortile* with arcades on two levels.

ROME, PALAZZO FARNESE. This monumental building was begun by Antonio da Sangallo, who carried out the greater part of the work – especially the lower storeys of the *cortile*. After his death, Giacomo della Porta built the loggia facing the Tiber and Michelangelo the somewhat heavier third storey. The murals by Annibale Carracci are famous.

ROME, ST PETER'S. In the middle of the 15th century, the plans were prepared for a huge new building to be erected on the site of the basilica of Old St Peter's, built above the presumed tomb of the Saint (ill. 46). Until 1626 the new structure gave employment to the most important architects of the age. Bramante, who was put in charge of the work in 1506, evolved the brilliant plan for a domed building arranged as a Greek cross. After Bramante's death (1514) there came a period of lively but, as it transpired, unfruitful discussion. Although such great masters as Raphael, Peruzzi, and both the Sangallos were engaged on the work, nothing decisive was achieved until Michelangelo took over in 1547. In principle, Michelangelo adhered to Bramante's plan but simplified it greatly and strengthened it structurally. His greatest achievement was the dome which, inter-

310

PIETER BRUEGEL THE ELDER: The Peasant Wedding

CORREGGIO: Madonna with the Basket

PARMIGIANINO: Madonna del Collo Lungo *(Madonna with the long neck)*

EL GRECO: Espolio *(Disrobing of Christ)*

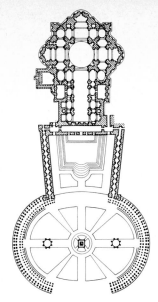

218. St Peter's, Rome,
aerial view from E.

219. St Peter's,
Rome, ground-plan

nally, is 390 feet high. Its imposing piers and the clean line of the cupola are among the greatest achievements of architecture. After Michelangelo's death (1564), work was continued by Vignola and Giacomo della Porta. Maderna added the nave in 1606. Bernini's colonnades in the piazza provide a splendid setting for the largest church in Christendom (ill. 218, 219).

ROSSELLINO, ANTONIO (1427–1479) and **BER-NARDO** (1409–1464). The Rossellino brothers were Florentine sculptors and architects of the Early Renaissance. Antonio's best-known work is the splendid tomb of the Cardinal of Portugal in S. Miniato al Monte in Florence. Other works by him are the reliefs of the Madonna (Berlin) and marble busts (London and Florence). Bernardo received a large number of commissions in Rome from Pope Nicholas V. When designing the tomb of the humanist, Leonardo Bruni, he placed the sarcophagus in a semicircular niche and thus set the pattern for wall tombs for his century.

SANGALLO. Two members of this family of Italian architects, which had a decisive influence on the architectural and artistic development of Rome for almost fifty years, are particularly distinguished. Giuliano da Sangallo (1445–1516), who was born in Florence, was the builder of the centrally planned S. Maria delle Carceri in Prato (cf. p. 260). A charming work by him is the Villa Reale at Poggio a Caiano; with its white loggias and terraces, it became a model for the Italian country house. Antonio da Sangallo (1485–1546), nephew of Giuliano and a pupil of Bramante, built, *inter alia*, the Palazzo Farnese (q. v.), and was for some time in charge of the rebuilding of St Peter's.

SANMICHELI, MICHELE (1484–1559) from Verona, was a Late Renaissance architect, who set his stamp on his native town in the 16th century (the town walls with the two ornamental gates, Porta Pallio and Porta Nuova). Of his secular buildings, the Palazzo Bevilacqua, with its rhythmical colonnades, and the Palazzo Canossa, with its double pilasters, have been much imitated.

SANSOVINO, ANDREA (1460–1529), whose real name was Andrea Contucci, was the Florentine architect responsible for the graves of the prelates, Girolamo Bassa and Ascanio Sforza, in the choir of S. Maria del Popolo, Rome. Instead of placing the graves in niches in the walls, he incorporated them in a triumphal arch. He also created the monumental 'Baptism of Christ' above the east door of the Baptistery in Florence.

SANSOVINO, JACOPO (1486–1570), whose real name was Tatti, was responsible not only for the Corner and Dolfin Palazzi in Venice but also for the splendid Library of St Mark, which is one of the most important Renaissance buildings in Italy (ill. 196). The Zecca (Mint) and the delicate Loggetta at the foot of the Campanile of St Mark's are also his. He later produced sculptured figures to decorate his own and other buildings in Venice (the statues on the roof of the Library of St Mark, the figures of the Evangelists in St Mark's; the colossal statues of Mars and Neptune on the steps of the Doge's Palace).

SARTO, ANDREA DEL (1486–1531). In his frescoes (the 'Madonna del Sacco' in the Santissima Annunziata and the 'Last Supper' in the Refectory of S. Salvi), in his altar-pieces (the 'Madonna delle Arpie' in the Uffizi) and in paintings (ill. p. 280), this Florentine painter of the High Renaissance used, by preference, a delicate, subdued chiaroscuro. His composition also has a soft, flowing, melodious line. Because of their accuracy, his crayon drawings earned him the name of 'Andrea senza errori' – the faultless painter.

SASSETTA (c. 1392–1451), whose real name was Stefano di Giovanni, was a Sienese painter whose religious paintings with their Gothic mould still belong to the medieval tradition; yet under the influence of the innovations of the Early Renaissance in Florence (Masaccio, q. v.) he attempted to achieve plastic treatment of figures and an effect of depth. One of his main works in Siena is the altar-piece of St Francis.

SCOREL, JAN VAN (1495–1562), a painter who was also an architect and musician, played a most important part in introducing the Italian Renaissance to Holland. A widely travelled humanist, he was for a time Raphael's successor as superintendent of the Vatican collections. His work – many altars by him were destroyed during the Reformation – attempted to fuse Venetian use of light and Raphael's classical forms with Dutch

315

realism. He was most successful in so doing in his portraits.

SIGNORELLI, LUCA (1445/50–1523). This pupil of Piero della Francesca strove in frescoes and altar-pieces to achieve monumental treatment of the human body. He is mainly known for his frescoes of the 'End of the World' in Orvieto Cathedral.

SODOMA (1477–1549), whose real name was Giovanni Antonio Bazzi, was the leading painter of the High Renaissance in Siena. His strength lies in his ability to capture a highly-charged incident (e. g. the 'Saint Sebastian' in the Uffizi), or scenes of passionate devotion. His painting tends towards the soft.

STEENWINKEL is the name of a family of Flemish artists who lived in Denmark and had a decisive influence on the architecture of the Danish Renaissance. Hans von Steenwinkel the Elder (c. 1545–1601) became Court architect. He collaborated in the building of the Kronborg near Helsingör and erected, *inter alia,* several buildings in the Italian Renaissance style for the astronomer, Tycho Brahe. Of buildings by his sons, Hans the Younger (1587–1639) and Laurens (1585–1619), the Copenhagen Bourse is of particular importance and is a jewel of Renaissance architecture in Northern Europe (ill. 220).

TINTORETTO (1518–1594), whose real name was Jacopo Robusti, is, by reason of his themes, the painter of the Counter-Reformation. In the matter of form, he is one of the great pioneers of Mannerism. Only his early works – they are mostly mythological in content – which show the influence of Titian, still accord with the classical law of harmony and beauty. Beginning with the 'Miracle of St Mark' (Venice/Accademia), he introduces a sense of movement which increases in the 'Passion of Christ' in the Scuola di San Rocco (Venice) and in the immense 'Paradise' in the Doges' Palace, and culminates in the extraordinary 'Last Supper' in S. Giorgio Maggiore. The composition disintegrates more and more into billowing masses which are fitfully lit by pale, ghostly light. Tintoretto had a strong influence on El Greco. But he points the way, too, to the magically lit world of Rembrandt; while the Impressionists on the one hand, and the Expressionists on the other, also owe something to his work. (Ill. p. 302)

220. Hans van Steenwinkel the Younger *and* Laurens van Steenwinkel, *Copenhagen Stock Exchange. Northern Renaissance building*

TITIAN (1476/77–1576), whose real name was Tiziano Vecelli, emigrated from the Dolomites to Venice. His life, which spans almost a century, covers in terms of historical development the period between the Early Renaissance and Early Baroque. The first period is taken up principally with devotional pictures; half-length figures, like the 'Madonna with Four Saints' (1505, Dresden) still recall his master, Giovanni Bellini. The second decade already sees world-famous works like the so-called 'Sacred and Profane Love' (Rome), which is strongly influenced by Giorgione and the 'Tribute Money' in Dresden (ill. p. 300). Only after Bellini's death (1516), does Titian begin to paint in a grand, independent manner. In the 'Ascension of the Virgin' (1518, S. Maria dei Frari, Venice) he creates a painting which is more grandiose than devotional and has an almost Baroque quality of pathos. In the 'Madonna with members of the Pesaro Family' for the same church, and in the 'Presentation of the Virgin in the Temple' (Venice/Accademia) the splendour of his palette, the flexible treatment of light, the crescendo and diminuendo of colour open up new vistas for painting. He largely neglects local colour and thereby achieves a kind of 'modelling', which Rubens and Velasquez developed and to which Delacroix and Cézanne were to turn. In the numerous portraits from this period he not only 'liberates' colour, but the whole art of painting – the brush strokes become open and have more impasto, the paint itself becomes something we experience. And these methods Rembrandt subsequently developed. In the 'Christ Crowned with Thorns' in Munich, painted when he was 95 years old, all these elements combine to produce one of the most stupendous of paintings – a work based on the emotional experience of an old man with a fiery temperament such as we find in no other painter.

TUDOR STYLE. A mixed Late Gothic and Renaissance style in England which took its name from the reigning royal House of Tudor (1485–1603). It was superseded at the beginning of the 17th century by the Palladian classicism of Inigo Jones.

TURA, COSIMO (1430–1495). Along with Francesco Cossa, Tura was one of the most important Ferrarese painters of the Quattrocento. A certain Late Gothic fussiness still lingers in his pictures together with a delight in curling lines and grotesques. His figures are highly volatile.

UCCELLO, PAOLO (c. 1400–1475), whose real name was Paolo Doni, was a Florentine painter of the Early Renaissance. All his life he was preoccupied with the problem of perspective, which he sought to apply in the composition of his paintings by means of a mathematical construction. He was one of the first artists to draw birds and plants from nature. His paintings of the Battle of San Romano (now in Paris/Louvre, London/Nat. Gall., and Florence/Uffizi, ill. p. 69), intended for the Palazzo Medici-Riccardi, earned him fame.

VASARI, GIORGIO (1511–1574). This versatile architect (e.g. of the Uffizi) and painter of Mannerist frescoes (Palazzo Vecchio, Florence), wrote in 1550 a series of biographies of the Italian painters of the previous 300 years. To-day it is the most important, if debated, source for the history of Renaissance art.

VENICE, LIBRARY OF ST MARK. This building in the Piazzetta has an extremely important function as a pendant to the Doges' Palace. It is two-storeyed, having arcades with Doric columns and a *piano nobile* with Ionian columns; its decorative style admirably suits the festive splendour of the city. Erected by Sansovino between 1532 and 1554 and decorated by Paolo Veronese, it is one of the best and most brilliant products of the Late Renaissance (ill. 196).

VERONESE, PAOLO (1528–1588), whose real name was Caliari, was born in Verona. He became the brilliant painter of the gay and splendid life of Venice. He delighted in painting an animated crowd of splendidly dressed men and women in spacious apartments and set them in the framework of biblical themes ('The Wedding at Cana', Louvre) and 'Christ in the House of Levi' (Venice/Accademia). He expresses his delight in the sensual brilliance of the world by such things as silk brocades, jewellery and splendid services; artistically, he expresses it by means of his finely graded palette, which has been admired throughout the centuries. A contemporary of the Mannerists, he embodied in the harmonious composition of his paintings the spirit of the Italian High Renaissance. (Ill. p. 301)

VERROCCHIO, ANDREA (1438–1488), whose real name was Andrea di Cione, is one of the universal geniuses of the Renaissance. His skill extended over the fields of sculpture and painting, woodcarving and goldsmith's work, music and mathematics. As a sculptor, he excels his Florentine contemporaries. Two of his most beautiful works are devoted to themes which Donatello had already handled with consummate artistry. His 'David' is no longer an idealized naked youth, but a figure with armour and sword. If Donatello's 'Gattamelata' shows us a wise strategist, in Verrocchio's equestrian statue of Colleoni we see a warrior chief looking imperiously into the distance (ill. 189). Further works by him include portrait busts (Lucretia Donati, in Florence), reliefs, funerary monuments, figures for fountains (e. g., the *putto* with the dolphin in the Palazzo Vecchio, Florence) as well as numerous small sculptures. Leonardo da Vinci was one of his pupils.

VIGNOLA, GIACOMO BAROZZI DA (1507–1573), was equally important as architect and theoretician in the Mannerist period. He built the Villa Giulia for Pope Julius in Rome with its original semicircular *cortile*. The most important of his works is the monumental, fortified castle at Caprarola, north of Rome. The design of the Roman Jesuit church, Il Gesù, became a pattern for later Baroque buildings (cf. p. 260, ill. 192).

VISCHER. Between 1453 and 1554 this family of metal-founders and sculptors left numerous important

221. VISCHER, *tomb of St Sebald in the Sebalduskirche, Nuremberg. Cast bronze*

works in Germany and Poland. Peter the Elder (c. 1460–1529) took over from his father, Herman the Elder, the family foundry in Nuremberg, which was established in 1453 and known as the Vischer workshop. He was responsible for the tomb of Archbishop Ernst of Saxony (Magdeburg Cathedral), and the statues of Theoderic and Artus for the Tomb of Maximilian in Innsbruck. In the case of the tomb of St Sebald (Sebalduskirche, Nuremberg), which is one of the most important examples of German Renaissance art (ill. 221), the basic structure is by Peter the Elder, while his two sons completed the tomb and decorated it with figures. Herman the Younger (1486–1517) probably worked on the three domed arches before he began his main work, the screen for the funerary chapel of the Fuggers in Augsburg, which is only partially preserved. Peter the Younger (1487–1528) produced the figures of children and the female figures supporting the candelabra which are entirely in the spirit of the Italian Renaissance. On his brother's death the youngest brother Hans (1489–1550) took over the workshop. He completed the Fugger screen and produced the Apollo fountain in the Market Square in Nuremberg.

WEYDEN, ROGIER VAN DER (c. 1399–1464), was born in Tournai where he studied under Robert Campin, who is probably the same person as the Master of Flémalle, and in 1436 became painter to the city of Brussels. Next to Jan van Eyck, he is the most important Flemish painter of the 15th century. During his journey to Italy in 1449–50 his work was greatly admired. Working in the Gothic tradition, he laid particular emphasis on draperies, which hang on his figures in a rich pattern of folds. The figures themselves lay bare their emotions by lively gestures (the 'Descent from the Cross', Escorial; the 'Adoration of the Magi', Munich, ill. p. 262). Unlike the van Eycks he concentrated more on over-all dramatic effect than on detail – his quiet portraits excepted.

317

Baroque and Rococo

222. *Sant' Agnese in Agone, Rome. Built by* Borromini *and* Rainaldi. *In the foreground the Fontana dei Fiumi and obelisk by* Bernini

The word 'Baroque' is of Romance origin and means 'irregular' or 'anomalous'. As applied to style in art it includes late Rococo and covers the period which begins with the supersession of Mannerism and ends with the rise of Classicism. This period extends approximately from 1600 to 1775.

By that time Humanism, the Renaissance and the Reformation had considerably lightened the burden of medieval constraint. The change had been accompanied by a progressive secularization of all walks of life and more independence of the sovereign power of the Church. But the Counter-Reformation movement, which set in about the middle of the 16th century, caused a reversal of these tendencies. The disorders of the wars of religion, which produced their worst effects during the Thirty Years' War, steadily diminished the economic and cultural importance of the middle classes. They relinquished the leading part which they had played during the Renaissance. The Church and the Princes recovered power. At the same time men began once more to take a deep interest in religion. The shock troops of the Counter-Reformation were constituted by the Order of the Jesuits, founded in 1534. The influence of this Order is still to be noted in the number of its churches still extant in Europe and in South and Central America.

In Spain the aims of the Counter-Reformation were allied with the idea of Spanish world-dominion. Spain endeavoured, by military violence, to force a decision in the Jesuits' underground campaign against Protestant Europe. The attempt failed with the loss of the Netherlands in 1581 and the rout of the Spanish Armada in 1588 by the rising naval power of England.

In England and the Netherlands these victories brought about, at the turn of the 16th and 17th centuries, economic progress and a consequent new cultural maturity. But Netherlandish art, as distinct from that of England and all the other European States, where secular and ecclesiastical absolutism determined – from Paris to St Petersburg, and from Stockholm to Rome – the aspect of art as of everything else, was supported by the broad masses of the people. It was given a general commercial value, to such an extent that pictures, for example, were accepted without hesitation as currency in case of need.

The dominant power in the 17th century was the France of Louis XIV. Its political absolutism affected the whole of public and spiritual life in Courts elsewhere, as though Versailles and its ruler, the 'Sun King', were the centre of the world. Every rank in society, each individual citizen, was allotted a fixed position in this 'planetary' system, where the monarch, enthroned at its centre in unapproachable majesty and a sort of divine perfection, subordinated the nation to his will. 'L'état, c'est moi,' he is said to have proclaimed – 'I am the State.' Even the greatest minds of the period did not dream of disputing the claims

Burgundian cabinet (16th century). Walnut overlaid with paint and gilt

Ceiling painting in the pilgrimage church at Steinhausen, *Württemberg.* DOMINICUS AND JOHANN BAPTIST ZIMMERMANN

GIOVANNI BATTISTA TIEPOLO: Asia. *Fresco on the stairway of the Residenz at Würzburg. Detail*

ANTONIO GRASSI: The Portrait-painter. *Viennese porcelain*

to omnipotence of an absolute monarch. In Molière's *Tartuffe*, when the plot seems to be thickening, towards the end, into a hopeless tangle, Louis XIV is brought on to the stage as an omniscient *deus ex machina*, who restores order with a single lordly gesture. All Europe was fascinated by the strictly regulated pattern of etiquette at the Court of Versailles. Frederick the Great wrote: 'There is no ruler, right down to the youngest representative of a subsidized dynasty, who does not imagine that he is some sort of a Louis XIV. He builds a Versailles, keeps mistresses and maintains armies.' This courtly absolutism obtained full recognition from secular art. The same artistic power and passion henceforward ruled in both secular and ecclesiastical spheres, where both types of patron, the absolute lay sovereign and the victoriously triumphant Church of the Counter-Reformation, vied with each other in the extravagant display of magnificence.

This pleasure in ostentation coincided with the delight of the age in theatrical performances. The meticulous ceremonial of the Court gave the character of a stage climax to the entry of the monarch. But the stage itself also celebrated his triumphs. The Theatre of the Jesuits, or the 'Caesarian Theatre' of the Habsburg emperors, the stately operas, produced at enormous expense, of the Court of Charles I of England, the Spanish Corpus Christi dramas, are all typical of the phenomenal heights to which passion for the stage had risen. England, France, Spain and Italy experienced, almost at the same time, a flourishing epoch of dramatic poetry. 'Grand' opera became the uncrowned queen of the period.

Life itself turned into a comedy and all the world into a stage. The ideal of human perfection was no longer the 'universal man', the versatile scholar of the Renaissance, but the 'honest man', the adroit horseman at home in all saddles, always in the fashion, whether in full-bottomed wig or stylized costume. It was no longer knowledge, but correct courtly behaviour, that counted.

It is one of the many paradoxical features of the age that this world-wide theatre, appealing to all the senses, sparkling and glittering in all the colours of the rainbow, also provided the scene for the irresistible advance of rationalism. The philosophies of such men as Descartes, Hobbes and Leibniz were associated with the observations made by Isaac Newton in the natural sciences. The figure of Newton affords a perfect example of the crystallization of the progress made in the 'exact' sciences, such as mathematics, physics and astronomy, since the Renaissance. Yet it was through this very penetration of the world and its phenomena by reason that in the 18th century the axe came to be laid to the root of the Baroque tree. While the emotional element in Baroque art was breaking up into the elegant and frivolous graces of Rococo, the intellectual movement of the 'Enlightenment' was already laying the foundations of a new cultural epoch. The great representative of this century was Voltaire, as Louis XIV had been of the previous one. The spirit of the Enlightenment, as it soberly, sceptically and with burrowing determination hacked away and exposed to the light the spiritual and political supports of the existing social order till in due course it tottered, is typified by such a work as the great French *Encyclopédie* in twenty-eight volumes. Outwardly it was a collection in alphabetical order of learned articles on philosophy, religion, literature, aesthetics, politics, economics, natural science and technology. But it contained a number of covert and skilful attacks on current spiritual and political doctrines. In the pastoral plays, novels and 'anacreontic' lyric verse of the Rococo period, in the minuets and serenades of its music and in the pastel shades of its painting the aristocratic culture of the past was once more attaining, though for the last time, an excessive refinement of polish. But the sheet-lightning of the Revolution was already perceptible in the writings of the encyclopaedists and their friends.

ARCHITECTURE

Ecclesiastical and secular absolutism, as patrons of Baroque architecture, determined the character of its designs, which reflected their own principles. In church architecture the tendencies of the late Renaissance, which had already begun to break down the classical harmony of buildings, formed a close

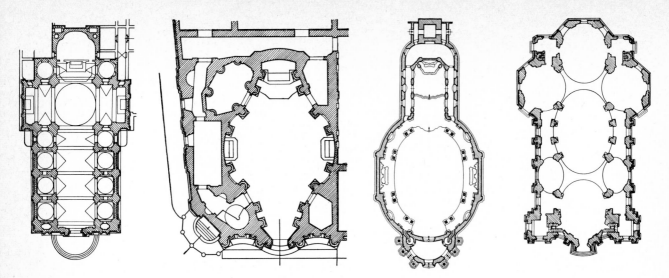

223. *Ground-plan with emphasis on the nave, issuing into the crossing: Sant' Andrea della Valle in Rome* (Maderna and Rainaldi) – *224. Elliptical ground-plan with alternation of concave and convex curves: San Carlo alle Quattro Fontane in Rome* (Borromini) – *225. Adoption north of the Alps of the elliptical structural scheme: pilgrimage church 'in der Wies'* (Dominikus Zimmermann) – *226. Interpenetration of elliptical and circular areas: pilgrimage church of the Vierzehnheiligen* (Balthasar Neumann)

alliance with the new conception of space developed as a result of the Baroque view of life. The Baroque architect started with the notion of a controlling total space, to which subsidiary spaces, as well as external construction and front elevation, were to be subordinated. The other arts, too, were taken into the service of this idea. Sculptors and painters contributed to the structure of a comprehensive work of art, governed in all its parts by the architect in charge of the whole undertaking.

In Italy this aspiration of Baroque style was fulfilled by Francesco Borromini. The interior walls of his churches are broken up into a series of separate niches of ample dimensions. The alternate concavities and convexities thus contrived produced a dynamic rhythm with wavelike effect. A similar rhythm was also applied to the front elevation. And finally, in order to extend it to the entire building, graceful lateral turrets were added to the cupola (ill. 222, 224).

Inside the church the most bewildering impressions of space were conjured up by exuberant decorations calculated to deceive the eye. They were provided by such costly materials as marble and ebony as well as by wood and plaster of little value. Such gorgeous decorative work was carried to extravagant heights beyond the Pyrenees in the style known as churrigueresque after its inventor Churriguera. He ornamented his surfaces with combinations of Baroque and Gothic with Moorish and even ancient Mexican and Peruvian motifs. His pillars, like his walls, were covered with several layers of a luxuriant growth of decoration (ill. 239).

Baroque church architecture came to a late flowering in Germany, where the ravages of the Thirty Years' War were succeeded by a passionate devotion to building in both urban and rural districts. Emperors and princes, ecclesiastical and secular potentates, engaged in deliberate mutual competition with a view to surpassing each other in this activity. At first foreign architects directed the work for a time. Then, about the year 1700, native builders began to make their appearance. The interlocking of space begun by Borromini in Italy led logically to an entirely free play of association between spaces filled with light and colour. Four lines of development can be traced in this connection.

The church of St Michael at München, with its emphasis on the nave, illustrates the 'Vorarlberg Cathedral Plan', which attempts an organic fusion of the barrel-vaulted, gallery-crowned nave and its chapel-recesses with the altar and choir space. The style was given splendid expression by the great South German architect Johann Michael Fischer.

A second architectural plan deals, as in Fischer von Erlach's Collegiate Church at Salzburg, with the old problem of the interpenetration of nave and central structure. This conception was tackled in the

Conventual Church at Weingarten and fully worked out – once more by J. M. Fischer – at Ottobeuren. The ground-plan is cruciform. Above the intersection of the nave rises a broad, low cupola. The transepts, equal in height and breadth to the middle aisle, thus expressly call attention to the intersection beneath the cupola, indicating its character as the controlling central space.

A third type of church, related to those of Borromini, extends the circular cupola-space so as to form an ellipse. It thus achieves the most natural amalgamation of the longitudinal nave and the central structure. South German architects have enriched this arrangement by a subtle introduction of light from concealed window-openings, as in Asam's Conventual Church at Weltenburg. Dominikus Zimmermann supplements the longitudinal oval of the inner wall by an additional surrounding row of pillars on the inside, which carry the vaulting. Light enters the oval inner spaces from all sides, creating an atmosphere both heartening and ceremonious in which to pray. The pillars of the inner circuit are, moreover, disposed in such a way that the visitor standing beneath the organ-loft remains unaware of the windows that admit the light (Wies and Steinhausen, ill. 225, p. 320).

The last line of development begins with Johann Dientzenhofer's church at the monastery of Banz. It ends with Balthasar Neumann's Pilgrimage Church of the 'Vierzehnheiligen' (1743–1772) which stands opposite the monastery. Contrasting with the sober external structure of the building, the interior consists of an alternation of interpenetrating elliptical and circular spaces. In the very middle of the church, and dominating it, stands the High Altar. It is at this point that the interplay of the various units of space begins. The Church of the 'Vierzehnheiligen' is also flooded with light from all sides, coming from great lateral windows hidden by the row of pillars extending along the middle aisle. The effect actually lends an insubstantial aspect to the material structure. The whitewashed pillars and pilasters, the gleaming gold of the stucco-work and the rich hues of the vast ceiling-painting, all contribute to the spell cast upon the pious pilgrim. (Ill. 226, 247)

Such ecclesiastical architecture was commissioned by the rich independent chapter-houses and abbeys engaged in rebuilding their monastic establishments and erecting numerous pilgrimage churches and chapels in open country. Their architects, Zimmermann and Dientzenhofer, the brothers Asam or J. M. Fischer, were originally domestic craftsmen and never ceased to operate as such.

Those who were originally rural artisans and remained to a great extent, in their art, associated with country life must be distinguished from those attached to the German princely Courts, who often came to architecture by way of the profession of 'Engineer Officer', as did Balthasar Neumann, Lucas von Hildebrandt and Daniel Pöppelmann.

But courtly Baroque architecture really originated in France. This type of architecture bears less relationship to Italian Baroque than to the palace-building of the Italian Renaissance, the theoretical principles of which, as laid down by such men as Alberti, Palladio or Vignola, had long found a second home in France. The French *Académie de l'Architecture* was concerned to maintain purity of style in structural design, just as its more famous sister institution, the *Académie Française,* superintended the use of language. When Lorenzo Bernini was invited to Paris by Louis XIV in 1665 to submit plans for the extension of the Louvre, the Italian's proposals met with determined opposition and were rejected in favour of those of Claude Perrault. The strict regularity of the latter's front elevation for the Louvre, arising from a single substructure, proves how literally French rationalism had interpreted the Italian theorists of the Renaissance.

A classical manner similar to that of France developed in England, where Sir John Vanbrugh (1666–1726) had been inspired by the palace at Versailles to erect buildings on a similarly huge scale at Blenheim, Castle Howard and Seaton Delaval. The two great English architects Inigo Jones and Sir Christopher Wren followed in the footsteps of Palladio, whose calm dignity of style evidently appealed to English taste (ill. 251). The country houses of the wealthy English nobility were equally inspired by

227. *View of the Palace and grounds of Versailles. Built by* Louis Levau *and* Jules Hardouin-Mansart, *Garden lay-out by* Le Nôtre *(copperplate by* Anton Averline *c. 1700)* – 228. *The Zwinger in Dresden (*Pöppelmann), *aerial view from S. E.*

Palladio's buildings. In England such mansions were surrounded by gardens designed to resemble natural landscape. William Kent (1685–1748) was the inaugurator of this novelty. The 'English Garden' gradually came to supersede the severely symmetrical lines of the Baroque park even in Central Europe.

But the most important secular buildings were the Baroque palaces. In these structures all the arts worked together for the glorification of absolutism. The Italian palazzo presented a forbidding, rigorously articulated façade and only opened out into a courtyard within. The palace, on the contrary, received its guests in a wide 'Court of Honour', which was, however, enclosed by railings to keep ordinary citizens at a distance. The front of the building no longer rose from the street itself but could be admired only by the courtiers admitted to the garden.

The palace of Versailles (ill. 227) magnified its proportions to the scale of a representative public building of great splendour, with rooms for more than ten thousand occupants. The enormous, tripartite Court of Honour and the impressive frontal elevation, 632 yards in length, facing Le Nôtre's famous gardens, with their geometrically arranged lawns and flower-beds, set an example of absolutist ambition in architecture which spread its influence far beyond the frontiers of France, till it reached St Petersburg itself. The vast design of the parks of such Baroque palaces took up so much space that they could not be confined within the cities and had literally to be forged out of the surrounding countryside. As many as 36,000 persons are said to have been simultaneously employed in the erection of Versailles alone.

Structures of dimensions similar to those of Versailles, at the gates of Paris, were established all over Europe. They included Schönbrunn at Vienna, Caserta at Naples, Peterhof at St Petersburg, Nymphenburg at Munich, Herrenhausen at Hanover and Ludwigsburg at Stuttgart. Ludwigsburg also provides an instance of the way in which whole new residential cities were built to surround the palace. The same thing happened at Mannheim (ill. 82), Potsdam and Karlsruhe. All these palaces are distinguished by a wealth of imagination in their architecture and use of space, developing and modifying the ideas of Versailles along independent lines (cf. Dresden Zwinger, ill. 228). Thus at the palace of Belvedere in Vienna, built by Lucas von Hildebrandt for Prince Eugene, the advancing and retreating lines of the façade diminish symmetrically in height from the centre to both wings, which terminate in corner pavilions (ill. 243). It is certainly a far cry from this development to its source in the massiveness of the Italian *palazzi* of the early Renaissance.

The interior of the Baroque palace, like its exterior, symbolizes absolutism. The long series of State apartments opening into one another in a straight line from door to door facilitates the ceremonious progress of the monarch, proceeding by prescribed stages, as though by clockwork. At Versailles the king's bedchamber is placed at the exact centre of the immensely long building, the other apartments being grouped round it like the honeycombs round the queen's cell in an apiary. The omnipresence of the divinely appointed ruler is represented in the Austrian and South German establishments of independent sovereigns

MICHELANGELO DA CARAVAGGIO: The Calling of St Matthew

PETER PAUL RUBENS: The Judgment of Paris

Nicolas Poussin: Bacchanalian Revel before a Term of Pan

Claude Lorraine: Morning Landscape (The expulsion of Hagar)

by the inclusion of a special imperial chamber furnished with lavish magnificence, as at Melk, St Florian and Schönthal. Staircases of vast proportions are generally a characteristic feature of the German palaces, as for example at Würzburg, Bruchsal, Brühl and Salzburg. They often occupy the entire width of the central section of the building. (Ill. 249, p. 321)

In Austria and South Germany even the library becomes a solemnly symbolic apartment. Costly cabinets of architectural proportions contain the treasured books which really played an important part in the courtly society of the time. For in order to succeed at Court it was necessary to prove oneself a cultured person, able to converse intelligently and wittily. We need only recall the famous 'round table' of Frederick the Great in this connection. Even in the wealthy monasteries special affection was lavished upon the libraries which were furnished with corresponding magnificence, as at Melk, Wiblingen and St Gallen (ill. 250).

The most impressive architectural features of a building therefore came more and more to be transferred to its interior. Henceforward the emotional aspect of Baroque gradually merged into the grace of Rococo. People grew tired of the stiff pomp of Baroque interiors. The walls of the rooms in a palace had still been treated, about 1700, in the same style as the outer front of the building. Massive mouldings projected downwards into the room. The wall surfaces were partitioned by pilasters and columns. But after 1720 the pilasters and columns were transformed into a mere framework, retreating, together with the mouldings, to the wall surface. The symmetry of the Baroque apartment and its massive symbolical splendour also yielded to ornamentation that was allowed to cover walls and ceiling with arrangements of shells (*rocaille*) and representations of fruits, flowers and climbing plants (ill. 70, cf. ill. 250). The charm of disproportion was discovered. Decorative pictures adorned hitherto empty surfaces. Wild animals peeped between the tangled foliage of painted jungles on the walls and took part in the general celebration of an unrestricted and graceful play of fancy. Miniature palaces replaced those of former days and were called by such names as Favorite, Eremitage or Sanssouci (ill. 248), like the summer residence of Frederick the Great, which introduced the style of 'Prussian Rococo', the king's personal contribution to architectural history. Rococo sounded the knell of the succession of great architectural styles that had flourished in Europe since the beginning of the Middle Ages. The last and most refined expression of the conception of a building as a comprehensive work of art are the designs of Robert Adam, who employed artists and designers in every field to execute his minute plans for the interior as well as the exterior of houses such as Syon, Osterley, Kenwood and Keddleston, which were severely classical in detail but were based on a Baroque conception of 'movement'.

SCULPTURE

The new, dynamic impulses of Baroque had already been applied in Mannerist sculpture. But they showed signs of becoming petrified in artistic formality. We may compare in this connection the 'Rape of the Sabines' by Giovanni da Bologna with Bernini's 'Saint Teresa'. In the former sculpture the figures are so closely interwoven in the ascending *figura serpentinata* that it seems as though the artist had imagined, as he worked, that the group was contained in an invisible hollow cylinder (ill. 200, 230).

The sculptor of the Baroque period obviously started from a different conception. While the movement of Mannerist figures remains restricted to a closed design, that of the Baroque sculptors' figures breaks out of this confinement into outer space. The saints are not longer represented as standing on their altars, but as positively being wafted heavenwards. The sculptors were

229. EGID QUIRIN ASAM, *Assumption of the Blessed Virgin from the High Altar of the Collegiate Church at Rohr, Bavaria*

230. BERNINI, *The Ecstasy of St Teresa. Altar group in the Church of Santa Maria della Vittoria, Rome*

231. GÜNTHER, *Annunciation group from the Conventual Church of Weyarn, Bavaria*

also able to treat their material in a special way, so as to lend it the appearance of animation and even of sensibility. Spanish sculptors like Fernández, Montañez and Cano attempted even more ambitious illusionary effects. In so doing they did not hesitate to endow their lavishly painted figures, mostly of wood, with real human hair, actual robes saturated in plaster, glass eyes and wax tears, their object being to increase the suggestion of lifelikeness and induce the beholder to participate in the experiences and sufferings depicted (ill. 246).

In sculpture Baroque individualism is particularly noticeable in the portrait busts of princes, which celebrate the power and the glory of these despotic personages. Bernini's portrait of the 'Sun King' (ill. 234) had an especially decisive influence on the subjects treated by the French sculptors, who took their orders from the absolutist Court. They could not, indeed, be induced to abandon the classical formula, except in the single case of Puget, whose works are rich in both internal and external dynamism. But the many portrait busts of Coyzevox manage to conceal all trace of a finer sensibility behind the frigid mask of courtly convention. This type of art continued to be practised in France until well into the 18th century, finding its outstanding exponent in Jean-Antoine Houdon. His impeccable technique could render permanent the most fugitive of facial expressions and his eye could penetrate the mask of the most conventional courtier. His portraits of Voltaire, for example, still define even to-day our common idea of the 'old man of Meudon' (ill. 233).

The Renaissance equestrian statue was also at first revived in France with considerable enthusiasm, as it was thought ideally suitable for the representation of the divine right of kings. Girardon's equestrian statue of Louis XIV and Falconet's of Peter the Great exemplify this feeling. But the most famous of the Baroque equestrian statues is not by a Frenchman but a German, Andreas Schlüter. His monument to the Great Elector is the most striking embodiment of absolute sovereignty in this medium (ill. 232).

The Baroque idea of a single, comprehensive, architectonic work of art, including painting, sculpture and incidental decoration, led to the execution of much decorative plastic work both in the interior furnishing and on the exterior elevations of ecclesiastical and princely buildings. Permoser's remarkable ornamental figures for the Zwinger Museum in Dresden may be instanced. The architects themselves were often also sculptors and workers in stucco, like Bernini and the brothers Asam.

In Egid Quirin Asam's work, in the heightened movement of his seemingly weightless figures, Baroque sculpture enjoyed a late flowering which Ignaz Günther carried over into the Rococo. In neigh-

332

232. SCHLÜTER, *statue of the Grand Elector in Berlin*   *233.* HOUDON, *seated figure of Voltaire. Marble*

bouring Austria at about the same time Raffael Donner, in both his secular and his church sculpture, steered Baroque emotion back into a more compact form. (Ill. 229, 231, 240)

A particular affection for the Rococo style was shown, especially in Germany, by potters. Such masters as Johann Joachim Kändler in Meissen, Franz Bustelli in Nymphenburg and Anton Grassi in Vienna created a number of graceful figurines, of shepherds and shepherdesses, harlequins and columbines, as well as countless groups of lovers from the Commedia dell'Arte plays. The frivolous elegance of these works mirrored the spirit of the age (ill. pp. 82, 322).

PAINTING

Baroque painting originated in Rome. In the year 1600 three masters were living there who were destined to influence Seicento painting in new ways. They were Michelangelo da Caravaggio, Annibale Carracci and Peter Paul Rubens. Caravaggio is the true forerunner of Baroque painting. He was the first to replace Mannerism by an increased and inexorable realism. When he was advised to study antique statues, he pointed in silence to the persons who were standing near him, thus implying that nature had already provided him with an abundance of models. The people in his pictures, as for instance his bald-headed apostle with the dirty finger-nails, and also the objects depicted, may be common enough in real life. But he lent his extreme naturalism a hitherto unprecedented power of suggestion by his revolutionary treatment of light, given a lateral direction and powerfully reinforced so as to bring out important centres of interest, and above all by his expert modelling. His pioneering works decided the general course taken by painting for the whole of the ensuing century. (Ill. p. 327)

Annibale Carracci, on the other hand, was concerned to establish a new classicism. At the Bologna Academy, which he founded, the taught his pupils to return to the painters of the High Renaissance. His frescoes at the Palazzo Farnese, gaily and vividly coloured mythological scenes, set an example for the wall painting of the Baroque period in its newly-built palaces, private residences and churches.

Carracci and the German, Elsheimer, between them created the 'ideal landscape' which had been foreshadowed by Giorgione. It is not a copy of reality in the sense of a literal correspondence with nature. On the contrary, hills, ruins and tall trees in full leaf are combined, in accordance with strict rules of composition, into an ideal landscape emblematic of a perfect world, regarded as identical with Arcadia, the paradise of shepherds and nymphs. Carracci's example was followed by the Frenchman Nicolas Poussin,

333

who lived in Rome; he 'built up' his landscapes and peopled them with 'heroic' scenes from ancient mythology. His compatriot, the Lorrainer Claude, who had also made his home in Rome, for his part followed atmospheric and light effects through to distant horizons (ill. pp. 329, 330).

There was a great difference between this style and that of the Dutch landscape painting of the same century by such masters as Hercules Seghers, Jan van Goyen, Solomon and Jacob van Ruysdael and Meindert Hobbema (ill. pp. 344, 345). Their pictures are documentary records of the domestic life of Holland. It was easy to recognise from them the scene depicted and the point at which the painter stood. Yet the 'realism' of this school is not its only interest. The pictures at the same time bear witness to the pantheistic feeling for nature which was expressed philosophically by the artists' contemporary, Spinoza of Amsterdam. Their powers of expression range from the lyrical character of Goyen's landscapes, fading into the distance under broad, lowering skies, to Jacob van Ruysdael's heroic, though somewhat melancholy, sentiment. At their best these paintings achieve a symbolic representation of the divinity of nature.

The joyous, triumphant splendour of Baroque art reaches its greatest heights in the work of Peter Paul Rubens. A Fleming born at Siegen in Westphalia, he made a pilgrimage, like nearly all Northern artists before him, to Italy. Tintoretto and Veronese had recently died there. Rubens took over the beauty of their colour with the same superb confidence with which he developed, in a manner all his own, the discoveries of Caravaggio, Carracci and Elsheimer, forging a new style of painting, colourful, optimistic, sensuous and revelling in the pleasures of mundane existence (ill. p. 328).

Just as Leonardo had summed up in his own person, during the High Renaissance, all the knowledge attained by the Italian and Dutch painters of the 15th century, so Rubens succeeded, during the Baroque age, in achieving a fresh synthesis of South and North. And just as the Italian High Renaissance had checked the influence of Dutch painting in Europe, so now Rubens restored leadership to the north of the continent. In order to be able to cope with the commissions that poured into his Antwerp studio from all directions, he gathered about him a staff of collaborators inspired by his own work. It was from this workshop that Anthony van Dyck came, to be summoned, as a subtle psychologist and born delineator of high society, to the post of Court painter to King Charles I and his cavaliers and ladies (ill. p. 335).

For Spanish art the 'Golden Age' began with the Baroque. Religious subjects had always interested Spanish painters more than any others; for centuries Spain had acted as a western buffer State between Christian Europe and Islam. The warlike and pious Spaniards demanded nothing of art but intervention on behalf of Christianity. 'Art has no other task', wrote Francisco Pacheco, the teacher of Velasquez, 'than that of showing mankind the way to faith and to God.' In consequence, it was mainly to the subject of the Christian martyrs that the Spanish painters devoted themselves with real fervour. For this theme permitted them to represent and glorify the strength of religious faith when put to the supreme test. In this spirit Ribera painted his pictures of martyrdoms with the same eloquent and inexorable objectivity as Zurbarán his dedicated saints and fanatically zealous monks. But an entirely different spirit seems to inform the typically cheerful artistic temper of Murillo. No one ever again lent the Mother of God such charm and benevolence – of a slightly sugary cast, indeed, but seeming to come straight from the heart of a simple man – as did the Andalusian master. (Ill. 37, pp. 352, 353)

But the greatest painter of Spain was destined to be Diego de Velasquez, Court painter to Philip IV. Inward emotion never affects his calm visual judgment; nor does he ever permit himself the intoxication with colour and sensuousness characteristic of Rubens, whom he nevertheless deeply reverenced. Velasquez depicted the society of the Spanish Court with undisguised objectivity, whether kings and princesses or those wretched, ugly beings, the Court dwarfs (ill. p. 351).

ANTHONY VAN DYCK: The painter Pieter Snayers

REMBRANDT: Hendrickje Stoffels

FRANS HALS: Fisher-girl

CAREL FABRITIUS: Self-portrait

The rise of political and economic power in Holland during the 17th century initiated, in the course of only three generations, the great period of Dutch painting. Based upon national self-confidence and material prosperity, art developed into a spontaneous expression of the character of the people. Religious subjects were henceforward only seldom attempted. The object was to adorn the private apartments of the citizens, and the artists therefore provided works likely to attract the taste of a purchaser. Concentration upon particular themes was the order of the day. Willem van de Velde painted chiefly ships, Jacob van Ruysdael landscapes, Paulus Potter animals and Jan Steen genre pictures.

The period opened under the sign of Caravaggio, which is clearly to be seen in the effective treatment of light by men like Hendrik Terbrugghen or Gerard van Honthorst. Yet Dutch painting soon acquired the independence exemplified by the work of Frans Hals. He painted nothing but portraits and had a penetrating eye for the peculiarities of human physiognomy (ill. p. 337). Besides many individual portraits he also specialized in the rendering of groups, where 'the solidarity of citizens associated in a common task becomes a symbol of democracy'. These works include the so-called 'marksmen scenes', representing with photographic accuracy and painterly skill the formal banquets and other meetings of the citizen militia. Rembrandt's picture of the marching-off of a company of musketeers, erroneously called the 'Night Watch' owing to the obscuring layers of varnish which for long covered it, is the most famous of such paintings. But in its deliberate and decisive departure from the usual pattern of an assembly in which all participants are entitled to equal rights, and in its concentration of the interest, this picture could not be regarded as a typical 'marksmen scene'. It was therefore declined by those who had commissioned the work.

Rembrandt represents the culmination of Dutch and European painting. Max Liebermann once remarked: 'When one sees a Frans Hals one longs to paint. But when one goes on to a Rembrandt one no longer wants to do so.' For Rembrandt was not content with the mere reproduction in paint of the material world of images, the mere rendering of external reality. His aim was the intensification and consequent spiritualization of the painter's experience, which remains only loosely tied to the outward aspect of things. Caravaggio's discovery of the effect of light falling in a single direction developed into the famous chiaroscuro of Rembrandt, which flashes out with special intensity at various illuminated points, while the colours in shadow lose their glow and fade into a warm reddish or brownish gold (ill. pp. 25, 336).

Special attention was given to those branches of Dutch painting which may be described as scenic, architectural and genre. While the former give us an exact picture down to the last detail of the towns, streets, houses, canals and churches of the 17th century, the genre paintings reflect the lives of the Dutch people. The traditional skill of the Netherlands in the reproduction of materials is shown in these pictures by the faultlessly painted details of curtains, carpets, silk, wool, furs and ornaments, of porcelain and glass as well as of the flesh of faces and hands. Freedom in the choice of subject naturally results in individual differences of conception as between the various masters. Jan Steen's inexhaustible fertility of narrative invention sees human life as one great comedy. Gabriel Metsu's dazzling colour-sense revels in expensive clothing. Terborch loves to depict, with the fastidious tact of a man of the world, the private apartments of young ladies. But the most exquisite contributions to genre painting were made by the two Delft masters, Jan Vermeer and Pieter de Hooch. The latter is a delightful story-teller, presenting scenes of middle-class family life with great affection and a high degree of realism. The lofty and spacious rooms in Vermeer's pictures have an atmosphere of dreamlike tranquillity with colour harmonies, in Claudel's phrase, of contrasted 'heavenly blue and transparent yellow'. (Ill. pp. 60, 346, 27, 70)

A conspicuous speciality of Netherlands painting is also the still-life, testimony to the hearty appetites of the citizens. Such pictures were eagerly bought by the bourgeoisie. They afforded artists opportunities for alluring experiments in colour organisation and composition (see ill. p. 71).

With the weakening of Dutch naval power towards the end of the 17th century, the native school of painting declined. At the same time, painting in France was beginning to assume the dominant position it has held in Europe ever since. In the age of Rococo it was devoted almost exclusively to the portrayal of courtly and aristocratic society. Arcadian landscapes are the setting, in Watteau's pictures, for the gay pastoral diversions of the ladies and gentlemen of French society in their *fêtes galantes*. Once more all the beauty and wealth of a doomed epoch shine out through the transparent, nacreous shimmer of their delicate colouring, with magical effect. Bathed in light and colour the old aristocratic civilisation makes its final bow. Watteau's humane undertones are renounced by François Boucher and Jean-Honoré Fragonard in favour of an increased refinement. A lightheartedness and graceful sensual enjoyment characterize their works (ill. pp. 360, 361, 359). A different mood, truer to reality and of decidedly middle-class outlook, was to be found, at the same period, in the paintings of Chardin. The richness of impasto in his still-lifes is a surprising anticipation of the characteristics of painting in the second half of the 19th century. The brilliant realism of William Hogarth, unequalled for humour and satire on canvas, also anticipates 19th-century developments (ill. p. 371).

Rococo painting in the rest of Europe also proved to be aristocratic in the sense of being dependent for its subjects on commissions from the nobility. In England, the polite composure of van Dyck's style had meanwhile formed a school and influenced the calm and 'noble' portraiture of such men as Reynolds and Thomas Gainsborough (ill. pp. 373, 374). The latter's landscapes, however, which he himself preferred to his portraits, and in which he was one of the first English artists to represent native rather than imaginary Italian scenery, communicate poetic and harmonious shades of feeling resembling Watteau's.

In the urban views of Venice by Canaletto and Guardi (ill. p. 362) the politically doomed republic of St Mark glittered once more with the brilliance of its public festivals, such as that of the marriage of the Doge to the Sea. It seemed as if the waning vitality of the Venetian lion was finally ebbing away in the painting of this century. At the Courts and in the Cabinets of Europe the Venetian ambassadors had long since degenerated into figures of marginal importance. Yet such a man as Giambattista Tiepolo could be made a universally honoured emissary, in the artistic sense, of his native city of Venice. He decorated churches and palaces, from Madrid to South Germany, with sparkling ceiling and wall frescoes (ill. p. 321).

Tiepolo brought to the highest perfection the illusive decorative painting of the Baroque age, begun in the first half of the 17th century in Italy by Pietro da Cortona. Before being taken up in Germany it had developed, especially in southern Italy, a distinctive style of wall and ceiling painting which came into its own in late Baroque and Rococo times. It was in this sphere that German Baroque painting, which was unable to produce any panels of importance, really achieved significant work, as in the interior church decoration by Cosmas Damian Asam or Dominicus and Johann Baptist Zimmermann. (Ill. p. 320)

The last representative Rococo painter is the Spaniard Francisco de Goya (ill. p. 354). But a new era is already perceptible in his prodigious output of both paintings and engravings. In his portraits of members of the Spanish Court he subjects the aristocracy to the pungent criticism of a mind naturally intolerant of disguise. The sweetness and grace of his first manner becomes transformed in the pictures of human malignity and the cruelty of war, with their visions of the abysmal depths to which the passions of mankind can descend. In these works he has already entered the epoch of the French Revolution.

THE GRAPHIC ARTS

The woodcut and the copper engraving had reached artistic perfection in the time of Dürer. But since about the middle of the 16th century, etching had become the dominant method of engraving. The copper plate underwent some further development in France after 1600, when Claude Mellan achieved

a special mastery of mannerist line engraving. His virtuosity enabled him, for example, to delineate a head of Christ in a single, unbroken spiral beginning at the nostril. A further variety of copper-plate engraving technique evolved during the 17th and 18th centuries in the form of stippling (cf. p. 51), in which the line is not cut into the surface of the metal with the burin but obtained by a system of dots punched close together. This method was used, in particular, for engraved portraits, which had a widespread popularity.

The copper plate, however, was only of outstanding importance as a means of reproduction. After a start had been made by Marcantonio Raimondi in Italy and Hendrik Goltzius in the Netherlands, Rubens, in the 17th century, had his paintings engraved on copper by his pupils and thus widely distributed. The French followed his example; a similar school of engraving was established by the successors of Watteau.

But meanwhile etching had become the dominant mode of engraving. It allowed the artist to work more freely than was possible by the previous methods, the chemical process by which acid eats into the metal being substituted for the slow ones of cutting or graving. The treatment with acid can be repeated several times over, thereby removing other parts of the ground of the plate as required. In this way the artist can obtain contrasting effects of great beauty and mutually graduate the foreground and background. He is also able to apply further treatment to the etched plate with a dry-point needle, to intensify the depth of shadow. These technical resources of the craft were not, of course, available at the outset. They had to be gradually discovered by experiment.

After a start had been made with etching in the 16th century, the Frenchman Jacques Callot devoted himself entirely, at the beginning of the following one, to the new art. Working in opposition to the classical taste then prevailing in France, he produced etchings remarkable for their imaginative quality and expert craftsmanship. In an age of enthusiasm for the theatre, Callot was especially fond of representing typical figures of the Commedia dell'Arte, the Italian form of extempore entertainment. But he also etched scenes of the Thirty Years' War, and drew beggars and hunchbacks, urban views and dancers, as well as freely invented *capricci,* with the needle. He thus introduced new subjects for etching, which had until then been almost exclusively concerned with landscape. 'Callot's manner' was thereafter identified with any kind of bizarre and complex fantasy. (Ill. 236)

But the greatest master of etching, superior to all who either preceded or followed him, was Rembrandt. There were important experts in landscape etching in Holland before his time, such as Buytewech and Seghers. Rembrandt, however, was chiefly notable for introducing new subjects into this field and revealing for the first time its full capacity for expression, through the simultaneous employment of a number of different techniques, such as the treatment of the etched plate with the graver and dry point. He thus transferred the chiaroscuro of his paintings to his engravings, thereby endowing his etched landscapes, portraits, biblical scenes and nudes with an expressive spiritual power hitherto unknown in the art (ill. 235).

Other painters of the 17th and 18th centuries also achieved considerable success in their etchings. In particular, Claude

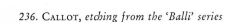

236. CALLOT, *etching from the 'Balli' series*

Lorraine, whose landscapes are suffused with light, deserves mention in this context as well as the Venetian, Tiepolo, with his *scherzi di fantasia,* in which, contrary to the practice of the Dutch etchers of landscape, who obtained their effects by working outwards from deep background shadow, he bathed his scenes in a shimmering radiance. In this sphere artists were repeatedly concerned to transfer their characteristic styles from painting to engraving.

The effort to achieve painterly effects eventually resulted in a new technique, the so-called aquatint (cf. p. 54), said to have been discovered by the Frenchman Jean Baptiste le Prince in 1768. It enabled artists to obtain facets of tone in chiaroscuro. The Spaniard Francisco de Goya was fond of employing this new method in his series of etchings. It was in this way that he produced the uncanny visions of the 'Caprices' and the 'Horrors of War', presenting mankind as in a grossly distorting mirror.

By the 18th century, etchers had long been busy with the illustration of books and the production of series of pictures dealing with a single theme. Immediately after the Thirty Years' War the German, Matthew Merian, had brought out the 'Urban Views', later to become so famous (ill. 245). His pupil Wenzel Hollar followed, with similar pictures of both town and country. In the 18th century the Venetian, Piranesi, etched his large-scale, romantic 'Views of Rome', while his compatriot Canaletto employed the same medium in his scenes of Venice, his native city. The German, Daniel Chodowiecki, bequeathed to posterity over two thousand prints of landscape, urban and genre scenes. He also illustrated almost all the first editions of the German classics from Klopstock to Goethe. Johann Elias Riedinger, again, specialized in equestrian, hunting and animal subjects. Finally, in England, William Hogarth had his popular series of satirical paintings (ill. p. 371), in which he pointed a moral by laying bare the vices of mankind, conveyed into the medium of engraving, thus facilitating the sale of these works to a wide public. Mention may also be made here of the invention by William Blake (1757–1827) of a system by which designs on copper, after the metal has been etched with acid, remain in relief and can be printed in colour; or the colour can subsequently be applied by hand.

Nearly all the engravings of the Baroque and Rococo periods are characterized by their picturesque style. The unique potentialities of expression thereby attained nevertheless led further and further from the essential 'art of line'. Thus a final stage was reached to go beyond which was for engraving to sign its own death-warrant. The ensuing period, that of classical art with its insistence on the circumscribed, brought about a return to fixed patterns and clear outlines, thereby introducing a new stylistic development in engraving.

THE CRAFTS

The Baroque ideal of a 'comprehensive work of art' led logically to a tendency to uniformity of style even in the furnishing of interiors and domestic utensils. The object was that each individual component should contribute to a general harmonious effect of splendour and dignity. These aims originated in France and were disseminated thence throughout Europe. The independent creative craftsman was replaced by the cabinet-maker, the Court purveyor who thought in terms of architectonic space and no longer designed separate articles of furniture but the entire equipment of particular rooms, as advertised in his sample-books. We may instance Ch. A. Boulle at the Court of Louis XIV (ill. 237, see ill. 27, ill. p. 81). Various rooms, differently furnished and planned, served a number of subsidiary purposes on the stage of Court life. The chambers of mirrors, whose sparkling walls and ceilings of glass confirmed the Court ladies and gentlemen in all the trappings of their dignity, are as typical of the age as the private museums of the monarchs for the storage of the valuable and rare objects either manufactured by skilled craftsmen or collected in the course of foreign travel.

Adriaen Brouwer: At the Tavern

Jacob van Ruisdael: The Mill at Wijk

MEINDERT HOBBEMA: The Avenue, Middelharnis

GERARD TERBORCH: Paternal Advice

The collectors' fever which infected both crowned and uncrowned heads gave the goldsmiths in particular plenty to do. Not only did the Church commission costly altar utensils but the secular eminences ordered ceremonial plate. The Baroque delight in glittering and resplendent objects led to an increased use of the precious metals at princely banquets. The articles thus employed were no longer separate items, each the work of a single artist, but whole dinner-services selected from those described in the sample-books and manuals supplied. They were commissioned from the big goldsmiths' factories situated mainly in Paris and Augsburg.

The glassworkers' art also contrived to contribute, after the middle of the 17th century, to the luxury of the festive board. Refinements in the production of crystal in Bohemia and flint-glass in England permitted more and more elaborate polishing and cutting, till finally the surface came to form a single network of sparkling facets, refracting light like a cut diamond.

In keeping with the representational tendencies of Baroque, increasing use was made of pictorial tapestries as wall-coverings in churches – Rubens' tapestries in Cologne Cathedral are an instance, – residential palaces and private apartments. From Brussels, where the art of tapestry-weaving had been of the greatest importance during the Renaissance, the ascendancy in this field passed to France, where the large factories of Paris, Aubusson and Beauvais wove their 'Gobelins' from designs by the great Baroque and Rococo painters.

The planning and decoration of interiors became more and more autocratic in the course of the 17th century, participating authoritatively in the transformation of Baroque into Rococo. Furniture lost its Baroque heaviness and was poised upon legs of slender elegance. Chests of drawers were reduced in size. Ponderous tables were replaced by small gilt-edged ones. Marquetry was enriched by the use of new materials, such as rosewood, ivory and tortoiseshell. That comfort was now placed before dignified ceremonial was evidenced by the elegant seating accommodation, small armchairs or sofas, with soft padding covered in silk, in which the occupants could nestle.

Porcelain, with which the century was infatuated, made a conquest of all Europe and cost its princely collectors vast fortunes. The first European china-factory, founded at Meissen in 1710, was followed by others in Vienna, Nymphenburg and Berlin and by those at Sèvres and Copenhagen, Chelsea, Derby and Worcester. Entire rooms were occupied exclusively by cabinets for porcelain. (Ill. pp. 82, 322, cf. ill. 74)

The art of eastern Asia became fashionable at the same time as porcelain. Apartments large and small were furnished with such *chinoiseries* as lacquered work, expensive silks and wallpapers. In association with the pastel shades of pictures by such artists as Boucher or Fragonard and the graceful convolutions of ornament on walls and ceilings, they contributed to the creation of that exquisite domestic environment of Rococo style in which the age of specifically aristocratic culture drew to its close.

237. Writing-desk by BOULLE, *made for the Grand Elector Max Emanuel of Bavaria. Inlaywork*

ALBANI, FRANCESCO (1578—1660). A Bolognese painter of the Carracci school who owes his renown chiefly to the way in which he exalted the grace and beauty of children in the numerous putti and amoretti of his mythological pictures (Dance of the Cupids, Milan Brera).

ALGARDI, ALESSANDRO (1602–1654), born in Bologna and trained by Lodovico Carracci and Giulio Conventi, was summoned to Rome as sculptor to the Curia by Pope Innocent X. His principal works are the marble tomb of Leo XI (St Peter's, Rome) and the impressive bronze of Innocent X (Palazzo dei Conservatori, Rome). In the great relief 'The Expulsion of Attila' (St Peter's, Rome) he subjected the strong movement of the groups of figures to a severely rhythmical composition. As an architect he designed the Villa Doria-Pamfili and the façade of S. Ignazio in Rome.

ASAM, COSMAS DAMIAN (1686–1739). Painter and architect. **ASAM, EGID QUIRIN** (1692–1756). Stucco-worker and sculptor. The two sons of Hans Georg Asam, trained in their profession from early youth, went to Rome in 1713, where they studied at first hand the language of forms of the Roman Full Baroque. Together they erected, from 1717 to 1721, one of their finest buildings: the monastic church of Weltenburg with the altar group of St George effectively lit by indirect means. They collaborated closely in the decoration of palaces and churches, held numerous appointments and enjoyed great repute. As well-to-do citizens, they were able to build, next to their residence in Munich, their own richly decorated Church of St Nepomuk. Furthermore, they excelled in decorating existing churches (Holy Trinity Church, Munich, 1715), and buildings erected by other masters (Osterhofen 1731, Weingarten 1718). Egid equipped the monastic church at Rohr with the magnificent sculptured altar-piece, 'The Assumption of the Virgin' (ill. 229). With the work of these two gifted brothers South German Baroque reached its zenith.

AVERCAMP, HENDRICK (1585–1634). This Netherlandish painter specialized in winter landscapes. He especially liked painting frozen Dutch canals and lakes, with crowds of gaily clad skaters.

BAEHR, GEORG (1666–1738). The most important work of this Dresden Guild Master was the Frauenkirche there (1726–38), which became the prototype of a Protestant preaching-house (ill. 238). In this perfectly proportioned church with a relatively simple ground-plan (130 × 130 ft) he succeeded in providing space for 3,600 people by skilfully arranging seven storeys of galleries. The interior dome was surmounted by a higher exterior one. Between the two domes a spiral staircase led up to the lantern. (Completely destroyed).

BANZ, MONASTERY. High above the valley of the Main and opposite the pilgrimage church of the Vierzehnheiligen stands the monastery of Banz which was begun in 1698 by the architects Leonhard and Johann Dientzenhofer and completed by Balthasar Neumann in 1753. The twin-towered church has a simple rectangular ground-plan, with extended choir; the interior, with its curved elliptic vaults and widely arched ribs, shows a great variety of fluid contours.

BERNINI, GIOVANNI LORENZO (1598–1680). Equally eminent as sculptor and architect. While in the service of the Pope, he designed St Peter's Square with its famous colonnades (1655–67), and also the elaborate bronze tabernacle above the Throne of St Peter inside the cathedral. In the Vatican, the Scala Regia and the equestrian statue of Constantine are by his hand. Bernini was also responsible for several notable fountains, such as the Fontana dei Fiumi (ill. 222) in the Piazza Navona, and the Fontana del Tritone. His outstanding ecclesiastical building is S. Andrea al Quirinale; the ground-plan is elliptical with chapel niches all around, and it has an elegantly curved atrium (1678). But it was the sculptor Bernini who, even more than the architect, led the Baroque to a zenith of expressiveness. His groups of figures in movement (Apollo and Daphne, Villa Borghese, Rome) represent a renunciation of the closed form of the Renaissance in favour of a looser pictorial treatment and a vigorous naturalism (cf. p. 327). The marble group of St Teresa (S. Maria della Vittoria, Rome; ill. 230) in its mystical exaltation becomes the prototype of the altar-sculpture of the Baroque. He also excelled in portrait-busts (Louis XIV, Versailles; ill. 234) and tomb-sculpture (Tomb of Urban VIII, St Peter's, Rome).

BIBIENA, GALLI DA. Fathers, sons and grandsons (e. g. Ferdinando, Giuseppe, Carlo) of this Italian family of artists vitally stimulated the theatrical architecture and stage decorations (movable backdrops) of the Baroque. Their designs, disseminated by engravings, influenced the building of theatres and stage-scenery all over Europe.

BLOEMART, ABRAHAM (1564–1651), is the founder of the so-called school of Utrecht, which was important for Dutch painting as the vehicle for Italian influences. He painted biblical and mythological pictures in bright and pleasing colours.

BLONDEL, JACQUES-FRANÇOIS (1705–1774). This architect, a native of Rouen, has left a number of great buildings in Metz (Town Hall, Parliament building, Bishop's Palace), Cambrai and Strassburg. In 1739 he

238. BAEHR, *the Frauenkirche, Dresden. Ground-plan*

opened his famous School of Architecture in Paris; in 1756 he became Professor at the Academy of Architecture. Besides a translation of Vitruvius he wrote several leading works on architecture.

BORROMINI, FRANCESCO (1599–1667). He and Bernini are the chief architects of the Full Baroque in Italy. Borromini's characteristic ground-plans of centrally planned churches, in which the enclosing walls have great fluidity, can best be seen in the churches of S. Carlo alle Quattro Fontane and S. Ivo, in Rome; into the latter he built a peculiar cupola, where the re-entrant angles of the ground-plan are carried up into the vault. Together with Rainaldi (1625–1650), Borromini built the Church of S. Agnese in the Piazza Navona. (Ill. 222, 224)

BOUCHARDON, EDMÉ (1698–1762). A French sculptor who acquired a thorough knowledge of classical art during a nine year's stay in Rome. An important commission (ten sculptures for S. Sulpice) brought him back to Paris. Both this work and the charming putti on the Fountain of Neptune at Versailles testify to his artistic talents. Among his later works, (besides portrait-busts and statues of saints) the great 'Fontaine de Grenelle' and the equestrian statue of Louis XV, destroyed during the French Revolution, are especially noteworthy.

BOUCHER, FRANÇOIS (1703–1770). In contrast to Watteau and Chardin, Boucher enjoyed quick success and worldly honours. He was Court painter in Paris and President of the Academy. In countless tapestries and ceiling-paintings he provided elegant Parisian society with what they wanted: a pleasing décor for their fashionable life at Court. He excelled in the rustic pastoral. (Ill. p. 361)

BOULLE, CHARLES ANDRÉ (1642–1732). This famous Parisian worker in ebony fashioned in his workshop the furniture for the Court of Louis XIV. It was inlaid with tortoise-shell, ivory and precious metals. He took his decorative motifs from the world of plants and animals (butterflies, flowers), but also created entire scenes. (Ill. 237)

BOURDON, SEBASTIAN (1616–1671). French Baroque painter. He got to know in Rome and Venice the work of Poussin and Claude Lorrain. His religious pictures and landscapes, which he painted in Paris and Stockholm (as Court painter to Queen Christina), testify to his personality and imagination.

BROUWER, ADRIAEN. This Flemish painter, who was born around 1605 in Oudenaarde and died at Antwerp in 1638, was a pupil of Frans Hals. The scenes of his pictures are taverns and barns, his subjects drinking, brawling and quarrelling peasants. (Ill. p. 343)

BRÜHL, AUGUSTUSBURG. Set in wonderful parkland near Cologne, this Baroque castle owes its origin to the love of splendour of Clement Augustus, of the House of Wittelsbach. The medieval castle, surrounded by water, was transformed into a building with three wings. It was designed by Johann Conrad Schlaun, who built it together with François Cuvilliés 1723–1734. The building owes its renown to the magnificent staircase in coloured marble, which Balthasar Neumann added 1743–1748.

BUSTELLI, FRANZ ANTON (1723–1763), was born in the Ticino and in 1763 became master of china-clay modelling for the Nymphenburg factory. The delicacy and wit of the Rococo found their perfect expression in his graceful pieces of porcelain. He arranged his figures mostly in charming pairs: Pierrot and Columbine from the Commedia dell'Arte, Shepherd and Shepherdess, Chinamen, Turks, etc. But his chief work is the life-size portrait-bust of Count von Haimhausen (Munich).

CALLOT, JACQUES (1592–1635), the eminent French designer and etcher, learnt the graver's craft in Italy where he stayed from 1609 to 1622. He executed the commissions of the Tuscan Court in Florence. On returning to his native Nancy he gave himself entirely to etching. Besides religious pictures, he portrayed original scenes from the life of the Italian people: 'Capricci di varie figure' and 'Balli', figures from the Commedia dell'Arte (ill. 236). He stigmatized the horrors of war in the 'Misères de la Guerre'. Callot placed the graphic arts on an equal footing with painting.

CANALETTO, 1. Giovanni Antonio Canale (1696–1768). Born in Venice, he specialized in scenes of his native city painted with great precision, showing canals, churches, palaces and bridges, usually enlivened by festive scenes ('Marriage of the Doge with the Sea'). In London, where he lived for a number of years, he was likewise appreciated for his masterly pictorial rendering of air, sky and water.

CANALETTO, 2. Bernardo Bellotto (1720–1780), nephew of Giovanni Canale, was also a popular painter of 'views'. In Vienna and in Dresden, as painter to the Court of the Elector of Saxony, later at the Court of Warsaw, he executed his precise city scenes, which he often repeated in the form of etchings.

CANO, ALONSO, known as el Granadino (1601–1667). This versatile Spaniard was active as painter, architect and sculptor (Court painter in Madrid, architect of the façade of Granada Cathedral). His wood-carvings, coloured by himself are characteristic examples of the 'naturalistic' style of Spanish Baroque sculpture (cf. p. 332).

CAPELLE, JAN VAN DE (1624–1679). An Amsterdam painter, noted for his portrayals of the Virgin Mary as well as for his winter landscapes. His beautiful sea-pieces are painted with perfect craftsmanship.

CARAVAGGIO, MICHELANGELO MERISI DA (c. 1573–1609), was one of the pioneers of Baroque painting. His fierce disposition drove him restlessly

239. CHURRIGUERA, *sacristy of the Cartuja in Granada*

from place to place (Rome, Naples, Sicily). His painting, dramatic and vigorous in its colour, not shunning
ugliness of mien, came as an antidote to the classicism
of the Brothers Carracci. His most vital discovery lay
in the contrasting changes of light and shadow, with
which Caravaggio created emphasis and sculptural
form. This famous 'cellar light' dramatizes a picturesque scene where brightly-lit figures are placed before
a dark background ('Calling of St Matthew', ill. p. 327;
'Entombment', Vatican; 'Conversion of Paul', Rome).
His pictorial manner strongly influenced Rubens, Velasquez and the 'Caravaggeschi' of the Netherlands
(Terbrugghen, Honthorst) and, finally, Rembrandt.

CARRACCI, ANNIBALE (1560–1609) with his brother
Agostino (1557–1602) and his cousin Lodovico (1555–
1619) founded an Academy in Bologna; here young
painters were trained practically (on the living model)
and theoretically (by aesthetic instruction). The study
of the great masters of the Renaissance was encouraged.
By doing so, the Carracci opposed Mannerism. Annibale, the most eminent of the three, professes in his
work a classical tendency within the compass of Baroque painting. He went to Rome in 1595 in order to
decorate a state-room of the Palazzo Farnese with
murals representing mythological subjects; he was
assisted by his brother Agostino and Domenichino, his
pupil. With these much admired frescoes he set the
standard for Italian decorative painting of the Baroque.
He became the founder of the 'ideal landscape', under
the influence of his Roman environment and mutual
contact with Adam Elsheimer (cf. p. 333).

CASTIGLIONE, GIOVANNI BENEDETTO (1616–
1670). This Italian painter and etcher from Genoa
specialized in biblical or mythological subjects that
offered him an opportunity of portraying animals.

CHAMPAIGNE, PHILIPP DE (1602–1674). The great
Champaigne Exhibition of 1952 confirmed anew the
importance of this Flemish painter who settled in Paris.
As portrait painter, he is absolutely sincere, since, as
opposed to the official art of his time, he shuns super-

ficial pose and seeks to plumb the character and the
spirit of his sitters (Richelieu, Louvre). His sacred
pictures reveal the artist's deep religious feeling ('Last
Supper', Louvre; 'Nun on her Deathbed', Geneva).

CHARDIN, JEAN-BAPTISTE SIMÉON (1699–1779).
A Rococo painter who did not indulge in 'effect' or
treat his pictures as part of a gay and light-hearted
game. Sober representations of reality, they show the
greatest refinement of colour-gradation and pictorial
manner. His still-life 'The Roach' contributed to his
election to the Academy, whose Treasurer he later
became. His subjects are interiors, genre pictures, still-
lifes. He was a keen observer of the simple life of the
housewife, and painted in broad brush-strokes and
large smooth planes ('Saying Grace', Paris; 'Girl peeling
vegetables', Munich, ill. p. 359). The more he advanced
in age, the simpler became his themes. In the end, a
tumbler, a tobacco box or a few onions sufficed as subjects for pictures of rarefied beauty. In his old age he
gave up oil-painting in favour of pastel, because of
his failing eyesight. His best pastels are self-portraits
and portraits of his second wife.

CHIAVERI GAETANO (1689–1770). An Italian
architect who designed the Catholic Court Church
(1738–1755) in Dresden (q. v., ill. 241).

CHIPPENDALE is the name given to a style of
furniture which originated with the English cabinet-
maker Thomas Chippendale (1718–1779). His text-book
The Gentleman and Cabinet-Maker's Director helped
it to become known throughout England and all over
Europe. Chippendale incorporated contemporary forms
as well as elements of the Gothic and of East Asian
art into his own style, whose products – above all,
comfortable chairs – he skilfully adapted to their
practical purpose. His favourite wood, mahogany, has
ever since been a staple of furniture-making.

CHODOWIECKI, DANIEL NIKOLAUS (1727–1801).
This artist, working in Berlin, was remarkably prolific
as an etcher (First Editions of Goethe, Claudius, Lessing,
Schiller, etc.; German translations of Sterne, Goldsmith). In his carefully executed pages he describes,
in a slightly moralising way, bourgeois Rococo society
in the Prussia of Frederick II.

CHURRIGUERA, JOSÉ DE (1650–1723). The significance of this sculptor and architect of the Spanish
Baroque lies in his special propensity for using the
decorative style. His influence in Spain was so strong
that it is customary to speak of Churriguerism as a
period style. Even though the attribution of many of
his works is contested (Town Hall and façade of the
Jesuit College, Salamanca), the architecture of the
tower and the interior decoration of the sacristy in
the Cathedral of Salamanca are certainly his, besides
a number of altars, tombs and decorative works. The
real magnificence of his style can be admired in the
sacristy of the Cartuja in Granada (ill. 239).

Diego Velasquez: The Infante Don Baltasar Carlos on Horseback

BARTOLOMÉ ESTEBAN MURILLO: The Young Fruit-seller

EPE DE RIBERA: The Holy Family with St Catherine

Francisco de Goya: Portrait of Doña Isabel Cobos de Porcel

CLAESZ, PIETER (1597–1661). Born in Haarlem, he belongs to the pioneers of Dutch still-life painting. Usually his still-lifes represent breakfast tables upon which he skilfully arranges only a few objects, chiefly pewter vessels. The component parts of his pictures merge into a characteristic brownish-yellow tone, which earned for them the name of 'unicoloured banquets'.

CLAUDE LORRAINE, actually named Claude Gellée (1600–1682), was born in Chamagne (Lorraine). Claude entered the workshop of the fresco painter Agostino Tassi in Rome at the age of 14. Like Elsheimer, Carracci and his compatriot Poussin, he developed his own (idyllic) form of the 'ideal landscape', distinguished from those of the others by its stillness and majestic calm. Claude often employed other artists to contribute small and undramatic mythological or Old Testament figures. He liked to use palaces, columns and trees to frame and confine his landscapes; and these move into his pictures from left to right, leading the eye into depth. But the vibrancy of light and atmosphere was what, above all, he sought to render, also in his etchings. The best of his numerous drawings are preserved in the British Museum. (Ill. p. 330)

CONINXLOO, GILLIS VAN (1544–1607). Leader of a group of artists who fled from the religious persecutions of the Spaniards in the Netherlands to Frankenthal in the Palatinate. A painter of landscapes, he transformed the 'panoramic' tradition of Patenir into a sober style, closer to nature.

COPLEY, JOHN SINGLETON (1738–1815). Born in Massachusetts, he became in early life the popular portraitist of the New Englanders. By the age of twenty he was an established portrait painter, and such works as his 'Paul Revere' show both his technical skill and psychological insight. In London, his native individuality was weakened by the influence of Romney, Gainsborough, Reynolds and West.

COQUES, GONZALES (1614–1684). This painter, who lived in Antwerp, was much in demand as a portraitist and became Court painter to the Governor of the Netherlands. The portraits by Coques convey nobility, not unlike those of his great compatriot van Dyck.

CORTONA, PIETRO DA (1596–1669). This Florentine painter and architect, whose actual name was Berretini, undertook to cover the enormous ceiling of the Great Hall in the Palazzo Barberini, Rome, with a large single composition, and thus to abandon the sectioning of the Carracci brothers. Vigorously modelled figures, representing the 'Triumph of the Barberini Family' rise up to Heaven, which opens above them. With this and other frescoes (Florence, Palazzo Pitti) Cortona created the model for the illusionistic ceiling-painting of the Baroque.

COUSTOU, GUILLAUME (1677–1746), showed himself in his sculptures to be closely related in style to his elder brother Nicolas (Marie Lescynska as Juno). But in his 'Horse Tamers' (commissioned for the Chateau at Marly but now at the bottom of the Champs Elysées), he created two over-life-size groups. Their restrained naturalism anticipates the formal language of Classicism.

COUSTOU, NICOLAS (1658–1733). Sculptor, born in Lyons and the nephew and pupil of Coyzevox. Abundant folds and demonstrative gestures characterize his marble statues of gods and princes, so typical of the Baroque style (Julius Caesar; Louis XV as Jupiter).

COZENS, ALEXANDER (c. 1710–1786), was born in Russia, trained in Italy and thence, in the middle of the century, entered the English Court as a drawing master. Besides teaching, he painted a number of landscapes in water colour of almost impressionist character (mostly in the Victoria and Albert Museum, London).

COZENS, JOHN ROBERT (1752–1799), son of Alexander. His importance in the history of art lies in the development of pure water-colour painting as an independent art. He derived the impressions for his water-colour landscapes, painted without the use of strong colours, from Italy and Switzerland. Their living quality lies in their atmospheric charm and in the gentle melancholy that broods over the quiet places which Cozens loved ('Lake of Albano', Manchester; 'Mountains of Elba', London).

CUVILLIÉS, FRANÇOIS, THE ELDER (1695–1768). An architect who became famous, above all, through his interior decorations which are fashioned in the richest Rococo style. His most important works are the Amalienburg (1734–37) in the Nymphenburg Park, the 'Reichen Zimmer' of the Munich Residenz, as well as the former Residenz Theatre (1751–53).

CUYP, AELBERT (1620–1691), was a well-to-do burgher of Dordrecht, son of the painter Jacob Cuyp, and painted the landscapes surrounding his native town. He preferred idyllic scenes, with grazing herds on the banks of the Meuse, paintings filled with the coloured reflections, the yellow and golden tones of the sun.

DESPORTES, FRANÇOIS (1661–1743). A painter of animals, renowned in his day, who glorified the royal chase in splendid pictures. He particularly liked painting racing greyhounds and hunting-dogs.

DIENTZENHOFER, CHRISTOPH (1655–1722). Baroque architect of Prague, ancestor of the Bohemian branch of the family. He created church interiors after the model of the Italian Baroque master, Guarini, with ornate walls and vaulting. In Prague he began the Church of St Nicholas (1703–11), which his son, Kilian Ignaz, completed.

DIENTZENHOFER, JOHANN (1665–1726). The Master of Bamberg is the most gifted scion of the Franconian branch of the Dientzenhofer family. In his Fulda Cathedral (1704–12), with the façade facing east, narrow two-storeyed chapels stand on either side of the barrel-vaulted nave, in rhythmical alternation with wider single-storeyed chapels. A dome with lantern rises over the crossing. The monastic church of Banz, influenced by the Bohemian church of the Dientzenhofer school, is attributed to him. But his masterpiece is Pommersfelden Palace which he built 1711–1718 for the Bishop of Bamberg, Lothar Franz von Schönborn. It is particularly renowned for its magnificent staircase surrounded by three-storeyed arcades.

DIENTZENHOFER, KILIAN IGNAZ (1689–1751). Baroque architect of Prague, and son of Christoph. Besides completing his father's Church of St Nicholas in Prague, he built a number of centrally planned churches with elliptical ground plan (Wahlstatt; Prague, St Nicholas in the Old Town, St John on the Rock; Carlsbad, St Magdalen; Gutwasser, etc.), as well as secular buildings in Prague and elsewhere.

DINGLINGER, JOHANN MELCHIOR (1664–1731). Court goldsmith to Augustus the Strong. In his big workshop in Dresden were manufactured the magnificent Baroque vessels for princely banquets, which were later collected in the 'Green Vault' of the Dresden Castle (e. g. Hercules-bowls), and figure-groups with their tiny enamelled and coloured figurines.

DOMENICHINO, IL, was the assumed name of Domenico Zampieri (1581–1641). Stimulated by Annibale Carracci and partly in conjunction with him, Domenichino painted numerous murals and ceilings in Naples and Rome (religious and historical subjects) which, incorporating landscape, show a clear and severe, almost classical composition (S. Andrea della Valle, S. Gregorio Magno, Rome).

DONNER, GEORG RAPHAEL (1693–1741). The outstanding Austrian sculptor of the Late Baroque. In his sculptured groups (often, also, lead casts) he combined the grace and lightness of the Rococo with the balance and harmony of an anticipated classicism. He was active, above all, in Vienna (fountain on the New Market), Pressburg (group with St Martin on the High

240. DONNER, *St Martin. Sculptural group in lead in Pressburg Cathedral*

Altar of the cathedral, ill. 240), and Salzburg (figures on the staircase of the Mirabell Palace, see ill. 249).

DOU, GERARD (1613–1675) was a pupil of Rembrandt during his stay in Leyden. He acquired from Rembrandt the expressive half-light of his small-size genre paintings. Dou was much celebrated in Leyden and his manner of applying paint taken as a pattern. More than 300 paintings by his hand are distributed over many museums of Europe and North America.

DRESDEN, COURT CHURCH. The architecture of this unique work by Gaetano Chiaveri is distinguished by its clear, graded construction, with its tectonic grouping of aisles, nave and tower. The latter is of almost Gothic transparency and lightness (ill. 241).

DRESDEN, ZWINGER. A gay and festively ornate work of architecture by Daniel Pöppelmann (1662–1736) surrounds the former Court of Tournaments by the city wall (Zwinger), which the Elector of Saxony, Augustus the Strong had erected 1711–1722 as a frame for his festivities (ill. 228). The open side of the court was meant to lead to a new palace building, which, however, was never erected. The gap was closed only in the following century when Gottfried Semper built the picture gallery. The delightful architecture blends with the rich ornament and the lively sculpture of Balthasar Permoser to make a perfect whole.

DUQUESNOY, FRANÇOIS (1594–1643), known as Il Fiamingo. This Flemish sculptor, a friend of Poussin, caused a stir in Rome by his marble statues of St Susanna (S. Maria di Loreto) and St Andrew (St Peter's), as well as by his small ivory figurines.

DYCK, SIR ANTHONY VAN, was born in Antwerp, 1599, and died in London, 1641. He was a pupil of Rubens and strongly influenced by the work of Titian during a stay in Italy lasting several years. He is important as a portraitist, first of the Genoese, then of the English aristocracy. In 1632 he became Court painter in London. Van Dyck's smooth brush-stroke reveals the painter's sensibility. The accessories of fashion, costume, jewellery, dogs and horses, are brilliantly perceived and rendered, yet one feels that the painter faces the sitter coldly, and shows no deeper interest in his individuality. He was responsible for a type which determined English portraiture for a century and a half – the courtly Gentleman or Lady (ill. p. 335).

EARLE, RALPH (1751–1801), is mainly remembered for one masterpiece, his full-length portrait of Roger Sherman, an American founding father whose signature appears on all four of the documents of American Independence. By placing his subject in a small chair almost facing the viewer, by emphasising his direct gaze and his stern but powerful features, Earle placed on canvas the man's entire character. Having worked for the English during the American Revolution, Earle deserted his wife and fled to England when the patriots' chances began to brighten. Here his style degenerated into

241. The Court Church in Dresden (CHIAVERI)

affectation, and it was not until his return to the United States that it regained any of its former vigour and power.

EINSIEDELN (Switzerland). The monastic church built here by Caspar Moosbrugger 1721–1725, the interior of which has a wealth of decoration, is composed of three centrally planned bays, the most important being the initial octagon. The convex façade, flanked by two towers, conforms admirably with the ground plan.

ELSHEIMER, ADAM (1578–1610), was born in Frankfurt, and went to Rome around 1600 via Venice. Excursions in the Campagna and the mountain country there may have been the stimulus for his landscapes, mostly painted upon small copper plates. He developed a very personal and 'poetic' style of landscape painting, with a special interest in light effects. The majority of his very small figures merge with the landscape to form a perfect unity. Elsheimer was highly esteemed by his friend Rubens and by Claude Lorraie for his part in creating the 'ideal' landscape. His impetuous landscape and figure drawings, as well as his etchings, form a valuable addition to his work as a painter.

FABRITIUS, CAREL (1622–1654). Only a few pictures by the hand of this pupil of Rembrandt's, who died young, are preserved. Their technical mastery, precision of perspective and transparent colours anticipate Vermeer (Self-portrait, Munich, ill. 338; Goldfinch, The Hague/Mauritshuis).

FEICHTMAYR (Feuchtmayer, Faichtmayr). The family of artists of this name from Wessobrunn provided a number of stucco-workers and sculptors in South Ger-

many during the 17th century. The most important members are Johann Michael (c. 1709/10–1772) who provided the decorations for the Baroque churches of Amorbach, Zwiefalten, Ottobeuren, Vierzehnheiligen and Bruchsal Castle, and Joseph Anton (1696–1730), active chiefly in the district around Lake Constance (Kloster Salem, Neubirnau, St Gallen).

FERNÁNDEZ, GREGORIO (c. 1576–1636), one of the chief Spanish sculptors of the Baroque, lived and worked in Valladolid. His painted wood-sculptures, like the works of his compatriots (Berruguete, Montañez, see p. 332), are exclusively devoted to sacred subjects, and attempt to translate deep religious feelings, such as the emotions aroused by Christ's Passion, into the plastic language of gesture (works especially in Valladolid).

FISCHER, JOHANN MICHAEL (1692–1766). Munich's industrious Baroque architect – his epitaph lists 23 monasteries and 32 churches – largely contributed towards forming the essential picture of the Bavarian Baroque. His main preoccupation was with centrally planned buildings flooded by light, sometimes with elliptical side-chapels or a sequence of centrally planned spaces, skilfully graded in size. St Anna am Lehel (Munich), the destroyed Franciscan church at Ingolstadt and Berg am Laim (Munich) are important stages in the evolution of his style. Outstanding is the magnificent church at Rott am Inn. Making use of other already existing plans, he created, *inter alia*, the churches of Diessen and Zwiefalten, distinguished by beautiful façades, and Ottobeuren, one of the finest German buildings of the Baroque (cf. p. 324).

FISCHER VON ERLACH, JOHANN BERNHARD (1656–1723). Italian-trained Austrian Baroque architect, and one of the strongest forces of the German Baroque. His great knowledge is recorded in the splendid work of engravings, 'Sketch of an Historical Architecture'. His plan for the Palace of Schönbrunn (which was abandoned or, at all events, very much simplified) is among the best architectural designs of the period. The most important works of the master in Vienna are: the Court Library, the Town Residence of Prince Eugene, and the Trautson Garden Palace (the two latter are remarkable for their staircase halls); in Prague, the Clam-Gallas Palace with impressively articulated façade. Among his sacred buildings the Church of St Charles Borromeo in Vienna (ill. 35) and the Collegiate Church in Salzburg, are distinguished by their spirited façades; while the concave front of the Trinity Church at Salzburg is more sober.

FLEGEL, GEORG (1568–1638), born in Olmütz, Moravia, a leading German still-life painter, was probably trained in the Netherlands. Later he founded a school in Frankfurt. He painted fruit, flowers, insects, fish, table and kitchen utensils, also some portraits (ill. p. 71).

FRAGONARD, JEAN-HONORÉ (1732–1806). A pupil of Boucher, this Parisian painter was one of the masters of the French Rococo. He was also influenced by Watteau and Tiepolo. His pictures reflect a carefree world; the colours are bright and evanescent, the brush-strokes delicate; 'Les Fêtes Galantes', the 'Genre Amoureux' are the themes of his gay and graceful art. His famous picture 'The Swing' (London/Wallace Coll.), is instinct with coquetry.

GAINSBOROUGH, THOMAS (1727–1788), was the equal of Reynolds as a portraitist of English Society. He, too, was in the tradition of van Dyck, but his colour is more airy, and his pictorial manner looser. With what ease Gainsborough could render aristocratic reserve is evident from the portrait of Mrs Siddons – a famous actress of the time. He paints with an almost impressionistic sparkle of colours: silken creases, rippling lace, flowers, feathers, glistening buckles (the 'Blue Boy', ill. p. 374). Gainsborough's landscapes – though they owe something to the Dutch and Flemish painters of the 17th century – point a way into the future. He was the first Englishman to try to see the English landscape with English eyes, and to paint it thus.

GIBBS, JAMES (1683–1754). Among this English architect's designs, which he published in book form, were those for London's churches of St Martin-in-the-Fields and St Mary-le-Strand. The Radcliffe Library (1737–47) in Oxford is probably his best work (ill. 242).

GIORDANO, LUCA (1632–1705), was called in his time 'Fa presto' – one who works fast. With obvious joy in his technical skill and craftsmanship, the Neapolitan master executed an astonishing number of oil paintings, besides numerous murals and ceiling frescoes, chiefly on religious themes (cupola fresco of the Assumption at S. Brigida, Naples). His perfect copies of older masters (Dürer, Veronese, Ribera) are among the first forgeries introduced into the picture trade.

GIRARDON, FRANÇOIS (1628–1715). Though technically more accomplished, this Baroque sculptor often borrowed the ideas of Lebrun in his statues, portrait busts and decorations for the palaces and gardens of Louis XIV (Gallery of Apollo, Louvre; Tuileries, Versailles, etc.). His most famous work, the equestrian statue in bronze of Le Roi Soleil, fell a victim to the French Revolution. Only a small copy is preserved.

GIRTIN, THOMAS (1775–1802). English water colourist and engraver. Of Huguenot descent, he lived mainly in London. He and Cozens were mainly responsible for bringing colour painting to its maturity. It was Girtin who turned from drawing outlines filled in with colour wash; by exploiting water colours to the full, he discovered the great potentialities they possessed. He developed a superb technique, which obtained surprising pictorial effects by strong contrast of light and shadow. For subjects, he preferred monastic and castle ruins (Kirkstall Abbey, London/Victoria & Albert Museum).

GONTARD, KARL PHILIPP CHRISTIAN VAN (1731–1791). A pupil of Blondel, who educated himself by his journeys to Italy and France, and never deviated from the clarity of French Classicism. His principal works are the so-called 'Communs' of the New Palace in Potsdam, the Marble Palace there and the domes of the two churches on the Gendarmenmarkt, Berlin, which were so well adapted to the city's planning.

GOYA Y LUCIENTES, FRANCISCO DE (1746–1828). The hot blood of this northern Spanish painter, born in a village near Saragossa, had led him in his youth to many an escapade; he even had to flee his country and tour Italy for a time with a troupe of bullfighters. Later, in Madrid, he quickly rose to fame. He soon abandoned his early style, which was still wholly Rococo and which he applied mainly to tapestry designing. As a painter, he worked in the tradition of Velasquez, but with less objectivity than the latter; he was wide-awake and aggressive. His paintings of 'Maja Nude' and 'Clothed' (1800–02) stand halfway between the 'Rokeby Venus' of Velasquez, and the 'Olympia' of Manet. Goya's pictorial manner became more and more restless. He chose his subjects chiefly from the world of tragedy, of the grotesque and the macabre ('The Bewitched', 1815, 'Kronos devours his Children'). Already his 'The Third of May' (1805) was almost an expressionistic picture. The commissions which he had to fulfill as Court painter to Charles IV were executed with merciless candour. Amongst them are splendid pictures of beautiful ladies (ill. p. 354), but he does not refrain from showing the sly faces of the most shameless royal family in Europe in all their corruption (Madrid/Prado). Goya was a moralist at heart; in his incomparable graphic work he castigates the brutality of the human race, especially the frightfulness of war, whose horrors and

242. The Radcliffe Library (1737–47) in Oxford, by JAMES GIBBS

Jean-Baptiste-Siméon Chardin: Girl peeling Vegetables

Antoine Watteau: ‚La gamme d'amour.‘ *Detail*

François Boucher: The Prophetess

FRANCESCO GUARDI: Canale di Cannaregio (*Venice*)

consequences he depicts by almost surrealistic means. With his cycles of etchings (Caprichos, Desastres de la Guerra, Tauromaquia, Disparates), he exercises a strong influence upon present-day art (Picasso), while his paintings inspired Delacroix, Daumier and Manet, in particular. After the return of the Inquisition, Goya left his country and died in Bordeaux. The greatest collection of his work is in the Prado, Madrid.

GOYEN, JAN VAN (1595–1656), is among the first important masters of Dutch landscape painting. His simple subjects are pictures of the misty seashore, with fishing boats fading into the seascape, but recognizable through the treatment of light which seems to filter the colours and make them transparent.

GRAFF, ANTON (1736–1813). A portrait painter who worked for the Dresden Academy and portrayed statesmen, poets and scholars. The portraits show their sitters (Lessing, Schiller, Metternich, etc.) in a natural pose, and an eye for the essential character. Graff painted almost exclusively half-lengths in dark, subdued tones. He left about 1,500 portraits and more than 300 delicate miniatures in silver point on parchment.

GRASSI, ANTON (1755–1807). This Viennese sculptor made numerous statues for the Palace of Schönbrunn, as well as portrait busts of the Emperor Francis I, Joseph II, Haydn, etc. He is best known for his activity as master designer in the Vienna porcelain factory. At first he made coloured figurines in the Rococo style (ill. p. 322), but, after a journey to Italy, tended towards Classicism with his groups in plain biscuit porcelain.

GRAVELOT, HUBERT FRANÇOIS, whose real name was Bourguignon (1699–1773), was a French artist, resident first in Paris, then in London, and one of the leading masters of book illustration in the 18th century. He designed vignettes and engravings, *inter alia* for Boccaccio's Decameron, for an edition of Shakespeare and for books by Racine and Voltaire.

GREUZE, JEAN BAPTISTE (1725–1805). His contemporaries were delighted with Greuze's bourgeois genre paintings with a moral ('La Malédiction paternelle', 'Le Fils Puni', Louvre). He also painted expressive, if somewhat sentimental, heads and half-lengths of young girls.

GRÜSSAU, MONASTIC CHURCH. A Baroque church in Silesia, whose interior with its angle pilasters, and a beautifully curved organ loft, makes an opulent impression. The façade, in particular, is arresting, with its concave and convex lines, curved mouldings and volutes.

GUARDI, FRANCESCO DE (1712–1793). A Venetian painter who was for long held in lower esteem than his compatriot and master, Canaletto; but in our century he has been assessed at his true worth. In subject matter he follows Canaletto in his city portraits, yet his pictorial manner is much freer and looser. He opposes the topographical precision of Canaletto by his brilliant sketches of Venice, which is evoked in the play of light and shadow upon the water. Through his interest in fleeting moods (also in his figure compositions), Guardi seems almost impressionistic. (Ill. p. 362)

GUERCINO, whose actual name was Giovanni Francesco Barbieri (1591–1666), was an Italian Baroque painter. He painted altar-pieces (St William of Aquitaine receiving the Habit, Bologna/Pinacoteca), ceiling frescoes (Rome/Casino Ludovisi), mythological paintings (Venus and Adonis, Dresden). He also left a large number of drawings (genre pictures, sketches of landscapes). Guercino's fluent style of painting, which relied upon contrasts of chiaroscuro and vigorous colour harmonies, was most effective in the works of his youth.

GÜNTHER, IGNAZ (1725–1775). The wood-carvings of this Bavarian sculptor, painted in the most delicate colours, belong to the most enchanting works of interior church decoration in southern Germany and Austria. His Madonnas and angels, and even his child-like putti, possess both nobility and an almost worldly charm. Rarely have the soaring movement and the aerial lightness of figures been so perfectly rendered in sculpture (ill. 231).

HALS, FRANS (1580/81–1666). Active in Haarlem, and one of the greatest of portrait painters. He observed acutely and painted his models, unhampered by an excess of intellect or reflection, in momentary poses, sparkling with life. His sitters owe the immediacy and liveliness of their expression to this same direct method of working. The strokes of his brush, which he wields with as much speed as certainty, are often visible. As the 'hand-writing' of his pictorial manner is transmitted in his paintings, people have come to refer to the 'impressionistic' touch of Frans Hals; indeed, the admiration for this painter was never greater than at the time of Impressionism (Liebermann). In the history of art, Hals is of special importance as a master of the group portrait. In his picture of 'marksmen' and 'governors' he eschewed the rigidity with which this traditional Dutch subject had hitherto been treated; his figures are shown in natural groupings as if in conversation, an effect that is further enhanced by a wealth of standards, sashes, armour and the like. Later, the vigorous colours are replaced by restrained black and grey tones. In his last great works, Hals – really an extravagant and bohemian character who, notwithstanding his successes, died in the workhouse – achieves depth and solemnity, especially in the moving picture of the old 'Regentinnen' in the Frans Hals Museum at Haarlem, where most of his best works are now to be found. (Ill. p. 337)

HILDEBRANDT, LUCAS VON (1668–1745). With the work of this Genoa-born Austrian architect and that of Fischer von Erlach, the German Baroque came into its own. While still a young man, he came with a recommendation to Prince Eugene to Vienna, and it was

243. LUCAS VON HILDEBRANDT, *Belvedere Palace in Vienna*

there that he constructed for his patron the Garden Palace of Belvedere (ill. 243), a palace for Prince Schwarzenberg, and the Daun-Kinsky Palace (1713–1716), whose grand stairway is designed as imaginatively as that of the Mirabell Palace in Salzburg, which Hildebrandt rebuilt in 1719 (see ill. 249). Among his great monastic buildings Stift Göttweig, near Krems, and Klosterbruck (Moravia) remained unfinished. A number of centrally planned churches derive from Hildebrandt, such as the massive domed church of St Lawrence at Gabel (Bohemia), St Peter's in Vienna, and also there the Church of the Piarists.

HOBBEMA, MEINDERT (1638–1709). A pupil of Jacob van Ruysdael, living in Amsterdam, he painted only his native countryside. Unlike his master, Hobbema did not idealize the scene, but painted it in loving detail, mostly shimmering in the sunlight. He shows the play of light upon trees, upon water-mills and farmsteads (The Avenue at Middelharnis, ill. p. 345).

HOGARTH, WILLIAM (1697–1764). A London artist, famous for his popular series of narrative picture-cycles, such as the 'Harlot's Progress', 'The Rake's Progress' (ill. p. 371), 'Marriage à la Mode'. He used his keen powers of observation to give an edge to social satire, thus providing an extreme contrast to the contemporary 'Fêtes Galantes' of the French Rococo. He produced these picture-cycles in the form of engravings, so that they spread far and wide. Hogarth was also an excellent portraitist.

HONTHORST, GERARD VAN (1590–1656). During his long stay in Rome, this Dutch painter was influenced by the art of Caravaggio, whose lighting effects for nocturnal scenes he adopted (Nativity; also pictures of banquets and concerts). In addition, Honthorst painted numerous portraits, especially later when he was Court painter in the Hague.

HOOCH, PIETER DE (1629–1677), lived in Delft and Amsterdam. He is considered the foremost genre painter after Vermeer. Deeply influenced by the latter, he painted, above all, scenes of comfortable Dutch domesticity (ill. p. 70). In his pictures of interiors light falls from lofty, and usually open, windows into the furthermost corners of quiet rooms with tiled floors, and through open doors it penetrates into other rooms.

HOUDON, JEAN-ANTOINE (1741–1828), is the last and greatest portrait-sculptor of the Rococo, whose later works anticipate Classicism (see p. 332). He made some 200 portrait-busts of statesmen, scholars, artists and generals (Mirabeau, Rousseau, bust of Voltaire and marble statue of Voltaire seated, ill. 233), all marked by sureness of form and psychological insight. His busts of women and children are also noteworthy.

JONES, INIGO (1573–1652). After an instructional journey which took him to northern Italy, and under the impact of Palladio's architecture, Jones dissociated himself from the Late Gothic Tudor style which lingered on in England; he helped to establish the Classicist trend of English architecture. His love of centrally planned cubic buildings can be seen in many of his works, especially in the Queen's House, Greenwich. Besides a number of country mansions, Jones made several plans for the Royal Palace of Whitehall, London.

JORDAENS, JAKOB (1593–1678). In company with Rubens and van Dyck, Jordaens is the third great Antwerp master of his time. Whilst Rubens inclined towards the grand manner, and van Dyck had aristocratic tastes, Jordaens remained the painter of an earthy world of peasant and burgher. He enjoyed painting vigorous scenes, full of joie de vivre, with boisterous banquets ('The Beanfeast'). Besides social gatherings, he painted a great number of mythological and religious pictures, where a predilection for genre-like scenes is evident.

KÄNDLER, JOHANN JOACHIM (1706–1775). Chief designer of the Meissen china factory from 1733, he was the creator of porcelain sculpture. In more than 1000 figures and groups of figures embodying the spirit of the Rococo (ill. p. 82), he thoroughly explored this art form and brought a fresh approach, *inter alia* to modern animal sculpture. Over a period of two years he created a number of portrait-busts of the Habsburg emperors, no taller than a span, to which Meissen chiefly owes its world reputation.

KALF, WILLEM (1619–1693). This Dutch still-life painter favoured compositions made up of only a few selected objects (embossed vessels of precious metal, valuable glass and bowls of faience with colourful fruit and shells). The effect is heightened by the mutual play of luminous colours against a background steeped in velvety darkness.

KEYSER, HENDRIK DE (1565–1621). A Dutch master, equally renowned as sculptor and architect. He erected a number of secular buildings, e. g. the East India Company's Offices and the old Stock Exchange in Amsterdam; the Town Hall of Delft. The prime examples of his church architecture are the Zuyderkerk and the Westerkerk in Amsterdam.

KNOBELSDORFF, GEORG WENZEL VON (1699-1753). Superintendent of the royal castles and gardens and friend of Frederick II. He trained in Italy and France, where he mastered the formal language of a sober Classicism as well as that of a sparkling Rococo. He assisted with the building of the palaces at Rheinsberg (1734–39), Charlottenburg (East wing, 1740–43) and Potsdam (1751). His finest achievement is the palace of Sanssouci (c. 1745–47, q. v., ill. 248).

LANCRET, NICOLAS (1690–1745). Influenced by Watteau, the French painter Lancret painted Court celebrations and theatrical scenes with a fine sense of colour. He distributed his 'Fêtes Galantes' over all four 'Seasons' (Louvre). Lancret's precise and detailed observation often gives his pictures realistic and genre-like features (life of the people, *inter alia*) which in their day were among the most popular of their kind ('The Ham Feast', Chantilly; 'The Hunting Breakfast', New Palace, Potsdam).

LARGILLIÈRE, NICOLAS DE (1656–1746). Except for a few history pictures and still-lifes, this Parisian painter devoted himself almost entirely to portraits. In friendly competition with Rigaud, the Court portraitist, he portrayed the middle class in more than 1500 pictures, toning down Rigaud's stately grandeur in favour of a more natural expression and giving his sitters a more informal pose (Family Picture, Bremen; Rousseau, Uffizi; Voltaire, Louvre).

LA TOUR, GEORGES DE (c. 1593–1652). A painter from Lorraine who was forgotten soon after his death, but whose rating in the world of art has recently been reassessed. His night-pieces with candle-light are characteristic: the stylized figures stand out calm and dignified in all their sculptural strength from the dark background. The light falls in concentrated shafts upon their faces and hands. In its homely simplicity it is a stimulating art, enhanced by an individual choice of colours (crimson and lilac). ('Nativity with Shepherds', Louvre; 'Sebastian mourned by St Irene' and the 'Holy Women', Berlin.)

LA TOUR, MAURICE QUENTIN DE (1704–1780). A French pastel painter who despised the conventional, rather sugary type of pastel painting of the Rococo and tried in his portraits to come to grips with the true character of his sitters (President de Rieux, Paris).

LEBRUN, CHARLES (1619–1690), was responsible for ceiling paintings and easel pictures, but excelled in the decoration of the royal palaces ('Premier peintre du roi'). His designs for furniture, tapestries, sculpture and objets d'art gave Court decoration the uniform stamp of the 'Louis Quatorze' style.

LELY, SIR PETER, born Pieter van der Faes (1618–1680), near Utrecht. Lely came to the English Court after the death of van Dyck and was acclaimed as his legitimate successor and knighted. He transformed the noble reserve of his predecessor into something appealing and sentimental. He often painted his models before a carefully arranged landscape background. His pictures are usually attuned to the harmony of a few contrasting tones – blue and yellow, grey and red – (Gallery of the 'Windsor Beauties', Hampton Court).

LEMOYNE, JEAN BAPTISTE (1704–1778), was one of the leading portrait sculptors of the 18th century.

His marble busts partake of both the demonstrative style of the Full Baroque (Montesquieu, Bordeaux) and the naturalistic (Fontenelle, Versailles). A large equestrian statue of Louis XV in Bordeaux was also by his hand; it was destroyed in the French Revolution. He excelled in making attractive terra-cotta busts.

LE NAIN, LOUIS (1593–1648), worked together with his two brothers, Antoine (1588–1648) and Mathieu (1607–1677), with whom he shared the same signature. It is therefore difficult to separate their works. Their paintings ('The Family of the Smith', Paris/Louvre) describe the life of peasant and artisan with earnest matter-of-factness. The portraits, too, reveal a calm and virile pictorial manner. The painters, who were born in Laon, worked chiefly in Paris, and from 1648 were members of the Academy there.

LESUEUR, EUSTACHE (1616/17–1655). Like his master Vouet, Lesueur painted picture-cycles in Paris of biblical and mythological subjects. He decorated the Hôtel Lambert with paintings of the Stories of Cupid (to-day in the Louvre). Clear, distinct composition and a certain spirituality characterize his pictures, painted in rather pale colours.

LEVAU, LOUIS (1612–1670). Architect to Louis XIV. Among his many works are the church of St Sulpice in Paris, which was begun in 1646 but completed only after his death, and the domed oval hall of the Quatre Nations College. After 1659 he enlarged the Louvre and after 1668 the Palace of Versailles. Other noteworthy secular buildings of his are the well-proportioned Hôtel Lambert in Paris, and above all, the magnificent Château of Vaux-le-Vicomte near Melun (1657–60).

LIOTARD, JEAN ÉTIENNE (1702–1789). Swiss painter, born in Geneva. He lived a restless life, wandering through Europe and the Near East. Besides light and graceful pictures in pastel, portraying the society of princely Courts, he left many red-chalk drawings of Orientals and of the Turkish landscape. His best-known pastel is the 'Chocolate Girl' (Dresden).

LISS, JOHANN, also Lyss, Jan (c. 1597–1629/30). Born in Holstein, Liss, despite his short life, ranks with Elsheimer as leading German painter of the 17th century. After training in Haarlem, he was from 1621 among the first painters in Venice, as was Elsheimer in Rome. He used a rich palette when painting his popular genre scenes or representations of mythological and biblical subjects.

LONGHENA, BALDASSARE (1598–1682). The leading Baroque architect of Venice, built the Pesaro and Rezzonico Palaces, the church of S. Maria dei Scalzi with its magnificent façade, and also the domed church of S. Maria della Salute (1630–56), so effectively placed at the entrance of the Grand Canal.

LONGHI, PIETRO (1702–1785). A Venetian painter who depicted the decadent Rococo society of his native city, often in a slightly ironical manner, evincing a

244. *The monastery of Melk by the Danube, western end and south frontage* (PRANDTAUER)

special liking for the fair Venetian ladies. He also painted good portraits, landscapes and hunting-scenes.

MADERNA, CARLO (1556–1629). The great Italian architect of the Baroque, who completed St Peter's in Rome (q. v.) by adding a nave to the centrally planned building. He also built the Roman churches of S. Giacomo al Corso and S. Susanna, as well as completing the important church of S. Andrea della Valle (ill. 223).

MANSART, FRANÇOIS (1598–1666). Famous French architect. He was responsible for one of the first outstanding works in the Louis XIV style: the Château of Maisons-Lafitte, near Paris. His most important building is the Val-de-Grâce Church in Paris, with its great cupola, which he began in 1645 and intended as a free imitation of the dome of St Peter's, Rome.

MANSART, JULES, or more correctly Hardouin-Mansart (1646–1708). As Court architect to Louis XIV, he inserted the Gallery of Mirrors between the corner-pavilions of the Palace of Versailles, built by Levau, and in 1678 began work on the wings. His most important work is the Dôme des Invalides in Paris, which became the landmark of the French metropolis (1675-1706). The word 'mansarde' (attic) is derived from Mansart. (Ill. 34, 227)

MARATTI, CARLO (1625–1713), belongs to the masters of the Late Baroque in Rome, with his monu-

245. MATTHEW MERIAN, *view of Würzburg. Etching*

mental altar-pieces and frescoes (also portraits and etchings). He is a master of the over-all composition, as seen in his 'Virgin and the Holy Man' in Ancona, where the figures are ranged above each other diagonally.

'MARKSMEN'S GUILD' PIECES, also Doelenstuck (Dutch *doele* – aim). Dutch painters of the 16th and 17th century prized these group-portraits which began by representing the members of a Marksmen's Guild in single portraits, placed side-by-side (mostly half-length pictures). Later, the composition was pictorially loosened and often based upon some action (Frans Hals and B. van der Helst). In this respect Rembrandt over-shot the mark, so that his famous 'Nightwatch' was no longer appreciated by its patrons, since the portrait character had been neglected.

MAULBERTSCH, FRANZ ANTON, or Maulpertsch (1724–1796). A painter and engraver, resident in Vienna from 1739, who decorated many churches and palaces of the Upper Danube. His wall and ceiling paintings as well as his altar-pieces, executed in luminous colours and characterized by the whirling movement of their figures, constitute the culminating point of Austrian Baroque painting (frescoes in Vienna, Court Chancery, Church of the Piarists, Assembly Room of the Academy; Prague Library Hall, etc.).

MELK MONASTERY rises on a high rock above the Danube and harmonizes superbly with the landscape. The complex of buildings by Jacob Prandtauer (1701–1736) is very impressive with its dome and twin towers, flanked by the great hall and library, which are connected by a gracefully curved gallery with a wide central arch. The court in front of the church is thus both opened up and enclosed. Behind the church, the courtyards of the 1050-feet-long buildings are axially planned. (Ill. 244)

MENGS, ANTON RAPHAEL (1728–1779). The study of Antiquity and his friendship with Winckelmann led this Dresden and Madrid Court painter to Classicism, after Baroque beginnings. His early Rococo portraits seem more lively than the frigid classicist ceiling frescoes in the Madrid Palace or in the Villa Albani, Rome ('Parnassus'). He set down his ideas on reforming art in a treatise, *Thoughts about Beauty and Taste in Painting,* which was much valued by the following generation of painters.

MERIAN, MATTHEW, THE ELDER (1593–1650), engraver and publisher who, though born in Basle, settled in Frankfurt. He owes his renown to the valuable city portraits which are of the greatest interest to the historian. His *Topographia,* in 30 volumes (continued by his sons), contains over 2000 views and plans. (Ill. 245)

METSU, GABRIEL (1629–1677). A Dutch painter whose single figures, portraits and genre pictures are highly prized to-day. His colours are exuberant, and he had a predilection for precious materials and robes.

MIGNARD, PIERRE (1612–1695). After a twenty years' stay in Rome, Mignard settled in Paris, where he became the antagonist and successor of Lebrun (q. v.). His chief painting is the gigantic fresco in the dome of the Parisian church of Val-de-Grâce. Of greater artistic merit, however, are his lifelike portraits (family portrait of the Grand Dauphin, Louvre).

MONTAÑEZ, JUAN MARTINEZ (1568–1649). The outstanding Baroque sculptor of southern Spain (Seville). He sought dramatic intensity of expression in order to give outward form to his religious emotion. He made crucifixes, Madonnas, statues and figures of saints (Seville Cathedral, S. Lorenzo), often making use of 'veristic' elements, such as robes filled in with gesso (see p. 332, ill. 246).

MUNICH, THEATINER CHURCH. The graceful façade by François Cuvilliés (1765–68), flanked by two towers, harmonizes well with the domed basilica by the Italians Agostino Barelli and Enrico Zuccali, which is about a century older.

MURILLO, BARTOLOMÉ ESTÉBAN (1618–1682). A native of Seville, Murillo was one of the most popular painters of the Spanish Baroque. He painted mostly Madonnas or the 'Holy Children', Jesus and St John the Baptist, in appealing beauty. However, in his genre pictures of youthful fruit-sellers (ill. p. 352) and beggar-boys (Munich), a strong realism can be noted, which Murillo was as capable of rendering as of painting idealized portraits and self-portraits.

NATTIER, JEAN-MARC (1685–1766). Many portraits of ladies by this French Rococo painter reveal the fascination of their beautiful models. The elegant ladies are seated in their boudoirs ('The Bath', London/Wallace Collection), or flower-wreathed before an idyllic landscape-backdrop (Marquise d'Autin, Paris). Often they are represented in mythological guise.

NERESHEIM MONASTIC CHURCH. This, the most mature work of Balthasar Neumann though not completed until long after his death (1745–92), consists of a sequence of domical bays. On the main axis there is a series of five ovals, on the transverse axis, three. The dome, which seems to float upon its four pairs of columns, is the crowning glory.

NEUMANN, BALTHASAR (1687–1753). A cannon-founder and artillery officer who attained to the respected position of chief town architect of Würzburg (q. v.). The Residenz there would alone suffice to establish his fame. Werneck Castle was another fine achievement. He built many splendid staircases, the most famous of which is in the Würzburg Residenz; others are in the castles of Bruchsal and Brühl (q. v.) and in the monasteries of Ebrach, Oberzell and Schöntal. In collaboration with Maximilian von Welsch, he added the domed chapel for the Schönborn family to the transept of Würzburg Cathedral. Neumann's most important ecclesiastical buildings are the monastic church of

246. MONTAÑEZ *Mater dolorosa. Painted woodcarving with inlaid glass teardrops*

Neresheim (q. v.) and the pilgrimage church of the Vierzehnheiligen (q. v.) which belong to the finest achievements of German Baroque architecture. (Ill. 226, 247)

NYMPHENBURG PALACE. The group of buildings, surrounded by extensive parks, grew 1663–1728 from a central building in the Italian style by Agostino Barelli, through a lengthening of the wings into an extensive complex 1770 ft broad. Scattered over the park are the small castles of Amalienburg, Badenburg and Pagodenburg, with their enchanting Rococo decoration.

OEBEN, FRANÇOIS (c. 1710/20–1763). French 'Ébéniste du roi', of German descent, who designed some elegant types of Rococo furniture (Louis quinze). The sumptuous writing-desk which he made for Louis XIV (Paris/Louvre), inlaid, and richly ornamented in bronze, is a world-famous masterpiece.

ORANGERY was the name given to buildings, or parts of buildings, where orange trees and other southern plants, which during the summer were placed out of doors, could spend the winter months. Sometimes they also contained ornate rooms for large festive gatherings of the Court (Versailles, Sanssouci, Hampton Court).

OSTADE, ADRIAEN VAN (1610–1685). Dutch painter and engraver from Haarlem, pupil of Hals and later influenced by Rembrandt. The subjects of his snug

247. *Pilgrimage church of the 'Vierzehnheiligen'* (B. NEUMANN)

and attractive genre pictures are: vagabond fiddlers, gay topers and dancers in rustic inns (works in Paris, Vienna, Leningrad). His brother Isaac (1621–1649) depicted similar scenes.

OTTOBEUREN, MONASTIC PILE. Following the erection of a group of buildings, divided by a longitudinal and transverse wing into three courts (1711–24) with splendid Imperial Hall and simpler Library, the planning of the church was undertaken by several architects. Owing to the nature of the site, this is aligned north and south; it is distinguished by a façade which curves boldly between the towers, and by the spreading arms of the transept – a combination of a longitudinal and a centrally planned building (cf. p. 324). The building was designed by Simpert Kramer and taken over by Johann Michael Fischer in 1748. The church was consecrated after completion of the interior decoration in 1766 (stucco: Johann Michael Feichtmayr; frescoes: Johann Jacob and Franz Anton Zeiller). The splendid Rococo interior is one of the highlights of South German Baroque architecture.

OUDRY, JEAN-BAPTISTE (1686–1755). This French painter began with still-lifes, but subsequently turned almost exclusively to animal and landscape painting ('The Farmstead', Louvre). He favoured the same subjects in his designs for tapestries (Louis XV at the Chase). As an illustrator he made drawings for the Fables of La Fontaine.

PARIS, DÔME DES INVALIDES. Situated in the centre of the vast complex of the Hôtel des Invalides, which Louis XIV had built for his veterans, this domed building, erected 1675–1706 by Jules Hardouin-Mansart, has become a dominant architectural feature of the French capital. The centrally-planned church is shaped according to strict geometrical laws of proportion and has a most effective façade (ill. 34).

PARIS, LOUVRE. The medieval city-stronghold of the French kings was replaced (1546–78) by a new building with cleverly articulated façade after the designs of the architect Pierre Lescot (ill. 212). Under Louis XIII the west wing was duplicated by Jacques Lemercier, but it was Louis Levau who completed the court as a whole at the time of Louis XIV. The imposing external frontage, facing east, was the work of Claude Perrault, 1665, who had to compete with Bernini. But the end wings belong to the 19th century, when parts of the ruined palace of the Tuileries were made use of. Nowadays the Louvre is the most famous of Parisian museums.

PARIS, PANTHÉON. The cruciform design (367 × 276 ft) groups four saucer-domes around a central cupola, surmounted by a lantern (interior height 272 ft, exterior height 384 ft), whose form derives from Bramante's model for the dome of St Peter's. The architect Soufflot put up a monumental portico in front of the entrance. The former church serves nowadays as a Hall of Glory.

PATER, JEAN-BAPTISTE (1695–1763). Like Watteau a native of Valenciennes, Pater was one of the masters of Rococo painting. By temperament he inclined towards a rather worldly and superficial rendering of amorous and playful scenes ('Rustic Feast', London, Buckingham Palace; 'Blind Man's Buff', formerly Potsdam). He also enjoyed depicting, in delicately painted interiors, the secrets of boudoirs and salons ('La Toilette', Louvre).

PEALE, CHARLES WILLSON (1741–1827), one of America's best painters, began his painting career by trading a saddle for lessons in portraiture. These produced such startlingly good results that a group of business men banded together and sent Peale to England to study under Benjamin West. On his return to the United States, Peale, an ardent patriot, immediately joined the Continental Army and painted its leaders, among them Washington. Peale's belief in complete realism, which he applied to his painting, enabled him to produce exceptionally perfect and lifelike likenesses. This almost photographic approach made him very popular and he painted many famous contemporaries, among them John Adams and James Madison.

PERMOSER, BALTHASAR (1651–1732). In 1689 Augustus the Strong appointed Permoser, a native of Upper Bavaria, Court sculptor to the capital of Saxony. Prior to this, the artist had spent 14 years in Italy; he introduced Italian Baroque sculpture into Germany. His masterpieces are the superb Baroque figures he carved for the Dresden Zwinger (much damaged by bombs in 1945). The two sculptures in Bautzen representing St Augustine and St Ambrose are also noteworthy.

PERRAULT, CLAUDE (c. 1613–1688). Parisian architect and sculptor. He successfully competed against Lorenzo Bernini, when a new east front was planned for the Louvre; this he began in 1667. With this splendid building, with its 28 Corinthian columns, Perrault laid the foundation of the classicist style of architecture in France. (Cf. p. 325)

PESNE, ANTOINE (1683–1757), was summoned in 1711 by the King of Prussia from his native Paris to Berlin, where he lived as Court painter until his death. He was portraitist to the Prussian Court and decorated its palaces (Rheinsberg, Charlottenburg, Sanssouci) which he adorned with mythological ceiling paintings. As the most important painter of the Rococo at the time of Frederick II, he strongly influenced contemporary painting in Berlin.

PETEL, GEORG (c. 1600–1634). A native of Upper Bavaria, Petel carved wood sculptures for numerous churches. Journeys to Antwerp brought him in contact with the Rubens circle. Petel was the first German sculptor to adopt the Baroque and his figures are emotionally conceived. He devoted much of his work to images of Christ crucified. With his masterly ivories he won fame in the field of miniature sculpture.

PIAZ(Z)ETTA, GIOVANNI BATTISTA (1682–1754), came to Venice from his native Pietra Rossa near Treviso. And here he promoted a beautiful and colourful second flowering of Baroque painting. His composition is clear and harmonious, his figures still have the sculptural strength of the Baroque. Yet his palette is lighter; there are delicate contrasts in the warm flooding light and in the shadows – the colours are those of the Rococo. Piazetta strongly influenced the young Tiepolo.

PIGALLE, JEAN BAPTISTE (1714–1785). The lively and graceful works in the spirit of pure Rococo of this French sculptor's youth, e. g. the 'Mercury Putting on his Sandals' (Louvre), were succeeded by portraits, busts, tombs and genre sculptures, where classicist tendencies are not always fully assimilated.

PIRANESI, GIAMBATTISTA (1720–1778), was probably born in Mogliano near Venice. He worked at first as an architect, before devoting himself entirely to engraving and etching. His well-known 'Vedute di Roma' give views of antique and Baroque monuments in the Eternal City; though the effects are heightened by the clever use of light and pitch-black shadows, the detail is accurately observed.

POTSDAM, NEW PALACE. The Palace with its plan related to the axis of the garden, was built by Büring and Manger 1763–1766. It combines Baroque magnificence with classicist austerity. The main front, surmounted by a cupola, diminishes on the garden side in elegant, one-storeyed galleries. Legeay and Gontard erected (1765–69) on the opposite side of the court two domed subsidiary buildings ('Communs') which are connected by a wide semicircular colonnade.

POTSDAM, SANSSOUCI. The small palace of Sanssouci lies above several terraces, intended for greenhouses, and amidst extensive parkland, ornamented with many dainty pavilions in the Far Eastern or Classical style. The palace, built 1745–1747 by von Knobelsdorff for Frederick the Great in the contemporary French style, derives its characteristic note from the domed central hall and from the caryatids of nymphs and satyrs, which in their imaginative treatment have only been surpassed by the architectural sculptures of the Dresden Zwinger. A semicircular colonnade is set before the court side of the building. The interior decoration is in the richest Rococo style. (Ill. 248)

POTTER, PAULUS (1625–1654). Potter repeatedly painted sections of landscapes beneath cloud-laden skies; sheep and cattle browse or lie placidly in the fields or stand before their troughs, closely observed to the smallest particle of their hide. Especially famous is the life-size 'Young Bull' (The Hague/Mauritshuis).

POUSSIN, NICOLAS (1594–1665), was born near Soissons. At the age of 30 he went to Rome and remained there to the end of his life – except for a two years' return to France. Yet in his sensibility this great painter always remained a Frenchman. Thus he did not

248. Sanssouci Palace in Potsdam (V. KNOBELSDORFF)

adopt the Baroque style of Caravaggio, but rather the manner of the Carracci and of Domenichino which he found more sympathetic; this led him to the classical tradition of Italy. He loved Raphael and he revered the Venetians; but it was Antiquity that he felt himself most drawn to (he copied the 'Aldobrandini Wedding'). In his carefully thought-out compositions (mythological, historical and religious scenes) all is clarity. The finished work does not betray any traces of the long and laborious process of maturing. Poussin's love of clear and well-proportioned beauty is best seen in his heroic landscapes (continuing the tradition of Carracci and Elsheimer, cf. p. 333), which are peopled by figures from classical mythology ('The Seasons', Paris). Ill. p. 329.

PRANDTAUER, JACOB (1658–1726). After having modelled himself in his younger days upon the Italian Carlone family, the master-mason from St Pölten soon faced the great architectural tasks of his time in a spirit of independence. Prandtauer helped in the building of the great monastic foundation of Kremsmünster and was responsible for all the significant portions of the two most prominent Austrian Baroque buildings – Melk (q. v.) and St Florian (q. v.). Ill. 244

PUGET, PIERRE (1620–1694). Baroque sculptor from Marseilles. By virtue of the vigorous and impetuous naturalism and the almost painterly movement of his figures and groups, especially the uncouth marble giants ('Milon', the 'Gallic Hercules', both Paris/Louvre), he is like a stranger among his classicist contemporaries. The originality and stature of his provincial genius were only recognised by later generations.

RAEBURN, SIR HENRY (1756–1823). Raeburn, who lived in Edinburgh, was the portraitist of Scottish society. He painted half- or full-length figures of his patrons, in their national costume and on horse-back, in parks, or hunting in the Scottish forests. This realistic and lively portrait-art is distinguished by a vigorous use of colour and a varied treatment of light (works in Scottish and London National Galleries). Ill. p. 372.

RASTRELLI, BARTOLOMEO FRANCESCO (c. 1700–1771). Born in Paris, of Italian descent, he was chief architect to the Imperial Court of Russia from 1736. In his building projects he sought to transform elements of Italian, French and German Baroque and Rococo

369

into a Russian national style (making ample use of coloured stucco). He made use of a large staff of assistants in St Petersburg (Winter Palace) and elsewhere.

REMBRANDT HARMENSZ VAN RIJN (1606–1669), was born in Leyden, the son of a miller. After his apprenticeship there and in Amsterdam, he returned to Leyden in 1626. Already in his first religious pictures he is a master of an effective and dramatized chiaroscuro ('Simeon in the Temple', The Hague/Mauritshuis). In addition, he was portraying and etching the heads of his family, drawn from life (Rembrandt's Mother, Wilton House), sometimes in certain guises ('The Money-changer', Berlin). When in 1631 Rembrandt settled in Amsterdam, his fame as a good painter preceded him. Then, after his marriage to the well-to-do Saskia of Uylenburgh ('Self-portrait with Saskia', Dresden), he became the favourite portraitist of the upper classes, who also commissioned group portraits ('Anatomy of Dr Tulp', The Hague/Mauritshuis). The mounting vigour of the successful artist found expression in the stronger colours he applied to larger pictures, which grew progressively in size and which he now liked to invest with dramatic narrative. He attired his figures in precious silks and satins, costumes and armour which he himself had collected ('The Blinding of Simon', Frankfurt). For a while, landscapes occupied most of his time ('Landscape with stone bridge', Amsterdam). The year 1642 brought a tragic turn of events: Saskia died, and the failure of the enormous group-portrait misnamed the 'Nightwatch' (12 ft 8 3/8 ins × 16 ft 5 5/8 ins), which broke out of the traditional framework, undermined his artistic and civic reputation. Rembrandt got into increasing financial difficulties, until in 1656 his house and all its art treasures were put up for auction. Yet his greatness grew in proportion to the independence which he now gained vis-à-vis the world. Apart from occasional portraits ('Burgomaster Six', Amsterdam; 'The Man with the Golden Helmet', Berlin), he again devoted himself almost entirely to biblical subjects in painting ('Jacob's Blessing', Kassel) and likewise in his etchings, which in tone values and graphic expression show a mastery since unequalled. The older and more solitary Rembrandt grew, the calmer and more serene became his art. Dramatic action gave way to a more restrained handling of scenes, and his earlier somewhat affected self-portraits developed into a serious and critical dialogue with the mirrored image (ill. 235). The once-vivid colours seem to yield entirely to the golden-brown, red, brownish-black and olive-green tones that are so characteristic of his later works. To this period after 1660 belongs a picture which seems to sum up one of life's basic relationships (Saul and David, The Hague/Mauritshuis); as moving are the magnificent group-portrait of the Syndici of the Clothmakers' Guild, the 'Staalmeester' (Amsterdam/Rijksmuseum), the portraits of Saskia's son Titus, the painterly homage paid to Hendrickje Stoffels (ill. p. 336), who was the devoted companion of the old and impoverished master; to these

may be added the beautiful 'Family Portrait' in the Brunswick Museum, outstanding for the freedom of its brushwork and the harmony of its three reds (ill. p. 25). At the time of his death in 1669 Rembrandt's work had grown to 700 paintings, 300 etchings and more than 1000 drawings.

RENI, GUIDO (1575–1642). Greatly respected in his native Bologna as well as in Rome where he spent much of his life, Guido was considered well into the 19th century as one of the most prominent Baroque painters of the Bolognese school. He executed frescoes and easel pictures of biblical and mythological subjects (Aurora, ceiling fresco in the Palazzo Rospigliosi, Rome). Half-length figures of Christ, the Virgin and saints occupy the greater part of his work (Ecce Homo; Mater Dolorosa; Lucretia); these are all characterized by the same uplifted eyes. The allure of Reni's work must have lain in the beauty and softness of his colour.

REYNOLDS, SIR JOSHUA (1723–1792). English Court painter from 1789 and for more than 20 years President of the Royal Academy, London. He is the first of the line of important 18th-century English portraitists. He, too, carried on the van Dyck tradition of depicting aristocratic bearing and treating all stuff or fabrics as precious. Soon he became the favourite painter of a society which sought to combine reserve with grace, informality with noblesse. He was in the habit of giving his patrons the foil of a quiet garden setting, painted in soft, luscious tones. Well-known works: Lady Crosby (priv. coll.); Duchess of Devonshire and her small daughter (Chatsworth); Lord Heathfield with the Key of Gibraltar (London); Nelly O'Brien (London) and Lady Cockburn and her children (London; ill. p. 373).

RIBERA, JUSEPE DE (1588–1652). Court painter to the Spanish Viceroy in Naples, who lived in Italy until his death. In order to give dramatic force to the realism of his religious pictures he made use of the pictorial discoveries of the Italians, e. g. Caravaggio's 'cellar light' falling from the sides (Holy Trinity, Escorial). His realism was compacted with earnest religious feeling and the passionate temperament of the Spaniard (St Sebastian, Berlin; St Andrew, Prado; Holy Family with St Catherine, Metropolitan Museum, New York; ill. p. 353, ill. 37).

RIESENER, JEAN-HENRI (1734–1806). Marie Antoinette's ebonist and cabinetmaker, born in Gladbach, carried on the workshop of his compatriot Oeben in Paris after the latter's death. His well-proportioned furniture with excellent decorations in bronze is characterized by its symmetrical forms.

RIGAUD, HYAZINTHE, actual name Rigau y Ros (1659–1743). In his day, Rigaud enjoyed throughout Europe the greatest fame as a portrait painter. With his sitters – aristocrats, scholars and artists – painted against a sumptuous background, he exactly met the taste of Louis XIV and his Court. Many of his pictures were painted with the help of assistants.

WILLIAM HOGARTH: The Rake's Progress. Scene III: The Orgy

HENRY RAEBURN: Portrait of Lieutenant-Colonel Bryce McMurdo

JOSHUA REYNOLDS: Lady Cockburn and her three eldest Sons

THOMAS GAINSBOROUGH: The Blue Boy

ROBERT, HUBERT (1733–1808). This French painter was given the soubriquet 'Robert of the Ruins' on account of his fanciful landscapes and architectural pictures, in which he invested with a poetic aura the magic of antique buildings. The foregrounds of these decorative scenes, painted with sure taste and colour sense, are enlivened by figures and groups in genre style.

ROCAILLE (Fr.: grottos, shells). A Rococo ornament, especially popular in France, in the form of finely shaped asymmetrical shells, which was also taken up, soon after, in Germany, especially in the South. (Ill. 70)

ROENTGEN, DAVID (1743–1807). This cabinet-maker's workshop in Neuwied, which he had taken over from his father Abraham, was world-famous. Its clients were the princes of Europe, the nobility, clergy and wealthy bourgeoisie. Where the model was successful, he often repeated some precious, inlaid and richly bronzed piece of gala-furniture, which he liked to provide with secret drawers.

ROLL-MOULDING. During the Late Renaissance and Mannerist period the plastic ornament of roll-moulding developed through the rolling-in of the edges or ends of coats of arms, scrolls, etc. (Floris-style; School of Fontainebleau), which was much employed as architectural decoration until the end of the Baroque. (Ill. 249)

ROMNEY, GEORGE (1734–1802). A contemporary of Reynolds and Gainsborough, he portrayed the beauties of the English Court and the Stage in the classicist style. He was considered, above all, a ladies' painter (Lady Hamilton) who knew exactly which of their attractions his clients wished to have emphasised (portraits in London National Gallery, Wallace Collection, Nat. Port. Gall., etc.).

ROSA, SALVATOR (1615–1673). Italian painter and graphic artist. Born in Naples, he lived and worked – with intervals in Naples and Florence – principally in Rome, where he became a Court painter, overloaded with commissions. He painted heroic-dramatic battle-pieces in tempestuous compositions, and landscapes, fantastic and eerie with rocky chasms. During his later period he ventured, not very successfully, to paint monumental history pictures and altar-pieces. Ninety etchings are preserved from his graphic work.

ROWLANDSON, THOMAS (1756–1827), who lived and died in London, was important as a graphic and water-colour artist. His town and country views (Naples, etc.), as well as his cycles of brilliant satirical caricatures of contemporary life ('The Dance through Life', etc.), were reproduced as coloured etchings by a carefully devised technique. Rowlandson also fittingly illustrated the works of the great English novelists (Fielding, Goldsmith, Sterne).

RUBENS, SIR PETER PAUL (1577–1640), was born in Siegen. His father was an Antwerp lawyer, exiled on account of the religious wars; later, he trained at Antwerp, first as a page for service at Court and finally as a painter. Rubens grew up to become one of those exceptional men whose worldly success did not affect

249. Roll-moulding on the staircase of the Mirabell Palace in Salzburg (L. v. HILDEBRANDT/DONNER)

their inward stature. This versatile man mastered the classics, the art of diplomacy and six languages. But his greatest achievement lies in his consummation of the Full Baroque. He is the greatest of all Flemish painters. During long years of wandering and apprenticeship in Italy, as Court painter to the Duke of Mantua (1600–1608) – when he absorbed many impressions from Mantegna, Michelangelo, Elsheimer, Caravaggio and, above all, Titian and Tintoretto, – he shed his early Mannerist style, derived from his masters in the Netherlands; extensive travel (Genoa, Madrid) and the assiduous study of Antiquity also contributed to this end. After 1608 he became Court painter to the Spanish Regent in Antwerp, also her political adviser and, in a sense, Secretary of State; in that capacity he was later to negotiate in Madrid and London the peace between Spain and England.

His first mature period begins after 1610 with the impressive 'Raising of the Cross' and the 'Deposition' (Antwerp Cathedral) and ends with the 'Last Judgment' and the 'Fall of the Damned' in the Munich Pinakothek. Already within this period the whole range of Rubens' subjects unfolds: battle pictures ('The Rape of the Daughters of Leucippus'; 'The Lion Hunt', Munich;) mythological subjects ('The Judgment of Paris', London, ill. p. 328); the first Bacchanales, full of intoxication and joie de vivre, with their fair, luscious female nudes, and portraits. In the quiet self-portrait with Isabella Brant (1609–10), he commemorates his youthful marriage. In the 1620's he reaches full maturity. Besides vigorous portraits, he continues to paint large compositions. They increase in movement, without seeming overloaded – pictorial inventions of the greatest compactness, and of euphonic colour, which reach their culmination with the enormous picture-cycle for Maria de' Medici (Paris/Louvre). The late style of the 1630's aims at still greater effects of colour, especially red (Altar of St Ildefonso, Vienna). Among his portraits the finest are those of his second wife, the youthful Helen Fourment ('The Fur Coat', Vienna). He painted her no less readily as a nude (Andromeda) than as St Cecilia (Vienna). The northern streak of this universal artist is most perfectly expressed in his landscape ('Steen Castle', 'Landscape with Rainbow'). Rubens maintained an enormous workshop which under his guidance decorated whole mansions with paintings. Among his most prominent assistants were for a time van Dyck, and, above all, Jan Brueghel, who painted the fruit and flowers, and Snijders, who painted the animals in his pictures. For these details he gave his assistants full freedom of action; nevertheless, the master's personality dominated the workshop. Among his countless works, about 500 are by Rubens' hand. Many of his paintings were engraved by the 'Rubens engravers', and spread far and wide.

RUYSDAEL, JACOB ISAACSZ VAN (1628/29–1682). An outstanding Dutch landscape painter of the 17th century, from Haarlem. He seems to lose himself willingly in the contemplation of transience and decay (marshy oakwoods, wintry wildernesses), and therefore he strongly influenced the German Romantics ('The Jewish Cemetery', Dresden). Besides these landscapes of mood, Ruysdael painted simple and quiet views of dunes, marshes and rivers, calm pictures in heavy golden-brown tones, with a minimum of movement, yet a maximum of feeling ('The Mill at Wijk', Amsterdam/ Rijksmuseum, ill. p. 344). Ruysdael's Scandinavian landscapes are also famous; these were inspired by Allaert van Everdingen (1621–1675).

RUYSDAEL, SALOMON VAN (c. 1600–1670), uncle of Jacob and also from Haarlem, belongs with Jan van Goyen to the first masters who painted landscape for its own sake. In his early period he favoured a greenish-grey tone, which covers the whole picture surface; later he worked with contrasting colours, and his nature-forms gained in firmness and precision. It is probable that his nephew the 'great Ruysdael' was trained in his workshop.

RUSH, WILLIAM (1756–1833). One of the earliest of important American sculptors, Rush was self-taught. He worked mainly in wood and clay. He was a founder of the Pennsylvania Academy of the Fine Arts (where one may see a fine plaster cast of an original pine-knot portrait Rush made of his own head). His major portraits include Washington, Franklin, Joseph Wright and Samuel Morris.

SALZBURG CATHEDRAL was erected 1622–55 by Santino Solari, and forms the grand overture to the Full Baroque in German-speaking lands. The apse and transepts – all with semicircular ends – are grouped around the dome, while the barrel-vaulted nave has side-chapels and galleries.

SANDRART, JOACHIM VON (1606–1688). Like Vasari and Karel van Mander, this German painter and engraver is known to posterity less by his artistic work than by what he wrote about art. In his *German Aca-*

demy of the noble arts of architecture, sculpture and painting, he dealt with aesthetic theory, followed by biographies of German and foreign artists.

ST FLORIAN (1698–1750) is, apart from Melk, the grandest monastic foundation of the Austrian Baroque. It is grouped around several courts. The main and southernmost court derives its special character from the architecture of the main complex of buildings in the centre of each wing. The southern wing contains the magnificent marble hall; the east wing the library, and the west wing the grand staircase which Carlo Antonio Carlone began and Jacob Prandtauer completed.

SCHLAUN, JOH. CONRAD (1694–1773). A leading Westphalian Baroque architect whose main works are to be found in Münster (Castle-residence, 'Erbdrosten-hof', church of St Clement).

SCHLÜTER, ANDREAS (c. 1660–1714). By way of Danzig and Warsaw (Vilanov Palace) the Hamburg-born Schlüter came to Berlin, where he was appointed Palace architect. The great square pile of the Berlin Castle (destroyed in the Second World War), a grand monument of the North German Baroque with its great pillared central court and magnificently appointed inner rooms (Parade Chambers, Knights' Hall), was in the main his work. He was no less accomplished as a sculptor than as an architect, and numbers among his works the 21 expressive heads of dying warriors on the Berlin Arsenal and the equestrian statue of the Grand Elector, the embodiment of absolute authority (now in the precincts of Charlottenburg Palace, ill. 232). Following the collapse of the inadequately supported Mint Tower, Schlüter had to leave Berlin in 1706. He died in St Petersburg.

SEGHERS, HERCULES (1589–c. 1645) a pupil of Coninxloo, stands at the beginning of Baroque Dutch landscape painting. He discarded the panoramic ordering in three successive picture planes (Patenir, q. v.) in favour of the tonal gradations of his poetic landscapes, spanned by the high vault of heaven. Through stylistic comparisons with his tinted landscape-etchings, many a work formerly attributed to other artists can now be ascribed to Seghers.

SNIJDERS (SNYDERS), FRANS (1579–1657). This Flemish painter was a close assistant of Rubens, in whose large pictures he often painted the flowers and fruit ('Garland of Fruit', Munich). He was a still-life specialist. On well-appointed tables he piles an abundance of fruit, vegetables, fish and venison, often animating the 'lifeless' subject by adding domestic animal or human figures. Snijders is accounted one of the most fertile painters of animals (mainly hunting-scenes).

STEEN, JAN (1626–1679). The lively imagination of this painter enabled him to cover the whole broad field of contemporary Dutch life with the gaiety of a Frans Hals. Open-air scenes and interiors came alternately from his brush and in their anecdotal variety offer ample opportunity for expressing his good humour and roguishness. He took delight in representing the fun of a noisy banquet ('Gay Company', The Hague/Mauritshuis; 'The Beanfeast', Kassel, ill. p. 60) or satirizing small human failings ('The Lovesick Maiden', Amsterdam). The narrative content of his pictures is so telling that their painterly quality, their wealth of colour and the superior handling of the composition are often overlooked.

STRAUB, JOHANN BAPTIST (1704–1784). This Court sculptor in Munich, who hailed from Suabia, was one of the foremost artists of the Bavarian Rococo. He adapted his altars and tabernacles most tactfully to the interior architecture of the buildings which were to house them (High Altar and side altars of the monastic churches of Ettal and Schäftlarn).

STROZZI, BERNARDO, known as Cappuccino (1581–1644). A Genoese painter who, motivated by religious enthusiasm, at the age of 17 entered a Capuchin monastery which, however, he left again in 1631. His exuberant painting, influenced by Veronese, was as tempestuous as his temperament. Genre scenes and biblical subjects are rendered in harmonies of vigorous colours which, in his adopted Venice, brought him high repute (pictures by him in Berlin, Vienna, Genoa).

STUART, GILBERT (1755–1828), is best known for his extraordinarily lifelike portraits, among which his paintings of George Washington are the most famous. Stuart began this tradition of vibrant and realistic portraiture at the tender age of fourteen when he travelled around the colonies with an itinerant painter. He became popular almost to the point of adulation, both in England and the United States, because of his phenomenal ability to catch the salient points of his subjects' character. So that he might better express a personality, Stuart even went so far as to match his backgrounds to the flesh tones of his sitters.

STUBBS, GEORGE (1724—1800). Stubbs, who was born in Liverpool, has always been considered a remarkable animal painter, but a recent comprehensive exhibition of his pictures, many of the most important of which had never before been shown, has established him as a major artist. He went to Italy in 1754 to study the old masters, but he preferred nature. An anatomist from childhood, he retired to a farm where he brought dead horses to his studio in order to execute from them the drawings which were the basis for his *Anatomy of the Horse,* published in 1766. This work revolutionized animal painting. Stubbs's greatest pictures are 'The Grosvenor Staghunt', 'Lord Rockingham's Racehorses' and 'The Hambletonian', all privately owned. They have a strength and weight attained by few; the modelling is superb; but what distinguishes them even more is a quality of aloofness, a sense of balance and serenity which are rare in English art and which relate Stubbs to Vermeer.

TENIERS, DAVID, THE YOUNGER (1610–1690). Born in Antwerp, died in Brussels. This extremely

250. THUMB, *monastic library at St Gallen*

fertile Flemish genre painter, always knew how to amuse a large public by his wittily rendered popular feasts and tavern brawls with soldiers and gambling scenes. Pictures by him are to be found in nearly all the large galleries.

TERBORCH, GERARD (1617–1681), grew up in a wealthy aristocratic environment and as a young painter visited many European countries. From 1646 to 1648 he painted a group-portrait of the diplomats assembled at Münster for the Westphalian peace congress. His education and career seem to have determined the contents and pictorial language of his paintings. He most enjoyed portraying aristocratic young ladies in precious robes of silk or velvet, making music, reading or writing, daydreaming in elegant interiors ('The Letter', Mauritshuis). In his paintings, too, he eschewed all garishness by the use of delicate colour harmonies. (Ill. p. 346)

TERBRUGGHEN, HENDRIK (1588–1629). During recent decades interest in this painter from Utrecht, who formerly was little noted, has become progressively livelier. Terbrugghen lived in Italy for ten years, and his pictures brought Caravaggio's perspective ideas to the north and prepared the way for the ascendancy of Dutch painting.

TESSIN, NICODEMUS, THE YOUNGER (1654–1728). During the years of his apprenticeship in Italy this Swedish Baroque architect came under the influence of Bernini and Fontana. Later, he preferred the more classical French School which harmonized better with the Swedish character. His most important building is the enormous, almost square castle in Stockholm, the outstanding monument of the Swedish Baroque.

THUMB, PETER (1681–1766). A Baroque architect from the Bregenz Forest (Vorarlberg) who collaborated with Franz Beer on the conventual church of St Urban (Switzerland) and also took a leading part in erecting the monastic church of St Gallen, which he built together with Bagnato. His most mature work, however, is the pilgrimage church of Birnau, Lake Constance, whose radiant serenity is enhanced by a wealth of Rococo decoration. (Ill. 31, 250)

TIEPOLO, GIOVANNI BATTISTA (1696–1770), represents the consummation of Venetian Baroque painting. He often enhances architecture by pictorial means, thereby gaining great spatial effects which have something operatic about them – spectacles of Court feasts such as the 'Banquet of Cleopatra' in the Palazzo Labia in Venice. Tiepolo's chief work, in which his son Domenico assisted him, is the great cycle of frescoes in the Emperor's hall and staircase of Balthasar Neumann's Würzburg Residenz. Allegorical representations of the continents of Europe, Asia, Africa and America adorn the staircase (ill. p. 321). Mythology, legend and exotic lore unite in a triumph of the Faith and an apotheosis of Art under the patronage of the prince-bishops from the House of Schönborn. Tiepolo's later works in the Palace at Madrid seem to dissolve in light and atmosphere, their hovering figures to disappear in ethereal space.

TISCHBEIN. Two members at least of this ramified family of painters of the 18th and 19th centuries deserve mention. Johann Friedrich August (1750–1812), who was apprenticed to his father Valentin and his uncle Johann Heinrich the Elder ('Kassel Tischbein'). His portraits with all their dependence on the cool English Court painters, retain much of the Rococo grace ('Leipzig Tischbein'). The famous portrait of Goethe in the Campagna (Staedel Institute, Frankfurt) is by his cousin Johann Heinrich Wilhelm ('Goethe – Tischbein'; 1751–1829).

TRUMBULL, JOHN (1756–1843), was the son of a colonial governor. At the age of twenty he resigned from the Continental Army, but did not desert the battlefield. He merely exchanged his sword for a brush and began to paint (at first under the tutelage of Benjamin West) the historic battles of the American Revolution and the memorable moments in the birth of a nation. Into extremely small canvases Trumbull compressed all the sweep and turbulence of war without losing accuracy and detail. His gift for perfect miniature portraits was fully utilized in these scenes, which were crowded with famous men. Both Washington and Jefferson recognised the importance of Trumbull's work and he was offered a sinecure as a private secretary which he refused.

VAN DE VELDE is the name of a Dutch family of painters of the 16th and 17th centuries. Adriaen van de Velde (1636–1672), a landscape artist, painted bright and friendly pastures with cattle resting and grazing. His elder brother Willem (1633–1707) depicted harbour scenes, naval battles and storms. He admirably succeeded in rendering light and atmospheric effects across the shimmer of water.

VELASQUEZ, DIEGO RODRIGUEZ DE SILVA Y (1599–1660), was, like Murillo, born in Seville, but spent his life as Court painter, gentleman-in-waiting and seneschal, chiefly in Madrid. His early works ('The Topers', 'Vulcan's Forge') still evince the stark realism and the harsh chiaroscuro of Caravaggio, who by that time had his following in Spain. Yet his very first journey to Italy (1630) brings about a change; the shadows assume colour, the light softens. Two pictures of the Medici Gardens in Rome, painted for his own pleasure, show a kind of *plein air* character, and such a loosening of the brushwork that they seem to anticipate Impressionism. But the Court painter had to submit to the will of his patrons and to paint chiefly portraits. Yet his sublime painterly skill ennobles even the insignificant figures of the King, the Infantes and Infantas by the beauty of his pictorial approach (ill. p. 351). Never before had the brush been used so lightly and impressionistically as in the portraits of the young princesses in their stiff and sumptuous ceremonial costumes of the Spanish Court. He never resorted to fussy imitation of material texture. As with Frans Hals, his brushwork remains visible, open and generous. And yet, at a certain distance from the picture every detail assumes plastic clarity. Perhaps he shows his greatest painterly skill and human sympathy in the portraits of the unfortunate 'Court jesters', who were kept by the Court like domestic pets – for here he felt unfettered by representational demands. His objective manner, eschewing all flattery, is admirable in his State portraits. That of Pope Innocent X, painted, entirely in reds, during the second Italian journey (1649–51), reveals the unpleasant yet energetic features so unequivocally, that the Pope complained of its excessive truthfulness. Among the large compositions, the early 'Surrender of Breda' (1634) is, in its chivalrous and conciliatory attitude on the part of the victors towards the vanquished, the most human and also the best organized battle-piece in the history of art. Its composition is mainly determined by the warriors' lances (hence the Spanish title 'Las Lanzas'). In the 'Maids of Honour' (Las Meninas, 1656) he created one of the supreme masterpieces of group painting, giving of his best in painterly skill. Finally, in 'Las Hilanderas' (1657), a picture which shows spinners at work in the dark foreground, and visiting members of the Court in the brightly lit background of a tapestry factory, Velasquez produced a work of exemplary artistic worth which at the same time is ethically without reproach. Almost all the principal works of Velasquez are in the Prado, Madrid; some are in Vienna and others in the National Gallery, London – where, *inter alia*, is the exquisitely painted 'Venus with the Mirror', until Goya the only female nude in Spanish painting.

VERMEER VAN DELFT, JAN (1632–1675). Only some 40 paintings by this master are known to us, and yet he ranks, as do Rembrandt and Frans Hals, as one of the very greatest painters of the Netherlands. Information about his life is scanty, and for more than 200 years he was even forgotten, until rediscovered during the second half of the 19th century. Vermeer is the painter par excellence of interiors; to these he entirely devoted himself, except for a few mythological pictures and the famous 'View of Delft' in the Mauritshuis, The Hague. The few human figures in his pictures are usually placed (or seated) in a room, of which only a wall, parallel to the picture frame, and the tiles of the floor are visible, clearly defined in the space. His female figures, mostly young, do not remain incidental, but are made to convey the general mood ('The Girl with the Pearl Necklace', Berlin; 'The Letter', Amsterdam; 'A Lady weighing Pearls', Washington; 'The Milkmaid', Amsterdam, ill. p. 27). Nothing disturbs the calm, harmonious intimacy of these scenes, steeped in a soft light falling from lofty windows, which invests Vermeer's rarefied colours, his favourite dark blues and warm yellows, with their intense radiance. The pleasure in painting detail and anecdote, which since van Eyck had characterized Dutch and Flemish painting of interiors, yielded in Vermeer's case to concentration upon only a few pictorial objects and to a calm and serenity worthy of being called classic.

VERSAILLES, PALACE OF. This residence of Louis XIV, through its combination of palace, town and gardens, became an architectural prototype of absolute monarchy. The road system radiates from the Cour d'honneur, and thus gives geometrical expression to the relationship between town and palace. The court of honour is relatively modest, since it derives substantially from the much smaller water-palace of Louis XIII. Louis Levau and Jules Hardouin-Mansart sheathed it (1668–1710), building the War and Peace rooms, and between these on the garden-front the magnificent Gallery of Mirrors. The central building, strongly projecting on the garden side and emphasised by its architectural articulation and sculptural decoration, was increased to a breadth of 1890 ft. This was effected by adding extensive wings, which enclose other inner courts. The palace chapel and theatre stand out among the richly decorated interiors. Gardens, planned just as generously, and integrated with the main building, are in keeping with the enormous palace (ill. 227).

VIERZEHNHEILIGEN. Opposite Banz, at the spot where the fourteen Saints are said to have appeared to a shepherd, rises the twin-towered pilgrimage church (1743–71). Balthasar Neumann erected its exuberant interior upon a relatively simple cruciform ground plan (ill. 226, 247). The nave surrounds the canopy of the shrine like a precious jewel, where once upon a time stood a modest Gothic chapel. Architecture, stucco work, fresco painting and ornament are happily blended.

VOUET, SIMON (1590–1649). This painter, whose work was much in demand, occupied a leading position in the contemporary artistic world of Paris. His pictures, of biblical and classical subjects, translate the 'Caravaggesque' painting of the Italian Baroque into French (St Louis, Dresden; Diana, Hampton Court). His beautiful half-lengths of the Virgin (one of them in the Louvre) deserve special mention.

WATTEAU, ANTOINE (1684–1721), was born in Flemish Valenciennes, and came to Paris at the age of 18. There, at the beginning of the century, his work already anticipated what was to become his artistic credo: to use light and shimmering colours, to achieve supple and spirited forms, to provide a sociable and amorous content (ill. p. 360). The themes of his pictures, reflecting the life of a sophisticated society, have been much imitated, but without awareness of the deeper substance of Watteau's art. He was a lonely and often a sick man, and his paintings are dreams of a fairer and gentler life, expressed in colour. A picture like 'The Embarcation to Cytherea' (two versions, Berlin and Paris) with the sparkling train of cavaliers and their ladies, is by no means a description of an experienced reality, but pure poetry, which glorifies the blissful encounter between man and nature. Other important works are: 'Gilles', Berlin; 'Trade Sign of the Art Dealer Gersaint', Berlin; 'L'Indifférent', Louvre; 'The Halt during the Chase', London. Watteau's paintings encouraged a number of engravers of his period to produce his work, which thus became widely distributed. His works, partly lost in the original, have been collected and edited by one of his admirers in almost 800 etchings.

WEINGARTEN, MONASTIC BUILDINGS. This Benedictine Abbey in Suabia has an enchanting church with convex façade, flanked by twin towers, and over the crossing a great dome with lantern. Cosmas Damian Asam painted the fine ceiling frescoes. The famous organ is the work of Joseph Gabler. The ideal plan for the monastic buildings did not materialize.

WELSCH, MAXIMILIAN VON (1671–1745). Franconian architect of the Baroque, and director of building in Mainz and Bamberg. Together with Neumann he built the Schönborn chapel in Würzburg Cathedral. His well-conceived plans – though they had to be largely modified – enabled him to participate in some important Baroque palace buildings, like Bruchsal, Pommersfelden, the Würzburg Residenz and the Fulda Orangerie.

WEST, BENJAMIN (1738–1820). A painter of historical, mythological and religious subjects, all of them executed in a heroic mould and in somewhat stereotyped colours. West was born in Springfield, Pennsylvania, the son of Quaker innkeepers. He credited friendly Indians near his birthplace, who showed him how they mixed the colours for painting their faces, with first interesting him in art. He became a successful portraitist before he was twenty, later going to London where he became the friend of George III (who helped him obtain many commissions), the successor to Sir Joshua Reynolds as president of the Royal Academy, the painter of more than 400 canvases in all, and the adviser of many young Americans studying in England, particularly Allston, Copley, C. W. Peale and Gilbert Stuart. Actually a mediocre (and didactic) painter himself, he nevertheless had an enormous influence on American artists, one of the most important of which was his execution of historical subjects in contemporary clothing instead of Roman togas – a radical departure for his day. His two best-known paintings are 'Death of General Wolfe' and 'Penn's Treaty with the Indians'.

VIENNA BELVEDERE. The garden palace of Prince Eugene, then situated outside the city-precincts of

251. WREN, St Paul's Cathedral, London

Vienna (1714–22), is one of the most charming secular buildings of the Austrian Baroque. It is Lucas von Hildebrandt's masterpiece. In spite of its simple ground-plan, a great sense of mobility is imparted by the great variety of roof-contours. (Ill. 243)

WIESKIRCHE. This pilgrimage church, situated in a magnificent landscape of the Lower Alps near Steingaden in Upper Bavaria, owes its origin to a miraculous statue of the Flagellation of Christ. The main elliptical interior is surrounded by a narrow ambulatory (ill. 225). In this building, his last (1746–54), Dominikus Zimmermann, the architect, combined the most mature ideas of his early works (cf. p. 325). Together with stucco workers from Wessobrunn and with his brother, the painter Johann Baptist Zimmermann, he decorated it with a wealth of Rococo splendour.

WILLMANN, MICHAEL (1630–1706). Court painter to the Grand Elector whose large frescoes in Silesian monasteries and the churches at Leubus and Grüssau made him the pioneer of ceiling decoration of the Late Baroque in eastern Germany.

WILSON, RICHARD (1714–1782), the English painter, settled in London after a long stay in Italy. The Roman Campagna, southern shores and his native Wales provided the subjects for his golden-tinted 'ideal' landscapes with ruins, castles and poetic vistas stretching away into the distance (Villa of Maecenas; Lake of Averno. Both in London/National Gallery).

WITTE, EMANUEL DE (1617–1692). Dutch painter of architecture and interiors. The latter were mainly of churches in Delft and Amsterdam, which are bathed in a painterly chiaroscuro through reflected light.

WOUVERMAN(S), PHILIPS (1619–1668). This Dutch painter concentrated upon horses and their riders in hunting and battle scenes. He used vigorous colours and strongly accented light, often placing emphasis upon the luminous white of a horse.

WREN, SIR CHRISTOPHER (1632–1723). After working as mathematician and astronomer, the great English architect turned entirely to designing buildings. His elaborate plan for the royal palace in Winchester was only partly executed. Hampton Court and Greenwich Hospital are well-known secular buildings by the master. After the Fire of London (1666), Wren, as supervisor of the royal buildings, built no less than 53 churches between 1670 and 1711. His chief work is St Paul's Cathedral, London (ill. 251), with its 360-foot dome and lantern evolved from Bramante's plan for the dome of St Peter's, Rome. Many of Wren's London churches were either destroyed or damaged during the Second World War.

WÜRZBURG RESIDENZ. This, the most imposing castle-residence of the German Baroque was built (1719–53) by Balthasar Neumann, jointly with the best Baroque architects like Maximilian von Welsch and Lucas von Hildebrandt, for the prince-bishop Johann Philip Franz of Schönborn. The lower part of the building still shows the severity of the French school, while the architecture of the upper parts becomes ever lighter and more exuberant, culminating in the graceful roof cupola on the garden side. The wings were enlarged by four inner courts which flank the Court of Honour. The lateral façades of the wings are emphasised by convex central projections. To the left of the entrance hall the grand staircase debouches. The Hall of the Emperor on the garden side and the vaulted ceiling over the staircase are adorned with magnificent Tiepolo frescoes (ill. p. 321).

ZICK, JANUARIUS (1730–1797). His ceiling paintings in Suabian churches (Wiblingen, Rot an der Rot) present a sharp contrast to the illusionistic fresco style of his father Johannes (1702–1762).

ZIMMERMANN, DOMINIKUS (1685–1766). This South German Rococo architect's strength lies in interior decoration, which with his brother Johann Baptist (1680–1758) he brought to a pitch of fabulous splendour. One of their finest achievements is the pilgrims' church of Steinhausen (Württemberg, ill. p. 320), a magnificent, slightly vaulted elliptical structure, whose inner garland of pillars forms an open ambulatory and thus gives the effect of lightness and unity. Together they also built the Church of Our Lady at Günzburg (1735–40) and – the finest product of their collaboration – the Wieskirche (q. v., ill. 225).

ZURBARÁN, FRANCISCO DE (1598–1664). Court painter to Philip IV, born in Estramadura, he worked in Seville and Madrid. He painted opulent portraits of the Spanish aristocracy, but religious pictures were his forte ('The Apotheosis of St Thomas Aquinas', Seville Museum), painted in the chiaroscuro style of the Baroque – influenced by Caravaggio – which assumes in him an expression of austere and fanatical faith. He painted devotional pictures of single figures, ascetic saints and monks, whose contemplative air animates their somewhat over-serious mien.

From Neo-Classicism
to the Impressionists

252. SCHINKEL, *the 'Neue Wache', Berlin, built in Greek Doric style*

'WHAT, ANOTHER REBELLION?' exclaimed Louis XVI on the morning of July 15, 1789, when told of the storming of the Bastille. He was given the famous answer, 'Sir, this is not another rebellion, this is the Revolution.' The French Revolution marked an important turning-point in history. Merging all the main aspirations of the Enlightenment in a single violent outburst, it swept away in a matter of weeks the privileges of the Church and of the Nobility. The Third Estate, subjugated by the feudal overlords in the 16th and 17th centuries, now demanded their rights. The armies of the Revolution nailed the words Liberty, Fraternity and Equality to their banners and carried them triumphantly across Europe.

The humanitarian ideals of the Enlightenment became the planks of a political programme. For example, the slave trade, tolerated by many European countries during the 18th century, was proscribed. The acceptance of the principle of equal rights led to the abolition of the privileges of rank and class. A commoner could now become an officer, a man without private means a magistrate or judge. In order to practise a trade it was no longer necessary to be a member of a guild. Peasants were no longer treated as serfs, and criminals put on the rack.

Men's standards of living underwent a basic change. Whereas the Church and the Nobility, so long entrenched, clung to the preservation of past institutions, the bourgeoisie of the 19th century ardently believed in progress. Technology and commerce, advancing by leaps and bounds, ushered in the first industrial revolution. The people were possessed by a craving for wealth and success, which to this day has continued to grow. Many of these trends, it must be admitted, did not clearly come to light until after the middle of the 19th century.

The people's revolutionary zeal at the turn of the century was still inspired by an idealism that had its roots in the 18th century. Dislike of the outmoded conventions of the Baroque period and of Rococo decadence and licence was already very widespread by 1750. This was the mood that engendered Rousseau's exhortation to go 'back to Nature', and encouraged the German 'Sturm und Drang' movement to exalt the individual man of genius. Schiller, in particular, was an ardent protagonist of this ideal of the 'whole man', whom he eloquently extolled in his poem *The Artists*, written in the year of the French Revolution. Byron and Carlyle were to follow in his steps, even if their ideals were less lofty.

It was the voice of a newly-orientated bourgeoisie that had awakened to a sense of its own destiny, and which was eager to take an active part in the building of a new world. In such a soil was nurtured the political liberalism of England and France, whose aim was to consolidate the rights for which the Revolution had been fought; in Germany, on the other hand, it blossomed forth as an unpolitical idealism – the idealism of German Classicism, which held that each individual was intellectually and morally an autonomous being.

Stimulated by the interaction of Romanticism and the Classical Revival, this upsurge of idealism manifested itself in the arts, though to varying degrees in different parts of Europe. The excavations at

381

Pompeii and Herculaneum in the mid-18th century turned men's thoughts to Antiquity. In the words of the French painter David – to whom we shall return – all Europe believed that the study of Ancient Greece could 'transform morals' no less than it could 'transform literature and art'. In 1764, Winckelmann wrote his well-known *History of Ancient Art,* in which he contrasts the 'noble simplicity and calm grandeur' of Ancient Greece with the 'irresponsibility, extravagance and impertinent fire' of the Baroque. Flaxman, Fuseli and Blake, in England, were, in their different ways, also influenced by the mood of the time.

The French Revolution recognised the great stylistic potentialities inherent in the Classical Revival. Napoleon took advantage of it, and, enhancing the effect to produce the so-called Empire style, used this as an expression of imperial power. Thus the Greek Revival, democratic in origin, became by infiltration the style of the Court and, later, of reaction.

The original aim, as we have seen, was to achieve a re-birth of Classical Antiquity, although re-awakening would perhaps be a better term. Nevertheless, the Greek Revival proved to be digging its own grave. Since it approached the arts from the viewpoint of archaeology and called upon them to copy Antiquity 'literally', it was bound to stifle all genuine creativeness in the artist. In place of originality we find nothing but flat, soulless imitation, sponsored by the academies of the 19th century.

The Romantic Movement had its beginnings at about the same time. Although the Brothers Adam and Sir John Soane were building in a strictly classical manner during the second half of the 18th century, English landscape-gardening was already based upon an essentially romantic conception, with clumps of trees to break up the old formal avenues. Macpherson's 'Ossian' was a brilliant imitation of old Celtic poetry and had great influence on the romantic poets that were to follow. The contrast grew more pronounced: whereas the Greek Revival tried to make all works of art conform to certain prescribed rules, the Romantic Movement radiated into the infinity of nature and developing history. The Greek Revival sought reality in a world from which the Romantics longed to escape.

The Greek Revival proclaimed that every one of the arts existed in its own right. Each was subject to its own laws and none should be allowed to merge with another. Sculpture is sculpture, and the drama remains the drama.

The Romantic Movement sought to redress this separateness; its supporters held that a work of art was a synthesis. Its musicians wanted to paint with notes and gave names to their compositions, a thing unknown in the past. In their landscapes, the Romantic painters tried to express in colour their own heightened awareness in the presence of nature, whilst Romantic poets gave their work musical nuances through the skilful use of words.

To those who supported the Greek Revival the world appeared as a well ordered place, the Romantics saw it as full of secrets and insoluble enigmas. The former saw in Greek Antiquity something valid for all time, the latter steeped themselves in the gloaming of a romanticized medievalism. The historical novel, the historical ballad, the historical painting, even the study of history itself, were largely inspired by the Romantics.

This preoccupation with their own past had strengthened the nationalistic aspirations of the peoples of Europe from the time of the French Revolution onwards and led – often through war and bloodshed – to the secession of individual countries from what had been associations of nations (Greece and the Balkan States) or to the formation of new States (Italy, Germany). The pent-up passions exploded in the two revolutions of 1830 and 1848 and helped the bourgeoisie to come into power. But the bourgeoisie had undergone a radical change since the turn of the century. Where it used to be cultured, with a strain of idealism, it was now concerned with material possessions – the kind of people we encounter in Balzac's *Comédie Humaine (Human Comedy).* A desire to make the world a better place and to improve mankind had yielded to *laisser-aller* and satisfaction with life as it was. The fundamental distinction between the new class and the ruling classes of an earlier age is the lack of tradition and real culture that characterizes the former. This is very marked in their relation to the arts.

Jean-Auguste Dominique Ingres: Odalisque

THÉODORE GÉRICAULT: The Raft of the Medusa

EUGÈNE DELACROIX: The March of the Teutons

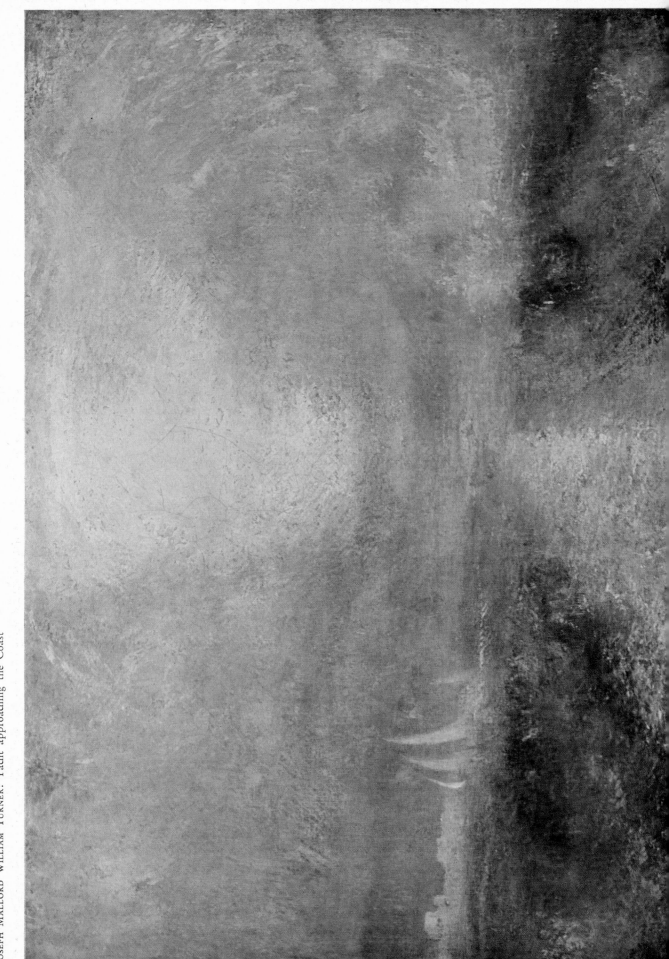

JOSEPH MALLORD WILLIAM TURNER: Yacht approaching the Coast

JOHN CONSTABLE: Weymouth Bay

WILLIAM BLAKE: Beatrice addressing Dante

The aristocracy and the wealthy patricians for the most part had a genuine understanding of art and were quite open to the views of others if they were expressed in a manner that was artistically acceptable. High court circles, for example, saw to it that Beaumarchais' *Marriage of Figaro* was staged for the first time, against the objections of the Censor, even though the play included a bold attack on the position held by the aristocracy.

We do not find a similar attitude in the middle class of 19th-century Europe. The gulf between art and society, which has still not been bridged, derives from this period. Most artists and poets are misunderstood by their age and become martyrs of public opinion. There was still a small élite, ready to help on these unrecognised artists, but for the majority art was merely a pleasant concomitant to life. The painter was required to produce pretty decorations for the walls, the writer effortless entertainment, the composer simple tunes for humming and the playwright plays with plenty going on. And did one really want to be uplifted by great works of art, one could always go to the museum. Indeed, the museum was a characteristic institution of the 19th century.

In such circumstances the artist was bound to feel isolated. He either took refuge in *l'art pour l'art* and treated the public's lack of understanding with contempt or he fought passionately for recognition of his work. An art that is rejected by society is bound to turn against that society sooner or later. A natural corollary is an alliance with the social movements that sought to mitigate the sufferings of the 'Fourth Estate' brought about by industrialization. Literature and the visual arts became vehicles for expressing the social conscience. The great European authors, Dickens, Tolstoy, Zola, great painters like Daumier or Millet, sculptors like Meunier, all dealt with the realities of existence, and all to a greater or lesser degree exposed the follies and injustices of their time.

Art, then, during the second half of the century was no longer in harmony with the economic and social ideas then current, but more often than not found itself at loggerheads with them. It would also be fair to say that art had grown to be in advance of its time, for most of the artists who were so despised or ignored during their lifetime eventually won recognition. What is more, out of this mood of conflict the new and changed art of our own day was to grow.

ARCHITECTURE

The re-awakened interest in Classical Antiquity encouraged architects, too, to make a new beginning. Palladio's classical style was studied with great enthusiasm in England and France already before the end of the Baroque period. Blondel and de Cotte in France, and Wren and Inigo Jones in England for the most part avoided Baroque exuberance. The Classic Movement in England began in 1730, although the affinity was rather more with the Renaissance – which had never intended to copy Greece and Rome literally. English architects (Wood, Adam, Chambers, Campbell) now went on pilgrimages to southern Italy and Greece, to survey Greek temples. The results of their researches were published in many large and elegant volumes. Neo-classicism took concrete form in England when Stuart, after a trip to Greece, built a Greek temple at Hagley in 1758. The remodelling of Keddleston by Adam in 1761 encouraged the movement, and the erection of the Bank of England by Soane, employing both Greek and Roman motifs, gave it authority. Winckelmann wrote, 'the springs of art have been tapped and to find them means going to Athens.' The Greek Revival was ranging back beyond Renaissance models to the Greek origins of the architecture of Classical Antiquity. Models for all types of structural and decorative features in the new style were to be found on the ancient sites. The bulging, elaborate façades of the Baroque were rejected in favour of plain, sober walls and clean outlines came back into favour for the buildings themselves. Columns – still architecture's noblest device – were now used in rows in front of buildings, with parapets, or surmounted by triangular gables. The dignity of the severe Doric manner in particular appealed

253. *Residence of the President of the United States of America, Thomas Jefferson: Monticello, Virginia. Adaptation of the antique Roman style*

to architects; it seemed to them ideal as a dignified means of offsetting the affectation of the Rococo.

In England, however, the style favoured by the Regency architects of the early 19th century was Ionic. Their work is a peculiarly felicitous and original adaptation of the Classic mode, in no way a slavish copy of antique example. There was a spate of building after the Napoleonic wars when, owing to the Industrial Revolution and the fact that there had been no sudden dispersal of capital as in other European countries, England was immensely wealthy. Regency architecture is a direct reflection of the taste of the Prince of Wales and his chief architect Nash, and to this it owes its individuality. The two major buildings of the period, Carlton House and the Royal Pavilion, the one purely Classic, the other a fantastic Hindu variation on the Classic theme are both stamped with the Regent's personality; Nash turned London into a stucco-covered, straight-fronted, Ionic city, while bow windows and verandahs, flat-pitched roofs and Ionic columns transformed Cheltenham, Clifton and Brighton.

It is characteristic of the Classical Revival that buildings were now associated with certain figurative ideas. When Langhans built his Brandenburg Gate in Berlin in 1797 and Schinkel his 'Neue Wache' (New Guard-House) in 1816, the Doric manner was meant to symbolize the Spartan spirit of Prussia; the classic façade of Jefferson's house in 1796 to express his veneration for the democratic virtues of the Roman citizen. (Ill. 252, 253)

The victory of the French Revolution had undermined the monarchy and the power of the Church. This also meant the end of the great architectural designs of the Baroque period: it is no longer church and palace that make the principal demands upon architecture. This role is taken over by the museum, preferably dressed up as a Greek temple (Schinkel's Altes Museum in Berlin, Smirke's British Museum, Klenze's Glyptothek in Munich), the theatre (Schauspielhaus, Berlin) and municipal buildings ('Greek' Thomson in Glasgow, Simpson in Aberdeen and many other examples throughout the British Isles).

If the Baroque architect made nature part and parcel of the composition, in which the royal residence should be the focal point, the designer of the Greek Revival went out of his way to hide the mansion in the artificial wilderness of a park. The gigantic palace with its long suites of rooms becomes a modest country house without any special trappings.

The interior also is simple and unaffected. The elaborate perspectives of the Rococo and the imaginative effects obtained by concealed lighting have gone. Strong colours, like ultramarine and red, glow from the recesses of the coffered ceilings and accentuate the white marble reliefs and medallions on the walls.

Several so-called revolutionary designs now make their first appearance, anticipating the architecture of the 20th century. The Frenchman Ledoux designed a house in the shape of a cube surmounted by four similar cubes to form a kind of tower. He designed another in the shape of a sphere, whilst his compatriot Boullé planned an enormous spherical tomb for Sir Isaac Newton. Gilly, a German architect, was in favour of cube-shaped houses and intended the Berlin Schauspielhaus to be a hexahedron, standing between two half-prisms of stone. But none of these designs got beyond the drawing-board. Their originators were ignored by their contemporaries and what might have become a genuine new architecture was not allowed to take root.

The purely classical phase in architecture did not last very long. The age, if it directed its attention to the past, was more interested in the art of the Middle Ages, with which it had closer ties, and so the neo-Gothic came into being. As early as 1750 Walpole built his mansion at Strawberry Hill in the Gothic

manner, and neo-medievalism soon spread. At the beginning of the 19th century, enthusiasm for the Gothic was as marked as had been the cult of the Greek Revival fifty years earlier.

Friedrich Schinkel, the great 19th-century German architect and probably the greatest exponent of the Greek Revival, dreamt of a Gothic national cathedral. Two designs of his exist for a certain Berlin church, one with a Gothic, the other with a Greek façade and interior decoration (ill. 276). But this very same architect also interested himself in new methods of construction and new building materials. Had the store which he designed for Unter den Linden in Berlin been put up, it would, with all its glass, have been the first modern commercial building. Schinkel's diverse buildings and designs already herald the medley of styles that was to be a characteristic feature of the century. It was quite usual for the leading architect to master several styles. Friedrich von Gärtner gave the same street in Munich three entirely different buildings. One was modelled on a triumphal arch, another on a Florentine loggia of the Renaissance, the third – the University – was built in the Romanesque manner.

This borrowing from the past partly resulted from the conviction that the outside of each building must suggest its function. The term 'architecture parlante' ('speaking architecture') was coined at that time. A monument to a great man had to reflect his essential nobility. Classical forms were considered most suitable for this purpose. The Gothic was preferred for churches, since church architecture in the Middle Ages symbolized the peak of Christian civilisation in the west (Gau's Sainte Clotilde in Paris). But the Early Christian basilica was also used as a model (the church of St Boniface in Munich).

The history of architecture was soon reduced to a catalogue of established styles to be used at will. Architects specialized in a particular style, and were entrusted with buildings that fell within their category. This often led to amusing complications. For example, after the old Houses of Parliament were burnt down in 1834, Sir Charles Barry's design won the competition for a new building. But, unfortunately, he had specialized in the Renaissance, whereas it was laid down that the building must be Gothic, since English democratic institutions owe their origin to the Magna Carta (1215). Barry therefore consulted Augustus Pugin, who designed the detail of the façade and the decorations for the interior. There can be no doubt that the magnificent silhouette along the river owes almost everything to Pugin. On the other hand, Barry's work can be seen at its best and most characteristic in the club buildings of Pall Mall. (Ill. 254)

A few words must be said about Pugin. He was convinced that Gothic methods could be applied to the buildings of his day and believed ardently in honest design and good craftmanship. He was a versatile man who, like William Morris, designed a variety of things besides buildings, and who is better known as a writer than as an architect. His brilliant caricatures of the work of his 'classic' contemporaries, his brilliant drawings and his all too few buildings prove him to have been a man of quite outstanding gifts. Pugin, who desperately fought the inhumanity of the machine age and the smugness and conceit of his fellow architects, went mad and died when he was only 39 years of age.

In England, many of the followers of the Gothic Revival wrought considerable havoc; but for this Pugin can scarcely be blamed. The leader of the movement was Sir Gilbert Scott, who as a young man won a prize for a Gothic church in Hamburg. Scott, whose own buildings are not without

255. *The Opéra, Paris* (GARNIER). *Built under the influence of Renaissance and Baroque forms*

a certain outré splendour (St Pancras Station, the Foreign Office) set about remodelling numerous English parish churches, each 'as it should have been built originally', with results that were little short of disastrous. In order to protect the past from the restorers and 'interpreters', William Morris and other founded the Society for the Preservation of Ancient Buildings. Morris maintained that a building must only be restored to preserve its fabric and that there must be no tampering with the design. The great Austrian architect Adolf Loos (see page 442) said that 'he who does not respect his own age will also have no reverence for the past.' This is an apt comment on the 'restorers' of the 19th century.

John Ruskin, the great pioneer of a genuine popular education in art, was not a true follower of the Gothic Revival, although some of his writings may suggest the contrary. Though a brilliant writer and art historian, his own designs (the Oxford Museum, among others) were disappointing.

The great German architect Gottfried Semper aptly described the architectural confusion he encountered everywhere: 'The young architect travels across the world, he stuffs his folders with tracings of every kind and goes home in the hope that there will very soon be orders for a Vallhalla à la Parthenon, a basilica à la Monreale, a boudoir à la Pompeii, a palace à la Palazzo Pitti, a Byzantine church or a bazaar in the Turkish manner.'

And indeed the orders came quickly enough. Conditions grew more and more chaotic after 1850. Whereas the previous 'architecture parlante' invariably confined each style to a certain type of building, everyone was now allowed a free hand. In Paris, the Madeleine and the Stock Exchange were given façades resembling that of a Greek temple. Theatres, railway stations, post offices and factories were made to resemble Romanesque basilicas or Renaissance or Baroque palaces. Even the exteriors of the vast new civilian barracks that came to characterize the mushrooming cities were happy-hunting-grounds for the imitators. (Ill. 272, 255)

Meanwhile, with their factories, bridges and lighthouses, English engineers were quietly paving the way to a new architecture. These were the progeny of the Industrial Revolution and in them the materials of the future, metal, glass and concrete were first used with logic and daring. As early as 1758 John Smeaton had built one of the landmarks of modern architecture, the Eddystone Lighthouse. Its functional design and its binding of cement allowed it to endure where the sea had smashed its predecessors. The first cast iron bridge was built over the Severn by Abraham Darby in 1779, in 1801 Thomas Telford submitted a design for replacing the old London Bridge with a single-arch metal span of 600 feet, and in 1836 Brunel built the Clifton suspension bridge, spanning 702 feet. Boulton and Watt constructed a seven-storey mill at Salford, Manchester in 1801 which was the forefather of all metal-frame buildings. Joseph Paxton's Crystal Palace of 1851 was built entirely of glass on a prefabricated metal frame. Paxton's example inspired the Galérie des Machines and the 1000-foot Eiffel Tower, both erected for the International Exhibition in Paris of 1889.

But it needed the new functionalism of the beginning of the 20th century to put an end to the continued aping of the past. Even so, as late as in 1912 the following order was issued in Cologne: 'New churches are to be built in the Romanesque or Gothic manner only. In our district, the Gothic style will prove more suitable. Of late, architects have tried to use later styles, even quite recent ones. In future no permission will be granted for such buildings except in very special cases.'

SCULPTURE

Sculpture also returned to the forms of Classical Antiquity under Winckelmann's far-reaching influence. The Italian, Antonio

256. THORVALDSEN, *Ganymede with the Eagle of Jupiter*

CASPAR DAVID FRIEDRICH: Evening Landscape

PHILIPP OTTO RUNGE: Self-portrait

KARL BLECHEN: Women bathing in a Wood

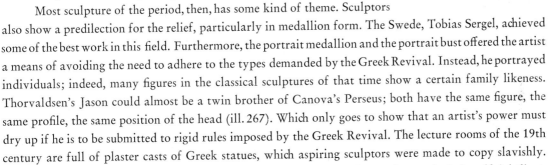

257. SCHADOW, *the Crown Princess Louise of Prussia and her sister Friederike.*
Marble

Canova, and the Dane, Bertel Thorvaldsen, are considered the leaders of
the Greek Revival. Both were idolized by their contemporaries, and the
European sculptors made pilgrimages to their Rome studios. Canova's
graceful figures are in sharp contrast to Thorvaldsen's more seriously-
conceived statues. Canova still has some of the joie de vivre of Boucher,
but there is certainly no trace of it in Thorvaldsen. Whilst Canova introduces movement into some of his groups, the Dane's statues are reduced to
immobility. What is more, Thorvaldsen's work is often instinct with historical and mythological symbolism. Anyone unconversant with Greek
mythology might conceivably derive some pleasure from his statue of
Ganymede and the Eagle (ill. 256), which approximates to a relief; but
only if he knows that Zeus, disguised as an eagle, carried off Ganymede,
can he plumb the sculptor's underlying intent – to represent the taming of
unbridled passion at the sight of pure beauty.

Most sculpture of the period, then, has some kind of theme. Sculptors
also show a predilection for the relief, particularly in medallion form. The Swede, Tobias Sergel, achieved
some of the best work in this field. Furthermore, the portrait medallion and the portrait bust offered the artist
a means of avoiding the need to adhere to the types demanded by the Greek Revival. Instead, he portrayed
individuals; indeed, many figures in the classical sculptures of that time show a certain family likeness.
Thorvaldsen's Jason could almost be a twin brother of Canova's Perseus; both have the same figure, the
same profile, the same position of the head (ill. 267). Which only goes to show that an artist's power must
dry up if he is to be submitted to rigid rules imposed by the Greek Revival. The lecture rooms of the 19th
century are full of plaster casts of Greek statues, which aspiring sculptors were made to copy slavishly.

Gottfried Schadow, a highly original sculptor of the time, vigorously attacked the official 'line':
'There is no such thing as ideal and beautiful humanity,' he claimed, 'there are only outstandingly handsome
human beings.' Although he made Greek Revival sculptures such as those for the tomb of Count von der
Mark, he was also able to produce highly individualistic groups such as 'The Princesses Louise and
Friederike' (ill. 257) and the monuments to the Prussian Generals in the Wilhelmstrasse in Berlin. Yet
Schadow's realism was abandoned by his pupil Rauch, who bowed to the taste of officialdom.

There was no genuine Romantic sculpture. This art form, with its trend towards clarity, and its
restricted size, did not appeal to the Romantics. But Romantic traits do appear from time to time.
Occasionally a statue or group is allowed to exceed all reasonable proportions, much to its detriment as
a work of art. The Statue of Liberty in New York Harbour and the Bavaria figure in Munich are Romantic
conceptions. And so is François Rude's 'La Marseillaise' (ill. 274) that petrified song of the Revolution.
Here classic restraint has gone by the board, to be replaced by an exaggerated appeal to the senses; instead
of clarity there is a plethora of details, held together only by the over-all artistic concept.

It is the idea of the Revolution, as represented by a woman, that gives life and substance to Rude's
figure. Without such a concept, all movement is reduced to empty gesticulation, as in the case of most of
the monuments of generals with drawn sword, fierce expression and 'significant pose'.

And yet even in the second half of the 19th century there were sculptors who were already paving
the way for a new art. One of them was Auguste Rodin. As a young man, he still made figures and
caryatids for elaborate house-fronts. But, on a journey through Italy, he saw Michelangelo's work and was
deeply affected by it. Although he could not avoid the usual run of commissions, his new method of
interpretating them assumes increasing importance. The 'Burghers of Calais' (1884–1888) was a monument
to the men who had surrendered voluntarily to Edward III of England in 1347 to save their city from
destruction (ill. 258). Another sculptor of the period would probably have put the six men on a pedestal

397

258. RODIN, *The Burghers of Calais*

in an idealized setting. Rodin placed his figures on a slab only 10 inches high and wanted them to stand in the middle of the market square. But his wish was ignored because the merciless realism of the group was too much for his contemporaries. Rodin was even suspected by some of having cast his figures from the living model. This powerful pictorial language, this revelation of an inner turmoil, already heralds Expressionism (see p. 457). But Rodin's treatment of surfaces, with its play of light and shadow, also produces effects that conflict with the firm, enclosing planes hitherto associated with sculpture, and are reminiscent of the contemporary art of the Impressionists (ill. 11).

Rodin's compatriot Maillol and the older German sculptor Adolf von Hildebrand approached their work from a precisely opposite angle. Here there is no emphasis on expression but a new monumentalization, an attempt to lead sculpture back to severer forms. Both aimed at continuing the classical tradition and by their efforts actually brought back to European sculpture at the end of the last century the disciplined treatment that had largely been lost during the Gothic Revival. (Ill. 270)

PAINTING

The Frenchman Jaques Louis David exhibited his painting 'The Oath of the Horatii' in 1785. It caused a sensation, according to a contemporary. 'For days it was just as though a procession were in progress. Princes and princesses, cardinals and bishops, priests, citizens and workmen all hurried to see it.' The picture was indeed revolutionary. The very theme itself came as a surprise. Rococo painters like Boucher or Fragonard had shown the aristocracy indulging in their 'innocent' games. David depicted a moment of Roman history, when three republican citizens swore undying allegiance to their country. The heroism and pathos of such a scene must, at that time, have had an overwhelming effect. But the use of colours and shapes was no less revolutionary. Rococo art loved pastel shades, delicate tints and dreamy blues, that shrouded an arcadian landscape in a misty haze. Here space is clearly circumscribed. The figures are sharply outlined, brilliantly lit and carefully grouped. Everything, down to the last detail, is ordered with the utmost precision. Three arches divide the canvas into three fields of equal size. The three brothers stand on the left, the father who is handing them their swords stands in the middle, the three mourning women are in the background. The artist's intention needs no explanation. He has portrayed a serious moment in the lives of men, not mere human dalliance. (Ill. 259)

David later became the painter of the Revolution and of the Napoleonic Court. He painted 'The Oath in the Tennis Court' and 'Marat Assassinated' for his Jacobite friends; for Napoleon he painted 'The Coronation' and pictures like 'The Distribution of the Eagles'.

Artists now no longer occupied themselves with landscape, genre pictures or still-life, but depicted dramatic moments in history or painted portraits of great men. The emphasis was on clean, clear forms, and superfluous detail was discarded. Clarity of outline was more important than colour. Schools of drawing now tended to supersede painting schools. Jean August Ingres (ill. p. 383), who was the

259. JACQUES LOUIS DAVID, *The Oath of the Horatii*

undisputed head of the Classical movement after David's death, once said to Delacroix who, as a Romantic, had neglected drawing for painting: 'Sir, drawing is a matter of decency, a matter of honour.'

The painters of the French Classic School did not interpret Antiquity in the same way as the German painters. For them, the study of – rather than a return to – Classic forms spelt purification of form. They wanted to lead the arts back to a natural and convincing beauty and did not obstinately insist on stating a theme. Ingres, in his 'Turkish Bath', did not attempt to create the atmosphere of the harem but to render a harmonious composition, formed by the skilfully handled outlines of beautiful bodies. Craftsmanship and technical perfection remained decisive for Ingres and for the other French painters of the Classic School.

The Germans had different views. Asmus Jakob Carstens, one of their leading painters, maintained that 'The choice of the theme and the degree of poetic feeling matter most in a work of art. If they are neglected, even the greatest skill will only produce something mediocre.' A work of art had to mean something, state something. Unlike the French, Carstens and his followers rejected the study of the living model. Nature, to him, seemed full of accidental deformities, and very remote from the perfect beauty of which he dreamt. He enthused about a golden age and gave his drawings allegoric titles like 'The Birth of Light', and filled them with the figures of his imagination.

The difference between the German and the French approach is even more pronounced in the Romantic School. The term 'heroic' is often applied to the French Romantics, to distinguish them from the German 'idyllic' painters. Artists like Géricault and Delacroix chose dramatic themes. Géricault painted Napoleonic cavalry officers in glittering uniforms on rearing horses, or the survivors of the 'Medusa' afloat on a raft (ill. p. 384). Delacroix illustrated the works of Shakespeare, Byron and Scott, as well as Goethe's *Faust*. He painted historical scenes (ill. p. 385) and evoked the coloured sparkle of the East in his pictures of lion hunts and equestrian games. He also depicted dramatic events like the 'Massacre of Chios' and 'Liberty leading the People' (the French Revolution of 1830), which were fresh in the minds of his contemporaries. The most significant factor is that these paintings are once again steeped in colour. Delacroix is in the great Baroque tradition, in that he largely dissolves outlines and surrenders himself to the spell of coloured light ('I do not paint a sword but its sparkle'). From Delacroix, who sought to bring the very paint to life, there is a direct path leading via Impressionism and neo-Impressionism to modern painting.

But the German Romantics wished to be more than painters. They felt themselves painter-poets and wanted the music of the spheres to sound in their pictures. They were in no way bound by tradition, but felt and acted as though with them art had begun anew. They held that such things could not be taught but could only be generated in moments of communion with the universe. Philipp Otto Runge (ill. p. 394) said: 'It is a vain hope that the public will ever understand us. A personal relationship is all we should aim at, and all that supports us.'

The Romantics loved to take refuge in the Middle Ages. The Nazarene School – given this name because of the manifest piety of many of its followers – wanted to step right out of the present, to live in an ideal world. The group (which included Cornelius, Overbeck and Pforr) went to Rome and set themselves up as the brotherhood of St Luke in the former monastery of San Isidoro. They not only wore 'Old German' dress and long hair, but actually tried to follow in the steps of Raphael. Although their art has hardly survived in its own right, we owe a great debt to them.

It was the Romantic German painters, and the English Pre-Raphaelites, who drew attention to the work of the early Italians, particularly the Sienese school. The Pre-Raphaelites (the original group, formed in 1848, consisted of Rossetti, Millais and Holman Hunt) were also partial to religious themes, though they transferred them to a contemporary setting. Neglected or ridiculed

260. ROSSETTI, *The Wedding of St George and Princess Sabra*

for many years – after they had been grossly overrated in their lifetime – we can now see that their contribution to modern painting is by no means negligible. (Ill. 260)

German Romantic art shows to best advantage in landscape painting (ill. pp. 393, 395). The painter is 'in communion with the universe', and the landscape becomes the mirror of the soul. Caspar David Friedrich never painted a landscape for its own sake, for he looked upon it as a vehicle for expressing his feelings. Friedrich's landscapes (ill. p. 393) are full of a deep and genuine piety. When looking at them, we find ourselves curiously attracted, since we tend to identify ourselves with one of the figures in the foreground, while our idealized self gazes into the heart of the picture.

The English school of landscape painting is based upon a totally different approach. Constable was not concerned with moods, but with a naturalistic presentation of light and colour. This was an important innovation and pointed the way to realism in painting. Before Constable, landscapes were always painted in the old tradition, particularly in the manner of Claude Lorraine, which adhered to rigid rules. For example, the foreground should have the brown tone of an old violin. It is told of Constable that he once placed a violin on the grass to demonstrate the difference in colour to a friend.

Whilst Turner's fantasies of light-steeped landscapes (ill. p. 386) were painted in the studio, or elsewhere under cover, Constable was one of the first to work in the open. His art was based on the study of nature and allowed him to apprehend the varied manifestations of light and to paint in a completely new manner (ill. p. 387) based on observation and not on intuition. He was thus strongly to influence Impressionism.

Classic and Romantic currents continued far into the middle of the 19th century and influenced the rise of neo-Romanticism and an Idealist school of painting. Puvis de Chavannes, one of the leaders of the 'monumental movement', achieved fame by virtue of such allegorical frescoes as 'Fancy' or 'Hope'. Here idealized human beings are presented in a harmonious landscape. A painter with a similar outlook is Anselm Feuerbach, who strove for a classic, timeless beauty in pictures such as his 'Iphigenia'. Arnold Böcklin (ill. 266), a Swiss of romantic temperament, brings the gods of Classical Antiquity to life in his landscapes. Hans von Marées (ill. p. 402), too, was one of the 'German Romans', as these three painters (together with the Nazarenes) were called because they had gone to live in Italy. His large canvases with their nude figures and dreamy landscapes still belong to classic idealism, although the severe grouping already foreshadows future trends and shows that he tried to solve the same problems as were to trouble Cézanne.

Nevertheless, the kind of art still favoured by State and Society and encouraged by German and French academies alike, was 'historical' painting – soon to lose what little vitality it ever possessed. Just as Sir Walter Scott, Dumas and Dahn provided the bourgeoisie with its reading matter throughout the century, and just as architecture repeated the styles of the past, so the 'historical' painters produced dramatic scenes from the past. A painter such as Delacroix showed that a bold treatment of colour can bring even a historical theme to life. The later 'historical' painters laid more stress on content and painted their pictures in a so-called 'studio-brown' or in 'gallery shades'. The canvases grew in size all the time and eventually even exceeded 'museum format'. The vast walls of the stairways and corridors in public buildings, too, were covered with frescoes. Those who painted 'only' landscapes or portraits had to be content with an inferior status. The artist found himself compelled to make concessions to the public taste – or his paintings remained unsold. Even a genius like Adolf von Menzel was appreciated only as a painter who evoked the age of Frederick the Great. His far more interesting 'realistic' paintings (ill. p. 404), like the famous 'Balkon-Zimmer' ('Balcony Room') were ignored. It is known of Corot that he made two versions of many of his paintings, one for sale, the other – painted as he wanted it to be – to keep.

Thus, the real development of painting took place independently of – and sometimes in conscious opposition to – public taste. It was the concern of only a few artists. A group of painters (Théodore Rousseau, Daubigny and others) dissatisfied with academic art, went to the village of Barbizon in the

Karl Spitzweg: The Cactus-fancier

Hans von Marées: The Dragon-killer

WILHELM LEIBL: Girl by a Window

ADOLF VON MENZEL: The Artist's Sister

forest of Fontainebleau, where they felt closer to nature than in Paris. In their paintings of the 'Paysage Intime' they followed the lead given by Constable and were in the tradition of the early Dutch masters, particularly Hobbema. Their landscapes were called 'intimate' because they only showed small sections of the countryside. Their canvases tell of fields and meadows, of coppices and single trees and of the peaceful rural life led by the people round Barbizon. Although they were still actually painted in the studio – being merely based on studies from nature – these pictures, with their heightened feeling for the natural scene, prepared the ground for a new approach. (Ill. p. 414)

Camille Corot is often regarded as a member of the Barbizon school although he did not officially belong to it. But Corot dedicated himself even more than they to 'tonal' painting. He claimed that a landscape is built up not only of lines but, above all, of 'light values' ('valeurs'); therefore he divided his landscapes into light and dark areas, bathed them in a silvery sheen and transformed them from mere reproductions of nature into carefully thought-out works of art (ill. p. 413).

When artists concentrate on landscape it is usually in protest against the prevalent bourgeois attitude towards art. This protest was particularly pointed in the case of Honoré Daumier. His drawings and lithographs are mentioned on a later page (see p. 407). He also belongs to those who discovered in the human toiler a theme for the painter. Daumier's 'The Washer-Woman', like Millet's 'The Gleaners' and Courbet's 'The Stone-Breakers' are among the first examples in this genre – to be adopted later by the young van Gogh and, in Germany, by Käthe Kollwitz. Everyday life is now introduced into painting. This 'realist' art seeks the truth and nothing but the truth. 'We want to observe the modern world, the only real world,' was how Courbet put it. The Classic and Romantic schools still sought to raise man out of the everyday world or to inspire him to noble deeds. Realism wanted nothing of the kind; indeed it called itself '*Sans idéal et sans religion* ('without ideals and without religion'). This passion for the truth was coupled in the case of the realistic painters with the greatest industry. Wilhelm Leibl, who, a generation later, painted the world of the Bavarian peasant (ill. p. 403), worked every day for three years at his famous painting 'Three Women in Church', compelling his models time and again to adopt the same uncomfortable pose. Courbet possessed a similar degree of devotion and perseverance. Just as, in his *Madame Bovary*, Flaubert – accused of immorality by a public which concentrated only on the story – was primarily concerned with the beauty and precision of his language, so Courbet regarded technique as much more important than the subject. Goya and Delacroix had already employed a freer and more buoyant style in their paintings. Now Courbet surrendered himself completely to beautifully toned colours, irrespective of whether or no they corresponded to actuality. (Ill. p. 415)

Edouard Manet forms the bridge from Courbet to Impressionism. To him, the themes matter even less. He sees the world as composed of coloured phenomena which the painter must co-ordinate in his mind's eye. In a picture like 'The Balcony' the actual face is of no importance. The painter is concerned only with the interesting contrast between daylight and the twilight which seems to swallow up the figures at the back of the room. Manet's discovery that things look different in daylight and indoors became one of the basic principles of Impressionism. (Ill. p. 416)

Manet was on terms of close friendship with the leading Impressionist masters. They, too, were at first harshly rejected. They were not admitted to the official annual exhibitions at the 'Salon', and their own private exhibitions – held from 1874 on – were sneered and laughed at by the critics. 'A grisly spectacle' was one comment, and the painters themselves were rated lunatics. Manet's 'Impression, soleil levant' ('Impression of the Sunrise') caused them to be dubbed 'Impressionists' as a term of abuse. Twenty years later this had become a very honourable title indeed and galleries and collectors fought to buy the works of Monet, Renoir, Sisley, Pissarro, Degas and Cézanne regardless of price. (Ill. p. 72, 417–420, 437)

Impressionist art was revolutionary because painters now worked for the first time in the open air. They discovered the full intensity of the light of the sun and the abrupt changes of colour that can be caused by a single cloud. They realized, in the words of a French critic, 'that the eye can only perceive coloured specks, that the specks change and dissolve all the time according to the reflection of the light.' The colour and form of an object, he went on to say, were perhaps realities to the mind, but for the eyes they were an illusion since there are only changing reflections of colours. The unexpected element had to be represented without first subjecting it to mental analysis.

The Impressionists, therefore, transform the flickering play of light into a wealth of small coloured dots and dashes. Broad areas of colour are replaced by a multitude of coloured specks, and these specks are only merged together by the eye of the beholder.

The Impressionists considered the treatment of light effects more important than naturalistic representation. They reproduced the 'impression' of objects, that which the eye perceives at a sudden glimpse. That colour can be broken down into its single components has been proved by the physicists. Working on this principle, the neo-Impressionists like Seurat (ill. p. 429) and Signac turned the more intuitive Impressionism into a 'science' of painting, introducing a new compactness into picture construction. Impressionism is of fundamental importance, too, where the choice of the theme is concerned. Since these painters now go out into the world, they find themselves also wanting to depict what they find there. They thus become the portrayers of contemporary life, as Baudelaire had dreamed they might when he said that the painter, the 'real painter', would be he who 'can make us see and appreciate how great and poetic are even we with our neck-ties and polished patent-leather shoes.' No theme was insignificant in the eyes of the Impressionists. They painted boats drifting on the Seine, a railway bridge spanning a river (Monet) and the life on the boulevards of Paris (Pissarro). The smoky railway station of St Lazare (Monet) and the ballet-dancers' dressing room (Degas) were as interesting to them as a spring day in an open-air café (Renoir). But they particularly liked to capture the impression made by objects in fast movement. Horse races and regattas, trains and carriages on the move were amongst their favourite themes. They were also particularly attracted to spotlighted scenes resembling camera-snapshots. (It should be remembered that photography had set out on its triumphal march during those years.)

The best works of Impressionism – the German painters Max Liebermann, Max Slevogt and Lovis Corinth (ill. pp. 28, 430, 431) later joined the movement although they never attained the completely unprejudiced vision of the French Masters – resulted from the painter completely abandoning himself to the moment. These men and women lived and re-created the world in its fleeting moods. It is entirely an art of the visual sense: impressions were to be caught, but not analysed and interpreted. This movement was carried to its logical conclusion in the 20th century through Expressionism and Symbolism. Paul Cézanne carried it a step further by giving his paintings a firmer structure. He sought to give permanence to what the Impressionist sees as evanescent and incidental, by treating space structurally and using enclosed areas of colour. 'Everything we see is untrue, disperses and is dissipated. Nature is always the same, but nothing we see of it remains. Our art must give nature the appearance of permanency.' Cézanne's art is the gateway to 20th-century painting.

THE GRAPHIC ARTS

The woodcut had been virtually ignored for over two hundred years. Towards the end of the 18th century Thomas Bewick discovered that box wood makes a very much stronger block than do other

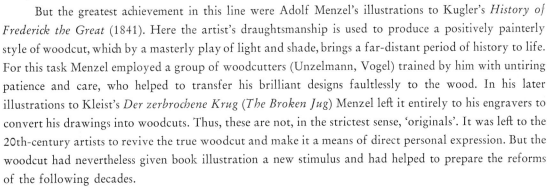

woods. Furthermore, he cut the lines across the grain, contrary to the earlier technique, thus producing the wood-engraving, which he used for his charming vignettes of birds. The book had rediscovered its old ally for purposes of illustration, the earlier line technique being also revived. Every Dickens reader is familiar with the woodcuts of Cruikshank and 'Phiz' (Browne). Gustave Doré illustrated Balzac's *Contes Drolatiques*, Rabelais' *Gargantua and Pantagruel* (ill. 262) and Cervantes' *Don Quixote*. Doré very rarely engraved the blocks himself; instead, he employed up to forty woodcutters and engravers, who copied his drawings. Indeed, scarcely any artists of the 19th century did their own engraving.

In Germany, the Romantics – particularly the Nazarenes – who took up woodcutting, based their work on John Flaxman's technique. Schnorr von Carolsfeld's Picture Bible, Peter Cornelius' *Faust* illustrations and Ludwig Richter's illustrations for *Grimm's Fairy Tales* are amongst the most important examples. A little later, Rethel adapted the theme of Holbein's cycle of woodcuts to the revolution of 1848, naming his cycle 'Also a Dance of Death'.

But the greatest achievement in this line were Adolf Menzel's illustrations to Kugler's *History of Frederick the Great* (1841). Here the artist's draughtsmanship is used to produce a positively painterly style of woodcut, which by a masterly play of light and shade, brings a far-distant period of history to life. For this task Menzel employed a group of woodcutters (Unzelmann, Vogel) trained by him with untiring patience and care, who helped to transfer his brilliant designs faultlessly to the wood. In his later illustrations to Kleist's *Der zerbrochene Krug* (*The Broken Jug*) Menzel left it entirely to his engravers to convert his drawings into woodcuts. Thus, these are not, in the strictest sense, 'originals'. It was left to the 20th-century artists to revive the true woodcut and make it a means of direct personal expression. But the woodcut had nevertheless given book illustration a new stimulus and had helped to prepare the reforms of the following decades.

Etching was the only other traditional graphic art form to achieve success in the 19th century. It was used by landscape-painters in England, France and Germany. A master such as Millet could make his etching of peasants at work, 'The Gleaners', even more convincing than the same theme on canvas. Two artists of the middle of the century call for special mention: the Frenchman Meryan and James McNeill Whistler. The former's views of Paris are still much coveted by collectors; the latter, who was no less famous for his sharp tongue than for his three thousand etchings, magically evoked in these the play of air and light over river landscapes by the use of tiny dashes and hooks (ill. 277).

But the greatest discovery of the 19th century in this field was lithography. Invented by the Austrian Senefelder in 1798, it allowed artists to convey their ideas directly to the stone, whether they were using pen, chalk or brush. Although Bonington, Whistler, Menzel, Krüger and, later, Liebermann and Slevogt often used this technique, its potentialities were most fully recognised in France, where it was further developed. Toulouse-Lautrec, in particular, made brilliant use of this technique, which Géricault and Delacroix had already used for their fine animal representations. Gavarni employed lithography for hundreds of topical illustrations in the journal *La Mode*.

But the undisputed master of the lithograph was Honoré Daumier, as his contributions to the weeklies *Le Charivari* and *La Caricature* show. Daumier is the exponent par excellence of political caricature. His irony stops at nothing. Cabinet Ministers, deputies and bankers are all brought before the tribunal of his art. Having

263. DAUMIER, *Le ventre législatif: The legislative paunch.* Lithograph

been imprisoned for the boldness of his attacks, however, he made the common man the butt of his satire. He hit upon the brilliant notion of deflating the self-importance of the world by dressing his bourgeois contemporaries as the heroes and gods of Antiquity, thus exposing man's smallness and pettiness, and making them a target for ridicule (ill. 263). Daumier was head and shoulders above all others in this technique. The very few contributions of the Impressionists, who were in any case more interested in colour and its problems, seem insignificant by comparison. Nevertheless, Toulouse-Lautrec, at the end of the century, gave the lithograph a new life through adapting it to colour (ill. p. 38). No doubt he was inspired by the coloured Japanese woodcuts which had been introduced into France shortly before. He perfected the technique of lithography in over 400 drawings. His posters and many small pieces describe the world of Montmartre and its bohemian life at the turn of the century. This artist believed in the utmost economy of means and became one of the great inspirers of the 20th-century lithograph.

THE CRAFTS

The simple, elegant Greek Revival rooms, too, called for a furniture different from that of the effete Rococo. People regarded this as a 'sensible' age and the fanciful, decorative and playful pieces of the past were discountenanced. Straightforward, practical designs were the order of the day. The curved legs were straightened out, the billowing fronts flattened. The painter David had his household goods based on antique models; they were upholstered in red, with coloured patterns offset by black palmettes in the style of Greek vases. Fashion, too, was now 'à la Greque' and society ladies like Madame Récamier (whose portrait David painted thus) wore Grecian robes. Vases of all sizes littered the drawing-rooms, and even the bronze fittings on the furniture were 'inspired' by such antique motifs as the lyre or the old 'meander' patterns, while along the edges ran key-fret designs. The Etruria factory, founded by Wedgwood in the 1770's, continued to make exact replicas of Greek vases and pottery varying in colour from blue and green to puce and black. The decoration of funerary urns was adapted to cheese dishes and coffee pots. Although the workmanship was often superb and the design not without a certain charm, the arbitrary use of such motifs already foreshadows the horrors of the Victorian age. Napoleon took the comparatively simple style of the First Empire and turned it into an elaborate Court display. Based on the monuments of Antiquity, wardrobes assumed vast proportions, and were given special bases instead of legs. Lions and griffins, even the Sphinx, were used as decorative adjuncts; these were either carved or made of metal.

But the splendour-loving Empire style, imitated at many of the Courts of Europe, died with Napoleon. After 1815 there was a return to simplicity. The furniture of the Biedermeier period, which now

came in, was undoubtedly influenced by English 18th-century designs. Chippendale and Sheraton had made well-designed yet comfortable pieces in mahogany. Biedermeier furniture breathes the same spirit. We find a similar simple elegance in the houses of the new Middle Class and in the palaces of the Aristocracy.

But a change set in around 1830, caused both by industrialization and the growing anarchy in the realm of the arts. Previously, furniture and articles of daily use had always reflected the style of the age in question. Now the styles of past eras were imitated in quick succession. At Art Schools the pupils were taught how to copy forms and ornament ranging from the Renaissance to the Biedermeier. This led to a decline in almost every craft. From 1860 onward, houses became furniture repositories. Their centre was the unused drawing-room with stuffed birds in glass cases, plush sofas and imitation flowers. All feeling for the genuine had gone.

William Morris (ill. 264), the followers of the so-called Art Nouveau and, later, the Bauhaus, led the way out of this confusion and brought about a renewal of the standards of craftsmanship.

264. *Tapestry from a design by* MORRIS

ABILGAARD, NICOLAI ABRAHAM (1743–1809), a Danish classical painter and sculptor, studied in Rome. In 1789 he became head of the Academy of Arts in Copenhagen. He had a preference for classical, historical and allegorical subjects as well as for themes from Norse sagas. He taught Runge and Thorvaldsen.

ALLSTON, WASHINGTON (1779–1843). A pupil of Benjamin West and of Gilbert Stuart, Allston is chiefly important in American painting for his efforts to paint romantic, subjective pictures. His large paintings, all done in the Renaissance manner, were failures, but his later work, done after he had settled near Boston in 1818, exhibits a subjectivity foreshadowing the Romantic movement which became as important to 19th-century America as did the Abstractionist movement of almost a century later.

ALT, RUDOLF VON (1812–1905). Like his father, Jacob von Alt, this Viennese artist painted mainly landscapes and architectural studies of Austria and Hungary – nearly always in water colour. With him, Viennese water-colour painting reached its greatest heights.

AUDUBON, JOHN JAMES (c. 1780–1851). The foremost painter of birds and wild-life in 19th-century America, Audubon, an ornithologist, studied in France but settled in Pennsylvania in 1803, then roamed the Midwest and South. His collected paintings of 'The Birds of America', done in water colours with an overlay of pastels and published in parts between 1827 and 1838, brought him wealth and fame by the fact that the paintings combine artistic talent with scientific observation.

BARYE, ANTOINE-LOUIS (1795–1875). The bronze sculptures of animals by this French artist are remarkable for their realism and picturesque animation. Barye was also a painter in oils and water colours.

BAZILLE, JEAN-FRÉDÉRIC (1841–1870). This French painter was one of Claude Monet's close friends and a pioneer of Impressionism. He was killed in the Franco-Prussian War of 1870, before his promising talent had come to full fruition.

BEARDSLEY, AUBREY (1872–1898). This highly gifted English draughtsman sought a new form of expression by depicting the human figure and exotic themes by means of an interplay of decorative stylized lines. In this manner, he illustrated a number of books (e. g. Wilde's *Salome*). He had, as a result, a strong influence on European book illustration, which was beginning to flourish once more at the turn of the century. (Ill. 265)

BINGHAM, GEORGE CALEB (1811–1879), was an American painter who produced many portraits and genre paintings. He grew up in the Far West and was able to depict its wide spaces and wild romantic quality as well as the daily life of the settlers, hunters

265. BEARDSLEY, *illustration for Oscar Wilde's 'Salome'*

and traders, with great fidelity in such typically 19th-century scenes as 'Fur Traders Descending the Missouri' and 'Daniel Boone Escorting a Band of Pioneers into the Western Country'. (Ill. p. 396)

BLAKE, WILLIAM (1757–1827). This versatile painter, engraver and poet, lived in London. His gifts were not assessed at their true value by his contemporaries and only the Pre-Raphaelites were to appreciate and interpret his mysteriously romantic works, in which art expressed symbols of higher truths. 'The nature of my works is visionary or imaginative,' he said. Blake invented his own tempera technique and a new method of printing for his prophetic books. As an illustrator, he was chiefly famous for his engravings for Dante, for the Book of Job and for his two great mystical poems *Milton* and *Jerusalem*. (Ill. p. 388)

BLAKELOCK, RALPH ALBERT (1847–1919). A self-taught painter who had studied to be a doctor, Blakelock, who was born in New York City, became a landscape painter noted chiefly for the melancholy subjectivity of his largely Western U. S. scenes, many of them darkly glowing canvases of moonlight and wilderness relieved by small figures of American Indians. Most of these were painted from memory and reflected more what the painter felt than what he had actually seen of the U. S. West. Unrecognized for years, he became insane in 1899 and was held in a New York State asylum until almost the end of his life. By that time his paintings were commanding enormous prices and a large number of additional ones were being forged. But Blakelock himself, except for works rendered with brushes improvised from matchsticks and hair in the asylum, never painted again.

266. BÖCKLIN, *Self-portrait with Death as fiddler*

BLECHEN, KARL (1798–1840). This Romantic painter's preference for hitherto undiscovered subjects – 'The Rolling Mill at Eberswalde' is the first picture of an industrial building in modern painting – and his particular interest in the most varied light effects, made him a precursor both of the Impressionists and of Menzel's realist painting. His importance was, however, only recognised in this century. In 1831, Blechen became Professor of Landscape Painting in Berlin. The drawings and sketches made during his Italian journey have a particular spontaneity (ill. p. 395).

BÖCKLIN, ARNOLD (1827–1901). Like Marées and Feuerbach, this Swiss painter belonged to the circle of the neo-Romantic or Idealist German artists in Rome. His symbolic landscapes – which are full of atmosphere and deal chiefly with themes from classical mythology, with fauns and nymphs, tritons and naiads – are, notwithstanding their invention, painted in highly realistic detail. It is largely due to this realism that his pictures had such a widespread influence during the early years of the German Empire. His early works ('Spring') still show a poetic concept of nature, which he later abandoned in favour of pure allegory. His 'Island of the Dead', with its cypresses taken from the Tuscan landscape (there are several versions) is famous. (Ill. 266)

BONINGTON, RICHARD PARKES (1801–1828), went to Paris when still a boy. He subsequently became a friend of Eugène Delacroix. In the 1820's he painted outstanding, limpid water colours, genre pictures and landscapes with harbours, beaches and street scenes. Bonington is considered to be one of the precursors of the Barbizon school. Several of his smaller paintings are in the Wallace Collection, London. (Cf. p. 407)

BOURDELLE, ANTOINE (1861–1929), was for a time a pupil of Auguste Rodin. He produced a series of reliefs, monuments and individual statues (e. g., of Beethoven), in which he combined expressive plastic form with the severity and power of Egyptian and archaic art.

BROWN, FORD MADDOX (1821–1893), was very close to the Pre-Raphaelite Brotherhood, although he never became a member. His early twenties were spent in Paris and in Rome, where he met Peter v. Cornelius, Johann Overbeck, Schnorr von Carolsfeld and other followers of the Nazarenes. His works include 'The Last of England' (Birmingham City Art Gall., smaller versions at London/Tate Gall. and Cambridge/Fitzwilliam Museum), 'Christ washing St Peter's Feet' (London/Nat. Gall.).

BURNE-JONES, SIR EDWARD (1833–1898), was – like his friend, William Morris – originally destined for the Church. But both decided to become artists and, under the influence of Rossetti, they joined the Pre-Raphaelites. In spite of their sentimentality, which was in keeping with the spirit of the time, Burne-Jones' pictures show a considerable talent – in particular a gift for colour, e. g., 'Cophetua and the Beggar-maid', 1884 (Tate Gallery, London). Along with Morris he later took up applied art, decorating furniture and illustrating books for the famous Kelmscott Press.

BUSCH, WILHELM (1832–1908). Behind the mask of the popular humorist, whom we see in his illustrated stories such as *Die fromme Helene* (Pious Helen), *Max und Moritz*, etc., he was in reality a pessimistic philosopher. His original and witty *Knittelverse* in which he mercilessly exposed human weaknesses, first appeared in the *Fliegende Blaetter* in 1859. His numerous small oil paintings in which he anticipates later pictorial discoveries in technique and the nature of colour contrasts (red-green) are less well known.

CANOVA, ANTONIO (1757–1822), had a revolutionary influence on sculpture similar to that exercised by Jacques-Louis David on painting (cf. p. 397). His studio in Rome became a place of pilgrimage and his neoclassical statues were admired and copied throughout Europe. He aimed at idealizing man in the classical manner and at eliminating everything spontaneous and natural from plastic form. The fact that the Pope had Canova's 'Perseus' (ill. 267) installed in the place of the Belvedere Apollo, which the French had removed to Paris, shows the high esteem in which his work was held.

CARPEAUX, JEAN-BAPTISTE (1827–1875). The main works of this French sculptor and painter are to be found in his native town of Valenciennes and in the Louvre. His sculptures, which are frequently arranged in groups as in the Louvre, the Paris Opéra and the fountain in the Luxembourg Gardens, soar upwards amid strongly contrasted light and shadow and are full of spontaneous, passionate, 'baroque' movement. Their creator is clearly a precursor of Rodin.

CARRIÈRE, EUGÉNE (1849–1906), was friendly with many French writers of his time (he did a portrait of Verlaine). He painted a number of portraits in warm, soft brown and his family groups show an exceptional gift for characterization. His lithographs are also important.

410

CARUS, CARL GUSTAV (1789–1869), was royal physician in Dresden (Court of Saxony) and a gifted natural scientist; as a philosopher he was in close contact with Goethe and Schelling. As a painter of romantic landscapes he followed his friend and teacher, Caspar David Friedrich (q. v.). Among his important theoretical works in which he evaluates and interprets the paintings of Friedrich, are *Letters on Landscape Painting*.

CASSATT, MARY (1845–1926). Unrecognized in her native U. S. during her lifetime, Mary Cassatt, who came from a wealthy Pennsylvania family but spent most of her life in Europe, was greatly influenced by Manet and Degas. Allying herself with the Impressionists, she learned from them to emphasise lighting over space and form in her paintings, and she also achieved a womanly touch in all her work. Her chief subjects were ladies at the tea-table or at the opera and numerous versions of mothers with their children, all of these being done with a remarkable sensitivity for everyday life and for pleasing colours. To-day she is generally recognised as America's most famous woman painter.

CHASSÉRIAU, THÉODORE (1819—1856), a Creole from San Domingo, was endowed with a strong talent, which matured early. He at first worked as a pupil of Ingres. Later he came closer to the romantic style of Delacroix. He attempted to weld together the particular qualities of his masters into a personal style, which unites Ingres's noble line with Delacroix's use of colour.

CONSTABLE, JOHN (1776–1837), was born in Suffolk. He was a pupil at the Royal Academy but it was among the trees and by the meadows and streams of his native landscape that Constable developed his surprising new way of looking at things, which expressed itself in a spontaneous, colour-flecked technique. Following in the steps of the Dutch masters, he had the courage to do what Thomas Gainsborough had already tried, namely to abandon the artificial composition of the 'ideal landscape' and to paint the sky, meadow, hill and pond as the eye sees them. All his life he attempted with great seriousness to reproduce the cool freshness and scent of the English landscape in blobs of colour which he was the first 19th-century artist to apply with the palette knife. He exercised an extremely strong influence on 19th-century painting, particularly through an exhibition in Paris in 1824 which caused a great stir. Constable's oil sketches, in particular the large, 6-foot 'Study for the Leaping Horse' and 'Study for the Haywain' are landmarks in the history of painting. (Ill. p. 387)

CORINTH, LOVIS (1858–1925), was born in East Prussia. After seven years of intensive study in Munich and Paris (Académie Julian), he painted his first pictures of importance at the age of thirty; in them the style of Leibl and Courbet still predominates. In 1900 he settled in Berlin and became, along with Liebermann and Slevogt, one of the leading German Impressionists. His palette now becomes lighter and his

267. CANOVA, *Perseus. Marble*

brushwork shows an unprecedented freedom, particularly in his female nudes, which combine an extremely sensual effect with an almost racy painting technique. His preference for epic subjects ('Lament for the Dead', 'Temptation of St Anthony'), his intense interest in the expression of the human face ('Graf Keyserling', 1901), his basically tragic concept of life, are all fundamentally far removed from French Impressionism. It is only a short step from Corinth to Expressionism – for example, to the expressionism of Kokoschka; this is evident in his moving late works such as the Walchensee pictures (ill. p. 28). These are visionary landscapes almost on the borderline of non-representational art.

CORNELIUS, PETER VON (1783–1867). Under the influence of early German art, this painter and philosopher evolved a very personal style. His first known works are the illustrations to the *Nibelungen* and to Goethe's *Faust*. During a stay in Rome he joined the Nazarene circle (q. v.). His monumental Christian murals (e. g., the 'Story of Joseph' for the Casa Bartholdy in Rome, now in Berlin) are particularly impressive; these enabled him to make full use of his draughtsmanship and dramatic power (cf. his cartoons for frescoes for a Royal mausoleum in which he produced his best work).

COROT, CAMILLE JEAN BAPTISTE (1796–1875). Corot's pictures are still instinct with the beauty and harmony of the 18th century, but they are painted in a technique which, in many ways, anticipates Impressionism. They resulted from a very carefully thought-out arrangement of light and shade, the painter adding spot after spot to his tone values to create an over-all colour value. From his journeys to Italy he brought back enchanting views of the classical scenes. But 'la douce et noble France' was closest to his heart – particularly his native district around Ville d'Arvay, where he painted the majority of his tranquil, poetic pictures (ill. p. 413). In the middle of the 19th century his pictures become more animated and include figures of

411

girls and nymphs. During his more mature period he painted extremely balanced and beautiful portraits of women. Later – because he felt unable to oppose the wishes of his clients and dealers, the quality of his painting deteriorated noticeably.

COTMAN, JOHN SELL (1782–1842). Cotman was born in Norwich and came to London about 1800. He was befriended by Dr Monro, the patron also of Turner and Girtin. He exhibited at the Royal Academy till 1806 when he returned to Norwich. In 1811 he succeeded Crome as President of the Norwich Society of Artists, founded in 1805. Subsequently he lived at Yarmouth and taught drawing there. Cotman painted both in oils and water colours and also etched and lithographed architectural subjects. Cotman's special contribution is to design. Both his remarkable water colours and his oil paintings are characterized by balanced masses of light and dark and by rich flat patterns. Cotman's abstract qualities of design and construction have only been appreciated in our own age; they could hardly be popular at the time and the artist was little noticed. He was relieved from the drudgery of teaching towards the end of his life when Turner helped him to get the post of drawing master at King's College, London.

COURBET, GUSTAVE (1819–1877). Along with Millet and Daumier, Courbet is regarded as one of the founders of modern realism. With sure judgment he selects from the variety of life and nature whatever he considers to be worth painting, and translates it in terms of his technically perfect craftsmanship. He paints forests in spring in tender colours and women sleeping on the banks of the Seine in the heat of the sun, snowy landscapes in the Alps and the dark ocean ('The Wave', Paris), and flower-pieces of lush splendour. Courbet places himself in the centre of the artistic universe in his huge picture 'The Studio'; together with the 'Burial at Ornans' – which is painted in an objective, serious style, – it is his chief work. The main attraction of his paintings is their absolute honesty, which was rejected, however, by his bourgeois contemporaries. But he stubbornly built his own pavilion for the 1855 World Exhibition and wrote over its door: 'Realism – Courbet'. This artist of genius was compelled to leave France for political reasons and died in Switzerland. (Ill. p. 415)

CROME, JOHN (1768–1821). 'Old Crome' is the first of the many great English landscape painters of the 19th century. He roved the countryside near his native city of Norwich with his sketch-book. In his water colours and paintings, he re-created in lovely fresh colours the spacious park landscape of England with its streams and meadows. The eye travels from the hills to the green fields; trees ravaged by the storm and romantic windmills stand out against a lofty, light-drenched sky, e. g., in 'The Poringland Oak' and 'Mousehold Heath' (both in the National Gallery, London).

CRUIKSHANK, GEORGE (1792–1878). The witty, biting caricatures with which Cruikshank castigated social evils in England were greatly feared by his contemporaries. He also illustrated almanacs and books, including works by Charles Dickens. He left more than 3000 woodcuts and etchings.

DAHL, JOHAN CHRISTIAN CLAUSEN (1788–1857). In 1824, this Norwegian landscape painter was appointed professor at the Academy in Dresden, where he was in close and friendly contact with the circle around C. D. Friedrich. Although he lived abroad, the subjects of his pictures, which are frequently painted in subtle shades of grey, are predominantly taken from the mountainous landscape of Norway. His works are to be found in Copenhagen, Stockholm, Oslo and Bergen.

DAUBIGNY, CHARLES-FRANÇOIS (1817–1878), belonged to the Barbizon school. His preference was for suggestive landscape, for gay, sunny woods, for flowering trees and the banks of the Oise and Seine, which he painted with a strong palette.

DAUMIER, HONORÉ (1808–1879), is one of the outstanding caricaturists of the 19th century. Working for the Paris reviews *La Caricature* and *Le Charivari*, he created in his thousands of lithographs a 'Human Comedy' of his time (cf. p. 407). His political satire was directed against the unhappy state of the empire under Louis Philippe, the citizen king, against the National Assembly (*le ventre législatif* – the 'legislative paunch' – as he called it), against judges and lawyers, etc. (ill. 263). When political satire was prohibited, he found a target for his caricatures in the middle classes and even in the world of Homeric epic, through which he satirised the neo-classical tendency of the period. In his drawings and woodcuts for book illustrations (e. g., for *Don Quixote)* and in those of his sculptures which have been preserved (e. g. Ratapoil) the satirical element also predominates. But his paintings, e. g. of washerwomen and insurrectionary scenes, which were fully appreciated only after his death, show the seriousness of his social conscience. Daumier's work influenced Cézanne and Rouault and has played an important part in the development of modern art.

DAVID, JACQUES-LOUIS (1748–1825). His 'Oath of the Horatii' is the first neo-classical work in French painting (cf. p. 398, ill. 259). It illustrates the manly republican spirit which David saw in Antiquity and which he wanted to renew in his own time. In addition to historical, mythological and contemporary subjects (the French Revolution, Napoleon), David painted a number of excellent portraits ('The Gérard Family', 'Madame Récamier', 'Napoleon on Horseback'). David exercised a great influence as a teacher and many artists from all over Europe gathered around him.

DAVID D'ANGERS, PIERRE-JEAN (1788–1856). This versatile artist, whose name derives from his birthplace Antwerp, was, like so many sculptors of his time, in close contact with Canova. In addition to

CAMILLE COROT: By the River

THÉODORE ROUSSEAU: River Landscape

GUSTAVE COURBET: The Quarry of Optevoz

EDGAR DEGAS: The Jockeys

Alfred Sisley: Avenue of Trees

CAMILLE PISSARRO: A Street in Rouen

Auguste Renoir: Girl in a Hat

numerous portrait statues and reliefs, he left a number of medallions and busts of contemporary French and German painters and poets (e. g., Friedrich, Tieck, Goethe, Schiller, etc.).

DEGAS, EDGAR (1834–1917), chose as his models chiefly seamstresses and ballet dancers. He was particularly fascinated by the latter because of their graceful movements and the acrobatic agility of their bodies. Whilst other Impressionists went to the country for their subjects, Degas preferred the ballet schools and seamstresses' workshops, dimly lit by flickering gas or candlelight. Whereas with Monet or Pissarro, the outline is dissolved in a shimmering play of light, with Degas the line acquires an almost classical quality. His friends painted the 'impression' of the moment, but Degas decided on his composition, which was usually an apparently accidental, arbitrary scene, before he started on a picture and first worked out every detail in sketches or studies. Pastel was his main love and for it he developed his own new technique based on experience of glazes in oil painting. In later years, until he became completely blind, he painted only from memory. However, even then he continued to work and produced small wax sculptures which show that he was not only a painter but also a sculptor of rank. (Ill. p. 417)

DELACROIX, EUGÈNE (1798–1863), is the 'romantic' of French painting – that is to say he did away with the linear neo-classicism of David. Colour is once more used as a means of expression; his models are Rubens and Veronese. He took his subjects from history (ill. p. 385), mythology or literature – Dante, Shakespeare, Byron, Goethe, the Bible, the Greek revolt against the Turks, and the French Revolution. After his journey to Algiers (1832) Delacroix's painting acquired an even more brilliant oriental splendour. His paintings of animals – in particular his magnificent pictures of lions which he painted after this journey – are famous. Delacroix was not only a painter, but also a draughtsman and illustrator. In his lithographs he succeeded in reproducing the romantic, dark, demoniac aspects of Goethe's *Faust* better than the German lithographers of the somewhat polite Biedermeier period. Delacroix was an invaluable inspiration to 19th-century painting, his influence making it at once more fluent and more picturesque. It was through him that the 'baroque' element of riotous colour and form was revived.

DORÉ, GUSTAVE (1832–1883), was born in Strassburg. He was one of the outstanding illustrators of the 19th century. He produced highly imaginative and original drawings for woodcuts to illustrate more than 30 works of world literature (Rabelais, Balzac, Münchhausen, etc.). In his Paris studio, Doré at times employed up to 40 assistants on his woodcuts. (Cf. p. 407, ill. 262)

EAKINS, THOMAS (1844–1916). Perhaps the greatest American realistic painter of the 19th century, Eakins, who was born in Philadelphia and attended Jefferson Medical College (where his lessons in anatomy were later to serve his painting well), was an uncompromising painter of things as they actually appear, insisting on the most painstaking detail in his finished paintings. His portraits (notably of Walt Whitman) show every wrinkle in the face; his paintings of singers and athletes always show them in action. A champion of realism, he introduced live models into the classrooms of the Pennsylvania Academy of Fine Arts when he became a teacher there, and he strove for a purely American art.

ETTY, WILLIAM (1787–1849), is best known for his paintings of the nude, and his merit is that despite its voluptuous character his work does deal with a subject scarcely ever attempted in English painting. A maked technical facility he owes to his master Sir Thomas Lawrence.

FANTIN-LATOUR, HENRI (1836–1904). Fantin-Latour was the contemporary, friend and portraitist of the French Impressionists, e. g. 'Manet's Studio at Batignolles'. His fantastic allegorical paintings were inspired by the music of Wagner and Berlioz. He also painted delicate flower-pieces, which were in great demand. (Ill. 261)

FEUERBACH, ANSELM (1829–1880), embodies in his life and work the longings and ideals of the cultured bourgeoisie of his time. He worked in Paris with Couture; there his tendency to classicism based on historical models was reinforced. From Paris, Feuerbach went to Rome and Venice and became more and more a 'Roman German'. His choice of subjects was decided by literary reminiscences – 'The Symposium', 'Iphigenia' and 'Medea'. He painted with cool, well-matched colours; his figures are large and are set in a dignified posture against a subdued background.

FLAXMAN, JOHN (1755–1826). English sculptor and illustrator, and one of the foremost promoters of neo-Classicism. His statues and relief models for Wedgwood ceramic ware show Greek influence. In his varied activities as an illustrator, he employed pure contour-drawing, such as is used in the making of antique vases.

FRIEDRICH, CASPAR DAVID (1774–1840), belonged, like Novalis and Philippe Otto Runge, to the same generation as Kleist and was, like them, a member of the North German Romantic school. The chief themes of his paintings were cemeteries, ruins of churches, the seasons of the year and the times of the day, all of which are symbols of the transience of things; in the same way he used ships at sea or in harbour as symbols of life (ill. p. 393). His native Baltic sea coast, the Riesengebirge and the Elbe valley with its rising mists, were the landscapes in which he felt at home.

FRITH, WILLIAM POWELL (1819–1909). Frith's paintings are remarkably naturalistic and detailed. 'Paddington Station' (London/Royal Holloway Coll.)

268. FUSELI, *Odin receives foreknowledge of the death of Balder*

and 'Derby Day' (London/Nat. Gall.) show his superb gift of observation, and are fascinating on that count alone.

FUSELI, HENRY (1741–1825), whose real name was Johann Heinrich Füssli, came from Zürich but lived mainly in London where he was very highly regarded. He was strongly influenced by Blake. In his illustrations for works of world literature such as Dante, Virgil, Shakespeare and the *Niebelungenlied* he displays figures in passionately exaggerated movement. His work shows a strong leaning towards phantoms and cruelty ('The Nightmare'). Ill. 268

GÄRTNER, FRIEDRICH VON (1792–1847), was director of the Munich Academy of Arts and Court architect to King Ludwig I of Bavaria. He had a preference for models drawn from the Italian Middle Ages and from the Early Renaissance. By his numerous public buildings he set his stamp on the Bavarian capital, e. g. the Feldherrnhalle, the Ludwigskirche, the Siegestor (Victory Arch) and the State Library.

GARNIER, JEAN-LOUIS-CHARLES (1825–1898), whose writings on theatre architecture aroused a considerable interest, built the theatre and the Casino at Monte Carlo, as well as the Paris Opéra, which he filled with all the splendour of neo-Baroque (ill. 255).

GAVARNI, PAUL (1804–1866), whose real name was Sulpice Chevalier, together with Daumier made the Paris political satirical review *Le Charivari* world-famous. Gavarni's witty and ironical drawings of the society of his time also appeared in other illustrated papers. He was a recorder of *moeurs* rather than a caricaturist and had a particular gift for witty drawings. Later in his career he turned increasingly to social problems. He left more than 3000 lithographs.

GÉRARD, FRANÇOIS, BARON (1770–1837), was Jacques-Louis David's favourite pupil and painted historical pictures and portraits in his master's neoclassical style. In his position as Court painter to Napoleon – and later to Louis XVIII – he visited all the Courts of Europe.

GÉRICAULT, THÉODORE (1791–1824). In the course of only 12 years of creative activity (1811–1823), which were interrupted by journeys to Italy and England in order to study, he produced – along with a vast number of drawings and sketches – paintings like 'The Raft of the Medusa' (ill. p. 384) and 'The Derby' (both in the Louvre). In them he achieves a successful synthesis of strict classical form with freedom of treatment and colour. His animal studies from nature contravert the view of the classical school that only man is a worthy subject for art. In his brilliant portraits of lunatics, he shows himself a master at portraying human faces on the borders of insanity; in these works he can only be compared to such of his contemporaries as Goya and Delacroix.

GREENOUGH, HORATIO (1805–1852), was the first American sculptor to come to Rome, where he was a student of Thorvaldsen. On his return, he introduced classical sculpture to the United States, where he produced the large seated statue of Washington for the Capitol, now in the National Museum, Washington.

GROS, ANTOINE-JEAN, BARON (1771–1835), was a pupil of David. To his classically inclined colleagues he said: 'You do not pay enough attention to colour.' He himself was inclined to use a stronger palette. His use of colour in his battle scenes – he followed Napoleon's army – and portraits had a considerable influence on French romantic painting (Delacroix and Géricault).

GUYS, CONSTANTIN (1805–1892), took part in the Greek War of Independence along with Byron. He travelled widely in Europe and the East as a newspaper correspondent and brought back a large number of sketches and water colours. Later he settled in Paris and worked constantly to perfect his technique. In his drawings, which he did from memory, and which were an important influence on the Impressionists, he portrayed the brilliant life of Paris under the Second Empire.

HASSAM, CHILDE (1859–1935). Boston-born, Hassam was both a painter and an etcher. A three-year stay abroad, where he studied in Paris with Jules Lefebvre and G. R. Boulanger, exposed him to Impressionism and influenced his ensuing work. He adopted the high-keyed colours of Monet and was the most outstanding of a group of painters called the 'Luminists'. 'Church At Old Lyme', 'Isle of Shoals' and 'The New York Window' are characteristic of his opalescent pictures.

HICKS, EDWARD (1780–1849). An itinerant Quaker preacher in Pennsylvania, Hicks was a self-taught painter who regarded his art as so unimportant that he gave his works away to friends, frequently along with a pious self-composed poem. He is best known for his superb primitive picture of 'The Peaceable Kingdom' the subject of which is taken from Isaiah and of which he painted as many as a hundred different versions, copying the figures of the animals and children from engravings of the Old Masters.

HILDEBRAND, ADOLF VON (1847–1921), was a sculptor born in Marburg who later became a friend of the painter Hans von Marées. Like the latter, Hildebrand strove to achieve rigid formalism in art; he wrote *The Problem of Form in the Plastic Arts.* What he aimed at was purified, timeless plastic form using the finest materials and purged of any romantic or neo-Baroque accretions (the Wittelsbach fountain, Munich, ill. 270). Hildebrand also produced portrait busts, reliefs and medallions.

HOMER, WINSLOW (1836–1910). A harshly realistic painter, Homer ist best known for his American coastal landscapes and his seascapes, many of which hang in museums throughout the U. S. Homer's work evades rigid classification. Self-trained and with keen powers of observation he became an excellent draughtsman and professional illustrator; and his dramatic realism, vigour, freshness and even grandeur make him outstanding among American painters. (Ill. p. 432)

HUDSON RIVER SCHOOL. This term has been given to the group of American landscape painters who worked in the Hudson River area during the period of 1826–1876. The romantic, poetic landscapes of Thomas Doughty (1793–1856), Thomas Cole (1801–1848) and Asher B. Durand (1796–1886) are in the tradition of those European painters like Both and Berchem, who had studied in Italy; they are formally composed and precise in detail. The later work of Doughty and Durand showed the influence of Constable and also of the Barbizon School. J. F. Kensett (1818–1872) is more markedly dependent on Constable. Albert Bierstadt (1830–1902) studied in Düsseldorf and his style is minute and painstaking even when dealing with grandiose scenes. Among the painters who were influenced by the Hudson River School were George Inness (1825–1894) who developed a freer, less detailed style and Frederick Edwin Church (1826–1900), a pupil of Cole, who was interested in the literal representation of nature.

HUNT, WILLIAM HOLMAN (1827–1910), was, along with Rossetti and Millais, one of the founders of the Pre-Raphaelites (q. v.). His religious and symbolical paintings are characterized by extreme realism. In his search for an exact background to his paintings Hunt travelled to Palestine. One of his best-known paintings, now in Oxford, is 'The Light of the World'.

INGRES, JEAN-AUGUSTE (1780–1867), who was the leader of the French Neo-Classicists after the death of his teacher David (q. v.), dedicated himself to a style of painting which depended on draughtsmanship for its effect. 'The simpler the lines and forms, the more effectively they reveal beauty and power,' he said. A long stay in Rome and Florence caused him to become an admirer of Raphael's art. Whatever he painted, whether mythological subjects, nudes (like his odalisques), or portraits (like that of Mademoiselle Rivière, in Paris), his interest is always in essential

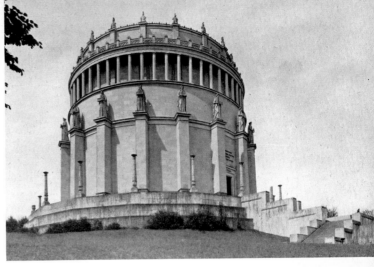

269. v. KLENZE, *The Hall of Liberation at Kelheim, Bavaria*

form. His drawing sets him in the forefront of the greatest portraitists. (Ill. p. 383)

JONGKIND, JOHAN BARTHOLD (1819–1891). Many years before the Impressionists, this Dutch painter was already attempting – by concentrating less on detail than on suggestion – to catch the movement of light, water and clouds in his landscapes and seascapes. He found the subject matter for his paintings near Grenoble and on the Dutch coast, even though his water colours and oil paintings with their strong, warm colour were not produced in the open but in the studio. He also was important as an etcher.

KLENZE, LEO VON (1784–1864), after training to be an architect under Friedrich Gilly in Berlin and visits to France, Italy and Greece, was appointed Court architect to Ludwig I. Like Schinkel, he sought to wed Northern and Greek elements, while re-interpreting Italian Early Renaissance ideas. Klenze quite changed the face of Munich by building there the Glyptothek, the Imperial Residence, the Alte Pinakothek and the Propylaea. (Ill. 269)

270. ADOLF VON HILDEBRAND, *Wittelsbach fountain in Munich, symbol of the healing power of water (the other side of the fountain depicts the destructive power of water)*

KRÜGER, FRANZ (1797–1857), was the main representative of the Biedermeier style in Berlin. His work consisted of realistic portraits which he produced for the Prussian and Czarist Courts as well as for rich Berlin citizens. In their day, his huge crowded pictures of military parades, in which everyone of rank or title is represented, were greatly admired. He was also famous for his many small paintings of horses and cavalry.

LANGHANS, KARL GOTTHARD (1732–1808), was one of the first classical architects in Prussia. He is chiefly known for the Brandenburg Gate in Berlin.

LATROBE, BENJAMIN HENRY (1766–1820). Though he was born in England, Latrobe is generally considered the first professional American architect. He came to the U. S. in 1796, was appointed surveyor of public buildings by President Jefferson in 1803 and, after the burning of the Capitol in the War of 1812, he was engaged to rebuild it. Credited with being the first to introduce the Greek Revival style into the U. S., Latrobe was the architect of many other buildings of national importance, including the Bank of Pennsylvania in Philadelphia, the Roman Catholic cathedral in Baltimore and many houses in Washington, Philadelphia and other eastern cities.

LAWRENCE, SIR THOMAS (1769–1803). Lawrence, the son of a Bristol innkeeper, was established as a portrait painter before he was twenty. He was elected A. R. A. in 1791, appointed Court painter in 1792 and elected R. A. in 1794. He had a facility resembling that of Sargent and much of his work is superficial; at his best, as in 'Queen Charlotte' (National Gallery) his brilliant technique is combined with a penetrating sense of period which to us sums up the age.

LEIBL, WILHELM (1844–1900), was born in Cologne and spent almost his whole life in the villages of Upper Bavaria among the peasants, village worthies and poachers, who were the models for his pictures (ill. p. 403). He painted with immense industry, reproducing every grain in the wood, every vein in the flesh and every thread in a dress, e. g. 'Three Women in Church' (Hamburg). A stay in Paris and the influence of Courbet were the inspiration of his free-style early works 'Frau Gedon' and 'The Cocotte' (Cologne). Later, he made a name for himself as a portrait-painter.

LEIGHTON, FREDERICK, LORD (1830–1896). Leighton spent most of his early life in Italy and later studied in Dresden and Paris. In his day, he was also considered to be a great sculptor. He was the principal neo-classical painter of the Victorian era – 'The Bath of Psyche' (London/Tate Gall.), 'Andromache Captive' (Manchester/City Art Gall.), – and enjoyed immense success. He was elected President of the Royal Academy and was the first painter to be raised to the peerage.

LIEBERMANN, MAX (1847–1935), was born in Berlin where he became President of the Academy. He was both painter and draughtsman and leader of the Berlin *Sezession,* founded in 1899. Along with Lovis Corinth and Max Slevogt, he was one of the leaders of German Impressionism. Important influences on him were Munkacsy in Paris and Millet in Barbizon. But the artistic home of his choice was Holland. Of the Dutch Old Masters he rated Frans Hals the most highly and had great respect for his work. His great early painting 'Women plucking Geese' is still inspired by the spirit of realism, but in the later 'Women mending Nets' or 'Woman with Goats' the palette and composition of the Impressionists can already be detected. His splendid pictures of the Wannsee (near Berlin) and of the beach at Scheveningen demonstrate the change to the full light of the open air. He was critically minded, a famous wit and the last great portrait painter of the *grande bourgeoisie,* to which he himself belonged. (Ill. p. 430)

MANET, EDOUARD (1832–1883), was one of the most important pioneers of modern painting. His boldness regarding both the objects and figures in his paintings from a purely pictorial point of view met with strong opposition from his contemporaries. A picture like his 'Déjeuner sur l'Herbe' (1863, Louvre) based on Raimondi's engraving after Raphael, with one naked and one half-dressed woman between two fully dressed men, produced the same storm of indignation as his 'Olympia' (after Titian) which was attacked by the critics as pornography but has to-day a place of honour in the Louvre. Manet continues in the great tradition of Velasquez, Goya and Titian. At the same time, however, he has an extremely unconventional concept of composition; for instance, in his 'Déjeuner à l'Atelier' (Munich) the eye is led from the principal figure in the foreground to various articles scattered about on the table and chairs, all painted with great virtuosity. Under Impressionist influence, Manet began to paint in the open air, e. g. 'The Boat' (Munich; ill. p. 416). But he was less interested in landscape than in his immediate surroundings in which man is always the centre of the composition, e. g. 'A Bar at the Folies-Bergère' (London/Nat. Gall.). Manet painted important portraits, e. g. of Zola and Mallarmé. Towards the end of his life, when his hand was crippled, he could only work with soft pastels.

MARÉES, HANS VON (1837–1887), strove to attain the gravity and simplicity of idealized large-scale painting. However, he was only once commissioned to produce a large fresco – for the Aquarium in Naples. He pursued his aims with great intensity, continually abandoning one solution after another and leaving much unfinished. From 1875 to 1887 he lived in Rome and found his spiritual home in Classical times. His paintings are mostly in subdued dark colours (e. g. 'The Golden Age', Munich). They deal with allegorical or mythological themes and repeatedly contain idealized nude figures in a broadly conceived landscape ('The Hesperides', Munich, or 'The Judgment of Paris', Berlin). His attempts to achieve a strict organization of his pictures are far ahead of his time. Marées also left an important collection of drawings. (Ill. p. 402)

271. MEUNIER, 'Industry' from the Memorial to Work, Brussels

MENZEL, ADOLF VON (1815–1905), was one of the most important German painters and illustrators of the 19th century. His motto was 'All drawing is good – to draw everything, even better'. He accordingly produced an extremely voluminous *corpus,* including thousands of drawings as well as paintings. He became best known for his illustrations to Kugler's *History of Frederick the Great* (400 drawings for woodcuts with strong chiaroscuro) and for his paintings on the same theme ('The Company at Dinner at Sanssouci' and 'Frederick playing the Flute', both in Berlin). With his 'Rolling Mill', the first important painting of the interior of a factory, Menzel founded realistic painting in Germany. Round about 1845, he produced a series of pictures which, in their feeling for the identity of objects, in their almost tangible reproduction of atmosphere and light, anticipate Impressionism by 40 years. These works first became known after his death through the memorial exhibition of 1905. (Ill. p. 404)

MEUNIER, CONSTANTIN (1831–1905). This Belgian painter began with religious themes and later turned to Impressionism. From 1886 onwards he worked as a sculptor. The muscular figures of his miners from the Borinage – the mining district around Mons – of his smiths and manual workers, are all clearly given a heroic aspect (ill. p. 271); Meunier did not seek to register any social protest. In 1939 a Meunier museum was opened in Brussels.

MILLAIS, SIR JOHN EVERETT (1829–1896). One of the founders of the Pre-Raphaelite Brotherhood, Millais entered the Royal Academy Schools in 1842 and won the gold medal and exhibited at the Academy when he was only seventeen. His first picture, 'Lorenzo and Isabella', was painted in accordance with Pre-Raphaelite principles and one of the most remarkable of Pre-Raphaelite pictures, 'Christ in the House of his Parents', a meticulously detailed work, was exhibited in 1850. Millais was elected A. R. A. in 1853 and his allegiance to the Brotherhood weakened. He entered upon the long series of popular paintings which bought him social success and have damaged his reputation to-day. Pictures such as 'The Blind Girl' (City Art Gall., Birmingham), however, show that at his best Millais was not only one of the most technically able of English artists but also one of the most imaginative and profoundly moving of 19th-century painters.

MILLET, JEAN-FRANÇOIS (1814–1875), a peasant's son from Normandy, became one of the Barbizon school. With deep religious seriousness he painted farm labourers at work or enjoying the quiet peace of the evening ('The Gleaners' and 'The Angelus', both in the Louvre). To-day, his drawings, which deal with similar themes, are preferred to his paintings, which are felt to be slightly too sentimental for modern taste.

MONET, CLAUDE (1840–1926). Monet's picture 'Impression, Soleil levant' caused a hostile critic to coin the term 'Impressionism'. Thus Monet became *the* Impressionist, but the derogatory name was applied to a whole group, consisting of Sisley, Pissarro, Renoir and Degas; now it has become a title of distinction (cf. p. 405). Monet was painted by Manet in his 'Boat on the Seine' (ill. p. 416). Thereafter, it became a symbol of the whole movement to work in the open air. To Monet the setting for the new style of painting was amid the play of natural light, the glitter and sheen of water (ill. p. 72), the atmospheric haze lying over sunny landscapes – as in his 'Summer's Day' (Stuttgart) – or among the houses of towns like London and Rouen. His tones are methodically analysed into pure colour in order to achieve the brightest possible ensemble. The individual object loses its importance as something to be accurately reproduced. Monet frequently painted the same object at different times of the day in order to catch the variations in light.

MONTICELLI, ADOLPHE JOSEPHE (1824–1886), who lived in Marseilles, found his personal style only in the last 15 years of his life. With something approaching obsession, he made his quiet landscapes and portraits into gleaming fantasies of colour. In so doing, he often calculated in advance the changes which would take place in the chemistry of his paint, so that their effect was only revealed many years later.

MORISOT, BERTHE (1841–1895), studied under Corot, followed the style of her brother-in-law Manet for a time, and then gradually turned away from the Impressionists' analysis of colour to a flatter use of paint.

MORRIS, WILLIAM (1834–1896), was an opponent of industrialization who attempted to reinstate handicrafts (cf. p. 436). Genuine materials and beautiful form combined with utility were all to be equally important. The workshop founded by him and his friends under the name of Morris, Marshall, Faulkner and Co. produced wallpapers, glassware, tiles and furniture to his designs; the group also undertook interior decoration. Morris revived the art of printing by hand with books from his Kelmscott Press, which are richly ornamented and set in old type-faces. Morris, who was also famous as a poet and social reformer, had a strong influence on the German *Jugendstil* (see Art Nouveau) and on the development of modern decoration. (Ill. 264)

NASH, JOHN (1752–1835). Although born in the mid-18th century, Nash is essentially a Regency architect, for his was the chief inspiration behind the Brighton Pavilion and it was he who planned the superb terraces surrounding Regent's Park (c. 1811) and Regent Street from the Quadrant at the Piccadilly Circus end to All Souls' Church, Langham Place. Though Nash's Regent Street buildings have been destroyed his surviving palatial blocks of stuccoed, classical architecture contribute substantially to the essential character of London. Nash's sense of unity in street architecture and his excellent use of stucco have never been surpassed.

NAZARENES. When J. Friedrich Overbeck and Franz Pforr, the leading members of the ascetically religious 'Brotherhood of St Luke' – a group of artists founded in Vienna in 1809 – moved to Rome, such similarly-minded painters already living there as Peter von Cornelius, Carl Philipp Fohr, Julius Schnorr von Carolsfeld, Joseph Führich, Philipp and Johann Veit, soon joined them. In order to bring art back to the 'way of truth' they drew their inspiration – as did the Pre-Raphaelites later – from Italian Christian art and the German art of the Renaissance, particularly Dürer. The group, who were in part converted to religion, attempted to carry on these traditions. They were not able, however, to give compelling artistic and formal expression to their message or their inner strivings. Their drawings – especially their studies for portraits – are more important than the well-known communal works, such as the frescoes in the Casa Bartholdy and the Villa Massimo, or their numerous landscape paintings.

OVERBECK, JOHANN FRIEDRICH (1789–1869), was one of the founders of the 'Brotherhood of St Luke' (see Nazarenes). His work lost its early freshness after his conversion to Catholicism in 1813, and became set in religious moulds.

PALMER, SAMUEL (1805–1881). Palmer began to exhibit at the Royal Academy at an early age. From 1826 to 1832 he lived at Shoreham, painting pastoral subjects in oils and water colours. With George Richmond, Edward Calvert and other painters he formed a group known as 'The Ancients', deeply influenced by Blake. It was during these years at Shoreham that Palmer produced the romantic paintings and wash drawings which are so admired to-day and which have influenced painters like Sutherland. After these years of high inspiration, Palmer's work lost its fire and originality and became almost entirely academic.

PARIS, THE MADELEINE. In 1806, on the instructions of Napoleon, the architect Barthelemy Vignon (1762–1846) began work on what was to be a Hall of Fame. The building, which has a peripteros (140 ft by 115 ft) borne by 65-foot Corinthian columns, was converted into a church in 1814 and completed by Huvé in 1842. (Ill. 272)

PILOTY, KARL VON (1826–1886). After training with Belgian and French historical painters, he became in 1874 director of the Munich Academy of Art, which flourished under his enlightened administration. His somewhat theatrical, highly coloured pictures have lost their appeal, though it must be conceded that a whole generation of painters benefited from his instruction.

PISSARRO, CAMILLE (1830–1903), the son of a French father and a Creole mother, was born in the Antilles. From 1855 onwards he lived in Paris. In his early works – realistic landscapes – the influence of Corot can be detected. Pissarro was the oldest and, in some ways, the leading figure within the Impressionist group; he was particularly close to Manet, Monet and Cézanne. After a period of classical Impressionist *plein air* painting, during which his most famous landscapes were produced, he temporarily adopted Seurat's neo-Impressionist theories (Pointillism). Towards the end of his life, he produced paintings of Paris, Rouen and other towns in bright and heartening colours (ill. p. 419).

POWERS, HIRAM (1805–1873). The leading neo-classical sculptor of the mid-19th century, Powers was born in Woodstock, Vermont. After making wax models for a Midwestern museum, he went to Washington, D. C., in 1835 to model portrait busts of President Andrew Jackson (now at the Metropolitan Museum) and others. Two years later he settled permanently in Italy, where his work was nourished by the classical environment of Florence.

PRENDERGAST, MAURICE BRAZIL (1859–1924), a quiet, shy enigmatic man, crept closer to Post-Impressionism (in 'Sunset and Sea Fog', 'Promenade', 'Gloucester') than any of his contemporaries. Born in Newfoundland, he sailed in 1886 to Europe, where he studied at the Académie Julian and the Académie Colarossi. He acquired mastery of the Impressionist technique but wilfully abandoned all except the tiny strokes of pure colour, which he built into dreamlike and gay tapestries whose naïveté was redeemed mainly by sensitive tonalities and an exquisitely personal sense of design.

272. The Madeleine, Paris (VIGNON and HUVÉ)

PRE-RAPHAELITES. In 1848, Rossetti, Hunt and Millais founded the Pre-Raphaelite Brotherhood, which found its spokesman in John Ruskin (q. v.). They took their models from the Italian art of the early 15th century. A noble subject, truthfulness to nature and extraordinary attention to detail were their cardinal tenets. The Brotherhood lasted only until 1851. Holman Hunt alone remained true to its principles. Ford Maddox Brown, though not a member of the Brotherhood, was sympathetic; Burne-Jones (1833–98) was the most prominent follower of the Pre-Raphaelites, and William Morris owed much to them. (Ill. 260)

PRUD'HON, PIERRE-PAUL (1758–1823), was more 'romantic' than 'classical' in outlook. His pictures, full of movement and internal tension, are dominated by picturesque chiaroscuro. His main works are 'The Rape of Psyche', 'Justice and Vengeance pursuing Crime' and 'The Empress Josephine' (all in the Louvre). Prud'hon's drawings are as important as his paintings, particularly his numerous studies of heads and nudes.

PUGIN, GEORGE AUGUSTUS WELBY NORTHMORE (1812–1852). Although the most brilliant writer amongst British architects, his buildings – of which few survive – are disappointing. Yet Pugin's importance can hardly be exaggerated. The first to attack the imitation of past styles, he demanded honesty of design sixty years before Adolf Loos. 'Gothic' building, to him, was honest building rather than the copying of particular features. Asked how a railway could be designed on Gothic principles, he replied that buttresses, supporting embankments and sturdy, stone-built bridges were no contradiction of the nature of the railway or of good architecture.

PUVIS DE CHAVANNES, PIERRE-CÉCILE (1824–1898), was unaffected by contemporary realism and Impressionism. He aimed at a renewal of large-scale wall painting and produced huge works in oil with allegorical themes which, when placed on a wall, give the impression of frescoes (e. g. in the Panthéon). His noble, beautiful, clearly defined figures have a solemn dignity as they move through an ideal landscape. The decorative side of his gifts had a great influence on Continental Art Nouveau.

QUIDOR, JOHN (1801–1881). Born in Tappan, New York, he studied briefly with John Wesley Jarvis. When Washington Irving's *History of New York* was brought out in 1809, it contained illustrations by Quidor. Recognised by a discerning few to have caught the satirical quintessence and the dramatic weirdness of such romantic writers of the period as Cooper and Irving, Quidor gained a reputation of some stature, but he was never widely appreciated his lifetime. Now he is regarded by many authorities as one of the finest early American painters, and his masterpiece, 'Rip Van Winkle at Nicholas Vedder's Tavern' (1839), remains one of the genuine treasures in the rich heritage left by American painters of the mid-19th century.

273. RAUCH, *King Frederick the Great of Prussia from the equestrian monument in Berlin. Bronze*

RAUCH, CHRISTIAN DANIEL (1777–1857). During his prolonged stay in Rome, Rauch closely followed the style of Thorvaldsen, whose classical influence can be clearly seen in his first important work, the marble tomb for Queen Louise. His monuments (e. g. Frederick II, ill. 273) and his busts (e. g. Goethe), have provided later generations with the definitive portrait of his sitters.

RENOIR, AUGUSTE (1841–1919). Along with Monet and Sisley, he belonged to the Impressionist school and was preoccupied with light and its coloured shadows. Later, after a period of Pointillism in the 'eighties, he returned to a classical concept of line in the manner of Ingres, but his painting soon became freer. His favourite colour is red in an infinite variety of shades, which are frequently too rosy (ill. p. 420). The colours of the Rococo boudoir have returned but they are healthier, more rural and more bourgeois ('La Maternité' and 'Girl with a Cat'). Renoir wished to make his fellow-men and himself happy in his art. In his old age, he still painted the olive groves and gardens of his house at Cagnes, even when his hands were crippled and the brush had to be tied on. The paintings of this period have a peaceful perfection and an untroubled confidence. Under his direction, a young assistant produced a number of works of sculpture (e. g. Venus). He himself was responsible for the portrait sculpture of his son Coco.

REPIN, ILYA YEFIMOVICH (1894–1930), was the most important representative of the new school of Russian realistic painting. After studying in Paris, he began by painting saints and then pictures of Russian life with large numbers of figures and a certain social content. His portraits of Russian poets and musicians, like Tolstoy and Mussorgsky, are penetrating psychological studies. The Tretvakov Gallery in Moscow contains more than fifty of his works.

427

274. RUDE, 'Marseillaise' (Chant du Départ). Relief from the Arc de Triomphe, Paris

RICHARDSON, HENRY HOBSON (1838–1886), was the first modern American architect. Although he was still inspired by historical models, such as the Roman architecture of southern France, he copied no particular style and did not indulge in pastiche. He succeeded in finding a new unity of architectural mass and function. He was trained in Paris under Labrousse. Among his later works are office buildings in Boston and Chicago in which he achieved something approaching a sky-scraper in brick.

RICHTER, ADRIAN LUDWIG (1803–1884), belonged to the German late Romantic school, and was for more than forty years teacher at the Dresden Academy. In spite of his love for Italy, where he spent several years, he was more at home with his native landscape, its myths and fairy-tales. He found a rich field of activity in book illustration in which he could develop all his gifts as a draughtsman. His *Memoirs of a German Painter* became almost as popular as his illustrations to fairy-tales.

RODIN, AUGUSTE (1840–1917), was the greatest French sculptor of the 19th century. He represents the Impressionist school in sculpture. He himself called form – which in his works is violent, flowing and fissured – an art of 'hollows and humps'. He did not wish to achieve smooth, rounded plastic form but sought to express spiritual tension and the impalpable qualities of sensibility and excitement by means of a surface on which there is a play of light and shadow. The 'Burghers of Calais' is the most impressive example of this, as are his figure of a youth – 'L'Age d'Airain' – and his numerous great sensitive portraits, e. g. of Balzac and Hugo (cf. p. 14, ill. 11, 258). Rodin felt that he was a latter-day Gothic artist and said that his true masters were the artists of the cathedrals. As an old man in the middle of the First World War he dedicated a hymn to the cathedrals of France.

ROSSETTI, DANTE GABRIEL (1820–1882). Rossetti – an Italian born in England – painted his early pictures while still wholly under the influence of the Pre-Raphaelite Brotherhood (q. v.), which he founded. Later, he developed his own highly imaginative style, in which he painted numerous visions of women and, in particular, scenes from the Life of Dante ('Dante's Dream', Liverpool). Ill. 260

ROUSSEAU, THÉODORE (1812–1867), was one of the leading figures of the Barbizon school, the group of painters who had settled in the little village of Barbizon in the forest of Fontainebleau in order to paint the silent world of the 'paysage intime' – small, remote, undramatic details of the landscape. Rousseau painted quiet corners of the woods, groups of trees and desolate swamps which have all the magic of the untouched countryside (ill. p. 414). Ruysdael and Hobbema and the realistic landscapes of Constable had the strongest influence on the Barbizon school, who in turn strongly influenced German realistic landscape-painting in the second half of the century.

RUDE, FRANÇOIS (1784–1855), born in Dijon, was trained as a sculptor in Paris. His style, which is powerful, impetuous and naturalistic, is linked to the Baroque by its use of form; it replaced academic classicism and had a great influence on 19th-century sculpture (cf. p. 397). His works include 'The Neapolitan Fisherboy' in the Louvre and the reliefs on the Arc de Triomphe (ill. 274).

RUNGE, PHILIPP OTTO (1777–1810), is, after C. D. Friedrich, the most important German Romantic painter. His aims were to break away from classicism and to bring new life into painting through a spirit of romantic symbolism. Such were the ideas which Runge wished to treat in a cycle of paintings called 'The Course of the Day', which remained unfinished. His theoretical opinions, as expressed in his letters, had a strong influence on the German Romantic school. Runge's pictures grip us by their straightforward technique and excellent portraiture ('The Painter's Parents' and 'Self-portrait' both in Hamburg; ill. p. 394).

RUSKIN, JOHN (1819–1900), learned to know and appreciate French Gothic and the Italian Quattrocento during his long journeys in Europe. He sought to revive this type of art, which, in his opinion, had not degenerated into mere craftsmanship, and thus became an ardent supporter of the Pre-Raphaelites (q. v.). In 1851 he published a book on the movement. He proclaimed a gospel of beauty which would derive its laws from exact observation of nature. He addressed himself with prophetic power to the English working class in *Fors Clavigera* (1871–1884), warning them against the dangers of industrialization.

RYDER, ALBERT PINKHAM (1847–1917), although he produced only 150 or so canvases during his life, stands in the forefront of the 19th-century American romantic painters. He painted and repainted small and

GEORGES SEURAT: La Baignade

MAX LIEBERMANN: Papageienallee

MAX SLEVOGT: The singer D'Andrade as Don Giovanni (The Champagne Aria)

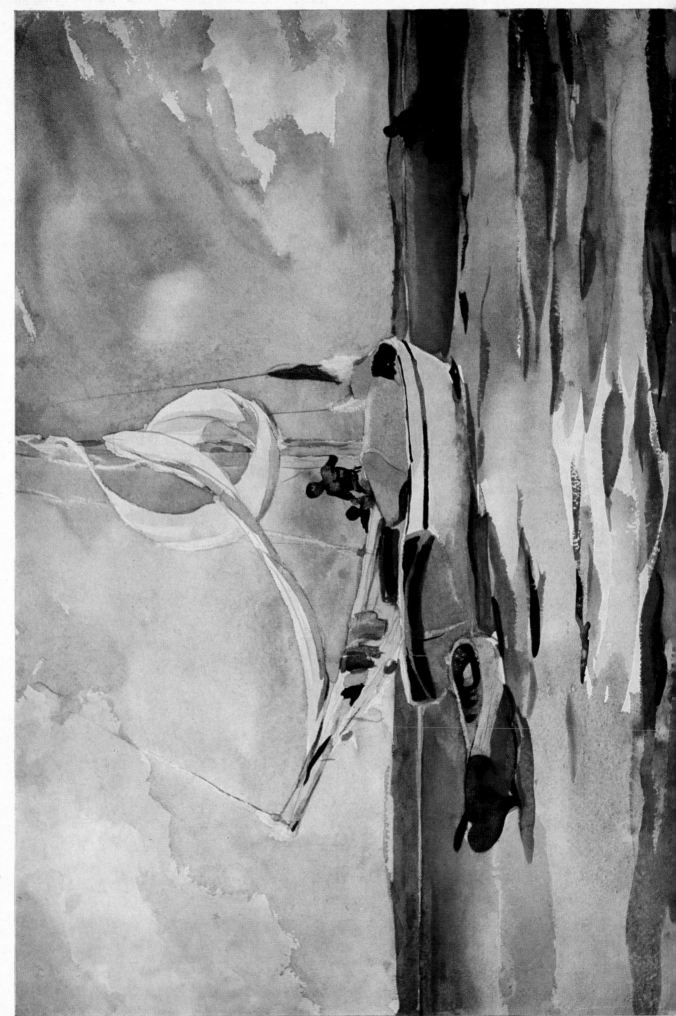

WINSLOW HOMER: The Sloop, Bermuda

dully-coloured, but nevertheless luminous and poetic, interpretations of moonlit scenes of land and sea (and also of romantic literary subjects) throughout his lifetime. As a result of his constant repainting – which he frequently did before the original paints had fully dried – most of his paintings are now cracked and yellowed. Some of his best-known and most characteristic works are: 'Toilers of the Sea', 'Death on a Pale Horse', and 'The Flying Dutchman'.

SAINT-GAUDENS, AUGUSTUS (1848–1907). Born in Dublin, Ireland, Saint-Gaudens became the foremost 19th-century American sculptor. He produced a galaxy of public statues in the U. S., all distinguished by a genius for plasticity and largely influenced by his training in France and by his knowledge of the Italian Renaissance. Among his chief works are the statues of Admiral Farragut in Madison Square, New York City; 'The Puritan' in Springfield, Massachusetts; and the Adams Memorial in Rock Creek Cemetery, Washington, D. C.

SARGENT, JOHN SINGER (1856–1925), was born in Florence, the son of American parents. He was much sought after by American and English society as a portraitist. His brilliant technique which was modelled on that of Velasquez, his sure eye for the salient features of his sitters, and his subdued colours earned him an immense success, all the greater perhaps because Sargent's grasp of character was superficial. His pictures are to be found chiefly in the Tate Gallery, in Paris and in New York. (Ill. 275)

SCHADOW, JOHANN GOTTFRIED (1764–1850). The works of this German sculptor are characterized by a keen appreciation of the living quality and the temperament of his sitters, whose natural movements he studied. This, and his sense of humour, precluded this admirer of Antiquity from indulging in the hollow pathos of the later classicists. The Quadriga on the Brandenburg Gate in Berlin numbers among his larger groups. (Ill. 257)

275. SARGENT, Portrait of Vernon Lee

276. SCHINKEL, The church in the Werder Market in Berlin. Water colour by Joh. Friedrich Stock, c. 1840

SCHINKEL, KARL FRIEDRICH (1781–1841), was the most important German architect of his day. Although he was a classical artist, he sought, because of his Romantic leanings, to give new life to Gothic. His talent was extremely versatile and he was active as painter, sculptor, stage designer and writer. His buildings, for example, the Old Museum in Berlin, are mostly strictly classical. (Ill. 252, 276)

SCHWIND, MORITZ VON (1804–1871), was born in Vienna but lived mostly in Munich. He was a painter and draughtsman who based his work on themes from history and fairy-tales. He produced a number of large and theatrical frescoes but his warm-heartedness, humour and imagination are better displayed in his smaller paintings, such as 'Des Knaben Wunderhorn' and 'Rübezahl', in his gay scenes from bourgeois life, such as 'The Honeymoon', or his book illustrations (e. g. to Mörike).

SEGANTINI, GIOVANNI (1858–1899), was born at Arco on Lake Garda. Using a technique of his own whereby he applied his colours unmixed in close thick strokes, he caught the clear pure hues and the transparent light of the Swiss and Italian Alps with their peasants and lake fishermen. Later he attempted to impart a deeper symbolical meaning to his pictures by the use of allegorical figures ('The Angel of Life'), but they were less well received.

SEURAT, GEORGES (1859–1891), is – together with Signac – the founder of neo-Impressionism, which is based on the statement by Charles Blanc that colours obey strict rules and can be taught like music. After a number of unconventional experiments in black and white in which line was abandoned, Seurat exhibited his first picture 'La Baignade' in the *Salon des Indépendants*. It is a large-scale work painted in dots of pure, unmixed complementary colours, which earned the new group the nickname of the 'confetti painters' (ill. p. 429). There followed 'Un Dimanche à la Grande Jatte' (1886), 'La Parade' (1887), 'Les Poseuses' (1888) and 'Le Chahut' (1890). It would hardly have been possible to bring the Pointillist vision more quickly to theo-

433

retical and artistic fruition – nor could it have been taken further. But that is not Seurat's only merit. What was more important for the future was the strictly ordered composition which he achieved in his last works and which represents his final break with Impressionism.

SIGNAC, PAUL (1863–1935). As a young man he joined the *Société des Artistes Indépendants,* of which he became president in 1908. He was a close friend of Seurat, with whom he drew up the neo-Impressionist programme. Signac worked from coloured sketches which he had collected in the course of his numerous and extensive journeys; his constant aim was to increase the high-lights to the utmost and to give durability to a chance impression.

SISLEY, ALFRED (1839–1899), the son of English parents, was born in Paris. Of all the Impressionists he was the calmest, the most modest and the most poetic. He painted almost exclusively landscapes – the banks of the Seine and Fontainebleau – in which he always attempted to achieve a soft harmony of tone values. Out of reverence for organic nature and the structure of things, he avoided the disintegrating tendencies of Impressionism. Sisley died poor and lonely without achieving fame in his lifetime. (Ill. p. 418)

SLEVOGT, MAX (1868–1932), was one of the chief masters of the German Impressionist school to which Liebermann and Corinth also belonged. After studying in Munich and Paris, he settled in Berlin in 1901 and became professor at the Academy in 1917. Brilliance and joviality both distinguish his pictures in which he cleverly caught the magic of a passing moment, a happy mood or a characteristic gesture ('D'Andrade as Don Giovanni', Stuttgart, ill. p. 431). His work as a witty and inventive illustrator is of particular importance, e. g. his lithographs for The Magic Flute or for Fennimore Cooper's *Last of the Mohicans.*

SPITZWEG, CARL (1808–1885), was a chemist before he took up painting. He found his favourite subjects in the dreamy world of the provincial small-town of his day, which he frequently depicted on cigar-box lids (ill. p. 401).

STEVENS, ALFRED (1817–1875), was active as painter, draughtsman, sculptor, craftsman and academic teacher. During his period of study in Rome, when he worked with Thorvaldsen, he took the great Michelangelo as his model. His monument to Wellington in St Paul's has been described as the most famous work of sculpture of the Victorian age.

SULLIVAN, HENRY LOUIS (1856–1924), is the most important of the American pioneers of modern architecture. He was one of the first to advocate the unity of form and purpose (Functionalism) and anticipated the Art Nouveau movement by producing a type of decoration which was not based on earlier models but discovered by himself. From 1874 to 1876 he studied in Paris. At first he followed the style of H. H. Richardson but in his most important buildings (e. g. his ware-

house for Carson, Pirie and Scott in Chicago, 1899), he was solving his problems in a way which is only a step from the architecture of to-day – of Gropius or Le Corbusier. His most important works are mostly to be found in Chicago, St Louis and Buffalo.

SULLY, THOMAS (1783–1872). Son of English Stage parents, Sully became one of the most famous American portrait painters of the nineteenth century. His subjects included Thomas Jefferson, James Madison, Andrew Jackson, Commodore Stephen Decatur, and the young Queen Victoria.

THOMA, HANS (1839–1924), was a peasant's son who worked as a house-painter before he attended the Academy in Karlsruhe and Düsseldorf. 'Perhaps', he said, 'we may regard art as a way of seeing order in the confused mass of impressions which our soul receives from the world.' The words reveal his clarity of outlook and his human modesty. Thoma produced his best work in lyrical landscapes of the Black Forest, the Upper Rhine and the Taunus, and in faithful portraits of his family. His work is distinguished by intense feeling for nature and a certain naïveté which is free of any false refinement. The allegorical and religious paintings he produced in the 'eighties under the influence of Böcklin, on the other hand, are pale and weak, and indeed his work, as a whole, shows great variations in quality. The lithographs which he produced in his old age gave new life to this art form.

THORVALDSEN, BERTEL (1768/70–1844). During a stay in Rome this Danish sculptor was led, by his experience of the art of Antiquity, to turn to classicism, of which he must be considered the most influential exponent after Canova (cf. p. 397). For modern taste his works, which are distinguished by their noble line, their calm and ease, are perhaps lacking in inspiration. In his day, they were considered the quintessence of perfection in sculpture. Thorvaldsen was overwhelmed with commissions from all over Europe. In Lucerne there is the 'Lion of Lucerne' hewn from the rock after a model by him; for Napoleon he produced a frieze of the campaigns of Alexander. His more than life-size statue of Christ imparting the benediction was one of the most frequently copied statues of the 19th century. All his important works – or casts of them – are collected in the Thorvaldsen Museum in Copenhagen. (Ill. 256)

TOULOUSE-LAUTREC, HENRI DE (1864–1901), was the last representative of a line stretching back to the Crusades. When he was fourteen he broke both his legs and was crippled for life. In order to have something to live for, he dedicated himself entirely to art. Degas and the Japanese coloured woodcuts had a decisive influence on him both as a painter and draughtsman. His 'Studio' was in the music-halls and pleasure haunts of Montmartre, such as the Moulin Rouge; his models were *chansonnières* and *cocottes;* the scenes he painted were cabarets, circuses and race-tracks. He caught and caricatured character with the same sharp observation as he painted the pointed, cheeky face of Yvette Guilbert, Jane Avril and La Goulue. In the 'nineties he began to take a special interest in colour-lithography of which he became the great master (ill. p. 38). He had an important influence on modern commercial art and, in particular, on the poster.

TRÜBNER, WILHELM (1851–1917), had marked talent, which developed early, and he produced a number of important pictures when still a young man. They were landscapes and portraits painted with thick brush strokes in the same dark tones and heavy colours as Courbet used; they were intended to be 'old masters'. His painting later became impressionistic – the air seems to acquire movement, the colour is looser and brighter. Trübner was influenced by Leibl (q. v.).

TURNER, JOSEPH MALLORD WILLIAM (1775–1851), left 21,000 sketches, water colours and oil paintings at his death. Unlike Constable, his painting was greatly praised by his contemporaries – particularly the brilliance and purity of his colours. Claude Lorraine, the painter of light, had a special influence on him. The ever-recurring theme of his painting is the atmosphere suffused by light in all its gradations – from the drab mist of London to the silvery blue sky of the South. This is so even when he peoples his landscapes with historical or mythological figures (ill. p. 386). His oils, though painted in the studio, were the result of a continual study of nature and a visual memory which has perhaps never been equalled. His greatness lies in his scope, his grasp of the essence of things and his power of creating an impression, with the merest suggestion of form. Turner's later works have only recently been appreciated and they have had great influence on the young painters of to-day.

UHDE, FRITZ VON (1848–1911), was an officer who resigned from his career in 1877 in order to devote himself to painting. Next to Liebermann, he is the most important representative of German early Impressionism and *plein-air* painting. Uhde came from a strictly Protestant family; in his large series of paintings of Christ, whom he sets among the peasants and artisans of his own day, he attempted to initiate a new school of religious painting. His portraits of children and of his family are more important artistically.

VERNET, HORACE (1789–1863), belonged to a family of painters. He himself painted genre paintings and battle scenes. His largest war paintings hang in Versailles. He was also noted for his woodcuts for L'Ardèche's *History of Napoleon*.

WATTS, GEORGES FREDERICK (1817–1904). Watts' career began at an early age. He exhibited paintings at the Royal Academy when he was only twenty and won the first prize in a competition for frescoes for the new Houses of Parliament, five years later. He then visited Italy, where he studied for three years. Apart from a large number of portraits – most of them now in the

277. WHISTLER, *San Biagio (No. 2) from the second Venice series. Etching*

London National Portrait Gallery – he painted allegorical subjects. The best known of these are 'Time, Death and Judgment', 'Sic Transit Gloria Mundi', and 'Hope' (all London/Tate Gall.). Watts was attempting to recapture, in the era of Krupps and Joseph Chamberlain, the antique grandeur of life in a vanished world. His subject pieces usually strike us as absurd, but his portraits put Watts in the front rank of English painters. They are shrewd and penetrating and yet retain something of the grand style of Reynolds.

WHISTLER, JAMES MACNEILL (1834–1903), was an Anglo-American who lived mostly in London and Paris. He was one of the first painters to recognise the importance of the Japanese coloured woodcut. His oil paintings and pastels, which dissolve more and more into impressionism, are composed in a musical tonality of colour ('Nocturne in Blue and Silver' and 'Arrangement in Grey and Black'). His architectural etchings of London and Venice are highly considered (ill. 277).

WILKIE, SIR DAVID (1785–1841). As early as 1806 a genre painting 'Village Politicians' by this young Scottish painter created a great impression in a London exhibition. His fame increased with every successive painting. He became President of the Royal Academy and finally succeeded Lawrence as Court painter, for which he received a knighthood. The genre painting remained his main strength. Like his artistic forebears, Ostade and Teniers, he painted rural scenes with great power. Thanks to clever composition, imaginative use of colour and fine modelling, Wilkie became one of the most important European genre painters of the 19th century.

ZORN, ANDERS (1860–1920). After travelling extensively, this Swedish painter and etcher settled in his birthplace, Mora, in the province of Dalarna. The artist's house, which is now a museum, contains many of his impressionistic *plein-air* nudes and scenes from Swedish peasant life. In his etchings, which are celebrated, the artist displays a virtuosity of technique which aims at dissolving contours in order to achieve the same open-air atmosphere as in his paintings.

435

Art in the Modern Age

278. *Lever Building, New York* (Skidmore, Owings and Merrill)

THERE IS NO DENYING that in the last hundred years the condition of civilised man has changed more radically than at any previous time. Inventions and discoveries, from the steam engine to the internal combustion engine, from electricity to atomic power, have led to the mechanization of industry which in turn has basically affected the social, economic and political structure of our society. A society of the masses has come into existence and is being buttressed by such mass means as the press, the cinema, radio and – latterly – television.

It is hardly surprising that these rapidly changing circumstances should have had their effect on the arts, too. Art has always been a highly sensitive instrument for registering any changes in the social order or in the ideas, beliefs and activities of man. One might ask whether it is possible for the creative faculty to exist at all in a mass-society, whether our mechanized world is the proper place for the production and enjoyment of a work of art. If it is true that calm contemplation is vital to the artist, does it not also follow that his whole being will protest most violently against an epoch in which the machine sets the pace, a pace that in its ruthless precision is the very opposite of that rhythm of life out of which art has hitherto grown?

Protests of this kind have been and are still being made on behalf of the arts. William Morris had in the sixties of the last century already tried, with commendable courage, to combat the effects of the machine age and the increase of mechanization, which he considered to be an evil to society. During his lifetime he never travelled by railway and, it is said, ostentatiously carried a spinning-wheel through the streets of London in defence of the old crafts. He founded a firm of artists whose hallmark was soundness of form and good craftsmanship. Together they designed and made all manner of furniture, fabrics, wall-paper, carpets, stained glass etc., in the belief that the artist, by also being a craftsman, could be saved from annihilation by the machine. The forms that Morris and his helpers chose for their products were inspired by the late Middle Ages, as was Morris's poetry. He wrote and decorated books with his own hand in the manner of the medieval monks, opposing the flood of popular mass-productions with the choice limited editions of the Kelmscott Press. The institution of technical schools in which studio and workshop were of equal importance was largely due to him. Morris's success was limited, however. His products never came within the means of more than a small public, and his ideas and achievements could not arrest the movement towards mass-production with its attendant social evils.

PAUL CÉZANNE: Mont Sainte-Victoire

PAUL GAUGUIN: The White Horse

Vincent van Gogh: The Church at Auvers

EDVARD MUNCH: Four Girls on the Bridge

The practitioners of the style known as Art Nouveau or *Jugendstil,* who in a sense developed Morris' ideas, fared no better. They attempted to replace traditional ornament by naturalistic forms, only to find that manufacturers got hold of their designs, and, with the help of the machine, turned them into hideous productions for the mass-market. The leaders of Art Nouveau soon realized that ornament had no place in the machine age, which demanded a new kind of simplicity with the emphasis on form rather than on decoration.

ARCHITECTURE

At quite an early stage this view found enthusiastic support from a group of people who, in contrast to the Arts and Crafts movement made full use of the machines and the means and potentialities of the new age. They were the engineers, who had never before contributed much to the arts and whose sole aim it was to produce functional, practical and durable works. They welcomed the new inventions and, above all, new materials such as cast iron, rolled iron, steel, concrete and ferro-concrete. At first their scope was restricted to the building of bridges and highways, but gradually it came to include more and more real architecture – a timely intervention, as the creative power of traditional architecture was beginning to wane.

When, in 1789, the French Revolution proclaimed a new world order, it brought to an end a continuous development in architecture that had lasted for a millennium. Baroque and Rococo had been the last truly original styles. They were succeeded by neo-Classicism which, however brilliant its achievements and exponents, still harked back to the historical past, that is, to the architecture of Ancient Greece and Rome. At the same time the effects of the French Revolution began to be felt. The difference between secular and sacred buildings virtually disappeared. The façade of a classical temple was used indiscriminately for a church (the Madeleine in Paris, ill. 272), a theatre, a national memorial, museum or ministerial building. The very age that revolutionized life as never before was tenaciously clinging to the past, studying, copying and practising its forms as if to commit every detail to memory. The Gothic Revival, a New Renaissance, a florid, re-hashed version of Baroque (Paris Opéra), a second Rococo (the buildings of Ludwig II of Bavaria) all made their appearance. Industry and international trade brought prosperity to a new section of the community, producing the characteristic trappings of a *nouveau riche* class. Factories, at least on the outside, simulated royal palaces, power stations were made to resemble castles, railway stations took the guise of cathedrals.

The appearance of the engineers in this general confusion was like a breath of fresh air. While the new-rich citizens built themselves sumptuous residences – at relatively low cost, since willing machines turned out in a few hours what it had once taken artists and craftsmen weeks to create, – while Morris attempted in vain to thwart that moloch, the machine, buildings arose whose like had never been seen before. They were structures with iron frames and glass walls and domes, designed by engineers: London's Crystal Palace by Paxton, the Chicago skyscrapers, the Galérie des Machines at the Paris Exhibition of 1889, and the famous Eiffel Tower,

280. The Bauhaus, Dessau (Gropius)

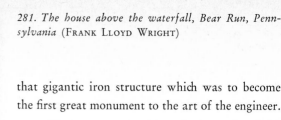

281. *The house above the waterfall, Bear Run, Pennsylvania* (FRANK LLOYD WRIGHT)

that gigantic iron structure which was to become the first great monument to the art of the engineer.

The movement could not be ignored and the more enlightened architects soon realized that if architecture was to become truly modern, free at last from the bondage of imitation and historical conventions, it was the engineers working with the new materials who must supply the inspiration. Former supporters of Art Nouveau, like architects Sullivan in Chicago, Otto Wagner and Adolf Loos in Vienna, and Peter Behrens (the AEG buildings in Berlin), began to study the ideas of the engineers and to work on similar lines. The balanced dimensions and harmonious proportions of their buildings, however, revealed the hand of the true artist (e. g. Otto Wagner's planning of the Vienna city railway). Le Corbusier, who was at first an admirer of Josef Hoffmann, the most important exponent of the Viennese *Jugendstil* and the first to go beyond it, apprenticed himself to the engineer Perret. This training fitted him for his role as the moving spirit behind contemporary architecture.

Walter Gropius, who was an equally important figure, was Behrens' pupil and assistant. At the age of thirty-one he was made principal of the Weimar School of Art, later known as the *Bauhaus*, to whose progressive activities designers all over the world are still indebted to-day (ill. 280). Gropius' first building, a factory of ferro-concrete and glass at Alfeld, stressed rather than concealed the link with engineering techniques. At the same time Gropius had the greatest respect for William Morris, whom he called one of the spiritual fathers of the *Bauhaus*. He included hand-crafts in the *Bauhaus* curriculum, considering them an important, even indispensable subject. But his weavers, carpenters, gold- and silversmiths did not aim at producing works of art, the time for that being past; instead, they sought to supply industry with good designs which would pass the test both of sound craftsmanship and of good art. Thus a new kind of artist, the industrial designer came into being. Hostility towards the machine ceased to exist, while respect for the craftsman was maintained. This synthesis was in keeping with the spirit of the age, more especially so since there were no engineers at the *Bauhaus* but only artists of great individuality and sensibility – Paul Klee, Lyonel Feininger, Oskar Schlemmer, to name only a few. The trend was unmistakable: the new epoch with its new social structure had to be accepted, but not its faults and weaknesses; these were to be offset by the creative freedom of the true artist. Architecture could once more become the mother of the arts; the *Bauhaus* would work in something like the spirit of the medieval guilds, while individual talent was able to develop and prove itself in collaboration with the team.

Indeed, architecture did become the first of all the arts to find public recognition, although the appearance of the new buildings was as unconventional as that of new sculpture and painting. But the impress of the deliberately personal, highly individual attitude that has characterized the other arts has always been less marked in architecture. In contemporary buildings complete harmony is achieved between their function and the artistic and technical means used. From the plain and sober style of English domestic architecture (Voysey, Norman Shaw, Mackintosh and others), from the corresponding pioneering works of the architects of Art Nouveau (Joseph Hoffmann, van de Velde, Behrens, Endell, etc.), and under the

442

282. *Ronchamp Church, France* (LE CORBUSIER)

influence of French and American engineer-designed buildings, there developed a uniform, lasting architectural style which has spread all over the civilised world. This style is marked by the absence of ornament and ostentatious façades in the earlier manner, and by construction and articulation of both the whole and the individual parts with simple geometric planes and solids rectangles, squares, cubes and prisms.

As a result of the organized use of new materials there was a trend towards buildings with an inner frame of vertical steel supports connected horizontally at the various floor levels and clad with glass walls. The strength of the supports made it possible to mount even the largest building on piles, thus for the first time taking the weight off the bottom storey, a device that completely did away with the heavy, pedestal-like base that had characterized all large formal buildings in the past. This removal of the base, which flouted all existing canons of art, was much criticized. Buildings were compared to balloons floating in the air and only connected with the earth by thin wires. However true this may be, it is not in itself a justification for criticism. Now that the aeroplane has enabled man himself to become airborne, such an impression of weightlessness in buildings, as if the force of gravity had itself been overcome, is surely not only technically justified but even of symbolic significance.

There is no lack of regional and climatic characteristics in modern architecture, nor of highly individual architects with a marked style of their own – Frank Lloyd Wright, Le Corbusier, Gropius, Mies van der Rohe and Oud, to mention but a few. But, as in the Middle Ages, modern architecture can draw on a common reserve of forms, and the teams in modern architects' offices use these in much the same anonymous fashion as the guilds did in earlier times. A sound architectural style is not judged so much by the 'personal note', the originality and subjective contribution of the architect, as by its all-round suitability to the demands of the moment; for architecture, unlike most other forms of art, is meant to be publicly enjoyed. Were architecture to set itself up in opposition to the social organism and all its manifestations, it would deny its own intrinsic nature. A block of flats or a government building, which lends character to the townscape in exactly the same way that a cathedral or royal palace did in the past, is an expression of modern mass-society. And it is among many-storeyed buildings of this type in particular that we find evidence of architecture having resolved in artistic terms most of the doubts and problems that still beset modern society (ill. 281, 282, 280, 279).

Nor would this be the first time that, at a period outwardly characterized by political chaos, insecurity and strife, art, and especially architecture, has spoken out in clear and harmonious language. The triumphs of classical art in Greece during the Persian wars and the art of the Italian Renaissance, when the country was convulsed by bloodshed and social upheavals, are two clear examples. Perhaps in our own day modern architecture, in which the parts have been perfectly blended with the whole, is the most hopeful evidence of man's urge for survival. Architecture has found a true style, it has become functional, which, in the strictest sense of the term, means that it is capable of fulfilling its purpose, whatever the difficulties.

PAINTING

A modern skyscraper can without difficulty house the entire population of a medium-sized village or a small town. People are living in closer proximity than ever before but, strangely enough, they do not feel the need to get to know each other. It is a curious paradox that this lack of contact is one of the characteristics of a mass-society in which the individual, by his own choice, is increasingly left to himself. Everyone is familiar with the feeling of utter loneliness that is commonly experienced in the midst of a crowd or in the busiest part of a large city.

It would be wrong, however, to see this isolation of the individual in a purely negative light. If it is one of the symptoms of our (Western) mass-society to insist more and more on the rights of the individual

443

– if, in fact, there is a growing emphasis on individualism – this also has its positive side. The increasing lack of privacy and standardization in our mode of living has resulted in a counter-movement, the desire to turn inwards and to live only according to one's own dictates, without paying too much attention to its effect on the outside world or the approval of society. This inward trend has found expression also in modern painting and sculpture.

The desire to turn in upon oneself is synonymous with rejection of the outside world. A good many of the changes that have taken place in modern art and that have so alarmed people can be attributed to this fact. If we consider the historical paintings and battle pictures of the last century, if we take a glance at certain national monuments, overloaded to the point of confusion with patriotic emblems, if we study the painting and sculpture of autocratic States, we have enough evidence to prove that many of the commissions given to the artist were not principally of an artistic nature but were intended to serve educational, propaganda and other ends. Gradually a reaction against the growing number of these commissions set in; it became the artist's endeavour to restrict, even to do away with, the secondary purpose of such works and to concentrate only on the intrinsic artistic problems they set. This reaction, which began already with Constable and Courbet, became more marked with the Impressionist painters who chose only the most simple subjects, preferably landscape and still-life. They rejected external, anecdotal elements in order to give the fullest possible expression to the inherent artistic message.

A purely individual approach with purely artistic means required close study of these means and their efficacy: it directed the attention towards form and materials and thus towards the very origins of art itself. Primitive and prehistoric art began to be studied and, soon after the turn of the century, rapidly gained in importance. Simple attempts at painting and sculpture by children were seen in a new light since they showed that much of the value of artistic activity lay in the actual process of creation, whereby the individual was freed from obsessions and repressions while satisfying the urgent need for self-expression. But in spite of such archetypal discoveries there was still a strong desire to explore new ground and to evolve an art that was suited to the changing conditions of modern times.

Out of this need three movements developed almost simultaneously in three different countries: Cubism in France, Futurism in Italy, and Expressionism in Germany.

With Expressionism the act of turning inwards focussed on the person of the artist himself. The artist considered it his task, even his mission, to reveal his own temperament, to state his personal attitude towards the world and to lay bare his apperceptions and his visions. This became an open declaration of war against Impressionism at the end of the 19th century. Impressionism had dedicated itself entirely to outwards appearances, even to the extent of excluding symbolism, that transmutation which was the real object of earlier art and was still to be found in Romanticism. Symbolism, even if as in the case of Caspar David Friedrich it took the form of a naturalistic landscape, transfigured the outer world by means of an inner poetic force. The Impressionists, on the other hand, were not concerned with any poetic or intellectual process but only with seeing and reproducing what they saw. Any inner voices had to be suppressed in order to represent the outside world not as one wished to see it but as it did in fact appear. This at least was the aim. But the act of seeing is in itself a subjective process which varies slightly from person to person. By shifting the emphasis a little, 'the way I *see* it' can easily become 'the way *I* see it'. This shift of stress demonstrates that it is equally possible to slide from Impressionism into Expressionism, and explains why most Expressionists went through an early Impressionist phase. The greater the tension between an artist's inner vision and the world around him, and the stronger his emotional reaction against the thing seen and his desire to transmute it, even to revolt against it, the more easily 'the way I see it' will become 'the way I experience it'. At this point the creative activity will have been given a new purpose which is no longer concerned with recording external *impressions* but with giving *expression* to an inner state of mind.

Paula Modersohn-Becker: Peasant Child

Ernst Ludwig Kirchner: Rising Moon on the Staffelalp

KARL SCHMIDT-ROTTLUFF: Poppy and Larkspur

FRANZ MARC: The Blue Horse

Augfust Macke: The Red Path

EMIL NOLDE: Rough Seas

The reaction against Impressionism manifested itself in two new movements: Symbolism and Expressionism. Symbolism centred mainly round Maurice Denis and the Nabis but it had already been evident in the work of Hodler although in a literary and poetic form rather than as visual art (cf. ill. 311, p. 462).

In Expressionism, the turning inwards is nearly always a protest against the rapid changes brought about by the machine age. During the early stages of our epoch the individual had not yet become reconciled to his changed surroundings and this resulted in a very unsettled state of mind. Van Gogh, who was not in the least interested in the technical achievements of his time, was tormented by the spiritual and material exploitation of man in the service of these achievements. Shattered by increasing materialism, lack of faith and cynicism, he became a missionary preacher in a Belgian mining community before ever he began to paint. Later, as a painter, he limned the tragic conflict of his times which became for him a destructive obsession (ill. p. 439).

Lack of harmony between a person and his surroundings must of necessity result in an awareness of contrast and conflict which has all the makings of tragedy; it is not surprising therefore that almost without exception the lives of Expressionist painters were tragic ones. The feeling of contrariness and frustration finds pictorial expression in an extreme tension of colours and forms. Not only van Gogh and Edvard Munch, the oldest members of the movement, but all Expressionist painters are more acutely aware of the tragedy of life than of its fleeting moments of harmony. Gauguin, who can also be numbered among the founders of the movement which later took root mainly in Germany, cut himself off from his age and civilisation and went to life among the Tahitians in the South Seas, thus hastening his own destruction. Such attempts at escape were common among Expressionist painters, although they were not usually as extreme as in Gauguin's case. Whereas there was a growing movement from the country to the big towns, painters sought out lonely places in remote districts. The members of the group known as the *Brücke,* formed by Expressionist painters in North Germany, settled near the mouth of the Rega, on the islands of the Baltic and in other equally remote spots. Painters of the *Blaue Reiter* group in Munich lived away from the city, in the country or in the mountains; Macke and Paul Klee did some of their best work in Kairouan, Tunis. Franz Marc withdrew not only from civilisation but from mankind, finding an escape in the world of animals which he considered purer and less tainted. He, and those working under his influence, had a nostalgic attachment to an archaic peasant art of a primitive type which had long ceased to exist in his day (ill. pp. 438–440, 446–9, 487).

Together with a desire for escapism went a strong religious tendency. Emil Nolde, after studying at first-hand the primitive cultures in the South Seas, retired to an island in the North Sea to paint biblical subjects. Karl Schmidt-Rottluff made woodcuts of the Passion cycle. Another Expressionist with pronounced religious leanings was Rouault, never entirely at home in his native France (ill. p. 473).

By turning towards religion – as indeed in any pictorial attempt to express an inner vision rather than reproduce external appearances – symbolic elements will necessarily be introduced. Symbolism reflects the underlying significance of a thing as the artist sees it, rather than its actual appearance. In this sense the art of the Expressionists is related in spirit to the Romantic movement at the beginning of the 19th century. There was the same desire to equate the inner with the outer vision, to make subject and object one. And already then there was a growing awareness that this could only be done by making use of the symbolic properties inherent in form, line and colour. Around, the year 1800, Goethe and Runge, in their treaties on colour, were enquiring into the symbolic properties of colours to which Kandinsky (ill. p. 488) and Hoelzel referred more than a hundred years later. In their work, Expressionist painters applied earlier discoveries in a logical and energetic manner. For example, in order to give blue more than a simple descriptive quality the colour had to be exaggerated, that is, intensified beyond its natural appearance in conjunction with a given object. Thus the Expressionist painter would render the

451

subdued English sky in a deep and luminous shade of blue (Kokoschka) that surpassed even that of the tropics, in order to convey the splendour of the heavens in symbolic terms. Similarly, Marc occasionally painted his horses an exaggerated red to make them appear as symbols of a vigorous natural life. If, on the other hand, he was using the same animal symbol to represent the creature in relation to the rest of creation, he would chose blue, the colour of distance, of the sky, of the universe itself. In his 'Tower of Blue Horses' the use of colour as a symbol and vehicle for inner expression is immediately intelligible.

Colours were now no longer applied to the canvas in a series of delicate broken hues, in the manner of the Impressionists, but boldly spread over large areas. This greatly increased the luminous quality of the paint, so that Expressionist pictures are almost reminiscent of the stained glass windows of medieval cathedrals. Just as the areas of colour there are separated by lead surrounds, so painters after Gauguin often enclosed areas of pure colour within a thick black outline. Form, which had become lost under a veil of colour in Impressionist painting, thus became firmly re-established.

Forms, objects and figures, too, became subordinated to, and transformed by, the artist's inner vision. The result was that departure from naturalistic representation of figures and objects which the layman so often rejects as being distorted or inhuman. But Grünewald and El Greco had already discovered that such distortion was the only way in which man could give expression to the unseen powers that afflict and torment him. To arouse compassion and even horror in the spectator was part of the artist's intention. This was nothing unnatural, but simply a logical development of a perfectly natural process. Heightened emotional states, such as great joy or great sorrow are expressed by laughter or tears, and the accompanying expression is so far removed from that of a naturally relaxed face that it can result in distortion, even caricature. The Expressionists' desire to heighten the expressiveness of such emotional states resulted in distortion not only of the face but of the entire body. It even transmitted itself to inanimate objects, because these did not appear for their own sakes but were meant to express part of the underlying creative intention.

Furthermore, the expression could be heightened by the omission of insignificant details, by simplification and restriction to essentials. For this reason the vigorous, unpolished technique of the woodcut was revived and played an important role at this time. Even lithography, as can be seen in the case of Munch, became more like the woodcut in character.

In their use of simplification and strong colours – that is, on the purely formal side – Expressionist painters had some affinity with the French group of artists who called themselves Fauves. But in their attitude of mind the two movements were entirely different. The tragic mood that underlies the work of the German movement is far less pronounced with the Fauves. The work of Matisse, their leader, is frankly decorative. His art, according to his own definition, was intended to bring pleasure into people's homes with its fresh, luminous colours. Criticism of his age, which is so marked a feature of German Expressionism, is absent from his work; he does not set out to stir up deep and violent emotions (ill. pp. 471–4).

In Italy a group of artists who called themselves Futurists emerged as leaders of the new movement in art. These differed from the German Expressionists in that they attempted to remodel art in accordance with the spirit of the new age, an age which the German movement had regarded with distaste, even hostility. The name of the group suggested that these young Italians were not merely concentrating on the present but looking beyond it into the future, which at that time (1909) was regarded optimistically as an era full of promise. Painting was to be given a new and modern dynamism. The movement in a picture was to be increased (by means of colour, line and form) to such a degree that it would be given what we now call 'tempo'. Encouraged by new scientific discoveries, artists dreamed of a fourth pictorial dimension, the dimension of time. Attempts were actually made to indicate the passage of time in relation to movement. With Russolo, for instance, there are hints of the same dancer appearing several times in one picture: there, one is made to feel, she sat, there she stood – one is aware of her movement about the

283. DALI, *Burning giraffe*   284. CHIRICO, *Anxious Muses*   285. ERNST, *Flautist. Woodcut*

room. An example of this simultaneous expression of a sequence of events separated in time which is typical of futurism, is a celebrated picture by Marcel Duchamp showing a figure descending a flight of stairs on which many pairs of feet are shown spreading fan-wise across the entire staircase.

Futurism ended with the outbreak of the First World War. Motion-pictures had by then found a completely new and striking solution for representing the passage of time in visual terms. But the treatment in the same picture of elements separated in time remained a characteristic of Italian painting for some time to come. *Pittura metafisica,* the group that formed around Chirico and Carrà, created works in which a longing for the classical past was combined with the spirit of modern times. Thus, classical statues would appear in startling combinations with parts of modern machinery. Throughout the war period and into the 'twenties these painters produced pictures in which realistically represented objects appeared in relationships that had no parallel in everyday life except perhaps in the realm of dreams. This gave them an unreal, supernatural air which appealed to the subconscious mind and startled the imagination into a heightened state of activity. A similar effect is obtained in the work of the Russian painter Marc Chagall, although it is there combined with a strong mystical and religious element. Chagall was one of the founders of the later Surrealist movement. (Ill. 284, pp. 475, 461)

Surrealism – the word first appeared in 1924 – could have been applied to Brueghel and Bosch, to Blake and Goya, even to Novalis and Hegel. In 20th-century painting, it is mainly associated with Max Ernst and Salvador Dali. It springs directly from *Pittura metafisica* but differs from it in this respect: the entire content and predominant creative principle of a work of art, according to the Surrealist Manifesto issued by André Breton, was now to be governed by the workings of the subconscious mind, 'the omnipotence of dreams and the free association of ideas, without the control of the mind and unhampered by any aesthetic or moral considerations'. The means to be used in art as well as in literature were to be 'automatic'. (Ill. 283, 285, p. 461)

The most significant influence on the future of painting, however, was French Cubism. This movement was not concerned with any reaction to social or political trends; its aims were purely artistic. Its main object was to solve the problem that had confronted painters at all times: how to represent a three-dimensional experience in two-dimensional terms and, going one step further, how to open up space on the flat surface of the canvas by purely artistic means, without recourse to the *trompe l'œil* devices of conventional perspective.

Cézanne had already pointed the way by proving that space and recession could be suggested by means of colour rather than by the illusionism of scientific perspective. But Cézanne had never really broken with the 19th-century tradition of naturalism. It fell to two great artists, Picasso and Braque, working in close association between the years 1909 and 1914, finally to reject this tradition by concentrating on the discovery of a purely pictorial realism. It soon became apparent that this could only be done by making the object itself unrecognisable. In representational painting the problems of suggesting space are comparatively easy to overcome. If the subject is a guitar player and the guitar partly obscures the body of the player, the spectator will be immediately convinced that he is confronted with an illusion of space. If, on the other hand, musician and instrument were to be reduced to a mere unintelligible arabesque, would he still be able to say whether the two forms were meant to appear one in front of the other or side by side? The Cubists destroyed the object as we know it in order to make certain that the spatial element, if it was to exist at all, was created not by external means and reasoning, but purely as the result of seeing, of recognising a certain relationship between forms and colours. And the experiment was successful. Cubist painting, although during its 'hermetic' stage it excluded the object altogether, created an infinite range of spatial illusions. To begin with, this was done by means of small cubes, later with simple superimposed flat areas. Thus a whole new field of opportunities was opened to painting. (Ill. 287, 305, pp. 503, 504, 486)

Reality as it appears to the eye had been discarded. But was this such a bad thing when, as the Cubists quite rightly said, reality is in any case different from what the eye perceives? Science has proved this to us. Nature herself has not altered, but we would see things very differently if we were to be given X-ray eyes or even the facetted eyes of insects; the earth appears entirely changed when seen from an aeroplane 30,000 feet above the ground; the microscope has opened up a new world of forms to the eye. Why not paint a table seen from above and from the side in one and the same picture, as the Egyptians did? Surely the result would be nearer the truth than a table drawn in perspective, where the further edge appears shorter without in fact being so. Why not paint a face so that front view and profile become visible at the same time? Everyone knows that it takes both views to give a proper idea of the appearance of a person – as criminal records show. Once we discard our prejudices and conventional habits of seeing, we will discover how much greater is the vitality and dynamic quality of such a painting. As for beauty, there is no reason why a fine profile in combination with a lively pair of eyes should not be beautiful, once we have got into the habit of seeing them together.

From the very beginning, Cubism concentrated almost entirely on the discovery of new pictorial means and possibilities, and in this it paved the way for artists and art students right up to the present day. Cubism also established the fact that abstract painting was feasible, although to arrive at this was never one of its aims. What we can say now is that, in spite of the disintegration of objects, Cubist painting shows such a variety of forms, such exciting use of space, such careful distribution of colours, such a balance of harmonies and discords – in short, such a wealth of visual experience – that it will always hold its own against an earlier landscape or still-life painting. Cubist painting does not 'go against nature'. Cristallography, for example, has revealed similar shapes and under the microscope combinations appear that resemble products of the artist's creative imagination when it works, not in imitation of nature, but like nature herself. That the object has not always been of primary importance has been demonstrated by still-life painters from Chardin onwards. Often their interest lay not so much in recording for posterity a few apples, a bunch of asparagus, a drinking glass or a pipe, but in using these objects to suggest a pleasing arrangement of shapes and colours. The works of Rembrandt already show large areas of so-called abstract painting. One has only to look in isolation at the garments of the child in his 'Family Portrait' (ill. p. 25), to find a piece of pure painting, infinitely varied in the application of paint and the distribution of the brush strokes, but not concerned with the naturalistic representation of the material as

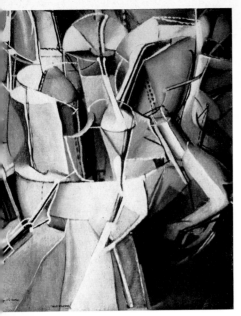

286. MARCEL DUCHAMP, *Le passage de la vierge à la mariée*

287. PICASSO, *Woman in a blue blouse*

288. DAVIS, *Owh! In San Pao*

such. In Impressionist painting, too, there is the strong suggestion of a gradual transition from representational to abstract painting. Seen from a certain distance, the Impressionist picture will give the illusion of a naturalistic world. From close to, however, recognisable forms disappear and we are left instead with bold brush strokes, seemingly arbitrary dots of colour, in fact pure and 'absolute' painting. But to the sensitive eye this is in itself pleasing and interesting.

A large group of abstract painting derives from these sources, although, as we shall see, abstract art has yet another, equally important origin. Kandinsky's early abstract 'improvisations' are in the Impressionist manner, rich in colour but not concerned with clearly defined forms. Such painting has lost nothing of its appeal to-day. In fact there is a movement in our very midst, Tachism, which has similar, purely painterly aims. In this kind of art the effect is based on the assumption that colours can in themselves produce certain emotional effects and experiences without reference to an object. The rise of this kind of painting had already been foretold by Adalbert Stifter, who related how deeply he was moved by the 'symphony of colours' in the sky during an eclipse of the sun. (Ill. 288, 325, pp. 488, 512)

But, as we have said, there is another kind of abstract art, of different origin. This art does not spring from an emotional source but from a highly disciplined intellectual approach in which the eye is still in rigid control. Cubist painters single-mindedly explored the laws of pictorial composition. They were not interested in representation or symbol but solely in creating a picture. There is little evidence that they had any positive attitude towards, any interest in, or aversion to, the new era with its scientific, technical and engineering discoveries.

After the end of the First World War, however, artists emerged – in Russia and Holland – who were greatly in sympathy with the new age. These had some affinity with a certain phase in the development of Cubism. They, too, set out to investigate the basic principles of pictorial composition. But they did not use the Cubist device of analysing form – breaking down objects. Proceeding with the thoroughness of engineers – hence the name Constructivism which was applied to the movement – they posed the question: what are the minimum requirements needed to fill a picture surface meaningfully? This is a matter of artistic economy, of reducing pictorial means to a minimum. Its logical consequence was a painting by the Russian artist Malevich showing a black rectangle, perfectly proportioned and balanced, on a white ground. The public, who thought the painting a hoax, was not slow to attack him, failing to understand that what Malevich had done was merely to formulate the starting-point for a new kind of artistic conception and representation in keeping with the spirit of modern times. A similar new

455

beginning had been made thousands of years before when the round huts that had suited certain geological conditions were first replaced by those of rectangular ground plan — an innovation to which all subsequent 'architecture' was indebted. Then, man had imposed an intellectual constructive concept on nature's own laws of growth and construction. And this is precisely what the Constructivists did (see pp. 488, 505).

Naturally, Malevich's rectangle was no more than a symbol, a point of departure. Mondrian, who designed his paintings with the same drawing-board accuracy, working in vertical and horizontal lines and filling-in the resulting rectangles in pale tones with a few primary colours, already achieved much fuller effects: a dynamic equilibrium of lines and rectangles supported by the careful distribution of a few bright colours (ill. p. 505). There is a strong link between paintings of this type and modern architecture with its articulation of carefully proportioned and balanced rectangles. Furthermore, Constructivists were aiming to create pictures in the same spirit of sober clarity that contemporary architects were trying to achieve. On the other hand, we cannot fail to see the effect these artists had on the face of the world around us to-day, from advertising posters to typography, from interior decoration to architecture. Later, this branch of abstract art became more dynamic, accepting diagonal lines and irregular and organic forms. But the underlying principle of excluding any kind of pictorial sign language remained. Coloured areas are carefully filled in. The artist endeavours to remain objective, aloof, in control, to move only in a world of pure form.

This did not necessarily mean using only geometric or abstract forms. Fernand Léger, in the early 'twenties, began this way, and he has often returned to his original practice. But he also found room in his paintings for man and the world around him, representing not the individual but rather a prototype of the whole modern race. This shows that Léger wanted – as do his followers – to give their art the character and impress of their own time and society, the mass-society in whose midst this art was created and for whom it is intended. Once it had become clear that the mechanical age was not the enemy of art, hostilities could cease. The fact that the painters in this group have worked mainly in conjunction with modern architecture, where they are most likely to meet the demands and approval of a wide public, shows that one branch of painting at least has successfully overcome the problems of segregation from the main stream of development. (Ill. p. 504)

THE GRAPHIC ARTS

It is not surprising that the trends that can be observed in modern painting are also evident in the graphic arts since in many cases the same artists have engaged in both. With the introduction of photo-mechanical processes for the purpose of reproducing original works in facsimile, the distinction between the artist who drew the design and the craftsman who hand-engraved it on wood or metal ceased to exist. The artist appropriated both functions, and engraving, woodcut, lithography and other graphic processes came to be used as means of artistic expression only, though modern graphic artists often rely on a first-class copperplate printer, such as Roger Lacourière in Paris, to whose workshop nearly every artist of any standing has found his way during the past twenty-five years.

The great revival of interest in engraving which is so conspicuous to-day owes its inspiration to two principal sources. First to the example of Gauguin and Munch, who were the pioneers in regarding the woodcut not as a means of translation or interpretation, as it had been in the past, but as a direct medium, the tool itself fashioning the design in the cutting; with them the woodcut had become an autonomous art. Their work heralded the remarkable achievements in this medium of the German Expressionists Kirchner, Heckel, Schmidt-Rottluff, Pechstein and Nolde. (Cf. ill. 289)

The second important influence on modern graphic design was the work of Ambroise Vollard, one of the most famous art dealers of recent times, who published his first book, Verlaine's *Parallèlement* with

lithographs by Pierre Bonnard in 1900. Vollard published twenty-seven books during his lifetime, and among those in preparation at his death was the magnificent *Georgiques* of Virgil with etchings by Segonzac. These books have been the main inspiration of the many artists who are now experimenting with new techniques. Among artists who worked for Vollard, using new techniques, Picasso and Derain achieved outstanding results. Picasso employed the sugar process aquatint for his fine series of thirty-one illustrations to the *Histoire Naturelle* by Buffon, a medium to which he was introduced by Lacourière. The process is the reverse procedure to normal aquatint in that the artist can work with black on white instead of white on black. Again, the colour woodcuts of Derain illustrating *Pantagruel* represent an entirely new use of the medium in Europe. Each illustration is printed from one block coloured by hand. The design is cut in white line and the background cleared, then the colours are applied separately to each portion with a brush.

It is from experiments such as these that the exciting modern use of mixed techniques has developed. Stanley Hayter, for example, who has had a profound influence on the younger contemporary graphic artists, works on metal plates which have been in part etched with hard or soft grounds, in part engraved, in part scooped out to yield prints which may be linear, tonal and shallowly embossed at the same time. Not only have old techniques like aquatint and mezzotint found renewed popularity and uses, but new processes like silk-screen printing are constantly being used to widen the artist's scope. The colour linocut has been brilliantly exploited by Michael Rothenstein and Edward Bawden. That reproduction has now been superseded as the final aim is demonstrated by the process of printing from glass (monotype), which yields only a single print.

It can be said that graphic reproduction in colour has become a favourite branch of modern art. Economy and control in the use and distribution of colour, which is one of the principal concerns of the modern painter, becomes for the graphic artist a necessity imposed by his processes. Artistic intention and practical result have therefore combined harmoniously in this field. This may in part account for its popularity and acceptance by the public. Well-known business concerns have commissioned large coloured lithographs from established artists which, being worked on directly by the artist concerned, bring original works to the man in the street in a very real way. In addition to this, methods of reproduction are relatively cheap so that original prints are available to a fairly wide public. The gulf between the modern artist and his public, which one hears so much about, can therefore be considered to-day as having been at least partially bridged by the graphic arts.

SCULPTURE

One can talk about the 'style' of a period where there is community of purpose linking the various arts, however different their individual problems. Considered in this light, there is a strong affinity between the sculpture of our time and modern painting and architecture.

Like the painters of the period, sculptors around the year 1900 had reached a stage of decadence from which they were attempting to break free in order to make a fresh start. The superb bronze sculptures of Auguste Rodin, with their roughly modelled surfaces, appealed to the eye rather than to that pure tactile sense which should form the basis of all plastic art. There is a constant play of light on his complex surfaces, breaking up the plastic unity of his forms for a more painterly effect which has been compared with contemporary Impressionism. This is an indication of the decadent state of

290. BARLACH, The Avenger

291. BOCCIONI, *Motion in space. Bronze*

such sculpture, since it is a fact that the more interpenetration there is between the different categories of art the greater the danger of exhausting and finally dissolving the individual character of each. It was as a reaction against this that Aristide Maillol, after the turn of the century, decided to resist current trends and seek fresh inspiration from the spirit of classical Greek sculpture (ill. 315). Succeeding sculptors went back even further, finding a new source of energy in the monumental sculpture of ancient times. Ancient Egyptian, archaic Greek and old Mexican sculpture was 'rediscovered' (though never directly imitated), as well as Negro wood-carving with its strong 'expressionist' features.

Already before the First World War there was an Expressionist movement in sculpture (Lehmbruck, Barlach) as well as a Futurist (Boccioni) and a Cubist (early Henri Laurens) one. The general trend of the times – to extract the fullest possible use from one's materials, to explore their special creative possibilities, and not to use them out of character – became particularly evident in 20th-century sculpture. Artists began to study the structure of rocks in their natural setting, to pay closer attention to the direction and appearance of the grain in wood, using them for special decorative effects. As in architecture, new materials were tried out. Malleable wire produced wire sculpture. Metal sculpture was wrought and welded (Gonzalez) rather than cast or embossed. Even synthetic materials like plastic were used in the service of a new sculptural idiom (Pevsner, Gabo). Ill. 314, 290–96, 306, 326

Paul Klee's resolution, to make his painting go right back to its origins ('*ganz Ursprung sein*') and begin anew through its own efforts, can equally well be applied to sculpture. This meant discovering the fundamental laws of plastic creation and applying them in similarly basic ways. The starting-point which Malevich and Mondrian had already formulated for painting had to be discovered for sculpture also. In prehistoric times this had been done by erecting some natural stone as a menhir or by giving symmetrical shape, and so a suggestion of tension, to a fragment of fire-stone. An example of a similar kind of process appears in Duchamp, who would take some bizarre prefabricated modern object, like a bottle-rack, mount it on a base and exhibit it under the title of 'Ready-Made'. Once it was dissociated from its functional purpose the object had to be judged entirely on the grounds of pure form and plastic effect, rather like the menhir, which was in a sense one of nature's 'ready-mades' transplanted by the human hand. The sculptor Brancusi presented an astonished and indignant public with an egg, carefully worked in marble and mounted on a base, which he called 'The Beginning of the World'. What he meant, of course, was the beginning of the world of plastic forms, and in this he was not claiming too much. The egg as a shape not

292. ARCHIPENKO, *Female torso. Bronze* – 293. LAURENS, *Sisters. Bronze* – 294. BRANCUSI, *Adam and Eve. Wood* – 295. BUTLER, *A Woman. Flexible iron*

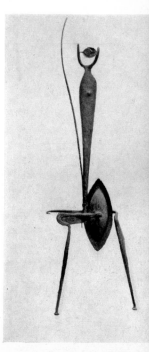

HENRI ROUSSEAU: War

JAMES ENSOR: Strange Masks

Marc Chagall: The Artist and his Model

PIERRE BONNARD: At the Window

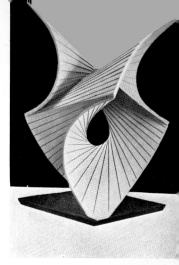

only satisfies our plastic sensibility but, tapering to a point at one end, as it does, comes much closer to symbolizing a sculptural beginning than the sphere with its complete lack of formal dynamic tension. This quality of tension is essential to any work of art, however primitive.

But neither Brancusi (ill. 294) himself nor sculptural development in general remained satisfied with such primitive forms. What they had done was to establish an important rule for the future. The measure of the true artist was to be his ability to concentrate on the essential, most direct means of expression, avoiding any unnecessary elaboration. If he was working from a natural subject, he was to concentrate on its basic structure and emphasise it boldly, as Cézanne had already urged the painter to do. The result would be a new monumental quality, which has indeed become one of the characteristics of modern sculpture. Furthermore, he was to work in accordance with the true requirements of his art. Therefore, in sculpture, which is a plastic, three-dimensional, art, it was important to preserve the essential tactile qualities and to present volumes in terms of space. As a result, modern sculpture is primarily interested in free-standing objects and sculpture in the round, while sculptural relief, so popular in earlier times, has declined somewhat in importance.

It is not surprising, then, that as a result of all this, sculpture too felt the need to dissociate itself from the object, to become abstract. In our introductory remarks on sculpture (see p. 15 f.) we have already shown that there are certain reasons for rendering nature and the human figure in abstract terms that apply to this art but not to painting. These rest on the assumption that a deliberate change made in the familiar appearance of a figure, such as the introduction of some element of deformity, will stimulate and increase our desire to move round it. It will arouse our awareness of its complexity and at the same time of its vitality – that ability to release energy in many different directions. (Ill. 297–299, 303, 310)

There is, however, another highly significant aspect of modern sculpture. This deserves special mention because it is peculiar to the art of sculpture and goes beyond anything that has yet been achieved in its history. It is the inclusion of space in the rendering of plastic form as a new source of creative energy.

There is no doubt that space can stake its claim in the realm of sculpture, the art of tactile sensations. Interior space and hollows both rely on the tactile sense, the sense used by the blind man to 'feel' the extent of a room by its limits. The hole through a stone, the cave in a hillside, emphasise the sense of the mass of which they form part by sheer contrast. 'A hole can in itself have as much shape – meaning – as a solid mass. The mystery of the hole – the mysterious fascination of caves in hillsides and cliffs' (Henry Moore). As an element in sculpture, space heightens the three-dimensional effect. (Ill. 15–17, 300, 302, 303, 310, 314)

Not in all epochs was this device used. Egyptian and Greek sculpture relied entirely on mass. It is true that medieval Gothic art was already aware of the creative possibilities of space, making extensive use of it in its sculptures and reliefs (Naumburg rood-screen ill. 23), but it never became an integral part of sculpture until modern times. Much of the startling appearance and unusual treatment of modern sculpture is accounted for by this inclusion of space.

Lehmbruck's figure 'The Fallen' (ill. 314) relies for its effect not only on the modelling of the body resting on its arms and knees, but also on the nature of the spaces between

296. PEVSNER, *Plane surface, a tangent emerges from the left curve* – 297. ARP, *Human – moon – ghost. Concrete* – 298. CHADWICK, *Moon from Alabama. Iron* – 299. KARL HARTUNG, *Plastic. Bronze*

300. ZADKINE, 'The city without a heart' (Rotterdam memorial). Bronze – 301. MARINI, Rider with outstretched arms. Wood – 302. CALDER, Lobster net and fish tails. Mobile of steel and aluminium

the limbs. The holes and cavities in Henry Moore's wood and stone sculptures (ill. 15–17) often contain another sculptured shape, exploring at the same time the relationship between kernel and shell. Many sculptors, including Moore, are interested in the group – father, mother and child, man and wife, a pair of runners (Gerhard Marcks) – which is again connected with the problem of space. The unity of a group emphasises the significance of the spaces between the individual figures: the spectator, though without conscious effort, is bound to become aware of them and to realize that they are not there by accident but form part of the design. (Cf. ill. 301)

Interest in the relationship between mass and space has given rise to a special new branch of modern sculpture: wire compositions. These, in a sense, rely on the combination of lines of tension confining and encompassing space, so that the figure itself becomes an element of space rather than of mass. But in an age where science is trying to prove that mass and energy are not, after all, two diametrically opposed forces – is even attempting to convert one into the other – this seems not only justified but natural.

The airy constructions of Alexander Calder, which quiver in the faintest breath of air, are a particularly characteristic and impressive manifestation of this. Mass and space have become a constantly interchanging concept, an element has been endowed with motion and, in Calder's own words, 'stands in a dynamic relationship to the other elements composing its world.' (Ill. 302)

Modern sculpture thus ranges from rough-hewn monumentalism to the most delicate and ethereal fabrications. If we consider painting with all its variety of method and idiom and see both arts against the background of, or encompassed by, modern architecture, we can only conclude that modern art is too complex to be summed up in a few sentences. There has seldom been so much freedom to experiment, so much courage to explore new ground as in our own epoch, and these qualities distinguish not only modern science but art as well. It is true that art is still beset by problems, still lacks the support of general understanding and agreement. But those who are bewildered by the diversity of its forms, by its pursuit of unknown, seemingly indefinite ends, must remember that this apparent confusion may be a sign of inner wealth. History has taught us that true culture is not marked so much by material possessions and power, by peace and calm, as by the complexity of its problems. That the art of to-day, in its transition from past to future, should show something of this same complexity is surely a tribute to its cultural significance.

464

AALTO, ALVAR (born 1898). A master designer of extremely functional (and extremely imaginative) buildings, Aalto, who is the foremost of modern Finnish architects, is responsible for many modern houses, factories, and public buildings in his native country and in Europe, the most notable of which are the library at Viipuri and an apartment house in Berlin. He first achieved fame as the designer of wooden buildings, but gradually he began combining wood with brick and with glass, copper and cement, thereby achieving a result which seems to spring naturally from the Finnish culture and which is superbly functional. He has also been a pioneer in evolving functional plywood furniture.

ABSTRACT ART. The name, perhaps not altogether apt, given to the type of art that has more or less turned away from the representation of nature. Since 1910 there have been paintings and sculptures which do not evoke reality as it appears in nature but aim at creating a visual experience by means of form, line or colour only. The term 'abstract art' is misleading because every work of art is in a sense an abstract of nature, i. e. it reproduces only one essential aspect of it, whereas in abstract art nature has no place at all. For this reason there have been attempts to substitute other designations, such as non-figurative, non-representational or non-naturalistic art. Abstract works of art may take reality as a starting point and transform it into abstraction or they may begin by using a non-representational (e. g. geometric) subject. Both approaches have been known in art since its earliest beginnings – in the field of ornament. But modern abstract art is distinguished from purely decorative art by superior intellectual aims, which are not satisfied with mere decoration. (For origins and types of abstract art see also pp. 454–6.)

ABSTRACT-EXPRESSIONISM is the term applied to one of the newest schools of art whose influence has become world-wide. Its American proponents, who descend from Kandinsky (and whose work is diametrically opposed to the precision and balance of Mondrian), include Jackson Pollock, Willem De Kooning, Marc Tobey, and numerous other contemporary painters, many of them living in New York City. Their style, which is a combination of the non-objectivity of abstractionism and of the personal viewpoint of expressionism – both of these being fused by this school to arrive at a new vision – is characterized by a vivid explosion of seemingly disjointed, unrelated, and often non-representational forms which are intended to convey emotion or symbolic meaning to the spectator.

ALBRIGHT, IVAN LE LORRAINE (born 1897). One of the most unusual of modern American painters, Albright, who was born in Chicago and still lives there, is famous for his canvases of bloated, horribly-veined human beings and of macabre still-lifes, all of these being executed with infinite patience and detail. Two characteristic paintings are: 'Into the World There Came a Soul Called Ida' (in which a bulbous and rotted old woman looks at her reflection in a mirror) and 'That Which I Should Have Done I Did Not Do' (the entire canvas being filled by a funeral wreath hanging on a grotesque doorway).

ARCHIPENKO, ALEXANDER. Sculptor. Born in Russia in 1887, he left Moscow and Kiev as early as 1908 to settle in Paris. He was the first to apply abstraction to sculpture. His favourite subject was the female figure which he simplified drastically, exaggerating its proportions until it was barely representational. After a period in Berlin (1920–1923) he settled in the United States where he is still active to-day. (Ill. 292)

ARP, JEAN. Alsatian. Born in 1887, Arp is one of the most versatile and interesting personalities in the world of art to-day. He is known as a painter, graphic artist, sculptor and poet (in French and German). In 1916 he was the moving force behind Dadaism (q. v.) which he logically carried over into Surrealism (q. v.). His art found its true expression in an abstract formal language employing elementary symbols reminiscent of primitive hieroglyphs. He produced woodcuts, collages (some together with his wife Sophie Täuber who died in 1943) and, above all, abstract sculptures. Notable among these is a bronze sculpture with the poetic title 'The Shepherd of the Clouds'. Both his origin and his work make Arp the most significant intermediary between contemporary German and French art. (Ill. 297)

ART NOUVEAU. A movement that originated in 1895 to counter the derivative conventions of 19th-century art. In Germany it derived its name *Jugendstil* from the magazine *Die Jugend* which proclaimed its ideas, but it became known in most other countries as Art Nouveau. It had its real origins in England under the lead of William Morris and others; in Germany its leaders were Otto Eckmann, August Endell, Hermann Obrist and Bruno Paul. Concerned at first with the use of new stylistic motifs based on abstract and plant ornaments (Beardsley), after 1905 the adherents of the movement brought a new objectivity to architecture (Voysey, Mackintosh) and design, thus becoming pioneers of the modern idiom. Though Art Nouveau fell into disrepute with the advent of mass-produced goods mainly as a result of commercial exploitation of many of the designs, there has of late been a revival of interest in the work of these artists who are now considered not only to have influenced the design of architecture and furniture but also to have brought certain ideas of importance to modern painting and sculpture. (Ill. 72, 264, 265)

BALLA, GIACOMO (born 1871). Italian painter and one of the founders of Futurism (q. v.) whose importance has only recently been recognised once again. His realization of the aims of this movement, to represent successive stages of action, was perhaps the most logical and artistic ('Centrifugal Force'), especially as shown in pictures painted between 1913 and 1916.

BARLACH, ERNST (1870–1938). Born in Holstein, Barlach was trained as a sculptor in Dresden and Paris. His early adherence to the *Jugendstil* (see Art Nouveau) ended in 1906 after a journey to Russia. From that time on his work became marked by a powerful expressionist monumentality manifested outwardly by emphasis on the act of production itself (the mark of the axe and the knife in wooden sculpture). Barlach derived his creative power from his deeply religious nature and his compassion for the sufferings and joys of mankind. He was also a pioneer in the field of the woodcut and lithography, as well as a poet whose expressionist plays *(Der tote Tag)* are as powerful in their effect to-day as when they were first written. In 1933 his art was branded as 'degenerate' in Germany because of the eastern features of his statues and his works were removed from museums and public places. (Ill. 290)

BAUHAUS. Founded by the architect Walter Gropius in 1919 in place of the Weimar School of Art. To-day its principles, which were to revolutionize the teaching of art, are universally recognised. Among the most important of these was the attempt to bridge the gap between pure and applied art, to place equal emphasis on all branches of the arts and crafts, and to strive for lucid, direct and functional forms (cf. p. 442). The fame of the Bauhaus owes much to the quality of the teaching staff which Gropius was able to attract. This included names like Feininger, Klee, Kandinsky, Schlemmer, Marcks, Moholy-Nagy and Mies van der Rohe. In 1925 the Bauhaus moved to new premises in Dessau designed by Walter Gropius, and this also marked the beginning of a new phase in its development. Certain romantic ideas associated with a revival of the medieval building confraternities, which still formed part of the Weimar programme, were dropped in favour of a completely modern attitude with strong leanings in the direction of industrial design. In 1933 Hitler closed the Bauhaus. But the ideas it had fostered have since spread across the world, and books published under its imprint after 1925 have helped to teach a younger generation of artists. (Ill. 280)

BAUMEISTER, WILLY (1889–1955). Born in Stuttgart, Baumeister was a pupil of Adolf Hoelzel whose interest in the science of colours was to provide him with an early grounding in the formal and theoretical aspects of painting. This proved of great value to his own work which tended more towards Constructivism (q. v.) and the painting of Fernand Léger than in the direction of Expressionism, prevalent in Germany at the time of the First World War. In his murals he successfully attempted a combination of relief and painting; later he specialized in completely abstract paintings with highly subtle colour gradations. During the period of the New Objectivity (q. v.) he produced portraits of sportsmen and other contemporary figures. In addition, he was strongly attracted to prehistoric art, using in his 'Eidos' paintings, a simple pictorial sign language (ideogram). He published his theories

on the creative activity in a book called *Das Unbekannte in der Kunst.*

BECHTEJEFF, VLADIMIR (born 1878). Russian painter. Together with Kandinsky, Jawlensky and Marianne von Werefkin, he founded the New Artists' Federation in Munich, some of whose members later formed the *Blaue Reiter* (q. v.) group.

BECKMANN, MAX (1884–1950). Of old North German peasant stock, he served as a member of the medical corps during the First World War where his art underwent a decisive change. From a descriptive Impressionist painter he turned into one of the leading German Expressionists. Between 1915 and 1933, when he was a teacher at the Städel School of Art in Frankfurt, he built up a pictorial world which reflected the tragedy of the times. The subjects of his etchings and paintings were taken from everyday life: the big city, circuses and fairs, coarse and vigorous themes which he used as symbols to hint at contemporary dangers. Although his later still-lifes are in a lighter key, his mood of gloom returned round about the period when he was branded as 'degenerate' (he lost his teaching post in 1933) and deepened during the time of the Second World War. In 1937 he left Germany with great reluctance to settle in Amsterdam, and ten years later moved to the USA. His many self-portraits tell us something about the course of his life and also reveal his uncompromising and militant spirit (ill. p. 498). As an artist his prolific output and vitality of expression triumphed over a hazardous existence and intense inner conflict. He completed 'The Argonauts', the last of seven great triptychs in which he freely interprets mythological themes or draws symbolical comparisons between real life and the stage ('Perseus', 'The Actors', 'Blind Man's Buff'), on the day of his death. This occurred while he was still at the height of his powers and at a point where age was beginning to temper his restless spirit.

BEHRENS, PETER (1868–1940). One of the founders and leaders of the German *Jugendstil* (see Art Nouveau) before it changed its course to become the New Objectivity (q. v.). Born in Hamburg, he was originally a painter but later excelled in every branch of applied art including carpet design and typography. He finally found his vocation as an architect. As the designer of the AEG buildings (1909) and the teacher of Le Corbusier and Walter Gropius, he must be considered one of the pioneers of modern architecture.

BELLOWS, GEORGE (1882–1924). An outstanding athlete all through his school years in Ohio, Bellows became one of the country's foremost painters of sports scenes and one of the prime figures in the so-called Ashcan school. Even Robert Henri, under whom Bellows first studied in New York, was amazed at the sense of animal action and perfect timing that Bellows brought to his painting – qualities which are perfectly exemplified in his first popular success, 'Stag at Sharkey's', where the action of two prize-fighters is arrested as in a speed photograph and where the lines and sweep of muscles are exaggerated to create a fury of movement. As Bellows grew older, his work deepened in insight. He lessened his contrasts, lightened his palette, and united people and landscapes in a serene and Impressionistic light.

BENTON, THOMAS HART. American painter, born 1889 in the state of Missouri. After studying at the Art Institute of Chicago he went to Paris in 1908, returning to the USA shortly before the First World War. In Paris he had been inspired by Cubism (q. v.) and this was reflected in his pictures and large murals in which he represented modern life, especially its technical aspects, with Cubist formality. During the 'thirties his attitude to painting completely changed. He renounced city life and returned to the Middle West where, no longer interested in modern developments in art, he painted rural scenes in a realistic, often slightly romanticized manner. He occupies a leading place among American regionalist landscape painters.

BERLAGE, HENDRIK (1856–1934). The first Dutch architect to break away from the derivative historical conventions of the 19th century. His Stock Exchange building in Amsterdam is one of the earliest and most important examples of a new trend in architecture which no longer relies on the imitation of traditional stylistic elements. Only the mouldings and decorations hark back to Romanesque and early North European motifs, although these are freely reinterpreted. Pure construction was as yet outside Berlage's reach.

BILL, MAX. Born at Winterthur, Switzerland in 1908, he has made his name in architecture, painting and, above all, sculpture. Sculpturally, he is most concerned with expressing abstract mathematical concepts in concrete terms. ('Mathematical thought in our time is not mathematics itself. It is the creation of rhythms and relationships, of laws which have a personal origin.') Well-known works in this field include his giant 'Continuity' (Zurich 1947), conceived as a smooth, continuous sheet curled and folded to envelop space. He built the Hochschule für Gestaltung at Ulm (1953–54) and was appointed its director. (Ill. 303)

BISSIÈRE, ROGER (born 1888). A French painter who, after achieving fame in the 'twenties, was comparatively unknown until in recent years a number of strange wall paintings, sometimes of a religious character, brought him into the public eye once more. He was awarded the Prix National for art in 1952. To-day as in the past, his pictures are distinguished by their sensitive colour effects, now achieved with the help of patches of material and coloured threads of wool in the manner of papiers collés.

BLAUE REITER, DER. Originally the title of a picture by Kandinsky, it became the name of an annual edited by Kandinsky and Franz Marc for the New Artists' Federation in Munich. This publication, containing essays by its members and reproductions of their work as well as contributions on such subjects as Negro masks, alpine peasant art, children's drawings and musical quotations showing the beginnings of the twelve-tone system, was of the greatest significance to the modern movement in art. Under the presidency of Kandinsky the association had already held a number of important avant-garde exhibitions including works by Picasso, Braque and the Paris Fauves (q. v.) when, in 1911, the president and a number of his friends decided to resign. They founded another, smaller group called *Der Blaue Reiter* (The Blue Rider) and which, besides Kandinsky, included Klee, Kubin, Macke, Marc and Gabriele Münter. Next to the *Brücke* (q. v.) it became the most significant movement formed during the period of German Expressionism (q. v.). Its aim was the combination of pure form with pure colour in art. The circle gradually came to include friends of members, such as Campendonk and Feininger, both painters, and the musician Arnold Schönberg. Exhibitions also presented the work of foreign artists (Henri Rousseau, Robert Delaunay and Jacob Epstein). The First World War put a stop to the activities of the group but later many of its members were reunited at the Bauhaus (q. v.) in Weimar where the work of the *Blaue Reiter* formed the basis for a new teaching programme. (Cf. ill. pp. 448, 449, 486–488)

BOCCIONI, UMBERTO (1882–1916). Painter and sculptor, and one of the leading exponents of Italian Futurism (q. v.). Both in his paintings (e. g. 'Elasticity', 1912) and his sculptures (e. g. 'Energy') he aimed at combining the movement inherent in such subjects as a rider or a man walking, with one of pure form. This he achieved by representing successive stages of action in a single image. (Ill. 291)

BOMBOIS, CAMILLE (born 1883). One of the French primitives, or 'Sunday painters', who had been cowherd, bullfighter, nightwatchman and railway ganger before he was discovered by Noël Bureau and Wilhelm Uhde. In his captivating and delightfully naïve style he has recorded each of these occupations since the age of sixteen. To-day he is working as an artist in Paris.

BONNARD, PIERRE (1867–1947). Although he has sometimes been called a Late Impressionist because of

303. BILL, *Rhythm in space. Plaster*

his preoccupation with light, the artistic origins of this great French painter must be sought elsewhere. Around 1890 he identified himself with the symbolist aims of the Nabis (q. v.), becoming associated particularly with the Intimist branch of the movement. His earliest work, which covered a variety of fields including poster design and crafts as well as his painting, showed leanings towards Art Nouveau. But once he had discovered his true style as a painter, as early as before the First World War, he kept to it until the end of his life. Certain subjects, such as landscapes, gardens with flowers, sailing boats, and in particular the female nude in various interior or exterior settings or in front of a mirror, are found again and again. They are not, however, treated in the Impressionist manner by being painted from nature but are composed 'from memory'. His pictures are the result of a gradual process of growth sometimes extending over several years until the final glorious iridescent harmony of colours was achieved. (Ill. p. 462)

BRANCUSI, CONSTANTIN (1876–1957). Born in Rumania, Brancusi received his first training in the local carpentry school. He won a scholarship to the Art Academy of Bucharest and having gained his diploma, made for Paris where he arrived in 1904. He remained there all his life except for a visit to India in 1937. His early work is academic. A change in his style occurred in about 1907 when he was influenced by Rodin ('La Muse endormie'). Shortly afterwards he felt the impact of African tribal wood sculpture ('The Chimera', 1918). From then on, Brancusi developed a monumental abstract style concerned with the relationships of material and volume, which achieves its clearest expression in the celebrated egg, the 'Sculpture for the Blind'. His earlier work was in wood, then as he became increasingly abstract he turned to other materials, handling them, especially metal, with a machine-like precision and polish. Brancusi's work has had a profound effect on the development of modern sculpture. (Ill. 294)

BRAQUE, GEORGES. Born in 1882, the son of a decorator, he is one of the most impressive personalities in modern art. He was associated with three important trends in modern painting in their early stages and made an important contribution to each: Fauvism (q. v.), to which he subscribed around 1905; the school of Cézanne, which he discovered for himself in 1908, and finally Cubism (q. v.), whose chief exponents he and Picasso became. Braque made some significant contributions to the evolution of Cubism, by introducing certain motifs (such as musical instruments and printed letters of the alphabet to echo reality) and by using new stylistic conventions (the *trompe l'oeil* imitation of materials such as wood and stone, familiar to him from his father's workshop). Even the name Cubism derives from Braque, whose painting was described by a critic in 1908 as being composed of small cubes. In the 'twenties his shallow surface style became more and more individual and still-life paintings

304. Buffet, *Self-portrait, 1952*

predominated. The paintings of this period, superbly composed and using colour in the most deft and subtle way, must be ranked among the great masterpieces of French art (ill. p. 503). Braque's wonderful colour sense, flexible line and pictorial harmony and control also characterize his later work – his coast scenes and recent large studio interiors. These latter mark the culmination of his researches into the interrelationship between form and space and in their free manipulation of objects and shapes reach 'a sort of intellectual non-existence which makes everything possible and right', to quote the artist's own words. 'Life then becomes a perpetual revelation. That is true poetry.' A large bird in flight is used as a recurrent theme in a number of these later paintings.

BRIANCHON, MAURICE (born 1899). Painter of landscapes whose delicate fashioning and intrinsic colour harmonies are sometimes reminiscent of Henri Rousseau. A modern in the best sense of the word, he avoids any ostentatious display of modernism. This moderation probably accounts for his popularity and success as a teacher at the Paris École des Beaux-Arts.

BRÜCKE. The pioneers of the Expressionist movement in painting were three architectural students from Dresden: Heckel, Kirchner and Schmidt-Rottluff. In 1905 all three took up painting and formed an association named *Brücke* (Bridge). As the name suggests, artists of different schools were welcomed. In this way Pechstein, Nolde (for a short time) and Otto Mueller from Berlin became members, while Paris and Finland were represented by Kees van Dongen and Axel Gallén respectively. The former established a link between *Brücke* and the Fauves (q. v.) whose artistic aims were in many ways similar (cf. p. 452). The German artists, however, led in the graphic arts. Under the influence of Gauguin and Munch their work, especially the woodcut, caused this branch of the arts to flourish in Germany; in which connection the name of Kirchner, perhaps the most eminent of the *Brücke* artists, should be mentioned. In 1911 the group moved its headquarters to Berlin. After an early unsuccessful exhibition in 1906 (held in a factory on the outskirts of Dresden) recognition followed in the years to come, culminating in a special hall (*Brücke-Saal*) devoted to them at the Cologne *Sonderbund* Exhibition of 1912. The group dissolved in 1913. A well-deserved tribute was paid to its achievement at the Venice Biennale in 1952. (Ill. pp. 446, 447)

BUFFET, BERNARD (born 1928). This Parisian painter has in recent years achieved an astonishing degree of success with his pictures, in a grey monotone, depicting human misery and anxiety. In 1948 he shared with Lorjou the Grand Prix de la Critique, since when he has been the recipient of numerous important awards. (Ill. 304)

BURCHFIELD, CHARLES (born 1893). An American painter who was born in Ashtabula, Ohio, who studied at the Cleveland Museum School of Art, and who spent a good many years supporting himself as a designer of wallpapers, Burchfield began his career as a romantic portrayer of nature in highly imaginative water colours ('The Night Wind'), then became a realist who was possessed of some satire and whose style was somewhat akin to Edward Hopper's ('Freight Cars Under a Bridge'). In recent years, he has returned to the portrayal of nature. By contrast with the Europeans, however, Burchfield paints all the movement of nature as he experiences it (his wind blows, his rain pelts, his snow swirls), and he has thus evolved a highly personal style of Expressionism.

BUTLER, REGINALD (born 1913). Originally an architect, he is now one of Britain's best-known sculptors. His work as a blacksmith during the war stimulated his interest in iron sculpture in the style of Gonzales. The model for his abstract 'Unknown Political Prisoner', which won first prize in an international competition in London in 1953, is an example of his work in this medium. To-day he is again more interested in modelling and produces expressionistic bronzes, often of the female nude. (Ill. 295)

CALDER, ALEXANDER (born 1898). This American sculptor began his artistic career as an engineer, which accounts for his early preference for metal and wire sculpture. Already in 1928, when he was living in Paris, he exhibited stabiles – riged metal constructions that were later succeeded by mobiles. The latter, delicate fabrics of wire mounted on a base or hung from the ceiling, only achieve their full effect when the wire arms and attached balls or thin flat pieces of metal are set swinging and rotating by a current of air. Mobiles are perhaps the most logical solution of an attempt to represent both time and space in sculpture. (Ill. 302)

CAMARO, ALEXANDER (born 1901). A German painter who represents the natural world as an improvised stage performance in which figures move about like puppets. A former dancer and partner of Mary Wigman he is now teaching at the Academy of Plastic Arts in Berlin.

CAMPENDONK, HEINRICH (1889–1957). A member of the *Blaue Reiter* (q. v.), he taught at the Academy in Düsseldorf and was later made a professor at the Rijksakademie in Amsterdam. As a painter, his style was influenced by Franz Marc and Chagall. He has also gained recognition for his powerful woodcuts which show both his inventiveness as an illustrator and his sensitive understanding of the medium.

CAMPIGLI, MASSIMO, was born in Florence in 1895. His work was related to French Cubism (q. v.) but his pictorial vision and his use of colour, which has a fresco-like quality, recall Etruscan wall paintings. The drawing of his figures has affinities with child art.

CARRÀ, CARLO (born 1881). An Italian painter who escaped from the noisy and agitated world of Futurism (q. v.) by going back to the work of Giotto and the Early Renaissance. He saw a kind of magic effect in perspective as used at that time, provided it was not combined with colour or aerial perspective (as in Impressionism). Treated in this way, objects appear isolated and are at the same time transformed in some strange and charmed way (Metaphysical Painting). The slightly cold and austere impression conveyed by this type of picture he later counteracted by using a meticulous and beautiful style of painting. (Ill. p. 475)

CÉZANNE, PAUL (1839–1906), was born at Aix-en-Provence. His early period is marked by restlessness and agitation: themes partly Romantic, partly Baroque are handled in a wild medley of thick colours. But in his 'Railway Cutting' (Staatsgalerie, Munich), still an early work, he is already groping towards a definite objective: solid construction and the creation of spatial effects by a receding sequence of flat, coloured planes without the use of scientific perspective. Although this was in direct opposition to the aims of the Impressionists who were then just beginning to form into a group, Cézanne, too, had first to pass through an Impressionist phase. His stay in Paris in the 'seventies, when Pissarro, Renoir and Monet became his friends, was marked by lighter colours and greater freedom in the handling of paint. After 1882, however, he secluded himself in the south of France, his home, becoming ever more eccentric and embittered through lack of success. This period of loneliness was the time of artistic fruition. In his landscapes, simple still-lifes, portraits of local people, self-portraits, and finally in his groups of card-players and bathers, all repeated again and again, he strove to 'realize' his vision. His aim was to reduce natural objects to their basic form, to represent volume and modelling by means of colour alone, without the use of shadows or perspective, and to achieve pictorial unity when combining flat and three-dimensional effects in the same painting. In building up his pictures Cézanne realized his aims both in his general construction and in his brushwork (the famous *touche de Cézanne*) the former by the use of receding vertical planes, the latter by the application of small rectangular colour areas. His discoveries, made during his solitary life in Aix and based on a tenacious adherence to the natural appearance of objects, were later developed by the Cubists – who had, however, to relinquish resemblance to nature in the process. Thus Cézanne's work, which combined traditional with revolutionary elements, became the bridge between two different artistic visions. To-day nearly all modern painters are in some way indebted to Cézanne. (Ill. p. 437)

CHADWICK, LYNN (born 1914). After experimenting with mobiles, this British sculptor turned to what he calls 'balanced sculptures', angular carapaces of metal incorporating a partially mobile component or a gob of coloured glass. These were followed by linear constructions in iron which paved the way for his recent solid figures built around 'armatures' of steel. A prize-winner in the 'Unknown Political Prisoner' competition of 1951, he has since frequently exhibited both in England and abroad. In 1956 he was awarded an International Sculpture Prize at the Venice Biennale. His sculptures have been acquired by many public collections in Europe and America. (Ill. 298)

CHAGALL, MARC (born 1887). The son of a poor Russian-Jewish herring merchant in Vitebsk, Chagall has achieved greatness without ever receiving any proper tuition. In his youth he was to some extent influenced by the work of the famous stage designer Bakst, but it was not until a small scholarship enabled him to move to Paris in 1910 that he found his own highly individual expression as a painter. In his dream-like pictures mystic and religious elements mingle with human experience and memories of childhood. Again and again he introduces such basic themes as birth, love and death. By the time he returned to Russia at the beginning of the First World War, he had already held an exhibition that was to have a decisive effect on German Expressionism (q. v.). Later, Surrealism (q. v.), too, claimed Chagall as one of its spiritual founders. Although the Bolshevik régime accepted him in the beginning, Chagall found it expedient to return to Paris in 1922. The war had left its mark on his work, which became harder in form and colder and more glaring in colour. But in his French paintings, notably his flower pictures and enchanting illustrations (Fables of La Fontaine), tenderness and grace returned once more. The Second World War and the persecution of his race brought on a return of melancholy resulting in a number of pictures of the Crucifixion. He sought asylum in America where his painting developed new and mysterious depths. In 1947 he returned to France once again and is now living and working in Vence. (Ill. p. 461)

CHIRICO, GIORGIO DE. Italian painter born in 1888. He had a conventional training in Athens and Munich and it was not until after 1910, when he had returned to Italy, that he began painting strange and mysterious compositions based on the new naturalistic Romanticism of Stuck and Böcklin. In these pictures familiar objects like window dummies, plaster busts, gloves, geometric shapes and bits of machinery are combined in interior settings or against a background of classical architecture in a completely unrealistic fashion. This was the birth of 'Metaphysical Painting' (cf. p. 453), the forerunner of Surrealism (q. v.). After the end of the First World War Chirico concentrated increasingly on the three-dimensional illusion of his painted scene, becoming the leader of a group that called itself *Valori Plastici* (q. v.). Towards the end of the 'twenties he dropped free invention in favour of more conventional painting, often in imitation of historical styles (e. g. Baroque). Ill. 284

COLLAGE. A term now generally accepted to define certain pictures or arrangements made in part or entirely of pasted pieces of paper, newsprint, wallpaper, reproductions, tickets or any other textured material, assembled in a manner totally incongruous when viewed in the light of ordinary visual experience. Sometimes the arrangement is combined with drawn, painted or three-dimensional passages. As a form of sophisticated artistic expression collage first appeared in about 1911 in the cubist works of Braque and Picasso, who introduced actual newspaper cuttings, laundry bills, stamps or bus tickets into their work partly for formal reasons, partly out of impatience with conventional artistic materials. The Dadaists (q. v.) used collage as a vehicle for their cynicism and mockery of contemporary pretensions.

The terms collage and *montage* are sometimes used interchangeably. Montage, however, is more often used of arrangements made entirely of sections of photographs or in connection with the technique of the motion-picture. The techniques of both collage and montage have greatly influenced the applied arts such as typography, illustration, packaging, window display and stage decoration.

CONSTRUCTIVISM. The term applied to visual representation by means of pure geometric forms, as practised after 1913 (cf. pp. 455–6). The trend originated in Russia with the paintings of Malevich, Tatlin and Rodchenko which relied entirely on rectangles, circles and straight lines; in manifestoes issued by these artists it was referred to as Suprematism, Constructivism and non-objective art. Constructivist ideas were taken up by the sculptors Naum Gabo and Antoine Pevsner and later became of special importance in the work of the Bauhaus (q. v.; Moholy-Nagy). At about the same time an independent Constructivist group was being formed in Holland (Stijl group), whose chief exponents were van Doesburg, Vantongerloo and, above all, Piet Mondrian who, in 1920, founded Neo-Plasticism. Jean and Sophie Arp in Zurich have also been connected with the movement, while contemporary representatives include Josef Albers in America, Diaz in Paris and Baertling in Sweden. Apart from its importance as a decorative element in architecture, Constructivism has made an international contribution to modern advertising art. (Ill. pp. 488, 505).

CRAIG, EDWARD GORDON (born in 1872). English stage designer and the first to break away from

HENRI MATISSE: Odalisque

GEORGES ROUAULT: Christ and the Fishermen

CARLO CARRÀ: The Boatman

the elaborate naturalistic conventions used in stage décor. He prepared the way for the 'stylized' stage. Worked in London, Berlin and Moscow where he had many pupils.

CUBISM. The aims of this highly significant modern movement in art have already been discussed at some length on p. 453–5, so that this note will be confined to giving a brief outline of its historical development. Cubism originated with Picasso and Braque who, after 1908, began to build up landscapes and figures with cube-like shapes, a method suggested by the paintings of Cézanne. They were soon joined by Juan Gris, Fernand Léger, Gleizes and Metzinger, and by the sculptors Laurens and Archipenko. In analytical Cubism (1910–1912) the subject, still taken from nature, was broken up into small facets (in place of the original cubes) and superimposed transparent planes *(plans superposés)*. This meant that objects became gradually less and less recognisable, a trend that ended with the complete obscurity of hermetic Cubism. In order not to sever the link with reality, however, Cubist artists introduced real materials like pieces of newsprint or bits of wallpaper into their pictures in the technique of *papiers collés* and collages. In its next, synthetic phase (1913/14) Cubism no longer took reality as a starting point but worked with free forms which did no more than faintly recall the world of natural objects. In other words if, to quote Juan Gris, analytical Cubism 'made a cylinder out of a bottle', synthetic Cubism reversed the process. The superimposed planes grew in size and, compared to the rather colourless pictures of the analytical phase, became brighter and sometimes deeply luminous (crystalline Cubism). The movement as such ended after 1915 but its artistic discoveries lived on in many different forms (cf. e. g. ill. 287, 305, 292, 293; p. 503).

DADAISM. In 1916 three poets, Tristan Tzara, Hugo Ball and Richard Hülsenbeck and the sculptor Jean Arp started a group which met at the 'Cabaret Voltaire' in Zurich. With humour, insolence, slapstick and trenchant irony they tried to ridicule contemporary culture and to poke fun at the hypocrisy of conventional behaviour. The word Dada was chosen by opening the dictionary at random. Before long the painter Max Ernst had joined the circle and other groups had formed: around Breton in Paris, Marcel Duchamp in New York, and Schwitters (known for his collages and as the editor of a publication called 'Merz'), in Hanover.

In its initial phase, Dadaism was quite clearly not interested in creating art but in breaking down the exaggerated esteem in which it was held. This nihilist phase, however, only lasted until 1922. Dadaism became the forerunner of Surrealism (q. v.) and many of its adherents, like Arp, Ernst and Schwitters, found no difficulty in making the transition from mere fooling to new and startling means of artistic representation.

DALI, SALVADOR (born 1904). A Surrealist painter, who was born in Spain, Dali has spent considerable

305. DELAUNAY, *St-Severin*

time in the United States, although he has recently returned to his native land. He has excited and exasperated people everywhere: in Madrid where he studied, in Barcelona at his exhibitions, in Paris, while making films, executing window displays, designing for the ballet, illustrating books (Lautréamont's 'Les Chants de Maldoror'), or writing them ('Hidden Faces', 'The Secret Life of Salvador Dali'). In 1929 he joined the Surrealists in Paris. His technical treatments of nightmares, hallucinations, delusions and other mental aberrations with their clear, coldly painted figures are often achieved with photographic exactness. His flamboyancy and addiction to publicity have added immeasurably to his reputation in the United States, where the subtle meanings behind his sensational canvases have not entirely eluded an amused public. 'Daddy-Long-Legs of the Evening – Hope' and 'Persistence of Memory' (with its famous limp watches) are characteristic. (Ill. 283)

DAVIS, STUART. His paintings are generally characterized by pure, fresh colours, by bold patterns, and by a certain carnival-like gaiety which is frequently redolent of jazz and of public signboards. Born in 1894 in Philadelphia, Davis moved to New York at the age of sixteen in order to study under Robert Henri. He worked first in an Impressionist, then in an Expressionist, style during his early years. By the 1920's his major work revealed a semi-Cubist style and, in fact, though he has moved through all the major modern styles, he, of all contemporary American artists, has been called the one who has been most influenced by Cubism. In 1938 he began to tend toward absolute abstraction, and there have been instances in which his work has approached complete non-objectivity. (Ill. 288)

DELAUNAY, ROBERT (1885–1941). At first closely linked with Cubism (q. v.), this Parisian painter extended the range of its subject matter by using themes like Gothic architectural interiors and the Eiffel Tower, as well as figures and still-lifes, for formal analysis. His greatest contribution, however, lay in his use of

477

colour. This he almost completely dissociated from subject matter and applied in strongly contrasting, luminous coats as the sole means of achieving rhythm, movement and depth. His method of superimposing transparent planes of colour *(plans superposés)* affected Cubism in its later stages and also had a strong influence on the German painters Marc and Macke who were Delaunay's close friends. Among his last works were ten large coloured reliefs for the Paris World Fair in 1937. Earlier he had used his art in the decorative and graphic fields by designing textiles and illustrating books, etc. with his wife and partner, Russian-born Sonia Delaunay-Terk. Apollinaire, trying to describe a new quality of tonal resonance in Delaunay's work, achieved by the emancipation of colour, coined for it the name 'Orphism'. (Ill. 305)

DEMUTH, CHARLES (1883–1935). This American painter, born in Philadelphia, studied at the Pennsylvania Academy of Fine Arts and, in Paris, was strongly influenced by Cézanne and Cubism (q. v.), resulting in his own work in a synthesis between Cubism and the Realist tradition. He worked mainly as a watercolourist and illustrator before, around 1919, turning to tempera and oil. One of the pioneers of modern American painting, he has a preference for architectural subjects, especially in the industrial field ('My Egypt', 1927). The Cubist-Realist style he developed was to become of great significance in American art.

DENIS, MAURICE (1870–1943). French painter. Together with Sérusier he became the leading theorist of the Symbolists (cf. Nabis). His training, which owed much to Puvis de Chavannes, Gauguin and Seurat, led him in the direction of mural decoration (frescoes in the Théâtre des Champs Elysées). But his real interest was the painting of religious themes for church interiors; these wall decorations he executed in the spirit of our own times with all the conviction of the devout Christian.

DERAIN, ANDRÉ (1880–1954), was born in Chatou. It is interesting to note that the early phase of his artistic career was also the most important one. Vlaminck, Picasso and Apollinaire were among his friends and he was a member of the Fauves (q. v.), excelling in the technique of rapid brush-strokes and vivid colours that characterized their work. Considered to have 'discovered' Negro art, he produced a work of the greatest significance with his 'Bathers' of 1907. In his later years he showed classical leanings and devoted himself to the study of the Old Masters. Although he gradually lost contact with progressive painting he must be considered one of its pioneers. (Ill. p. 472)

DESPIAU, CHARLES (1874–1946). A French sculptor who originally worked in the impressionistic style of Rodin. Later his forms became firmer and more disciplined and his sculpture tended more towards an adherence to type, in the manner of Maillol. His subjects remained animated, however.

478

DIX, OTTO. Born 1891 near Gera. He already had an eventful artistic career behind him when he became a teacher at the Dresden Academy in 1927, a post from which he was dismissed in 1933. Like George Grosz he used painting as a moral weapon directed against war and its social consequences, which he either described with crude and exaggerated accuracy ('verism') or reduced to caricature. After passing through a Dadaist phase Dix became interested in the New Objectivity (q. v.), tempering its style with a leaning towards Romanticism, the work of Runge, and the Old Masters. After the end of the Second World War an expressionistic quality once more showed in his paintings which were frequently of religious content.

DOESBURG, THEO VAN (1883–1931). A versatile and talented artist who not only founded the Dutch Constructivist 'Stijl' movement and remained the inspiration behind it, but also published poems, plays and art-historical articles. As a painter his concern was to keep in close contact with modern architecture and he produced his best work in this field (e. g. mosaic floors, stained glass windows, and wall decorations). Until 1923 his art was completely devoid of any naturalistic elements and, like Mondrian who was painting in the same spirit, he used only straight lines and right-angles. Later he began to admit less rigid basic forms. His ideas on design became of significance to the Bauhaus (q. v.) both in its Weimar and Dessau periods.

DONGEN, KEES VAN. A Dutch painter, born 1877, he moved to Paris when still a young man in his twenties. In 1905 he joined the Fauves (q. v.) and before the First World War produced some of his best work in the style of this group. As a member of the *Brücke* (q. v.) he also kept in close touch with German painting. Later he became much sought after as a fashionable portraitist.

306. DUCHAMP-VILLON, *Little Horse. Bronze*

DOVE, ARTHUR G. (1880–1946). Claimed to be the first of the Abstract painters, Dove, painting in America (he was born in Canandaigua, New York), was ahead of Kandinsky in Europe in breaking away from all direct representational reference to his subject matter. By 1910 he had painted his geometrically-formed 'Abstraction No. 2' of the landscape near his home.

DUCHAMP, MARCEL. French artist, born in 1887, the son of a notary. Like his brothers Jacques Villon the painter, Duchamp-Villon the sculptor, and his sister, the painter Suzanne Duchamp, he has achieved international fame. His 'Nude descending a Staircase', painted in 1912, was still strictly Futurist in manner. He is also known as the inventor of the 'Ready Made' (cf. p. 458) and, after his move to New York in 1915, became the inspiration behind American Dadaism. For eight years he was engaged on a composition in glass and metal 10 feet high, which is now considered to be his most important work. He has also tried his hand at abstract films and, apart from his artistic activities, practises journalism. From 1942–1944 he helped to edit the avant-garde American magazine *VVV*. (Ill. 286)

DUCHAMP-VILLON, RAYMOND (1876–1918). French sculptor and brother of Marcel Duchamp. His 'Little Horse' of 1914 (ill. 306) occupies a place half-way between nature and the machine. By logically applying Cubist theories of form to sculpture and by combining organic and mechanical rhythms in visual terms Villon erected a milestone in the history of modern sculpture.

DUFRESNE, CHARLES (1875–1938). A French painter whose talent for flat surface decoration has found full expression in his murals (Palais de Chaillot, École de Pharmacie, Paris) and designs for tapestries.

DUFY, RAOUL (1877–1953). Born in Le Havre. He dropped his early Impressionist manner when he came into contact with Fauve (q. v.) painting. After joining the group, he found himself in special sympathy with the decorative element in their art which he developed further and was able to apply when he became textile artist for the fashion designer Poiret. He also revealed a gift for monumental wall decoration which was brilliantly displayed in the 'Hall of Electricity' at the World Fair in 1937. But his talents are best shown in his landscape paintings. Even when done in oil these retain the freshness of his water colours and their bright colours heighten the feeling of exuberance which they express. His subjects, too, are festive and gay: e. g. streets decked with flags, sailing regattas and race-meetings. Dufy's success (he was awarded the Biennale prize in 1952) did not affect his modest and unassuming personality, nor did he allow a lingering and eventually fatal illness to cast a shadow over his painting. (Ill. p. 474)

DUNOYER DE SEGONZAC, ANDRÉ (1884–1955). A French painter whose work cleverly steered a course

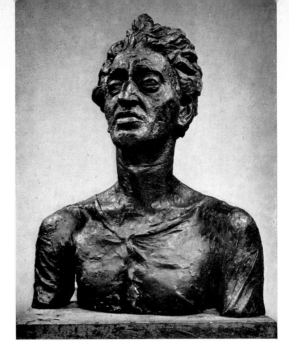

307. EPSTEIN, *Jacob Kramer, 1921. Bronze*

between Impressionist disregard for firmness of construction and Expressionist forcefulness in execution. His luminous water colours are particularly attractive examples of his style. He also produced a remarkable number of etchings.

ENSOR, JAMES (1860–1949). This Belgian painter hardly ever left his home town, Ostend, and also resisted foreign influences in his painting. His leanings towards the weird and supernatural, as evinced in his predilection for ghosts, skeletons and masquerades, show him to be a direct descendant of Brueghel and Bosch. They also make him a forerunner of Expressionism (q. v.), the strong colours and desire for distortion of whose protagonists he shares. (Ill. p. 460)

EPSTEIN, SIR JACOB. Born in New York in 1880, the son of Polish parents, he has lived the best part of his life in England. After specialising in sculptures with a strong tendency towards abstraction ('Genesis', 'Adam'), often grotesque and on a massive scale, he gradually inclined towards a more realistic though still modern style. He is now known above all for his fine portrait busts in bronze in which the texture of the material and the rhythm of the modelling are used towards highly artistic ends (ill. 307).

ERNST, MAX. Born in the Rhineland in 1891, Ernst is considered to be the most serious and profound of the Surrealist painters and, according to André Breton, has 'the most magnificent haunted brain of to-day'. Before joining Breton's circle he passed through a Dadaist phase (with Arp in Cologne), like many other Surrealists. In his frottages (in which a pencil is rubbed over paper resting on surfaces like floorboards, leaves, etc.) he found an interesting technical process which, by almost mechanical means, yielded graphic formations to stimulate the imagination and encourage further visual discoveries. He also produced collage cycles by cutting out pieces from a variety of old woodcuts and pasting them together in such a way that they formed new and independent imaginative combinations. In America, where he stayed for more than ten years, he gradually matured into a painter. His poetic and intuitive powers blended elements from the phenomenal world with those of his own imagination to produce dreamlike fantasies. He is now living in France once more. (Ill. 285)

EXPRESSIONISM. In its widest sense the term describes the kind of art, already found in late medieval times in Germany and in the work of Grünewald and El Greco, in which a desire for heightened expression leads to the distortion of natural proportions. The word was, however, first used in connection with modern art in which expressive and intensifying formal means are used to their utmost limits. In its narrowest sense the term Expressionism is usually applied to such German groups as the *Brücke* (q. v.) and the *Blaue Reiter* (q. v.), to artists such as Nolde and Beckmann, and to those who prepared the way for them, like van Gogh and Munch. (Cf. pp. 444, 451–2)

FAUVES, FAUVISM. The word *fauves,* which means 'wild beasts', was first used in 1906 by a critic describing an exhibition of work by a revolutionary group of young French painters. These included Matisse, Derain, van Dongen, Dufy, Friesz, Vlaminck and Rouault. Unlike the Impressionists, the Fauves did not use colour by carefully grading it and distributing it in minute quantities, but by spreading it across large, unbroken areas. In this way surface shapes received greater emphasis and the state of heightened intensity that accompanies the act of creation was immediately conveyed (cf. p. 452). The quality of violence inherent in the use of strong colours and the desire to distort objects accounts for the name of the movement whose origins are usually traced back to Gauguin. After 1907 its members ceased to work as a group but Matisse, their leading exponent, remained true to its aims although his youthful 'wildness' gradually lessened. (Ill. pp. 438, 471–474)

FEININGER, LYONEL (1871–1956). Born in New York, of German parents who, both musicians, wanted him to take up the same profession; but in spite of his considerable talent Feininger decided to study painting – in Hamburg, Berlin and Paris. Originally a caricaturist, he later came into contact with the Cubists, Delaunay and the *Blaue Reiter* (q. v.) group. Already before the First World War he found an individual mode of expression (not unrelated to the art of Paul Klee) in paintings of seemingly transparent rainbow hues in which he transformed Cubism (q. v.) in a poetic and romantic way (ill. p. 486). He joined the Bauhaus (q. v.) in 1919 and kept up the association until its dissolution in 1933, although towards the end he was no longer a member of its staff. In 1937 he returned to America and after this date his sensitive atmospheric paintings, hitherto mostly of old German towns, began to feature the skyscrapers of New York.

FRESNAYE, ROGER DE LA (1885–1925). A French painter who participated in every modern trend from Symbolism (q. v.) to Cubism (q. v.). Later he produced mostly landscapes and still-lifes of a more traditional character but structurally these owe much to his earlier Cubist phase.

FRIESZ, ÉMILE-OTHON (1879–1949). In his youth this painter from Normandy was friendly with Dufy whose career was in many ways similar to his own. Originally a member of the Fauves (q. v.), he later applied his art to cartoons for carpets and also collaborated with Dufy in his murals for the Palais de Chaillot. His best work comprises his landscapes of La Ciotat (where Braque also painted) and such portraits as that of the poet Fernand Fleuret.

FUTURISM. The short history of this Italian movement in art began with a number of resounding manifestoes. In 1909 Marinetti published one on behalf of the poetry of the future (hence the name Futurism), which was followed in 1910 by another signed by such painters as Balla, Boccioni, Carrà, Russolo and Severini. These painters, who were adherents of the neo-Impressionist school of Seurat, formulated a new set of aims which included, above all, the representation of action (cf. p. 452–3). The manifestoes attacked tradition and the museums, and in their provocative tone and exaltation of power bore the seeds of future Fascism. But the artistic manifestations of the movement were on a more serious level and revealed many new possibilities in the field of visual representation. Apollinaire, Marcel Duchamp and Picabia were converted to its aims and the German painter August Macke also came under its influence. The movement as such ceased to exist after the beginning of the First World War.

GABO, NAUM (born 1890). A Russian-born sculptor living in America, whose real name is Naum Pevsner. He is the brother of Antoine Pevsner to whom he is also related as an artist (cf. p. 458). In his days as an architectural student in Munich he met Kandinsky and, later, Archipenko. He discovered his real métier in Oslo in 1914: the formal representation of space in sculpture. To this end he often uses transparent materials like plexiglass. His constructions do not bear much resemblance to sculpture in the old sense for, like Calder with his mobiles, he created an entirely new departure in three-dimensional representation.

GAUGUIN, PAUL (1848–1903). A Parisian by birth, Gauguin grew up in Lima. After a period at sea and some years on the Stock Exchange in Paris he gave up his job and, with complete disregard for his own future and that of his family, took up painting. From that time on he spent a restless existence, moving between Paris and Brittany, Martinique, Tahiti and finally the Marquesas (ill. p. 438) where he died in extreme poverty. Like Cézanne he reacted against Impressionism. His interest, however, lay not in creating effects of space by pictorial means but in evolving a flat decorative style that relied on the use of strong, pure, and not necessarily naturalistic colours. Outlines were emphasised and treated in an ornamental manner while figures were represented in attitudes of repose. His Tahitian men and women are often invested with a ceremonial dignity and represented with symbolic rather than real attributes. Thus Gauguin anticipated both the Symbolism of the Nabis (q. v.), and the Expressionist movement. He also brought back to the woodcut the severe quality with which we are familiar to-day.

GIACOMETTI, ALBERTO (born 1901), is a Swiss sculptor who lives in Paris. His ghostly elongated bronze figures with their spindly arms and legs are related to Surrealism.

GILL, ERIC. Born at Brighton in 1882, he made his name both as a sculptor and as an engraver. Some of his carvings are marked by a slightly grotesque element, but on the whole his sculpture is characterized by economy of expression and a fine simplicity ('The Crucifixion', Tate Gallery, London) and, especially in his later work, there is a preference for religious subjects. He is also known as the designer of a modern style of lettering named after him.

GILLES, WERNER (born 1894). A pupil of Feininger at the Bauhaus he has spent most of the last twenty years in Italy (Ischia). His painting, which has been developed against this background, represents a symbolical world in which northern imagination is blended with southern, classical forms and a nostalgic feeling for Classical Antiquity. Southern landscapes and mythological material, often simplified to the point of abstraction, are re-created in lyrical colours. (Ill. 308)

GLACKENS, WILLIAM JAMES (1870–1938). A member of the Ashcan School, the group of painters who favoured intimate city genre as a subject, Glackens started out primarily as an illustrator. His paintings were adversely influenced by the dark and limited palette of Robert Henri. In 1906 he went to Spain, and it was here that his painting was liberated to admit the sunlight of Impressionism more natural to his talent. His subject matter also changed from brooding city studies to opalescent nudes done by placing colours close together so that they mixed in the eye of the beholder.

GLEIZES, ALBERT (1881–1953). A Parisian Cubist painter who, like Villon, Metzinger and other exhibitors at the Salon of the *Section d'Or,* attempted to

represent animation in pictorial terms. He was mainly interested in the human figure. After 1917 his pictures showed an increasing preoccupation with religious subjects. He is also known as the author of an important monograph on the theory and practice of Cubism.

GOGH, VINCENT VAN (1853–1890). Son of a Calvinist preacher from Groot-Zundert in Holland, he was, like Cézanne, to herald a new epoch in painting. In his youth his strong social convictions made him work as a missionary in a Belgian mining village, a venture which ended in complete failure. He withdrew into himself more and more, and began to draw and paint. His earliest pictures, painted in sombre tones, represent such themes as weavers, peasants and 'Potato-eaters'. An important change took place in 1885 when he saw his first Japanese woodcuts and came into contact with the work of the Impressionist painters in Paris. His colours became lighter and more varied and in less than two years he painted 200 pictures. But neither the technique of the Impressionists nor the *pointillism* of Seurat and Signac who were his friends, was able to give adequate expression to his turbulent nature with its intense desire for self-revelation. In 1888 he went to Arles in Provence. There the fierce light of the sun revealed to him a landscape composed entirely of primary colours, and these yellows, reds and blues he squeezed straight from the tube on to his canvas or applied in vigorous, curving brush-strokes. During this period he created his best pictures: portraits, interiors of his simple home and studio, the night-café at Arles, sunflowers and the local landscape, a theme which he repeated over and over again with the vision of the Expressionist. He was visited by Gauguin but the two quarrelled and separated. A first bout of insane fury, directed against himself, was followed by further periods of mental derangement marked by melancholy rather than violence. He finally committed suicide at Auvers-sur-Oise where Dr Gachet, commemorated in several portraits, had looked after him and befriended him. In his last months he produced hundreds of paintings and drawings which, in their firm and confident construction, give only the barest hint of pathological disturbance, and which inspired a generation of younger artists. But until the time of his death only one of his pictures was ever sold. Van Gogh's deeply moving letters to his brother Theo bear testimony to the lifelong sufferings of this troubled genius. (Ill. p. 439)

GONZALES, JULIO (1876–1942). Born in Barcelona, Gonzales was trained as a blacksmith, his father's trade, before taking an evening course in painting at Barcelona Art Academy. It was not until 1908 that he began to devote himself almost entirely to sculpture. With his wrought iron sculptures, usually of female figures handled in a severely abstract idiom, he became the much-admired leader of a school whose exponents include Butler in England, Jacobsen in Denmark, David Smith in America and Lardera in Italy. It was Gonzales who, round about 1930, introduced his compatriot Picasso to metal sculpture.

308. GILLES, Lament of Death

481

GORKY, ARSHILE (1904–1948). His importance stems chiefly from the fact that he was one of the first of the Abstract-Expressionists. His painting is characterized by a style of abstraction which is free, non-geometrical, mysterious, and curiously alive. Born in Armenia, he studied at the Polytechnical Institute in Tiflis (Georgia) and went to the US in 1920. Studying engineering at Brown University, he turned to painting in his spare time. Though his productive artistic career lasted little more than sixteen years, his individuality of expression has had enormous influence on the whole school of Abstract-Expressionism.

GOTTLIEB, ADOLPH (born 1903), is perhaps the strongest individualist among contemporary American painters, both in style and personality. Although he studied briefly in Paris, Berlin and Munich in 1921–1922, Gottlieb, who was born in New York, is primarily a self-taught artist influenced by Abstract-Expressionism but never affiliating himself with any school of painting. In rebellion, he invented what he calls the pictograph. This is simply an arrangement of inter-relating patterns and motifs and forthright designs for the sake of the medium itself. Gottlieb never starts from nature but rather from the materials with which he works. As in 'Red Sky', he merely makes a statement about disparate elements, dividing the canvas in two, with red in one section and black in the other. Any connection with nature is therefore *ex post facto*. Gottlieb's ambition is to transfer feeling to canvas without the interference of an established image.

GRAVES, MORRIS (born 1910). It was in San Francisco that Graves, an American painter who was born in Oregon, discovered the art and philosophy of the Orient and found that they perfectly suited him. From his study of Oriental painting, sculpture and bronzes he arrived at a decorative and intensely disciplined linear style of great delicacy. From Zen Buddhism he drew the insights, paradoxes and mystical symbolism that give meaning to his canvases. All his paintings contain established personal symbols, mostly of animals. As in 'The Preening Sparrow', he unites message and style in a flat, linear design, Chinese in its delicacy and precision. The sparrow is calmly enjoying himself on the wing of a bird of prey while both ignore the eclipsed sun overhead. The purpose of his picture, according to Graves, is to allow the beholder to explain himself to himself, and to relate himself to the harmony of the universe.

GRIS, JUAN (1887–1927). A Spanish painter whose real name was José Victoriano Gonzalez. In 1905 he moved to Paris and met Picasso who had his studio in the same building. Gris played a vital role in the development of Cubism (q. v.), particularly in its transition from the analytical to the 'synthetic' stage which he furthered both by his theories and in practice. His work is characterized by cool, restrained colours and a certain element of severity which may explain why he did not achieve the recognition due to him until com-

309. GROSZ, *Funeral of the poet Panizza*

paratively late in his career, in the 'twenties. During these years Diaghilev commissioned from him the décor and costumes for several operas *(La Colombe, l'Education Manquée)* and ballet performances. A lecture on the scope of painting given by Gris at the Sorbonne was received with enthusiasm and translated into several languages.

GROMAIRE, MARCEL, was born in 1892 of a French father and a Flemish mother. The figures in his paintings are framed by severe black outlines resembling the leading used in medieval stained glass. But this does not detract from the vitality of his workmen and card-players and the natural eroticism of his female nudes. Apart from his paintings Gromaire also works on a smaller scale, designing tapestries and Sèvres porcelain.

GROPIUS, WALTER (born 1883). The pioneering Berlin architect who, after acting as assistant to Peter Behrens until 1910, a year later built the Fagus factory at Alfeld an der Leine, which can be called the first truly modern piece of architecture. In 1918 he was appointed Director of the Weimar School of Art and in the following year founded the Bauhaus (q. v.) whose entirely novel ideas on the teaching of art have since been recognised the world over. In 1925 the Bauhaus moved into new buildings at Dessau designed by Gropius (ill. 280). Three years later he left to start a private architectural practice in Berlin. In 1934 he emigrated to England and in 1937 took up a post at Harvard University. By now one of the most eminent architects of our time, he carried out an extensive building programme in America, some of it in partnership with his former pupil Marcel Breuer. Meanwhile the ideas which had been tried out at the Bauhaus and which he had so eloquently advocated steadily gained ground, being taken up by, *inter alia*, Yale University, Illinois Institute of Technology and Brooklyn College. It is an indication of his vitality that, apart from his teaching and architectural work, Gropius has also found time to engage in journalism.

GROSZ, GEORGE (born 1893). A German-born painter who began as a caricaturist and, after the First World War, produced a large number of lithographs in which he exposed post-war conditions with ruthlessness and biting sarcasm. His graphic series 'Faces of the Ruling Class', in which the style of drawing is in itself aggressive, attacked militarism, philistinism, bureaucracy and capitalism with equal venom. Since 1933 he has lived in New York, where he at first turned to water colours of the city and to Baroque still-lifes. During the Second World War he began painting symbolic, terror-filled, anti-war pictures which are among the most powerful of their kind. (Ill. 309)

HARTUNG, KARL (born 1908). Sculptor and professor at the Academy of Plastic Arts in Berlin. Creatively he stands somewhere between Brancusi and Henry Moore, combining the former's extreme formal abstraction and smooth surfaces with the latter's inclusion of space by hollowing out his material. A master of abstract monumental figure sculpture as well as of small and vital plastic representations developed from simple basic shapes, Hartung is one of the leading exponents of contemporary German sculpture. (Ill. 299)

HECKEL, ERICH. This painter, born in Saxony in 1883, was one of the founders and most active members of the *Brücke* (q. v.) group, as well as being among the most important representatives of German Expressionism. This is particularly true of his work as a graphic artist, a field in which he excelled during the early part of his career, especially as an exponent of lithography and the woodcut. As a painter, his Expressionist fervour gradually diminished after 1920: his landscapes, still-lifes and portraits after this period, painted in a quiet vein, are distinguished by delicate colours and a sensitive appreciation of nature.

HEPWORTH, BARBARA. Born in Yorkshire in 1903, she studied first at the Royal College of Art, London

310. HEPWORTH, *Figure (Requiem). Walnut*

311. HODLER, *Disillusioned souls*

and then in Florence and Rome. She held the first of her many exhibitions in 1928, in London, and joined the '7 and 5' Group in 1931. In 1951 she executed two large sculptures for the Festival of Britain. A colour film 'Figures in Landscape – Sculpture of Barbara Hepworth' was first shown in 1953. One of Britain's outstanding sculptors, Barbara Hepworth has works in the Tate Gallery and the Victoria and Albert Museum in London, as well as in many public and private collections in Europe and America. Her abstract or semi-abstract sculpture, which relies less on the use of organic forms than that of Henry Moore, shows a great interest in formal problems and the relationship between different forms and objects. By piercing her shapes and by the use of stringed figures she has added to her range of expression. In spite of her non-naturalistic approach she is deeply interested in nature, an interest which she expresses in abstract terms by, among other things, the introduction of colour. (Ill. 310)

HITCHENS, IVON. Born in London in 1893, Hitchens studied at the St John's Wood and Royal Academy Schools. Like Barbara Hepworth, he was a member of the '7 and 5' Group and of the London Group. He paints landscapes and flowers using oil as fluidly as if it were water colour. His pictures give an impression of the utmost freshness and spontaneity, but this is usually the result of several versions of the same subject each tending farther and farther away from representationalism while preserving the essential character of the scene or objects. Hitchens is represented in the Tate Gallery and in provincial and American collections.

HODLER, FERDINAND (1853–1918). A Swiss painter whose leanings towards Symbolism and use of line as an ornamental as well as an expressive ingredient relate him closely to the European *Jugendstil* (see Art Nouveau). The element of pathos which characterizes his work and which even in his best paintings ('The World-Weary', 'Disillusioned Souls') does not always ring quite true, also shows his kinship with this movement. The naturalistic models' heads of some of his figures often contrast sharply with their measured movements and idealized dress. Hodler became the idol of Symbolists in Switzerland and even more so in Germany, although to-day his 'non-literary' pictures, like his distant views of alpine landscapes, are more popular. (Ill. 311)

483

HODGKINS, FRANCES (1870–1947). A New Zealand painter who, after 1900, lived in England and France. She won recognition in 1925 with her first one-man exhibition in London, and became a member of the '7 and 5' Group. She worked mostly in gouache, but occasionally in oil. Apart from a few early portraits, she painted mainly still-lifes and landscapes of a poetic quality which, in later years, became less and less representational.

HOFER, CARL (1878–1955). The firm construction of this German painter's early landscapes shows the influence of Cézanne. Two journeys to India also left their mark on his paintings with figures of young girls resembling each other like sisters and imbued with a certain spiritual quality. But after the First World War the lyrical element in his work gradually disappeared and the beginning of the Hitler régime saw such paintings as 'Drummer', 'Prisoners' and 'The Watchers' which were already filled with forebodings about the future. The feeling of uneasiness and suspicion lingered on in his work even after the end of the war and was expressed by such symbols as masks and demons. He was Director of the Academy of Plastic Arts in Berlin.

HOFFMANN, JOSEF (born 1870). As architect and exponent of the crafts he was the leader of the Viennese *Jugendstil* (see Art Nouveau). But the '*Wiener Werkstätte*', which he founded in 1903, already went far beyond the aims of that movement. In those early years of the century the simplicity and functionalism of his furniture and buildings (Palais Stoclet, Brussels) already proclaimed the modern trend in design.

HOFMANN, HANS (born 1880), is probably equally renowned as a teacher and as an artist, and has influenced thousands of pupils, among them such American painters as Larry Rivers, Giorgio Cavallon and George McNiel. Even in his formative years in Paris and Munich, Hofmann, a Bavarian with a Germanic taste for philosophy, was searching for a satisfactory theory behind his painting. His philosophy of painting conceives the universe as a field of forces, the plane of the canvas being meant to cut through it as a slice of space so that space exists on either side of it. The thing to be striven for, according to Hofmann, is the third dimension – a dimension expressed as the balancing pressures and counter-pressures of the universe. To achieve this balance, natural shapes are ignored in favour of movement of line and interplay of light and colour. Depth is suggested by tensions between violent colours, textures and shapes.

HOPPER, EDWARD (born 1882), is a realistic American painter whose predominant scene is of everyday small-town or big-city life, always done somewhat harshly and with certain overtones of criticism. A disciple of the 'Ashcan' school of American painting, Hopper became famous at the age of forty-three – only after he had struggled for years to achieve an unmistakable originality in his work. Born in Nyack, N. Y., he was influenced by Impressionism during two years which he spent in Paris (1906–1907). By comparison with the style of the Impressionists, however, Hopper's lighting is exceedingly glaring. His works – bearing such self-descriptive, realistic titles as 'Sunlight on Brownstones' and 'Manhattan Bridge Loop' – are characterized by a suppression of detail and by a flat use of paint.

JAWLENSKY, ALEXEJ VON (1864–1941). Russian-born and a former Czarist officer, Jawlensky studied painting before joining the New Artists' Federation in Munich. He remained on friendly terms with the *Blaue Reiter* group (q. v.) after it had split off from the Federation and, in 1924, joined Klee, Kandinsky and Feininger to form the '*Blauen Vier*' (the 'Blue Four'). Matisse with his free use of colour had a strong influence on his painting but his own application of this freedom, and one perhaps more suited to his Russian temperament, was to mystical and symbolic rather than decorative ends (like Chagall). Eventually he limited his subject matter entirely to the human face which he represented in heightened colours and in a kind of symbolic pictorial shorthand. (Ill. p. 485)

JOHN, AUGUSTUS. Born in Tenby, South Wales, in 1878, John studied at the Slade School in London from 1894–1898, where he distinguished himself by his masterly drawing. During the early part of his career he established almost a new genre with his portraits of gipsies, peasants and vagabonds whom he encountered on his wanderings through England. These, as well as his landscapes with and without figures, his still-lifes and portraits all reveal a deep interest in the visible world. But in some of his large murals (e. g. 'Lyric Fantasy') he gives more play to pure inventiveness. John has never been much influenced by contemporary movements in art, relying more on a spontaneous and deeply intuitive gift for creating works that seem to reflect his own powerful personality. He is perhaps best known for such masterly portraits as 'Madame Suggia', 'Robin', 'Bernard Shaw' and 'James Joyce'.

JUGENDSTIL. See Art Nouveau.

KANDINSKY, WASSILY (1866–1944). Born in Moscow, Kandinsky was a lawyer and economist before, at the age of thirty, he decided to take up painting. His academic and philosophical training was to stand him in good stead, especially since it never interfered with his creative sensibility. While studying art in Munich he met a number of progressive young painters with whom he soon became more intimate. Together they founded the New Artists' Federation, some of whose members later formed the *Blaue Reiter* group (q. v.) under his leadership. In 1910, a year of vital importance in his development as an artist, Kandinsky painted his first abstract picture and wrote his book *Concerning the Spiritual in Art (Vom Geistigen in der Kunst)*, a brilliant exposition of the principles underlying his own work and modern painting in general. From that time on, his own career can be divided into three almost completely distinct phases. The first

Alexej von Jawlensky: Portrait of a Girl

Lyonel Feininger: Gelmeroda

Paul Klee: Death and Fire

WASSILY KANDINSKY: Division-Unité

of these was marked by an abstract form of Expressionism shown in his so-called 'improvisations', with their calligraphic brush-strokes. These, though not representational, are reminiscent of landscapes. His second phase, the result of his meeting with the painter Malewich, was characterized by stricter forms and the use of geometric symbols in place of the earlier splashes of colour. After his appointment to the Bauhaus (q. v.) in 1922 he further developed the organization of his paintings into circles and geometric crystalline structures. In 1933 he went to Paris where he stayed until his death. Here the beginnings of his third phase, which represented a synthesis, emerged: his forms lost their geometric severity and became more organic; his colours and compositions lightened in mood and 'a cool romanticism' (to use one of Paul Klee's phrases) which harked back to the beginning of his career also marked the end of his work. This has been of the greatest significance to modern art. (Ill. p. 488)

KIRCHNER, ERNST LUDWIG (1880–1938). This German painter occupies an important position in the history of modern German art both as an artist and as the founder and inspiration behind the Expressionist *Brücke* (q. v.) movement. In contrast with other members of the group, his energies and powers increased steadily until the time of his death. During the early stages of his career he was influenced by Negro sculpture and old German woodcuts. He was himself a sculptor and also made an important contribution to the development of the modern woodcut (both in black-and-white and colour) and woodcut illustrations (Chamisso's *Peter Schlemihl*). With their angular, broken forms his paintings, based first on themes from the metropolis, later on alpine life and scenery, reflect a tragic outlook and a feeling of great loneliness. During the last years of his life there was an increased tendency towards abstraction and the simultaneous representation of an animated figure seen from a number of different viewpoints, in the manner of Picasso. But the new vision was never completely realized. (Ill. p. 446)

KLEE, PAUL (1879–1940). Born in Switzerland, Klee has become one of the greatest names in 20th-century art. Perhaps his most significant and revolutionary contribution to painting lay in the creative method itself. This was not, as in all earlier painting, based on a definite preliminary idea but sprang from some formal suggestion, a few splashes of colour, some lines drawn intuitively, all according to the mood of the moment. These first subjective utterances made an immediate objective impression on the painter which called for completion in a certain way. Thus the initial subconscious artistic act was succeeded by 'pictorial thinking'. Any material suggestions and associations that arose in the process were not rejected but welcomed for the further ideas they might evoke. Not until the very end was the title chosen, the 'baptism' of the picture being the final creative act. This interplay of pure contemplation and an exact knowledge of the laws and possibilities of pictorial composition opened up a new path in painting which has since found many adherents. But none of Klee's followers have ever rivalled him in artistic inventiveness or intensity of feeling.

There is a marked affinity between Klee's creative method and certain types of musical composition. Klee himself was an excellent musician who played the violin and was at one time undecided whether to make music his career. Eventually he went to Munich to study painting, joined the *Blaue Reiter* group (q. v.) and became friendly with Kandinsky. Later, in 1912, he went to Paris and met Picasso and Delaunay. Not until 1914, after a journey to Tunis with Macke, did he first explore the possibilities of colour. His first exhibition opened in Munich in 1920; in the same year he was invited to join the Bauhaus (q. v.) in Weimar where he produced his *Pedagogical Sketchbook*, a poetic synthesis of his experiences as teacher and artist. His appointment to the Academy at Düsseldorf in 1931 ended with his abrupt dismissal two years later. He returned to Switzerland and continued to work with unfailing energy (his artistic output runs into thousands of pictures). But in the course of time he dropped his earlier tendency towards the grotesque and whimsical. His colours became more contrasting, his lines hardened into rigid angular ciphers. During the last two years of his life there is an unmistakable undertone of tragedy in his work. (Ill. p. 487)

KOKOSCHKA, OSKAR (born 1886). A revolutionary Austrian painter who, in the course of his artistic career has gradually modified his unorthodox ideas in favour of older traditions. In his youth he wrote plays ('*Murder – Woman's Hope*', 1908) in which he treated Strindbergian themes with Expressionist intensity and the same penetrating insight that he applied to probing the inner life of the sitters in his portraits. During his years as a professor at Dresden, from 1919 on, and in the course of his travels in Europe and Africa after 1924, he concentrated on landscape painting in which equal emphasis was laid on capturing the unique and individual character of the scenery and on the process of creation itself. Although Kokoschka often heightens his colours in an Expressionist manner, his landscapes, as well as his later work, maintain a link with the colour tradition of the Old Masters, from Tintoretto to Delacroix. Drawing, which his paintings scarcely call for since they rely largely on colour, was never neglected by this artist but developed quite independently in his graphic work which found its culmination in his portrait lithographs. After making his home both in Vienna (1931) and in Prague (1934), whence he was driven by invading German armies, he lived in London until 1953. He has now made his home by the Lake of Geneva but continues to travel and is also conducting courses in painting at Salzburg. Still predominantly a painter of portraits and landscapes, he made a surprising departure with his vast composition 'Thermopylae' (1954). Ill. p. 497

KOLBE, GEORG (1877–1947). A German sculptor who, under the influence of Tuaillon in Rome, gave up

489

312. KOLBE, *Standing figure (South Sea Maiden). Bronze*

313. De Kooning, *Woman with bicycle*

painting in favour of sculpture, going a stage beyond the classicism of Tuaillon and the naturalism of Rodin. But while the heads and bodies of his bronze nudes bear the stamp of individuality and the physical reality of his models invests the substance, Kolbe still maintained on over-all classical repose and unity of form. He produced his best work when using this individual blend between tradition and innovation, the most popular being his famous 'Dancer' (1912) at the National Gallery in Berlin. (Ill. 312)

KOLLWITZ, KÄTHE (1867–1945). This distinguished German graphic artist was born in East Prussia, but lived in Berlin from 1891 onwards where, both in her life and her art, she became the champion of the poor and oppressed. Her early illustrations of historical themes ('The Weavers' Revolt', 1898, 'The Peasants' Revolt', 1908), and later, her scenes taken mainly from the life of the working class in Berlin, show her virtuosity in every graphic medium. In her many self-portraits she also reveals a serious desire for self-knowledge. Apart from her graphic work she produced sculptures in an idiom related to Barlach.

KOONING, WILLEM DE (born 1904). Since the death of Jackson Pollock, De Kooning has taken his place as the leader of the Abstract-Expressionists in New York. Painted in comparatively sombre colours, his works, though the first impression is one of chaos, are nevertheless controlled. Recently he has begun to introduce human forms into his paintings, thereby influencing a large group of followers who are eager to move from pure abstraction into more representational art. De Kooning, of Dutch parentage, was born in Rotterdam and came to America in 1926. A house-painter, he did not turn to abstract art until the mid-

1930's. His first one-man show in 1948 was the result of a long struggle to discover and understand fully the nature of his own creative impulse and brought him immediate fame. (Ill. 313)

KUNIYOSHI, YASUO (1893–1953). This painter, though born in Japan, lived in America from 1906 on. In his work, Eastern and Western elements are both represented – the former by the subject, which is often oriental, the latter by the painting style. His early pictures, in which objects drift about without regard for realism or perspective, recall Chagall. His later work is marked by a strong Surrealist element.

KUPKA, FRANK (François Frantižek, 1871–1957). A Czech painter, Kupka came to Paris early in his career after spending some time in Prague and Vienna. By 1911/12 he was producing completely non-representational pictures which placed him among the earliest abstract painters. Although he single-mindedly continued along this path, his name was almost completely forgotten for many years. Two retrospective exhibitions of his work (Prague 1946, New York 1951) revived interest in him.

LAURENCIN, MARIE (1885–1956), was a Parisian painter who wrote poetry in her youth. Her pictures of graceful, large-eyed, slender-limbed young girls have a poetic as well as a purely feminine appeal. Although she grew up in Montmartre, the home of Cubism, she remained aloof from artistic trends and developed her painting purely according to her unfailing taste and artistic insight.

LAURENS, HENRI (1885–1954). A French sculptor who, with Archipenko, was the first to join the Cubist (q. v.) movement in 1911. In his work, in which natural objects are hardly recognisable, he tried as far as possible to exclude all non-sculptural elements, especially the effect of light, using colour to emphasise formal contrast. After 1925 he reintroduced human and organic forms, which he modelled in severely abstract terms, using curving contours to achieve vitality and dynamic expression. (Ill. 293)

LE CORBUSIER (born 1887). Under this name, the Swiss architect Charles Édouard Jeanneret has won an international reputation. Originally trained as a copper-plate engraver, he has continued to work as a painter and graphic artist, making a considerable contribution to post-Cubist painting. His real genius, however, is revealed in his architecture. His 'DOMINO Houses' (1915) and 'Pavillon de l'Esprit Nouveau' (1920), in which he first gave expression to his revolutionary ideas about modern living, have had far-reaching effects on our surroundings to-day. His greatest interest lies in domestic architecture. As a pupil of the engineer and architect Auguste Perret he was equipped to make the fullest use of modern constructional techniques and materials in the service of brighter living with emphasis on air, light, sun and, above all, space, to which the past had never attributed enough importance. Rooms leading into each other with moveable partition walls are one of his favourite devices. The character of his individual houses (Weissenhof settlement, Stuttgart 1923) is carried over into his huge blocks of flats (Marseilles 1952, Berlin 1957) which, with their two-storeyed maisonettes, have been dubbed 'vertical towns'. They all prove that his work is not governed by functionalism alone but relies on an artistic consideration for form. His endeavour is to achieve a precise and monumental interplay of form within light (Swiss Pavilion of the University City, Paris 1930) and a tense, dynamic rhythm of plastic forms (church of Notre Dame at Ronchamp, ill. 282). Corbusier's influence on modern architecture cannot be exaggerated. A fitting tribute was paid to his lifelong preoccupation with the problems of civic architecture when he was entrusted with the planning of Chandigarh, the capital of the Punjab .

LÉGER, FERNAND (1881–1955). This French painter, the son of a Normandy farmer, went, in 1900, to Paris where he passed through several phases, including Impressionism. Finally, taking Cubism as his starting point, he systematically developed his own style which may well point the way to future painting more than we realise to-day. With their simple harmonies of blue, yellow and red, his pictures are characterized by precision, control and meticulous composition. Although he shared with the constructivists the determination to eliminate all specifically individual traits from his paintings, he nevertheless used a wide range of forms and was interested in natural objects. Machinery, cogged wheels, etc. play an important part in his art, and in the 'twenties man himself was made to look like a machine ('The Mechanic'). But progressively his human beings were endowed with classical features and warmth (musicians, acrobats, youths with bicycles). Landscape motifs, too, which had been used in his early work, reappeared. Like Matisse, Léger wanted his art to express joy, but in this case it was a feeling of confidence in the modern machine age. His optimism about the world he lived in also prompted him to put his talents to practical use in producing murals, tapestries and mosaics (and sculpture) in conjunction with architecture. As a mural painter he was represented at the World Fair in Paris in 1937, and he further showed his versatility by designing the stained glass windows for the church at Audincourt. Léger has had a considerable influence on art outside France, e. g. on international poster design. (Ill. p. 504)

LEHMBRUCK, WILHELM (1881–1919). German sculptor, born in Duisburg. After training in Düsseldorf, he went to Italy and Paris in 1906. There he evolved his highly expressive, contemplative and expressionistic style, in which volume is tapered down to a minimum and limbs and bodies become slender and elongated almost as in Gothic art (the over-life-size figure of a 'Kneeling Woman'). Although there is a certain delicacy, even a trace of sweetness especially in the expressions of his female figures, the over-all effect of his bent forms and inclined heads, weighed down as if by some

invisible load, is one of tragedy ('The Fallen', 1915–16; ill. 314). Lehmbruck also produced some excellent litographs and etchings.

LEVINE, JACK (born 1915). A fighting, satirical painter, Levine, who was born in South Boston, Massachusetts, paints sermons of social protest with a barbed wit and an evident sense of morality. Characteristic is 'Welcome Home', which he painted after serving in the Second World War and in which stiff-shirted, gluttonous diners are shown enjoying a luxurious repast, completely oblivious to the tragedy of war. All his paintings are aimed at man's injustice, his meanness, his poverty. His style is firmly based on a study of the traditionalists, with overtones of Expressionism.

LEWIS, PERCY WYNDHAM (1884–1957). British painter and writer, and one of the pioneers of modern art in England. He was a member of the London Group, originator of the Vorticist movement which attracted painters and writers around the beginning of the First World War, and editor of its periodical *Blast*. His own painting, which like Vorticism owes much to Cubist and even more to Futurist influence, was never restricted to a single representational style, embracing both abstraction and portraiture ('T. S. Eliot').

LHOTE, ANDRÉ (born 1885). A French painter and theorist who has written a number of important books about painting. A great admirer of Cézanne, his main interest both in theory and in practice has been the representation of space without using perspective or destroying the characteristic flat surface appearance of the picture.

LIPCHITZ, JACQUES (born 1891). French sculptor, born in Lithuania. In Paris his style, modelled on Cubism (q. v.), passed from a hard and angular phase to a softer manner with greater emphasis on modelling. In America, where he has lived since 1941, his abstract compositions cast in bronze have made a particularly powerful impression, even on the younger generation.

LISSITZKY, ELIEZER (1890–1941). A Russian painter and member of the Constructivist (q. v.) movement, Lissitzky's individual method was to combine simple geometric surface patterns with three-dimensional designs. His influence was especially great in Germany.

LURÇAT, JEAN (born 1892). A French painter who has travelled widely and has a large range of interests. He is known principally as a designer of tapestries (e. g. for the church at Assy), a medium in which he has used

314. LEHMBRUCK, *'The Fallen'. Stone*

315. MAILLOL, *The Mediterranean. Stone*

old techniques and infused them with new life. His decorative Expressionist style relies on strong colours and a simple symbolism (ill. p. 100).

LUTYENS, SIR EDWIN L. (1869–1944), was born in London, studied at South Kensington and was in private practice by the time he was twenty. His principal works are the government buildings in New Delhi, including the Viceroy's Lodge, the British School in Rome, the Cenotaph, Whitehall, innumerable country houses and the preliminary plans for Liverpool Roman Catholic Cathedral. Lutyen's work is based on the Renaissance and Georgian styles, but he used these styles to create an original and highly individual architecture. He was the last great exponent of the European tradition, built up by classic, medieval and Renaissance masters, of architecture as a fine art; he was the last architect of the age of humanism.

MACKE, AUGUST (1887–1914). Macke is now considered one of Germany's most important modern painters. In spite of his short career (he only had five full years as a painter), he left a considerable output. Macke was greatly stimulated by a stay in Paris and especially by the work of his friend Delaunay. In his paintings of hat shops (e. g. in the Hanover Museum) he represents action taking place simultaneously in different places. This Futurist device is combined with extraordinary skill in the handling of abstract design based on reflections in the shop windows. After 1909 he became friendly with Franz Marc and this association proved fruitful to both artists. Macke was one of the leading members of the *Blaue Reiter* (q. v.) and helped to organize the famous *Sonderbund* Exhibition in Cologne, at which modern German art made its first important public appearance. In 1914 he went to Tunis with Paul Klee and the Swiss painter Moilliet. There a fortnight's stay yielded 37 water colours which were to prove as significant for German 20th-century art as Dürer's water-colour landscapes had been in their time. In the last few months before joining

the army he produced 35 oil paintings, making up a total of 500 works in this medium completed by the time of his death. These pictures possess the same luminous quality of colour, used without shadows, that we find in the work of Marc, although Macke did not share his friend's brooding preoccupation with mysticism. (Ill. p. 449)

MAGNELLI, ALBERTO (born 1888), is one of Italy's leading abstract painters, who has been influenced especially by Léger. His art is related to Constructivism (q. v.) in that it avoids any suggestion of personal expression in the application of paint, but it does not limit itself rigidly to straight lines and geometric precision. Magnelli has fully realized his avowed purpose to invest his painting with 'fire and expression'. A Florentine by birth, he has for many years lived in Paris.

MACKINTOSH, CHARLES RENNIE (1868–1928), architect and painter born in Glasgow, where he studied, later visiting France and Italy. His designs had great influence on Continental architecture, particularly in Germany, Holland and Sweden. The whole modern movement in architecture owes much to him. His Glasgow School of Art building was an early and successful attempt to combine the decorative and the structural; he also designed the Music Room, Vienna.

MAILLOL, ARISTIDE (1861–1944). This sculptor from the south of France began as a painter and designer of tapestries. He only turned to sculpture after 1900 as a result of a temporary eye complaint, a decision that was to have far-reaching effects. Not interested in the 19th-century approach with its over-emphasis on gestures, or the style of Rodin with its 'humps and hollows', its reliance on light and striving after painterly effects, Maillol reverted to a controlled synthesis of plastic forms. His subject was almost always the female nude in a standing or sitting position, strong and amply proportioned in a spirit akin to that of Classical Antiquity (ill. 315). A journey to Greece in 1906 confirmed Maillol in his feeling of kinship with the classical tradition. By excluding all elements that were not 'purely sculptural' in the sense of being appropriate to a tactile art, he became the founder of a new school which aimed at going back to first principles in sculpture. In addition to his plastic work Maillol also produced superb drawings and woodcuts (illustrations for *Daphnis and Chloë* and Ovid's *Ars Amandi*).

MALEVICH, KASIMIR (1878–1935). The principal representative of Russian Constructivism (q. v.), or 'Suprematism' as he called it, a movement that originated between 1913 and 1915. Malevich exhibited a painting in Moscow which consisted of nothing more than a black rectangle on a white ground, followed in 1919 by another representing two white squares on a white ground (Museum of Modern Art, New York). With these paintings he was performing a symbolic act: he was pointing to the fundamentals of pictorial representation from which, step by step, further simple pictorial forms could be developed (cf. p. 455). Malevich was in Paris in 1912 and in Germany in 1926. After that he went back to Russia where he ended his days in an atmosphere of constant hostility and great poverty.

MANESSIER, ALFRED (born 1911). A French abstract painter and former architectural student from Paris, who owes much to his older friend Bissière. He has been using his art more and more in the service of ecclesiastical architecture and has produced stained glass windows for a number of churches (e. g. in Hem near Roubaix, Arles and Basle).

MANZU, GIACOMO (born 1908). A leading Italian sculptor from Milan. Originally influenced by Rodin and Degas, he also has affinities with Marini. His interest lies in his searching study of character which, in the treatment of facial expressions, often leads him to the borders of caricature.

MARC, FRANZ (1880–1916). Until 1909, this German painter experimented with a variety of styles (Impressionism, *Jugendstil*, the art of van Gogh) without finding a way out of the confusion that characterized this critical period in the history of art. His friendship with August Macke, which began around 1909/1910, for the first time opened his eyes to the potentialities of colour as an independent element in composition. This discovery he immediately applied in a symbolical way ('blue is the masculine, yellow the feminine principle', etc.). His ideas soon found a supporter in Kandinsky who, with Marc, became one of the founders of the *Blaue Reiter* (q. v.). But it is Marc who has always been rightly considered the true exponent of this movement. Although he made a careful study of Cubist (Delaunay, Picasso) and Futurist ideas, his own deeply poetic nature converted these new representational methods into a kind of personal mysticism. What he wanted to show in his painting was the essence of being in its true setting – against the rhythm of nature and the harmony of the cosmos. This concept led him to depict animals, since these creatures, unlike man with his dual nature, had still not severed their link with a fundamental and harmonious state of existence. In trying to realize this vision Marc was not interested in the external appearance of his animals although he had by then investigated this aspect in a large number of studies. What he sought to do was to portray their deeper significance and to fit them into a larger cosmic pattern ('Tower of Blue Horses', 'Fate of Animals', 1913). In the course of time Marc discovered that this feeling of order within order as well as the suggestion of cosmic forces could be achieved equally well by means of colour and form alone, a realization that in the end inevitably led him towards abstract painting ('Forms in Combat', 1914). (Ill. p. 448)

MARCKS, GERHARD (born 1889). German sculptor, born in Berlin. His figures, which in the firmness of their modelling show something of the classical Greek feeling for physical form ('Maya', 1951), are also invested with a spiritual quality which ranges from the lyrical to the intensely expressive. The latter is especially evident in the church of St Catherine at Lübeck where he continued a row of figures begun by Barlach (ill. 316). Marcks is also a graphic artist of some standing, known particularly for his severe woodcuts (Orpheus illustrations and Africa series).

MARIN, JOHN (1870–1953). A member of the Stieglitz group and of the famed '291' gallery in New York. Born in Rutherford, New Jersey, he became one of America's leading water-colourists after several years of study in Paris. Marin's paintings, though representational, possess something of the quality of Abstract-Expressionism. Painting scenes chiefly on the coasts of Maine and of New Jersey, Marin achieved an almost ecstatic style of tilting planes and stenographic symbols (in order to use as few details as possible). Toward the end of his life he concentrated on oils, but he is best remembered for his watercolours. (Ill. p. 476)

MARINETTI, FILIPPO (1876–1944). This Italian was the ideological leader of Futurism (q. v.). He wrote the movement's manifestoes, gave many rousing lectures in Italy, France and Russia and was one of the literary forces behind modern art. Although his propaganda methods were often noisy and showy, he rendered a great service to 20th-century art by helping to free it from conventional forms and out-dated formulae.

MARINI, MARINO (born 1901). In the work of this sculptor from Pistoia in Tuscany certain features of old Etruscan sculpture seem to have come to life again, overshadowing even his affinity with Rodin, Rosso and Martini who influenced him in his youth. With his portraits ('Stravinsky'), female dancers and riders, of

316. MARCKS, *The Man of Sorrows. Figure from the church of St Catherine, Lübeck. Ceramic*

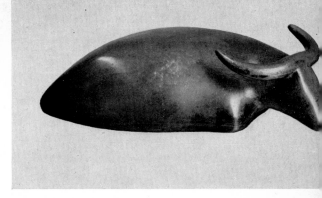

which especially the latter sometimes add an almost aggressive expressiveness to the customary severity of his forms, he ranks among the most significant sculptors of the present age. Apart from his over-all control of large forms Marini is also greatly interested in working on a small scale, animating his surfaces with rough textures and incised lines to give the effect of tattooing, etc. To heighten his effects he often paints his sculptures, including his bronzes. Since 1940 he has been a teacher at the Brera Academy in Milan. (Ill. 301)

MARQUET, ALBERT (1875–1947). A French painter from Bordeaux who numbered Matisse among his early friends in Paris but did not participate in the latter's turbulent Fauve period. To his atmospheric landscapes Marquet lent a Late-Impressionist tonality. He found his subjects mainly along the Seine and in international ports such as Algiers, Naples, Stockholm and Hamburg.

MARSH, REGINALD (1898–1954), was perhaps America's most prolific painter of the 20th century. He painted more than 1,000 paintings and produced an undisclosed number of drawings, nearly all of them of New York City. Marsh strove to do for modern New York what William Hogarth had done for 18th-century London: to record the era. He was born in Paris, the son of artists. Whereas his compatriot, John Koch, has shown the glossy side of New York, Marsh concentrated on the rough and seamy (e. g. 'Why Not Use The 'L'?' and 'Negroes On Rockaway Beach'), and he was not above exaggerating his subjects on occasion and stooping to meaningless superficiality.

MASEREEL, FRANS (born 1889). A Belgian by birth and a painter as well as a writer, Masereel is at his best with woodcuts in which illustration is treated in an Expressionist manner. These reveal his remarkable inventive powers as well as his brilliant and appropriate handling of the medium.

MASSON, ANDRÉ (born 1896). This French painter, who lives in Provence, was a Surrealist and member of André Breton's circle. His later work is sometimes in the Expressionist, sometimes in the calligraphic style. Apart from an erotic symbolism he also makes frequent use of bird and plant motifs.

MATARÉ, EWALD (born 1887). German artist. Originally a painter and pupil of Corinth, he continued to produce water colours and coloured woodcuts even after turning to sculpture in 1918. In both fields he has concentrated mainly on animals which he reduces to their basic forms. His work includes the new doors for Cologne Cathedral (1949). He was until 1954 a professor at the Düsseldorf Academy. (Ill. 317)

MATISSE, HENRI (1869–1954). This French painter has played a vital part in gaining a new freedom for 20th-century art and, more particularly, colour. This he used almost without reference to subject, applying it in pure, strong hues. In the creation of space, too, he no longer relied on conventional perspective as this

would have broken up the surface unity which he tried to achieve, but came to depend more and more on colour. Although he derived from Cézanne in this respect, Matisse's work is distinguished by its luminous colours which in his years as leader of the Fauves (q. v.) became even more vibrant. Intensity of expression was, however, only a passing phase with him. He tried to guide his art more and more towards 'balance, purity and moderation', comparing it to an easy chair in which one could relax. Thus in his painting – of women, flowers and fruit – he created beauty of a high decorative order, while professedly seeking to express joy. Matisse's influence was widespread and he had many followers outside France. His graphic work, too, and his drawing which relied on pure, unbroken line had a marked influence all over the world. But his serious and noble nature also fitted him for work on a more monumental scale, shown by the murals he carried out for the Barnes Foundation (1930) and, towards the end of his life, by the wall decorations and stained glass for the chapel at Vence (1949–51). He was over eighty when he discovered yet another new representational medium: large collage decorations in which objects were reduced to pictorial symbols in the most logical way. Matisse was born at Cateau (northern France) and when he was not travelling (he went to Germany, Spain, Russia, America and Tahiti), lived in Paris and Nice (ill. p. 471).

MENDELSOHN, ERICH (1887–1953). Architect, and one of the leaders of the New Objectivity (q. v.) in Germany, to which, after his early imaginative and original phase ('Einsteinturm', Potsdam) he turned after coming into contact with the Dutch Stijl group. He emigrated to the USA in 1933 and there became one of the leading industrial architects.

METZINGER, JEAN (born 1883). French painter, born in Nantes. He joined forces with Cubism (q. v.) as early as 1910 and substantially participated in its development right up to the final stage in which still-life themes, still strictly subordinated to the laws of shallow surface composition, were treated in heightened colours. Metzinger now lives in Paris.

MEYER-AMDEN, OTTO (1885–1933). This Swiss painter studied with Hoelzel in Stuttgart 1909–1912 and developed his abstract, non-representational style. Later he tried to blend this with his mythical and religious attitude to life.

MIES VAN DER ROHE, LUDWIG (born in Aachen in 1886). This German architect was a pupil of Bruno Paul and an assistant to Peter Behrens. In 1921–25 while working for the 'Novembergruppe', Mies van der Rohe abandoned Neo-Classicism in favour of houses designed as machines for living. He designed five projects in which he emphasised flowing space instead of confining such space within the normal cube-like room shapes. Under the influence of the Dutchman Berlage, he also came to believe that the elements used in a building should be emphasised in its construction. These are ideas he carried into all his later work. In 1927 he was put in charge of the Weissenhof Settlement in Stuttgart, a model housing project in which famous architects from all over the world participated and which for the first time applied steel construction to domestic building. In 1929 he designed the Barcelona Pavillon, using his theories of free-floating space. Later he became the most consistent exponent of glass and steel-frame construction. Director of the Bauhaus (q. v.) from 1930–33, he emigrated to Chicago in 1938. Here he built the Farnsworth house, a glass building raised off the ground and designed to cage space and yet to give a feeling of weightlessness. Since 1946, he has been the head of the architectural department of the Illinois Institute of Technology. His latest work, in collaboration with Philip Johnson, is the striking Seagram Building in New York. (Ill. 279)

MILLES, CARL (1875–1955). Popular Swedish sculptor and creator of many decorative memorials ('Sun Singer'), fountains (Triton Fountain) and statues. In 1932 he went to America to take up a post as professor of sculpture at the Cranbrook Academy in Michigan.

MINNE, GEORG (1866–1941). A Belgian sculptor whose mystical nature led him to renounce naturalism at an early stage. In his sculpture, mostly of slender young male and female figures, he combines the purity

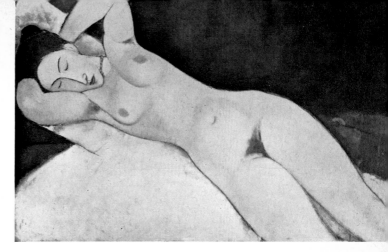

319. MODIGLIANI, *Reclining nude*

of line characteristic of Art Nouveau (q. v.) with the aims of Early Expressionism. His work impresses by virtue of the deep sincerity and complete individuality it reveals.

MIRÓ, JOAN (born in 1893). A follower of van Gogh in his youth, this Spanish painter practised Dadaism for a time and belonged to André Breton's Surrealist circle. He has designed costumes and décor for the Diaghilev Ballet (with Max Ernst) and the Ballets Russes de Monte Carlo. Important exhibitions of his work have been held in Paris and New York. His own characteristic and now world-famous style did not emerge until the 'forties. In this, Miró went right back to the origins of arts as manifested in the work of primitive peoples, Indians, Eskimos and children. But he brought to it an artist's instinct sharpened by many years of practice. With childish and naïve assurance he set down his hieroglyphs and pictorial symbols: different signs for the sun, the moon, plants, animals and man, applied in strokes and spots and with strong primary colours of yellow, red and blue, preferably on a green or black ground. In his pictorial conception and the endeavour to create out of pure contemplation Miró is related to Paul Klee. But in character their work is entirely different. Miró is a monumental artist who, unlike Klee, prefers to work on a large scale. Furthermore, his ideograms, which seem to spring from some dim primeval past, often have a sharp, direct and cruel quality. In this respect Miró is closer to his compatriot Picasso who, like him, seems to have something of the ancient Spanish-Catalonian inheritance in his blood. (Ill. 318)

MODERSOHN-BECKER, PAULA (1876–1907). A German painter who helped German art to break with Impressionism and the tradition of lyrical naturalism, thus being the first to prepare the way for Expressionism (q. v.). A member of the artists' colony at Worpswede, she was friendly with Rilke (whose portrait she painted) and married the Worpswede painter Otto Modersohn. In order to see Worpswede in the right perspective she went to Paris five times and was deeply affected by her contact with Cézanne and Gauguin. As a result her art underwent a complete change and her passion for 'great simplicity of form' was kindled. In her still-lifes and portraits, especially, she

318. MIRÓ, *Acrobats in the night-garden*

495

has left some masterpieces which express her clear artistic vision, cut short by her early death. Her letters and diaries, which are a moving tribute to her profound humanity, are also invaluable for the light they shed on the state of art at that time. (Ill. p. 445)

MODIGLIANI, AMADEO (1884–1920). This Italian painter was the son of poor Jewish parents. At the age of twenty-two he went to Paris where he lived a restless and tragic life among a small circle of devoted friends (Kisling, Pascin, Soutine) in Montmartre, finally dying of tuberculosis. His grave and sensitive female nudes and his melancholy portraits reveal the influence of Cézanne and Negro sculpture, absorbed and transformed by his unique genius. True to the central Italian tradition and like its earlier exponent Botticelli, he placed greater emphasis on the melody of line than the harmony of colours. This endeavour to express the tangible reality of forms finds even more direct expression in some of his sculptures ('Head of a Woman', Tate Gallery, London), which he created under the influence of Brancusi, than in his drawing. (Ill. 319)

MOHOLY-NAGY, LÁSLÓ (1895–1946). A Hungarian, he took up painting and other experimental Constructivist art forms in about 1920, as a result of his meeting with Malevich and Lissitzky. His media included photography and films. Invited to join the Bauhaus (q. v.) in 1923, he became one of its most influential teachers, especially in the field of industrial design, architecture, typography and poster art. In 1934 he emigrated to Amsterdam, whence he moved on to London (1935) and Chicago (1937). There he founded the New Bauhaus (later the Institute of Design).

MONDRIAN, PIET (1872–1944). This Dutch painter was the chief representative of the Constructivist (q. v.) movement and its most consistent and sensitive exponent. He began his career as a landscape painter but on going to Paris in 1912 he came under the influence of Cubism (q. v.). After 1914, when he was back in Holland, he began to produce pictures made up of vertical and horizontal lines rhythmically distributed on a neutral (grey or ochre) background. In 1917, together with van Doesburg, he founded the magazine 'De Stijl' and became the progenitor of neo-Plasticism (q. v.). This established a severe and formal style resting on the dualism of simple vertical and horizontal units in black on a white ground, with the addition of a few primary colours. It depended entirely on the harmonious balance of proportions which were considered the fundamental requisite of visual representation. In this respect neo-Plasticism was also of immense significance to modern architecture and has had a profound effect on our surroundings generally. After 1940, when Mondrian emigrated to America, his painting (Boogie-Woogie series) lost some if its static severity and began to admit stronger rhythmic effects to compensate for his earlier rigid exclusion of all individual sentiment. (Ill. p. 505)

MOORE, HENRY (born 1898). English sculptor, born in Yorkshire and trained at the Leeds School of Art and the Royal College, London. One of the greatest living exponents of modern sculpture, he has shown the most profound grasp of the problems that confront this art to-day; he has, furthermore, proved his genius for sensing and expressing the complex inner relationship of their various aspects. In his early phase he sought to win back for sculpture the effect of square mass and 'block rhythms' in a style whose forms were not unrelated to Egyptian and Mexican sculpture. Realizing how vastly important in a work of art is the actual material used, he has explored the potentialities of stone, wood and bronze with equal sensibility. The inclusion of space, which has been the main concern of modern sculpture has also found an eloquent advocate in Moore, who said that the first time he pierced a hole through a stone was a revelation to him. He represents the mass-space relationship in a number of ways: in closely-knit groups ('Mother and Child'; 'Family Group'); in more loosely connected figural or abstract shapes; in hollowed-out mass (core-shell relationship); or in the stringed concave figure ('The Bride'). He is a master of massive sculpture in the round and stresses the three-dimensional quality in order to give his work increased vitality (cf. p. 464). Moore has also done some remarkable drawings and gouache paintings (his shelter scenes during the Second World War). Ill. 15–17

MORANDI, GIORGIO (born 1890). An Italian painter whose work does not follow any one school. He was born in Bologna, which he has never left. There, with care and patience, he composes his still-lifes consisting of a few bottles and bowls, seeking like Cézanne some middle way between faithful description and the autonomous laws of pictorial composition. The severe tectonic ordering of his pictures is softened by gentle and lyrical colours. Morandi's work, which seems to be imbued with the same kind of Italian humanism that we find in the art of Giotto or Piero della Francesca, has won him a considerable reputation.

MOSES, GRANDMA (real name Anna Mary Robertson). America's most famous contemporary naïve painter. A farmer's wife, born in 1860, she did not begin to paint until her seventy-seventh year. Since then she has produced a large number of lively pictures of rural life with a strong anecdotal interest. Her work is now extremely popular. It has been reproduced on textiles and Christmas cards and her paintings have been shown at the Museum of Modern Art in New York.

MOTHERWELL, ROBERT (born 1915). Critic, lecturer and editor, as well as one of the important Abstract-Expressionists, Motherwell has succeeded in clarifying the often irrational theoretical verbalizations of contemporary painters, thereby establishing himself as a high priest of American Abstract art. Born in Aberdeen, Washington, he began painting seriously at an early age. Upon graduating from Stanford, he studied

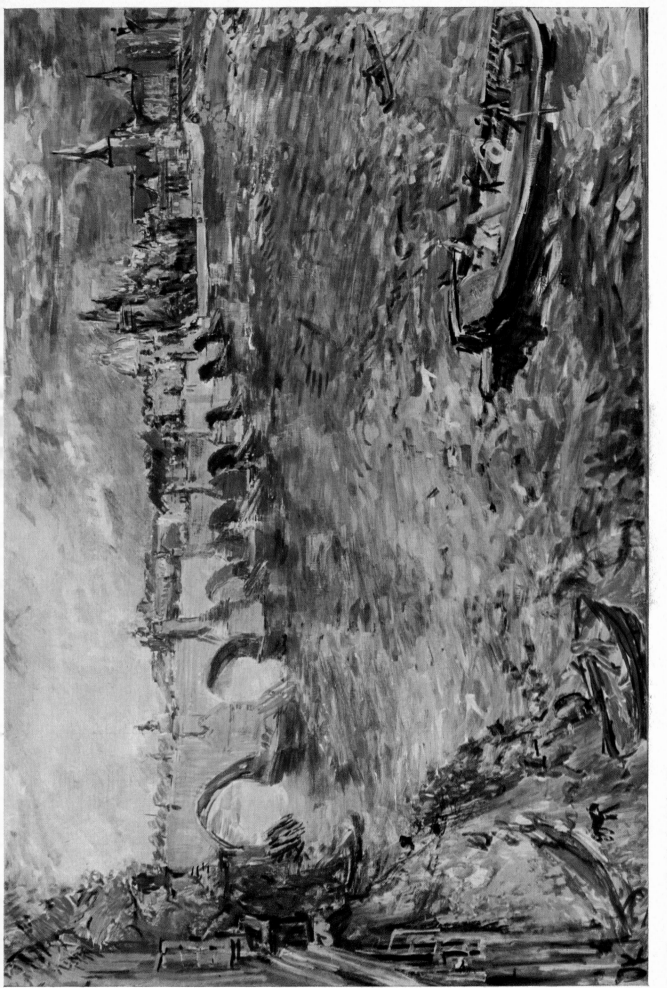

OSKAR KOKOSCHKA: The Charles Bridge, Prague

MAX BECKMANN: Self-portrait with Sculpture

philosophy at Harvard, aesthetics with David Prall. After a year's study in Paris, he began in 1938, while in Mexico with Roberto Matta, the Chilean Surrealist and architect, to work in 'automatic Abstract art'. Since Motherwell believes that 'drawing is a matter of internal rhythm', he does not work from models. His large canvases entrust their major effects to hypnotic symbolism, the language of the subconscious.

MUELLER, OTTO (1874–1930). A German painter from Silesia, who trained as a lithographer. His coloured work in this medium includes a series on gipsy life which, because of his own gipsy ancestry, he could depict with sympathy. In 1910, when he was in Berlin, he became a member of the *Brücke* (q. v.), where his subdued use of colour (he liked to work in tempera on canvas) relates him most closely to Heckel.

MUNCH, EDVARD (1863–1944). A Norwegian painter who, like Cézanne, Gauguin and van Gogh, was one of the pioneers of modern painting. His own natural disposition and the atmosphere of misfortune and misery in which he grew up made him see life as a constant threat, a war of the sexes, a long-drawn-out tale of sickness and death. It was beyond the scope of Impressionism, which was in its heyday when Munch first went to Paris in 1885, to give expression to such feelings. But by some fortunate chance the young painter met van Gogh who was then completely unknown and made a deep impression on him. An exhibition of Munch's works in Berlin in 1892, which caused a public scandal, already showed Expressionist features, and later his paintings took on a more direct form of expression in which emotional states were revealed by means of colour and form alone (e. g. the crashing diagonals in 'Fear', the flame-like white spot in 'The Cry', and the black tree-tops in 'Threat'). In this respect his art was completely original. After he had recovered from a nervous breakdown in 1908, Munch's painting became lighter. The figures in his murals at Oslo University (1909–1915) are surmounted by a giant sun. The next three years, which he spent in seclusion on his Norwegian farm, avoiding all contact with people, found him using the wonderful Northern landscape as his predominant theme. Munch had a considerable influence on German Expressionism (q. v.) in its various forms – as manifested in the work of Emil Nolde or that of the *Brücke* (q. v.). The revival and revitalization of the woodcut and other branches of the graphic arts, too, owes much to his efforts. (Ill. p. 440)

NABIS. The Hebrew word for 'prophet'. The name was assumed by a group of artists who incorporated Symbolist and decorative aims in a Post-Impressionist style of painting. The chief inspiration of this group (consisting of the painters Bonnard, Vuillard, Maurice Denis, Vallotton, Roussel, and the sculptor Maillol) was Gauguin, personally known to Paul Sérusier, who was its originator in 1889. The Nabis were also connected with the journal *Revue Blanche,* which was a

320. PAUL NASH, *Pillar and Moon*

platform for the literary symbolism of such writers as Mirbeau, Fénéon, Fagus and Apollinaire. The painters found their spokesman in Maurice Denis. The group broke up, however, in 1897 after Bonnard and Vuillard had already left it. (Cf. ill. p. 438, 462)

NASH, PAUL (1889–1946). An English painter of international standing. He was trained at Chelsea Polytechnic and in the years after the First World War, when he was made an official war artist, gradually evolved his own highly individual style, in which landscape subjects predominated. In his work the tendency towards simplification and emphasis on geometric design ('design considered as a structural pursuit'), which owed something to Cubist influence and persisted all his life, was blended with a touch of Surrealism into a poetic and dreamlike vision of nature, rendered in cool but delicate colours. He was at his best as a landscape painter in water colour or oils, whether depicting the *genius loci* of some part of southern England or placing an object (a pillar, a fallen tree trunk, a wrecked aeroplane) in mysterious juxtaposition with a landscape setting. In his own words, he was constantly trying to 'find new symbols to express our reaction to environment'. Many of Nash's aims are expressed in the manifestoes issued when in 1933 he formed 'Unit One', an uncompromisingly English movement joined by painters, architects and sculptors. Nash, whose brother John is almost equally well-known as a landscape painter, also produced still-lifes and, especially during the earlier part of his career, theatre designs, textiles, wood-engravings and book illustrations. He was again made an official war artist in the Second World War. (Ill. 320)

NAY, ERNST WILHELM. A German painter, born in Berlin in 1902 and a pupil of Carl Hofer, whose early style relates him to Edvard Munch. He only turned to abstract painting after 1945, and in their violent colours and splintery forms these works are even more 'expressionistic' than his Norwegian pictures of the Lofotens. Since 1950 his palette has become lighter and his paintings have acquired a restful and harmonious quality. (Ill. p. 511)

NEO-PLASTICISM is a Dutch geometric-abstract movement in painting, sculpture and the applied arts. It was begun by Mondrian who during the years 1912

499

to 1914 systematically carried the earliest Cubist compositions to their logical conclusion and painted pure form and pure colour. His work had far-reaching effects on modern art, not only on painting and design but also on architecture. He himself wrote, 'neo-Plasticism both in painting and the plastic arts has its own inner laws and may be considered as preparing the way for the architecture of the future.' In 1915 Mondrian's principles were adopted by van Doesburg and Bart von der Leck and in 1917 van Doesburg founded the periodical 'De Stijl' which became the rallying point of the neo-Plasticists. They included Cok, Oud, Huszar, Wils, Rietveld, van Estered and Vordemberge. Their aim was to influence and transform life by means of art and architecture, and it was the reforming character of neo-Plasticism that utterly differentiated it from Cubism which was exclusively concerned with formal values.

NERVI, PIER LUIGI (born 1891). The work of Nervi, an Italian-born architect and engineer who is one of the greatest contemporary masters of concrete construction, is related in spirit to the work of Freyssinet, Perret and Maillart. He introduced new ways to vault vast open spaces with his ribbed, reticulated and corrugated systems of reinforced concrete, from which have emerged wonderful forms and patterns (half-spirals, trapezoids, Y-shapes; audaciously cantilevered roofs and tiers) which are based on an equilibrium of stress and tension and which employ gracefully soaring buttresses as supports. Among his many daring and original works are the Stadium at Florence, the Hangars at Orbetello, the Exhibition Halls at Turin, the UNESCO building in Paris (designed in collaboration with Breuer and Zehrfuss), the Pirelli Office Block in Milan, the Tortona Saltwarehouse, the Military Academy Swimming Pool of Livorno, the State factory at Bologna and the Kursaal Restaurant.

NESCH, ROLF, was born in Oberesslingen, Germany, in 1893. Since 1945, he has become internationally known as a graphic artist, working mainly in colour. He produces his effects by combining bits of wire, iron rings, gauze and other materials into grotesque shapes which he then welds on to a plate (montage printing). Since 1933 Nesch has lived in Norway, first in Oslo and, since 1951, in Aal.

NEUTRA, RICHARD (born 1892). A Viennese architect who emigrated to the USA as early as 1923. Like Frank Lloyd Wright he is particularly interested in integrating the modern dwelling, especially the private house, into the surrounding landscape. He has made extensive use of large areas of glass walling and of the balloon-frame skeleton (houses in Texas and southern California) to achieve elegance, light and a feeling of lightness. His concern with the individual requirements of each house is in direct opposition to any tendencies towards standardization in modern architecture.

NEW OBJECTIVITY, THE. The term 'Die Neue Sachlichkeit' was first used in 1924 by Dr Hartlaub, Director of the Mannheim Art Gallery, to describe a new tendency of realism with a social flavour in German art. 'Die Neue Sachlichkeit', or the New Objectivity, reflected conditions at the end of the First World War and during the early post-war period: it expressed on the negative side disillusionment, cynicism and despair, on the positive side 'enthusiasm for immediate reality – the result of a desire to take things entirely objectively on a material basis without immediately investing them with ideal implications.' The extremes of the negative side were represented by the Verist painters (Georges Grosz, Otto Dix, Max Beckmann in his early work) who voiced their feelings of disgust with contemporary life in a clinically detailed realism that was often shocking and brutal. The characteristic dry, matter-of-fact style of the New Objectivity artists, their rendering of subjects on a small scale and observed at close range, was also in a way a reaction against the vast generalities, powerful emotions and religious intensity of the Expressionists. After its early phase of political and social criticism the New Objectivity continued in various guises both in art and literature right until the beginning of the Nazi régime.

NEW REALISM. The name given by certain critics to a group of young artists who do not paint abstracts or conventional landscapes, flower pieces and still-lifes, but concentrate on their immediate environment. This sometimes, but by no means always, includes sinks, wash-basins, dustbins or kitchen tables crowded with groceries, so that the English members of this group have been labelled the Social Realists and the 'Kitchen Sink' school, while their American counterparts have been called the 'Ashcan' school. Their pictures and their subject matter reflect the mood of the decade 1950–60 just as clearly as Abstract-Expressionism. The principal New Realist painters include John Bratby, Jack Smith and Edward Middleditch in England; Reyberolle, Mineaux and their followers in France. All these painters share with the abstract painters of their generation, such as Sam Francis and De Kooning, the urge to work on a large scale. Size is necessary and significant for them, though there is no obvious explanation for this.

NICHOLSON, BEN (born 1894). English abstract painter and son of Sir William Nicholson. Having made Cubism (q. v.) its starting point, his art was much influenced and enriched by Piet Mondrian. His pictures and coloured geometric reliefs have made him the chief representative of non-figurative painting in England. Nicholson lives in Cornwall.

NICHOLSON, SIR WILLIAM (1872–1949). This English artist was born in Newark-on-Trent. A successful and popular painter of portraits and still-lifes, he has also achieved international fame as a graphic artist, and the posters which he and James Pryde produced under the name of 'The Beggarstaffs' heralded the modern idiom even before 1900.

NOLDE, EMIL (real name Emil Hansen, 1867–1956). German artist born in Nolde, near the Danish frontier, of old peasant stock. The importance of his contribution to modern art lies in his 'emancipated colour', intensified to serve as a vehicle for expressing basic emotions. The turning point in his career came in 1906 when he met Munch and was invited to join the Brücke (q. v.). He stayed with the group for a year but, partly as a result of visiting Paris, was already evolving a style of his own in the form of an Impressionism with heightened colours and affinities with van Gogh. After 1908/09 his work took on a new monumentality. This was the period of his religious paintings, the most important works in German Expressionism (q. v.): the triptych of 'St Mary of Egypt' (1912), 'The Entombment' (1915) and others. In these pictures distortion of physical features to portray spiritual agony took on a new intensity. A journey to the South Seas (1913/14) provided fresh material for the primitive expressiveness of his art. His subjects at this time included landscapes, seascapes, social satire and flowers. He also produced hundreds of water colours which, though more transparent than his oils, showed the same concentrated energy of violent colours. Parallel with all this his graphic output increased and included woodcuts, etchings and coloured lithographs. (Ill. p. 450)

O'KEEFFE, GEORGIA (born 1887). She was discovered by the sensitive and sophisticated Alfred Stieglitz who, in 1916, was busy introducing Cézanne, Toulouse-Lautrec, Rodin and Matisse to a slowly awakening US. Born in Sun Prairie, Wisconsin, Miss O'Keeffe has spent much of her life in the Southwest, which serves as the subject of many of her landscapes. She studied at the Art Institute in Chicago, the Art Students League in New York, and the University of Virginia. In the 1920's she abandoned Abstraction to develop an immaculate Cubist-Realist style, intensely Puritanical in its sharpness and bareness. Miss O'Keeffe, who is America's most important woman painter after Mary Cassatt, is most famous for her enlarged and realistic flower studies (lilies, irises and hollyhocks), which are done in brilliant colours and are often surrounded by whitened, surgically-pared bones and skulls. The backgrounds sometimes reveal the New Mexican mountains that she loves so well, and where she now lives.

OUD, JACOBUS JOHANNES PIETER (born 1890). Dutch architect. He became a member of the constructivist Stijl group in Holland and has done especially good work with modern blocks of flats and terrace houses in which logical planning is combined with a simple elegance of form (Weissenhof Settlement, Stuttgart; terrace houses in Hook of Holland). From 1918 to 1933 he was chief architect of the city of Rotterdam where he supervised an extensive programme for the building of dwelling-houses. He is now practising as an architect in Wassenaar (Holland).

OZENFANT, AMÉDÉE (born 1886). In 1918 this French painter and Le Corbusier drew up the first manifesto of the Purist movement which aimed at ridding Cubism (q. v.) of its decorative elements, and from 1921 until 1925 the two artists edited the famous journal *L'Esprit Nouveau*. Here and elsewhere (London 1935–1938, later in New York) Ozenfant distinguished himself as a writer on the theoretical aspects of art. In New York he became the director of a well-known art school. Some large murals in the Musée de l'Art Moderne in Paris are among the outstanding examples of his work as a painter.

PASCIN, JULES (real name Julius Pincas, 1885–1930). Like Toulouse-Lautrec, Pascin was a superb draughtsman and found inspiration for his paintings in the life of the cafés. Born into a well-to-do Bulgarian family, Pascin travelled in Austria, Germany, Paris and America, eventually settling down in the Paris of the 1920's. Most of his paintings were produced after 1920. Prone to work in environments of confusion and disorder, Pascin nevertheless painted with an authority and charm that recalls the masters of the 18th century, who appealed to him. His 'Prodigal Son', 'The Judgment of Solomon' and 'Salome' express a personal mysticism strangely blended with eroticism. He drew through sheets of carbon paper to obtain his nervous, linear rhythms and contours. Although success had already come to him, Pascin was found hanged in his studio in the summer of 1930.

PAUL, BRUNO (born 1874). This German artist began as an illustrator for *Simplizissimus* and in the later phases of the *Jugendstil* (see Art Nouveau) turned to furniture design, finding inspiration in the honest and craftsmanlike traditions of the Biedermeier style. He was the first artist to design factory-made furniture. Paul also did some important work on the interior decoration of ships. He now lives in Düsseldorf.

PECHSTEIN, MAX (1881–1955). A German painter who joined the *Brücke* (q. v.) at Dresden in 1906 and became its most easily intelligible and least troubled representative. In 1911, having been president of the *Neue Sezession* in Berlin for a year, he was responsible for the group's move to the capital. His love for the art of the primitive peoples, which he shared with other Expressionists, took Pechstein to the South Pacific in 1914 and during these years he did his best work. Later his creative powers waned noticeably.

PERMEKE, CONSTANT (1886–1951), was the earliest and most powerful of the Belgian Expressionist painters. At his happiest when working on a large scale, his painting is unpolished but sincere. His subjects include peasants and fishermen of a rudimentary type recalling the Flemish Baroque, seascapes and harbour scenes composed in a simple, unsophisticated manner. Permeke worked in Antwerp, Ostend, and Jabbeke near Bruges.

PEVSNER, ANTOINE (born 1886). Russian sculptor. After being introduced to Cubism (q. v.) in Paris in 1911, he joined the Constructivist circle of Malevich and Tatlin in Moscow in 1917, together with his brother

Naum Gabo. From that time on both brothers became interested in three-dimensional construction, sometimes based on algebraic formulae, and the use of such synthetic materials as plexiglass. Pevsner later left Russia, going first to Berlin, then to Paris where, since 1946, he has been one of the leading members of the 'Salon des Réalités Nouvelles'. (Ill. 296)

PICABIA, FRANCIS (1878–1953), was a Spanish artist who lived in Paris, New York and Barcelona. In the course of his life he sampled Impressionism and Cubism, was one of the most inventive Dadaist and Surrealist artists and painted both in the abstract and representational manner. Himself a gifted painter, his significance lies mainly in his ability to stimulate ideas in others. Hans Arp said of him that he was the Christopher Columbus of art but that he sailed without a compass.

PICASSO, PABLO, was born in 1881 in Malaga, Spain. Although he has now lived in France for fifty years, Picasso has never disguised his Spanish origin in his art. The world's most famous contemporary painter, he has embraced a whole range of artistic influences in his time, from primitive art to the work of Ingres and Delacroix. His unique genius has, however, given an individual stamp to everything he has done. Picasso was a child prodigy who at the age of fourteen was already producing work of exhibition standard, painted in the style of the Old Masters. His first original phase, known as the 'Blue Period', began soon after 1900 and lasted until 1904. The paintings of this time were characterized by their deep blue background colour which lent such themes as poverty, loneliness and anguish ('The Tippler') symbolic overtones. In his 'Pink Period' (1905/06) the mood softened to one of gentle melancholy (families of acrobats, young female nudes on rose or terra-cotta backgrounds). Although these works were much admired, Picasso did not hesitate to change his style abruptly after coming into contact with the forceful idiom of Negro masks. From these he learned the power of expression that lay in distortion and departure from natural representation. In 1907 he painted 'The Young Ladies of Avignon' (New York), a milestone in the history of art in that this picture, which outraged public opinion, already foreshadowed Cubism (q. v.). In the years that followed, he and Braque, basing their discoveries on a study of Cézanne, systematically explored the path leading to this goal. Picasso's shabby studio, the Bateau-Lavoir in Montmartre, became the focal point of the movement. After 1917 he admitted another pictorial world besides that of Cubism, suggested by the work of Ingres and based once more on natural appearances, harmony and delight in living. This was the beginning of his Classical Period which lasted from 1920–1925 (subjects – Mother and Child, Women Bathers). Around 1930 his work showed the influence of Surrealism (q. v.) and at the same time his Spanish Expressionism manifested itself again in the form of violent distortion. The miseries of the Spanish Civil War and the general atmosphere of foreboding in the 'thirties found expression in his vast 'Guernica' (1937), a painting whose symbolism was meant to shock and serve as a warning against terrorism, violence and war. Picasso remained in Paris until the end of the Second World War and created his over-life-size sculpture of 'The Man with a Lamb'. Then, bidding Paris farewell with some paintings of the city, he moved to the south of France (Antibes, Vallauris). Here a new spirit of joy entered his art ('La Joie de Vivre: a Pastoral Scene'), expressed in paintings, sculptures, lithographs and ceramics in their thousands. He continued to paint landscapes, still-lifes and portraits in which his children and their mother formed a recurrent theme. His picture 'The Korean Massacres' shows him making a protest against that war, while in two giant paintings of Peace and War, executed in 1953 for a chapel ceiling, he uses a monumental symbolic Expressionism to show human existence vacillating between the two extremes of happiness and shame. Picasso has had the most profound influence on 20th-century painting. Whether we admire or intensely dislike his work, we cannot ignore it. (Ill. 287, p. 506)

PIPER, JOHN (born 1903). This English painter became well-known during the Second World War with his vivid and poetic pictures of bombed and ruined buildings. After an early abstract phase he turned back more and more to the English romantic landscape tradition. He is especially fond of architectural themes and has also done some highly imaginative designs for the stage.

PISIS, FILIPPO DE (1896–1956). A popular and prolific Italian painter, whose favourite themes are landscapes and portraits which he paints in a loose Impressionist style.

POLIAKOFF, SERGE. Russian painter, born in Moscow in 1906. Since 1924 he has lived in Paris, where he is now one of the most successful abstract painters. Although he uses simple geometric forms he does not, like the Constructivists, sacrifice either the personal quality of paint applied in rough brush-strokes or the pleasant effects produced by the materials used.

POLLOCK, JACKSON (1912–1956). A leading, if not *the* leading exponent of the New York school of Abstract-Expressionism, Pollock achieved wide fame throughout his native US and throughout Europe by means of his unique technique of dripping paint on to unstretched canvases which he tacked either to a wall or to a floor and worked at from all sides – thereby, he said, achieving an otherwise impossible intimacy with his work. He developed his abstract style in the mid-1940's, and soon his work achieved the wild, violent appearance of swirling, non-representational, labyrinthine patterns which became his unmistakable trademark. Born in Cody, Wyoming, Pollock first studied under Thomas Hart Benton and, later, at the Art Students League in New York. (Ill. p. 512)

Georges Braque: Still-life

Fernand Léger: Yellow Flowers

PIET MONDRIAN: Tableau I

PABLO PICASSO: Landscape

PORTINARI, CANDIDO (born 1903). The fame of this Brazilian painter has spread to Europe. In his work, including his vast murals, he always takes reality as a starting point (e. g. life among the people on the outskirts of Rio de Janeiro). Thereafter it undergoes a metamorphosis in which muted colours and stylization reminiscent of Egyptian and prehistoric times evoke different worlds and ages. One might apply the term 'magic realism' to his art.

PRAMPOLINI, ENRICO (1894–1956). An Italian painter who belonged to the Futurist (q. v.) movement and added a large number of his own manifestoes to those published officially.

RAY, MAN (born 1890). This Philadelphia-born painter and photographer was among the founders of the Dadaist (q. v.) movement in New York, working predominantly in the photographic medium. Between 1921 and 1940 he lived in Paris where he was one of the most admired avant-garde photographers. After his return to America (he now lives in Hollywood) he again took up painting. Ray's work also includes a number of Surrealist films.

REDON, ODILON (1840–1916). A French painter, who always relied more on the world of dreams, fantasy and a subjective reinterpretation of reality than on exact observation. For this reason he was an outsider among his own generation of Impressionists and was only fully appreciated by the Post-Impressionists who looked on him as a pioneer and prophet. Redon excels as a colourist (e. g. his much sought-after flower pieces) and as a lithographer ('Dans le Rêve' cycle).

RIVERA, DIEGO (1886–1957). A Mexican painter who, in spite of his European training and contact with Cubism, has preserved the national character of his painting. For the last twenty years he has concentrated on large murals and frescoes in which he combines the artistic traditions of the Maya civilisation with a richly coloured style and revolutionary themes from history.

ROHLFS, CHRISTIAN (1849–1938). The son of a Holstein farmer, this German painter became a teacher at the Academy of Art in Weimar when he was still quite young, later moving to a teaching post at Hagen. Throughout his life he was ever ready to tackle new problems or participate in new discoveries. He went through an Impressionist phase and then joined the Expressionists. Although a whole generation older than they, he became one of their chief representatives, both as a painter and as a graphic artist. His wonderful flower-pieces and visionary townscapes (Soest) relate him to Nolde, with whom he worked for a time and whose robust energy he countered with a more highly refined sense of colour. This found its full fruition in the sublime water colours and pastels of his old age.

ROSZAK, THEODORE (born 1910). Roszak began as a painter of the Romantic-Realist school of Bellows and Luks, moved on into the Surrealism of de Chirico, and, in his search for the relation between form and content, finally ended a sculptor. By 1930 he had become a disciple of Constructivism and the belief in the importance of the artist as a leader in the modern industrial world. In this style he created 'Chrysalis', a machine-like and perfectly balanced work. From here his work became more and more Expressionistic, as exemplified by such titles as 'Anguish' and 'Surge', and it is only with his later style that he finds the correct blend between formal Constructivism and Abstract-Expressionism which for him integrates form and content. His most notable type of sculpture in this recent period is that in which he uses a crescent shape opposed by a mass of jagged projections, as in 'The Spectre of Kitty Hawk'. He likes to work mainly with welded metal.

ROUAULT, GEORGES (1871–1958). Though he lived and died in Paris, Rouault appears as an isolated figure in French art. Whilst he was strongly influenced by Daumier and although he did for a time become a Fauvist (q. v.), his pessimistic, serious and religious nature was basically not in harmony with the decorative tendencies of that movement. Temperamentally he can more easily be related to the German Expressionism of the *Brücke* (q. v.) and the art of Emil Nolde and Max Beckmann. This is true at least of his early period in which he painted human misery, prostitutes, clowns and religious scenes in sombre tones which, with their luminous colours surrounded by broad black outlines, are reminiscent of medieval stained glass windows. Rouault had in fact been trained as a glass painter and restorer and is responsible for the windows in the church at Assy (1948). In his later works, which still deal with the same themes, he expresses compassion rather than protest. His many half-length figures have something of the mystic quality of icon-painting. Rouault's pessimistic nature is also revealed in his graphic work, e. g. his etchings 'Miserere' and 'Guerre', which recalls Goya. (Ill. p. 473)

ROUSSEAU, HENRI (1844–1910). This popular French painter was until 1869 a saxophone player in a military band. In 1871 he became a customs officer (hence the nickname 'Le Douanier'), a post from which he retired in 1885 to devote himself to painting in Paris. A true primitive in the sense that he had a natural bond with painting and was overcome with terror at the sight of the tigers which he painted from memory, he was also a genuine 'naïve' artist whom no teaching could have helped because his rich pictorial imagination was entirely untroubled by any problems. Thus his work came as a revelation to modern art which was just then concerned with exploring the origins of visual representation. Meanwhile Rousseau, with touching innocence, continued to portray his neighbours, the streets of Paris, mysterious jungles, lions and flamingoes, or his allegory of war with its echoes of Uccello. The assurance of his compositions sprang from instinct, his wonderful colour schemes were entirely original. Gauguin, Pissarro, Seurat, Signac,

321. SCHLEMMER, *Interior (Roman figures)*

Léger and many others became his friends. In 1908 Picasso gave his famous banquet in Rousseau's honour. Wilhelm Uhde prepared a monograph about him, while Apollinaire (whose portrait he painted) wrote a poem in charcoal on his tombstone which the sculptor Brancusi engraved in the poet's own handwriting. (Ill. p. 459)

RUSSOLO, LUIGI (1885–1947). Venetian painter and one of the founders and foremost exponents of Futurism (q. v.). He had originally studied music and actually tried to reproduce accoustic effects and screens of sound in painting ('Bruitism').

SCHARFF, EDWIN (1887–1955). Born in Ulm, Scharff is one of the most significant figures in German sculpture, combining in his work monumentality of conception with sensuous warmth (over-life-size sculpture of 'Pandora'). He also distinguished himself as a teacher at the academies of Berlin, Düsseldorf and Hamburg.

322. SHAHN, *'Reconstruction'*

SCHLEMMER, OSKAR (1888–1943). German artist, born in Stuttgart. A pupil of Adolf Hoelzel, he was invited by Gropius in 1920 to become head of the departments of sculpture and scenic design at the Bauhaus (q. v.) in Weimar. His paintings depict people, not unlike Fernand Léger's mechanical puppets in appearance, arranged in choreographic fashion within an organized space. But unlike Léger, Schlemmer invests his world, which lies beyond realism, with more spiritual, strongly romantic features (the artist was once very much influenced by the Romantic painter Philipp Otto Runge). Ill. 321.

SCHMIDT-ROTTLUFF, KARL (born 1884). German painter, born in Rottluff near Chemnitz. He studied architecture in Dresden, like Ernst Ludwig Kirchner and Erich Heckel with whom he founded the *Brücke* (q. v.) in 1905. Schmidt-Rottluff's work stands out in German Expressionism (q. v.) by virtue of its monumental style, shown in cube-like landscape compositions and the angular character of his woodcuts (e. g. the Passion cycle). Later, the heroic mood and violent colours gave way to a more delicate and sensitive approach, as in his water colours of simple landscape details, still-lifes and branches of blossoms. Under the Nazi régime his work was condemned. He was appointed to the Academy of Plastic Arts in Berlin in 1947. (Ill. p. 447)

SCHWITTERS, KURT (1887–1948). Schwitters, whose home was in Hanover, became the leader of German Dadaism (q. v.) in 1920. Keeping up a constant flow of ludicrous nonsense in his periodical *Merz* (1923–1932), his poems of 'Anna Blume' and his lectures 'Sonate in Urlauten', he also revealed before long his serio-comic and genuine artistic talent. This took the form of fanciful and poetic collage pictures which evoke the world of Paul Klee and have recently attracted the attention of art connoisseurs all over the world. Schwitters moved to Norway in 1933, and died in England.

SÉRUSIER, PAUL (1864–1927). A French theorist and painter whose meeting with Gauguin in 1888 provided him with ideas and material that led to the formation of the Nabis (q. v.) in Paris. In his painting he struck a balance between symbolic and ornamental representation. Sérusier published his theories in a book called *ABC de la Peinture*.

SEVERINI, GINO (born 1883). Italian painter from Cortona, who was a Futurist and signed the movement's manifestoes. In his work he combined the aims of Futurism – to represent themes connected with movement – with the *pointillist* technique of Seurat. Later he alternated between abstract art and a representational style in the classical manner. Severini is now director of a school of mosaic in Paris.

SHAHN, BEN (born 1898). An American painter who has become famous for his canvases of social protest, Shahn, who was born in Russia and who grew up in a Brooklyn slum, is a firm believer in harsh realism.

One of his first paintings was 'The Passion of Sacco and Vanzetti' (in which the coffins of the two condemned men lie satirically in front of the judges who sentenced them). Influenced by the French Abstract painters (from whom he learned to flatten his figures, to make full use of the surface of the canvas, and to simplify his forms geometrically), Shahn has been a WPA artist, has done posters and frescoes (and government posters during the Second World War). At times his paintings show their dependence on photographic prototypes (and he does indeed keep a collection of candid camera shots for this purpose), but he is an exceedingly inventive painter, a superb draftsman, and, at times, a lyrical quality is evident in his work. (Ill. 322)

SICKERT, WALTER RICHARD (1860–1942), son and grandson of Danish painters, born in Munich. His mother was English. The family settled in England in 1868 and Sickert studied for a short time at the Slade School, then worked in Whistler's studio. In 1883 he went to Paris where he was chiefly influenced by Degas whose interest in Sickert's work lasted until his death in 1917. Sickert worked principally in London, Dieppe, Venice and at Bath. During the 'nineties he was associated with the founder members of the New English Art Club and later with the Camden Town group which in 1917 was enlarged and re-named the London Group. Sickert represents a link between English and French painting, applying a French technique to the interpretation of dull days and dark interiors in the mean streets where he usually liked to rent rooms. He was skilled in suggesting atmosphere, both mental and physical – generally a disillusioned, if not tragic atmosphere. Among his most personal productions are 'La Giuseppina', 'Resting', and 'The New Bedford'. He is represented in the Tate Gallery by 'Despair', 'Venice and the Old Campanile', 'Dieppe', 'The Café des Tribunaux' and other works. Examples of his work are also in the Luxembourg.

SINTENIS, RENÉE (born 1888). A popular German sculptor who has been professor at the Academy of

323. SINTENIS, *Polo player. Bronze*

Plastic Arts in Berlin since 1947. Her small bronzes recall Rodin's animated style of modelling, while her larger figure sculptures ('Daphne', 1930) and portraits (self-portrait, 1931) evince a considerable depth of feeling. (Ill. 323)

SLOAN, JOHN (1871–1951). A principle member of the famous 'Ashcan' school, Sloan ('McSorley's Bar', 'In The Wake of the Ferry' and 'Back Yards, Greenwich Village') remains truer to the Ashcan credo than does the work of most of the other artists in that school. Born at Lock Haven, Pennsylvania, he studied at the Pennsylvania Academy of the Fine Arts. During his twenties he was illustrating newspapers. Sloan's vintage period as a painter (1900–1912) is characterized by the grey tonalities and gay accents of the Ashcan school, from which he subsequently departed in order to paint more varied subject matter and to work in a higher key. In the 1930's he became involved in problems of form, resulting in many studies of glazed nudes.

SMITH, DAVID (born 1906). A Midwesterner, Smith, who was born in Indiana and who came to New York at the age of twenty-one, is one of the important innovators in contemporary American sculpture, being second only to Calder in point of time. His sculptures, which often show a kinship to modern industrial forms, are generally free-standing, open, mobile-like metal structures, frequently relieved by touches of Surrealism. Originally a painter, Smith began adding wood and other foreign materials to his canvases. In this connection he has written: 'My student period was involved with painting. The painting developed into raised levels from the canvas. Gradually the canvas was the base and the painting was a sculpture.'

SMITH, SIR MATTHEW. Born in 1879 at Halifax, he studied painting at the Manchester School of Art and at the Slade School, after which he went first to Brittany then to Paris, where he joined the school of Matisse. After serving in the First World War, Smith returned to France and lived for the most part in the south. He has settled in England only since the Second World War. He is an outstanding colourist, using glazes as no other modern painter has done. His pictures have the brilliancy, the deep translucency of stained glass. With Matthew Smith colour is not used, as with Cézanne, to create form, but as an end in itself. It is used with a boldness, flourish and variety which make him unique among English painters. His work is further characterized by largeness of scale, audacious simplification and forcefulness of composition; his subjects are limited to flowers, nubile girls, plump fruits and an occasional landscape. He is well represented in the Tate Gallery, London.

SOULAGES, PIERRE (born 1919). One of France's leading abstract painters. Artistically he is related to Hans Hartung and Gérard Schneider but differs from them in that his work is characterized by firmer construction and occasional geometric severity.

509

324. SUTHERLAND, *Entrance to a lane*

SOUTINE, CHAIM (1894–1943). Like Marc Chagall Soutine came from a humble Russian-Jewish background and went to Paris with the help of a small scholarship. There he learnt most from the Old Masters and became an intimate friend of Modigliani. His eerie, visionary landscapes and his touching and melancholy portraits were not properly appreciated until after his death. Since then they have been increasingly and deservedly admired.

SPENCER, STANLEY (born 1892), has lived all his life, except during the four years of the First World War, at Cookham, in Berkshire. He studied at the Slade School from 1910 to 1914. Spencer is a narrative painter, unique to-day, in a subdivision of the greater class to which Giotto belongs. His pictures fall into two groups, those dealing with Bible texts or with private mythologies, such as 'Sarah Tubb and the Heavenly Visitors', and the landscapes, portraits and studies of flowers which are purely documentary statements of fact. What gives Spencer his special flavour is that he interprets the Bible in terms of Cookham. Yet his major work, one of the great creative works of the century, was the result of his experiences as a Red Cross orderly and later as a soldier in Macedonia in the First World War – the paintings in the Memorial Chapel of Burghclere near Newbury, which he finished in 1933. They show soldiers working, digging, map-reading, erecting tents, building dams, folding blankets, washing lockers and finally in the 'resurrection' on the East wall, laying down their burdens, depositing their crosses with Christ and wandering slowly off towards a high distant horizon.

SPRINGER, FERDINAND. Born in 1907 in Berlin, Springer went to Paris and became a French subject. He worked as a graphic artist before turning to abstract painting and four of his engravings illustrating the Tao-te-ching were officially commissioned for tapestries. Springer lives at Grasse near Cannes.

SURREALISM. Surrealist painting sprang from discoveries relating to the hidden desires and unconscious processes of the mind (cf. p. 453). Its forerunners were Metaphysical Painting *(Pittura Metafisica)* as in the work of Giorgio de Chirico and Carlo Carràs, and Dadaism (q. v.). The movement found its literary representative in André Breton, whilst its most notable painters have included Max Ernst, Salvador Dali, Yves Tanguy, Man Ray, and, for a time, Joan Miró and Jean Arp. (Cf. ill. 283, 284, 285, 297, 318, pp. 461, 475)

SUTHERLAND, GRAHAM. English painter born in London in 1903. After training for a year as an engineer in the Midland Railway works at Derby, he went to the Goldsmiths School of Art in London where he began to produce the etchings which were his chief medium for many years. As a painter his style was formed under the influence of William Blake, Samuel Palmer and the Surrealists, and his vision, in conjunction with a deep interest in nature, led to the creation of works of fantasy dominated by plant and insect forms. During the Second World War he painted scenes of devastation and also became interested in the representation of human beings (ironworkers and coal-miners). He has worked on religious wall paintings (church at Northampton, 1944–46), and in recent years has produced several forceful portraits (Sir Winston Churchill, Somerset Maugham, Lord Beaverbrook). His work represented England at the Venice Biennale in 1952.

SYMBOLISM. In its narrower sense a term applied to an artistic movement around 1885–1890 which was concerned not so much with describing things as with hinting at their meaning. In painting, it centred mainly round the Nabis (q. v.) who gathered round Paul Sérusier and Maurice Denis and found inspiration in the work of Puvis de Chavannes; in poetry it was represented by Mallarmé, Valéry, Stefan George and Hofmannsthal, appearing there in a purer form than in painting where there was always the danger of slipping into a decorative or illustrative style. (Ill. p. 462)

TACHISM (Fr. *une tache,* a spot). The name recently given to a form of painting that is not concerned with natural representation or conscious composition and, above all, avoids any suggestion of static construction. Instead, it relies on the more or less unconscious manipulation of colour as a result of the natural movements of the hand. Leading names in Tachism are Wols in France, Pollock and Sam Francis in America, the young Danish painter K. R. H. Sonderborg, and possibly Goetz and Schultze in Germany and Alan Davie in England. The Tachist method is gaining ground, especially among the younger generation. (Ill. p. 512)

TANGUY, YVES (1900–1955). A poetic Surrealist, Tanguy, who was born in Paris but became an American citizen before his death, was a painter of imaginary but precise forms which look as if they come from a dream-world or the depths of the sea. A thoroughly

Ernst Wilhelm Nay: With feathery green

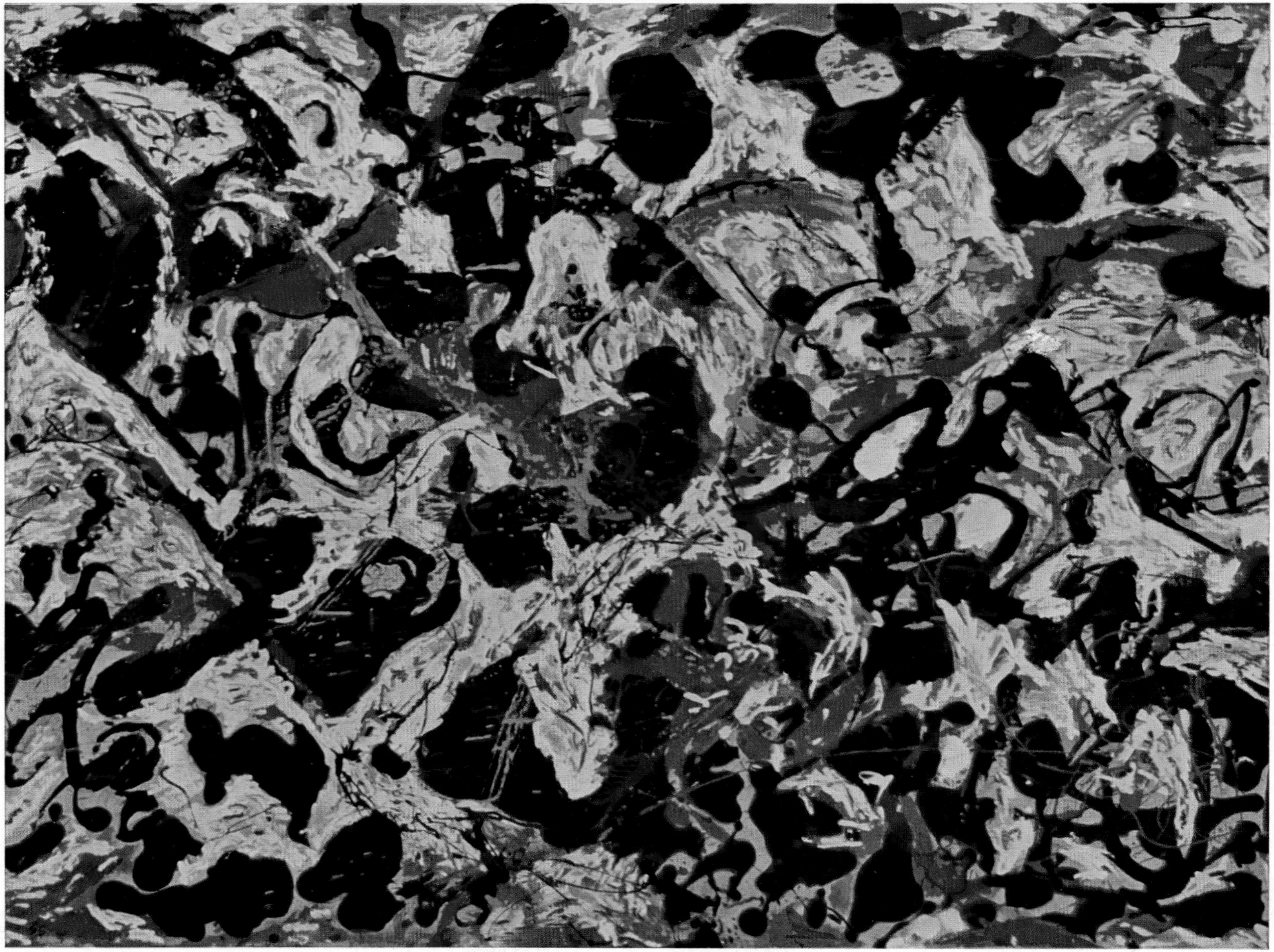

Jackson Pollock: Search

original painter, Tanguy, met the Surrealists in Paris in 1925, and began exhibiting with them. He left Europe in 1939, stayed for a while in California, then settled in Woodbury, Connecticut, where he died.

TATLIN, VLADIMIR. Born in Moscow in 1885, he is one of the first and most important of the Russian Constructivists, and was producing three-dimensional forms in glass, wood and metal as early as 1913. He strongly influenced Antoine Pevsner and Naum Gabo. His best-known work is the design for 'A Monument to the Third International' (1919) which was intended to be more than 1300 ft high and anticipated later wire sculpture. Tatlin lives in Moscow where he is a commercial artist.

TOBEY, MARK (born 1890). At first a Chicago mail-order house catalogue illustrator, Tobey, who was born in Centerville, Wisconsin, left Chicago for New York, then studied in Europe and in the Orient under the Chinese Teng Kwei and finally returned to Seattle to live. Through the Chinese influence he has developed his famous 'white writing', a style of painting which combines occidental art with oriental calligraphy – and which has influenced many subsequent painters. His paintings are, as a result, multiple spaces of dark colours, surrounded by mazes of white lines, the whole being abstract in style and symbolizing, as Tobey believes, 'a higher state of consciousness' which is analogous to the effect of music. Tobey has developed a delicate style admirably suited to the chief inspiration of his paintings: the electricity-bathed nights of American cities.

TOSI, ARTURO (born 1871). Italian landscape painter whose art, like that of Filippo de Pisis, is deeply rooted in the Italian tradition and in Impressionism. The contribution of these artists to modern painting rests in their supreme refinement of painterly means of expression. Tosi's Late-Impressionist work is marked by a delicately poetic and lyrical mood.

UTRILLO, MAURICE (1883–1955). Son of Suzanne Valadon the French painter, and adopted son of the Spaniard, Miguel Utrillo, he is one of the strangest figures in the history of art. Already as a boy he was addicted to alcohol and, until his phenomenal success in the 'twenties, led a dissolute vagabond existence. But in spite of his undisciplined nature, lack of proper training and state of constant dissipation he painted some magnificent pictures at this time. Later, when he became an officer of the Légion d'honneur and a prosperous, respectable citizen, his artistic inspiration rapidly waned. His paintings are related to the Impressionism of Pissarro, but for all their delectable colours and technical sophistication they reveal an element of innocence and naïveté which makes it possible to think of Utrillo as a primitive painter in certain respects. His principal themes are the street corners of Montmartre and the smaller French towns (Villejuif).

VALADON, SUZANNE (1867–1938). French painter and mother of Utrillo. She had been an acrobat and the model of Puvis de Chavannes, Renoir, and Toulouse-Lautrec, when Lautrec and Degas encouraged her to try her hand at drawing and painting. Her pronounced talent for the precise linear interpretation of objects and especially of the female nude also distinguishes her oil paintings which, apart from a certain and possibly coincidental resemblance to Matisse, are entirely original in conception and feeling.

VALLOTTON, FÉLIX (1865–1927). A Swiss painter who moved to Paris in 1882. Interested for a time in the Symbolist movement of the Nabis (q. v.) whom he joined, he later concentrated on nudes and portraits of an almost caustic realism. He also distinguished himself as a graphic artist, especially as an exponent of the woodcut which he helped to revitalize. His decorative use of line influenced Art Nouveau (q. v.).

VALORI PLASTICI was the name of an influential art periodical founded in 1918, in which the problems and ideas of the painters of *Pittura metafisica*, and later of neo-Classicism, were discussed.

VANTONGERLOO, GEORGES (born 1886). This Belgian sculptor was one of the most active members of the Constructivist Stijl group, before he settled in Paris in 1927. By translating the geometric forms of Mondrian into three-dimensional designs he produced configurations of cube-shaped forms which, in their disposition and proportions had a fruitful effect on contemporary architecture.

VELDE, HENRY VAN DE (1863–1957). A Belgian artist from Antwerp who began as a neo-Impressionist painter but soon turned entirely to the applied arts, adapting van Gogh's curvilinear style to the decorative linear idiom of the Art Nouveau (q. v.). His industry as one of the main champions of this movement, both in theory and in practice, was astonishing. He applied himself to architecture (Folkwang Museum, Hagen), the designing of carpets, industrial publicity and even women's fashions, with style and untiring energy. Under his leadership the Weimar School of Art became a progressive institution and, in suggesting Walter Gropius as his successor, he indirectly helped to call the Bauhaus (q. v.) into life. Van de Velde ended his days in Switzerland.

VIANI, ALBERTO (born 1906). A leading Italian abstract sculptor, living in Venice. Viani is a pupil of Arturo Martini and follows the style of Jean Arp. His subjects, always organic, are usually based on the female form which he reduces to abstract terms. He was awarded a prize at the 1948 Venice Biennale.

VIGELAND, GUSTAV (1869–1943). This popular Norwegian sculptor worked in the tradition of Rodin. A number of his sculptures have been assembled in the Vigeland Museum in Oslo and it is in that city, too, that his principal monumental works can be seen (Frognerpark: the bridge with 58 over-life-size statues, the fountain and the 'monolith' incorporating 120 carved figures).

VILLON, JACQUES (real name Gaston Duchamp, born 1875). Brother of Marcel Duchamp and Duchamp-Villon, the sculptor. He began as a Cubist and was the founder of the 'Section d'Or', the avant-garde group which, as its name implies, was concerned above all with ideal proportions (the 'golden section'). Villon's painting retained a pronounced constructional element; never completely non-figurative it reduced natural themes to kaleidoscopic surface shapes, relying on colour for spatial effects. After several stays in America the artist settled in Paris.

VIVIANI, GIUSEPPE. Italian painter, born 1899 in Pisa where he is still living to-day. He has been much influenced by de Chirico. Viviani works mainly as a graphic artist and his etchings are much admired.

VIVIN, LOUIS (1861–1936). One of the best-known of the French primitive painters. After being pensioned off from the post office in 1922 he devoted himself entirely to painting. His themes were predominantly views of the city of Paris which he recorded with faithful naïveté. Vivin was discovered by Wilhelm Uhde.

VLAMINCK, MAURICE DE. Born in Paris in 1876, of Flemish ancestry. One of the foremost representatives of Fauvism (q. v.), he hated the restrictions of tradition and was also an enthusiastic racing cyclist. Vlaminck's passion for art was kindled in 1901 by van Gogh and he became a close friend of Derain. At this time he produced magnificent landscapes whose violent colours and turbulent feeling did not abate until after 1907, when he was passing through his 'Cézanne Period'. His later work, which is based on a more realistic formula, completely lacks all the earlier forcefulness.

VOLLARD, AMBROISE (1865–1939). French art dealer and collector who, like Daniel Henry Kahnweiler, rendered a lasting service to modern art by his encouragement and support of artists ranging from the Impressionists to Picasso and Chagall. At the risk of causing a scandal, he arranged first exhibitions of the work of Cézanne (1895), Picasso (1901) and Matisse (1904). In his capacity as publisher of graphic works he befriended Degas, Toulouse-Lautrec, Rodin, Redon, Bonnard, Rouault, Picasso, Chagall and others. Many artists, among them Renoir, Bonnard, Cézanne, Picasso, Rouault and Dufy, expressed their gratitude by portraying him.

VOYSEY, CHARLES F. ANNESLEY (1857–1941). British architect and one of the pioneers of modern building. He concentrated almost entirely on modest private houses but within these limitations developed a homely, personal and functional style. Continuing the tradition of William Morris and Norman Shaw, Voysey and such architects as Charles Rennie Mackintosh and Edwin

325. WINTER, *The temple gateway*

Lutyens strove to bring to domestic architecture a new freshness and simplicity of form. These qualitites are also evident in Voysey's interiors.

VUILLARD, ÉDOUARD (1868–1940). A French painter who joined the Nabis (q. v.) in 1889. After that, his development was strongly influenced by his friend Bonnard whose art his own resembled in many ways without, however, attaining the same rich colour effects. Like Bonnard an 'Intimist' painter, he too concentrated on simple, everyday subjects within the home, painted in warm colours. Vuillard is also of importance as a graphic artist and mural painter (Palais de Chaillot, Paris 1937; Palais des Nations, Geneva 1939).

WAGNER, OTTO (1841–1918). A Viennese architect who was one of the earliest champions of modern architecture in the spirit of the machine age. With his elevated and underground railway system in Vienna he met a contemporary challenge by combining iron construction with *Jugendstil* (see Art Nouveau) ornamentation. The Savings Bank building in Vienna (1905) and the hospital at Hütteldorf (1904–1906) show his use of a direct and functional style of architecture which freely admits the retrograde influence of his own pupils Josef Hoffmann and Josef Olbrich and the Viennese architect Adolf Loos.

WEBER, MAX (born 1881). Although Weber (America's earliest pioneer in Modernism) is fundamentally opposed to formal Abstraction, he was in 1912 the most important Abstractionist in the nation. Son of a tailor and born in Russia, Weber studied art at Pratt Institute and in Paris where he cultivated the friendships of Picasso, Cézanne, Rousseau and (his master) Matisse. Depending upon 'the great ancients of all races and climes' for inspiration and incentive, his religious nature became thoroughly evident during his mid-thirties when he turned to themes of prayer and contemplation and to pictures of women which were suggestive of passages in the Bible. His later work is characterized by a freely distorted Naturalism which is at once intimate, subtle in colour, complex in composition and extremely well organized. 'The Geranium' (1911), 'Tranquility' (1928), 'Hasidic Dance' (1940), 'Latest News' (c. 1940) and 'Three Literary Gentlemen' (1945) are fine examples of his work. (Ill. 289)

WINTER, FRITZ (born 1905). Winter began life as an electrician and miner and later became a pupil at the Bauhaus (q. v.). After his release from captivity in Russia in 1949 he quickly rose to the front rank of German painters. His pictorial vision in some respects resembles that of Hans Hartung but his work is more colourful and, for all its abstraction, more easily related to human experience, creating a mood in a truly romantic sense. Since 1955 Winter has been a professor at the Academy in Kassel. (Ill. 325)

WOLS (real name Wolfgang Schulze, 1913–1951). Born in Berlin, he trained as a violinist before studying art at the Bauhaus (q. v.). In 1932 he went to Paris where he worked as a photographer. Wols did not begin to paint until 1940, when he was in the south of France. He returned to Paris in 1945. His unusual pictures, composed of minute particles of colour and form, and giving the impression of having been created in a trance, pointed the way to Tachism (q. v.).

WOOD, GRANT (1892–1942). This American painter studied at the Art Institute of Chicago and the Académie Julien. A journey to Munich in 1928, which brought him into contact with Netherlandish and Old German painting as well as the New Objectivity (q. v.), was decisive for his future development. After that time he painted portraits and scenes from everyday American life with a cool, hard realism ('American Gothic', Art Institute of Chicago).

WOTRUBA, FRITZ. Born 1907 in Vienna, he is Austria's most outstanding contemporary sculptor. The human quality of his figures has had to yield to the rhythm of the medium, which emerges as the dominant element. But in return for this his understanding of the natural properties of stone and his artistic exploitation of its basic structure are such that, while turning man into stone he imbues stone with life. Wotruba emigrated to Switzerland in 1938 and in 1945 became a teacher at the Vienna Academy where he had studied. (Ill. 326)

WRIGHT, FRANK LLOYD (born 1869). The famous American architect served his apprenticeship under

Louis Sullivan, who was himself a pioneer of modern architecture, and with his department store for Carson, Pirie and Scott in Chicago (1899–1904) erected the first purely functional skyscraper of the skeleton-frame type (cf. p. 443). Wright himself specialized in domestic architecture and his revolutionary ideas in this field have had far-reaching effects. By 1900 he was building houses whose interior space was conceived as a single unit in which walls were introduced to afford 'protection against storm and heat only when needed'. Treating each house as an individual problem, he tried in his designs to reflect something of the owner's personality while at the same time achieving a feeling of harmony between the building and its natural setting. That this could lead to an expressionistic form of architecture is indicated by his 'House above the waterfall' (Pennsylvania, 1937). And indeed the element of drama, demonstrated by the rhythmic stress of building unit and support, is evident also in his industrial architecture (Laboratory Tower for the Johnson Wax Company, Racine) and even more so in his ecclesiastical buildings (Wayfarers' Chapel, Palos Verdes, 1951). A completely new approach is represented by Wright's design for the Solomon R. Guggenheim Museum, which is conceived as a continuous spiral expanding into widening circles as it rises. (Ill. 281)

YEATS, JACK B. (1871–1957), painter and writer, born in London, lived and worked in Ireland. A brother of the poet W. B. Yeats, he studied at the Westminster School of Art under Fred Brown. He captured the spirit and atmosphere of Ireland as no other painter has done, in expressionist, astonishingly vital pictures of horses, the theatre, legendary themes and wild landscapes. He has great stylistic affinities with Kokoschka. His best work is in the galleries of Dublin and Cork, but he is also represented in the Tate Gallery, London.

ZADKINE, OSSIP. Sculptor, born 1890 in Smolensk, Russia. In 1909 he went to Paris where, apart from a stay in the USA (1941–1945), he has been living ever since. Apart from his Cubist sculpture, he has also produced a massive memorial to the devastated city of Rotterdam ('City without a heart', 1952/53, ill. 300). He is a teacher at the Académie de la Grande Chaumière.

ZIMMERMANN, MAC (born 1912). One of the few serious German Surrealists, he is especially successful as a graphic artist when representing the bizarre and fantastic. He taught at the Dessau Academy for a short time (1946), went to Berlin until 1949 and now lives in Munich.

ZORACH, WILLIAM (born 1887). Zorach, who is best known as a sculptor, was born in Lithuania, but he was brought to America by his parents at the age of four. His sculptures, though they are of classic, monumental style, exhibit a personal flair, shedding reality and taking on a spiritual feeling as in his 'Spirit of the Dance', a kneeling figure cast in aluminium which he executed for the Radio City Music Hall in New York.

326. WOTRUBA, Reclining figure. Cement casting

Art outside Europe

ISLAMIC ART

327. *The Sultan Ahmed Mosque in Istanbul (built beg. 17th cent.)*

When Mahomet conquered his native city, Mecca, in A. D. 630, he achieved his life's ambition. World-wide conversion had never entered his mind, yet scarcely was he dead than the most learned of his followers set down those 114 sections of the Koran that call for divinely ordained world conquest. Thirty years after Mahomet's death, Islam extended as far as the Caspian Sea and Afghanistan. Arabia, Persia, Syria, Egypt and Libya all acclaimed Allah and his prophet. The Caliphs of the Omayyad dynasty moved their capital from Medina to Damascus. Islam had become a world power.

The new faith was spread by the enthusiasm and devotion of its followers rather than by fire and sword. The Caliphs, contrary to popular belief, were very tolerant. Although non-Muslims were taxed more heavily, they were not in any way persecuted. The artists of the newly conquered countries were set extensive tasks, regardless of their religion. Syria and Egypt had belonged to the Byzantine Empire and Byzantine civilisation was to experience a last great flowering under the Omayyad rulers (661–750). Islamic art developed by gradual stages from the art of late Antiquity. The Great Mosque in Damascus and the façade of the desert palace of Mchatta in Jordan (now in the Islamic section of the Berlin Museum) alike testify to this.

The new faith was not limited to any particular race. The ruling dynasties – originally Arab – were at times Persian, at others Turkish. The Abbasid rulers succeeded the Omayyad Caliphs in Asia Minor and made Baghdad their capital in 758. The splendour of Harun-al-Rashid's court in the city is reflected in the 'Tales from the Arabian Nights'. Persian influence now became very marked. Persia had been under Sassanian rule before the Islamic conquest and the Abbasids, having absorbed Sassanian civilisation with its strongly marked Byzantine and Persian traits, continued to use Sassanian methods of government. This applied equally to Egypt, even after that country had become politically independent – like several other territories – in the 10th century.

Although the Muslim empire disintegrated during the Abbasid rule, this did not prevent Islam from spreading rapidly. It reached Russia and Siberia in the following centuries and flourished in India under the Mughal Emperors (1526–c. 1800); the Seljuk Turks began their attacks on Constantinople and the Balkans, which their Ottoman successors brought to a successful conclusion, reaching the gates of Vienna in 1683.

Western Europe had been invaded almost a thousand years earlier. The Moors conquered Spain in 711, crossed the Pyrenees and might have been a great danger to the West, if they had not been defeated

516

by Charles Martel in the battle of Tours and Poitiers in 732. Spain was governed by the Caliphs of Cordova from 756 onwards.

Spain, also, is evidence of the tolerance of Islam. Spanish Visigothic artists – even those that remained Christians – were widely employed, and many Muslim buildings bear the stamp of their artistic tradition. The new mixed style was called 'Mozarabic' and persisted for a long time. It must be mentioned in fairness to Spain's Christian rulers that they proved far more tolerant than is generally conceded, after their final victory over the Muslims – Granada, the last bastion, fell in 1492. Arab artists then worked for Christian patrons and the new mixed form of art, the Mudéjar style (q. v.) – in a sense the Mozarabic style in reverse – showed many Islamic features.

Sicily, too, provides an example of the peaceful co-existence of the civilisations of East and West. The island had been conquered by the Mohammedans in the 9th century and by the Normans in the 11th. A mixed Norman-Arab culture developed there from 1060 onwards and the Norman kings did not hesitate to entrust Muslim artists with important tasks, such as the ceiling frescoes in the Capella Palatina in Palermo.

Considering the great differences between the Mohammedan races, we may well ask how a specific 'Islamic art' could come about at all. But the integrating power of religion – notwithstanding the tolerance shown to other cultures – must not be underrated. It was all the stronger by virtue of the fact that Islam – contrary to the West – did not distinguish between religious and secular rule. In consequence, there was no fundamental difference between sacred and profane art. Styles – named not after peoples or epochs but after dynasties – continued much longer than in the West. The Arab language formed a universal link. In the past, every Muslim between Kashmir and Gibraltar knew Arabic. He had to know it, because the Koran was written in Arabic and was not allowed to be translated. It was to no small degree the Koran, with its later commentaries and supplementary rules, which – if not from the outset, at least progressively later – determined the character of Islamic art. It is an art that has an unmistakable unifying quality which shines clearly through differing racial traits.

ARCHITECTURE

The appearance of the mosque, the most important building of Islam, is determined by prescribed rules. In the days of Mahomet, the sanctuary was nothing but a fenced-in courtyard with fountains for the prescribed ritual ablutions. This plan has not changed fundamentally since the time of the Omayyad Caliphs. The courtyard, with its fountain in the middle, is surrounded by colonnades. The minaret (q. v.), whence the muezzin calls to prayer five times a day, rises above it. The façade of the mosque proper, which has a central prayer hall with a flat or vaulted ceiling, forms one side of the courtyard. The mosque at Cordova, one of the oldest and most magnificent in existence, contains a veritable forest of pillars to isolate the worshippers from each other and to give a sense of enclosure conducive to calm and concentration. In the Osman style, the domed mosque blossoms into great splendour at the close of the Middle Ages, as at Edirne (Adrianople). But, in principle, all mosques are alike. There is an arched prayer recess (mihrab) in the east, the pulpit (mimbar) is near-by. In very large mosques there might also be a 'dikka', a platform where the 'unnam' reads the Koran and intones the prayers. Stalls do not exist; the faithful kneel on the prayer carpet. Lamps, often made of pierced and damascened brass, hang from the ceiling. There is none of the equipment

328. Medrese of Bey Kait in Cairo (built 1475, 2nd Mameluke dynasty)

so characteristic of churches in the West, apart from the supports for the Koran, the 'kursi', which are no different from ordinary household furniture. (Ill. 29, 327)

The lay-out of the palaces of Islamic rulers is also clearly defined. There is always a division into three parts: the public portion (meshnuar), a private section (the divan), and the living quarters (the harem). If, to mosque and palace we add the two kinds of mausoleum (the qubba and the tourbé), and the medrese (q. v.), we have outlined the entire field of monumental Islamic architecture. All these buildings are made of brick, the traditional form of construction in the Near East (ill. 343, 328).

SCULPTURE AND PAINTING

Monumental sculpture and figure painting, the most characteristic forms of Christian art in the West, are unknown in Islamic art. The representation not only of the Godhead, but of all living creatures was forbidden under the Abassid rulers, and Islamic art – entirely non-representational, therefore, – had to prove its vigour in ornament and pattern. Although this law was not interpreted too literally – it could always be argued that it was not contained in the Koran, – it had the most far-reaching effect. Religious statues are unknown; where figures are introduced at all in secular art, they are shown as different from nature as possible. 'If you want to show figures, make them like flowers,' was the advice given by theologians. Men and animals therefore become part of the pattern in Islamic ornament and, reduced to their basic form, appear very stylized, as in the animal carpets of the Safavid period (16th to 18th centuries). Next to geometric patterns, stylized plant motifs enjoyed great popularity. Here, too, the laws of nature were deliberately disregarded. In the split palmette (see Arabesque; ill. 68), leaves send out shoots, stems grow from blossoms. It may be added, in this connection, that the art of gardening had flourished in Spain under the Moors, in medieval Turkey and in Persia; Islamic artists knew very well what these plants really looked like. But abstractions of natural forms stimulate the imagination, because they allow an infinite number of variations on simple themes.

Occasionally – as under the Ottoman rulers – miniature painting, one of the most impressive chapters of Islamic art, was exempt from the ban on depicting the human form. But even here, in a minor art devoted to illustration, there is no imitation of nature, no perspective; the figures are arranged in a linear and purely decorative manner. The earliest outstanding miniatures are the work of the artists of the school of Baghdad (12th and 13th centuries) and of Indian artists of the same period (the legend of Kalila and Dimna). Later, some of the finest miniatures were produced in Mughal India and in Persia – the illustrations to the poems of Firdusi, the Hafiz Divan and especially the miniatures painted under Safavid (17th century) rule belong to the most beautiful works of art of this kind. There the artists' names sometimes appear, although this is very unusual in the art of Islam where no individual masters are otherwise mentioned. These include the renowned Bihzad (c. 1500), as well as Aga Mirak, Sultan Muhammad and Riza Abassi (c. 1630). Ill. p. 521

Islamic miniatures usually contain writing, thereby undoubtedly increasing their ornamental appearance, since Arab characters possess a decorative quality which is only equalled by the writing of the Chinese. Indeed, Arab calligraphy appears everywhere as decoration, in the arts as in the crafts (cf. ill. 329). The visitor from the West can enjoy looking at the walls of the Alhambra (q. v.) in Granada in the same way as at any other work of art, whereas the Moslem can also 'read' them, delighting in their poetry as well as in their splendour. Calligraphy at its most beautiful was practised in Samarkand under the rule of the Persian Samanid dynasty in Samarkand (9th/10th cent.). In secular buildings Islamic culture, in particular that of the splendour-loving Persians, produced a colourful and comparatively realistic wall painting, representing, say, in the princely palaces the deeds of the rulers (ill. p. 522).

THE CRAFTS

It is not surprising that Islam, having its origin amongst nomad tent-dwellers, gave great attention to the textile arts. There is no need to stress the great importance of the oriental carpet; many cities and whole provinces of the East such as Tabriz, Bokhara, Smyrna, Shiraz and others have become famous in the West for their export of carpets, which has continued to the present day. The most outstanding Persian carpets were made during the Safavid dynasty. Under the rule of the Ottoman Turks, Cairo and Ushak became the chief carpet suppliers of the Sultan's court (1400–1750). Brocade and silk weaving also achieved great fame at that time. (Ill. pp. 99, 531)

But despite the great achievements described above, the artists of Islam were at their most successful when they created articles of daily use. Islamic craftsmen, well organized into guilds, stimulated by the keen competition in the Bazaar, and working under the gaze of the public, are among the finest in the world. The ban on gold and silver vessels – in force from the early days of Islam – merely spurred them on to devising ways and means of making simple materials simulate costly ones. Bronze vessels, weapons and ornaments of all kinds were inlaid with gold and silver wire (damascened, q. v.), a technique still practised in Toledo to-day (ill. 329, 349). Already under Abassid rule, glazed vessels were coated with a further glaze that gave them a metallic sheen, recalling gold or silver (the so-called lustre technique, q. v.). Gilt and enamelled Islamic glass was highly coveted everywhere, as were objects of cut rock-crystal, a form of art that did not offend against any religious rule. The potter supplied not only vessels, but also tiles for inner and outer walls of buildings. The ceramic art of Islam has excelled at various times: a magnificent ware with black and red decoration on a white ground was produced in Samarkand under the Samanid dynasty; equally outstanding wares were made at Rhages, Sultanabad and numerous other places, in the 13th century, in Egypt in the 14th, and throughout Persia in the 17th. Often, the Persian potter freely interpreted the work of his Chinese contemporaries and thus produced works of a vigour, which, perhaps, is sometimes lacking – indeed unsought – in Chinese pieces. A fine polychrome pottery, lavishly decorated with stylized flowers, was also made in Turkey in the 16th and 17th centuries (well represented at the Victoria and Albert Museum and the British Museum, London). Decorative wood carving also flourished down the centuries in Islam, where fabric printing saw an early development.

Wherever we look, we find the articles of everyday use in the Islamic world decorated with such taste and such splendour, that medieval stories about the marvels of the East are not hard to explain. The European of to-day still feels as if he were in Aladdin's cave when he visits the collections of Islamic art in the museums.

INDIAN ART

'Indian Art' is only a small part of 'Art in India'. Large sections of the Indian people have been Mohammedan for centuries and here, as elsewhere, Islam knew how to lift the arts from their racial affiliations to make them subservient to its religious needs. It was necessary, therefore, to refer to Indo-Islamic art in the chapter on Islamic art, although it is often – geographically – very close to Indian art proper. But wherever we see a mosque next to a Buddhist or Hindu temple, we realize the enormous intrinsic contrast between Islamic and Indian art; in the one case, there is the fundamental hostility of Islam to the image, in the other, the Indian's inherent joy in giving spiritual and cosmic forces material form. One is a richly ornamented linear art, the other the result of visualizing things in their essentially plastic aspect. Indian art, as we can still admire it to-day, consists chiefly of sculpture. This sculpture is entirely original and cannot be mistaken for that of any other continent. We still marvel at its vast extent and huge dimensions – there are reliefs that continue for miles – and perhaps ask ourselves how it was possible for the so differently orientated art of Islam, with its fundamental hostility to sculpture, to have made any headway in this country. But here the sequence of history was favourable, for classic Indian art had already passed its zenith when Islam gathered strength in India in the 12th century.

Indian art goes far back into Antiquity. The earliest surviving examples belong to the 3rd century B. C. and are made of stone. But we must assume the existence of a very much older art whose monuments were not carved from stone but from wood, a material that could not survive the ravages of the Indian tropical climate.

Indian civilisation ranks amongst the oldest in history, although this was not known until the sensational English and American excavations of the twenties and thirties of this century. These led to the discovery of the Indus culture and proved that Sind and the Punjab provinces already had a highly evolved civilisation between 3000 and 4000 B.C., which was not even surpassed by the coeval Egyptians and Sumerians, with whom there are certain links. There were cities (Mohenjo-daro, Harappa), built on a geometric plan, with houses of brick and an excellent water supply. Writing was also known, although it has not yet been deciphered. A wealth of terra-cotta idols and stucco and soapstone reliefs bear witness to the development of sculpture. It is not known what races inhabited these cities and this early phase, which was not destined to endure, is therefore not considered part of Indian history proper.

Indian history only began with the invasions of the Aryans, who came from the north in about 1000 B.C. They brought the Vedic religion with the nature deities to India: Agni, the God of Fire, Indra, the God of Lightning and of Battles, Varuna, Mitra and others. It was no longer a primitive religion, as the Vedas show; the gods already represented an abstract concept and personified a spiritual principle, Rta, or Truth. The later transformation and humanization of this nature-religion on Indian soil thus already had its origin in the Vedas. Four new religions were to appear: Brahmanism, Buddhism, Jainism and Hinduism (neo-Brahmanism). They all delighted in the arts and in the representation of the human form. Indian art – like the art of the Christian West – drew its strength from religion, and to such a degree that a real understanding demands some knowledge of Indian religious systems and creeds.

Brahmanism clung to the caste system, introduced by the immigrants, and strengthened it further. It is based on the belief in the transmigration of souls (reincarnation). A trinity (trimurti) consisting of Brahma, the Creator, Vishnu, the Preserver, and Siva, the Destroyer, stands at the top of the hierarchy. Brahma is often shown with four heads, facing north, south, east and west, respectively. His attributes are the alms bowl and the lotus flower. He is transported by the 'Vahanan', the swan, on which he stands. Vishnu, who is shown with four arms, carries a shell, a lotus flower, a discus and a club. He can appear in any of the following ten incarnations: fish, turtle, boar, dwarf, a composite man-lion, but also in pure human form as Krishna, the hero and philosopher, as two forms of Rama, the subject of many legends, or as the Buddha. Siva usually appears as a dancer with four or even ten arms. He carries snakes in his hair and a torch (Vajra) in his hands. But he is also shown as the loving husband and father with his wife Parvati. Many demons (Yaksas) and deities of nature assemble around this trinity.

Buddhism rebelled against this all-too physical character of the world of the Brahmanic gods. At first it did not accept a supreme being and attributed reincarnation to all gods. This great movement towards an entirely new concept of the world of the gods began with Gotama, the Prince Siddharta, who was called the Buddha (the Enlightened One), around 560 B.C. Siddharta himself left his family and his possessions and lived in poverty. He taught that life is suffering and that enlightenment alone can bring redemption. The ultimate aim of action was to attain the merit which led to freedom from the eternal transmigration of souls in Nirvana (annihilation). As enlightenment can only be achieved by renouncing

520

Persian miniature (c. 1430) from the manuscript 'Baisunghar's Shahnamah': Tribal hunt in the presence of Prince Baisunghar

Persian wall painting in the palace of Chibil Situn, Isfahan (c. 1642—1666): Resting

the pleasures of this world, many monasteries were built and beggar-monks, who were also missionaries, travelled all over the country. Buddhism became the national religion under Asoka (274–232 B.C.). The new faith spread to Tibet, China, Japan, Korea and South-East Asia, where it has continued until the present day. It is remarkable that Buddhism should have lasted but a short time in India, the country of its origin. It had already lost its importance by the 3rd century A. D. and had practically disappeared by the 7th.

Jainism also arose as a protest against the over-developed ritualism of Hinduism at about the same time as Buddhism in the 6th century B.C., and was at one time widespread, but suffered a decline in popular taste because of its ascetic ideas. The Jains erected whole temple-cities in the mountains of the North, in particular at Mount Abu. The Jains believe that their faith was founded by a succession of 24 Thirthankanas (saints) of whom the last Vardhamana, called 'Mahavira' (great hero) or Jina (the victor) was historical and contemporary with the Buddha. He is usually shown in Yogi posture and can only be distinguished from the Buddha by his attributes, such as the cobra hood umbrella above his head.

It is understandable that the masses of India could neither appreciate nor 'live' Buddhism. Brahmanism had never died and had persisted amongst the people even when Buddhism was the national religion. It later celebrated new triumphs as neo-Brahmanism or Hinduism. The world of its gods was enlarged even further with various nature-deities, but some Buddhist features were retained. The Buddha himself was venerated as an incarnation of Vishnu and Buddha's and Jina's identity with Siva was declared one of the tenets of the new religion. Hinduism experienced its golden age, and Indian art its classic period and maturity, between A. D. 300 and 800; that is, during the Gupta dynasty (until A. D. 600) and the two following centuries.

ARCHITECTURE

The age of Buddhism was also the formative period of Indian art. The earliest surviving examples belong to the reign of Asoka, when Buddhism had become the national religion. Asoka himself is said to have erected 30 animal pillars, of which ten survive as a worthy and monumental inauguration of Indian sculpture. These memorial pillars (stambhas, q. v.) usually carry on their slender shafts animals such as crocodiles, elephants and, above all, lions. Various details – particularly the recurrent bell-shaped capital – show Persian influence. Monumental stone buildings also appeared for the first time during Asoka's reign. The most important amongst them is the Buddhist temple (stupa, q. v., ill. 330). Its shape suggests its derivation from the tumulus, the earliest kind of burial mound; it has, however, been transformed into a dream-like edifice, whose carefully devised structure personifies both symbol and pure idea. It consists of a flattened hemisphere, standing on a square platform and is sometimes surmounted by a wooden umbrella, which can either be interpreted as the symbol of princely power or as the Bodh-tree that sheltered the Buddha when he received his enlightenment. It is surrounded by the stupa screen, which – although made of stone – clearly owes its form to a wooden structure. Though later lavishly decorated, early stupa screens – as at Sanchi – are still free from ornament. The gates there (5th or 4th century B.C.), however, are carved in magnificent reliefs, the most important of which show scenes from the life of the Buddha. Animals, plants, demons, the old and by then already legendary deities – even Indra with the Vajra appears – are given ample space. The characteristics of all later Indian sculpture are already fully developed. (Ill. 350)

The Stupa remained the most important form taken by the Buddhist temple, although a tower-like, slender form was later introduced in the border regions of India. How much it was intended as a pure symbol of the Buddha himself is proved by its appearance in diminutive form on burial grounds

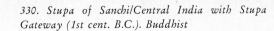
330. Stupa of Sanchi/Central India with Stupa Gateway (1st cent. B.C.). Buddhist

and as a reliquary shrine in the Chaitya halls (q. v.), where it replaced the altar. Such Buddhist assembly halls – hollowed-out caves – still survive in fairly large numbers from the early days of Buddhism. They have been hewn into the rock with infinite care and devotion and recall so many features of timber construction (e. g. at Karli), that the existence of a free-standing wooden prototype can be taken for granted. A wealth of sculpture and ornament endows these grottoes with a fairy-tale splendour. Extensive wall paintings also occur. The cave temples of Ajanta (q. v.) reveal how a revived Brahmanism was able to creep into these originally Buddhist halls, to continue and complete the work – particularly where the paintings are concerned – begun under Buddhism. There is no real break with tradition (ill. p. 532).

But Hinduism also developed its own temple forms. We can distinguish three geographically separate groups. In North India, the temple is dedicated to Vishnu and comprises a cell-like sanctuary (the cella), surmounted by a tower in the shape of a slender cone (the Sikara). It further includes an assembly hall, open to all sides, called the Mandapam. The walls and the massive roof are covered with abstract architectural ornament and sculpture in high relief (Khajuraho). Indian art abhors the plain surface, a dislike deeply rooted in the Hindu attitude to the cosmos. All-over ornament is a symbol of unity, of Man as he forms part of all Creation.

The Hindu temple in South India is more extensive. Small temples, halls, baths and loggias are grouped around the Sanctuary. The gate-towers, wholly covered with sculpture and ornament, make an overwhelming impression. Often, these temples took hundreds of years to build (Tanjore), although some of the largest in the South (Madura, Siringam) only date from the 17th and 18th centuries. (Ill. 331, 344)

We find both types combined in Central India (in the Deccan). The cella, surmounted by the stambha of South India, is usually built on a star-shaped plan, the lay-out being similar to that of the northern temples (Halebid).

But the old cave, or grotto, temples endure. The Brahman Elephanta (q. v.) temple on an island near Bombay is one of the finest examples. Indeed, the Brahmanist South went considerably further. The rock was not only hollowed out to form a hall, but was also carved from the outside, until it had the appearance of elaborate buildings and towers, like the famous Kailasa at Ellora. In these 'monolithic' temples the landscape is, as it were, turned into architecture in a manner we no longer find anywhere else in the world.

Other forms of this architecture developed in the border regions of India, Ceylon, the islands of the Indonesian archipelago, the Himalayas and in Buddhist Tibet. The tapering stupa became a finely pointed tower in Burma and Siam. A feverish building activity under the Khmer Kings in Cambodia, between the 9th and 12th centuries, culminated in such masterpieces as the terraced temples of Angkor Thom (q. v.) and Angkor Vat. An altogether different type of temple, the pagoda, emerged

524

331. The Great Temple of Tanjore/South India (11th cent.). Hindu

in the Himalayan kingdom of Nepal, which was once said to possess more temples than houses. The pagoda (q. v.) comprises a number of storeys of diminishing size, built upon a square base with four steep flight of steps, each storey having widely projecting roofs. The roofs are straight, and not curved like those of the otherwise similar Chinese pagoda. There is a clear link with China, although the origins of this type of building are still obscure.

SCULPTURE

Indian architecture is unthinkable without sculpture, as the pre-Christian Sanchi Stupa (ill. 330, 350), clearly showed. But apart from the animal pillars of Asoka's reign, sculpture in the round was unknown in the early Buddhist period. The impressive seated or standing (i. e. teaching or meditating) Buddha-figures – to our minds so characteristic of Buddhist art – only appeared several centuries after the death of the Buddha. Originally, the stupa was his only monument. Nor does he appear in the numerous reliefs showing scenes from his life; at the most, his footsteps might be carved into the stone. The monumental Buddha-figure did not appear until the time of Christ's birth and was obviously strongly inspired by the work of Greek sculptors of the Hellenistic period. A colony of Greek sculptors would seem to have existed in Gandhara (q. v.) on the North-West frontier since the time of Alexander the Great. Here we find the earliest Buddha-statues, dating from the first centuries A. D. Many of their features still recall the Greek god, Apollo, although the Indian spirit soon triumphed over all Western influence. Meditating Yogi-style, and given a nobility and delicacy of body that banishes all thought of an earthly nature, the Indian Buddha becomes the exalted symbol of moral greatness. The long ear lobes signify that he is listening intently to the secrets of the cosmos, the jewel on the forehead represents the third eye of inner vision.

The Buddha-figure, in its serene calm, seems lifted out of the world of sensual pleasure we normally associate with Indian sculpture. But gods, demons and human beings were never formed in slavish imitation of nature. Attention to the structure of the skeleton, to anatomical accuracy and a firm stance – all of great importance in Greek art – was also utterly alien to Indian sculpture. And yet, Indian figures pulsate with life. The women in particular, with the curves of their wide hips, their narrow waists and their full breasts, are an expression of loving attention to the rhythm that pulsates in all living Creation. Siva's triumphal dance leads us into dionysian realms, where demonic vitality reigns (ill. 332). Trimurti, the three-headed composite being of Siva, Vishnu and Brahma, represents the all-embracing unity of all cosmic existence; this also is the message of the narrative reliefs we find everywhere on the walls of the temples – at their most magnificent on the still well-preserved walls of the stupa of Borobudur in Java. The mile-long reliefs were carved at the end of the 8th century A. D. In them, Indo-Aryan, Buddhist and Brahmanistic legends interweave and, while transporting the initiated into the world of the gods, they at the same time reveal the unaffected charm of the Javanese people.

PAINTING

The warmth and richness of Indian art is enhanced by colour. Painting undoubtedly played an important part in Ancient India, although very little survives. But the frescoes in the cave-temples of Ajanta (painted between the 1st and 7th centuries A. D., and partly preserved) compensate for many losses (ill. p. 532). Perspective was unknown, but vigorously drawn outlines and a wealth of contrasting colour have produced a style that reflects fully the Indian love of telling a story.

Very much later, this early fresco style experienced a renaissance, after a manifest waning of interest in painting. In the 16th century the artists of the Rajput school (named after the Rajasthan province) painted miniatures on paper in the style of the Ajanta frescoes. Their work shows the influence of Islamic miniature painting, which, closely associated with Persian artists, had flourished in India under the Mughal Emperors from the 16th century (ill. p. 533). The Rajput tradition has continued up to the present day. Members of the Tagore family of artists, in particular, have tried to revive it. But there can be no doubt that painting, compared to sculpture and architecture, plays only a very subordinate part amongst the arts of India, when seen as a whole; whereas in China and Japan, it established a leading position amongst the other arts already in very early times.

THE ARTS OF THE FAR EAST

If the arts of China and Japan are described in a single chapter under this heading, our justification is not only the need for concise treatment, but the very nature of the development of Far Eastern art itself. China is the motherland of Japanese art. In the Far East, just as in Europe, art refused to be politically or racially confined. There, as in the Christian West, religious considerations largely contributed to this unity of purpose. Buddhism reached Japan via Korea, bringing Chinese civilisation in its train. A number of outstanding achievements of a national character must be conceded, and these will be mentioned in due course. But the strikingly similar development of the arts – over centuries – in this vast region is far more surprising than are the occasional divergencies.

The free expression of individual personality, which is such a decisive factor in European works of art, never counted for much in the Far East. There, a human being is not only part of society, of his class, but is also the slave of his family to a degree that Western peoples find it hard to conceive. The 'family', in China and Japan, includes not only the living relatives but also the dead, who form part of it for all time. Ancestor-worship has the absolutism of a religion and since it directs the gaze into the past rather than into the future, customs, one established, rarely change. The result, on the positive side, is a harmonious and homogeneous culture; on the negative side, a severely limited range of expression.

Confucianism, given to the Chinese by Confucius (Kung-fu-tsu), in the 6th century B.C., encouraged this development. Confucius did not found a religion, as is so often assumed; he created an

332. The god Siva as cosmic dancer (c. 12th cent.). Bronze – 333. Kwannon in the Chugu-ji Temple near Nara/Japan (mid-7th cent.). Wood – 334. Sakyamuni Buddha in the Jingo-ji Temple near Kyoto/Japan (8th cent.). Laquer carving in the Kanshitsu technique

elaborate system of ethics and a social order that remained unchanged for many centuries It regulated by law and custom all aspects of everyday life from the cradle to the grave, even down to details like 'the right way to wear one's hat or to lie in bed'.

But a decline into formalism was prevented by what were, more strictly speaking, the religious faiths. Taoism was based on the teachings of Confucius' contemporary Lao-tse, who lived in the Yang-tse-kiang valley. Although Taoism appeals to the individual, and to the soul within him – as all religions do – its aim is to induce humility rather than self-glorification. Lao-tse taught loving devotion to nature, to plant and beast, the clouds, the wind and to the entire universe.

Various mystic traits of this religion later facilitated the coming of Buddhism, which was brought to China by Indian missionaries in the first centuries of the Christian era. The teachings of Zen – a special form of Buddhism – have much in common with Taoism, above all, the pantheistic concepts which make man strive for union with a divine spirit that informs all living things. Zen Buddhism appeared in China in the 6th century and was later also of great importance to Japan.

The periods when Far Eastern art flourished coincide with those when the religions flourished. The T'ang dynasty (618–907), the golden age of Chinese art, corresponds with the time when Buddhism embraced the whole of China. The ensuing, scarcely less splendid, Sung period (960–1280) was greatly stimulated by Zen Buddhism, which was then gaining ground. In the years between, there were decades when Buddhism was opposed and Confucius' code of ethics was considered sufficient – it was also a time of anarchy and iconoclasm that, beginning round 800, has on its conscience the destruction of innumerable works of art of the T'ang dynasty.

The Sung dynasty was ended by the invasion of Mongolian tribes, who set up a new dynasty, the Yüan (1280–1368). The Ming dynasty (1368–1644), trying to restore China's former greatness by going back to T'ang traditions, did not succeed in even approaching the glories of the T'ang period. After a thousand years, Chinese art was coming to an end. It lived entirely on the past during the Ch'ing or Manchu dynasty (1644–1912), when a flourishing export trade was carried on with the West, where Baroque art, with its 'chinoiseries' was highly receptive to Eastern influences.

But the door to the East was closed. Japan cut herself off from the mainland under the Tokugawa rulers and their military vassals, the Samurai. While the earlier development of Chinese and Japanese art had run more or less parallel, the Japanese now brought what they had inherited from China to a new and independent fruition. The Japanese woodcut enjoyed great popularity and spread far and wide. It also crossed the seas, where it was to open new vistas to the tired art of the West by way of Impressionism and the Art Nouveau movement.

ARCHITECTURE

China's recorded history begins in the 2nd millennium B.C., but no surviving examples of her architecture date from such a distant past. Although building regulations – virtually unchanged to the present day – already existed during the Chou dynasty (1122–255 B.C.), nothing survives. The famous Great Wall of China with its arched gates and towers, which enclosed the 'Middle Kingdom', can undoubtedly be counted an impressive work of architecture, but it dates from no earlier than the Ch'in dynasty (255–206 B. C.). Also, the Ch'in rulers, who gave China her name, were Tartars and not Chinese, and showed their contempt for Ancient Chinese civilisation by burning every book they could lay their hands on.

Far Eastern buildings are mostly timber structures and therefore very much at the mercy of the ravages of time. The earliest extant examples are found in Japan – proof that the Japanese actually surpassed the Chinese in craftsmanship and in the preservation of the past, although form and

527

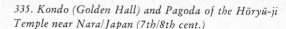
*335. Kondo (Golden Hall) and Pagoda of the Hōryū-ji
Temple near Nara/Japan (7th/8th cent.)*

architectural concept undoubtedly derived from
China. The Japanese Hōryū-ji temple near Nara
can thus be described with every justification as a
typical example of Chinese architecture. Chinese
descriptions and illustrations of buildings of much
earlier centuries point to the same type, thus
suggesting great antiquity and a persevering adherence to the same forms that seems stange to
Western minds. (Ill. 335)

Indeed, architecture in the Far East is the
most conservative of all the arts, the art least anxious to give up a successful and established style.
Whether sacred or profane, public or private, monumental architecture in China, and therefore in
Japan, retains the same basic design down the centuries. Temple and palace alike are built as wooden
halls above a stone base or terrace. Their most characteristic feature is the – frequently double – curved
roof with widely projecting eaves. It is a typical frame structure, i. e. the roof is carried by wooden
uprights. The walls, often of brick, merely fill the gaps between the uprights and have no supporting function. Ornament, and particularly colour, are widely employed. The colour depends on the owner's rank
and is laid down by law; yellow roofs, for example, denote imperial buildings. The main halls are
divided into several aisles.

Neither the Chinese nor the Japanese like a number of self-contained rooms under one roof.
Instead, we find in the temple or palace precincts a number of single-roomed pavilions of varying size,
but always of the same type. Above them towers the tall pagoda. It is a development of both the Indian
síkhara and the stupa (see p. 523), whose superstructure of 'umbrellas' has become the multiplicity of
roofs so characteristic of the pagoda tower and, with it, of the Chinese and Japanese scene. Though
occasionally built of stone, the pagoda even there betrays its origin as a timber structure. (Ill. 335)

This also applies to another type of building, likewise suggesting an Indian origin: the memorial
arch, called in China *p'ai-lou*, in Japan *torii*. Built either as a memorial to an ancestor or to commemorate a famous man, it recalls the gates of the Indian stupa surrounds although it has the characteristic
curved Chinese roof. All these types of building reached Japan from China via Korea with the eastward spread of Buddhism. The earlier Japanese Shinto temple gradually gave way to the Chinese pagoda.
The way the Chinese strove to combine dignity and beauty in a simple form with the utmost economy
must have impressed and carried conviction at all times. Thus, in China, unlike anywhere else, Islam
refrained from building mosques and minarets, using instead the Chinese temple in its original form
for its own purposes.

The geography of their country caused the Japanese to vary the design of the Chinese pavilion
in a visually effective manner, by making the walls even lighter and turning them into sliding partitions.
The constant danger of earthquakes accounts for this variation, which also gave the Japanese house an
air of great delicacy and charm. Its attractiveness is further heightened by the verdant garden – a feature
of every Japanese house – with its luxuriant climbing plants, which often hide the buildings to such an
extent that it is hard to tell the dividing line between indoors and outdoors when the walls are pushed
back. In their penchant for the merging of architecture with the landscape, the Japanese even surpass the
Chinese. Colours of buildings in Japan are therefore less bright than in China and a fine natural wood
is often left exposed. Undoubtedly, the Japanese in their perfect taste and their unfailing sense for
interior decoration – even in the simplest dwelling – are far in advance of all other civilisations, not only
of Asia but also of the West. Unquestionably, the Japanese house has been a great inspiration to the
leaders of the modern movement in architecture, and to designers of interiors everywhere.

528

SCULPTURE

The fructifying influence of Indian art is even more clearly marked in the sculpture than in the architecture, although several impressive examples of Chinese sculpture date from the time before the coming of Indian Buddhism. A number of monumental animal figures in granite – horses, buffaloes and lions – of the Han dynasty (206 B. C. – A. D. 220) must be considered typically Chinese, since these forms, used in the same spirit, recur again and again down the centuries, from the winged lions at the tomb of Hsiao Hsiu near Nanking (6th cent.; ill. 336) and the avenue of elephants of the Ming Emperor Hung Wu (c. 1400) to the imperial tombs in Peking in the 19th century. To the Han period belong also cavalcades of horsemen and teams of horses, carved in silhouette-like relief, although their linear treatment suggests that they are substitutes for lost – although attested – frescoes rather than real sculpture.

Free-standing sculpture of the human figure came in with Buddhism. It appears in China in the 4th century, in Korea soon afterwards, and is found in Japanese art from the 6th century onwards. Cave-temples of the Wei dynasty (c. 500) at Yün-kang in North China – these temples, also, are of Indian origin – are insignificant as architecture, but are of the greatest importance to the student of early Chinese sculpture. Here we find the world of Indian mythology, the Buddha with his retinue of saints and Boddhisattvas (the 'Buddhas-to-be'), and sometimes even the many-headed Hindu gods with their profusion of arms.

But the Chinese spirit soon effected a transformation. Their figures seem more detached and more spiritual than in India, where sculpture – with the exception of the Buddha statue – always betrayed a certain delight in the senses. It is characteristic that one of the Boddhisattvas should have taken on female form in China and become the delicately-featured goddess Kuan-yin – called Kwannon in Japan – who shares many traits with the Christian Madonna, the more so when she is shown with a child in her lap.

The serenity and noble expression of two 7th-century figures of Kuan-yin – one standing, one seated – in the famous Hōryū-ji temple near Nara in Japan, go to show how high a level of accomplishment the lost bronze and wooden sculptures of China must have attained (ill. 333).

Here, during the golden age of the T'ang period, Buddhist sculpture was mostly of stone. High reliefs, carved in the rock, show Buddhas of enormous dimensions (up to 300 ft high). But these are exceptions. Mostly, the recesses contain figures arranged in groups of five. The unadorned Buddha, tall and serious, stands in the centre, flanked on either side by a follower and a Boddhisattva, the latter lavishly bedecked and of lively gesture. At the gates stand fierce muscular monsters who, not much later, appear in Japanese art as the warriors of heaven. We can thus see the gradual transition from an 'incorporeal' serenity to a readiness to give battle in this world.

Japan now belonged completely to the domain of Chinese civilisation. The Chinese method of administration was introduced in A. D. 645; Chinese was the official language of the Court and many Japanese employed Chinese sculptors. But techniques had to be different, since the island kingdom lacked stone. Besides bronze sculpture, the so-called kanshitsu statuary was evolved. By this method a frame of wood or basketry is wound with strips of fabric, to which layers of lacquer are applied and moulded. Much of this type of thing has been preserved in Japan, whereas it has vanished from China (ill. 334). We find magnificent portrait statues of priests, whose features prove Japanese artists of the time to have been brilliant observers of nature.

Naturalism is a characteristic of the T'ang period. In China, secular tomb-figures like the stone horses of the emperor

336. Winged Lion on the Sepulchral Way of the Hsiao Hsiu at Nanking/China (6th cent.). Stone

T'ai-tung (627–650), whose movements are reproduced in great detail, and which even show the characteristic features of their breed, acquired great realism. This applies even more to the numerous small figures of the time. Next to animal sculptures of every kind, we find servants, grooms, water-carriers – in fact, the entire range of characters from the life of the people. These figures are made of bronze, terracotta or a glazed stoneware that already approaches porcelain in its composition.

This flourishing culture faced collapse in the 9th century. Only in Japan, which periodically cut itself off from China from 893 on, was development continued along these lines towards a form of 'baroque', to which China – having by now overcome her crisis – also found her way during the Sung period. Animation and 'baroque' intensity even laid hold of the delicate figure of Kuan-yin. Fierce warriors, of cast iron, appeared in China, while the Japanese produced peerless character studies of human passions in the form of masks for their dancers. A stylistic phase, corresponding to our European Rococo was reached in the Kwannon of Kuramadera. The Japanese Kamakura period (1192–1338) once again produced several great schools of sculpture, whose works could easily be mistaken for examples of European Baroque art, were they not precisely dated; here, artists like Kokei, Unkei and Tokiyori Hojo are but the leading names. The passing of these men, however, saw the sculpture of the Far East come to gradual end, paling in the shadow of mere imitation of its former glory.

PAINTING

The Chinese had possessed a script since the late prehistoric period, i. e. since the third millennium B.C. Developed from the pictograph and always written with pen and brush, their characters differed from the very beginning from all other forms of writing. They never regarded writing merely as a means of communication; it was an art that needed long and arduous years of training. Mere legibility never sufficed. The rhythm of the brush strokes, the beauty of the painted characters – regardless of their meaning – were quite as important. Chinese painting, furthermore, is a development of writing with the brush. The greatest Chinese painters were also the greatest calligraphers, besides being poets, philosophers or priests. It was by means of painting that the élite and the most cultured people expressed themselves. In the hands of the Chinese or Japanese, the ink brush, whether dry or wet, whether hesitantly or boldly used, from the thick stroke to the finest hairline, from the deep black blob to the most delicate hue, could express every sensation, every emotion. Far Eastern ink painting became one of the most moving testimonies of all time to man's gift of interpretation through the arts. (Ill. 38)

Such painting has nothing in common with the European easel picture that hangs on the wall in its solid frame. Oriental artists painted exclusively on silk or paper and preserved their work in a scroll, rolled vertically (Kakemono) or horizontally (Makimono). Only the former could be hung up. Sometimes, the sheets were folded and bound into an album. Fans, trays, screens and sliding doors were also painted with scenes and landscapes. Picture galleries were unknown. The pictures were kept in a chest and were taken out to be studied, intently and reverently, from time to time. (Cf. ill. pp. 534, 539, 540.) But the Far East also knew a form of painting more akin to that of the West. Fresco painting on a monumental scale had been practised since the days of the Han dynasty. Chinese sources speak very highly of it. This art was later given a new impetus with the coming of Buddhism, but practically nothing has been preserved. We can judge from the paintings in the 'Kondo', the Golden Hall at Nara (A. D. 711) in Japan, how great are the losses of works of art whose existence is known only from literary sources. The Chinese, who treasured painting above all other arts, have for centuries kept careful records of the artists and their works. Thousands of names have thus been preserved, but in most cases not a single work survives. This applies to the whole period between A. D. 265 and 960, which Chinese historians consider to be the classic age of painting. The greatest Chinese painter is said to have been Wu Tao-tzu (700–760), though

Persian carpet from Kirman. 19th century

Indian wall painting from the temple of Ajanta (7th century): Indra, King of the Heavens, with heavenly nymphs

Indian miniature from a manuscript of the Mahabharata (Mughal painting, Akbar period, 1556–1605): Krishna holding up Mount Govardhan to protect the faithful from the rain-showers of the angry god, Indra

Chinese handscroll painting on silk. Sung dynasty (960–1280). Detail: Spring morning at the palaces of Han

only a few copies of his work, of a later date, have come down to us. So it is, too, with the highly esteemed Ku K'ai-chih (344–406), who was the first painter to master every subject, from the Buddhist fresco to the portrait. Various instruction manuals from the beginning of the 6th century also prove that painting in China was already developed to a very high degree during the T'ang dynasty. The Chinese artist's motto: 'spirit harmony, life's motion' (Sir Arthur Waley's trans.) – meaning, the spirit means more than facility, vitality more than naturalistic representation – might well be applied to the art of all times and continents.

Painting flourished during the T'ang dynasty as never before or since, which can, indeed, be said of every sphere of Chinese culture. It was the time of great lyric poetry, of the poets Li Tai-Pe and Tu Fu – of ink painting, which from then on can legitimately be regarded as the poetry of the pen and the brush. Wang Wei was both a famous poet and a great painter and so a worthy representative of an age in which Lo Yang and Ch'ang-an were the focal points of the intellectual life 'not only of China, but of the globe'. During the T'ang dynasty, mountains, trees and waterfalls were used for the first time in history to create paintings of 'mood and atmosphere'.

Li Ssu-hsün (671–720), who achieved great depth in his landscapes through colour perspective, ranging from deep green in the foreground to the most delicate blue in the distance, and Wang Wei, who was one of the first to master the 'lyric' landscape done entirely in shades of grey, must be considered the best and – where later generations of Chinese artists were concerned – most influential painters, although no authenticated works from their hands survive.

T'ang art enjoyed a later flowering in Japan during the Fujiwara period (897–1195). Again, poetry and painting developed together. A highly civilised Court encouraged competitions for short lyric poems and small pictorial sketches, as a kind of superior party game. This they could do, since every painter had to adhere to certain prescribed rules – whatever his individual outlook – with which all educated Chinese or Japanese were acquainted. Sixteen ways of drawing mountains were permitted, and similar rules applied to the treatment of water and other motifs. We can see that there was no question of naturalism, but rather a kind of meditaion using the symbols of landscape. The Japanese Yamato school (11th and 12th centuries) produced works of the highest order. Portraits, chronicles of war and many genre scenes from the life of the Japanese people – in their earthy humour often bordering on caricatures – now appear in addition to landscape.

The Sung period had meanwhile begun in China, and painting made great strides. What is virtually a renaissance of the art of earlier centuries manifests itself in enormous temple frescoes. Votive pictures on silk begin to appear. Painters excel in nature- and landscape-painting (ill. p. 534), which are more enchanting than ever. A phantom flight of wild ducks, a bird on a rocky ledge and, above all, mist-veiled ravines with the small and humble figure of a lonely traveller meditating on the cosmos are favourite themes, painted in grey monochrome with unexcelled mastery. Nothing prevents us from seeing the great painters of the age personified in those small figures sunk in meditation: Li Ti, Chao Ta-nien, Ma Yüan . . . there are too many great names to enumerate. This matchless love of nature was in due course strengthened and refined by the influence of Zen Buddhism. To be one with Nature remained an unfulfilled longing of the Romantics of the early 19th century; to the Chinese – so it would seem – it was a natural state. God lives in all Creation. 'The branch drooping in the fog, the butterfly on a blossom, the beggar in the filth of the courtyard – they all are Buddha,' said the painter Hsia Kuei. And when Sung art, in its turn, experienced a last flowering in Japan after it had come to an end in China, it was the Zen priest Sesshū (1420–1506, q. v.) who led painting once more to great heights.

The Ming dynasty tried hard to revive the spirit of the past in its painting, as in all the other arts (ill. p. 540, cf. ill. p. 539); but, notwithstanding many fine works, the profundity and earnestness of the T'ang and Sung periods were never again achieved. Japan cut herself off from China – whose artistic

energies seemed exhausted – during the Tokugawa period (1614–1868) and developed in the coloured woodcut an art that has come to be greatly appreciated in the West. The coloured woodcut is a development of the ancient Chinese woodcut technique.

Moronobu (1638–1717) is often considered the inventor of the coloured woodcut – erroneously, although he is undoubtedly one of its pioneers. Here, too, the inspiration came from China. The delightful Chinese colour prints of the 'Hall of Ten Bamboos' (q. v.) are of somewhat earlier date (1627–1643). Like the Chinese 'Mustard Seed Garden' (1679–1701), they are among the finest examples of all graphic art. But Japanese artists like the lyrically-disposed Harunobu (1725–1770) and Utamaro (1753–1800), the great Sharaku (died 1795) who portrayed actors in magnificent dramatic poses, the versatile and popular Hokusai (1760–1849), Hiroshige (1797–1858), Toyokuni (1768–1825) and many others, have given the woodcut an importance it never possessed amongst the arts of China. Indeed, the coloured woodcut has justly been called the 'real national painting of Japan'. Its importance is seen to be all the greater when it is remembered that it inspired research as well as admiration in Europe. Sinology and the study of Oriental art only began seriously in the West when Manet and others bought and cherished Japanese woodcuts (ill. pp. 540, 541).

THE CRAFTS

No survey of the arts of the Far East is complete without mention of the crafts. The Chinese and Japanese belong to the finest craftsmen in the world. Their favourite materials since earliest times have been bronze, jade, pottery and lacquer.

The forms are largely based on the ritual bronze vessels of the Shang-Yin dynasty (1766–1122 B.C.). Their beautifully balanced shapes have ever since influenced Chinese art. Their forceful animal decoration – the dragon, one of the important symbolic beasts of China, already appears at that time – became more naturalistic in Han art, which is seen to be linked with the animal bronzes of the Scythians and other nomad tribes from the vast region between the Altai mountains and the Pontus. The political contact – Tartar warriors repeatedly made themselves the rulers of the Middle Kingdom – is also clearly reflected in art. (Ill. 337)

Ritual offerings and ornaments were fashioned in jade (q. v.) as early as in the Chou dynasty. This evocative stone was also used for small vessels, and the invention of porcelain was to no small degree due to attempts to obtain the resonance of jade in a material that was both more easily accessible and less hard to work. A striking revival of the art of jade carving occurred as late as in the 18th century, when a waxy glow, the so-called 'mutton fat' appearance, was produced with great skill.

Glazed and painted pottery had also been treasured since early times, although not for nearly as long as jade and bronze. The Ch'ai Emperor's expressed wish for porcelain to be made 'as blue as the sky, as clear as a mirror, as thin as paper and as resonant as jade' led to great improvements already before the Sung dynasty. His wish was fully granted. The whole world was amazed by Chinese porcelain; its impact, and the consequences it had, on 18th-century Europe are too well-known to need further mention. (Ill. p. 547)

The lacquer used in the arts of China and Japan is the resin of the lacquer tree (Rhus vernicifera). Extremely hard, it is applied in several layers to a carefully worked wooden vessel and can be modelled, inlaid or painted. (Ill. 334, p. 542)

The textile arts must not be forgotten. The brocades of the kimono, worn by the actors of the Japanese No drama, are admirable examples of silk weaving at its best.

A highly evolved feeling for the beauty of a rare object is as natural to the Chinese or Japanese as a sense of form and good taste. Nothing illustrates this better than the story of a Japanese ruler who once had himself invited to visit a garden in order to admire the beauty of a rare flower which grew there in great abundance. When he arrived, he found the garden stripped of all its plants. White pebbles and sand had taken their place. Furiously, he entered the tea room, where his rage was turned to joy: in the toko-no-ma, the picture alcove, stood a bronze bowl of the Sung dynasty with a single blossom in it – it was the queen of the entire garden.

THE ANCIENT CIVILISATIONS OF AMERICA

While there was continuous contact down the centuries between the civilisations of Europe, the Middle East and Asia, the American continent had remained completely isolated until its discovery in the 10th century. The origin of its indigenous populations has not yet been explained. Amongst the many theories put forward, immigration from Asia via the Bering Straits at the end of the last Ice Age, i. e. about 10,000 years ago, seems the most likely explanation. It is generally accepted that the vast continent was untouched by the civilisations of the West until its discovery by Columbus, even though Viking or Irish fishermen reached the shores of North America from time to time. Nevertheless, a civilisation evolved in Central and South America which, in its spiritual, artistic and political aspects seems in some ways akin to those of the Ancient World – perhaps most to those of Ancient Egypt. But recent research has also discovered certain affinities with South Asia.

Like circumstances result in a similar development. Just as a prosperous agriculture was possible in the Nile region when the State took charge of irrigation and drainage, so good living conditions could be achieved in the American tropics, provided the threat of the encroaching jungle (Maya region) or the dangers of frequent, prolonged drought in arid regions (the highlands of Mexico and Peru) were combatted communally. Thus there arose in these regions organized communities of varying size and power, supported by an agriculture based on maize, during the first centuries A. D. Moreover, those civilisations had reached quite an advanced stage of development, even though they belong nominally to the Stone Age, when stone was used for weapons and tools. Although metals, including gold and silver, were known, they were used almost exclusively for adornment. The results of excavations indicate that the archaic stage of these civilisations probably dates back to the time between 1500–1000 or 500 B.C. (the Olmecs in Mexico, the Chavín culture on the coast of Peru).

The two distinct areas of civilisation of Meso-America and South-America gave rise to several important parallel and successive cultures (cf. ill. 338). The term 'Meso-America' was coined for the cultural areas, in contrast to the geographic term 'Central America', since the frontiers of the two regions are not identical.

Meso-America: the Maya in Guatemala, Honduras and Yucatan; the Teotihuacan (or classical Toltec civilisation), Toltecs and Aztecs in the highlands of Mexico; Zapotecs and Mixtecs in Southern Mexico.

South America: Tiahuanaco and Inca in the highlands of Peru and throughout the entire cultural region; Early Chimú (Mochica) and Chimú on the north-west coast; Nazca on the south-west coast; the gold countries of Columbia and Costa Rica in the North.

338. The Ancient American civilisations

The main difference between these two great cultural regions – apart from the contrasted development of their architecture – lay in the fact that the two Central American peoples possessed an elaborate, carefully worked-out calendar and hieroglyphic writing, while the peoples of South America had a complicated system of statistical reckoning, and were more advanced in the working of metal (bronze) and in the breeding of animals.

Government in the Ancient American civilisations was originally theocratic – as in Ancient Egypt. That is to say, there was no difference between religious and secular power and the ruling dynasties traced back their origin to certain gods or were themselves looked upon as deities. Religious concepts were closely linked to natural phenomena. The Sun God (Tiahuanaco and Inca) and the Moon God (Mochica) took pride of place amongst the numerous gods and demons of the South American pantheon. The Central American peoples usually conceded equal status to several deities, such as the gods of rain, wind, fire, maize, etc. These, again as in Ancient Egypt, were represented as creatures compounded of human and animal forms or of various animals. Quetzalcoatl, or the 'Plumed Serpent', the symbol of wind and rain or of the sky – in the language of the Maya, Kukulkan – is one of the most familiar figures of Central American mythology (cf. ill. 339).

Everyday life and art in all early American civilisations were largely, indeed entirely, determined by religious concepts. The 'cities' were probably at first nothing more than temple-cities, the size and splendour of their buildings being for the benefit of the gods alone. They were only gradually converted into human settlements with houses built of stone (in place of sun-dried bricks) and fortifications against hostile neighbours. At the same time, they became economic centres and thereby fertile ground for the growth of luxury amongst the leading strata of the people and for the display of great wealth and wordly splendour. The Spanish conquerors, arriving at the beginning of the 16th century, found both Aztecs and Incas at this stage of development.

CENTRAL AMERICA

When in recent times the spades of archaeologists brought to light so many astonishing and unexpected works of art of the Ancient American peoples, the cultural level and, above all, the antiquity, of these civilisations were at first grossly overrated. These errors have since been rectified, and the earliest clearly datable Mayan civilisation is seen to have flourished between A. D. 450 and 900. After a decline, probably caused by civil wars, a new upward swing – which for some years was under strong Toltec influence – began round 1000. But internecine wars amongst the leading rulers of the federation of Mayan States brought about a new decline prior to the Spanish conquest in 1527.

A separate cultural epoch, the Teotihuacan, developed parallel to that of the Maya in the highlands of Mexico and reached its zenith in the 6th century A. D. It was followed by the Toltec civilisation (9th to 12th cent.), which was in turn succeeded by that of the Aztecs in the 14th century after an interregnum of various smaller warrior tribes. Although the Aztec empire was at the peak of its political power at the time of the Spanish conquest, its civilisation never equalled that of the greatest period of the Maya.

The architecture of Ancient America is truly striking from an operational point of view alone, since beasts of burden and the wheel did not exist. The pyramid temple was the most important type of building. The Pyramid of the Sun at Teotihuacan covers an area about 700 feet square and is over 200 feet high. These structures, made of rammed earth and faced with stone slabs, are terraced and – in contrast to the Egyptian pyramids – merely form the base of the actual temple which stands on the flattened summit. The walls of the temple, too, usually comprise a core of rammed earth faced with stone slabs (ill. 339). In the main, therefore, the walls are thick, especially if they also have to support the

Page from album by the Chinese master Lu Yüan *(18th century): Group of trees*

CH'IEN CHU *(1508–1572): Seascape. Chinese
ink and colour on silk*

HOKUSAI *(1760–1849): The poet Toba goes
into exile. Japanese colour woodcut*

TOYOKUNI *(1769–1825): Young lady at her toilet. Japanese colour woodcut*

Screen of Coromandel lacquer. East Asian work, c. 1720

heavy corbel table so characteristic of Mayan architecture. The interior (cella) is usually of very modest proportions. The temple chiefly owes its distinction to an elaborate decoration which may consist of relief (usually coloured), mosaic, or frescoes, in the interior often also of gold and silver. The luxuriant opulence of Central American ornament finds its counterpart only in India.

Almost everywhere in Central America we find walled-in playing fields for ritual ball games in the temple areas, the ball being considered the symbol of the sun.

As in all other early civilisations, architectural sculpture played an extremely important part. Free-standing sculpture was practically unknown, apart from occasional monoliths, such as the gigantic Olmec basalt heads (15 feet high) and numerous stelae decorated with calendric symbols, hieroglyphs and reliefs. Giant caryatids, made in four parts and representing realistic 16-feet-high warrior figures, were peculiar to Toltec art. A characteristic feature are the pillars with feathered shafts, the base being formed by a serpent's head: they are symbolic of Quetzalcoatl, or Kukulkan, to whom a series of important temples were dedicated, as for instance the warrior temple ('El Castillo') at Chichen-Itzá (ill. 339).

Reliefs, the chief form of sculpture, were either carved into the façades of the temples or modelled in stucco. Animal figures – symbols of the gods – take pride of place; often, there are beasts (jaguar and eagle) carrying human bodies or hearts in their gaping maw. But there are also narrative relief friezes in the manner of the frescoes of the time, showing processions of warriors, etc.

Mosaic also appears as wall decoration (Mitla, Chichen-Itzá, Uxmal, etc.), probably as the result of Toltec influence. Carefully prepared stones were set in cement to form patterns, for the most part geometric.

Wall painting has an essentially narrative character. The themes – religious scenes, scenes of battle and even events from everyday life – are shown in an essentially linear and two-dimensional manner without any perspective, as in child-art, and afford a very good insight into the mode of life and beliefs of this ancient civilisation. A particularly important find was a wall painting in the Mayan temple at Bonampak, showing scenes from a religious campaign (ill. 340).

Where small-scale painting and drawing were practised, in manuscripts – whose paper was made of raffia and coated with a fine layer of whitewash – and, above all, in pottery, we find a great mastery of line; the curves of the body are brilliantly expressed by means of mere outline, while foreshortening also is occasionally used.

The potter's wheel was unknown, as were glazes. Black and yellow motifs and white and brown drawings were very popular. The Aztec 'wax resist' technique of decoration is characteristic: the drawing in wax is laid on a white background, coated all over with black and then heated. The wax melts away with the colour that is on it and reveals the white ground, which now produces the drawing proper (negative painting).

The next most important of the minor arts of Ancient Mexico after the making of gold ornaments is stone-carving. One cannot but admire these outstanding craftsmen who fashioned masks and small statues with the most primitive tools, out of the hardest crystal and out of stone-like marble,

543

340. *Maya wall painting from Bonampak (c. A. D. 800): sacrificial scene*

obsidian and onyx. Turquoise was used very widely, particularly for incrustations and mosaic on ornaments. Human skulls – human sacrifice played an important part in the ritual of the Aztecs – thus treated are well known (ill. p. 548); there is a fine specimen, encrusted with turquoise and obsidian, in the British Museum, London.

SOUTH AMERICA

After the decline of the archaic Chavín civilisation, three new focal points are clearly discernible in the cultural regions of South America in the middle of the 1st century A. D. These were the Mochica culture of the early Chimú empire in the North, Nazca and Ica in the South, and Tiahuanaco on Lake Titicaca. The Tiahuanaco cultural epoch was at its zenith between A. D. 600 and 1000. From about 1000 onwards, it spread over vast regions of the highlands and finally flourished on the coastal plain. The Inca, whose empire at the time of the Spanish conquest included the entire regions of Peru, Bolivia, Ecuador, Chile and the West of the Argentine, did not consolidate their power until the middle of the 15th century. Like the Aztecs, the Inca absorbed the highly evolved civilisations of the conquered tribes. The Inca State, with all its ramifications, was an astounding achievement, and the conquering Spaniards were almost at a loss to describe the greatness, splendour and wealth of this civilisation.

What was found by way of testimony to their architecture within the lava walls of Cusco and within the granite walls of the Inca city of Machu Picchu was striking indeed (ill. 345). There were. pyramid temples like those of Mexico, but also palaces with baths, fountains and terraces. The long mountain roads – the 'royal roads' of the Inca – were so well planned, that the designers of modern highways still benefit from what they have to teach.

In contrast to Central American architecture, the walls of Peruvian buildings were made of large polygonal or square stone blocks without any binding. Architectural sculpture existed, but was comparatively rare. In the civilisations of the Andes, walls and façades were usually left plain and owed their effect entirely to the size of the megalithic masonry.

As in Mexico, the few surviving dried brick – adobe – buildings of the coastal cultures also include terraced pyramids (for example, the Temple of the Sun at Moche).

The comparatively rare examples of stone sculpture in South America – giant statues and reliefs – belong, like the very ancient, still unidentified, finds at San Augustín in Colombia (ill. 14), mostly to the Chavín and Tiahuanaco cultural epochs (reliefs on the Gates of the Sun).

Sculpture plays a far greater part in pottery. The Mochica culture, in particular, attained an exceptionally high standard in this sphere. Its naturalistic figured vessels are seen at their best in the so-called 'portrait vases' – vessels with human features and stirrup-shaped spouts – which in their proximation to life and nobility of expression compare favourably with the ceramic art of any age (ill. p. 553).

Not only shape but decorative painting was of great importance in pottery. In this respect, too, the Mochica vessels are outstanding. As well as being aesthetically satisfying, the bi-coloured scenes from mythology, war and everyday life tell us a great deal about life in Ancient Peru. The painted vessels of the Nazca and Tiahuanaco – at times very different from each other – are brilliant in colouring, but far less naturalistic. They show, principally, stylized animal and plant forms, and highly decorative mythic symbols (ill. p. 553).

Like Mexican sculpture, Peruvian pottery had a great influence on modern European art – Picasso's pottery is not unrelated to the ceramic arts of Peru.

Wall paintings (such as those in the Temple of the Moon at Moche) and textile motifs are very similar in style to the painted decoration on pottery. Woven and embroidered textiles found in tombs – well-preserved through the dry alkaline soil – are admirable examples of this type of art (ill. 341).

544

But, above all, the Spaniards coveted the almost unlimited treasure of gold and silver work, and were prepared to endure all the hardships of arduous journeys to attain it. With the conquest of the Chimú Empire, the Inca had become the inheritors of a highly evolved art of metalwork – beaten gold and silver, various methods of casting, alloys of gold and copper (called guanin or tumbaga) – which they had developed into a style of their own, characterized by simplicity and generosity of form. But the gold countries proper lay to the North, in the region of the Chicha peoples (Colombia, Panama, Costa Rica, Nicaragua). The various tribes evolved a series of very individual styles of gold-smith's work, which ranged from elaborate realism to strong stylization and geometric ornament (ill. p. 554).

This great proclivity for the crafts has remained one of the most characteristic traits of the indigenous peoples of America. The painted pottery, the basketry and the textile arts of the North American Indians are no less interesting. But these belong to so-called 'primitive' art and not to the great early civilisations.

PRIMITIVE ART

Primitive art is not prehistoric art, although the two have much in common. Most of humanity passed beyond the hunting and fishing stage, and learned how to cultivate the land and, finally, by discovering how to write, stepped into the light of history. Many races and tribes have still not done so. They remain at a prehistoric level and would probably stay there, if modern civilisation were to leave them alone. The different 'primitive' races of to-day represent in their religion, their customs and their art all the stages of the history of man. But all have one feature in common: primitive races throughout the world are 'animistic', i. e. they think of nature as inhabited by souls and spirits, who have to be contacted and, if possible, mastered by magic. This can be done through the fetish, an object of magical properties, which can both ward off spirits and help to gain their favour. Dance, accentuated by masks and fantastic costumes, serves the same purpose. Ancestor worship is widespread and often linked with totemism, the belief in a personal relationship between man and animal. Ancestor- or totem-poles play an outstanding part in the religion and in the art of these peoples. Everywhere, social and religious life are inextricably linked.

The simplest forms of primitive art are the tattooing and painting of the body. The African pygmies know no other kind of art; but it is also found amongst primitive peoples at a more advanced stage of their development. The urge for colour, everywhere, is irrepressible. It does not necessarily lead to painting as we understand it; this is the exception rather than the rule in primitive cultures. The man- and animal-pictures of the bushmen of the Kalahari desert south of the Congo, who stand on a very primitive level, recall Palaeolithic cave paintings and the rock paintings of eastern Spain.

But these hunters and nomads, and the peoples of North America, have no sculpture, although this usually takes the most important place in primitive art. Thus, when we speak of Negro art, we usually mean sculpture – in this case mostly wood sculpture. The primitive sculptor naturally prefers materials that are easily come by and are simple to work.

The African continent in particular, with its rich inheritance of the arts of past civilisations, supplies an excellent view of the development of primitive art.

It must be realized that out of 1200 identifiable culture groups (Negroes and Pygmies), only about 180 had produced works that could be classed as sculpture or painting at the turn of the last century. Negro art, as already mentioned, is chiefly sculpture; in its character and approach, it is in harmony with other forms of primitive art. It never copies nature. The aim is, certainly, to reproduce reality,

but primitive peoples, like children, do this by emphasising characteristic forms. The essential parts are never absent; but head, limbs, breasts, etc. are treated as separate entities and are joined without regard to natural proportions. Such deviations from nature can almost shock at times by their forcefulness. No wonder that Negro sculpture, which is so highly 'expressive', was discovered and admired by the Expressionists. Undoubtedly, this quality is desired and consciously accentuated by virtue of the function of certain objects, as in the case of the mask and the fetish. But although Negro art at times seems very close to the work of latter-day Western Expressionists, it differs from it fundamentally in that Negro sculpture (as primitive art generally) is not primarily an individual artist's interpretation. It is firmly rooted in a tradition passed on from generation to generation. Naturally, this awareness of tradition is an obstacle to any quick changes in style, as are the limitations on the Negro artist set by technique and material.

Everything is made of one piece only. Saw, nails and glue are unknown or disdained. The basic material is the tree trunk. Pole sculpture, then, appears as a stylistically early form of Negro sculpture. Examples in which the basic character of the pole largely survives therefore mark an early development; those where the wood is cut into more deeply and where the pole is to some extent 'dissolved' in sculptures, a mature and 'late' phase. (Cf. ill. p. 548, ill. 347)

But the effect of even the simplest pole sculpture is heightened by painting, and by the addition of hair, fabric, shells, pearls, feathers, etc. These 'real' materials make up for anything such sculptures – which are also painted ('polychrome style') – may lack in the way of naturalistic representation. Unpainted figures ('monochrome style'), in Negro sculpture, characterize a comparatively advanced level of culture and seem to have appeared at the same time as the casting of bronze. (Cf. ill. 348, 347)

Bronze casting presupposes a more elaborate social order. We speak in this case of a 'court' art, and semi-urban cultures, guided by powerful rulers, existed even before European colonization. The Yoruba culture in the Sudan (5th to 10th centuries) produced terra-cotta and bronze sculpture, as did the Benin culture, a development produced by Yoruba colonization. Benin art (ill. 342) between the 12th century and the British conquest in 1897 can be divided, stylistically, into at least five phases. Other centres of similarly advanced 'court' art were found in the Cameroons and in the southern and eastern Congo. The Akan on the Gold Coast even knew how to cast gold.

The free-standing human figure – and this applies to primitive art in general – is of only minor importance in primitive sculpture. Primitive art is mainly decorative, and the wood-carver applied his skill mostly to the decoration of objects such as door posts, chair backs, head rests, weapons, sceptres, combs, spoons, etc. Here we find the transition to applied art. The gift for ornament and a proficiency in crafts, especially basketry and occasionally also weaving, are the most characteristic features of all primitive art, and the outstanding achievements of individual races or cultures can easily be distinguished.

Similar conditions and materials have made the arts of all the Arctic peoples rather alike. Works in bone, fur, hide, bark and, less frequently, wood, are characteristic of these races of hunters, fishermen and reindeer keepers. All their work is remarkably naturalistic.

The art of the Ainu, a Palaeo-Asiatic, non-Mongolian people – the aborigines of the Kurile Islands, Hokkaido, and the southern part of Sakhalin, – includes moustache-like tattooing on the faces of women, carved grave-posts, bas-reliefs cut in wood and a wealth of Japanese-influenced ornament.

In India, primitive art now occurs hardly anywhere except amongst the populations of the Orissa region, West Bihar and the Nilgiri Hills; it includes pole sculpture in stone and wood, of a rather archaic character.

Chinese covered jar. 'Famille noire' porcelain. Early Ch'ang Hsi period, 1662–1722

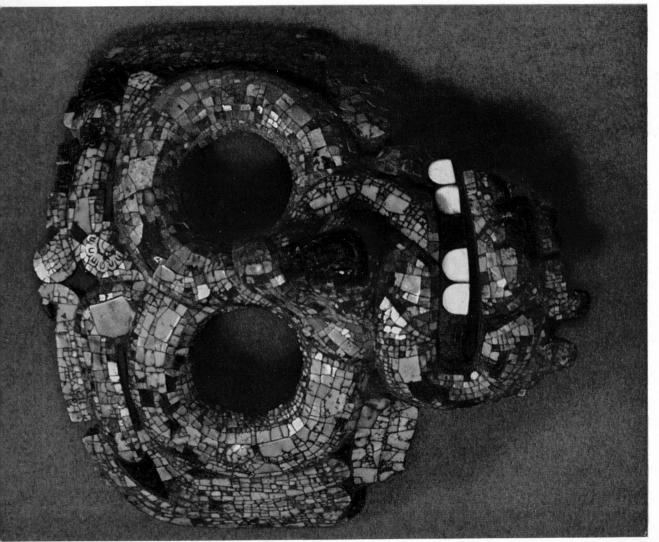

Turquoise mosaic mask of Tlaloc (?), an Aztec deity. Aztec civilisation, early 16th century

Dance mask from the Mpongwe tribe of the Gaboon, French Equatorial Africa (19th century). Painted wood

The Naga tribes in the Assam hills, whose art has survived to the present day, are of Indonesian origin. Their tomb figures, frequently life-size, recall the much smaller statuettes with pointed hats, typical of the sculpture of the Nias tribes. – In the Indonesian Archipelago, the Bataks of Sumatra have produced an outstanding art. Apart from pole sculpture, we find bronze casting by the *cire perdu* method. A remarkable form of sculpture of a rather Cubist character occurs in the Philippines and, in somewhat less abstract versions, in Nias, Singapore, Celebes and Borneo.

The art of Oceania (Melanesia, Micronesia and Polynesia) is more varied and richer in style than the primitive art of any other region, although there are certain common traits, based on race, economic conditions and religious life (ancestor worship, fetishism, etc.; ill. p. 556).

The wood carvings of New Guinea – both free-standing sculpture and articles of everyday use – are only equalled by African Negro sculpture at its best and by the art of North-West America. Tombara, an island in the Bismarck Archipelago and the principal art centre of New Ireland, is the home of pigmented memorial statues, which were carved from chalk, kept in special houses, and destroyed after some time had passed. These houses demonstrate the merging of architecture and sculpture in a truly exemplary manner (ill. p. 555). The *uli* and the *malanggans* are types of wooden sculpture, the former commemorative images of chiefs, the latter a variety of wood carving, decorated with motifs derived from human forms, animals, fishes, etc. These served the cult of the dead, of the sun, the moon and so on, and are also painted. Micronesian art, too, is essentially sculptural. Brilliant naturalistic wood carvings belong to the island of Yap; abstract cubist sculptures, to the south-east of the Caroline Islands.

Central Polynesia – Samoa, Tonga and Fiji – has produced little sculpture, in contrast to the border regions where the former inhabitants of Easter Island created monumental stone figures (ill. 346). The characteristic statuettes of this region are carved in toromiro wood, to whose texture they owe their bent shape. Fiji, Tonga, Hawaii, Tahiti and the Marquesas have produced an essentially cubist sculpture. In New Zealand, the Maori – who are also famed for the spiral pattern of their tattoo marks – have used similar ornamentation in magnificent wood carvings.

Drawing and engraving occupy an important place in the art of the aborigines of Australia. While similar in this respect to African Bushman art, the latter is more differentiated, more subtle and of stronger expression. Engravings on rocks and vessels already show the transition to the relief.

American primitive art comprises every stage of development and every form of expression. Except within the orbit of its ancient civilisations, there is practically no sculpture in Central and South American art, which therefore mostly finds expression in making all kinds of natural objects into ornaments. Coloured feathers, fruits (gourds, etc.) are of great importance in this connection. Woven and plaited articles often owe their beauty in no small degree to abstract geometric ornaments. The women of the Pueblo Indians are noted as outstanding potters and the colourful decoration of their pottery has symbolic significance. The Indians of the plain have great talent for drawing, and sculpture occurs in the early stages.

The Iroquois still make grotesque and highly expressive wooden masks. In their preliminary forms these masks are carved on the living tree so as to retain some of the forces of nature to keep away evil spirits. The North-West American Indians of the coastal regions show an exceptional gift for sculpture and drawing. Their totem- and house-poles – poles carved with the family crest – and their sometimes jointed masks, with features both human and animal, are what might be described as archetypal examples of the close link that once existed between the art and religion of all races. (Ill. 348)

But their religion, as mentioned at the outset, determines the rhythm of the life of primitive peoples, and it is at the root of their music, dance and poetry, no less than of their visual arts. It is hard indeed to say whether the so-called 'primitive' peoples, apparently so different from us, have really lagged behind the 'civilised' races in their manner of experiencing the world within and around them.

343. *The 'Court of the Lions' of the Alhambra in Granada/Spain (14th cent.)*

AJANTA. The ceilings and walls of the chaityas and viharas of the Ajanta caves (four cave-temples and 22 halls hewn into the rock) are decorated with magnificent Buddhist frescoes (ill. p. 532) and sculptures, dating from the 1st to the 7th century A. D. The paintings, on plaster, show scenes from the life of the Buddha and from the Jatakas (popular tales of the former incarnations of the Buddha).

ALHAMBRA (Arabic: 'Red Castle'). The Alhambra was the palace of the Moorish rulers of Spain at Granada. It comprises a series of palatial buildings, erected in the 13th and 14th centuries, and covers a vast area nearly two miles in circumference. The 'Court of the Lions', with 12 black marble lions supporting the basin of the central fountain (ill. 343), and the 'Court of the Alberca' are perhaps the most famous of the numerous arcaded courts and halls. Both the layout and, above all, the treatment of its interior, basically influenced Islamic architecture in Spain and throughout the Western part of the Muslim world (see Maghrib). The characteristic features of the Alhambra style are the lavish geometric decoration of the walls – here, two-dimensional ornament assumes an architectural function – and the use of calligraphy for its ornamental qualities. Another important element of this style are the so-called 'Azulejos' (Spanish: *azul* – blue), i. e. polychrome and elaborately patterned tiles, which were used for facing the lower portion of the inner walls of the Alhambra. The Alhambra vases illustrate the Moorish artist's penchant for repeating zones, borders and friezes in a horizontal manner.

ANGKOR THOM. Angkor Thom, with its central sanctuary, the Bayon temple, was the capital of Cambodia during the reign of the Khmer kings (9th to 12th cent.). The 12th-century Angkor Vat outside the city walls is a three-storeyed terraced temple dedicated to Vishnu. Monumental rock carvings with mythological scenes decorate the inside of the surrounding wall of the first terrace.

ASOKA. The exact dates of the reign of the Mauryan emperor Asoka are not clearly established. He probably ruled between 274 and 232 B.C. Under Asoka, Buddhism – hitherto despised – became the official religion. The earliest examples of Indian Buddhist art, the memorial columns or stambhas (q. v.), date from Asoka's reign. These edict pillars – as they were also called after the inscriptions they bore – had bell-shaped capitals and were surmounted by animal figures. The life-size elephant, carved from the living rock, and the relief fragment of the 'Squatting Girl' belong to the same period. In its perfection Buddhist sculpture during Asoka's reign remained unique – despite many later outstanding achievements – and suggests Western Asiatic, Bactro-Persian influence.

AZTECS. Tenochtitlan, the capital of the Aztec Empire (c. 1430–1521) was completely destroyed during the Spanish conquest. It had stood on the site of the present Mexico City. The Aztecs (cf. p. 538) adoped the Toltec pyramid temple in a somewhat simplified form, dispensing in particular with the rather over-elaborate decoration of the façade. They are also said to have achieved notable engineering feats (irrigation systems, aqueducts for piping drinking water, etc.).

BARK PAINTING. This form of painting is one of the principal arts practised by the aborigines of Australia. Stylistically, there is a distinction between the bark paintings of Eastern Australia (spirals, waves, etc.) and those of Western Australia (diamond patterns, squares, meander patterns). Although ornament is entirely geometric, bark painting depicts scenes from the everyday life of the aboriginal artist. Animals are shown 'transparent', with muscles, stomach and spine displayed as fully as possible. This is sometimes referred to as the 'X-ray style'. Bark painting has been carried on until the present day and experts can identify the work of individual artists without much difficulty.

BASKETRY. This is one of the most important crafts of the North-West American Indians, who have no pottery. Their baskets – made by a tight twining technique – are frequently decorated with wool or coloured grasses in a manner reminiscent of embroidery.

BENIN. The bronzes (figures and reliefs; ill. 342) of Benin (Nigeria) are amongst the finest examples of metal casting in primitive art. They are made in the *cire perdu* – 'lost wax' – technique, a method widely used in Europe and the Far East. European influence, according to some leading scholars, cannot be ruled out. Indeed, some authorities would not call Benin art 'primitive'. The kingdom of Benin was founded by the Yoruba people at the beginning of the 14th century B.C. Terra-cotta heads, found in the holy city of Ife, are characteristic of the Yoruba style in their life-like realism. The influence of Yoruba art extended as far as Lake Chad, where small bronze figures have been found in increasing numbers since 1930, besides somewhat coarser sculptures and clay vessels decorated in relief. The bronze reliefs of the classic phase of Benin art already show a tendency towards abstraction. This characteristic feature of African art developed even further in wooden sculpture, where the form often seems to merge completely into pattern. Benin bronze, being rather yellow, is often described as brass. Another important centre of metal casting was the Ashanti region of Ghana, the former Gold Coast. Many of the Ashanti figures are rather small and were used to weigh gold dust. Modern bronzes from Ghana, the Central Sudan and the Cameroons are debased tourist products.

BHUVANESWAR. This city is one of the oldest religious centres of India. The name means 'Lord of the Universe'. Like Benares, Bhuvaneswar was considered, by devout Hindus, to be the seat of the Gods and was therefore visited by pilgrims from all over India. The tower of the Mukteshvara temple – one of the city's numerous magnificent temples – has no peer in the architecture of any other civilisation. (Ill. 344)

BIDRI WARE. A technique – named after the Indian city Bidra – of inlaying a black, non-oxidising alloy of tin or zinc and copper or lead with gold and silver.

BIHZAD (1468–1515) was the greatest and the most famous of the Persian miniature painters. He has been called the 'Raphael of the East'. He was in charge of the famous Herat Academy (q. v.) and contributed greatly to the development of a national Persian style.

BOAR INCARNATION OF VISHNU. The group of Vishnu – shown in his boar incarnation as he rescues the Earth, Bhumi, from the cosmic ocean – at Udayagiri in Bhopal is probably the earliest Hindu rock sculpture. Vishnu also appears in nine other incarnations, namely, as a fish, a turtle, a man-lion, a dwarf, as 'Rama with the axe', as Rama, hero of the Ramayana, as Krishna, and as the Buddha in his most recent incarnation. Vishnu's tenth incarnation – when he will appear as a white horse – has not yet materialized.

BONE SCULPTURE. Bone sculpture is a characteristic form of Eskimo art. It occurs especially in regions (Alaska) where figures are carved in wood although it is found amongst all Eskimo tribes. At first, it probably served to decorate weapons or tools; independent sculpture came later.

BOROBUDUR, the most important Buddhist temple precinct in Java, contains the largest stupa in Indian architecture. Its core is formed by a stone-faced earth mound, supporting four oblong and three circular terraces. These rise to a total height of 115 ft. The side

344. Hindu Temple in Bhuvaneswar/Orissa, India (c. 1000 B.C.)

of the lowest terrace is 364 ft long. With its more than 500 statues, some 1400 bas-reliefs and 72 bell-shaped towers, it is an impressive sight.

BRICKWORK, DECORATIVE, is a contribution of northern and north-eastern Persia to Early Islamic art. All kinds of patterns are obtained with bricks or by means of a combination of brick and stucco. Some of the most famous examples are the brick and stucco mosaics at Nakhshivan in western Persia and the Baghdad Gate at Raqqa in Syria.

BRONZE VESSELS. Ritual bronze vessels occupy an important place in Chinese art. They were made for use in the ancestral sacrifice or to commemorate an important event, such as an official appointment, and have mostly been found in tombs. A Han bronze, now in the British Museum, was discovered amongst some Roman remains in England. These bronzes take the form of either food or wine vessels. Some of the most important forms are the ku, a trumpet-shaped wine vessel; the ting, a three- or four-legged food vessel; the li, a food vessel with three hollow legs; the yu, a wine vessel not unlike a coal-scuttle with a lid (ill. 331); the sauce-boat shaped i; the kuei, a round food vessel with two (later three) handles; the three-legged cone-shaped chueh, a wine vessel with two lips at its rim; and the tsun, a wine vessel of almost any shape, often in the form of an animal. Most scholars divide Chinese bronzes into three groups: the first, or archaic, phase lasted from the beginning of the Shang-Yin Dynasty to the 10th century B.C.; the second, or Middle Chou, which followed, continued until the middle of the 7th century; the third, or Huai, extended from the 7th century until the beginning of the Han Dynasty (c. 200 B.C.). The Huai style derives its name from the Huai river valley where bronzes of this type were first found. Many of the bronzes we see to-day are copies made during the Sung dynasty (A. D. 960–1127) or later.

CALABASH. A calabash is the wooden shell of a gourd. Their round, bottle-shaped or flat form makes calabashes natural models for pottery. The material is ideally suited for all kinds of decoration by carving, poker work or engraving. Pierced work also occurs. Sometimes, several techniques are combined and used in conjunction with colour, thus producing very elaborate effects. Quite often, the calabash is covered completely with beads, feathers or leather. In West Africa and the Cameroons, calabashes are frequently decorated in poker work. South and East Africa have produced magnificent examples of bead decoration.

CANTON, already one of the most important cities of South China in the 3rd century A. D., has always been a centre of the export trade, first to Persia and the Arab world, later to Europe. T'ang wares – sent to Persia from Canton – were copied in the Middle East as early as in the 9th century. Chinese lacquer was made especially for the European market from the 17th century onwards and was widely copied in Europe. In the 19th century, the Chinese made an exceptionally inartistic, over-decorated porcelain in green and pink enamels and heavy gildings, for the European market. Much could be written about Chinese export wares, both for Europe and for Siam and the Middle East. Many Sung celadon dishes were exported, as were the red and green – occasionally also blue and white – Swatow dishes of the Ming period. The Chinese, at all times shrewd judges of human nature, knew the taste of their foreign customers only too well. Dishes of vigorous shapes with, at the most, little ornament and free, yet stylized drawing went to Persia, Siam and Borneo; Europe received Cantonese porcelain. Perhaps the unprepossessing faces of the figures that adorn every Canton saucer, cup and teapot were meant to express some of the contempt the Chinese must have felt for everything European after the looting of the Summer Palace. Canton enamels – also heavily decorated – were often inspired by European models.

CELADON. This term is applied rather vaguely to a large class of Chinese monochrome ware – mostly of the Sung and early Ming dynasty – ranging in colour from a neat brown through a variety of greens to skyblue and almost white. The glaze is often cracked. First made in Korea and North China – in the Honan province – celadons were brought to great perfection in the South after the Sung Court had fled thence in 1127. The Percival David Collection in London contains one of the finest collections of celadons in the world. All the most famous types, such as the sky-blue Ju ware, the almost grey Ko and the nearly white Kuan with the cracks in the glaze stained brown – all Imperial wares – are represented there. The word 'celadon' is of French 18th-century origin and derives from the light green coat of an actor who played the part of the shepherd Celadon.

CEYLON. This island off South India contains many important early Buddhist remains, some dating from the time of Asoka, which coincides with the beginnings of the Sinhalese Empire. The two most important cities – both now in ruins – were Anuradhapura (the capital, until A.D. 726) and from the 12th century onwards, Polannaruwa. Ceylon was never conquered by Islam and therefore presents the picture of a purely Indian civilisation.

CHA-IRE. These are bowls of a grey or yellowish stoneware, covered with a thick brownish-black glaze, in which the dried tea leaves are kept. They appeared first in the 12th century A.D. The Japanese attribute the invention of this ware – which is used in the tea ceremony – to Kato Shirozaemon (q. v.), called Toshiro.

CHAITYA. The word 'chaitya', in its literal sense, means a mountain, or an earth mound. It is also applied to venerable objects, such as stupas, reliquaries and relics. Chaitya halls are Buddhist temples, hewn out of the living rock; as a rule they contain a stupa, and the interior is divided up by a series of carved columns. Some of the most famous examples are at Karli (c. 78 B.C.), Ajanta (q. v.) and Elephanta (q. v.).

CHA-NO-YU. This is the name of the tea ceremony, which was introduced in Japan with Zen Buddhism in the 13th/14th centuries. Tea was the means of acquiring purity of thought and nobility of feeling. The tea room and the tea equipment therefore had to cater for these needs. In consequence, the followers of the tea ceremony became severe judges of aesthetic matters. Their opinion had great influence on the craftsmen who made the utensils for the tea ceremony (lacquer and metal artists and potters) and spurred them on to great achievements. The tea equipment is an entirely original Japanese contribution to the potter's art and is of much earlier origin than Japanese porcelain (see Kato Shirozaemon).

CHATRA. The chatra, originally a honorific umbrella surmounting the dome of the stupa, has had a far-reaching influence on the architecture of the Far East. The roof of the Pagoda (q. v.) is but one example of the numerous transformations it has undergone. In its narrower sense, the term is used for pavilions with bell-shaped roofs.

CHAVÍN CULTURE (c. 1200 B.C.–A. D. 200). Named after the site of Chavín de Huantar in the northern highlands of Peru, where extensive ruins, including three-storeyed temples and monumental stone reliefs were found. It is the oldest civilisation of South America and includes the entire cultural region of Peru.

CHILKAT. The Chilkat, a branch of the Tlingit (an Indian tribe of the north-west coast of America) are oustanding weavers. Their blankets, made of the wool of the mountain goat, have designs woven into them in black, yellow and greenish-blue. These designs, however, are not characteristic weaving patterns but motifs used in wood carving and painting, such as the symmetrical profiles encountered on totem-poles (see Pole Sculpture).

CHIMU. The Chimu empire – the largest of the kingdoms of Ancient America – on the west coast of Peru, developed between the 13th and 15th centuries in the area of the Mochica culture and soon extended far beyond it. The ruins of Chanchan, the ancient capital, cover more than 8 sq. m. The city with its streets, squares, pyramid temples and palaces was originally divided into ten districts by enormous walls, whose remains are still standing. As throughout the entire coastal region, air-dried bricks were used. Chimu pottery and goldsmith's work were both of high quality.

CHINOISERIE. This term originally applied to a trend in Late Baroque and Rococo decorative art (especially in France), which was inspired by an enthusiasm for the newly discovered crafts of the Chinese. To-day, when there is no such stimulus, any imitation of Chinese objects and motifs is called a chinoiserie.

CHI PAI-SHIH (1863–1958). The greatest Chinese painter of our time, and known in his own country as the 'master of all masters', Chi Pai-shih painted landscapes, flowers and animals in the ancient Chinese tradition. His work is permeated by his great love of nature.

Peruvian portrait vase in the form of an Indian head (Moche district)
Top left: Painted pottery (Nasca district)
Left: Pottery with fish and snake motifs (Coastal Tiahuanaco style)

Ornamental breastplate of the Chibcha of Ancient Columbia. Beaten gold with chased human figure

Modern Negro painting from Poto-Poto, French Congo

Tambaran house (house of spirits) from the Uluppu district, Maprik mountains, New Guinea. The façade has giant faces painted on it, representing the spirits. On the beam near the bottom ancestors are represented

Helmet-dance mask from New Ireland (Melanesia, South Seas). Wood, carved and painted, eyes made of jewels, hair made of plant fibres

Mask commemorating a dead man, from New Ireland (Melanesia, South Seas). Wood, carved and painted

CHUNG. See Bronze Vessels.

CLOUD BAND. A highly stylized ornament that has been used in Chinese art since the Han dynasty; it has only a superficial resemblance to clouds, and is probably of symbolic origin.

COROMANDEL WORK. This type of lacquer work is named after the coast of Coromandel (in the gulf of Bengal), although it actually originated in China. The lacquer is carved and painted, the raised surfaces forming the design. Coromandel work was frequently used for folding screens, etc.

DAMASCUS. After the transfer of the Caliphate from Medina to Damascus, the city became the capital of the Omayyad rulers in A.D. 661. The Great Mosque, built in 735, is the first truly monumental building of its kind. It was built on the site – and with the materials – of the former Christian church of St John (consecrated in 379). The work of artists and craftsmen who still had their roots in the Byzantine tradition, it is one of the oldest and most important examples of Early Islamic architecture. Damascening (q. v.), the famous technique of inlaying metal, also owes its name to Damascus, as does damask, a monochrome fabric of silk, linen, wool or cotton, whose pattern is produced by a special method of crossing warp and weft.

DESERT PALACE. The caliphs of Damascus used to build themselves winter palaces in the desert. The most famous examples are Qusayr 'Amra, at the northern end of the Dead Sea, and Mchatta. The former contains frescoes of a vaguely mythological character in the Hellenistic manner. No other example of such extensive fresco decoration in a pre-Romanesque building has yet been discovered, either in the East or in the West. Mchatta represents a different type of building, namely the Hira, or enclosure, of which it is the earliest example. It is the most famous of the palaces of the Omayyad Caliphs. Most of these desert palaces covered an enormous area. The sides of one of the largest – Balkuwara, near Samarra – measured three quarters of a mile.

DYNASTIES, CHINESE. The history of China is divided into the reigns of twenty-four dynasties, and Chinese works of art are broadly classified according to these dynasties. They are Shang-Yin 1766–1122 B.C.; Chou 1122–255 B.C.; Ch'in 255–206 B.C.; Han 206 B.C. – A. D. 200; Three Kingdoms 220–265; Chin 265–317; Eastern Chin 317–420; Northern & Southern Dynasties 420–589 – this includes, amongst others, the Northern, Eastern and Western Wei dynasties (385–557); Sui 589–618 (although a short dynasty, it is important in the development in Chinese Buddhist sculpture); T'ang 618–907; Five Dynasties 907–960; Sung 960–1127; Southern Sung 1127–2180; Yüan 1280–1368; Ming 1368–1644; Ch'ing or Manchu 1644–1912.

ELEPHANTA. The rock temple at Elephanta, on an island near Bombay, has been called the Indian Parthenon. The enormous statue of Trimurti, the Brahmanist Trinity, dominates the central portion of the temple. The cave, with its sculpture, is a fine example of the sense of the grandiose and love of the colossal that characterized post-Gupta sculpture.

ELLORA. Like Elephanta, Ellora (or Ellura) is famed for its Siva statues (especially Siva Nataraja, Lord of the Dance.

FEATHERWORK is an important branch of primitive art. One of the finest examples is the bust of the Hawaiian war-god Kukailimoku, which is made of the feathers of rare birds. This technique produces an effect of great splendour and was therefore also used for royal cloaks (yellow), the cloaks of chiefs (yellow and red) and those of priests (red) as well as for ceremonial collars and helmets. Featherwork was widely practised not only in the South Seas (in particular, Polynesia), but also on the American continent, where the Aztecs of Ancient Mexico made pictures from coloured feathers. The Indians of South and Central America developed various methods for attaching feathers and also used them in connection with a wealth of other materials.

FETISH. A fetish is a figure endowed with magic properties, and any object considered to be 'magic' can become a fetish in certain parts of Africa. Fetish figures were often made to order for a special purpose. They cannot compare as works of art with memorial statues or statues connected with ancestor worship.

FRIDAY MOSQUE. The giant mosque was first built in Persia under Abbasid rule (750–1258). It enabled thousands of warriors from surrounding camps to assemble there on a Friday in prayer. The Friday mosques – also significantly known as camp mosques or Djami el Askar – thus expressed the military power of Islam as well as the devotion of its followers.

FUR MOSAIC. The Eskimos of Greenland and Alaska frequently decorate their clothes in appliqué style with pieces of fur or hide (dog, seal or reindeer) either dyed or in its natural colour.

GANDHARA, to-day a province of Afghanistan, is famous in the history of Indian Art for its sculptures. In the art of Gandhara, Hellenistic forms combine with Buddhist piety, and it has therefore also been referred to as Graeco-Buddhist art. Its beginnings are generally attributed to the 1st century B.C., and it had more or less disappeared by the 5th century A. D. Gandhara art is chiefly noted for its two types of the Buddha image, the teaching and the meditating Buddha. The former is shown standing, the latter seated. Every example of the Buddha image known to us is based on the life and past incarnations of the Buddha in some form. In Gandhara art he was for the first time presented as a human being and not as symbol.

GORODAYU SHONZUI was a Japanese potter, who visited China at the beginning of the 16th century to study the making of porcelain. He brought back with him some of the clay used in porcelain manufacture in the hope of establishing this craft in Japan. But he was

557

thwarted for lack of a suitable local clay. It was a Korean potter, Ri Sampei (q. v.), who eventually succeeded a century later in doing so.

GUPTA DYNASTY AND PERIOD. The Gupta period, named after the Gupta rulers of Northern India (4th to 7th centuries A. D.), was the Golden Age of Indian Art. Some of the finest examples of Indian sculpture, such as the red sandstone Buddha at Matura, belong to this time. It was an age in which the two great Indian religions – Buddhism and Brahmanism – existed peaceably side by side. All the arts flourished, and such examples as have come down to us possess a gay and almost Dionysian quality. (Ill. p. 532)

HERAT ACADEMY. The Herat Academy was founded by the Timurid ruler Baisunghar at the beginning of the 15th century. Its most renowned member was Bihzad (q. v.). The masters of the Early Islamic schools of Basra and Baghdad had continued to practise miniature painting in the time-honoured, highly formal tradition: picture and calligraphy were closely interwoven, the colours were used according to aesthetic principles and for their symbolic content. The painters of the Herat School broke with this tradition by painting naturalistic miniatures, isolated from the text. The subjects were mostly portraits and scenes from Persian legend and history. (Ill. p. 521)

HILL JAR. A hill jar is a glazed earthenware vessel of the Han period. It is of cylindrical shape, with a lid in the form of a mountain.

HIRAME (Golden Lacquer). This technique consists in embedding gold dust in the lacquer. The earliest examples of this type of lacquer work date from the Fujiwara (after 858) and Heike (876–1185) periods.

HSIA KUEI. Like his contemporary Ma Yuan, Hsia Kuei – who was active in the first quarter of the 13th century – ranked as a leading painter of the 'Romantic' landscape, which relies for its effect on restraint rather than dramatic intensity. One of Hsia Kuei's most famous works is 'Ten Thousand Li of the Long River', a 35-ft-long scroll.

HUAI. See Bronze Vessels.

HUANG CH'ÜAN (died 965) is considered by the Chinese to be the greatest flower painter of the Early Sung period. He is thought to be the founder of the famous Sung academy.

INCAS. The stone structures of Cuzco, Cajamarca, Saccsaihuaman and Machu Picchu, in the highlands of Peru, and Pachacamac, on the coast, all date from the Golden Age of the Inca Empire (1438–1527) in Peru. The walls are made of carefully dressed stones, joined without any mortar or metal clamps (Tiahuanaco, q. v.). The entirely smooth or rusticated surfaces are without any ornament and rely for their effect only on the arrangement of the small, trapeze-like openings for doors and windows.

INRO. The inro is a small box for medicines and the like, worn by the Japanese dangling from the belt of

345. Buildings of the Inca city of Machu Picchu (Uplands of Peru)

their traditional dress. It is attached to the belt by a silken rope and held in position with the netsuke (q. v.).

JADE. The term 'jade' is applied to two kinds of minerals, nephrite and jadeite. The former is a silicate of magnesium and calcium, the latter a silicate of sodium and aluminium. Both are very hard and can only be worked with the dust of minerals of an even higher degree of hardness. Jade – called 'yu' by the Chinese – occurs in Burma, Khotan and Yarkand (both in Turkestan), in Siberia, New Zealand, South America and even Europe, although it has rarely been of interest to craftsmen outside the Far East, India, New Zealand and South America. Apart from Chinese jade carvings, fine pieces were made in Nughal, India. Unlike Chinese examples these are often studded with precious stones.

JAVA possesses some of the finest examples of Buddhist and Hindu sculpture and architecture. Here, Buddhist sculpture flourished and developed (Borobudur, q. v.) after the decline of Buddhism in India. In eastern Java, Brahman art produced gigantic sculptures, such as the Durga of Candi Singasari.

KAMAKURA BORI. This term is used for a type of wood-carving in relief, which has been practised in Japan since the Kamakura period (1192–1338). The figures are successively covered with black and red lacquer in such a fashion that the black still shows through the red.

KATO SHIROZAEMON, also called Toshiro, has become an almost legendary figure in the history of Japanese civilisation. According to tradition, he visited China in the 12th century in the company of the Zen priest Dogen to study the ceramic arts. He, his descendants and his numerous pupils are credited with the invention of the cha-no-yu (q. v.). Kato Shirozaemon at first used Chinese materials; later he found a suitable Japanese clay. The glazes – in imitation of the Sung tamokkü – are rather thick and are black, dark brown, chocolate and yellowish-grey.

KOFTGARI. This term is used in India for Persian damascening (q. v.) techniques. There are three types, the so-called 'deep' koftgari (for steel, which is treated with fire after damascening, to make it blue), 'simple koftgari' (where the steel is inlaid without any further treatment) and 'false koftgari' (when gold is melted into the engraved pattern).

KOSE NO KANAOKA. An outstanding Japanese landscape painter of the second half of the 9th century, Kose No Kanaoka has often been classed with the famous Chinese artist Wu Tao-tzu. He was the most important painter of secular themes in an age when art was still almost entirely in the service of Buddhism.

KUDU. This is a popular decorative feature in Indian architecture. The kudu, which is shaped like a lotus leaf, is of Vedic origin.

KUFIC. Islamic artists exploited the decorative qualities of this highly angular form of early Arabic writing to the utmost, as they did the many other Arabic and Persian scripts.

KURSI. These are folding trestles, often made in two parts, for supporting the Koran during the service in a mosque. Elaborately carved in hardwood and inlaid all over with ivory, metal and mother-of-pearl, they embody the principles of Islamic decoration to the highest degree.

LACQUER. Chinese lacquer dates back at least to the second half of the 2nd century B.C.; quite possibly it was known much earlier. It is made from the juice of the lac tree (Chinese: ch'i shu) and can be dyed almost any colour. The traditional lacquer colours are black, red, brown and yellow. The core, usually of thin wood, is coated with layers of lacquer at intervals of several months. When the lacquer is of the required thickness, the design is carved into it. The article is then given another coat of lacquer and is often dried for years before it is offered for sale. Lacquer will withstand damp to an extraordinary degree. Lacquer objects well over 2000 years old have been found in flooded tombs in a state of perfect preservation. The centre of Chinese lacquer manufacture was Szechwan. (See also: Canton, Coromandel Work, Hirame)

LI LUNG-MIEN (died 1106), whose real name was Li Po-shih, was a calligrapher and a painter of landscapes, Confucianist themes and animals. His favourite subject was horses. Regarded as the greatest Chinese painter next to Wu Tao-tzu (q. v.), he was essentially a cultured amateur without any 'professional' training.

LUSTRE WARE. The ban on the use of precious metals (q. v.) forced the craftsmen of Islam to look for substitutes. Lustre was produced by applying a layer of iridescent colour to the glaze. The vessel was then fired again in a muffle kiln (see Ceramics). Gold, silver, ruby lustre, etc., are named according to the colour and material used.

MAGHRIB. The Maghrib is the name applied to the West of the Islamic world. The centre of the art of the Maghrib, i. e. Moorish art, was Andalusia, where Abder-Rahman – having fled Syria in 755 – founded an empire with Cordova as the capital. Moorish art is a synthesis of Islamic, Byzantine, Hellenistic and Spanish elements. One of its most characteristic products is the Alhambra (q. v.), Granada. (Cf. ill. 29, 343)

MAMALLAPURAM. The great 8th-century relief of the Descent of the Ganges at Mamallapuram near Madras is a unique example of rock sculpture. It is 90 ft long and 30 ft high, and comprises human figures (often life-size), groups of animals and scenes from mythology, which have been carved on the face of an enormous boulder near the sea-shore.

MARKS, EMBLEMS, etc. Marks, on Chinese porcelain, can be of many kinds. There are reign marks, or nien hao, with the name of the particular Emperor; date marks, giving the exact year; honorific marks, being marks in praise of a particular piece; hall marks and marks of dedication and good wishes (ill. 74a). There is also as variety of symbols, including the eight Buddhist emblems and the eight precious things. The former comprise the bell, the conch shell, the State umbrella, a canopy, the lotus flower, a covered vase, two fishes (for a happy married life) and a knot, the emblem of longevity. So many different symbols are there, however, that even the experts, who have spent a lifetime amongst Chinese porcelain, keep coming across new marks. Marks, which rarely, if at all, go back to before the Ming dynasty (1368–1644), are usually inscribed under the glaze in blue or above the glaze in red. Chinese potters frequently put the mark of an earlier reign on their work, not with the idea of deceiving, but as a tribute to the ceramic arts of a prior age. Such marks are often found on wares of the Wan-li period (1573–1619), which sometimes bear a Hsüan-te nien hao, and on Ch'ien-lung (1736–1795) pieces. Marks on Japanese porcelain and pottery are basically very similar to Chinese marks.

MARUYAMA OKYO (1733–95) is considered to be the leading painter of the realistic school of the late Tokugawa period (cf. p. 536). He was strongly influenced by European art.

MASKS have, at one period or another, been common to almost every civilisation. The Iroquois Indians of North America, significantly, call masks 'false faces'. Their masks are carved from the living tree, so that they, too, shall be alive. Masks probably originated in tattooing (q. v.), body-painting, animal disguises and the worship of skulls. Animal masks are mostly associated with hunting peoples, ancestor masks with agricultural races. There are all manner of masks, made from every kind of material, though the basic material is wood. The inhabitants of New Britain incorporate portions of skulls, and Iroquois add human hair. Feathers, beads and the like are also used. Some masks merely cover the face, some the entire head; others, again are set upon the head like a hat. Styles can only be classified within a particular region, though within each region they will be governed by traditional art forms. (Ill. p. 548, 556)

MAYA. It is still a mystery why the Maya suddenly abandoned the temple cities of the 'Old Kingdom' in the 10th century and built new, fortified towns further east on the Yucatan peninsula. Maya culture never again flourished as it had done in the Old Kingdom. The temple cities (Uaxactun, Tikal, Copan, Palenque, Bonampak, etc.) with their pyramid temples, enclosures for ritual ball games, observatories and palaces are believed to have been wholly monastic settlements. The cities of the New Kingdom (Chichen-Itzá, Uxmal, Mayapan), where palaces predominated, had an essentially secular character. Architectural sculpture and frescoes (ill. 340) now frequently dealt with scenes from everyday life. A strong Toltec influence is noticeable, particularly in the Temple of the Warriors ('El Castillo') at Chichen-Itzá with its pillars in the shape of plumed serpents. Other important buildings of this period are the observatory at Chichen-Itzá ('Caracol') and the 'nunnery' at Uxmal. In sculpture, the Maya produced a type of stele ('milestones' of time), which was erected at fixed intervals. Apart from complicated calendric symbols, these stelae were decorated in reliefs of a symbolic and religious character. In the ceramic arts, the Maya surpassed all the other peoples of South America by virtue of their figure vases and the narrative painting on their pottery.

MEDRESE. Although the medrese, or madraseh, is a type of mosque of purely Persian origin, it was largely introduced to the Islamic world through the Sunnite Turks and the Mongols. A famous example is the Madraseh Ulugh Beg in Samarkand (Turkestan), which was built between 1447 and 1449. Literally, the word means a school of law and Islamic theology, and the medrese originally did – and still occasionally does – serve this purpose. (Ill. 328)

MINARET. A slender tower, usually with a gallery, from which the muezzin calls the faithful to prayer in the Islamic East. The minaret probably originated in the watch- and grave-towers of the Middle East. The name is derived from 'menara' (Arabic 'where fire burns'), thus suggesting that it may have been inspired by a famous light-house, the Pharos of Alexandria. (Cf. ill. 327)

MIRRORS. Chinese and Japanese mirrors were originally made of metal. They were discs, without any glass. Often, they are elaborately decorated with the motifs characteristic of the period. After the T'ang dynasty, earlier motifs were more often copied, although original designs are still found occasionally as late as in the 18th century.

MISHIMA. A technique of inlaying pottery with strips of clay before glazing, and mostly used in Korea.

MIXTECS (c. A. D. 800–1521). Important examples of Mixtec art were discovered in the Ancient Mexican ruins of Monte Alban and Mitla (formerly religious centres of Zapotec civilisation). These finds include a tomb treasure, consisting of gold and silver articles set with precious stones and stone mosaics on the façades of the palace at Mitla.

MOCHICA. The 135-ft-high Temple of the Sun at Moche (on the west coast of Peru) was the religious centre of the Mochica or Moche culture (at its peak between A. D. 600 and 1000), which was distinguished above all by its superb pottery. (Cf. p. 544 ill. p. 553)

MOHAMMEDAN BLUE. A term used in China during the Ming dynasty for cobalt, which – in its best quality – could only be obtained from the Mohammedan West. Blue was of such importance in Chinese ceramics from the Yuan dynasty onwards, that quality was considerably affected when supplies of cobalt were short.

MUDÉJAR STYLE. The Mudéjars are Moors who were allowed to stay in Spain after the end of Arab rule. Muslim artists thus worked for Christian patrons and produced a mixed style with both European and Islamic features. This happened very gradually, parallel with the Spanish re-conquest of the Iberian peninsula (11th to 15th cent.). The influence of the Mudéjar style is most noticeable in textiles (knotted carpets, silk brocades), pottery (Paterna) and architecture (the Alcazar of Seville, Estramadura, etc.).

MUGHAL PAINTING. Mughal painting is contemporary with Rajput painting and has its roots in Persian illumination. It was essentially a secular Court art. Babur, the Turkish conqueror of India and the founder of the Mughal dynasty (1526) had Persian miniatures copied. His son Akbar set up a school of Court painters, whose greatest teachers came from the school of Herat. Mughal painting, in contrast to Rajput painting, shows strong European influence. (Ill. p. 533)

NARA. From 710 to 794, Nara (cf. ill. 335) was the capital of Japan. Nara art, pertaining to this period, has an almost entirely Chinese character. Although Buddhism became the official religion during those years it did not displace Shintoism. The discovery of large deposits of copper ore made the production of bronze much easier and greatly influenced sculpture. Indeed, the Japanese sculptors of the time produced outstanding bronze figures (such as the Yakushi Trinity in the Kondo of Yakushi-ji (whose central statue measures nearly 15 ft) of a kind quite unknown in China. Besides wooden statues and coloured pottery figures – often life-size – the Japanese also evolved a dry lacquer technique called kanshitsu or chia-chu, by which enormous figures could be made, whose size seems quite out of proportion to their weight (the 10-ft lacquer Kwannon at Shorin-ji, *inter alia*). The same method was also used for the masks worn in a ritual dance, called Gigaku. One of the most interesting collections of works of the T'ang dynasty (A. D. 618–907) is the Shoso-in (temple treasure) at Nara. It contains thousands of articles of every kind, including weapons, armour, mirrors, textiles, etc. It is not known whether these were made in China or by Chinese craftsmen employed at the Japanese Court.

NETSUKE. These are ornamental buttons carved from wood, ivory or some other comparatively precious material. They serve to attach the inro (q. v.) to its silken cord. Netsukes of the 18th and early 19th centuries often represent magnificent examples of carving and are true works of art in miniature. Few other objects are so essentially Japanese. Collectors all over the

world treasure netsukes quite as much as Japanese sword guards (see Swords).

OCEANIA. Ancestor worship is practised throughout Oceania (Melanesia, Micronesia, Polynesia). The most important object is the ancestor figure, which can be made of wood, stone, raffia fabric or chalk. Some of the most interesting examples are the vigorous and stylized wood sculptures of the Uli (southern New Ireland), and the painted and carved boards, human figures and masks, which are classed together under the name of *malanggans* (nothern New Ireland). This term is derived from Malanggane, which is the name of a festival held annually between May and July in honour of the dead. The ceremonial seat (Sepik), ancestor boards and masks (Sulka, Baining and Buka masks on the Solomon Islands, various types in New Caledonia) are also considered personifications of the souls of ancestors. Closely related to these masks – and frequently used as such – are painted and decorated ancestor skulls, which are either made of the front portion of the skull and the jaw (New Ireland) or the skull only (New Guinea). Animals, birds or reptiles – the crocodile, the cassowary or the turtle in Melanesia, a fish in eastern Polynesia – can also represent the souls of ancestors. Such symbols are also used to decorate weapons, buildings, boats, etc. The art of Oceania ranges from realism to geometric ornament (cf. p. 549). On Easter Island huge stone figures are to be found – there are now two fine examples in the entrance hall of the British Museum – in the style of primary pole sculpture. Their origin is still debated. (Ill. 346, pp. 555, 556)

PAGODA. The term pagoda is used for the temples of South-East Asia and China. The form of the pagoda is derived from the Indian stupa (q. v.) and was first developed in Burma. There are various types of pagoda. A feature common to many – but by no means all – is the upward-curving roof. Among the most important are the Wild Goose Pagoda, Ch'ang-an (701–705), which is a seven-storeyed tower, the Sat Mahal Pasada, a 12th-century tower in Polannaruwa (see Ceylon), and the pagoda at Hōryū-ji, Japan, said to have been built by

346. Giant figures on Easter Island/South Seas. Stone

the Koreans at the beginning of the 7th century. Pagan, the capital of Burma, became one of the centres of the Buddhist world in the 11th century – after the conversion of King Anawratha to Buddhism – and contained some magnificent pagodas, as did Rangoon, where relics of the Buddha are enshrined in the Shwe Dagon Pagoda.

PEKING, rebuilt several times on different sites, has been one of the important administrative centres of China since the early days of Chinese history. Part of it is formed by the Imperial City, which includes the Forbidden City with the Winter Palace. The Winter Palace, begun during the Ming dynasty (1368–1644) is one of the greatest works of architecture of any civilisation. The 'Altar of Heaven', within the precincts of the 'Temple of Heaven', is a good illustration of the effect of symbolism on Chinese architecture. It consists of a three-tiered circular marble terrace, enclosed by a double wall with a circular inner and a square outer portion, thus symbolizing Heaven (round) and Earth (square).

PHOENIX. The phoenix, or feng huang, has been a common motif in Chinese art since the Han period. It appears especially on textiles and on pottery.

POLE SCULPTURE. This term is used for works of sculpture carved out of natural objects basically cylindrical in shape, such as a tree trunk or an elephant's tusk. There are two kinds of pole sculpture: primary, and secondary. In the former, the subject is shown at rest, in the latter in movement. Realistic, or naturalistic developments of secondary pole sculpture were probably due to European influence. The principal regions of primary pole sculpture are the western Sudan, the north-eastern and equatorial areas of the Congo, and Melanesia. Secondary pole sculpture is also to be found in these parts of Africa, as well as in the vast region between the Pacific and the Atlantic, throughout the forests of the Sudan, the Congo and along the coast of Alaska and British Columbia. Some of the liveliest and most interesting examples are the 'cubist' works of the Tlingit and the Haida of the north-west coast of America. Totem poles, too, are a product of North America. Often tree-high, they stand in front of Indian dwellings or support the eaves. They are carved and painted with highly stylized figures of the inhabitants of the house and their protecting spirits and animals (a belief in a relationship between a family and certain spirits, less frequently between individuals and certain animals, is the essence of totemism). Such figures, which have lost their original form and have become integrated into a kind of ornament, are characteristic of the

561

art of the north-west coast. Reduced to two dimensions (on the walls, skin, clothing, etc.), they become rather flattened and symmetrical. An animal or bird is shown in double profile, as if it had been split in two and opened out. Many of these poles also display heraldic devices and are known as heraldic poles. (Ill. 347, 348)

PRECIOUS METALS, THE BAN ON. According to the orthodox interpretation of the Koran, the faithful were to be rewarded in Paradise with vessels of gold and silver. The ban on precious metals was based on this belief. It is quite possible that this ban was really caused by a shortage of gold and silver. Islamic artists discovered the most splendid substitutes, such as damascening (q. v.) and lustre (see Ceramics). Ill. 329, 349

RAJPUT SCHOOL. While India was ruled by the Islamic Mughal dynasty, the wealthy Rajput princes encouraged a school of miniature painting, whose followers tried to carry on the old Hindu tradition (c. 1500–1800). The centres of this school were Rajasthan (with the cities of Jaipur, Jodhpur and Jamma) and Pahari (with Basohli and Kangra) in the north-western Himalayas. The Rajput, or Rajasthani, artists – who were not able to free themselves completely from the influence of Mughal painting – aimed at large, simple forms in the manner of the fresco. Legends from the life of Krishna were a favourite theme.

RAKU. Raku ware has been made by fourteen generations of the Raku family since the 16th century. Raku pottery – always bowls – is used in the tea ceremony. The colour is usually black, sometimes also red or white. It is a coarse ware, often with a rough, pitted glaze. Undoubtedly, Raku pottery is far more characteristic of Japan than the rather horrible egg-shell tea cups made since the last century for the Western market. It is probably of Korean origin – similar wares were known in China during the Sung dynasty – since colonies of Korean potters had been brought to Japan in the reign of the Emperor Hideyoshi.

RI SAMPEI. A Korean potter, Ri Sampei was the first to discover deposits of porcelaneous clay in Japan (17th century). He founded the first Japanese porcelain factory at Arita in the Hizen province.

RIZA AL'ABBASI (c. 1598–1643). A native of Tabriz, Riza was one of the best-known miniature painters of Safavid Persia (17th. cent.) and calligrapher to Abbas the Great. The work of Riza and his school is naturalistic in the extreme. Individual figures of courtiers, etc. were a favourite subject.

SATSUMA. Although well known in Europe as an over-decorated, heavily gilt and enamel-painted ware, the type used by the Japanese is very different. It has rough glaze in black, greenish blue or flambé, reminiscent of the stoneware made in the Kwantung province of China from the late Ming dynasty onwards.

SESSHŪ (1420–1506). A landscape painter, Sesshū was the most famous master of Japanese ink painting.

SHEN CHOU (1427–1509) was the landscape painter par excellence of the Ming period and one of the greatest Chinese artists of all time.

STALACTITE VAULTING. This is a characteristic feature of Islamic architecture and can be seen at its best in the mosques of Isfahan. The term is derived from the stalactite-like projections on vaults of every size. Since few branches of the arts are less affected by the imitation of nature than Islamic architecture, it would be a mistake to regard stalactite vaulting as an attempt to copy actual stalactites.

STAMBHA. Stambhas are memorial pillars, meant to recall events in the life of the Buddha. With their bell-shaped capitals, surmounted by animals, they achieve a very high degree of workmanship. The stambha of Sarnath (from the reign of Asoka) stands where the Buddha taught for the first time.

STUPA. The earliest type of a Buddhist religious building. It originally consisted of a series of umbrella-shaped structures of different heights, made of wood, brick or stone. The basic form is believed to be derived from the Indian funeral mound. Originally, the stupa was a monument, erected in places hallowed by a visit of the Buddha or a Boddhisatva. It was also a reliquary shrine, where sacred objects or texts might be preserved. One of the outstanding examples is the Great Stupa at Sanchi, India (ill. 330, 350). The monumental Stupa at Borobudur (q. v.) in Java is essentially Indian in its outline. The towers and terraces of Burmese and Siamese stupas are characteristic of the architecture of South-East Asia.

SU SHIH (1036–1101). One of the great artists of the Sung dynasty, Su Shih (also called Su Tung-p'o), was not only an outstanding painter and calligrapher but a poet-philosopher, like his friend Li Lung-mien.

349. *Persian jug from Khurasan (12th cent.). Bronze with damascening*

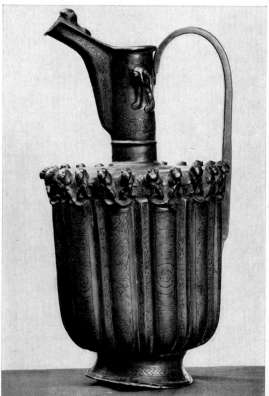

350. *Apex of the North Gateway of the Great Stupa of Sanchi/Central India (1st cent. B.C.). Stone*

SWAMIN STYLE. Objects decorated in the Swamin style (carvings, textiles, metalwork), an almost Baroque manner, originating in Southern India, are frequently covered with figures from Indian mythology. The term 'Swamin' means lord, master or hero.

SWORDS. Swords – and indeed weapons of almost any description – have always been eagerly coveted by collectors, both in the West and in the East. The Japanese swordsmith has from earliest times been a craftsman of the highest order. The tsuba, or guard – the portion between handle and blade – was probably the first section of the sword to be decorated. The fuchi, an ornamental metal collar at the base of the handle, immediately behind the tsuba, and the kashira, a metal cap at the upper end of the handle, are scarcely less important. Sometimes, a small knife, the kozuka, is worn in the same scabbard. The kozuka, which is also decorated, is inserted through a small opening in the tsuba. Metal ornaments fastened to the handle by the cord wrapping, or itomaki, are called menuki.

TAJ MAHAL. The Taj Mahal, near Agra in Central India, is a sepulchral monument of white marble, which Shah Jahan had erected (1630–48) in memory of his favourite wife, Mumtaz Mahal. A magnificent example of the Moghul style, it ultimately derives from the formal gardens and pavilions of Persia. The name of the architect-in-chief was Ustad Isa; but the undertaking was a supreme instance of co-operative endeavour and combined labour, for Shah Jahan brought together master-masons from Delhi, Kandahar and Mooltan, a specialist in dome construction from Constantinople, designers of cupola-spires from Lahore and Samarkand, graphic artists from Syria, mosaicists, carvers, garden planners and experts in hydraulics from India, the Orient and Central Asia. (Ill. 351)

TAPA. This is a Polynesian word, meaning a barkcloth, and is made by beating the bast of various trees (mulberry, fig, breadfruit, etc.) with a special instrument. Although this fabric is also made in tropical Africa, South America and Indonesia, the peoples of Oceania are the undisputed masters of the technique. They are also the most advanced in the decoration of tapa, for which they use a method of block printing. Painted tapa is not met with very frequently, and figural work is the exception rather than the rule. Here, as elsewhere, the geometric ornament predominates.

TATTOOING. The word is derived from tatau, a Samoan expression, meaning 'to beat'. Next to painting and scarring, it is the most popular form of 'decorating' the body – and is by no means confined to the so-called primitive races. To get the colour under the skin, the tattoo artist uses small, sharp tools, with which he can often cover the entire body with lasting decoration. Patterns denote membership of social groups. Painting is probably the earliest form of decorating the body. It is possible that the practice of opening the skin and producing permanent scars by inserting foreign bodies in the wounds first suggested the idea of tattooing.

TEN BAMBOOS, HALL OF. This is an illustrated manual of painting, written in 1627 by Hu Yueh-tsung. An equally important work is the 'Mustard Seed Garden', which was first issued in 1679 by Wang Kai. Two further series followed in 1701 and a fourth, comparatively inferior, one appeared in the last century.

TEOTIHUACAN (Aztec: 'Seat of the Gods'). The Ancient Mexican temple city of Teotihuacan was the centre of a flourishing civilisation between A.D. 200 and 800. Its most famous buildings are the Pyramid of the Sun, the Pyramid of the Moon – the two largest Mexican pyramid temples – and the so-called Temple of Quetzalcoatl. The Pyramid of the Sun, which almost equals the Cheops pyramid in size (200 ft high, the uppermost platform over 130 ft square) and the smaller Pyramid of the Moon are both faced with stone slabs and plaster. The façade of the Temple of Quetzalcoatl, by contrast, is lavishly decorated with butterfly sculptures (the Butterfly God was an Aztec deity), heads of plumed serpents and snake reliefs.

351. *Taj Mahal near Agra/Central India (1630–1648)*

THAI STYLE. The name is derived from the Thai people, the ancestors of the inhabitants of modern Thailand, or Siam, who ruled a large kingdom – including parts of Cambodia – in the 14th century. Buddhist votive plaques in clay show some of the characteristic features of the Thai style: slim, lithe figures (e. g. a Buddha stepping forward) standing in a niche.

TIAHUANACO CULTURE (at its peak between A. D. 600 and 1000, though it began at about the time of the Birth of Christ). The ruins of Tiahuanaco (12,200 ft above sea level) on the southern shore of Lake Titicaca in the Andes occupy an area of roughly a sixth of a square mile. The famous Gateway of the Sun is a 10-ft monolith, decorated in symbolic and highly stylized relief. It is part of the Calasasaya, a large square surrounded by 90 monolithic stone pillars. A characteristic feature of Tiahuanaco architecture is the use of copper clamps for joining the carefully squared stones. The stylization found in Tiahuanaco reliefs also occurs on pottery and textiles (ill. p. 553).

TOBA SOJO (1053–1140). The Buddhist priest Toba Sojo, also known as Kakuyu, was an outstanding master of caricature. Some of his paintings take the form of animals, others of human beings. Such painting has been named Toba-e after him. Toba Sojo was also one of the great religious painters of his day.

TOLTECS. The Toltec capital, Tollan, with its pyramids and temples, two enclosures for ritual ball-games, an excellent street drainage system and numerous palaces, stood on the site of modern Tula, north of Mexiko City. Excavations have shown that its architectural sculpture strongly resembles that of the Toltec-influenced Mayan buildings at Yucatan. The Temple of the Morning Star with caryatids and snake pillars (the symbol of Quetzalcoatl) seems an exact replica – or even the model for – the Temple of the Warriors at Chichen-Itzá (ill. 339). Toltec culture spread south to the Maya through migrations (11th cent.), although it did not lose its influence in Mexico, where it was to provide the basis of Aztec civilisation.

TSUBA. See Swords.

TSUN. See Bronze Vessels.

VIHARA. Literally, 'a place where time can be passed pleasantly'. In India the term is applied to a hermitage, an abbey, a simple monastic dwelling or a shrine. If viharas are grouped, we speak of a sangharama. The sangharama is supposed to be modelled on a Nomadic camp, where tents surrounded a square, as monastic cells surround a courtyard.

WAMPUM. The Iroquois, Algonkin and Huron Indians of North America make beads – called wampum – from a variety of shells. These beads – whose natural colours are white and a deep mauve – were used for decorating belts. The ornament often had symbolic significance.

WANG HSI-CHIH (321–379). The most famous of Chinese calligraphers, Wang Hsi-chih is said to have changed the style of k'ai shu, the official Chinese writing.

WANG WEI (699–759). A contemporary of Wu Tao-tzu, he painted landscapes in the spirit of Zen Buddhism.

WU TAO-TZU (700–760). The name of Wu Tao-tzu has become almost legendary. He was one of the outstanding painters of the T'ang period. Over 300 paintings of the capitals Lo-yang and Ch'ang-an have been attributed to him, although – as in the case of most Chinese painters before the Sung dynasty – no actual work from his hand survives.

YAMATO-E is a typically Japanese form of narrative painting on scrolls. These are sometimes as much as 100 ft long. The greatest master of this art form – which was developed during the Fujiwara period – was Fujiwara Mitsunaga (second half of the 12th century). The themes were chiefly chivalry and romance. (Ill. 352)

YÜ. See Jade.

ZAPOTECS. Numerous catacombs, pyramid temples and palaces of the Ancient Mexican Zapotec culture (c. A. D. 300 to 1000) have been discovered in the former religious centres of Monte Alban and Mitla. Zapotec pottery includes the characteristic 'funerary urns', which are incense burners with highly expressive human figures.

352. Yamato-e painting from the Heian Period (11th cent. A. D.)

INDEX

Figures in bold type indicate glossary entries; an asterisk precedes the page numbers of colour plates; Ill. denotes black-and-white illustrations. A = architect, Gr = graphic artist, P = painter, S = sculptor

566

New Objectivity **500**
New Realism **500**
New York, Lever Building Ill. 278
New York, Seagram Building s. Mies van der Rohe 495
New York, Solomon R. Guggenheim Museum s. Wright, Frank Lloyd 515
Nias Tribes 549
Niaux s. Rock painting 167
Nicholas of Verdun 197, **237**; s. Tournai Cathedral 248
Nicholson, Ben **500**
Nicholson, Sir William **500**; s. Book plate 42
Nicias 135, **163**
Nicolo dell'Abbate 297
Niello 75; ill. 51
Nike (Victory), Temple of, s. Athens, Acropolis 145; ill. 118
Nineveh 103, 110, 111, **163**; ill. 92, 93, 95
Niobid painter **163**; ill. 110
No Drama 536
Nolan, Sidney (b. 1917) Austr. P
Nolde, Emil 451, 456, **501**; * **450**; s. Woodcut 98
Nollekens, Joseph (1737–1823) Engl. S (portr.) 86
Nördlingen, St George's Ill. 61
North-west American Indian Art 549; ill. 348; s. Bark painting 550
Notke, Bernt **237**
Noyon Cathedral 199
Numismatics **75**
Nuremberg, St Lawrence's **237**; ill. 161, 182; s. Krafft 232
Nuremberg, St Sebald's (Sebalduskirche) s. Stoss 247, Vischer 317
Nymphaeum **75**
Nymphenburg Palace 326, **367**
Nymphenburg porcelain 343; ill. 78; s. Bustelli 349, Porcelain 79

Obelisks 15, 120, **163**; ill. 12, 20
Obrist, Hermann (1863–1927) Germ. Gr and S, s. Art Nouveau 465
Oceania 549, **561**; * 555, 556; ill. 346
Odeon (Odeum) Ill. 118; s. Theatre Architecture 93
Ochre 24
Odo von Metz Ill. 143; s. Aix-la-Chapelle Cathedral 214
Oeben, François **367**; s. Furniture 56
Oeser, Adam Friedrich (1717–1799) Germ. P, S and Gr
Oeuvre: an artist's entire creative work
Ogee Ill. 43 h
Oil painting 29, **75**
O'Keeffe, Georgia **501**

Olbrich, Josef (1867–1908) s. Wagner 514
Oliver, Isaac **308**
Olmecs, Ancient Mexican civ. (500 B.C.–A. D. 300) 537, 543; ill. 338
Olympia **163**; ill. 22, 85, 95, 100
Olympia, Heraion 129; ill. 101
Olympia, Temple of Zeus 133, 207, 22, 85, 100; s. Pheidias 166
Omphalos Apollo **164**
Opisthodomos 128; ill. 100; s. Temple 92
Orangery **367**
Orcagna, Andrea 209, **237**; ill. 159
Orchestra Ill. 118; s. Theatre architecture 92
Orders **75**, 128; ill. 62
Orley, Bernaert (Barend) van (1492–1542) Fl. P, s. Tapestry 92
Orlik, Emil (b. 1870) s. Stage design 88
Ornament **76**; ill. 60, 63–72, 78, 249; s. Rocaille 375
Orphism s. Delaunay 478
Orvieto Cathedral 202, **237**; s. Maitani 234, Orcagna 237, Pisano, A. 238
Oseberg Treasure **164**; ill. 69; s. Germanic art 155
Ostade, Adriaen van **367**
Ostendorfer, Michael (c. 1490–1559) s. Danube school 295
Ottobeuren: Monastic pile 325, **368**; s. Fischer, J. M. 358
Ottonian 10
Oud, Jacobus Johannes Pieter 443, **501**
Oudry, Jean-Baptiste **368**
Overbeck, Johann Friedrich 399, **426**; s. Nazarenes 426
Ozenfant, Amédée **501**

Pachacamac Ill. 338, 341; s. Incas 558
Pacheco, Francisco (1564–1654) 334
Pacher, Michael **237**; ill. 84
Padeloup, Antoine Michel (1685–1758) s. Bindings 40
Paderborn Cathedral 202, 209; s. Rogerus von Helmarshausen 244
Padua, Arena Chapel 212; * 179; ill. 177; s. Giotto 225, Pisano, G. 243
Paeonius 134; s. Olympia 164
Paestum **164**
Pagoda 525, 528, **561**; ill. 335
P'ai-Lou (Chinese = memorial arch) 528
Painted Pottery **164**; ill. 89
Pala d'Oro 184, 197, **237**
Palermo, Cappella Palatina 189
Palette Knife **77**

Palissy, Bernard (1510–1589) 291, 308; ill. 214
Palladio, Andrea **308**, 325, 389; ill. 215; s. Theatre architecture 93, Jones, Inigo, 364
Palma, Jacopo (Palma Vecchio) **308**
Palmer, Samuel **426**
Palmette Ill. 66, 110; s. Ornament 76
Palmyra **164**
Palos Verdes, Wayfarers' Chapel s. Wright 515
Panini, Giov. Antonio (1695-1768) It. P
Pantheon, Rome 141, **164**, 173; ill. 113, 129
Papiers Collés, s. Cubism 477
Parchment **77**
Paris, Matthew (d. 1259) 212
Paris, Dôme des Invalides **368**; ill. 34; s. Mansart, J. 366
Paris, Eiffel Tower 392; 441; s. Iron structures 65
Paris, Galérie des Machines 392, 441; s. Iron structures 65
Paris, Louvre 266, 325, **368**; ill. 212; s. Perrault 368
Paris, Notre Dame 199, 207, **237**; ill. 30, 33
Paris, The Madeleine 392, **426**, 441; ill. 272
Paris, Opéra 391, 441; ill. 255
Paris, Panthéon **368**
Paris, Ste-Clotilde 391
Paris, St-Etienne-du-Mont s. Rood 85
Paris, Ste-Chapelle 200, 210, **238**; ill. 153
Paris, Stock Exchange 392
Paris, Swiss Pavilion 491
Paris, UNESCO building s. Nervi 500
Parler family A and S, s. Schwäbisch-Gmünd 245, Ulm Cathedral 248
Parler, Peter 209, **238**, 268; ill. 160; s. Schwäbisch-Gmünd 245
Parma Cathedral and Baptistery s. Antelami 214
Parma, Teatro Farnese s. Stage design 88, Theatre architecture 93
Parmigianino 282, 284, **309**; * 313
Parrhasius 136, **165**
Parthenon 17, 130, 133, **165**; ill. 102, 118, 130; s. Acropolis 145
Pascin, Jules **501**
Pasiteles **165**
Pasquino group **165**
Pastel drawing 31, **77**; * 420
Pasticcio (pastiche) s. copy 52
Patenir (Patinier), Joachim 281, **309**
Pater, Jean-Baptiste **368**
Patina s. Restoring 85
Paul, Bruno **501**

Pavilion: Small circular or polygonal building Ill. 228
Paxton, Joseph (1801–65) 392, 441
'Paysage Intime' 405
Peale, Charles Willson **368**; s. Silhouette 87
Peale, Raphaelle (1774–1825) US P
Pechstein, Max **501**
Pediment Ill. 62
Pegged mosaic **165**
Peintre graveur 31; s. Copper Engraver 51
Peking **561**
Pencil drawing 31; ill. 39
Pen drawing 31; ill. 40
Pendentive 53; s. Dome 52
Penni, Giovanni Francesco (1488–1528) s. Stucco 90
Pentimenti **78**
Perez family s. Borassá 220
Pergamum 127, **165**
Périgueux, St-Front 176, 187, **238**
Peripteros 130; ill. 99, 100, 118; s. Temple 92
Peristyle **165**
Permeke, Constant **501**
Permoser, Balthasar 332; **368**; s. Dresden, Zwinger 356
Perpendicular Style 201, **238**; ill. 169; s. London, Westminster Abbey 133
Perrault, Claude 325, **368**
Perret, Auguste (born 1873) s. Le Corbusier 490
Perroneau, Jean Baptiste (1715–1783) Fr. Gr (portr.)
Persepolis 113, **165**
Persian art, 113 f.; * 106
Persian book illumination * 521; s. Herat Academy 558
Perspective 30, **78**; * 37; ill. 73
Perugia fountain 209; s. Pisano, N. 243
Perugino **309**; s. Orvieto Cathedral 237
Pesne, Antoine **368**
Petel, George **368**
Peruzzi, Baldassare (1481–1535) Ital. A and P
Peterborough Cathedral 188, **238**
Peterhof (Leningrad) 326
Peto, John Frederick (1854–1907) US P
Pevsner, Antoine 458, **502**; ill 296; s. Constructivism 470
Pevsner, Naum, s. Gabo, Naum 480
Pewter **78**
Pforr, Franz (1788–1812) 399; s. Nazarenes 426
Pheidias 133–4, **166**; ill. 102, 130; s. Acropolis 145, Gold and Ivory statues 156, Olympia 163, Parthenon 165, Propylaea 167

LIST OF COLOUR PLATES

MONOCHROME ILLUSTRATIONS: MUSEUMS AND GALLERIES

SOURCES OF ILLUSTRATIONS

In-text illustrations: Aerofilms Ltd., London (1); Alinari, Florence (17); Foto Alpenland, Vienna (1); Prof. Alsdorf, Sprötze (1); D. Anderson, Rome (1); W. Andrews, New York (2); Archiv f. Kunst u. Geschichte, Berlin (1); Kunstarchiv Arntz, Stuttgart (29); L. Aufsberg, Sonthofen (10); Bredol-Lepper, Aachen (1); British Features, Bonn (2); F. Bruckmann KG, Munich (2); Deutscher Kunstverlag, Munich (12); Photographie Giraudon, Paris (1); W. Hahn, Dresden (2); Prof. Hassenpflug, Munich (1); L. Hervé, Paris (1); Verlag Hoffmann & Campe, Hamburg (1); O. Hoppe, Brunswick (1); Karfeld-Verlag GmbH., Düsseldorf (1); W. Kohlhammer Verlag, Stuttgart (11); Lever House, New York (1); E. Lieseberg, Hanover (1); Foto Marburg, Marburg/Lahn (81); H. Morscher, St. Gallen (1); Nordisk Pressefoto, Copenhagen (2); Fr. A. Praeger Inc., New York (4); H. Reclam, Stuttgart (1); Rembrandt-Verlag, Berlin (9); roebild, Frankfurt/M. (2); J. Roubier, Paris (1); G. Schaffert, Creglingen (1); Dr. F. Stoedtner, Düsseldorf (12); G. Straicher, Goslar (1); W. Tietze, Brunswick (1); Ullstein, A.G., Berlin, from *Propyläen Kunstgeschichte* (5); Wehmeyer, Hildesheim (1); H. Wiegandt, Frankfurt/M. (1); L. Windstosser, Stuttgart (1); Prof. Winter, Diessen (1); Dr. P. Wolff & Tritschler, Frankfurt/M. (2); Berlin, Staatl. Museen (3); Brunswick, Kunstverein (1); Brussels World Exhibition 1958 (6); Hamburg, Museum f. Kunst u. Gewerbe (1); Hanover, Kestner-Gesellschaft (1); Cologne, Rheinisches Museum (1); Munich, Bayer. Nat.-Museum (2); Paris, Archives Photogr. des Monuments Historiques (6); Rome, Archivi Fotogr. Gall. Mus. Vaticani (1); Rome, Deutsches Archäologisches Institut (1); Rome, Museo Nazionale di Villa Giulia (1); Vienna, Österr. National-Bibl. (2).

Colour plates: Prints or blocks were supplied by: H. Abrams, Amsterdam (pp. 182, 327); Alinari, Florence (pp. 149, 162); F. Bruckmann KG, Munich (pp. 204 a, 262, 415, 450 from Nolde, *Aquarelle und Zeichnungen*); Buchheim-Verlag, Feldafing (p. 420); Büchergilde Gutenberg, Zurich (p. 540); Dumont Schauberg, Cologne (pp. 191, 488, 505); Urs Graf-Verlag GmbH., Lausanne (p. 180); Franz Hanfstaengl, Munich (pp. 241, 253, 280, 290, 344, 351, 374, 448); Hirmer Verlag, Munich (p. 115, 116, 121, 122); Hannov. Druck- u. Verlagsgesellschaft mbH., Hanover (pp. 38, 311); Hoffmann & Campe, Hamburg (pp. 150, 320); Holbeinverlag, Basle (p. 105 a); Iris-Verlag, Laupen/Berne (pp. 204 b, 228); Woldemar Klein, Baden-Baden (pp. 28, 475, 506); W. Kohlhammer AG, Stuttgart (pp. 59, 242, 287); London, British Museum (p. 106 b); New York Graphic Soc., Greenwich (pp. 27, 362, 461, 472, 474, 504, 522); R. Piper & Co., Munich (p. 252); Die Piperdrucke Verlags-GmbH., Munich (pp. 72, 299, 300, 336, 417, 471); Rembrandt-Verlag, Berlin (p. 314); J. Roubier, Paris (p. 106 a); Les Editions Skira, Geneva (pp. 216, 227, 240).

For their kind permission to use picture material thanks are also due to: Artia-Verlag, Prague, and Verlag W. Dausien, Hanau/M. (p. 240, from Matejcek-Pesina, *Gotische Malerei in Böhmen 1350—1450*); University of Dublin, Trinity College (p. 180); Galerie Günther Franke, Munich (pp. 498, 511); Galerie Gurlitt, Munich (p. 385); Mr. Bernh. Koehler, Berlin (p. 448); New York, Metropolitan Museum of Art, The Cloisters (p. 216); New York, Sidney Janis Gall. (p. 512); Stiftung Seebüll Ada und Emil Nolde (p. 450); Oslo Kommunes Kunstsamlinger (p. 440); Mr. Heinrich Reclam, Stuttgart (Ill. 259); Mrs. E. Schürer-v. Witzleben, Seeshaupt (p. 204 a); Mr. Bernh. Sprengel, Hanover (p. 450); Stuttgarter Kunstkabinett (p. 447); for reproduction rights, S. P. A. D. E. M. Paris and Cosmopress, Geneva pp. 72, 100, 417, 420, 459, 462, 471, 473, 474, 506 and 6 in-text pictures.